EVERYBODY
(INCLUDING ELIZABETH TAYLOR)
HAD A POINT OF VIEW ABOUT
ELIZABETH TAYLOR

"She is one of the most misunderstood and underestimated people of our time."

—**Truman Capote**

"Nobody on earth is better company than Elizabeth Taylor, more lively, more fun, and more of a three-ring circus. When I began seeing her, she was fifty-five and better than ever. The year was 1986. She had divorced Senator John Warner and shed all that weight that John Belushi lampooned on Saturday Night Live. For Elizabeth, looking great was the best revenge."

—**George Hamilton** in *Don't Mind If I Do*

"She was a femme fatale. I was an homme fatale. We made a fatal combination. She told me she wanted to marry me, but she was still a struggling actress at the time. I told her she couldn't afford me."

—**Porfirio Rubirosa** to Elsa Maxwell

"Let's face it: My life seems to lack dignity."

—**Elizabeth Taylor**

"Elizabeth was a committed wife—at least for the first week."

—**Lana Turner**

"Elizabeth's favorite pastime was celebrity gossip. Her definition of celebrity included royalty, world leaders, writers, artists, and musicians, and the occasional Greek billionaire. She needed gossip as fuel to shock at dinner parties. She had to know who was sleeping with whom, who was great in bed, and who was not, and who was well hung. The gay secretaries were especially good at collecting that necessary information, especially Richard Hanley, whose years at MGM had made him a sexpert on the entire film industry."

—**Vicky Tiel**, *It's All About the Dress*

"I lied about being a virgin on my wedding night. Actually, my first sexual experience was giving John Derek a blow-job when I'd just learned to walk, which is only a slight exaggeration. I was very, very young at the time, and he was a child molester."

—**Elizabeth Taylor** at a dinner party in Gstaad in 1968

"Elizabeth should have acquired more jewelry and fewer husbands. But who am I to cast 'stones,' dah-link?"

—**Zsa Zsa Gabor**

"That Krupp diamond is far too vulgar to wear in public."

—**Princess Margaret**

"After Elizabeth and I smelled each other out, we became two fast friends. Bitches in heat recognize each other."

—**Laurence Harvey**

"My troubles all started because I have a woman's body and a child's emotions.

—**Elizabeth Taylor**

"I was torn in my loyalties between two goddesses—Bessie May and Pussy."

—**Monty Clift**, using his nicknames for Elizabeth Taylor and Marilyn Monroe

"I called Elizabeth Taylor and told her that Monty Clift was being held a prisoner in his apartment in New York. He got involved with this dangerous hustler. He's bringing in guys who want to fuck Monty and charging them a hundred dollars a lay. You've got to come and rescue him."

—**Truman Capote** in Key West

"What is this, a memory test?"

—**Elizabeth Taylor,** responding to the justice of the peace at her wedding to Larry Fortensky when he asked her the names of her former husbands.

"You know, an actress can learn to hate Elizabeth Taylor."

—**Patricia Neal**

"I often fucked actors who liked to fuck each other—Peter Lawford, Monty Clift (well, I tried at least), Rock Hudson, James Dean, Paul Newman. Or, actors who other actors wanted to fuck—namely George Hamilton, Robert Wagner...do we have all night?"

—**Elizabeth Taylor**

"No raise. Now get out. You're such a whore."

—MGM's casting director **Benny Thau** to Elizabeth Taylor after denying her request for a pay raise

"Burt Lancaster raped me that night back in April of 1961 after we'd won our joint Oscars for Butterfield 8 and Elmer Gantry. Well, it wasn't rape exactly, but a gal can pretend, can't she?"

—**Elizabeth Taylor** in 1975

"Elizabeth Taylor got to sample my noble tool when we made Reflections in a Golden Eye together. Burton found out and was seriously pissed off, probably because I didn't fuck the sod himself."

—**Marlon Brando** to Carlo Fiore

"Drugs have become a crutch. I wouldn't take them just when I was in pain. I needed oblivion, escape...I was hooked on Percodan and of course, I could drink everybody under the table. I had a hollow leg. My capacity to consume was terrifying. I didn't even realize I was an alcoholic."

—**Elizabeth Taylor**

"I guess in time all of us fucked her. I know Sammy did. So did Frank. So did Peter, a long time ago. Joey Bishop was the only one who didn't join the rat race."

—**Dean Martin** about Elizabeth Taylor

"What did you expect me to do—sleep alone?"

—**Elizabeth Taylor** to Hedda Hopper

"The trouble with Elizabeth Taylor is that she always envied my sex appeal. She just didn't have it, and I did."

—**Marilyn Monroe** to Clark Gable

"I have written a sequel to The Wizard of Oz about a 60-year-old Dorothy returning to Oz and I'm talking to Elizabeth Taylor about starring in it. She told me she wants to play the role, and she would be perfect for it."

—**Rod Steiger,** 1998

"Yes, it's true. On that infamous night I recited the Gettyburg Address at the Lincoln Memorial wearing nothing but a mink coat. Ask Halston. He was the designer who dressed me."

—**Elizabeth Taylor**

"In this Age of Vulgarity, marked by such minor matters as war and poverty, it gets harder every day to scale the heights of true vulgarity. But given some loose millions, it can be done—and, worse, admired."

—**The New York Times** on the Taylor/Burton roadshow

"I know I'm vulgar, but would you have me any other way?"

—**Elizabeth Taylor**

"Does it matter what Maureen Stapleton weighs? Why the hell does it matter what I weigh? It's nobody's damn business what I weigh, but talking about it seems to be a national pastime. And that pisses me off!"

—**Elizabeth Taylor**

"I visited her in London in the hospital when she had that trachotomy. She had what looked like a silver dollar in her throat. I couldn't figure out what held it in place, and it surprised me she wasn't bleeding or oozing. A few nights later, I went out with Eddie Fisher. The next afternoon, Elizabeth told me that Eddie thought I was trying to make a pass at him. At that moment, she played a trick on me and yanked at the plug in her throat, spurting out champagne—I'd brought her a magnum of Don Perignon—all over the hospital room. I thought I was going to pass out."

—Truman Capote

"After I married Mike Todd, he invited Eddie Fisher into our bedroom and pulled the sheet off me, exposing my nude body to Eddie. I think he really wanted a ménage à trois. There are those who say we had one."

—Elizabeth Taylor

"She had the face of an angel and the morals of a truck driver. We'd make love three, four, five times a day. We'd make love in the swimming pool, on Mexican beaches, under waterfalls, in the back seat of a limousine on the way home from a party. There was nothing more erotic than a moonlit beach and Elizabeth Taylor."

—Eddie Fisher

"Did I seduce Mike Todd's son and Peter Lawford's son? I wouldn't put it past me."

—Elizabeth Taylor

"I think Elizabeth is having an affair with Sammy Davis, Jr., but she dismisses the notion, joking that 'just over five foot tall' Sammy couldn't reach that high."

—Richard Burton

"Do you want to know some people I screwed that most people don't know about? Ardeshir Zahedi, the Iranian ambassador to the United States. Would you believe that Swedish boxer, Ingemar Johansson? Ronald Reagan, Errol Flynn, John and Bobby (guess who?), Prince Aly Khan."

—**Elizabeth Taylor,** overheard by the author in 1961, in a bar in Portofino

"If you leave me I shall have to kill myself. I love you. There is no life without you."

—**Richard Burton** during his second divorce proceedings
from Elizabeth Taylor.

"I hung up the phone after Mike Todd told me he was in love with Elizabeth Taylor. I had been...taken. When I wasn't looking, I was delivered the knockout punch. I felt jilted. I should have seen it coming. He fell in love too fast. Like that phone call from Moscow to Marlene Dietrich when she was still big news. Like that circus act when he got Marilyn Monroe to ride the pink elephant at Madison Square Garden. And now Elizabeth Taylor beckoning with her little pinkie."

—**Evelyn Keyes** in her memoir, *Scarlett O'Hara's Little Sister*

"In May of 2000, I was critically ill with pneumonia and had a near death experience. I was on the other side, like in a tunnel, and I was with Mike Todd. I held onto him and he said, 'You have to go back now. You have things to do and I will be here.' I wanted to stay with Mike. He was my one true love."

—**Elizabeth Taylor**

"Elizabeth Taylor was the last of the great glamour stars. She was the longest running soap opera in history, and represented all the allure and tragedy that attracts people to Hollywood."

—British director **Michael Winner**

"I'm old and I'm tired and I've represented everyone from that cunt Bette Davis to Elizabeth Taylor and Richard Burton. Everyone wants to know my secrets. Okay, I'm dying and out of harm's way now, so I'll tell you a few —Burton said he liked to fuck Fisher's ass better than he did Elizabeth's. She screwed Ronald Reagan, John F. Kennedy, Bobby Kennedy. Tallulah Bankhead masturbated Elizabeth at the dinner table one night. Marilyn Monroe went down on her one night in Las Vegas. Elvis Presley fucked Elizabeth and wanted to do a movie with her. She had a three-way with Monty Clift and Marlon Brando. And I'm only just getting wound up."

—Talent Agent **Robert Lantz**

"I get pissed off with all the talk of the great love story of my husband Richard Burton and Elizabeth Taylor. Yes, they were in love, but they divorced twice. That means their marriages didn't work. I'm still very bitter about the torch Richard carried for that woman."

—Richard Burton's widow, **Sally Hay**, in 2011

"Richard Burton fucked me long before he did the honors with you."

—**Noël Coward** to Elizabeth Taylor on the set of *Boom!*

"I knew she would be devastated, shattered by the death of Burton, but I didn't expect her to become completely hysterical. I could not get her to stop crying. She was completely out of control. I realized how deeply tied she was to this man, how vital a role he played in her life. And I realized I could never have that special place in her heart she keeps for Burton. For me, the romance was over, and I told Elizabeth that."

—**Victor Luna**, Mexican Attorney

"We have been fighting and have been fighting for over a year now over anything and everything. I dread it at night when she has had her shots of drugs and is only semi-articulate. When she moans and groans in agony, I simply become bored. What is more frightening is she has become bored with everything in life. I have always been a heavy drinker, but now I'm drinking twice as much. The upshoot will be that I'll die of drink while she'll go on blithely in her half-world."

—**Richard Burton** in his diary, 1969

"Being with Elizabeth Taylor is like sticking an eggbeater in your brain. I loved her, and I think she loved me. But on the practical level, she was not the woman I needed in my life. With her, there was a great deal of maintenance. This is not a woman who gets up in the morning and fixes breakfast. By the time she comes downstairs for breakfast, it's time for dinner. Her life is built completely around Elizabeth, and she needs a man to service her life 24/7."

—Robert Wagner

"In our last chat, I told Elizabeth that getting old is really shit. She said, 'It certainly is. It certainly is, Debbie. This is really tough. I'm really trying to hang in there.'"

—Debbie Reynolds in 2011

"She told me that there had never been a time in her life when she wasn't famous."

—Barbara Walters

"We just stopped communicating. Why was every guy she befriended gay?"

—Larry Fortensky

"'Stay with me,' Elizabeth said. Curling up close, spoon fashion, I wrapped my arms around her and looked at the room I found myself in. A woman's bedroom. So inviting. So frightening."

—Frank Langella, in his memoirs

"She was a great broad."

—Whoopi Goldberg, commenting on the death of Elizabeth Taylor

ELIZABETH TAYLOR

THERE IS NOTHING LIKE A DAME

ELIZABETH TAYLOR
THERE IS NOTHING LIKE A DAME

DARWIN PORTER

ELIZABETH TAYLOR
THERE IS NOTHING LIKE A DAME

by Darwin Porter

THANKS FOR THE MEMORIES

THIS BOOK IS DEDICATED TO

DICK HANLEY

&

RODDY MCDOWALL

*AND TO A CAST OF THOUSANDS, FRIENDS AND FOES,
WHO SHARED GOOD TIMES AND BAD TIMES
WITH DAME ELIZABETH*

CONTENTS

ENTERTAINMENT ABOUT HOW AMERICA INTERPRETS ITS CELEBRITIES

The Films of Elizabeth Taylor

A Lifetime of Achievement

There's One Born Every Minute, Universal, 1942, D: Harold Young, with "Alfalfa" Switzer, Peggy Morgan, Hugh Herbert.

Lassie Come Home, MGM, 1943, D: Fred M. Wilcox, with Roddy McDowall, Donald Crisp, Edmund Gwenn, Dame Mae Whitty, Elsa Lanchester, Pal (Lassie).

Jane Eyre, 20th Century Fox, 1944, D: Robert Stevenson, with Orson Welles, Joan Fontaine, Margaret O'Brien, Peggy Ann Garner, Agnes Moorehead.

The White Cliffs of Dover, MGM, 1944, D: Clarence Brown, with Irene Dunne, Alan Marshal, Dame Mae Whitty, Peter Lawford, Van Johnson, Gladys Cooper, Roddy McDowall.

National Velvet, MGM, 1944, D: Clarence Brown, with Mickey Rooney, Donald Crisp, Angela Lansbury, Anne Revere.

Courage of Lassie, MGM, 1945, D: Fred M. Wilcox, with Frank Morgan, Tom Drake, Selena Royle, George Cleveland.

Cynthia, MGM, 1947, D: Robert Z. Leonard, with George Murphy, Mary Astor, S.Z. Sakall, Gene Lockhart, James Lydon, Spring Byington.

Life with Father, Warner Brothers, 1947, D: Michael Curtiz, with William Powell, Irene Dunne, Edmund Gwenn, ZaSu Pitts, James Lydon.

A Date With Judy, MGM, 1948, D: Richard Thorpe, with Wallace Beery, Selena Royle, Jane Powell, Robert Stack, Carmen Miranda, Xavier Cugat, Scotty Beckett, Leon Ames, George Cleveland.

Julia Misbehaves, MGM, 1948, D: Mervin LeRoy, with Greer Garson, Walter Pidgeon, Peter Lawford, Cesar Romero, Mary Boland, Nigel Bruce, Lucile Watson.

Little Women, MGM, 1949, D: Mervin LeRoy, with June Allyson, Peter Lawford, Janet Leigh, Margaret O'Brien, Mary Astor, Lucile Watson, Rossano Brazzi.

Conspirator, MGM, 1949, D: Victor Saville, with Robert Taylor, Robert Flemyng, Honor Blackman, Thora Hird.

The Big Hangover, MGM, 1959, D: Norman Krasna, with Van Johnson, Leon Ames, Gene Lockhart, Selene Royle, Rosemary DeCamp.

Father of the Bride, MGM, 1950, D: Vincente Minnelli, with Spencer Tracy, Joan Bennett, Don Taylor, Billie Burke, Leo G. Carroll, Russ Tamblyn.

A Place in the Sun, Paramount, 1951, with Montgomery Clift, Shelley Winters, Anne Revere, Keefe Brasselle, Raymond Burr, Shepperd Strudwick.

Love is Better Than Ever, MGM, 1952, D: Stanley Donen, with Larry Parks, Josephine Hutchinson, Tom Tully, Ann Doran.

Ivanhoe, MGM, 1952, D: Richard Thorpe, with Robert Taylor, Joan Fontaine, George Sanders, Emlyn Williams, Finlay Currie, Feliz Aylmer, Robert Douglas.

The Girl Who Had Everything, MGM, 1953, D: Richard Thorpe, with William Powell, Fernando Lamas, James Whitmore, Gig Young.

Rhapsody, MGM, 1954, D: Charles Vidor, with Vittorio Gassman, John Ericson, Louis Calhern.

Elephant Walk, Paramount, 1954, D: William Dieterle, with Dana Andrews, Peter Finch.

Beau Brummell, MGM, 1954, D: Curtis Bernhardt, with Stewart Granger, Peter Ustinov, Robert Morley.

The Last Time I Saw Paris, MGM, 1954, D: Richard Brooks, with Van Johnson, Walter Pidgeon, Donna Reed, Eva Gabor, Kurt Kasnar.

Giant, Warner Brothers, 1956, D: George Stevens, with Rock Hudson, James Dean, Carroll Baker, Jane Withers, Mercedes McCambridge, Sal Mineo, Chill Wills, Dennis Hopper.

Raintree County, MGM, 1957, D: Edward Dmytryk, with Montgomery Clift, Eva Marie Saint, Lee Marvin, Nigel Bruce, Rod Taylor, Agnes Moorehead, Walter Abel, Tom Drake.

Cat on a Hot Tin Roof, MGM, 1958, D: Richard Brooks, with Paul Newman, Burl Ives, Judith Anderson, Jack Carson, Madeleine Sherwood.

Suddenly, Last Summer, Columbia, 1959, D: Joseph L. Mankiewicz, with Katharine Hepburn, Montgomery Clift, Mercedes McCambridge, Albert Dekker.

Scent of Mystery (*Holiday In Spain* in British release), Michael Todd, Jr., Productions, 1960, D: Jack Cardiff, with Denholm Elliott, Peter Lorre, Paul Lukas.

Butterfield 8, MGM, 1960, D: Daniel Mann, with Laurence Harvey, Eddie Fisher, Dina Merrill, Mildred Dunnock, Betty Field, Jeffrey Lynn.

Cleopatra, 20th Century Fox, 1963, D: Joseph L. Mankiewicz, with Richard Burton, Rex Harriosn, Hume Cronyn, Roddy McDowall, Martin Landau.

The V.I.P.s, MGM, 1963, D: Anthony Asquith, with Richard Burton, Louis Jourdan, Elsa Martinelli, Margaret Rutherford, Maggie Smith, Orson Welles, Linda Christian, Rod Taylor.

The Sandpiper, MGM, 1965, D: Vincente Minnelli, with Richard Burton, Eva Marie Saint, Charles Bronson, Eduardo Tirella, Tom Drake.

Who's Afraid of Virginia Woolf?, Warner Brothers, 1966, D: Mike Nichols, with Richard Burton, George Segal, Sandy Dennis.

The Taming of the Shrew, Columbia, 1967, D: Franco Zeffirelli, with Richard Burton, Michael York, Cyril Cusack, Michael Hordern.

Doctor Faustus, Columbia, 1967, D: Nevill Coghill, with Richard Burton, Andreas Teuber, Elizabeth O'Donovan.

Reflections in a Golden Eye, Seven Arts, 1967, D: John Huston, with Marlon Brando, Brian Keith, Julie Harris, Robert Forster.

The Comedians, MGM, 1967, D: Peter Glenville, with Richard Burton, Alec Guinness, Peter Ustinov, Lillian Gish, Paul Ford.

Boom!, Universal, 1968, D: Joseph Losey, with Richard Burton, Noël Coward, Michael Dunn.

Secret Ceremony, Universal, 1968, D: Joseph Losey, with Mia Farrow, Robert Mitchum, Peggy Ashcroft, Pamela Brown.

The Only Game in Town, 20th Century Fox, 1970, D: George Stevens, with Warren Beatty, Charles Braswell, Hank Henry.

Under Milk Wood, Altura Films, 1971, D: Andrew Sinclair, with Richard Burton, Peter O'Toole, Glynnis Johns,

X, Y, and Zee (*Zee & Company* in British release), 1972, D: Brian G. Hutton, with Michael Caine, Susannah York, Margaret Leighton.

Hammersmith is Out, Cornelius Crean Films, 1972, D: Peter Ustinov, with Richard Burton, Beau Bridges, Leon Ames, George Raft.

Night Watch, Avco Embassy, 1973, D: Brian Hutton, with Laurence Harvey, Billie Whitelaw, Robert Lang.

Divorce His, Divorce Hers, ABC-TV, 1973, D: Waris Hussein, with Richard Burton, Carrie Nye, Barry Foster.

Ash Wednesday, Paramount 1973, D: Larry Peerce, with Helmut Berger, Henry Fonda.

The Driver's Seat (aka *Identikit*), Avco Embassy, 1974, D: Giuseppe Patroni Griffi, with Ian Bennan, Guido Mannari.

The Blue Bird, 20th Century Fox, 1976, D: George Cukor, with Ava Gardner, Jane Fonda, Robert Morley, Cicely Tyson.

A Little Night Music, New World Pictures, 1977, D: Harold Prince, with Hermione Gingold, Lesley-Anne Down.

Winter Kills, Avco Embassy, 1979, D: William Richert, with Jeff Bridges, John Huston, Tony Perkins, Sterling Hayden, Eli Wallach, Dorothy Malone, Ralph Meeker.

The Mirror Crack'ed, EMI Films, 1980, D: Guy Hamilton, with Rock Hudson, Tony Curtis, Kim Novak, Edward Fox, Geraldine Chaplin, Angela Lansbury.

Malice in Wonderland, ITC,TV-, 1985: D: Gus Trikonis, with Jane Alexander, Richard Dysart, Joyce Van Patten.

There Must Be a Pony, Columbia TV, 1986, D: Joseph Sargent, with Robert Wagner, James Coco.

Il Giovane Toscanini, Cathago Films, 1988, D: Franco Zeffirelli, with C. Thomas Howell, Sophie Ward.

Sweet Bird of Youth, NBC-TV, 1989, D: Nicolas Roeg, with Mark Harmon, Valerie Perrine.

The Flintstones, Universal, 1994: D: Brian Levant, with John Goodman, Rosie O'Donnell.

These Old Broads, ABC-TV, 2001, D: Matthew Diamond, with Debbie Reynolds, Shirley MacLaine, Peter Graves, Joan Collins.

CHAPTER ONE
Born Into a *Ménage à Trois*
BABY ELIZABETH

The chimes of Big Ben announced to London that it was two o'clock in the morning. At this cold moment in February, a pea-soup fog had fallen over the city, obscuring early morning traffic on the Thames. Prostitutes still walking the streets of Soho, in what is known as "the desperate hour," referred to it as "Jack the Ripper" weather.

In a black sedan, a doctor, Charles Huggenheim, sped rapidly north through nearly deserted streets. He was heading for Hampstead, where an urgent call had summoned him to the house of an American couple. A former stage actress was about to give birth.

With the screech of his brakes, the doctor parked and rushed to an open door at 8 Wildwood Road in Golders Green, where two anxious men stood. He did not have time to determine which one was the father, as the nanny directed him up the steps where the sounds of pain led him to the master bedroom.

A little baby girl, weighing 8½ pounds, entered the world at exactly 2:30 that morning. It was a relatively smooth delivery. Before the baby was born, the mother had told him, "Two years ago I had a boy. He was called a Botticelli angel. I know this one, boy or girl, will be even more beautiful."

Almost immediately after the delivery, Sara fell into a deep sleep. She didn't even see the child before the nanny took her away.

Dawn had broken across the London Heath before Sara woke up. The morning sun had chased away the nightmarish fog.

On her left, her husband, Francis Taylor, held her hand. "You've come through, precious one," he said in a soft voice. On his right, Victor Cazalet, a conservative Member of Parliament, held her other hand. "The three of us have a healthy baby daughter," he told her, squeezing her hand.

Francis was her husband, Victor was her lover. Not only that, but Victor was also the lover of her husband. She'd never known that any two men could be that devoted to each other. As only her closest confidants were aware, she did not really know which one was the father of her newborn.

In a weak but determined voice, she said, "For appearance's sake, Francis will be the father. As for you, Victor, we'll make you the godfather. I know that both of you will love the girl like she was your own blood." After receiving assurances from both men, she asked them, "Would you please bring in our little girl?"

Francis went for the infant in the nursery. While he was gone, Victor leaned over and kissed Sara on the lips.

"Oh, my darling man, you've given Francis and me such a wonderful life. You've made us a part of your world. You're the only person Francis has ever loved. He's devoted to you and your every wish. I, too, love you with all my heart. I know you'll bestow your love on our beautiful daughter and take care of her, too."

"That I promise, and I don't have to tell you and Francis that I'm a man of my word."

As he was saying that, Francis came back into the bedroom, holding the newborn girl swaddled in a pink blanket. At bedside, he stood beside Victor, giving him a long, lingering kiss. "Okay, Daddy, present our girl to its mother."

Victor very gently took the baby and lowered her to Sara's outstretched arms. "May I present Elizabeth Rosemond Taylor Cazalet?" he asked.

The morning sun streaming in had brightly lit the bedroom. Sara reached for her newborn, taking her in her protective arms.

For the first time, she gazed lovingly into her baby's face. Suddenly, her own face became one of shock and horror. "Take her away!" she shouted at Victor. "It's not my daughter. The hairy little thing is the newborn of a money at the zoo!"

Victor quickly retrieved the bundle and passed her immediately to Francis, who carried her from the bedroom back to the nursery and the nanny.

"The doctor assured me she won't always look that ghastly," Victor said.

8 **Wildwood Road** in Golders Glen, Hampstead, near London, site of Elizabeth Taylor's birth in 1932

"In a few months, all that hair will fall from her body—at least that's what happens in most cases. Nature itself will cure these genetic defects."

The cries coming from the nursery sounded more like a screaming rage.

Only a handful of people took note of the historic date of February 27, 1932, and that birth of this ghoulish little girl. But this pathetic little creature with a head far too big for its narrow shoulders would eventually be hailed as "the world's most beautiful woman."

A lifetime of tragedy and triumph awaited her in the more than seven decades that followed, decades that would evolve into a new millennium not yet born.

Elizabeth Taylor would both enchant and appall the world she'd so awkwardly entered.

Besides her unusually colored eyes—a curious shade of violet—she would become known for her breasts. A Welsh actor and her future husband, Richard Burton, would refer to them as "apocalyptic. They will topple empires before they wither!"

***

When Elizabeth Taylor became an international star, Sara vicariously lived her daughter's life. Stardom had been the dream of Sara herself.

Born Sara Viola Warmbrodt on August 21, 1896, she was the daughter of Samuel Warmbrodt, an émigré laundry manager who'd been trained as an engineer. In the milltown of Arkansas City, Kansas, he'd married Anna Elizabeth Wilson, a talented singer and pianist, whose own dream of an artistic career had been abandoned when she became a housewife.

By the time Sara was only eight years old, Samuel claimed that his beautiful daughter had a "bloodthirsty ambition." Dropping out of high school, she set out to pursue her goal, taking the train to Los Angeles and changing her name to Sara Sothern, "because it will look better on a theater marquee."

In California, she met a "swishy actor" [her words], Brooklyn-born Edward Everett Horton, who had established a stock company presenting theatrical performances in Pasadena. He would become famous in the movies of the 1930s, for which he was known for saying, "Oh, dear," in numerous films. His face, with its beaked nose, looked "in perpetual pain," as the critics said, and he had a jittery voice.

Horton cast Sara in a minor role in *The Sign on the Door* (1922), a play by Channing Pollock. In 1929, the drama would be adapted for the screen and retitled *The Locked Door.* It included a role for Barbara Stanwyck as one of her first films.

A THESPIAN MOTHER: Views of **Sara Warmbrodt** (aka Sara Sothern) in 1916 (*top photo*) and 1926 as *The Little Spitfire*

3

Pollock was so impressed with Sara's acting that he cast her in a key role in his next play, *The Fool,* (1922-23). She played a fifteen-year-old crippled girl, Mary Margaret, a modern-day interpretation of Mary Magdalene. The play was about faith healing, which appealed to Sara, who had been brought up by her mother as a Christian Scientist. At the finale, a crippled Sara throws her crutches away and shouts, "*I kin walk!*"

The critics attacked it, but evangelical audiences adored it. The play received so much attention that it attracted Alla Nazimova as a member of the audience. Nazimova was enjoying a brief reign as "The Queen of MGM" in spite of her gunboat feet and pumpkin-shaped head. Born in the Ukraine, she lived in a mansion on Sunset Boulevard called "the Garden of Alla."

Backstage, after one of Sara's performances, Nazimova swept down like a bird of prey onto the more innocent Sara, dazzling her with her appearance in a peacock gown. "I saw a brilliant actress in the making on the stage tonight," she told Sara.

By that weekend, Sara was living with Nazimova at the Garden of Alla. The movie queen was known for seducing young women. Some of her earlier involvements had included sexual and emotional flings with Natacha Rombova, wife of Rudolph Valentino, and Dolly Wilde, the niece of Oscar Wilde, described as "the only Wilde who likes women."

Nazimova arranged a screen test at MGM for Sara, which she directed herself. Although at the time, she still had considerable influence, no director found Sara worth even a minor role in any of their silent films.

Through Nazimova, Sara met her first "beau," Franklin Pangborn, a member of Nazimova's stage company. The effeminate actor would enjoy a long career in films, becoming known for his droopy puss and his "hands on his hips" style of acting, indicating his disapproval of the antics being played out before him. Critics called him "the screen's most effete fussbudget."

There couldn't have been much of a romance between Sara and Pangborn, as he was known as one of Hollywood's most stately homos. Nazimova disapproved of the relationship. "What do you want with that mincer? My more masculine actors go to his dressing room for fellatio."

By modern standards, Pangborn is hailed as "a gay stereotype of the 1930s." Over the years, Sara occasionally encountered him in Hollywood. The actor lived in Laguna Beach with his devoted mother and his partner, Gavin Gordon.

As the years went by, Sara would have a number of discreet affairs with women, although she confined most of her adulterous relationships to men.

Nazimova liked to dominate her young *protégées,* and Sara was a very self-determined woman with an independent streak.

When an offer arrived to star opposite James Kirkwood, Sr. on Broadway for a repeat of the role she had played in *The Fool,* Sara told Nazimova good-bye and took the train East.

Kirkwood had made his film debut in 1909, and was both a director and an actor, playing leads for D.W. Griffith and later directing Mary Pickford, who also became his lover. Before his death in 1963, he would be involved with more than two hundred films, either as an actor or as a director.

[Ironically, Kirkwood Srs.' son, James Kirkwood, Jr., would one day write a novel, *There Must Be a Pony,* in which Elizabeth would star, in 1986, for Columbia TV, opposite Robert Wagner, her former lover.]

Critics labeled *The Fool* as "religious buncombe" and even attacked the audiences who went to see it. "Their favorite tune is *Onward, Christian Soldiers,*" wrote one columnist. In time, however, five million devout believers would attend performances of *The Fool.*

The play became so successful that it was taken to London, opening in September of 1924 at the Apollo Theatre, starring Henry Ainley, the lover of a very young Laurence Olivier. Sara retained her role as the crippled girl. The critic for *The Times* attacked it as a "religious orgy."

On Sara's free night, she went to see "the toast of London," Miss Tallulah Bankhead, starring with Nigel Bruce and C. Aubrey Smith in *The Creaking Chair.* The noted playwright, Emlyn Williams, said of Tallulah's voice, "It is a timbre steeped as deep in sex as the human voice can go without drowning." Sara came backstage to congratulate Tallulah on her performance, and they were seen an hour later driving out of town together in Tallulah's new emerald-green and cream-colored Talbot Coupe, heading to a country house in Surrey that C. Aubrey Smith allowed Tallulah to use for sexual trysts.

Sara arrived at the theater the following night "a little worse for wear."

Ironically, Sara's future daughter, Elizabeth, would take over roles previously performed on Broadway by her mother's lover, Tallulah.

Later in life, when Francis Taylor met Tallulah, the outspoken Alabama belle said to him, "I've had your wife. You're next!"

During her London stay, although Sara did not build up the massive lesbian cabal of fans that Tallulah did, numerous female admirers awaited outside the theater door for a glimpse of her every night.

As the playwright, Channing Pollock said, "These baritone babes were clamoring for bits of Sara's frock or locks of her hair as souvenirs."

When *The Fool* closed in London, Sara went back to New York, where her career wound down as she appeared in one flop after another. In the late summer of 1925, she starred on Broadway as Colette in *The Dagger,* a play which critic Alexander Woollcott defined as "childish rubbish."

Meanwhile, Pollock had written a new play called *The Enemy,* and Sara desperately wanted to play the lead. But Pollock preferred Fay Bainter instead.

Sara sent him what Pollock later called "the most vulgar, venomous, and vicious letter in the history of the theater." Perhaps daughter Elizabeth inherited her famous potty mouth from her mother.

In October of 1925, Sara appeared in a featherweight musical called *Arabesque.* Bela Lugosi was ridiculously cast as a lecherous sheik, for which he was laughed off the stage. But in 1931, he made a marvelous film comeback as *Dracula.*

Three days before Christmas of 1925, Sara opened in *Fool's Bells,* which ran for five nights. It was a fantasy in which she played a character trying to bring solace to a hunchback, evocative of Charles Laughton in *The Hunchback of Notre-Dame.* Unwilling to abandon her hopes of working as an actress, she made two more attempts at stardom, opening on February 22, 1926 in *Mama Loves Papa,* a matrimonial farce that was ridiculed in the press. Her final stage appearance was in August of 1926 when she starred in a pallid comedy called *The Little Spitfire.* It sputtered out at Broadway's Cort Theater.

By then, Sara had decided that she wanted to play another role—that of the wife of a successful man. Nearing thirty, she went with her roommate, Leatrice Loyale, to El Morocco, a nightclub where wealthy clients pursued showgirls.

In the club, she was seated two tables away from a handsome man about her own age and an older, distinguished-looking gentleman who appeared to be his patron, possibly his lover. She studied the younger man's face carefully, as it looked familiar. She finally concluded that it was Francis Taylor, whom she'd known back in Arkansas City.

Tugging at her roommate's sleeve, she said, "The night is young, but I'm getting older every minute. Let's go over to that table and say hello to these guys. I know the younger one. He doesn't know it yet, but I'm going to marry him."

***

Francis Lenn Taylor, who may have been the father of Elizabeth, was born in Springfield, Illinois on December 18, 1897, the son of Francis Marion Taylor and Elizabeth Mary Rosemond. Later, his parents moved to Arkansas City, Kansas. To earn a living, the senior Francis became what was known at the time as "a commercial gent" (i.e., a traveling salesman). Eventually, he left the road to settle down in Arkansas City, where he opened a lucrative private express mail messenger service.

Young Francis inherited the good looks of his tall, rugged father, who had a bloodline that was both Scottish and Irish. Unlike his more outgoing father, the son was shy and introverted.

In school, many girls found him very good-looking and tried to strike up a conversation with him. He was polite but definitely not interested. Any free time he had was spent with football hero Randolph Parrafin, whom he affectionately called "Randy." Three years older than Francis, Randy had almost a devoted slave in Francis, who spent whatever money he had on presents for the football athlete. On many days, Randy ate both his own packed lunch and part of Francis' paper-bagged lunch as well.

One summer, Randy took Francis for a six-week camping trip through the Ozarks. But for his senior year, he dumped Francis and took up with the school's beauty queen, Marcia Rothermere. Randy had no more time for Francis. After he was graduated from school, the older boy married Marcia and moved with her to Kansas City.

Sara, a year older than Francis, befriended him. Romance didn't seem a factor. Sara seemed to console Francis, as each of them plotted various ways to get the hell out of this bleak Kansas landscape. Each of them dreamed of life in Hollywood or New York.

Sara was the first to leave, abandoning Francis, who felt lonelier than ever. But he was rescued by the arrival of his uncle, Howard Young. Uncle Howard was a rich art collector, who had married Mabel Rosemond, the younger sister of Francis' mother.

Howard had made a small fortune from his lucrative business of retouching and tinting family photographs and selling them in gold-colored oval frames. With the profits, he'd invested in the booming oil well business of Texas and Oklahoma.

Newly rich, he'd opened an art gallery in St. Louis, specializing in Old Masters from Europe, which he sold to the *nouveaux riches* of the Middle West. For some reason, Howard took to Francis, virtually adopting the sixteen-year-old. "He became like the son I never had," Howard said. "When you looked into the sparkling blue eyes of his, the day was yours. He was a handsome and charming boy, but he knew nothing of art. I talked to him about art for hours at a time, and he absorbed everything I said like a sponge."

Before Howard ended his family visit, he'd convinced Francis to drop out of school and go to St. Louis with him as his secretary.

Francis' parents were jealous that Howard had taken their son from them, but his mother said, "Howard can give you all the advantages in life we can't."

The father was more cynical. "There's something about your brother…well, something unnatural," he said to his wife. "I can't put my finger on it."

"Don't be a silly old goose." Elizabeth Mary responded. "Howard was always artistic."

Francis learned how to run an art gallery so quickly that Howard invited him to come and live with him in New York, and help him operate the Howard Young Art Gallery at 620 Fifth Avenue.

As an art dealer, Francis was an immediate success. Many of his older women clients preferred to be waited on by him, and he was often presented to their eligible daughters, but he showed no interest,.

Howard objected to the nights when Francis would disappear into the taverns of Greenwich Village, often not arriving back home until nearly dawn.

Francis admired his uncle and listened to stories of how he'd come out of Ohio, arriving in New York without a penny. By the time he was eighteen, he'd accumulated half a million dollars, which was a fabulous fortune in those days. Eventually, he found himself in the position of selling Old Master paintings to the Ford and Fisher families of Detroit.

At the time of Howard's death in 1972, he left an estate of $20 million, none of which went to Elizabeth. He claimed that his movie star relative already knew how to make her own money.

When he wasn't working, Francis lived in luxury, visiting his uncle's vacation homes in Westport, Connecticut, and in Minocqua, Wisconsin. In winter, he made frequent visits to Howard's mansion on Star Island, Florida. Various young men from New York also accompanied him on his vacation trips. On one trip to Florida, Francis met one of Howard's closest friends, Dwight D. Eisenhower.

Back in New York, Howard told Francis that he wanted to expand his galleries and was negotiating for a location in the exclusive Mayfair district of London. He wanted Francis to manage it, but only if he'd break from running around with a "rough gang of boys from the Village" and take a wife, presumably as a means of settling into marital bliss. "As the director of a major gallery in Mayfair, you must look very respectable to the rich Brits who are investing thousands of dollars in a piece of art," Howard advised.

That night, Howard invited Francis to El Morocco to celebrate. With the challenge of a marriage in front of him, Francis was dressed immaculately for the occasion, sporting a pair of horn-rimmed glasses and a well-tailored suit in midnight blue with gray pin stripes.

When Sara and her friend, Leatrice, came over, Francis, of course, remembered her from their days together in Arkansas City. Both Sara and Francis had changed and matured.

At first, after learning that she was an actress, Howard objected to Sara, even though she told him that she was giving up the theater.

Sara and Francis resumed the friendly intimacy they'd enjoyed as teenagers, and began to date each other after their reunion at El Morocco. He took her to the theater, to art exhibitions, and for long walks in Central Park. The pressure to marry was strong for Francis, who talked it over with Sara. In fairness to her, he warned her that it might be a marriage based on love and respect, but she was told not to expect passion—"Perhaps sex every three months or so." Attracted to the idea of the good life he held out for her, and having no other career options, she eventually accepted his proposal of marriage.

They were married at the Fifth Avenue Presbyterian Church, with Howard standing in as best man. The date was October 23, 1926.

After a brief honeymoon, the couple moved into a Manhattan apartment Howard rented for them at 55 West 55th Street.

Sara was dazzled to learn that Howard was going to finance a three-year honeymoon for them. With the understanding that the newlyweds would be based in London, Howard would orchestrate, and pay for, an extended tour of the capitals of Europe, including Budapest, Paris, Rome, Vienna, Berlin, Florence, and Venice. They were instructed to purchase Old Master paintings, with the understanding that they'd be shipped back to New York, where Howard would peddle them to wealthy art collectors at inflated prices.

Sara by now had informed Francis that within the confines of their marriage, she would be the boss. When she became angry with him, she reminded him that she could have been a great star had she not abandoned the theater to marry him.

During their long, drawn-out honeymoon, Sara spent many a night alone in her hotel suite, as Francis sampled the night life of various capitals, often in the company of handsome young men.

On one occasion, Howard joined the newlyweds in Paris. His nephew was candid in his confession, telling his uncle that he was experiencing sexual difficulties with Sara. "I find men exciting, but I am not excited by the female body, except when it is depicted in art. We do go to bed on occasion, but it is not something I look forward to."

One of their sexual unions was fruitful, however. When Sara and Francis settled more permanently in London, she announced that she was pregnant.

After settling into an unsuitable residence, Sara found her dream house on the edge of Hampstead Heath. She recorded in her diary that in the yard, "the tulips were almost three feet high, with forget-me-nots, yellow and lavender violas, flaming snapdragons, rich red wallflowers, and a formal rose garden terraced down to the Heath."

Francis Lenn Taylor later in life. He had been described as having "a leonine head, lake-blue eyes, and thick dark lashes that spoke of adventure in faraway lands."

Their first child, a startlingly beautiful boy, was born in 1929. They named him Howard in honor of their patron, Howard Young.

At 35 Old Bond Street, Francis had immediate success with his art gallery, often catering to rich American tourists visiting London. Among less important work, he was selling paintings by Constable, Reynolds, and Gainsborough.

One slow, rainy afternoon, a handsome, gregarious bachelor, politician, sportsman, and art collector came into Francis' gallery. He seemed to exude charm.

"Mr. Taylor, I presume," he said in a cultured, aristocratic British accent. "I am Victor Cazalet. I collect art." He paused, studying Francis carefully. "And other things that amuse me."

Victor Cazalet
A Member of Parliament

and his sister,
Thelma Cazalet-Keir

***

Those who believe in love at first sight can point to Francis Taylor and Victor Cazalet to prove their case. Victor admired the paintings in Francis' gallery so much he purchased three valuable ones that afternoon. Victor's political enemies also spread the rumor that he purchased Francis, too.

After Francis closed the gallery, he had drinks with Victor at The Dorchester, followed by a lavish dinner at a private supper club in Mayfair. Francis called Sara, telling her that he wouldn't be home that night, as he was spending it with a very important new client.

At Victor's flat the following morning, his butler served his boss and Francis breakfast. Francis was attired in one of Victor's satin robes. Apparently, the conservative Member of Parliament and the art dealer found in each other what each of them had been searching for for such a long time. From that morning forth, until World War II drove them apart, Victor and Francis became almost inseparable.

That night the two new lovers dined with Sara in Mayfair, Victor finding her a total delight. He obviously was pleased at how accepting she was of his newly formed relationship with her husband. Victor had a small bisexual streak in him, and soon he was bedding both Francis and Sara, but not at the same time. Most of his nights were spent in the arms of her husband.

"My brother practically adopted Sara and Francis, and they were seen everywhere together," claimed Victor's sister, Thelma Cazalet-Keir, who was also a Member of Parliament, one of the first women to occupy such a position. Advanced in thinking and outlook for a woman of her time, Thelma was understanding about her brother's need for love, either from Francis or Sara. She never disapproved of his friendship with the Taylors, and often spoke of it to family and friends. It is because of her that future Elizabeth Taylor fans have an insight into what was going on before her birth.

Victor introduced both Sara and Francis into the closed door world of *tout* London, as they met financiers, politicians, the literati, theatrical stars, and the ruling class of lords and ladies. "My brother took Francis everywhere—and sometimes Sara was included," Thelma said. "They visited great country houses of Victor's friends. Francis—and Sara, too—got to see a slice of Britain that would more or less disappear when World War II came. Victor lavished presents on Francis, even giving him a red Buick when you didn't see any red vehicles on the road, except for fire trucks.

Victor stook only five feet three and since childhood had been nicknamed "Teenie." Even though short of stature, he was a towering figure in Britain, numbering Winston Churchill and Anthony Eden among his closest friends, and Queen Victoria herself as his godmother. When Elizabeth was born, Churchill, at least on one occasion, bounced her on his knee. When she met Eden, she would invite him to ride her favorite horse. The horse objected, tossing the famous British leader into a rose bush.

One morning, Victor invited Francis to a junk shop along Kings Road in Chelsea. It was one of those occasions that happens about as often as the average person wins Lotto.

With his keen eye for art, Francis spotted a portrait of a man which appealed to him. Victor purchased it for him for five pounds.

The next week, Francis called in three experts who examined the picture, *Portrait of a Man,* and defined it as having been painted by Frans Hals the Elder (c. 1580-1666), a Dutch Golden Age painter who is best known today for his portraits.

The valuable painting, years later, was owned by Francis' daughter, Elizabeth Taylor, who was advised by art experts to value it at $2.3 million. *Portrait of a Man* became the cor-

Portrait of a Man
by Frans Hals the Elder

nerstone of her personal collection of world-class masterpieces.

Victor was a close friend of Dame Rebecca West (1892-1983), who was defined by one writer as "the greatest woman since Elizabeth I." During her youth, West was a fiery suffragette and socialist, and, as she matured, she became one of the foremost publicly famous intellectuals of the 20th Century.

When Victor invited Francis to spend an afternoon with Dame Rebecca, she later said, "Francis was one of the handsomest men I'd ever met—a leonine head, lake-blue eyes, and thick dark lashes that spoke of adventure in faraway lands."

In the late 1930s, Victor took Francis and their newly born daughter, Elizabeth, to spend an afternoon in the country with Dame Rebecca. Elizabeth always remembered meeting this formidable woman. In later life, after Elizabeth had become a public advocate in the struggle against AIDS, she said, "Dame Rebecca was a kind of role model for me. I decided that before I died, I wanted to be known for something other than collecting diamonds."

Victor became so enamored of Francis, and of Sara as well, that he presented them with a country home, Little Swallows, which was a fourteen-room, 16th-Century gatekeeper's lodge located on his 3,000-acre country estate, Great Swifts, near Cranbrook, Kent. The home had been named after the birds that lived outside young Elizabeth's bedroom window. Locals referred to it as a haunted house, and it was immortalized in the Jeffry Farnols novel, *The Broad Highway*.

When Howard Young flew to London and learned about Francis' close relationship with Victor, he invited both young men to go with him on an art-buying spree in Paris. Howard joined them on wild nights on the town, as they patronized such clubs as *L'Elephant Blanc, Scheherazade*, and *Monseigneur.*

"Those two couldn't hold their firewater," Howard later revealed to his close friends in New York. "They kissed and held hands. They giggled and nibbled ears. They even danced together. Their behavior was acceptable for Paris, but, as I warned them, such antics surely would not be tolerated in Britain, where Victor was a leading member of the Conservative Parliament. What would Winston Churchill say?"

During a visit to Little Swallows, the distinguished art critic, Charles R. Stephens, said, "Victor and Francis were very, very close. One would start a sentence and the other would finish it. It was all too apparent that these two men were in love, but in the art world of London, I was accustomed to such liaisons."

Allen T. Knots, who worked at the time as an editor at Simon & Schuster in New York, visited Little Swallows as a house guest. "In the middle of the night, I got up to use the bathroom. Out in the hallway, I saw both Victor and Francis chasing after each other. Each of them was totally drunk and jaybird naked. Victor and Francis occupied the master bedroom, and Sara slept in an adjoining room." This was revealed by Knots to Robert Rhodes James, Victor's biographer.

Often, Victor was away on some political event. When he was not in London, Francis was seen with a tall, handsome, blonde-haired twenty-year-old, Marshall Baldridge, who worked as his assistant in Francis' art gallery. Francis was about twenty-five years older than Baldridge

During the late 1930s, Dame Rebecca said, "Victor was a man of great charm, but as an intellect, he was definitely a featherweight. He could be incredibly naïve." She cited his strong support of General Francisco Franco and his Fascists during the Spanish Civil War.

In Rome, Cazalet said, "I'm very impressed with Benito Mussolini. The government of Italy is a one-man show, and law, order, and prosperity reign supreme today." In 1937, he visited a concentration camp in Bavaria, and later cited it for being "quite well run with no undue misery or discomfort. The prisoners seemed quite content."

But after that, just before the outbreak of World War II, Cazalet, along with Winston Churchill, opposed the appeasement of Adolf Hitler by Britain's Prime Minister Neville Chamberlain. Victor also became the leading exponent in England for the promotion of a Jewish homeland in Palestine. He was most sympathetic to the plight of the Jews throughout history. He wrote, "If I were a Jew, I would cling onto the idea of a sovereign state for all I was worth."

Often, Victor and Francis preferred to spend weekends in London, with Sara and their son, Howard, stashed in Kent. The two men attended concerts together and often saw plays in the West End.

On one occasion, they met a handsome and charismatic young actor, Laurence Olivier, and became intimate friends with him. A bisexual, Olivier often spent nights with Francis and Victor in their London flat. Olivier's envious chief rival, John Gielgud, spread stories about how the three young men were involved in a *ménage à trois*.

When he heard these rumors, Victor denounced Gielgud as "a silly old queen. He's no doubt jealous that he's not included."

During the summer of 1931, Sara prepared a special dinner for Victor and Francis in London at the home near Hampstead Heath. She had an announcement to make.

At the end of the dinner, when the men sat in the library enjoying their brandy, she came in to tell her secret. "I visited the doctor today. We are going to have an addition to our family. Surely no little infant in all the world could be blessed to have two such wonderful fathers."

top photo: **Baby Elizabeth, Sara,** and brother **Howard**
bottom photo: **Baby Elizabeth** with a guardian.

CHAPTER TWO
The Girl With the Violet Eyes

Sara Taylor completely distorted her version of Elizabeth's birth when she wrote an article for *McCall's* in 1954. "As the precious bundle was placed in my arms, my heart stood still. There, inside the cashmere shawl, was the *funniest* looking baby I had ever seen! Her hair was long and black. Her ears were covered with a thick black fuzz and inlaid into the sides of her head. Her nose looked like a tip-tilted button, and her tiny face was so tightly closed it looked as if it would never unfold."

Sara also declared that Elizabeth went ten days before opening her eyes. "That's poppycock," claimed Thelma Cazalet-Keir, Victor's sister, who had been appointed as the child's godmother. "I visited the day after the birth. Her eyes were not only wide open, they were as blue as a summer day."

In time, the child would become celebrated for her violet eyes.

After leaving the Taylor home, Thelma reported back to the Cazalet family. "That is definitely Victor's child. I think she should be named Elizabeth Taylor-Cazalet."

The little girl was born with a genetic mutation—distichiasis, *aka* a double set of eyelashes. Child actor Roddy McDowall would later recall that during the making of *Lassie Come Home* (1943), the director called out, "Get that girl off the set—she has too much eye makeup on, too much mascara."

Back in the makeup department, it was ascertained that Elizabeth was wearing no mascara at all. "That double set of eyelashes was the real thing," Roddy said.

Elizabeth also had a localized form of hypertrichosis, which in the cases of most babies with the condition disappears after they're three months old. However, in Elizabeth's case, this chromosomal abnormality would sometimes re-occur, especially on her arms, and she'd have to have excess hair removed by electrolysis. One morning, her then-husband, Richard Burton, said he woke up in the dark and reached for his wife. "Bloody hell, I thought I'd gone to bed drunk with a fucking monkey."

The excess hair on Baby Elizabeth's body soon faded away, and she began to be viewed as a very beautiful young girl, except for her big head. When she was old enough to form an opinion of herself, she said, "What a podge! A big head set on a dumpy body." And although her adult face would be universally applauded, her body often drew mixed reviews.

Her birth in 1932 was registered in the very unfashionable blue collar district of Hendon, bordering chic Hampstead. Years later, Elizabeth would claim that she had been born in Hampstead, although her future husband, Richard Burton, would remind her, "Ducky, you were just a low-rent girl from Hendon."

As she grew older, her brother Howard called her "Lizzie the Lizard." From then onward, she always hated to be called "Liz." All of her friends knew to refer to her as "Elizabeth." She was furious in 1995 when C. David Heymann published a thick (and well-respected) biography of her and entitled it *Liz*.

An art patron, Philip Beaver, purchased two valuable paintings from Francis at his Mayfair gallery and was invited back to Golders Green for dinner. He recalled the night. "I saw them socially, and both Sara and Francis looked unhappy. Francis drank a lot. I don't think he wanted to be a family man. He spent most of the evening talking about Victor Cazalet. There was a story making the rounds of Mayfair that Francis had once been arrested in a gents' toilet for inappropriate behavior. Their son, Howard, was a classic beauty. I was shown Elizabeth in her cradle. She was a strange little thing, with lashes so long they'd have looked more appropriate on a Soho tart. She still had her baby hair and a thick downy pelt. Who would have thought that such a little creature would grow into one of the world's most glamorous women?"

As each passing year went by, Elizabeth grew into the dark-haired beauty that she was to become. Victor doted on her, buying her expensive presents. In many way, he seemed more like a father to her than Francis.

When Elizabeth turned three years old, she came down with her most serious illness to date, a harbinger of many afflictions that would haunt her for the rest of her life.

Hearing that she'd been running a fever of 103°, and how desperately ill she was, Victor drove through "buckets of rain" for ninety miles to reach her side. He stayed with her, often sleeping with her in his arms and doctoring her himself, until her fever broke. According to his biographer, Robert Rhodes James, after three weeks by her side, ignoring his commitments, both business and political, he finally left. But he formed a bond with her that would last forever, even beyond his death.

With money provided by both Victor and Howard Young, now back in New York, the Taylor family lived an upperclass life, with a full-time chauffeur, three maids, a private chef, and a nanny. Victor and Francis made frequent commuter flights to Paris, where they bought fashionable frocks "for our little daughter."

When Elizabeth was old enough, Victor bought her her first horse, which she named "Betty." She rode it around his 3,000-acre estate. Later, she would claim that, "My greatest happiness as a child was riding Betty through the woodlands of Kent."

"I had the best of both worlds," Elizabeth later said. "The lovely countryside of Kent and that beautiful home in London where I would wander through the Heath every afternoon."

In a touch of irony, the Hampstead house where Francis and Sara lived had previously been owned by Augustus John, the Welsh painter who before World War I was known as the leading exponent of post-Impressionism in Britain.

In London, his work was compared to that of both Matisse and Gauguin. A great deal of his fame rested on his style of portraiture, which was both imaginative and extravagant. By the 1920s, he'd become Britain's leading portrait painter, interpreting subjects who included T.E. Lawrence (the famous Lawrence of Arabia), Tallulah Bankhead, George Bernard Shaw, and Thomas Hardy.

When Augustus John moved out of his Hampstead house for other digs, he'd abandoned several of his paintings, leaving them still hanging on the walls. Francis seized them as his property and shipped them to New York, where Howard Young sold them at exorbitant prices.

Acclaimed English portraitist **Augustus John** (*right figure, above*) with the then-toast of London, **Tallulah Bankhead,** and his portrait of her

Francis and Victor often visited John, who had a habit of not finishing and discarding paintings that displeased him. Several times, Francis discreetly rescued them from the garbage and quietly sent them to New York where they, too, brought high prices. Francis, in fact, is interpreted today as the dealer who was most instrumental in making John famous among consumers and critics in America.

In spite of Francis' exploitation of John, the two men became friends. Francis was astonished at

John's "insatiable sexual appetite," as the artist himself defined his condition. "My appetite has destroyed the women who love me best," John told Victor and Francis. As art critic Brian Sewell said, "He was driven to draw the women whom he bedded, and bed the women whom he drew."

Many of John's drawings were of beautiful nudes. Introduced to Elizabeth when she was six years old, he asked Sara and Francis if he could paint her. Both of them were overjoyed, and so was Victor. However, when Sara learned that Elizabeth would have to pose in the nude, she objected.

Years later, in Hollywood, Elizabeth would express her deep regret. "I should have posed bare ass for Augustus. My God, that painting today would be worth millions."

When she came of age, Elizabeth attended school at Byron House, which was known for being "snobbish and strict" and reserved for children of only the finest families. She rebelled at the green cotton smock she was forced to wear like the rest of the girls. "I don't ever want to dress like the rest," she told her teachers. "When I grow up, I will wear only clothes designed just for me."

Elizabeth also studied dance at the Vacani Dance School on Brompton Road, run by Pauline Vacani and her daughter, Betty. Years later, in Hollywood, Elizabeth claimed that she attended school with the Princesses Elizabeth and Margaret Rose. But that wasn't quite true. For the royal sisters, a private instructor was sent to teach dance to the girls at Buckingham Palace. Betty denied

The **Duchess of York** (Elizabeth Bowes-Lyon, later Queen Elizabeth, the Queen Mother) in 1935 with her daughters, **Elizabeth** and **Margaret Rose**

that Elizabeth ever studied ballet at the school, as she'd later tell interviewers. "We didn't teach ballet to girls that young. Elizabeth learned dance routines such as tap, polka, and such social dancing as the waltz."

Members of the royal family did, however, attend an end-of-semester recital. The Duchess of York (later to become Queen Elizabeth, wife of George VI) attended, bringing the royal daughters, Elizabeth and Margaret Rose. After her presentation, Elizabeth (Taylor), dressed as a butterfly, remained on the stage by herself, curtsying and taking bows until the stage manager was forced to draw the curtain. Sara later recalled the incident. "I had given birth to a ham."

Before she left England for America, Elizabeth did meet Margaret Rose on two other occasions when they were very young. "She gave me my first ciga-rette—called a fag—to smoke. I smoked it, or rather choked on it, and we talked about boys. Margaret and I were very advanced for our age, and we were think-ing about the opposite sex when most girls our age were still nursing their dolls."

Sara noticed this early interest in boys. "Elizabeth was maturing too fast."

Francis told both Victor and Sara, as well as Thelma, that there was no cause for alarm. "Haven't you heard of childhood sexuality? Five-year-old kids can show an interest in sex. If you don't believe me, go sign up for a session with Anna Freud. She practices in London and is said to be an ex-pert on child sexuality."

Elizabeth and Margaret Rose would meet again officially on several more occasions.

In addition to introducing Francis and Sara to leading members of English society and pol-itics, Victor also introduced them to prominent Americans living in London. In 1939, none was more famous than Joseph P. Kennedy, U.S. Am-bassador to the Court of St. James's.

At one point, Victor had suggested to Am-bassador Kennedy that he should have his por-trait painted by Augustus John. Victor invited Rose Kennedy and the Ambassador for a visit at Francis' Mayfair art gallery, knowing that he could make the arrangements for such a portrait.

A deal was never struck, but Fran-cis bonded with the Ambassador and Mrs. Kennedy. The expatriate Ameri-cans got along so well that the ambas-sador invited Sara, Francis, and Victor to a lavish party at the American Em-bassy on Grosvenor Square in Mayfair.

This was reciprocated by an invi-tation from Victor for the Kennedy family to spend a Sunday at his sprawl-ing estate in Kent. It was on this occa-sion that a seven-year-old Elizabeth Taylor met the handsome and charis-matic John F. Kennedy, who was

Top photo: Young **JFK** in 1937, and *(bottom photo)* the future Ambassador to the Court of Saint James's, **Joseph Patrick Kennedy** ("Papa Joe") and his wife, **Rose Fitzgerald Kennedy**, in 1938

twenty-two years old at the time.

Elizabeth would often discuss that afternoon with her friends in Hollywood. "I thought Jack was handsome, tall, rich, and on the prowl. For the first time, I cursed myself for being so young. When he flashed that smile at me, I melted."

JFK and the young Elizabeth went horseback riding together. "I knew he wanted to be spending his Sunday with an older and more beautiful girl, but he was very gracious to me, although I could see that the look in his glazed eyes was far away."

Elizabeth later said that before the day ended, "I became very bold. Before we got back to Victor's home for dinner, I said something that must have amused him to no end. I told him that when I grew up, and that would be sooner, not later, I planned to marry him. When he looked at me with a most doubtful expression, I told him 'Even if you've not the kind of man who wants to get married, I plan to make you my boyfriend.'"

"You mean, you and me...lovers?" he asked.

"That's right. "You and me."

In spite of her young years, Elizabeth turned out to be clairvoyant.

Two views of **Baby Elizabeth**:
left photo: Intuitively preparing for *National Velvet*, and
right photo: a class portrait from 1937. Five-year-old **Elizabeth** is the fourth figure from the left.

CHAPTER THREE
Elizabeth's Imaginary Parents:
SCARLETT AND RHETT

When the British government, in the spring of 1939, began passing out gas masks to Londoners, Sara Taylor decided it was time for Francis to evacuate Elizabeth and Howard to the relative safety of "Fortress America." Even Ambassador Joseph P. Kennedy at London's American Embassy advised them to leave as soon as Francis could close down his affairs.

Francis could not stand the thought of being torn away from Victor Cazalet, but his British lover demanded that he go. Victor's close friend, Winston Churchill, had told them, "Hitler will not be appeased even if we offered him Southeast England. He'd then demand all the British Isles." Francis agreed to send Sara and his children back to the U.S., but told Victor that he wanted to stay with him in London during the upcoming war, which Victor was convinced could break out at any minute.

Victor and Francis were at London's Victoria Station to escort Sara, Howard, and Elizabeth off on the first stage of their departure aboard the *SS Manhattan,* scheduled for an eight-day crossing to the port of New York. Elizabeth always remembered her last Sunday in London, as Victor held her hand, showing her the trenches being dug around Hyde Park.

Aboard the vessel, Elizabeth, her mother, and her brother were made painfully aware of the oncoming war. Most of their fellow passengers were Jews fleeing the Nazis

Baby Elizabeth with her older brother, **Howard**

21

in Austria and Germany. Elizabeth heard much talk of Hitler's takeover of the hopelessly outmaneuvered Czechoslovakia.

Before her departure from London, Elizabeth had cut out a picture from *The Times* showing three smiling faces—the Joseph P. Kennedys, Sr. and Jr. and the dashing John F. Kennedy. She took her mother's scissors and cut away the ambassador and his oldest son. She then attached the picture of young JFK to her cabin wall.

Noticing this unprecedented interest, Sara penned a letter back to Francis in London. Before the ship reached New York, she'd write him a total of eight letters, each posted upon the ship's arrival in the New World.

In one of them, Sara wrote, "Elizabeth is not only showing an interest in boys, but in young men such as that divine Jack Kennedy, the ambassador's son. What happened on that horseback ride they took? At Elizabeth's age, I was not interested in boys, but in my new doll, or in my new dress. I fear we can expect the announcement of an early marriage for our only daughter. As for Howard, he is so beautiful, I have to keep a constant watch on him to protect him from some of the passengers, who appear to me to be pedophiles."

For Elizabeth, a life-changing event occurred as the *SS Manhattan* sailed across the watery North Atlantic grave of the *Titanic*. As part of their onboard entertainment, the passengers were shown a film, *The Little Princess* (1939), starring Shirley Temple, then one of the world's leading box office sensations. It was the story of a motherless daughter placed in an exclusive girls' school while her father goes off to fight the Boers. After his death, the money for her school is cut off, and she is relegated to the role of a servant.

Throughout the film, seven-year-old Elizabeth sat mesmerized, watching Temple. Over breakfast the next morning, Elizabeth announced to Sara, "When

Diva rage from a seven-year-old: **Shirley Temple** as *The Little Princess*

we get to Hollywood, I plan to become a child star. I would be so much better than that goody-goody, curly haired, chubby-cheeked lollipop sucker. She just cries out, 'I'm adorable…Don't you think so too?' She makes me sick at my stomach. I read in a movie magazine that she's four years older than me. That means she'll soon be too old to play the part of a five-year-old. Someone's going to replace her. You're looking at her—namely, me. I'll give the little tart one thing, though. Her legs are better than mine."

Apparently, Sara was shocked at such talk from one so young—and by such determination and ambition.

***

Arriving in glamorous pre-war New York, Elizabeth was enthralled. No one seemed to be worried about war clouds looming over Europe.

After four days, the Taylors traveled by train to California.

Sara had faced a choice of living in California or New York, and she'd already had the experience of living in both states. Her happier and better days had been spent in Los Angeles, where she'd enjoyed her greatest success as an actress. She still associated Broadway with her series of theatrical flops. Publicly, she said that she wanted to be close to her family, who had moved to California. But there was apparently another reason, a secret she may have kept to herself. She wanted to help her strong-willed daughter in rising to the rank of a child star.

Once there, they were driven to a chicken farm owned by Sara's father in San Gabriel. Neither Sara not Elizabeth could tolerate the place, both of them longing for the excitement of urban life. "After we left," Elizabeth recalled, "I swore I'd never look at another egg as long as I lived."

Sara's father drove Elizabeth and Sara in a pickup truck to Los Angeles, where they found a temporary house rental for $75 a month. Elizabeth later jokingly recalled to her friends, "I made a grand entrance into Hollywood smelling like chicken shit."

Sara was later accused of becoming a stage mother from hell, pushing her daughter into a film career. Sara denied that. "Later on, that might have been true, but in the beginning, my daughter was determined to become the next child star, replacing Shirley Temple. It was her idea. She turned on the charm with anybody who might help her. I wrote Francis that our daughter was seven years old going on thirty."

Francis eventually managed to tear himself away from Victor and their life together in London and departed to join his family in California. Reunited at last, Francis opened a branch of his increasingly well-known art gallery at the Château Élysée in Hollywood, but soon moved it to the dramatically more upscale Beverly Hills Hotel, on its the lower level, with easy access to the hotel's outdoor swimming pool. Art lovers Vincent Price and Edward G. Robinson were among his early patrons.

Elizabeth settled into a daily routine: After finishing classes at The Willard School, a private day school near Pasadena, Elizabeth was driven to the gallery, where she studied her lessons, hoping to spot movie stars out by the pool. She remembered that James Mason was the first film star she spotted. He was a bit tipsy when she went up to him. "You're very beautiful," he told her. "Come back in ten years, and I'll make mad, passionate love to you."

23

The talk in Hollywood at the time involved the filming that had recently begun on *Gone With the Wind*. The novel the movie was based on was a best-seller by Atlanta's Margaret Mitchell.

After the producer, David O. Selznick, evaluated such stars as Ronald Colman, Errol Flynn, Gary Cooper, Basil Rathbone, and (unbelievably) Humphrey Bogart, he'd settled on a reluctant Clark Gable for the male lead of Rhett Butler.

Selznick's search for the film's heroine, Scarlett O'Hara, had ignited a nationwide talent hunt. Many of the contenders were already established stars, and included an aging Tallulah Bankhead, Miriam Hopkins, Paulette Goddard, Joan Crawford, Katharine Hepburn, Joan Bennett, Joan Fontaine, Susan Hayward, and (unbelievably) Lucille Ball.

Finally, Selznick discovered "my Scarlett," in the person of a relative newcomer to U.S. audiences, Vivien Leigh, a British beauty and a lover of Laurence Olivier, who was also in Hollywood at the time, preparing for his signature role in *Wuthering Heights*. Elizabeth had previously encountered Olivier in London, where he had often been intimately associated with Victor and Francis.

Gone with the Wind
and the role Baby Elizabeth didn't get:

Two views of Victoria Regina Butler ("Bonnie Blue") as played by Elizabeth's rival, **Cammie King.**
Top photo: With **Clark Gable** and *bottom*, with a disinterested **Vivien Leigh**

In her (very vanilla) memoirs, published in 1964 under the title of *Elizabeth Taylor by Elizabeth Taylor,* she said, "I would be out with my mother shopping, and people would come up and say, 'Your daughter looks *so* much like Vivien Leigh! Go to Selznick's studio and have her tested for Vivien Leigh's daughter.' Of course, each time, I was thrilled."

Elizabeth learned that the role of Victoria Eugenia, also known as "Bonnie Blue," the daughter of Rhett and Scarlett, had not yet been cast. When she learned that the role involved riding a pony, she said, "The part is mine. I know how to ride. MGM won't have to give me riding lessons."

Elizabeth was encouraged and, to some degree, sponsored in her bid for the role by three famous Hollywood players—Vivien Leigh,

24

Greta Garbo, and gossip maven Hedda Hopper.

Knowing how much his daughter wanted the role, Francis telephoned Olivier, his former lover, and invited him to visit, with Vivien, the Taylor family at their home in Beverly Hills.

Although they arrived an hour late, "Larry and Viv" dazzled seven-year-old Elizabeth. Years later, she would often recall meeting this romantic couple. "Each one, both Larry and Vivien, was more beautiful than the other. I couldn't decide. Right there and then, I wanted to grow up to look just like Vivien."

Over drinks, Vivien told Elizabeth's parents, "Your daughter is stunningly beautiful. If I had a daughter, I would want her to look just like Elizabeth. I'm going to beg David Selznick and George Cukor to cast her as Bonnie Blue."

Olivier had brought along a script that laid out the young character's part. Elizabeth might have been disappointed at how small the role was, but she thanked Olivier and Vivien profusely and said she'd await word about whether MGM would grant her a screen test.

Elizabeth was told that within the context of the film, Rhett Butler would kiss Bonnie more frequently than he'd kiss Scarlett. "I know what I'm going to do," Elizabeth told Sara. "When Clark Gable leans over to kiss me good night, I'm going to grab his cheeks and give him a sloppy one. I know the director will cut it out of the picture, but for the rest of my life, I can claim that I got my first screen kiss from Clark Gable himself. I hope his mustache doesn't scratch me."

Nothing ever came of Vivien's offer, and Elizabeth harbored a grudge against her for the rest of her life.

Many years later, Elizabeth felt a sense of triumph when she was called in to replace an emotionally unstable Vivien Leigh in *Elephant Walk*, most of which had already been filmed in Ceylon (Sri Lanka) before Vivien had a complete mental breakdown. Released to theaters in 1954, the film still depicted Vivien in its long shots, with all of the close-ups rather awkwardly completed, months later, by Elizabeth.

A few days after her inaugural meeting with Vivien at her parents' home, Elizabeth was in her father's gallery when Greta Garbo walked in to evaluate the kind of art Francis was selling.

Noticing Elizabeth, Garbo turned to Francis and said, "What a divine child you have. She is far too beautiful for the movies."

Greta Garbo *(photo above)* to young Elizabeth: "You're the only girl in Hollywood I would even consider."

Hearing that, Elizabeth approached Garbo. "Oh, ma'am. My father took me to see you and Robert Taylor in *Camille*. You are the most beautiful woman in the world."

"How very kind, in spite of your misjudgment," Garbo responded.

"If you ever make a movie that calls for your daughter, let me play her," Elizabeth pleaded.

"You're the only girl in Hollywood I would even consider," Garbo said. "But I think, at the moment, you'd be ideal cast as Vivien Leigh's daughter in *Gone With the Wind*. Tomorrow morning I will call Louis B. Mayer and recommend you."

"Oh, thank you, *thank you*," Elizabeth said, kissing her hand.

"What lovely manners," Garbo said to Francis. "Your daughter must have grown up in Europe."

Elizabeth never knew whether Garbo recommended her or not. At the time, Garbo was filming *Ninotchka* (1930), with one final movie to go, the disastrous *Two-Faced Woman* released in 1941 as her farewell to the screen. Neither of these movies contained a suitable role for Elizabeth.

Elizabeth would encounter Garbo again. In 1958, shortly after the death of Mike Todd, Elizabeth's third husband, the widow was receiving mourners in the den of her home. Suddenly, Garbo appeared before her. She placed a gentle hand on the new widow's. Into her ear, she whispered, "Be brave!" before disappearing.

The columnist, Hedda Hopper, remained young Elizabeth's last chance for the role of Bonnie Blue. Hopper was a friend of Victor Cazalet and his sister, Thelma Cazalet-Keir.

Hopper was already throwing business toward Francis, having herself purchased one of Augustus John's study of gypsy heads. She introduced him to Douglas Fairbanks, Jr., Nelson Eddy, and David O. Selznick, who purchased a drawing by John for $150, for which Francis had paid nothing. E l i z a b e t h was sick that day and had not attended school, nor had she been at the art gallery at the day's end. "It was one of the disappointments of my life that I was not at the gallery the day Selznick arrived."

Nonetheless, Hopper suggested in her column that Elizabeth was a dead ringer for the role of Scarlett O'Hara's daughter, adding, "although she has never acted professionally." But as events unfolded, the dream of transforming Elizabeth into a juvenile replacement for singing star Deanna Durbin and/or Shirley Temple backfired, at least temporarily.

Sara had maneuvered Hopper into inviting Elizabeth to her home for an audition in her drawing room.

In a memoir, Hopper later evaluated the audition like this: "The young girl, her face clouded with worry and tears about to fall, sang a sweet song, 'The

Blue Danube,' in a weak and thin voice. As she sang, she nervously fingered her hair and stared into space. It was one of the most painful ordeals I have ever witnessed. Finally, I told Sara to let the child be a child, and not try to force her into the movies."

Despite that pronouncement, Hopper would later take credit for "discovering Elizabeth Taylor."

With money coming in from the gallery, and still subsidized to some degree by Howard back in New York, Francis eventually moved his family from Pasadena to the more fashionable community of Pacific Palisades, where their neighbors included Norma Shearer, the former queen of MGM, and Darryl F. Zanuck. In Elizabeth's dancing classes, she made friends with Judy and Barbara Goetz, the grandchildren of Louis B. Mayer, who would soon become her boss.

In Sara's words, Elizabeth ended up with a broken heart when Selznick and George Cukor cast four-year-old Cammie King in the small but pivotal role of Bonnie Blue.

In 1944, five years after the elaborate 1939 release of *Gone With the Wind,* Cammie's mother brought her daughter for a visit with her movie star friend Irene Dunne during the filming of *The White Cliffs of Dover.* Alongside Dunne, Elizabeth Taylor was appearing in that movie with Roddy McDowall.

Cammie recalled, years later, "When I met Elizabeth, I realized what a rude and ill-mannered girl she was. She looked me straight in the eye and told me, 'I could have played Bonnie Blue so much better than an ugly, gawky thing like you.' Then she turned and walked away."

In the mid-1990s, in a glut of regional nostalgia, the 60-something-year old Cammie King was signing autographs, dressed in an antebellum hoop skirt in the parking lot of a supermarket in the town of Washington, Georgia. There, the author of this book asked her about Elizabeth Taylor coveting her iconic role of Bonnie Blue. Cammie responded, "Even as a young girl, Elizabeth Taylor was far too brazen to play an innocent girl like Bonnie

THREE HOLLYWOOD PLAYERS:
A ferociously ambitious stage mother **(Sara**; *left figure above*);
Baby Elizabeth groomed and camera-ready; and
(right figure) the infamously egomaniacal gossip columnist and
former B-rated actress, **Hedda Hopper.**

Blue. She was much more at home cast as a whore in *Butterfield 8.* Esther Williams, not Elizabeth Taylor, was my screen idol."

Ironically, in 1957, MGM tried to replicate the box office bonanza associated with *Gone With the Wind* with the release of the big-budget Civil War epic, *Raintree County,* starring Elizabeth and Montgomery Clift. For her efforts, Elizabeth won an Oscar nomination as Best Actress, but *Raintree County,* beset with troubles throughout its filming, never approached the pathos and popular appeal of *Gone With the Wind.*

Despite her loss of a role in *Gone With the Wind*, Elizabeth continued to follow, with deep interest, the career of Clark Gable, and reciprocally, he saw most of her pictures, including *National Velvet.* To the press, he later defined her role as "The best ever performance given by a juvenile."

By the late 1940s, Elizabeth was voicing violent objections to anyone daring to call her "a juvenile." She wanted to play adult roles opposite MGM's leading males. She desperately wanted to escape that awkward period that Shirley Temple had endured between playing pre-teen girls and becoming an adult.

Louis B. Mayer became aware of how Elizabeth had filled out, and how she appeared on screen as an actress far more mature than her actual age. An audacious idea was proposed: Elizabeth would appear on screen opposite Clark Gable as his love interest in an upcoming picture. But Mayer needed to be convinced, and he persuaded Gable to appear in a screen test to see how the unlikely pair would emote.

Later, after Mayer viewed the results of that test, he referred to it as "grotesque," and ordered all copies of it burned.

That screen test, however, lay in Elizabeth's future as a late teenager. Back with her parents in Hollywood during World War II, she became a fast-rising child star, graduating not only from young girl roles but from Hollywood boys to Hollywood men.

It would be an arduous journey.

CHAPTER FOUR
Mother's Little Dividend
INVADES HOLLYWOOD

Film critic Barry Monush accurately described the decades-long film career of Elizabeth Taylor like this: "For the most part, she was merely competent, sometimes inadequate, and now and then above average, with occasional instances where she rose most brilliantly to become something special."

But how did it all begin?

Elizabeth made her first appearance on the screen in a highly forgettable B-list comedy, *There's One Born Every Minute,* released by Universal Pictures in 1942. From such a box office disaster, one of the most publicized movie careers of all time was launched.

Before signing with Universal, she'd toured the studios at MGM, comparing it to a garden party with "happy child actors running and playing." She wanted an association with the top-tier MGM instead of with some second-rate studio turning out B-list comedy/horror films like Abbott and Costello's *Hold That Ghost* (1941), which she'd recently seen. Sara, however, had warned her, "Sometimes, movie stars don't have a choice of studios, but take what is offered, including pictures they don't want to make."

Elizabeth's career got a jump start when Andrea Cowden—the wife of J. Cheever Cowden, CEO of Universal Studios—made a happenstance visit to the Howard Young Gallery in Beverly Hills, where she met Francis. Through Francis, she purchased $20,000 worth of Augustus John sketches and paintings, some of which Francis had stolen from the trash can of the Welsh painter.

On the wall of the gallery, Sara had affixed a photo of her daughter next to a photographic portrait of Vivien Leigh. Andrea commented on the similarities of their features. That casual remark catalyzed an invitation from Sara to the

Cowdens for tea at the Taylor home in Beverly Hills. "Tea" turned out to be filet of beef Wellington with caviar, followed by a fresh raspberry parfait.

Dressed in frilly clothing, Elizabeth was brought out after dinner. Sara had spent most of the day grooming her. J. Cheever Cowden seemed stunned, pronouncing her "the most beautiful girl I've ever seen."

Francis later recalled, "Cowden put his money where his mouth was." On April 21, 1941, he signed Elizabeth to a five-month contract at Universal, with a salary of one-hundred dollars per week.

In the project that evolved out of all this, *There's One Born Every Minute* (1942), Elizabeth appeared briefly onscreen with the film's star, Carl ("Alfalfa")

Switzer, a refugee from the *Our Gang* comedies. In the 1970s, decades later, on television's *The David Frost Show*, Elizabeth claimed that in her screen debut, "I played a beastly child who runs around slinging rubber bands at fat ladies' bottoms."

Known for his specialty of singing off-key, Switzer ("Alfalfa") was dark haired, freckle faced, and known for his foul mouth. He taught Elizabeth "every curse word I'd need until the end of my days." Perhaps Alfalfa should be blamed for the origins of her soon-to-be-infamous potty mouth.

Alfalfa was the first to experience what became known in Hollywood as "the Liz Taylor curse." In the years ahead, many of her co-stars would die prematurely. Of course, Elizabeth had nothing to do with these early deaths, including those of Montgomery Clift and James Dean. Even so, gossips labeled her as "The Black Widow." Hedda Hopper once wrote, probably with bitchery, "The best way to die before your time is to get cast in a Liz Taylor picture."

Years after his career had peaked, on the night of January 21,

Top photo, inset: **Carl Switzer ("Alfalfa")** "He taught me every curse word I'd need."

Lower photo: **Baby Elizabeth**, aged ten, in *There's One Born Every Minute*

1959, the forty-year-old Switzer went to the Mission Hills, California, home of Moses ("Bud") Stiltz as part of an effort to collect a $50 reward that Stiltz owed him for retrieving his lost dog. Both men had been drinking, and the encounter ended in a single gunshot wound. Switzer ("Alfalfa") was fatally wounded as a bullet desecrated his genitals.

In the enquiries and trials that followed, Stiltz was absolved of all charges, claiming he'd killed the actor in self-defense.

Dan Kelly, the casting director at Universal, sat through Elizabeth's film debut. He reported back to his bosses, "Her eyes are old, and she just doesn't have the face of a kid. In fact, she has nothing at all. Give me Margaret O'Brien any time." On Kelly's recommendation, Universal did not renew Elizabeth's contract after the inaugural five months.

***

The Taylor household was a sad and gloomy place during the early 1940s. After the U.S. officially entered World War II in December of 1941, affluent patrons no longer invested heavily in art. The Taylors hoped that their daughter's acting career might recoup some of their much-needed income.

At this point, Howard Young, Francis' uncle and patron, no long contributed to their welfare, although he did offer a twenty percent commission on any art work Francis sold within his gallery. Otherwise, he did not send checks, perhaps figuring it was time for the Taylors to survive on their own merits.

The mood brightened when Victor Cazalet announced that the British government had instructed him, as part of a secret mission, to visit New York and California during the late spring of 1943. Francis flew from Los Angeles to New York to be on hand to greet Victor. The two men booked a suite at Manhattan's Waldorf Astoria Hotel, where neither of them emerged for the first twenty-four hours.

After concluding his business in Manhattan, Victor accompanied Francis to Los Angeles, where Sara met them at the airport with hugs and kisses. Victor was taken to their new home in Beverly Hills, where he moved into a bedroom with Francis. Sara had her own bedroom.

Casting director at Universal, about Baby Elizabeth: "Give me Margaret O'Brien any day."

Above: **Margaret O'Brien**

Elizabeth's "Daddy" was as loving as ever to "my precious daughter" when she arrived home from school. Victor seemed delighted when Sara falsely told him that Elizabeth had signed a lucrative seven-year contract with Universal. "She also has a spectacular film coming out." Elizabeth's picture with Alfalfa had not yet been released.

When Francis wasn't monopolizing Victor, Elizabeth doted on him, hugging and kissing him and sitting on his lap. Francis had recently tended to be cold and distant to her, sometimes slapping her when he got drunk. Victor was just the opposite, showering affection on her. He'd just arrived from war-torn London, but still, he had brought her some of her favorite sweets, purchased at Fortnum & Mason's before his departure.

During his days in Los Angeles, Francis drove Victor around for various speaking engagements where he reported on the progress of the war.

Victor's speeches, based partly on his standing as a godson of Queen Victoria, drew A-list audiences, members of which included English-born Greer Garson, who was at the time the virtual Queen of MGM, as well as Mary Pickford, Basil Rathbone, and Robert Montgomery.

During their evenings together, Victor urged all of the Taylors to return to London when the war ended, assuring them that victory was almost certain, even though at that time in 1943, the war was going badly for the Allies.

Victor assured Elizabeth that the British film industry would undergo a great renaissance after the war ended. "You'll be an even bigger star in England than you would here in this horrible town dedicated to glitz and glamour."

Elizabeth would always remember Victor's tearful farewell. "Father just clung to him like he'd never see him again. I felt sorry for him that day and in the days to come. I knew how much he loved Victor. He never shared that love with Sara or me, but gave it all to Victor." Even though she was only nine years old, Elizabeth was a very perceptive child. She told Sara that "Victor and Francis are stuck together like glue."

That was not said with any disdain. From an early age, Elizabeth seemed very accepting of homosexuality, although she surely knew little about the inner workings of such relationships. She'd later say, "Love of one's fellow man is too precious a gift to be outlawed in any way."

Her knowledge of heterosexuality was also extremely limited during those days as well, although that was about to change.

A few short weeks after Victor's return to a war-torn Europe, the Taylors were notified of

Victor Cazalet
(left figure in foreground)
on May 24, 1943, six weeks before his death, receiving Polish government documents from **Stanislaw Grabski** *(right)*, an outspoken opponent of the Nazis and a key figure in Poland's government-in-exile.

his death. On the foggy morning of July 12, 1943, his Liberator bomber, returning from a trip to the Middle East en route to London, stopped for refueling at Gibraltar. The plane crashed almost immediately after takeoff, going down in the harbor. On board was General Wladyslaw Sikorski, the Prime Minister of Poland in exile. Victor was functioning at the time as his aide. Charges of the plane's sabotage were never proven, although speculation was rampant.

Victor's death made headlines in London's *Daily Mail,* with journalist Ward Price writing that Victor "was one of the gayest and most versatile figures in public life."

Throughout the rest of her life, Elizabeth maintained her contacts with members of the Cazalet family. Victor's niece, Sheran Cazalet, asserted, "Elizabeth always arrives dressed in black in honor of Victor's long-ago death. No plunging *décolletage*—she knows I don't allow that."

No one missed Victor more than Francis. After Victor's death, he retreated to his blackened-out bedroom, surviving mainly on whiskey and an occasional cup of broth. Both Elizabeth and Sara could hear his cries of anguish at night. On two occasions, Sara had to summon doctors when he threatened suicide. After Francis emerged from his dank cell, he was colder and more distant than ever. He would never allow the mention of Victor's name within earshot.

To Sara, Francis seemed a lost cause. She turned all her energy toward the promotion of Elizabeth's stalled career, inviting any possible contact she'd made with members of the film industry to their home in Beverly Hills, into which they'd moved after a brief period in Pacific Palisades. The Mediterranean-style villa would be Elizabeth's final residence before she left home to marry Nicky Hilton.

Francis Taylor
with four-year-old **Baby Elizabeth** in 1936
on the sands at Brighton

While Sara worked behind the scenes to promote Elizabeth's career, she, along with her brother Howard, attended Hawthorn Elementary School, a short distance from her house. Fellow classmates mocked the British accents of both brother and sister.

Elizabeth's agent, who believed in her as "yet-untapped talent," was none other than Myron Selznick, the brother of David O. Selznick, who had rejected Elizabeth as a candidate for the role of Bonnie Blue in *Gone With the Wind*.

On her tenth birthday, Elizabeth invited some of her friends to her parents' home, where Sara had purchased a large birthday cake. As Elizabeth blew out the candles, she said, "Here I am, only ten years old, and already washed up in the fucking movies."

Sara seemed (or pretended to be) shocked at the use of Elizabeth's language. But she'd have to get used to it. One of the film industry's most unrepentant potty mouths was coming into bloom.

Every morning over breakfast, before Elizabeth went off to school, Sara told her, "You're going to be a movie star. Any day now, we're going to meet the right man who will award you a contract. You're growing more beautiful every day. Someone in Hollywood is going to take note, someone, somebody, some day."

Sara spoke the truth to her ten-year-old daughter. Her stardom at MGM, a studio that had previously rejected her, was growing brighter and more visible. It came about through a chance encounter.

Samuel Marx, a producer at MGM, lived on the same street in Beverly Hills as the Taylors. At night, he was an air-raid warden supervising government-mandated blackouts which were regularly enforced in an era when an air attacks from Japan were envisioned and feared. Francis also volunteered for duty, and he and Marx often talked about Francis' daughter, Elizabeth.

One night, Marx told Francis that he'd had to fire a young Maria Flynn, who had previously appeared with Ingrid Bergman in *Intermezzo (*1939*)*. Flynn had, prior to her dismissal, been scheduled for a role in a movie, at the time under production, called *Lassie Come Home*. As it happened, the role of Priscilla, the granddaughter of an English duke (played by Nigel Bruce), was up for grabs.

Describing Flynn, Marx told Francis, "When we filmed a test, she (Flynn) stood a foot taller than our young male lead (Roddy McDowall)," Marx said.

Baby Elizabeth: "I could have done it better as Dorothy."

Photo above: "that horrible"
Judy Garland
from *The Wizard of Oz*

"We can't have that. I've seen your daughter, and she seems right, if she can act. Another thing…The part calls for a British accent. That, Elizabeth has."

Francis hurried home that Friday afternoon and told Sara, who immediately dressed Elizabeth for a visit to MGM. It was nearly 6pm when they arrived for a meeting with the film's then-novice director, Fred Wilcox, but Sara couldn't wait for Monday morning.

On the way to MGM, with Sara piloting a secondhand Chevrolet with a weak battery, Elizabeth kept saying, "Oh Mommy, Mommy, I'm going to be a bigtime movie star. MGM has all the big stars—Clark Gable, Greta Garbo, Katharine Hepburn, Spencer Tracy, and that horrible little girl, Judy Garland, who did such a bad job in *The Wizard of Oz*. I could have done it so much better as Dorothy."

Wilcox always remembered Elizabeth's arrival on a set at MGM. "Her mother had dressed her in a purplish cape, which colored her eyes," he said. "I may have started all this shit about her eyes being violet. She was beautiful, very dramatic, very theatrical. I cast her on the spot. I was doubly lucky when I saw how she bonded with Lassie. She just assumed it was a female dog. But Lassie was a male dog named Pal. The collie became known on the MGM lot as the only star who could play a bitch better than Bette Davis."

"I thought the mother, Sara, was a nanny," Wilcox said. "I'd heard that Sara was once a great beauty, but she looked like the stocky matron type in 1942."

"The collie was getting ninety dollars a week," Wilcox said. "We raised the dog's salary to $250 a week. We signed Elizabeth for $75 a week."

Louis B. Mayer approved of the arrangements, although his early assessment of Elizabeth was dismal. "No dimples like that Shirley Temple twat. No voice like the Judy Garland lez. No voice like the goody-goody Jane Powell, who sings so sweet on radio. And Taylor can't cry on command like Margaret O'Brien. But sign her up anyway. We'll see what the limey little bitch can do."

Lassie and **Roddy McDowall** in
Lassie Come Home (1943)

E.T. and **Lassie** in
The Courage of Lassie (1946)

Rare for a B picture, *Lassie Come Home* was shot in color. Neither Marx nor Wilcox liked the way Elizabeth looked in color. Marx wanted to dye her hair blonde. "In color, her hair photographed as blue-black. She wore too much mascara, or so I thought. Actually, they were her real lashes. I told Sara to pluck them, but she refused. I also wanted to remove that mole on her face. I even wanted to change her name to Virginia Taylor. But Sara and Elizabeth refused all my requests. Finally, I said 'to hell with it. Photograph her the way she is.'"

On the second day of shooting, ten-year-old Elizabeth met another child actor, Roddy McDowall, who, at the age of fourteen, had already been in a hit called *How Green Was My Valley* (1939).

"That god damn collie is going to steal the picture from us," were his first words to her.

The friendship that formed between Elizabeth and Roddy would last a lifetime.

Each of them shared their most private secrets with each other, and as the years went by, those secrets became more scandalous than ever.

"I was enchanted with Elizabeth the moment I saw her," Roddy later recalled. "What a beautiful child, but her head was almost that of a young woman, an incredible sight. I introduced her to fellow cast members Elsa Lanchester and Dame Mae Whitty, two old ball crackers."

Elizabeth told Roddy that, "My mother, Sara, will stop at nothing until I'm a household name. My brother Howard is even more beautiful than I am. At first, Sara tried to promote him as a child star. She and my father, Francis, got into a bitter fight. He accused her of trying to peddle Howard to a producer who is known for molesting children. Howard would have none of it. The Botticelli angel shaved his head bald the day he was to be screen-tested."

Jerry O'Connell, a friend of Roddy's and a journalist for *Show* magazine, later said, "With gay men later in her life, Elizabeth would play a mothering role, but with Roddy, he was the one she could lean on."

Sara allowed Elizabeth to attend weekend parties at Roddy's house, where she would sip lemonade and talk to his friends. They included a young Robert (R.J.) Wagner, her future lover and co-star.

Elizabeth confided to Roddy, "I stopped being a child the moment I started making movies. I became the bread-winner in the family. When Francis got drunk, he batted me around quite a bit, taking care not to ruin my face for the camera, though. I think he was jealous that I was bringing more money into the family than he was."

When not working on the MGM lot, Elizabeth as a budding child star appeared in newspaper and magazine ads promoting Lux Soap, Whitman's Sampler Chocolates, and Luster-Creme Shampoo.

After screening an early version of *Lassie Come Home,* Mayer called Elizabeth into his office, instructing Sara to wait outside. "I sat on his knee," Elizabeth later told Roddy. "His chubby hand traveled north to Alaska."

Roddy was delighted with such sophisticated dialogue from "a child who grew up before her time, as I did."

Mayer signed Elizabeth to a seven-year contract at MGM, with a salary which started at $100 a week and which steadily increased to $750 a week.

"That's just the beginning," Sara told her daughter. Clairvoyantly, she predicted that one day, Elizabeth would be earning a million dollars per picture.

Roddy was among the first to whom Elizabeth would confide her sexual secrets. She told Roddy that

John Derek

36

she'd fallen in love with "the world's most beautiful boy," at school. He was six years older than her. His name was Derek Harris, and he wanted to become an actor, too.

"He's the most gorgeous thing God ever put on this planet," she told Roddy. "One day, we'll be the screen's greatest team of lovers."

One weekend, in desperation, Elizabeth turned to Roddy, who had already told her that he was sexually mature for his age. He'd been having sexual relations with older boys since he'd turned twelve.

"I'm going to lose Derek if I don't start having sex with him—he warned me," she said. "I want so much to hold onto him, but I don't want to have a baby."

"Yes, having a baby at the age of eleven would be a scandal, wouldn't it?"

"You've got to help me," she pleaded. "What am I to do?"

"Don't despair," he told her. "There are ways to keep a guy satisfied without getting pregnant. I'll show you how I satisfy guys. I do certain things to a boy, and they really enjoy it. You can, too."

"Show me what to do," she said. "I'll do anything to hold onto him...anything but *that.*"

"We'll go upstairs to my bedroom, where we can have some privacy," he said. "Believe me, I'm not into doing this with a girl. Just imagine me as a teacher. Better yet, imagine we're two actors rehearsing for a role. After you've learned your lessons, you can invite Derek over, and you guys can slip away to the cabana out back. That way, you can put to use what I'm about to teach you."

"Oh, Roddy, show me...show me," she pleaded. "I'll always be grateful to you."

And so she was.

Myron Selznick, agent and talent scout, recognized E.T.'s talent

Louis B. Mayer, head of MGM, did not

WHEN INGÉNUE DIVAS CLASH
(THE NIGHTMARE OF TRANSITIONING TO ADULTHOOD)

The Crushes and Romantic Sagas of the teenaged Elizabeth seemed to closely parallel those of the adolescent
SHIRLEY TEMPLE.
Was the competition deliberate, and who was the predator?

Starlettes
at War

Four views of **Shirley Temple** with *(clockwise from upper left):* **Ronald Reagan, John Derek,** her philandering husband **John Agar,** and **Clark Gable**
Inset photo: Shirley's nemesis, **Elizabeth Taylor**

CHAPTER FIVE
And They Called It "Puppy Love"
LOLITA DOES HOLLYWOOD

After shooting *Lassie Come Home,* MGM had no immediate film for Elizabeth. To make money on the studio's $100-a-week investment, she was hired out to 20th Century Fox for $150 a week. MGM profited $50 weekly from the exchange. Fox was remaking the Charlotte Brontë classic, *Jane Eyre,* having scheduled it for a 1944 release. An earlier version, starring Virginia Bruce and Colin Clive, had been shot ten years before at (the relatively unfashionable and usually low-budget) Monogram Pictures.

The Fox version of 1944 would star Joan Fontaine as the mature Jane Eyre, with Orson Welles co-starring as Rochester, his part greatly enlarged from that of the original character as envisioned in the novel by Brontë.

Jane Eyre is the Victorian Gothic tale of an orphan girl who grows up to become a governess in a mysterious (and mysteriously tormented) household in an isolated manor house on the moors of northern England. At Fox, it was helmed by Robert Stevenson, an English film writer and director who is best remembered today for the Julie Andrews musical *Mary Poppins* (1964), for which he was nominated for an Oscar as Best Director.

Elizabeth was cast opposite other child stars who included Margaret O'Brien (who played the role of Adele Varens) and Peggy Ann Garner, who was cast as Jane Eyre as a young girl. Elizabeth was not impressed. She surprised Stevenson with her rather adult pronouncements about each of her rivals. Elizabeth referred to Garner as "a blonde wisp of nothing," predicting she'd soon fade from the screen and would end up selling real estate in the San Fernando Valley. A critic had defined O'Brien as "desperately appealing." Elizabeth satirized that assessment: "She's desperate all right. Her phony French accent is ruining the movie."

Because, like many other child actors at the time, she had dropped out of public school as a means of fulfilling her film commitments, Elizabeth was forced to attend MGM's one-room schoolhouse on the studio lot. "I hated it," she later recalled. She also didn't like being bossed around. Even as a twelve-year-old, she referred to Louis B. Mayer as a tyrant. "Everybody was afraid of him. Not me. I defied him and refused to let him push me around. Judy Garland never talked back. She just followed studio orders. They pumped pills into that poor girl to keep her awake or to put her to sleep—and to keep her slim. Judy was an eager, loving person and went along with their plan, which ultimately destroyed her. I wasn't going to let Mayer do that to me."

Elizabeth was cast as Helen Burns, a pre-teen who became a friend of the young Jane Eyre (as played by Garner) in the orphanage. Sara fought with Stevenson to get Elizabeth's part enlarged. He complained to Fox about it, and as a reprimand to Sara, the studio dropped Elizabeth's name from the film's credits. A critic for *The Hollywood Reporter* later interpreted that omission as "regrettable."

Years later, when Elizabeth showed the movie to her children on TV, she painfully ascertained that her role, and all the footage associated with it, had been cut to make way for commercials. Elizabeth's performance was restored in later releases, and many diehard fans still remember her portrayal of the tiny, sickly, orphaned waif.

As writer Gina Barreca put it:

"Elizabeth Taylor was no Helen Burns. It seems as if she did every damn thing she ever wanted to do: Made soap-opera appearances as well as defining the characters of Tennessee Williams so entirely that every actress following her in these roles has had to wrestle with Taylor's portrayals; she married the men she wanted, sometimes several times; she ate what she wanted and had clothes made to fit her rather than trying to fit into some outfit a thirteen-year-old waif who weighed as much as Helen Burns could wear; she was amazing in Butterfield 8, even though the rest of the cast was awful; she made her way, barging through life (even when she wasn't playing Cleopatra) and made the world hers."

Young Elizabeth *(right)* interprets a small role in *Jane Eyre.* **Peggy Anne Garner** *(left)* snagged the bigger role, playing Jane Eyre as a young girl.

In *Jane Eyre,* Elizabeth, as punishment, had her hair cut on screen for the first time, and she portrayed her first deathbed scene.

She would always remember the first day Orson Welles showed up on the set, arriving with his entourage four hours late. Evoking a 16th-century European monarch, he referred to his staff as "my minions."

Elizabeth told Garner, "In a few years, I'll follow Orson's example, arriving on set with my hairdresser, my secretary, my make-up artist, my costume designer, perhaps a paid lover, and most definitely, one of the many husbands I plan to marry. I'll put on a bigger show than Orson."

Welles was introduced to Elizabeth, finding her utterly fascinating. As he'd later recall, "When I read Vladimir Nabokov's *Lolita,* I understood his characterization because of my contact with Elizabeth Taylor as a child. I had never encountered anyone like her. She was unbelievable."

He invited her to sit on his lap, and they chatted pleasantly. When it was

time for her to go, he grabbed her and sloppily kissed her, inserting his tongue into her mouth. As she'd later tell Roddy McDowall. "I've never tasted a man's tongue before." Welles would be the first of many more male tongues she'd taste in her future.

As Elizabeth was leaving, Welles called to her, "Come back and see me in three or four years."

He was sincere about that invitation. After she'd evolved into a "full-busted woman" in Welles' view, after she'd celebrated her fifteenth birthday, he spotted her in the MGM commissary. "I have never found myself attracted to young girls." Perhaps his memory was sketchy. He seemed to have forgotten that he'd first seduced Judy Garland when she was only fifteen, and he'd also seduced a very young starlet who had recently changed her name to Marilyn Monroe.

"Elizabeth Taylor had something that transcended age," Welles claimed. "I will never forget how she moved down the commissary table, holding her food tray. I lusted for that young girl and felt, for the first time in my life, like a dirty old man."

As Elizabeth would later tell Roddy,

Two views of **Orson Welles**
Top photo: in 1938
Lower photo: in 1949

"Orson invited me back to his dressing room that afternoon in 1949. He said he was going to make a new film, and he had a role in it that would be my most important part to date. I guess I knew what he was going to do. I wouldn't call it rape, but he forced himself on me. I didn't enjoy the experience. Actually, he hurt me."

Years later, in 1969, when Elizabeth was dining with Welles at Maxim's in Paris, both of them laughed at that experience of long ago.

"I did to you what I had done to me when I was a teenager," Welles told her. "From my earliest years, I was the Lillie Langtry of the older homosexual set. Everyone wanted me. I'm sorry that film role I held out for you didn't come about. But you must understand: I always seduce actors I plan to work with. I make them fall in love with me."

"You didn't in my case, Big Boy," she told him. "I don't mind a certain exchange of body fluids when a man and woman are making love. But a whole bucket of spit—that's a bit much."

"Rita always liked it," he said. He was referring, of course, to his second wife, screen goddess Rita Hayworth.

He spent the rest of the evening in the *belle époque* setting of Maxim's telling her about his recent adventures. "I just returned from Morocco where I seduced the number one concubine of the Pasha of Marrakesh. Then I stopped off in Rome, where a gypsy taught me how to walk with a chicken between my legs."

***

One snowy night in 1996, at the Palace Hotel in Gstaad, in Switzerland's Bernese Oberland, Elizabeth Taylor was hosting a drunken dinner party that lasted until two o'clock in the morning. She was, as she put it, entertaining "a cabal of European trash."

As the champagne flowed after dessert, she proposed a party game. Each of the guests would describe his or her first sexual experience. "Tell it like it is, good or bad, male or female," she instructed. "I'll be the last. It's the privilege of the host."

Many of the men relayed the details of an early homosexual encounter; three of the women named dear old Dad, and one Austrian countess cited a rape from a German baron.

When it was Elizabeth's turn, she mocked her biographers, who had claimed that she had been a virgin at the time of her wedding to her first husband, Nicky Hilton. "Like hell I was. I was already a regular little Lolita before then. I got broken in by an actor, Derek Harris. You know him as John Derek. I think I was about twelve years old, but John has always been famous for his taste for 'quail.'"

In her informal 1964 memoir entitled *Elizabeth Taylor,* Elizabeth was more delicate: "At school, I had my first crush. There was the most beautiful boy— to me, then, like a god. One day, we were going down the corridor, and he tripped me, then picked me up and said, 'Hi there, beautiful.' Oh, you can't imagine. I was in such ecstasy. I went to the girls' room and just sat there dreaming. His name was Derek Harris. Later, he changed it to John Derek."

At her Gstaad dinner party, she continued her confession:

"The event occurred in a little dressing room Roddy McDowall had beside his pool," Elizabeth said. "All his other guests were in the main house enjoying Roddy's Sunday buffet. John slowly removed my clothes. He marveled at the size of my breasts, which would have put a grown woman to shame. Then he did a striptease for me. My heart was beating practically out of my chest. For the first time, I was confronted with a male penis. Remember, we didn't have porn on TV in those days. I was flabbergasted."

Sipping her champagne and enjoying center stage, she said, "John told me 'if I'd play with it, it would grow.' He didn't lie. It grew and then grew some more. Roddy had sorta warned me what to expect, but that was nothing compared to experiencing the real thing. John was a master teacher. He told me to 'make like it's a lollipop.' In less than fifteen minutes this rock hard toy I had just discovered—the male penis—erupted with all this white sticky stuff. I didn't want to get it all over me, much less taste it. But John could be very commanding. During all the time I knew him back then, we never did it in the missionary position. Another young man would have the honor of deflowering me. Sunday afternoons in Roddy's cabaña became a ritual for Derek and me. I learned how to do it without choking. But, alas, my competition moved in, although I had a hell of a lot more to offer."

Producer David O. Selznick had already locked both Derek and Shirley Temple under contract. He cast them in two of his most popular movies. In *Since You Went Away* (1944), Derek played Temple's boyfriend. The picture was a big hit, starring Claudette Colbert, Jennifer Jones, and Joseph Cotten. Selznick also cast Temple and Derek in his next picture, *I'll Be Seeing You* (1944), starring Ginger Rogers and—once again—Joseph Cotten. Whereas Elizabeth at the time was still a juvenile, she nonetheless coveted both roles, Temple was struggling to move beyond her image as a child star into more mature roles.

Temple, at age sixteen, was four years older than Elizabeth, but Elizabeth was confident that she could summon the reserves to play an older girl. Selznick, motivated perhaps by the fact that he had Temple already "locked down" and under contract at the time, turned Elizabeth down once again, having previously rejected her for the role of the daughter of Rhett Butler and Scarlett O'Hara in *Gone With the Wind.*

I'm growing more beautiful every day," Elizabeth told her parents and studio officials at MGM. "Temple has lost her cuteness. A few years from now, I'll look even more gorgeous, and she'll look like a housewife from Pasadena."

Suddenly, Derek was no longer available for his Sunday afternoon sex trysts with Elizabeth. He hardly saw her anymore. Roddy told her that Selznick had ordained that his two rising stars be seen together in public for publicity purposes, and that Derek was dating Temple both privately and publicly, escorting her to events which included movie premieres.

"Derek has become a male whore, selling it for ten dollars a session," Roddy claimed. "Spencer Tracy is one of his best customers."

At first, Elizabeth seemed shocked. "Don't be a silly goose. Only women are whores. How can a man be a whore? It's impossible."

"Elizabeth, my dear, we have to continue with your sex education," Roddy said.

To Roddy, she admitted that she was heartbroken. "When I turned sixteen, I planned to marry Derek. I didn't count on *Rebecca of Sunnybrook Farm* taking a sail on *The Good Ship Lollipop.* Damn the bitch!"

Sara showed Elizabeth an item in the paper, in which Selznick described how Temple was in the process of entering the second phase of her career. He predicted that as an adult performer, she would exceed her box office success as a child star.

"That's bullshit!" Elizabeth said. "I will grow out of my child star roles and become the biggest box office attraction in the world. I'll become on the screen what Louis B. Mayer likes to call a 'siren.'"

In 1988, when Elizabeth read Temple's memoirs, *Child Star,* she became seriously "pissed off" at what the former 1930s box office champion had written about John Derek.

Temple had referred to him as "a self-important young man who had pleasing features, perhaps a little too sensitive for my taste. With a shock of dark hair cascaded artfully over his forehead and his suit shoulders padded to disguise a rather delicate frame, he made a highly photogenic companion."

"To hell with her," Taylor said about Temple. "I knew every inch of John's body. Take it from your mother. That young man didn't need padding anywhere on his body."

In her memoirs, Temple had other observations to make about Derek, dismissing his acting and comparing it to "a wooden post." She did admit to engaging in necking with Derek, but claimed that she soon grew weary of it. "I was not courageous enough to enter into a sexual liaison."

Derek continued to function as Temple's escort, however. She recalled that on her fifteenth birthday, he took her to lunch at the expensive Rue Restaurant.

"But when the bill arrived, he excused himself to go to the men's room." According to Temple, Derek inaccurately asserted that he was the illegitimate son of Greta Garbo, but Temple knew differently. His mother was Dolores Johnson, a minor actress married to Lawson Harris, a songwriter.

As Temple relayed in *Child Star*, Derek would occasionally use a dangerous-looking knife to furiously stab the air, supposedly aiming it at invisible enemies. Years later, in a summation of her relationship with Derek, Temple claimed, "Not every girl gets to neck with a knife-wielding bastard."

Despite her rejection of him, Derek really didn't want to give up on Temple. She recalled that he once pursued her when she went on a family vacation to Palm Springs. "He was like a stalker, spending the night in a sleeping bag in the desert near where I stayed. He was lurking around possessively to see who I was dating."

Actually, it was Derek's presentation of two oil paintings—one offered to Elizabeth, another to Temple—that ended both relationships. Temple recalled that her oil painting was "a macabre gift—a bluish face entwined in a surrealistic background of green seaweed. In his mystical, watery depiction, Mother instantly saw a symbolic likeness between the disembodied face and mine. She forbade me to see John again."

Watching as the competition burns and sinks:

(photo above)
Shirley Temple
in 1944,
at age 16, before retiring
completely
from films in 1950 at the
age of 22

Elizabeth was given an even more ghoulish painting. Her severed head was floating underwater in a bed of slimy seaweed, the victim of a flesh-eating octopus who was devouring what was left of her nude corpse. When Sara discovered the picture hanging in Elizabeth's bedroom, she ripped it from the wall and burned it.

"I don't want my daughter dating such a sick young man," Sara told Elizabeth and Francis. "He looks like such a clean-cut young man, but I fear he's really a psycho."

Derek's parents also became alarmed at their son's "dark side," and sent him to a psychiatrist. Reportedly, the analyst determined that Derek harbored a secret desire for sex with very young girls—definitely underage—and that he suffered from a distinct sense of sexual confusion, based perhaps on his pastime of renting his body to older homosexual men.

Although Temple dropped Derek, Elizabeth furtively continued her encounters with the handsome young actor during the next two years. It was "a sometimes thing," Roddy said. "They often saw each other at my house and never went out in public together. She kept it a secret from Sara, who seemed terrified of Derek."

Years later, Derek would surface once again in Elizabeth's life during the late 1950s. Having lost his allure as a matinee idol, he wanted to reactivate a fading career. He approached Elizabeth, asking her to use her clout to get him cast as the second male lead in *Butterfield 8*.

She recalled spending a night with him. "After all those years, we finally got around to doing it in the baby-making way," she told Roddy. "He screwed the hell out of me, and I loved it. I wanted to keep him on for an occasional roll in the hay, but he got really pissed off at me when I recommended Eddie Fisher for the role he wanted in *Butterfield 8*. My loss."

For the rest of his life, Elizabeth followed Derek's career, including his marriages to Ursula Andress and Linda Evans. He entered another phase of his career when he met a sixteen-year-old, Mary Cathleen Collins, whom he later married and renamed Bo Derek. She achieved fame in Blake Edwards' film *10*. During the course of his respective marriages, Derek photographed all three of his wives for their appearances in Hugh Hefner's *Playboy*.

As a mature woman, at one of Roddy's drunken parties, Elizabeth laughed about her relationship with Derek. "He didn't mind sharing the charms of his young wives with a wolf pack of horny males. But I'll always be grateful to him for teaching me how to suck cock."

***

In the mid-1940s, Elizabeth appeared briefly in *White Cliffs of Dover* (1944), the story of an American, Susan Dunn, a role played by Irene Dunne, still a big star at the time, who headed a cast that included such formidable talent as Dame May Whitty and Gladys Cooper. Dunne (as Susan) visits England, falls in love with and marries Sir John Ashwood, played by Alan Marshal, "the poor man's Ronald Colman." World War I breaks out and, pregnant, she loses her husband, and shortly thereafter gives birth to a son (played by Peter Lawford). During World War II, her son is wounded at Dieppe. As American troops march victoriously through London, her son slips into a coma and dies. Directed by Clarence Brown, it was definitely a weeper.

Elizabeth had only two scenes in this tribute to British heroism in wartime, most of them played opposite Roddy McDowall. He played Susan and Sir John's son as a young boy. In the movie, Roddy falls in love with Betty Kenney (Elizabeth), the daughter of tenant farmers on the Ashwood estate.

During the filming, even at this early age, Elizabeth developed a crush on Peter Lawford, a romantic complication which would gnaw at her throughout most of the 1940s, especially when Lawford began an eight-month affair with

Lana Turner. Elizabeth told Roddy, "He looks handsome in his pictures, but he's much prettier in real life."

"I'm warning you," Roddy said to her, masking jealousy with a smile. "Keep your hands off him, bitch. He's mine!"

"All yours and Lana Turner's," she said.

Lawford was the latest of Turner's many lovers. They included or had included Robert Taylor, Clark Gable, Victor Mature, Tony Martin, Howard Hughes, Buddy Rich, and Frank Sinatra, as well as two future U.S. presidents, John F. Kennedy and Ronald Reagan. At nineteen, she'd married bandleader Artie Shaw and filed for divorce four months later. With her latest husband, Steve Crane, Turner had given birth to a daughter, Cheryl. Having husbands, however, never stopped this *femme fatale* from enjoying affairs on the side.

Lawford, a bisexual, was also having an affair with Roddy, but during the course of the filming, he also began a long-enduring affair with Tom Drake, a wholesome-looking "boy next door" type who played a dying American soldier in *The White Cliffs of Dover*.

The entire cast, especially Clarence Brown and his co-producer, Sidney Franklin, gossiped at lunch about the many young love affairs blossoming around the set. Irene Dunne and Alan Marshal were also keen observers of the mini-dramas. Elizabeth usually remained silent, but eagerly absorbed whatever was indiscreetly revealed in her presence.

The gossip, especially its gay variations, particularly intrigued another actor, Van Johnson, who played a minor role in *The White Cliffs of Dover*. Before the shoot was over, he, too, managed to attract the sexual and romantic attentions of Lawford.

British-born Jill Esmond, playing a minor character, Rosamund, in the film, had recently been dumped by her husband, Laurence Olivier, in favor of Vivien Leigh. One day, at lunch, she told Elizabeth and Dunne, "My advice to established actresses or to aspiring ones is to never marry an actor. It's bad for your health."

When Elizabeth heard that Clarence Brown's next project involved directing *National Velvet,* she diverted her attention away from Lawford to focus on him directly. Enid Bagnold's novel, *National Velvet,* originally written in 1935, had been kicked around MGM for years.

The story's theme celebrates the capacity of ordinary people, especially women, to accomplish great things. Set in the 1920s, it's the story of a 12-year-old English girl named Velvet Brown, who rides her horse to victory in the Grand National Steeplechase. Velvet, in the novel, at least, is a high-strung, nervous child who passes credit for her eventual victory on to the horse she famously rides through various obstacles both on the racecourse and off. At one time, *National Velvet* was viewed as a possible vehicle for thirty-year-old Katharine Hepburn, who would, it was believed, convincingly portray a twelve-year-old.

Margaret Sullavan was also considered for the role, as was Vivien Leigh. Finally, MGM settled on Elizabeth's nemesis, Shirley Temple, but Darryl F. Zanuck at Fox wouldn't release his money-maker from her contract.

Elizabeth read Bagnold's novel five times, telling Brown, "I was born to play Velvet Brown. I've been riding horses since I was four years old. And I've spoken with a British accent most of my life."

When Valentine's Day came, according to Brown, Elizabeth sent him a "mushy" card. "The little Jezebel pubescent was practically making herself available to me in case I harbored secret desires as a child molester. Of course, I knew what the card meant: It meant she wanted me to star her in *National Velvet.*"

To her horror, Elizabeth was shown an item in *Variety* which asserted that Pandro S. Berman, the producer of *National Velvet,* was going to order a nationwide talent search for a young girl to play the title role. He predicted that the search would be as big as that of the national hunt conducted in the late 1930s for an actress to play Scarlett O'Hara in *Gone With the Wind.*

The perky young Elizabeth swung immediately into action, demanding that Sara drive her to MGM. When she got there, she instructed her mother to remain outside as she barged into Berman's office without an appointment. "What's this shit about a nationwide search to find some snotty-nosed kid to play Velvet? You're looking at Velvet right now."

As Berman would later tell Brown and Louis B. Mayer, "The force and power in that voice—and the language she used—was like no eleven-year-old girl I knew. I suspect that Elizabeth Taylor is a midget disguised as a young girl."

Berman told her she was wrong for the part. "You're too small for the role, much too short. Maybe if you could grow three more inches in height…And I'm afraid I have

Studio executive **Pandro Berman** *(top photo)* gets bothered by a Hollywood Lolita

lower photo: Horsing Around with *Velvet*
left to right: **Jackie Jenkins, Elizabeth Taylor,** and **Mickey Rooney**

to bring up a delicate point. During the steeplechase, Velvet is disguised as a boy, but the audience has to know she's really a girl. How shall I put this diplomatically? We need to cast a girl with some semblance of tits on her."

"I couldn't believe what happened next," Berman told Brown. "That young girl standing before me ripped open her white blouse. She wasn't wearing a training bra, and she flashed her bosom in front of me. Jane Russell in *The Outlaw* had bigger breasts, but this little vixen had a small pair of world class knockers on her at her age. I'm a tit man myself, and I know women's breasts. I'd guess a size B cup."

"But it's what she said that floored me," Berman claimed.

"I've got the boobs, you fucker, and I'm going to star as Velvet Brown."

"'And so you are,' I told her," Berman said.

The next day, MGM announced that Elizabeth Taylor had been granted her first starring role as Velvet Brown in the upcoming motion picture, *National Velvet.*

The beginning of one of Hollywood's most enduring legends was birthed that day.

Velvet Goes National
Elizabeth Taylor with **Mickey Rooney**

John Derek in 1956:
"Thank Heaven for Little Girls"

Hollywood News of 1944!!
Starring with the Stars in *White Cliffs of Dover!*
The eleven-year-old Anglo-American *ingénue*
ELIZABETH TAYLOR

Irene Dunne

Alan Marshal

White Cliffs: "The sentimental tale of one woman's unwavering courage in the face of two world wars."

Dame May Whitty

Gladys Cooper

Elizabeth Taylor exchanging secrets with **Roddy McDowall**

CHAPTER SIX
How Hollywood's Last Superstar Made HER DEBUT

There is a moment within her 1944 film, *National Velvet,* when Elizabeth Taylor, playing Velvet Brown, and disguised as a male jockey, faints after learning she has won the legendary Grand Steeplechase in an English racing event attended by the Queen.

Summoned to the scene, a doctor unbuttons her racing silks. With no hint of the irony of the famous cleavage to come, he pronounces to bystanders, "It's a girl!"

The story may be apocryphal, but pint-sized Mickey Rooney, her co-star, was said to ask, "Where did a little girl like you grow boobs?"

"They didn't grow on trees," was Elizabeth's sharp response.

Rooney could hardly have been impressed with Elizabeth's boobs-in-the-making. He'd just emerged heartbroken from a marriage with the sultry MGM beauty, Ava Gardner. To a journalist on the *Hollywood Reporter,* he'd rhapsodized over Ava's breasts. "She had these big brown nipples which, when aroused, stood out like some double long golden California raisins."

To fill out for her role, Elizabeth had put herself through a hard regime, using "fast-grow creams" and performing rigorous daily exercises. She was aided not so much by Sara, but by Liz Whitney, who was married to the industrialist and socialite, Jock Whitney, known for seducing some of the most famous women of the 20th century, including Tallulah Bankhead.

"I was like a surrogate aunt to the eleven-year-old," Liz Whitney said. "In Hollywood, we were called 'Big Liz' and "Little Liz.' To play the role of Velvet, Elizabeth desperately wanted to increase her bust size more than she worried about her horse-riding scenes. In addition to a truckload of cosmetic creams, she ate huge meals. She also read avidly from the dozen or so books I gave her on chest development."

In her 1987 memoir, *Elizabeth Takes Off,* the star recalled those heavy breakfasts she used to eat at Tipps Restaurant in Los Angeles: Two fried eggs, hamburger patties, hash-brown potatoes, and a stack of silver-dollar pancakes covered with maple syrup. And I *never* put on an ounce."

In the three months that preceded the actual filming of *National Velvet,* which began shooting in February of 1944, Elizabeth claimed she grew three inches and put on ten pounds of weight, which contradicted her claim of not adding an ounce.

"I willed myself to grow into the part."

When shooting began, she found that Clarence Brown once again had been assigned to direct her.

Brown had been personally selected by Louis B. Mayer. Previously, Brown had guided Greta Garbo through seven of her films. Of Elizabeth, he said, "There's something behind her eyes you can't quite fathom. Something Garbo had."

Sara and Elizabeth tangled with Brown during the first week of the shoot when he demanded that she cut her beautiful long hair. Both mother and daughter refused, but Brown insisted.

In desperation, they turned to Hollywood's best-known hairdresser, Sidney Guilaroff, who would later loom large in the life of Marilyn Monroe. Author Ellis Amburn called Guilaroff "the crotchety, queenly, Metro makeover genie, who'd given Garbo, Greer Garson, Joan Crawford, and Norma Shearer their distinctive looks while serving as their father-confessor."

Guilaroff saved the day by concocting a perfect wig that matched Elizabeth's hair color. He was able to fit it tightly over her scalp. When she showed up on the set, Brown gave her his hearty approval and continued with the picture. He learned the truth when she appeared at the wrap party with her hair down to her shoulders. He knew, of course, that she didn't grow that long hair overnight, and that he'd been tricked by a clever hair stylist. "Are the boobs fake, too?" he asked her.

"That's all me," she told him. "Feel them if you don't believe me."

"A brazen little thing," Brown said. "At times this twelve-year-old sounded like a tart on Times Square."

Rooney, twenty-three at the time he met Elizabeth, was the former box office champion at MGM, known especially for his Andy Hardy series. In spite of her age, Rooney was rumored to have begun an affair with Elizabeth.

This appears not to be true. If Rooney had seduced Elizabeth, as some reporters maintain, he might have written about it in his candid memoir, *Life Is Too Short,* unless he wanted to face a belated charge of child molestation. Rooney was very outspoken about admitting previous affairs, and was, perhaps, the only star to praise Marilyn Monroe as "a great cocksucker" in a memoir.

A lot of the gossip may have stemmed from an item in Sheilah Graham's column. A rival of both Louella Parsons and Hedda Hopper, Graham was the first columnist to cite Elizabeth, in print, as part of a romantic link.

Graham claimed that two very young MGM stars, Elizabeth Taylor and Judy Garland, had lost out to another MGM star, Ava Gardner, in the race for Rooney. She claimed he was "one of Hollywood's most prized lovers." This incited a rival columnist, James Bacon, to suggest, "Maybe everything about Mickey isn't sawed off."

What is strange about Graham's column is that Ava and Rooney had already married and separated, and that she was already deep into a pattern of dating other men. Surely, Graham must have known that, yet the item ran in newspapers across the country anyway.

On meeting Rooney, Elizabeth had seemed to measure her new height against his shortness. She told Brown that she was glad he was only "titty-high," which was a gross exaggeration, of course, but showing what, as the years passed, evolved into a wicked sense of humor. The director was amused with her choice of words. After making that remark to him, he called her "Sugartit" throughout the remainder of the shoot.

On the set, Elizabeth bonded with "King Charles," the horse she would ride in the film. Named "Pi" in the movie, he was a splendid, chestnut-colored gelding that was the grandson of the famous Man o' War. He wore a white star on his forehead and had three "white socks." Rooney warned her that the horse was downright mean, but Elizabeth wasn't afraid. She even took to riding him bareback.

The script called for her to take a fall off Pi. She insisted on doing the scene herself, but she hit the ground with such a thud that she bounced back off the turf. This accident would cause her tortuous pain throughout the rest of her life, and it was not treated properly on the set of *National Velvet*. Three years later, when she took another fall, a spinal X-ray revealed that two of her vertebrae had jammed into each other because of that initial impact in 1944.

In snagging the role of Velvet, Elizabeth and Sara had exaggerated her ability as an equestrienne. "She had trouble staying seated on an active mount," claimed Egon Mertz, and instructor at the chic Riviera Country Club, where Elizabeth took lessons. "She was much better riding Snowy Baker."

Mertz was referring to Reginald Leslie ("Snowy") Baker (1884-1953), the Australia-born actor matinee idol and former champion boxer, who in semi-retirement worked at the Riviera. He would get down on his hands and knees on the floor of the clubroom. A red leather saddle would be placed on his back, and he'd put a rope into his mouth instead of reins. Elizabeth would mount him and crack her crop on his muscled back, and he'd bolt ahead like a racehorse. "She'd ride him screaming like a drunken cowboy at the rodeo," claimed Mertz.

Irene Dunne, who had appeared with Elizabeth in *The White Cliffs of Dover,* had been invited to the Taylor home on Elm Drive for tea. "I was flabbergasted," she later recalled. "There were large framed pictures of Elizabeth in every room, and just tons of mother-daughter photo-

graphs. At least ten scrapbooks lay on the coffee table filled with interviews and photographs of Elizabeth. In the hallway and in the living room were mounted costumes on store mannequins that Elizabeth had worn in films. I couldn't imagine what all this adulation was going to do to the poor child. In spite of all this praise and attention, she still had beautiful manners and was so polite, a lovable youngster."

Elizabeth got along with her co-stars, except for Anne Revere, who would win a Best Supporting Actress Oscar for portraying Velvet's mother. According to Revere, as stated to Clarence Brown, "This Taylor girl reminded me of a mechanized midget with buck teeth, content to go through the motions without the slightest hint of feeling."

Although Revere was not impressed, Sara noted that a lot of other women were paying "undue attention to my daughter."

Sara began to follow Elizabeth into the women's toilet, fearing that one of the lesbians working at MGM would attempt to molest her daughter. Elizabeth rebelled at such strong parental control, later claiming, "I felt like I was living under a microscope."

Fortunately, Elizabeth had Roddy in her life. Knowing that he was a homosexual, Sara trusted him to be alone with her daughter. When Elizabeth wanted to slip around and see a boy, Roddy served as her "beard."

top photo: Australian boxing champ **Snowy Baker**, "the first male Elizabeth ever rode."

lower photo: **Irene Dunne**

54

Ironically, attempts at child molestation were not unfolding within the ladies' toilets at MGM, but right from within the Taylor household.

Roddy had been a frequent guest at the Taylor home in Beverly Hills, but during her filming of *National Velvet,* he'd stopped coming over and met with Elizabeth only at his own home. One Sunday afternoon at one of his cookouts, she asked him why he no longer visited.

He bluntly told her why: He said that one Saturday evening when the Taylors were entertaining guests, he went to their bathroom to take a leak. "As you know, there are no locks on the door. As I was pissing, the door opened. It was Francis. I thought he wanted to use the bathroom and that he'd excuse himself to wait until I had finished by business. Hell no! He barged right over to the toilet bowl and stared at me in mid-piss. He'd told me he'd always wanted to see my dick, which he'd heard was one of the biggest in Hollywood. He propositioned me and asked me to go with him to the bushes in your backyard for a quick blow-job."

"If it had been anyone but your father, I might have said yes," Roddy told Elizabeth. "I rarely turn down a blow-job. But I just couldn't do it with the father of my best friend. The thought made me sick."

He might have been surprised at how calmly Elizabeth received the news. She later told him, "I've known about my father for a very long time. You were a guest in our home. I must apologize for him."

After Roddy confessed what had happened with Francis, Elizabeth showed up on the set of *National Velvet* looking rather dour. Her spirits were brightened when she was invited to lunch with the novelist Enid Bagnold, who had created the original character of Velvet. Enid later said that she found Elizabeth "a sheer delight, but very, very old for her age."

Enid told Elizabeth that she had originally sold all rights to *National Velvet* to Paramount for a flat fee of $8,000. "Not realizing that I'd have to pay American taxes, I spent all the money and then ended up having to shell out $2,000 to the U.S. government."

At the end of the shoot of *National Velvet,* Elizabeth approached Pandro S. Berman and asked if he would make her a gift of the horse, King Charles, to whom she had become attached. He explained to her that since it was the property of MGM, he would have to ask Louis B. Mayer. At that point, based on having watched *National Velvet,* Mayer was convinced that Elizabeth was going to become a big star. "She could play Dracula's daughter and people would line up at the box office," the studio mogul predicted. "Give her the god damn horse. I heard it's become lame anyway."

Presented with the horse, Elizabeth decided to make permanent her policy of asking rewards at the end of filming. In the future, she'd request an expensive gift from the producer, and she usually got it.

One day, the columnist Sidney Skolsky asked her about this. She was very blunt in her answer, knowing that he wouldn't dare print her response. "One night after William Holden fucked me, he told me that all actors are whores, selling their bodies. Well, this is one whore who is not opposed to a few gratuities."

The gift of the horse occurred in 1944. Elizabeth thanked Berman profusely. However, years later, at the debut of discussions about producing *Butterfield 8* in 1959, he encountered a very different Elizabeth, a woman jaded and sophisticated. "Aren't you the guy who gave me that horse I rode in *National Velvet?*" she asked.

"Yes, I'm afraid I am," he told her.

"You son of a bitch," she said. "I'm still paying for feed for that god damn nag."

After her encounter with Berman, Elizabeth told Sara, "I've heard that MGM without Berman has been compared to an American flag without the stars. But frankly, to me he looks like Mr. Magoo wanting to throw me down on the casting couch."

Opening during the Christmas season of 1944 at Radio City Music Hall in Manhattan, *National Velvet* was a smash hit. Although Rooney was the star, Elizabeth garnered most of the praise.

Time magazine commented on her "pre-adolescent sexuality" on the screen. As far as it is known, this was the first time the press had discussed sexuality as it related to underage Elizabeth. Before her death, half the trees in Canada would fall to create the newsprint absorbed by articles addressing her sexuality.

Enid Bagnold attended the premiere of *National Velvet* in London, describing it as "a glossy version of my story." Later, she was horrified to read reviews of her work in the American press. One journalist asserted that "*National Velvet* is about sex, the story of a virgin on the dawn of puberty, who is in love with her horse."

Another book critic referred to the novel as "juvenile pornography" and cited a passage from the book to prove his point:

"The horse sprang to the surge of her heart as her eyes gazed between his ears at the blue top of the flint wall. She bent slightly and held him fast and steady, her hands buried in the flaming mane, firm on the stout muscles of his neck."

In her eighties at the time, Bagnold was

Enid Bagnold, horrified at the reviews generated by the filmed version of her novel, *National Velvet*

56

appalled by such observations. "Balderdash!" she said. "What's next? They'll be talking nonsense about girls and goats."

Regardless of one's individual perception of *National Velvet,* the movie was a smash hit—and so was its star, Elizabeth Taylor.

From coast to coast, and abroad, especially in war-torn England, the word was out: MGM had a new star shining to prove its claim that it had more stars than there are in Heaven.

***

As Elizabeth entered her teens, she spent most of her time concentrating on becoming a woman. To capitalize off the box office success of *Lassie Come Home,* Mayer forced her to film a sequel, *Courage of Lassie,* which was released in 1946. Director Fred Wilcox helmed a cast that included Frank Morgan, Harry Davenport, and George Cleveland. Elizabeth related particularly well to the distinguished white-haired "old man" of the Silent Screen, George Davenport, who had played Dr. Meade in *Gone With the Wind,* back in 1939.

During the filming of *Courage of Lassie,* Elizabeth was reunited with the collie, Pal, which was actually a male dog playing a bitch. Originally, the film was entitled *Hold High the Torch* and later renamed *Blue Sierra* until Mayer found out. "You fuck!" he told Wilcox. "Get *Lassie* in the title."

Before the summer of the film's release in 1946, it had been retitled *Courage of Lassie.*

During his reprise movie, "Pal" was assigned the name of "Bill" and arrives onscreen shell-shocked after accompanying British troops into the trenches of World War I. "Most of my dialogue consisted of me standing around crying out, 'Oh Bill' every ten seconds," Elizabeth remembered, years later. "It was my last movie with a quadruped as my co-star. I wanted to appear opposite hot, hung, and hunky he-men." [Roddy had recently taught her the meaning of the word "hung," which subsequently became one of her favorite words.]

In the film, she was cast opposite Tom Drake, who had had a brief role in *The White Cliffs of Dover.* Since then, he'd achieved fame as "the boy next door" opposite Judy Garland in *Meet Me in St. Louis* (1944). In the reprise of the Lassie movie, he played the soldier who had trained "Bill the Collie" to become a killer.

Elizabeth might have preferred a more virile beau, but Drake was handsome enough. We can assume that Elizabeth was indulging in hyperbole when she used the word "spread-eagled" in what she said about him later: "He was very sweet and soft-spoken. I did go after him, but he wouldn't kiss me even when I spread-eagled myself before him."

At Roddy's Sunday afternoon barbecue, she poured out her frustrations to her trusted friend and confidant. She'd later recall, "I've never seen Roddy so angry. I thought he was going to burst several blood vessels."

"That bitch!" Roddy shouted. "That *cunt!* That *WHORE!* I'd love to cut off his balls if I can find them. Guess what Miss Priss has done? He stole Peter Lawford from me. Those two get oral with each other night after night."

She was shocked. Not only did she learn that she didn't have a chance with Drake, but that he was sleeping with the handsome young actor upon whom "I have the ultimate crush." She commiserated with Roddy throughout the rest of the afternoon. "Ah, Hollywood. What's a girl to do? For Peter, I've had to compete with Lana Turner and you, my dearest friend. That's painful enough. Now Tom Drake. In the future, when I fall for a guy, I've got to be realistic. In Hollywood, with the most beautiful girls and the most beautiful boys in the world, it's doubly hard for a girl in love to battle both guys and dolls for her man."

"Get used to it," he warned her. "Hollywood is the most competitive town in the universe. The only time we can be sure that the object of each of our affections isn't sleeping with someone else, male or female, is when we're actually in bed alone with them."

"I can't wait to grow up," she said. "I'm so fucking young, my age is against me. Why aren't there more child molesters out here?"

"Don't rush it," he told her. "Wait just three years, and then every guy in Hollywood will want to plug you."

"Three fucking years?" she asked. "Are you out of your bloody mind? I can't wait that long. I want it now!"

She urged Roddy to line her up with a hot date. She'd been attracted to a young actor, Darryl Hickman, at one of Rodney's Saturday afternoon cookouts. "Give him my phone number, and see if he'll ask me out on a date. Tell him I'll let him fuck me if you'll go out with me."

Ever since Hickman had appeared in *Grapes of Wrath,* Elizabeth had had a fantasy about him.

Roddy called her two nights later. "Forget about Darryl. He told me he's considering entering a monastery. Those monks aren't even allowed to jerk off."

"Oh, fuck that!" she told him. "In all of Hollywood, aren't there any real he-men who lust for a hot young pussy?"

"Oh, Elizabeth, I'll have to wash out your mouth," he said. "No wonder Sara makes you wear a chastity belt."

In her 1987 memoir, *Elizabeth Takes Off,* she wrote, "I wanted to be a woman. I had a small waistline which I'd squeeze even smaller, knowing that it accentuated my bust and hips. I flaunted an hourglass figure at a stage when most young girls were still developing."

Sidney Guilaroff, her hairdresser, testified to her success. He recalled eating lunch with Pandro S. Berman in the MGM commissary a year after casting Elizabeth as the little girl in *National Velvet*. "When Elizabeth walked in to have her lunch, Berman was flabbergasted at the transformation of her body. Seeing her new look, he told me, 'I think I could go to jail for that!'"

That afternoon at the commissary, Elizabeth was still at the stage where she was going around the tables asking for autographs from all the big MGM stars, such as Lana Turner (who drove her into jealous fits), Judy Garland (whom she envied), and Hedy Lamarr (who she wanted to replace as the most beautiful woman in the world). She spotted Katharine Hepburn involved in a deep conversation with Spencer Tracy. She walked over to her table and asked, "May I have your autograph, Miss Hepburn?"

She recalled Hepburn's reaction. "She granted me the autograph, but did not stop talking. Nor did she even look at me. The lezzie [a new word taught to her by Roddy] would later want to have a lobotomy performed on me."

Elizabeth was referring, of course, to her 1959 picture, *Suddenly, Last Summer,* in which she co-starred with Hepburn and Montgomery Clift.

"That was the last day I ever asked anyone for an autograph," Elizabeth said. "From then on, I let other people ask *me* for an autograph. There was no reserved seating in the commissary. I ended up sitting at table between Clark Gable, my idol, and Marjorie Main. I felt that both of these established older stars would like to get into my panties, which at the time were pink silk."

***

The domestic details of Elizabeth's home in Beverly Hills changed in 1944, as she found out when a studio limousine deposited her at Elm Drive. Usually, Sara was with her, but not today.

Going into the living room, Elizabeth found Sara busily reorganizing their possessions. "We're moving out this weekend. I have rooms for us at the Riviera Club until I get our beach cottage in Malibu in order."

"Have we lost the house?" an alarmed Elizabeth asked. She'd later relate the details of this dramatic saga in her life to Roddy.

"For the moment," Sara said, "Francis and your brother, Howard, will stay on here. You see, my dear, Francis has found a replacement for Victor Cazalet. He's fallen in love with Adrian, and they are going to live together." Like the rest of Hollywood, Elizabeth was aware of Gilbert Adrian, the legal husband of the film star, Janet Gaynor, whom he'd wed in 1939, entering into a "lavender marriage" with the costume designer.

Elizabeth knew Adrian because he'd designed the famous costumes for *The Wizard of Oz*. In time, over the course of a long and celebrated career, he would design gowns for more than 250 films.

At MGM, he'd earned his fame by designing gowns for Greta Garbo, Norma Shearer, Jeanette MacDonald, Jean Harlow, and Katharine Hepburn. He'd designed costumes for Joan Crawford in twenty-eight films, creating those signature outfits with large shoulder pads, launching a nationwide fashion trend.

"Oh, Mommy, I want to meet him!" Elizabeth said, offering no sympathy that Francis had walked out on his family for the love of another man. Perhaps because of her father's long relationship with Victor, Elizabeth was accustomed to such an arrangement.

"Your father wants you to come over Sunday to have lunch with him and his new friend."

"What should I call him?" Elizabeth asked. "I called Victor 'Daddy.'"

"Think of Adrian as a surrogate stepfather," Sara said. "In his case, 'Daddy' would not be appropriate. Perhaps 'Uncle Adrian.'"

Sara may have been surprised at how casually her daughter treated the news of her separation from her father. Later, Elizabeth would tell Roddy, "It was no big deal for me, no special loss. Hell, I've been fatherless for years anyway. I'll not miss his slapping me around. I don't know this Adrian person, but in a way, I can't blame my father."

"And why not?" he asked.

"Who wouldn't like cock?"

"Elizabeth, the way you talk sometimes makes me forget you're still a little girl."

Before the afternoon ended, Sara delivered another bombshell. "Tonight, I'm entertaining a gentleman caller for a light supper. I'd like you to make an appearance, looking your very best, and then I'd like you to toddle off to bed. You can eat before he gets here."

"Do I know him, Mommy?" she asked.

"No, darling, but you will. He's Michael Curtiz, the director."

"I know him," she said with a certain glee. "He won an Oscar directing Bogart in *Casablanca*. He was married to Errol Flynn's wife, Lili Damita. God, how I wish I could marry Errol."

The Grand Days of Hollywood Couture:

top photo: Francis Taylor's new love interest, **Adrian**, and

lower photo, a **"fitted suit"** the designer conceived and commercialized in 1947.

"I already know that," Sara said. "In your bathroom, I noticed that those pictures of Clark Gable have gone down and were replaced by pictures of Mr. Flynn. You and he might hit it off. He's famous for seducing underage girls."

"Oh, Mommy, Mr. Curtiz directed that wonderful film, *The Adventures of Robin Hood*. Errol looked wonderful in those green tights. I think he's the handsomest man who ever lived. Do you think Mr. Curtiz will introduce me?"

"You little vixen," Sara said. "You'll meet Errol Flynn over my dead body."

"Oh, Mommy, you try to spoil every thrill for me," Elizabeth said. "I hope I'm not going to have to remind you that I've become the bread winner of the family."

Those words, painful as they were, must have hurt Sara a great deal. But she moved ahead, issuing orders and clarifications to Elizabeth: "Michael is married to Bess Meredyth, an unhappy union like mine with Francis. She's an actress—not much of one—and a screenwriter…ghastly."

Elizabeth spent what remained of the afternoon preparing for her "audition" in front of Curtiz. Over the previous few weeks, she'd brought home various cosmetic creams, shades of lipstick, and face powders from the makeup department at MGM. She'd also borrowed three gowns from wardrobe that were adjusted to fit her perfectly, in case a boy called to ask her out. One was a strapless black velvet evening gown that plunged practically to the crack of her buttocks. Roddy referred to that dress as "anal-colletage." She'd also, since discovering the joys of perfume, made off with three expensive bottles of it, including Chanel no. 5.

For the finishing touches, she painted her fingernails and toenails scarlet. She chose golden earrings the size of curtain rings. "They bring out the gypsy in my soul," she said. She tightened a black patent leather belt around her waist so snugly, she could hardly breathe, but by doing that, she made her rapidly growing breasts so much larger.

Curtiz arrived on the doorstep carrying the present of a toy doll, but when he first gazed upon Elizabeth, he met what he later remembered "as a former child star hell bent on becoming the next Hedy Lamarr. She'd made herself up like the most expensive whore in a bordello, catering to those johns who liked their fresh flesh." He'd meant to say "their flesh fresh," but he often juxtaposed words.

As she sat in the family's living room with Curtiz, Elizabeth ignored Sara's signals to get up and leave.

"I loved *Mildred Pierce*," she told Curtiz. "You're such a brilliant director. Getting a good performance out of Joan Crawford…what a miracle man you are."

Curtiz appeared startled at the words coming out of Elizabeth's mouth. Her line about Crawford was something Bette Davis might say, not a little girl.

"I'll always regret that I was not old enough to play Vida in the film," Elizabeth said. "I know I could out-bitch Ann Blyth. I felt she was very sweet and just play-acting at being a bitch."

Still ignoring Sara's signs of dismissal, Elizabeth pumped Curtiz for information about Errol Flynn: "He's my favorite movie star. He's so dashing, so handsome, so athletic. Could you tell me about him?"

"I'm afraid all the stories I know about Flynn don't belong in a children's verses of book."

"He means, 'book of verses,'" Sara said.

"I know what he means, Mommy!" Elizabeth said, growing impatient with her mother. "Would you introduce me to him?"

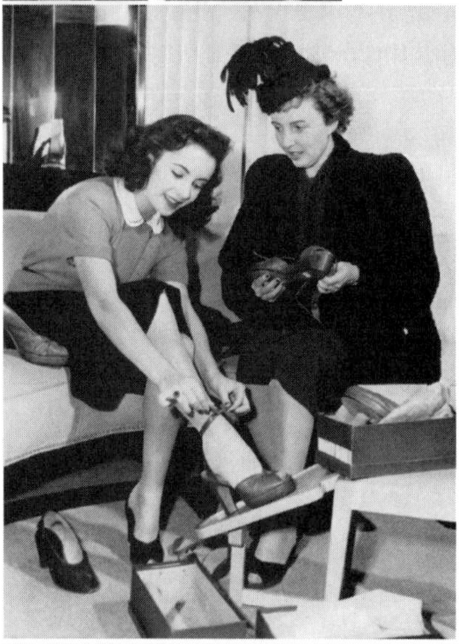

Curtiz looked at Sara. "That depends on your mother."

"Let's make a deal," Sara said. "You won't get to meet Flynn, but I'm sure Michael can get you an autographed photo to put over your bed."

"That I can do," Curtiz said. "It's safer that way. After all, Flynn is always going around singing, 'Thank God for Little Girls.'"

Elizabeth must go to bed now," Sara interjected. "It's way past her bedtime."

As she was practically shoved out the door, Elizabeth made one last request. "Oh, Mr. Curtiz, would you please see that a role for me is written into your next picture?"

"My dear, sweet girl, I fear I don't direct pictures for child stars."

Ironically, one of Elizabeth's upcoming movies would be directed by none other than Curtiz.

***

At her Sunday lunch with Francis and Adrian, her brother, Howard, was nowhere to be seen, and she didn't ask about him. Throughout the meal, she virtually ignored her father and concentrated on the costume designer instead. He won her heart when he told her, "I can't wait for you to grow up so I can start designing gowns for you."

How to Handle One's Parents:
Michael Curtiz *(top photo)* at around the time he began dating **Sara Taylor** *(right figure in lower photo),* who's helping her daughter, **Elizabeth,** accessorize.

"The sooner the better," she told him, "and don't be afraid of a little *décolletage*. I've been introduced to Edith Head. The lez taught me the word *décolletage*.

"I've stuffed many a *brassière* in my time, but in your case I don't think I'll have to."

She was eager to hear his stories about working with all the big stars. Whatever name she brought up, he had to story to tell.

"It was because of Garbo that I said goodbye to Louis B. Mayer and MGM," Adrian claimed. "When the war came and her lucrative European market dried up, Mayer wanted to convert her into a sweater girl, a real American type like Lana Turner. I told Mayer that 'when the glamour ends for Garbo, it also ends for me. She has created a type. If you destroy that illusion, you destroy Garbo on the screen.' Garbo bolted from MGM, and I went with her."

"As for Joan Crawford, she begins every fitting the same way. She strips off all of her clothes and says, 'Okay, Big Boy, here's what you've got to work with.'"

"As a man, you must be so tempted," Elizabeth said.

"Kid, you've got a lot to learn," Adrian said. "Give me Francis Taylor any day."

Francis seemed embarrassed at this kind of talk, and tried to change the conversation to Elizabeth and her career.

An hour later, Adrian informed Elizabeth that his wife, Janet Gaynor, would be arriving soon with her "husband," Mary Martin.

If Elizabeth was shocked by the use of the word "husband," she tried not to show it. She couldn't wait to tell Roddy about this luncheon. Her friend and confidant would want to know every juicy tidbit of gossip.

Elizabeth had heard of Janet Gaynor, who stood only five feet tall, but had never seen any of her movies, including *A Star Is Born* (1937). She'd been told that Gaynor had won the first Oscar for Best Actress in 1928 and had appeared in Silent Pictures.

When Gaynor and Martin arrived, Elizabeth tried to ingratiate herself with both women, focusing first on Gaynor and making use of her recently acquired information.

Gaynor looked astonished when Elizabeth told her, "Francis said you were the youngest actress to win an Oscar and that you were only twenty-two. I will wait until I'm twenty-three to win my first Oscar so I won't beat your record."

"That is so kind of you, you adorable thing," Gaynor graciously responded.

When Elizabeth talked to Martin, she discovered that she had another husband, Richard Halliday, yet was herself sometimes identified as the "husband" of Gaynor. Roddy would have to explain all these grown-up relationships to her more thoroughly.

After lunch, Elizabeth sat with Martin, the Broadway singing star, in the garden, while the other three made lemonade. "I hear you're a fabulous singer," Elizabeth said. "There's a rumor I'm going to sing in my next picture. Perhaps you'll give me singing lessons?"

"Just listen to Bing Crosby records," Martin advised. "That's what I did. Hollywood doesn't know quite what to do with me. I'm in town to make a picture called *Night and Day* (1946).

"Is there a part in it for me?" Elizabeth asked.

"Not that I know of," Martin said. "But I can offer you something else. A real prize. I have a divine boy, Larry Hagman, by my first husband. I think you and he would make an ideal couple.

"I'd like to meet him," she said.

"He has great legs," Martin added.

"If only I did." Elizabeth would later tell Roddy that whereas the legs of the female are usually commented on, those of males elicit less scrutiny. He'd inform her that in Hollywood, a man's legs often get as much attention as a woman's, at least during private encounters.

"I'll have Larry call you sometime," Martin said. "You're old enough to date now. When Larry turned fourteen—he's two years older than you—I sent him to boarding school. But he started drinking a quart of whiskey a day. He's on this ranch right now, being rehabilitated."

Elizabeth seemed generally pleased with her father's new living arrangements, but as noted by all the adults who knew her at the time, she always tried to press for a favor from any actor, director, or producer she met. Adrian was no exception.

When Francis was talking in the garden with Martin and Gaynor, Elizabeth moved in with a very special request. "I've given you Francis," she said, perhaps shocking Adrian at how brazen she was for one so young. "Now I want you to give me something. I want you to duplicate those red-sequined ruby slippers you made for Judy Garland in that Oz picture. *Please, pretty please!"*

Within a month, the red slippers arrived and Elizabeth loved wearing them. Then one night after Sara had a bitter fight with Adrian over Francis, she tossed the slippers into the garbage.

As late as 1990, Elizabeth was still lamenting the loss of those ruby slippers. "My god, the damn things would be worth a fortune today, and Sara threw them in the garbage."

In 1949, when Elizabeth, with Nicky Hilton, attended one of Martin's signature performances of *South Pacific* (1949) on Broadway, she went backstage to congratulate her. Upon leaving, and out of earshot of Nicky, she whispered to Martin, "I've seen your son's picture. He's gorgeous. Tell him I'm still waiting for that phone call from him."

64

"But you've got the Hilton boy now for a beau," Martin said.

"A girl can't have too many beaux," Elizabeth said. "When you wear one out, there's always the next in line."

"Smart thinking, girl," Martin said, kissing her good night.

***

After the commercial success of *National Velvet,* both Sara and Elizabeth expected that she'd be besieged with film offers, but nothing was forthcoming. A rumor floated around the studio that Louis B. Mayer was about to cast Elizabeth in a musical.

Growing impatient, Sara took Elizabeth to Mayer's office, where they met Ida Koverman, his executive assistant, who had previously functioned as former U.S. President Herbert Hoover's campaign secretary in California. She was to some degree like a gatekeeper protecting Mayer from unwanted intrusions. However, the studio mogul agreed to see Sara and Elizabeth.

He was in a bad mood that morning.

In a memoir, Elizabeth recalled, "Mayer looked rather like a gross, thick penguin. He had huge glasses, and he had a way of looking at you that made you feel completely squashable. You felt his vitality, but you also felt his enormous arrogance, his ego, his overbearing, his driving personality. To know him was to be terrified of him."

Elizabeth's memory and her reality of that era didn't match. That morning, she was not yet terrified of Mayer, and at her young age, she dared to confront him.

Sara launched into the meeting by immediately saying that she'd heard that her daughter was going to be cast in a musical that required her to sing and dance. "I think you should hire a singing coach and a dancing coach for Elizabeth right now, since all her time is going to waste."

Mayer tossed aside the contracts he was reviewing and turned on Sara. "How dare you come into my office and tell me how to run my business. You and your daughter are guttersnipes. I took you out of the gutter, and I can send you back there. You're so god damn stupid you don't even know the day of the week."

Then the unthinkable happened. Not since John Gilbert slugged Mayer had an MGM star confronted him. Elizabeth barged over to his desk. "Don't you dare speak to my mother that way. You can go to hell and shove MGM up your dirty asshole."

Then, in tears, Elizabeth ran from the office. Outside, she collided into the arms of Richard Hanley, Mayer's devoted homosexual secretary.

He held her in his arms and comforted her. "Now, now, Elizabeth," he said.

"Whatever happened will fade away. Why don't you take the advice of Scarlett O'Hara and think about it tomorrow?"

He escorted her to her dressing room, firmly holding her hand. Once in the room, he dried her tears and kissed her forehead. "If something goes wrong tomorrow, you can always count on me. I'll be there for you."

"I'm going to hold you to that promise," she said. Perhaps without realizing it, Elizabeth had just begun one of the most vital relationships of her life, having discovered a friend and a confidant "until death do us part."

In the meantime, Mayer had summoned Koverman to his office and told her what Elizabeth had said to him. Koverman heard Sara pleading with the mogul not to fire her daughter. "She's just an impetuous little girl," Sara said.

"Bring that nasty little brat back in here," Mayer ordered Koverman. "Tell her I'm demanding an apology—not tomorrow, not later, but NOW! Get to it."

Koverman trailed Elizabeth to her dressing room, where she was preparing to leave the studio. "Mr. Mayer demands that you come back and apologize."

"Why don't you tell your Mr. Mayer to kiss my ass," she said. "On second thought, not that. That would get him too excited."

"Why you little bitch," Koverman said. "Mr. Mayer never forgives, never forgets. You're washed up at MGM. Too bad you couldn't keep your damn trap shut. He could have made you a big star. Now he'll see to it that no other studio hires you."

Shocked, startled, and filled with horror, Elizabeth faced the reality of what she'd done to herself. She ran into her toilet, slamming the door behind her. Koverman heard the sound of glass breaking.

Having previously been involved in some fifteen suicide attempts at MGM, Koverman knew what the sound of breaking glass meant.

Elizabeth Taylor was slashing her wrists.

Louis B. Mayer with **Elizabeth Taylor**
In spite of her demure smile,
she detested the mogul.

CHAPTER SEVEN
Coming of Age:
WHAT'S LOVE GOT TO DO WITH IT?

In the ambulance on its way to the hospital, Dick Hanley was at Elizabeth's side after she'd slashed her wrists in the dressing room at MGM.

"I'm here for you," he whispered in her ear. "You'll pull through."

Rushed into emergency, Elizabeth was resting in her private room only an hour later. Her wounds were superficial. The doctor told Hanley that she'd merely "scratched" her wrists with the glass and that the wounds would soon heal.

As Dick sat by her bed, Sara barged into the hospital room. "Oh, my darling, my poor darling! They didn't tell me right away."

Very patiently, Dick explained Elizabeth's condition to Sara, who at first seemed to resent his intrusion into her daughter's life. But when he was interrupted by a call from Louis B. Mayer, and when Sara overheard Dick's remarks to the studio mogul, he won Sara's heart.

When he was able to speak, Dick explained how he had the situation at the hospital under control. "Under no circumstances can we let the press find out that Elizabeth slashed her wrist because she was fired. God, I can just see what the press would make of that. But I'll see that they don't find out."

"I'll get MGM publicity on it to squelch this thing," Mayer shouted.

"In case anybody asks, we can say it was Elizabeth's first onslaught of menstruation. No one had explained to her what that meant. She panicked. She's no longer a little girl, and no one instructed her about the changes likely to occur in her body."

"I'll buy that god damn lie," Mayer said. "The papers won't print it. Stay at the hospital. Don't let anybody see her, and don't allow her back on the lot until her wrists have healed. Who in hell does she think she is? Lana Turner? Tell her that her suicide attempts should come when, say, Frank Sinatra leaves her standing pregnant at the altar and her career is about to go up in flames."

During the next forty-eight hours, the only person Dick let into Elizabeth's room included Sara as part of regular afternoon visits; a very concerned Francis; brother Howard, who told his sister she was crazy; and Roddy McDowall.

Roddy liked Dick so much he even made a date with him for sometime "after this blows over and Elizabeth is safe and stable again."

Roddy sternly lectured Elizabeth. "Don't you ever let me hear you pulling shit like this again?"

When Sara came to visit during her final afternoon in the hospital, Elizabeth used her suicide attempt to demand concessions from her mother. Whereas Sara would have kept her in child roles for as long as possible, Elizabeth was demanding more grown-up parts. Elizabeth told her that as the breadwinner of the family, she could no longer be chaperoned day and night. She announced that she was going to start dating and that she would refuse any curfew imposed upon her.

Sara was more or less forced to give in to her, but warned her daughter, "You must not have sex with these boys coming into your life. Perhaps a kiss on the cheek when they're saying good night on your doorstep, but it mustn't go beyond that in any way."

Later, Elizabeth confided to Dick, "Roddy has taught me how to have sex with boys without getting pregnant."

"Roddy should know," Dick said with a wink.

She smiled at him and took his hand. "So, your date with Roddy last night was successful?"

"And how!" he said. "God has been very good to Roddy."

During her incarceration in the hospital, Elizabeth got to know her new friend. At the time Elizabeth met Dick, he was in his mid-thirties, having come to Hollywood from Indianapolis, where his Irish father worked for the railroads. "I came to Hollywood because I fell in love with Clark Gable on the movie screen and wanted to meet him," Dick said. "One day at MGM, I found myself standing next to Clark at a urinal. That day, I lost my passion for him."

"My passion for Clark has dimmed, too," she said. "After seeing Errol Flynn as Robin Hood, he's become my imaginary new lover."

***

While Elizabeth was still in the hospital, Dick picked up the phone to hear an unexpected caller. The phone call had originated in San Simeon, that multi-million dollar palace the press baron, William Randolph Hearst, had built for his mistress, actress Marion Davies, on a mountain overlooking the California coast.

Through her close link with the Hearst gossip maven, Louella Parsons, Marion had learned that Elizabeth was in the hospital.

"This is Marion Davies," the voice on the phone said to Elizabeth, "calling to wish you a speedy recovery and also to congratulate you. Last night, Willie and I saw *National Velvet*. He adored the picture, but mostly, he adored you. You really touched the old man's heart. In spite of his reputation, at heart, he's a silly sentimental fool."

"Oh, Miss Davies, I'm so honored to speak to you. Roddy McDowall has been to San Simeon and told me so much about you."

"This empty shell!" Marion said. "It needs to be livened up on the weekends, and Willie wants to invite you up. Come Saturday morning, we'll send a limousine for you. And, for God's sake, bring a date—preferably a hot one—and not that mother of yours."

"A date? You mean a real date and not a chaperone?"

"Yeah, why not? Marion responded. "I hear you're grown up…well, almost."

"I'm getting there," Elizabeth said. "I known Mr. Hearst likes to run pictures of actresses in bathing suits in his newspapers. I hope in a few months, if my breasts keep growing at the rate they are now, that I'll be posing for one of his photographers."

"I'd bet my left tit that you will. It's time you got out in the world. Hell, when I was your age, I'd have five *beaux* a week on Broadway. We called them 'Stage Door Johnnies.'"

"Oh, please, Miss Davies, tell me how I can go about getting *beaux*. I bet I could have no better teacher than you."

"Sure, kid, I know the ropes. Just ask Gable, Chaplin, Old Joe Kennedy. They'll tell you."

After chatting for another ten minutes, a thrilled Elizabeth put down the phone, turning to Dick, who had listened to every word. "I've been invited to San Simeon as the guest of Mr. Hearst and Miss Davies. It'll be my first outing as a grown-up. I'm allowed to bring a date, but don't tell Sara. I'll tell her I'm going there alone without her being my god damn chaperone. How am I to get my cherry popped when she's hovering over me?" She looked up at Dick with a great intensity on her face. "I've got to know something. Just how much power do you have with the young male stars at MGM? I mean, you being the one who decides who can go in to see Mayer."

"Except for the established stars like Gable, I can get the younger ones to unzip for me on request," he said. "They're usually willing to do anything to get ahead."

"That's what I thought," she said. "I want you to call Peter Lawford. Tell him he's going to be my date during our weekend trip to San Simeon. Tell him he'll also be sharing my bedroom."

"Your wish, my command!" Dick said.

***

Elizabeth always remembered the limousine Marion Davies sent to carry her, with Peter Lawford, to San Simeon to party with William Randolph Hearst. "It was large enough for eight couples to have intercourse, with enough room for everyone to be comfortable while going at it," she'd later tell Dick.

En route, driving north from Los Angeles along the coast, Lawford entertained her with stories of the filming of *Son of Lassie* (1945). In this dog picture, he and June Lockhart had played the adult versions of the characters that Roddy McDowall and Elizabeth had portrayed in *Lassie Come Home.*

"I know the dog adored you, but to me, he was a vicious bastard," Lawford claimed. "That collie, playing a female in the picture, hated me and growled every time I came near him. But the script called for intimate scenes between us. The director ordered me to put raw meal under my arms and on my chest. My face was also rubbed with raw hamburger, freshly ground."

"That's how I got the animal to show love for me. Love, hell! The god damn dog was eating me alive. He almost cannibalized me!"

As she would later tell Dick, Elizabeth learned for the first time that Lawford had very limited use of his right arm because of a childhood injury with shattered glass. "I did everything to hide that from the director," he said. "In *Lassie,* I even did my own swimming in the treacherous waters of the Columbia River. I was left to my own devices, although every safety precaution was provided for Lassie to keep him from drowning. I was housed in a bedroom that must have been a maid's closet, but Lassie was given a two-bedroom suite. Instead of *Son of Lassie,* Mayer should have titled the picture *Son of a Bitch.*"

lower photo: Media baron
William Randolph Hearst with
Marion Davies
upper photo: the Hearst Castle's
entrance

Speaking of bitches," he said. "When my mother, the divine Lady Lawford, went to see the movie, she said that because of my long shaggy hair, she couldn't tell me apart from the dog."

"That's all behind you now," Elizabeth assured him. "You're going to the top. I just saw the latest copy of *Modern Screen*. You've been named the most popular actor in Hollywood."

"I know," he said. "I bought one-hundred copies of that magazine."

She wanted to get to know him better, and they shared their experiences of growing up in Britain. His memories were so very different from hers. He claimed he lost his virginity when he was only ten years old to a thirty-five-year-old governess who fellated him to climax. "Other governesses and two chauffeurs also used me for their sexual purposes," Lawford claimed.

He told Elizabeth how much he hated his mother, Lady May, who was known as "Mother Bitch" in Hollywood. "She once went to Mayer and told him that I was a homosexual and asked him if he could get 'treatment' for me. I had to bring in Lana Turner for confirmation that I was not a homosexual."

Elizabeth later told Dick, who confided to Roddy, "Since the talk had gone sexual, I told Peter that I was still a virgin, giving a broad hint that I was ready to change my status. To me, Peter was a gorgeous doll, the latest in the sophistication I long to acquire. Everyone in Hollywood knew I had a crush on him. I figured that since he'd been dumped by my friend Roddy, that he was up for grabs. But he didn't even hold my hand or try to kiss me. If I'd been a boy, I would have simply unzipped and said, 'Go for it, Peter!'"

When Dick first met her, he was astonished at Elizabeth's style of talking. "I think you're an old soul," he told her. "You've lived lives before. Cleopatra, Helen of Troy. Your love of horses must stem from your life as Catherine the Great. When the empress couldn't find men in the Russian army endowed enough to accommodate her, she went to the royal stables."

"I was not the Empress of Russia, but I was Cleopatra," Elizabeth said. "I was also Madame de Pompadour."

Roddy revealed to her that Lawford had told him that he thought Elizabeth was beautiful. His exact words were, "Even at her age, Elizabeth is an exquisite creature. Everything about her face is perfect— those eyes, those long dark lashes, her smile, her hair. I'd be a liar if I denied a certain sexual attraction."

Armed with that information, Elizabeth decided to "take the bull by the horns" (her words).

"But what, exactly, does 'take the bull by the horns' mean?" Dick asked her.

"During my last week at MGM, I sat one early

Julia Misbehaves:
Elizabeth Taylor with
Peter Lawford

71

morning in make-up with Judy Garland," Elizabeth said. "I'd heard that Spencer Tracy had taken her virginity when she was only fifteen. Of all the women at MGM, Judy seemed the best person to ask for advice. 'Just how do you get a man to fuck you when you're still jail bait?' I asked her. She said she uses a technique that is almost certain to work unless a guy is homosexual. 'Just grope him! Start feeling him up. Under the table, at a restaurant, on the dance floor…anywhere!'"

"Since I was in this huge black limousine, and since I had a long drive ahead of me, I followed Judy's advice," Elizabeth claimed. "I groped Peter, and it produced the desired results. Before he knew what was happening, I was all over him, kissing him. Right there in that car, I lost my cherry, an expression I've only recently learned from Roddy."

"How did you like it?" Dick asked.

"Not all that much," she said. "It hurt at first, and it was real messy. I soiled my dress. We didn't have any protection. For all I know, I might be carrying Peter's child right now."

Dick told her not to worry about that, because at MGM, Mayer frequently assigned him the task of accompanying whichever of his female stars might at the time need an illegal abortion.

He also told her that from what he'd heard, Lawford was not an appropriate candidate for the assignment of taking her virginity. "A more skilled lover would have aroused more passion in you. George Cukor told me that Peter was a lousy lay. Intercourse doesn't interest him so much. He prefers oral sex instead."

Over the years, a long list of Lawford's intimates would agree with Cukor, including June Allyson, Noël Coward, Merv Griffin, Robert Walker, Lucille Ball, Anne Baxter, Dorothy Dandridge, Ava Gardner, Judy Garland, Rita Hayworth, Judy Holliday, Van Johnson, Janet Leigh, Sal Mineo, Kim Novak, Lee Remick, Clifton Webb, Jane Wyman, and Keenan Wynn. Author Mart Martin also added some categories of other names to that list—"lots of college girls, starlets, 'beach bunnies' he met while surfing, and prostitutes who knew Lawford as an excellent $50 oral sex trick, and 'call boys,' male hustlers, young male extras, and studio messenger boys."

Elizabeth promised Dick, "I'm going to try again and again. I realize now that the sex act should not be judged by just one bad experience. Perhaps it's like an actor's performance in a movie. Some men are great, some are mediocre, and some are rotten."

"By God, she's got it!" Dick said, kissing her lightly on the lips.

She told him that she still considered Lawford very attractive. "I'm not giving up on him. I'll pick up more experience with other men, and then maybe teach him a trick or two to make him a better lover."

"Good luck with that," Dick said.

***

When Elizabeth and Peter Lawford took that long uphill drive to San Simeon, both of them would witness the end of an era. Marion Davies and William Randolph Hearst were on the verge of abandoning their beloved castle. Its high elevation was bad for his failing heart.

They were already planning a move into a newly acquired mansion, details of which were being organized by Marion, off Benedict Canyon in Beverly Hills. Although Marion had arranged its purchase for only $120,000, it had originally been built in 1927 by Milton Goetz for one million dollars.

Led to their sumptuously decorated bedroom by servants, Elizabeth and Lawford were told that Marion would receive them for lunch and both she and Hearst would enjoy their company at dinner too. In the meantime, a guide would be made available to show them around the grounds of the estate, including a chance to see the Hearst collection of wild animals.

This visit marked the first time that Elizabeth would sleep alone in a bedroom with a man other than her brother Howard.

The butler told her that their bedroom had once been occupied by Clark Gable and Carole Lombard. Later, a rather drunken Marion would give them more juicy details, claiming that Claudette Colbert and Marlene Dietrich had also spent the night in the same room, making wild, passionate love.

Both Lawford and Elizabeth were shocked when they greeted Marion at her luncheon, at which Hearst himself was conspicuously absent. The blonde, spunky star, a former beauty in the Ziegfeld Follies, was a ghost of her former self. She'd once captivated Winston Churchill and Lord Mountbatten, but now she was no longer mobile. She'd taken to heavy drinking again, which had caused her legs to give way. Two nurses attended to her.

William Haines was a fellow guest at the luncheon table, along with his lover, Jimmy Shields, a union which Joan Crawford had once described as "the happiest marriage in Hollywood." Elizabeth and Lawford didn't know who they were. Haines had to tell them that in 1930, he'd been the number one box office attraction in Hollywood.

"I'm an interior decorator now," Haines told her. "Louis B. Mayer fired me because I wouldn't give up Jimmy. I'm Cranberry's best friend. Mayer fired her, too. If you'd like to meet her, I'll arrange it."

Marion explained to Elizabeth that Cranberry was Haines' nickname for Crawford.

Haines was straightforward and rather bold. He said, "I'm predicting an early marriage for you two. I hope you let me decorate your new home—that is, if you're partial to Empire furnishing and rococo accents. I owe everything to W.R.; he taught me about antiques. When I met him, I didn't know the difference between a *jardinière* and a pisspot."

Marion inquired about the accommodations of her guests. Elizabeth responded that she and Lawford were "living in luxury."

Haines said that he was happy with Jimmy now, but he recalled how displeased he was when Marion had first invited him to San Simeon back in the 1930s. "Marion extended an invitation to Gary Cooper and Anderson Lawler and assigned them a room together. She didn't know at the time that I was chasing after Coop. Anderson and I got into a big fight over who'd sleep with Coop. He won."

After a tour of the grounds and a siesta, Elizabeth woke up to discover Lawford performing oral sex on her. She offered to do the same for him, or at least that was what she later told Dick Hanley, but Peter responded, "later, tonight."

At long last, before dinner was served, they were summoned into the library to meet W.R. Hearst. She didn't know what to expect, but was shocked to see this once fabled press baron now moving deep into his 80s, and seemingly fading away. His eyes, which seemed to stare right through her, were surrounded by deep purple rings, which made them seem far larger than they were. The strain of a failing heart was clearly reflected in his withered face. Yet his mind was still sharp, and Marion told them that he still wrote a weekly editorial.

He praised Elizabeth's love of animals, as reflected by her performance in *National Velvet*, and she told him she was thrilled to see the animals on his estate, and how well they were being treated.

Disgraced matinee idol
William Haines (left)
with **Marion Davies**

"One of the reasons I fell in love with Willie was because of his love for animals." Marion said. "He once rescued an injured seal who'd washed up on the rocks right below the castle. One time he found a mouse trapped in a *jardinière,* and Willie brought it cheese and crackers until it ran away one day."

"I've seen all the stars of Hollywood come and go, and I predict you'll become one of the big ones," Hearst told Elizabeth. He made no such prediction for Lawford. "My only regret is that I will not be here to guide you through a spectacular career."

Elizabeth noted that Marion, in spite of her own physical wreck of a body, was very attentive and protective of Hearst. Years later, Elizabeth would tell Richard Burton that Hearst reminded her of King Lear from Shakespeare's play. At one point over dinner, he expressed his mistrust of his sons. "They're gold diggers, and I want Marion protected from these scheming beasts."

Marion seemed almost embarrassed that Elizabeth and Lawford were visiting during the final hours of their reign over San Simeon. At one point, she said that she and Hearst used to invite as many as fifty guests for the weekend. "Those were the days," she said. "Gloria Swanson, Louella Parsons, Jean Harlow, Norma Shearer, Irving Thalberg, Errol Flynn, Jack Pickford, Eleanor Boardman, Adolphe Menjou and his wife Katharine, Bebe Daniels, Damon Runyon."

Despite Hearst's obvious annoyance when she brought up the subject, Marion claimed that in 1934 during a visit to Berlin, Hearst had even invited Adolf Hitler for a visit. "Of course, that was before we knew what a mean guy he was, killing all those Jews."

"And all those poor homosexuals," Haines added.

Hearst retired to bed early, and Marion asked the two couples to join her in the library, where she amused them with stories about the Golden Years of Hollywood. "I saved John Gilbert's life one afternoon when he was going to walk into the ocean and drown himself after Greta Garbo dumped him."

"Tell them about all the men who seduced you," Jimmy Shields said to Marion.

"Oh, Jimmy, they don't want to know that. But, since you insist, I remember them all. Charlie Chaplin, Clark Gable, Joseph Kennedy…even Rudolph Valentino, but he was mostly into guys."

"I've had Gable, too." Haines added.

"Yes, we know," Shields said, frowning at him.

Marion continued: "I once asked that halo-haired Albert Einstein why he didn't get a haircut. At another time, Billy here challenged me to seduce Calvin Coolidge, and I took the bet. He was a teetotaler. When he came to visit, I offered him a glass of Tokay wine, telling him it was only fruit juice. He drank four glasses and told me it was the most refreshing beverage he'd ever tasted. I didn't really get him drunk enough to seduce him. But Grace Coolidge told me that the first time she spotted her future husband was through a bathroom window in a house in Northampton , Massachusetts."

"Grace told me that Coolidge was jaybird naked and shaving with his hat on, so his hair wouldn't fall down over his face," Marion said. "Grace also claimed that after her sighting of him that morning, she decided she was going to marry him. I was always told that still waters run deep, but in Silent Cal's case I never got to find out."

"But it certainly sounds like you weren't deprived," Lawford said.

Before midnight, all the guests retreated to their bedrooms. Lawford stripped down and joined a naked Elizabeth in bed, asking her to "Go down on me."

She obliged, as she would later confide to Dick Hanley.

After a Sunday morning breakfast at ten o'clock, both Elizabeth and Lawford thanked Hearst and Marion profusely. Elizabeth kissed Hearst goodbye on the lips, since she'd decided that physical intimacies between Marion and Hearst had ended before the attack on Pearl Harbor.

Marion was wheeled out into the foyer for a final goodbye. She told Elizabeth and Lawford, "When you guys want some privacy, you can have the use of my guest cottage in Beverly Hills. No one will find you there. There's also a big swimming pool. You can invite your friends over to use it. I'm sure Willie would love to sit by the window, listening to the sound of young laughter again."

In the limousine retracing its steps south to Los Angeles, Lawford complained that visiting San Simeon was like a pilgrimage to a mausoleum.

Elizabeth differed, claiming, "I adored them. Let's don't be too harsh. I fully expect one day to end up in a decaying Hollywood mansion with pictures all over the place showing how I looked in the 1950s and 60s. Every evening, I'll show my old movies."

Without knowing it, Elizabeth had eerily evoked the plot of an upcoming film, *Sunset Blvd.,* in which Gloria Swanson played a faded star of the silent screen, Norma Desmond. But when Elizabeth made that prediction, *Sunset Blvd.* was only a germ in the brain of Billy Wilder.

***

Louis B. Mayer quickly rescinded his order to fire Elizabeth, and called Dick Hanley with the news. Mayer had been in serious negotiations with Sara. The end result was that Elizabeth would be lent out to Warner Brothers for a key role in *Life with Father* (1947), a film that would star William Powell and Irene Dunne. The director? None other than Sara's new lover, Michael Curtiz.

When Dick relayed this news to Elizabeth, she was delighted. She'd be reunited with the Taylor's family friend, Irene Dunne, and she'd be directed by the eccentric but well-respected Curtiz. "I'll force him to bring Errol Flynn onto the set!" Elizabeth vowed to Dick.

She was less than thrilled when she learned that her onscreen boyfriend would be played by James Lydon, a young actor known for his screechy voice and adolescent portrayal of Henry Aldrich in the Henry Aldrich movie series filmed throughout the course of World War II. She would later say, "Jimmy and I have about as much chemistry together as Marjorie Main and Clark Gable."

"Even before the filming of *Life With Father*, I had already switched my bobbysoxer allegiance from Frank Sinatra to Vic Damone. I had pictures of Errol Flynn pasted in my bathroom and a framed studio portrait of Vic Damone beside my bed. At night, I practiced French kissing Vic on my satin-covered pink pillowcase."

Between *Courage of Lassie* (1946) and the five-month shoot of *Life with Father,* Elizabeth breasts grew very large and very fast for a teenager as young as she was. "I wasn't quite up there with Jane Russell yet, but I came in with a 35" bust by the time I turned fifteen. I found that nothing excites a man, even a middle-aged man, more than a teenage girl with large busts."

"The 1940s after the war was a time of Pretty Girls and Varga Girls," Elizabeth recalled. "A girl was supposed to have melons for breasts and sticky sweet, scarlet-red lips, ideal for a man's cocksucking fantasies. Someone in makeup suggested that a 'Joan Crawford mouth' should be painted on me. Because Curtiz knew Crawford so well, I asked him if I could be introduced to her at some point. Who better to paint a Joan Crawford mouth on me than the star herself? Curtiz promised he'd arrange a meeting between us."

In *Life With Father,* Elizabeth found herself co-starring with Powell and Dunne in a comedy set in New York of the 1880s. MGM was getting $3,500 a week from Warner Brothers for her services, five times her salary at MGM. Elizabeth played a girl who wins the love of the household's oldest son, Lydon, whom *Variety* would later describe as "effective as a potential Yale man."

Powell noted that Elizabeth was "swiftly maturing," and Dunne feared that "she is growing up too fast for her own good."

Elizabeth had her own comments about the stars. "Irene is a lovely creature, charming and polite. But it's time she started playing matrons. As for Powell, what in hell did Jean Harlow see in him?"

During filming, Sara hovered over Elizabeth as if she were a rare Tiffany gem. She even took her home when she developed a pimple or had the semblance of a cold coming on.

"Yet in spite of this, I managed to slip away from Sara enough to have a back alley life," Elizabeth told friends at one of Roddy's Sunday afternoon parties. "My mother never really knew what I was up to. Roddy was my beard on many an occasion. So was Dick Hanley. Sara knew they don't like girls. I also got help from 'mainstream adults' like Marion Davies and Michael Curtiz, who criticized my mother for holding on to me too tightly."

As Errol Flynn would tell anybody who asked, Curtiz was a tyrant on the set. One afternoon, when Sara was away, Curtiz was shooting a scene between

Lydon and Elizabeth. "I told you not to eat lunch," he shouted at Lydon. "Actors who eat lunch are drowsy all afternoon." Then he not only denounced Lydon, but got so angry at him he kicked his ass, toppling the juvenile over a box.

"I nearly broke my spine," Lydon recalled. "What a bastard!"

Curtiz then turned his fury on Elizabeth, calling her a "big tit, two-bit whore." In tears, she ran screaming from the set to her dressing room, where she bolted herself inside. Curtiz stood before the locked door, calling in to her, "Son of a bitch, Elizabeth. Stop fucking crying. You break my heart. Cut the shit."

Fortunately, the director and his star had made peace by the time Sara arrived back from lunch.

Elizabeth didn't resent the affair of Sara with Curtiz. On many a night, Sara was away somewhere with her lover, leaving Elizabeth at home with a maid. Elizabeth quickly learned that the maid could be bribed, allowing her to slip away for some off-the-record rendezvous with her *beau du jour,* as she referred to the various young men she met secretly.

"I wanted a more grown-up role than the girl I played in *Life With Father."* Elizabeth said. "but since Mayer didn't fire me, I continued in that gauze-wrapped cotton candy cloud that was MGM in those days. Mayer remained a tyrant, but I never set foot in his office again after that fight we'd had. Even when he summoned me, I wouldn't go. I did, however, show up at his annual birthday bash at MGM with a fake smile plastered on my face. We both hated each other."

"I got by better than his gay actors did at the time," she said. "There was a whorehouse across from the studio. Mayer made the gay guys go over there and fuck the whores as a means of proving their manhood."

Writer Jhan Robbins summed up Elizabeth's life at this point. "She belonged less to her family than to a studio, to agents, publicity people, photographers, costumers, directors, coaches, makeup artists, fan clubs, and her huge, adoring, and insistent public. Elizabeth, one might say, no longer had a career—rather, the career had *her."*

Confronted with the absence of her real father, she turned more and more to her agent, Jules Goldstone, using him as a kind of surrogate daddy. "Unlike Sara, Jules was eager for me to play more adult roles on the screen. Off screen, he contributed to my juvenile delinquency. He was pinning most of his hopes on me to make it big, even though his other major client was my former director, Clarence Brown."

Goldstone also represented the humorist, James Thurber.

"Goldstone worked to get me roles and to arrange things. I wanted him to line up dates for me and to convince Sara that they were strictly for MGM publicity purposes. The first man Jules sent to my mantrap was a handsome young actor named Marshall Thompson."

Hailing from Illinois, Thompson was known for his boy-next-door good looks.

At first, Elizabeth didn't want to date Marshall because she'd read that he had wanted to become a priest. Elizabeth told Goldstone, "I don't want a date who'll listen to my confessions. I want a young man with whom I can commit sins."

For her first meeting with Thompson, she dressed to imitate Jennifer Jones in *Duel in the Sun.* She put on a large pair of hoop earrings, and wore a peasant blouse with a full skirt with a cinched waist. At some point later that evening, Thompson sang "Golden Earrings" to her, a song by Frankie Lane that around that time was on *The Hit Parade.*

Thompson was seven years older than Elizabeth. On their first official date—an attendance at the premiere of *The Yearling* (1940), a sensitive tale of a young boy's attachment to a deer—Sara insisted that Thompson's mother accompany them as a chaperone.

"We managed to dump his dear ol' mom early in the evening and sneak off together," Elizabeth said. "When he first kissed me, I practically had to blast open his mouth to get my tongue inside. He wasn't an expert on French kissing. But by the time Christmas came around and he took me to a Yuletide dance, we kissed beneath the mistletoe. God, had he learned his lessons. I felt his tongue at the bottom of my throat. After that night, I came up with a nickname for him: HOT LIPS!"

Later, Elizabeth was seen with Thompson dining at the Trocadero and dancing at the Cocoanut Grove. Sometimes at later sightings at that nightclub, they would have drinks with Peter Lawford, who seemed intent on seducing Thompson himself.

Photoplay, the most popular movie magazine of its day, staged a Hollywood party in honor of Elizabeth, who arrived with Thompson as her escort. Pictures of the party were lavishly featured in the magazine's next issue, which arrived on the desk of Louis B. Mayer. Examining the pictures of his rising young star, he exploded in fury. He called Dick Hanley into his office and dictated a memo to Howard Strickling, his chief of publicity.

"Miss Taylor with her plunging neckline looks like a teenage whore flaunting her wares. That is, of course, an accurate portrait of who she is, but it's not the squeaky clean image we're promoting here at MGM. See that this doesn't happen again. When Miss Taylor goes out in public, warn her that she must keep her tits covered."

Elizabeth and Thompson frequently talked about appearing as young lovers together on the screen. She discussed the possibility with her agent, Jules Goldstone, who presented it to Benjamin Thau at MGM. He told Goldstone that

Thompson did not have "an image that's masculine and virile enough for Elizabeth. Mayer and I are thinking about co-starring her with either Clark Gable or Robert Taylor."

Goldstone reminded Thau that Taylor was nearly forty years old and that Gable had been born in 1901.

For the next few weeks, Elizabeth and Marshall showed up every Sunday afternoon at Roddy's house, retiring at around four o'clock to his cabana.

Then one afternoon, Roddy introduced her to one of his recent lovers, another handsome young actor named Richard Long. Roddy assured her, "Dick accommodates both sexes." Elizabeth soon realized that she was more attracted to Long than she was to Thompson, but she had to compete with Merv Griffin for Long's favors.

"I had to fight off Griffin to get my nails into Richard's gorgeous flesh," she told Roddy. "I got him before he ended up playing the son to Ma and Pa Kettle in all those hillbilly flicks. Dick was a real gentleman in bed, perhaps too gentle. I think that both Dick and Marshall represented the kind of all-American boys who girls were marrying at the end of the war, heading for the suburbs to raise kids."

"In bed, both of these young men were sufficient in their way, but hardly adventuresome. No variation. Actually going to bed with either of them was like getting the same fuck twice."

"I drifted away from both Marshall and Dick when I found more intriguing partners," Elizabeth confessed.

After a brief fling with Long's gym buddy, Rock Hudson, an actor who would become Elizabeth's close friend, Long married Suzan Ball, a cousin of Lucille Ball. But Suzan died of cancer a year later.

Elizabeth with **Marshall Thomson**

Some time after Suzan's death, Long called Elizabeth, hoping to rekindle some passion in her, but she politely turned him down. Ironically, he married Barbara Thompson, and became the brother-in-law of his former competitor for Elizabeth's affections, Marshall Thompson.

In 1974, after multiple heart attacks, Long died at the age of forty-seven. Too preoccupied to attend the funeral, Elizabeth sent flowers.

"Marshall and Dick treated me well," Elizabeth recalled to Roddy. "They were boys you had a hot dog and a coke with and I was dreaming of champagne and caviar.

Actually, I wanted men who stood for danger. Take Errol Flynn, for example. Dick or Marshall would take a girl to bed, perform adequately, and then want to go to a football game. I wanted to be ravished by a lover who would take me to darkest Africa and do unspeakable things to me."

"I knew both Francis and Sara Taylor," Thompson recalled years later to columnist James Bacon. "They trusted me. Perhaps that trust wasn't well founded, since Elizabeth and I were doing it. When Francis died in 1968, I went to the funeral. Elizabeth showed up with Richard Burton."

"Burton stormed over to me like he wanted a fight," Thompson said. "He was drunk. 'So you're the bloke who gave Elizabeth her first screen kiss,' Burton said. Then Elizabeth came up behind him. 'No, Richard, Marshall gave me my first offscreen kiss.' Then Burton glared at me. 'That makes it even worse,' he said."

"If looks could kill, I would have been buried that day with Francis," Thompson said. "I found it hard to believe that a world class whore like Burton, who had fucked half the pretty boys and half the beautiful women on the planet, would actually be jealous of me after all those years."

"After the funeral ended, I stood and watched as Elizabeth and Burton got into a long stretch limousine. At that time they were the most notorious couple on the globe. Why was Burton jealous of me? After she dumped me, she had a string of affairs and adventures with all sorts of men who would make our little fling look like a scene from Shirley Temple's *Rebecca of Sunnybrook Farm.* Elizabeth, that darling little girl from *National Velvet,* had grown up to become a world class adventuress."

***

From March of 1945 until the summer of 1947, MGM had no film roles for Elizabeth. At this strategic stage of her career, she was desperately searching for more mature roles and not just waiting around for MGM to assign her her next picture.

She telephoned her agent, Jules Goldstone, every day. If MGM didn't have a part for her, perhaps Paramount or Warner Brothers did. She was almost certain that Louis B. Mayer would lend her out, since MGM had previously made sizable profits by doing that.

One role that appeared on the horizon with a part she felt was suitable was *That Hagen Girl,* a script written by Charles Hoffman and based on a novel by Edith Roberts.

The soap opera plot involved a small town's small-mindedness. A teenaged girl, Mary Hagen, is ostracized because gossips think she is illegitimate. When a lawyer, an older man called Tom Bates, arrives in town, the gossips assume (incorrectly) that he is the girl's father.

A handsome young hunk, ultimately played by Rory Calhoun, pursues the Hagen girl, but she falls for the older character, the lawyer, instead. He rescues her from a suicide attempt after she jumps into a roaring river. Bates professes his love for her and gives her a reason to live.

Ronald Reagan, whose career at the time was in a steep decline, read the script and (wisely) rejected it. The casting department at Warners insisted, however, promising him that if he accepted the role of the lawyer in *That Hagen Girl,* they'd eventually assign him a lead role in another, yet-to-be-determined outdoor adventure picture. Despite his objections to playing romantic scenes with a teenager, (he was thirty-six years old at the time) Reagan accepted the deal.

Elizabeth wanted Goldstone to get her the role of the Hagen girl before filming on another project (*Cynthia;* 1947) began. When she learned that Reagan's friend, actor/politician George Murphy would be cast in the film with her, she enlisted his help in her campaign to get the role opposite Reagan in *That Hagen Girl.*

A few days later, Reagan, partly because of Murphy's intervention, called Elizabeth and invited her to dinner at an apartment in West Hollywood. She noted that he pointedly did not invite her to his home, which he still shared with his estranged wife, Jane Wyman.

Elizabeth was picked up by her agent, Goldstone, and delivered to the apartment in West Hollywood. In distinct contrast to the plan which had been presented to Sara, Goldstone would not be at the dinner, but would retrieve Elizabeth shortly before midnight to take her back home.

Elizabeth would relay the details of what happened that night to dozens of her friends, but not until after 1980, when Reagan was elected president of the United States, beating the incumbent president, Jimmy Carter.

***

A few weeks after her dinner with Reagan—the details of which are relayed within this chapter's next scene—he called her with news that the studio had rejected her bid and had cast Shirley Temple, an older teenager, in the Hagen role instead. Temple would play the role as part of a loan-out from David O. Selznick.

"I was terribly disappointed that my nemesis had been cast opposite Reagan," Elizabeth said. "But it was only one of many casting disappointments I'd experience in my future."

She followed the news of this troubled film as it was made. She'd read that Temple interpreted her role as *That Hagen Girl* as "my lip-smacking chance," even though Shirley's domineering mother, Gertrude, had warned her that "Reagan is long on quips and short on talent."

Reagan's onscreen involvement with a younger actress was already raising concern, but at least some of his fears had been assuaged by Cary Grant, who had reminded him that earlier that year (1947), Grant had appeared in a romantic plot co-starring Shirley Temple in *The Bachelor and the Bobby Soxer*. Grant reminded Reagan that he was seven years older than he was. "And I pulled it off," he said.

Nonetheless, during the filming of *That Hagen Girl*, Reagan informed its director, Peter Godfrey, that he found it embarrassing to play a romantic lead opposite Temple because of the seventeen-year- difference in their ages. "I find such relationships repulsive."

Tersely, Godfrey reminded Reagan that "my own wife is young enough to be my daughter." In embarrassment, Reagan retreated.

One of his scenes required that Reagan jump into a roaring cold river to rescue Temple from her suicide attempt. When he has her safely on shore, he declares his love for her. It was a difficult shot, requiring lots of time and several takes.

In the wake of his immersion in the freezing waters, Reagan, hovering near death, was hospitalized at the Cedars of Lebanon Hospital with viral pneumonia and a constant temperature of 104°. Elizabeth sent flowers. During his hospitalization, Reagan received the unfortunate news that his wife, Jane Wyman, had suffered a miscarriage.

Temple, during the slowdown in filming caused by Reagan's hospitalization, despite strenuous dieting, kept gaining weight. Finally, a doctor informed her that she was pregnant.

That Hagen Girl had its sneak preview in Pasadena. In disguise, Elizabeth was escorted there by Marshall Thompson. She was hoping that the film would be a disaster, and her wish, indeed, came abundantly true.

During the scene in the movie when Reagan tells Temple, "I

The role that Elizabeth was glad she lost,and the role that another child star was sorry she got: *That* (horrible) *Hagen Girl*

lower photo: Its co-stars,
Ronald Reagan and **Shirley Temple**,
who shocked viewers with its
"appearance of unrebated incest."

love you," the audience screamed, "OH NO!!" Because of their reaction, the studio opted to cut that pivotal scene from the film's final version.

Later that evening, Elizabeth told Thompson, "With me in the role, the audience would have believed that Reagan really loved the Hagen girl. But despite her age, her fans still think of Miss Temple as a little curly haired moppet. As I told Reagan, audiences won't accept a love affair between Miss Lollipop and him. I was right."

"I learned a lesson from watching *That Hagen Girl,*" Elizabeth confided to Thompson. "Shirley Temple probably destroyed her chance to *segué* from being a child star to a teenaged actress. I'm not going to let that happen to me. Also, there is absolutely no chemistry between Reagan and her. Reagan knows, however, that there *is* chemistry between us—but I can't go into that right now. I don't want to shock you. You're far too young."

Time magazine denounced the picture, claiming, "Moviegoers with very strong stomachs may be able to view an appearance of rebated incest as a romantic situation."

Temple told the press, "As movie kissers go, Reagan was good."

Reagan said, "After the cuts, it was left up to the audience to decide if I married Shirley, traveled with her doing naughties, or adopted her."

Unlike Temple, based on the dinner she had shared with him in that apartment in West Hollywood, Elizabeth could evaluate firsthand Reagan's performance in bed—and not just as a kisser. But she would wait for him to become President of the United States before she "dined out" on stories about his performance in the boudoir.

***

During the 1980s, Elizabeth did not like Reagan's policies, and was horrified at his utter silence on the subject of the AIDS epidemic sweeping across the globe like the Black Plague of the Middle Ages.

For the first time, she began speaking publicly about his seduction of her when she was a teenager back in the Hollywood of the late 1940s. Often, under the influence of a champagne buzz, she'd have her dining companions laughing and amused at social venues that stretched from Rome to Gstaad, from London to New York and on to Los Angeles.

She recounted how her agent, Jules Goldstone, drove her to a secret little apartment in West Hollywood. "I never knew if this were Reagan's fuck pad—or else the apartment of a friend of his," she said.

Ostensibly, shrouded at the time in studio intrigue, she had arrived to lobby for the role of Mary Hagen in the box office disaster *That Hagen Girl,* a part that eventually went to the older Shirley Temple.

"I thought he might have invited me to a restaurant, but he preferred this small flat," Elizabeth told Frank Sinatra's guests in Palm Springs one night.

"Reagan opened the door wearing an apron. He complimented me on how beautiful I was—and how grown-up I looked. Then he offered me a drink and invited me into his dimly lit living room, where the music of Doris Day could be heard. I later found out he was also pursuing Miss Day."

"The table was already set with candles. He invited me into the kitchen, where he'd made a salad. He pointed out five kinds of lettuce he'd purchased at the Farmers' Market. Our meal that night included juicy hamburgers, his favorite. He told me he'd ground the beef himself."

"Reagan was treating me like a grown woman, and that thrilled me," Elizabeth said. "Of course, I was still a child at the time, but I didn't want to be treated like one. Back in those days, he was still quite handsome and had a good body, at least according to the standards of the time, which were hardly the buff standards of today. A few years earlier, he'd actually posed for beefcake photos."

"I tried to act as sophisticated as I could, even though he was old enough to be my father. We talked a lot about the script of *That Hagen Girl*, and he had serious doubts about his own role within it. We bonded over our mutual concerns for our careers. I was trying to cross the bridge between child star and adult roles, and he was trying to hold onto his role as a leading romantic figure as he moved into middle age in the 1950s. Neither of us wanted to be a footnote in some survey of movies of the 1940s."

"He was a pretty good cook, and he'd bought the world's most delicious rum-laced chocolate cake with 'drunken' cherries on top. I volunteered to help with the dishes, but he told me a maid would come to clean up in the morning."

"We sat on his sofa, and I could tell he wanted to get it on. But he seemed reluctant to make the first move, probably because of my age. I finally took Judy Garland's advice and became the aggressor. God, I wished they'd been casting *Lolita* around that time...I could have won an Oscar playing the nymphet. When he found my tongue down his throat and my hand massaging his goodies, he was mine for the night."

"Once I broke the ice, he took charge," she claimed. "After a heavy make-out session on the sofa, with a lot of fondling of my breasts, we went into the bedroom, where he stripped me. He was somewhat reluctant, but he finally removed his clothing. When he dropped his boxer shorts, I was pleasantly surprised. By then, I knew that God did not create all men equally, and that he was hung better than average. He put on a condom—he called it a 'rubber'—and assured me that it was the most expensive on the market, so I didn't have to fear getting pregnant."

"Let me give credit where credit is due," she said. "It was the longest running fuck I'd ever had up to that point. I didn't exactly time it, but it went on for at least forty-five minutes. It wasn't the greatest lay of my life, but it ranked up there with the best of them. He seemed very concerned with my own satisfaction, and I liked him for that."

"As soon as he'd shot off—finally—he rushed for the showers. He was the cleanest smelling man I've ever known, unlike Richard Burton, who was often smelly and stunk like a brewery. Reagan must have enjoyed it, because he called me ten days later for a repeat."

"I turned him down because at this point I had been introduced to the one star in Hollywood who was better in the sack than any other. But that's a story for another day."

Elizabeth's story has been dismissed by some of her critics and fans, some of whom believe that her oft-repeated recitation was a politically motivated fabrication intended to embarrass President Reagan.

However, when actress Piper Laurie published her memoirs, *Learning to Live Out Loud,* in 2011, Elizabeth's rendition became far more plausible.

In *Louisa* (1950)*,* the then-teenaged Piper was cast as Reagan's daughter. She wrote that Reagan seduced her during the shoot. In her case, she was not only a teenager, but a virgin.

So the possibility of Reagan's seduction of young Elizabeth was not out of character. There were numerous other stories about Reagan's seductions of young women—girls, really—that circulated about him during his years in Hollywood, stories which were amplified and expanded after his election as President.

When Elizabeth's former lover, Frank Sinatra, got together for booze and laughs, he always told her that he'd seduced two First Ladies and that she'd been sexually intimate with two U.S. Presidents.

"The big difference between them," she jokingly recalled, "was how long each of them was in the saddle. I much preferred the second president's politics to those of Reagan. But, in all fairness to Reagan, this other president (JFK) had one big drawback. He was a two-minute man."

Piper Laurie

CHAPTER EIGHT
"The Most Beautiful Woman in the World"

The 1947 film, *Cynthia,* cast Elizabeth in her first role as a maturing adolescent, marking a major transformation from the child star of *National Velvet* to her emergence as a beautiful young woman—that is, a very young and a very beautiful woman. Beginning with this movie, two titles were bestowed on her by the Hollywood press machine: "Princess of Hollywood" and "The Most Beautiful Woman in the World."

For the first time, she appeared on the cover of *Life* magazine. Throughout her life, she would pose for more *Life* covers than any other actress. *Cynthia* would also mark her first screen kiss, a chaste smooch from James (Jimmy) Lydon, whose World War II Henry Aldrich film series had provided competition for Mickey Rooney, who, after his marriage to Ava Gardner, was hardly convincing any more as the youthful, innocent Andy.

Cynthia, whose story was based on Viña Delmar's Broadway flop, *The Rich, Full Life.* was promoted as "a teenaged version of *Camille.*" Its plot centered around a sickly, sheltered teen beauty who rebels against overprotective parents, played by Mary Astor and George Murphy. Cynthia finds a boyfriend, Lydon, who takes her to the senior prom, giving her a good night kiss—pretty innocent stuff for an actress who one day would be called "The Serpent of the Nile."

A *femme fatale* reduced to mother roles, Astor wrote about Elizabeth in her memoir, *Life on Film,* and had additional, more provocative, comments to make about her in private to fellow cast members. "Elizabeth was cool and slightly superior," she wrote. "There was a look in those violet eyes that was somewhat calculating. She was quite sure of what she wanted and was quite sure of getting it."

When Elizabeth, in later years, read that, she said, "What an acute observation from the Astor bitch. It's amazing that she was so perceptive, considering she was drunk every day."

Throughout the shoot, Astor battled the bottle. After the filming of *Cynthia* ended, she entered rehab, as would Elizabeth herself in the years to come.

In later interviews, Astor was more revealing of her feelings. "Elizabeth had begun taking sedatives to calm her nerves. She appeared on set very high strung and brittle and snapped at you if you dared speak to her. Like Cynthia in the film, Elizabeth required a lot of sick leave. I think she had already begun to take herself too seriously and to believe her press clippings. She was preparing for the melodramatic lifestyle that would follow in her later years. My God, she was only fifteen and ordering her mother to leave the set and go home. The cast learned why. After work, Elizabeth was seen driving away with John Derek, even Errol Flynn. And in the 1930s, *I* was called a scarlet woman. Errol should have been dating me—not Elizabeth."

Elizabeth understood the character of Cynthia and even gave advice to the screenwriter and director, according to George Murphy. "She wanted to move into the adult world far too soon. I felt guilty setting her up with Ronald Reagan. I loved Ronnie dearly, but when it came to women, he could go too far. My God, in a year or so, he would be pursuing Marilyn Monroe. Of course, there are worse things than screwing Elizabeth Taylor and Marilyn Monroe."

The director of *Cynthia* was Robert Z. Leonard, who had in the 1920s married the blonde silent screen vamp, Mae Murray, famed for her 1925 portrayal of *The Merry Widow*.

"From what I'd observed, Elizabeth Taylor was turning into a little whore, and Sara seemed none the wiser," Leonard claimed to Mary Astor and George Murphy. "Of course, I could be wrong. Privately, Sara may have known everything that was going on and was just maintaining a pristine public image. Everybody in Hollywood did that. Elizabeth was complaining to the press that boys were intimidated by her fame and were too afraid to ask

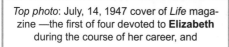

Top photo: July, 14, 1947 cover of *Life* magazine —the first of four devoted to **Elizabeth** during the course of her career, and

Lower photos: Co-workers who were less than enchanted by the antics of young Elizabeth: *left :***Mary Astor**, and *right:* Director **Robert Z. Leonard**

her out on a date. That was pure bullshit. No dates! Hell, she was sucking off John Derek and doing God knows what with Errol Flynn. I can't believe how many writers fell for Elizabeth's line. Here she was, hailed as the most beautiful woman in the world, and complaining that men wouldn't go out with her—in Hollywood, of all places! I would have fucked her myself if she'd picked up on my signals."

Leonard would have been a bit old for Elizabeth, as he'd been born in Chicago in 1889. She was pleased to be working with such an experienced director, who had been nominated for Oscars for helming *The Divorcée* in 1930 and *The Great Ziegfeld* in 1936.

When introduced to him on the first day of the shoot, Elizabeth said, "Oh, Mr. Leonard, I've researched your career. Here you are directing Jimmy Lydon and me in a silly little romance when you once directed Clark Gable and Greta Garbo in *Susan Lenox (Her Fall and Rise)."*

"I want to grow up fast, even faster than I'm doing," she told Leonard. "I know I'm very young, but have the emotions of a woman twice my age. I want to create a world for myself away from my parents and MGM."

"What kind of a world would that be?" Leonard asked.

"A world filled with men, lots of men," she said, smiling.

Her remarks were tamer in the summer of 1947 when she went on a radio show hosted by Louella Parsons. She bluntly told the gossip maven, "I want to become a great actress. But mostly, I want to snare a husband. Boys my own age bore me."

Privately, she told Parsons. "I'll be auditioning several *beaux* over the next few months until I find the man most suited to me."

When Parsons quizzed her about the estrangement of her father and mother, she ducked the question, claiming that both of her parents were busy pursuing their own careers.

Cynthia was shot out of sequence, and the kissing scene with Lydon was one of the first to be filmed. Leonard also directed and filmed Elizabeth's kissing scene at the end of the movie. "She's not well versed in pucking," he said. "The difference on film between her early kiss and the film's concluding kiss was day and night. By the end of the shoot, Errol Flynn had taught her everything she ever knew or wanted to know about sex. She should always be grateful to her sexual mentor."

Lydon wasn't all that excited by the kiss. "It was almost a half-century ago," he said, "and people are still talking about it. At the time, I didn't view it as a milestone. It felt more like a handshake. Elizabeth also sang a song in the movie. Her voice was a bit shrill, rather reedy, if you ask me."

During the filming of *Cynthia,* Sara changed her position about wanting Elizabeth to prolong her role as a child star, as Mickey Rooney had done. When she saw how Shirley Temple was failing at the box office as a young adult, Sara insisted on major changes in Elizabeth's appearance. "She deliberately encouraged her to dress far older than she was, and to show bosom," according to Lawford.

`Spencer Tracy observed her in the MGM commissary. "Every day she showed up revealing her tits. It gave even older guys like me hard-ons."

The First Lady of the United States was not impressed. Harry Truman's wife, Bess, invited Elizabeth and other stars to the White House to attend a March of Dimes campaign. Making a stunning entrance, Elizabeth arrived in a black velvet dress, cut very low, a white fur coat, and a pair of seamless black nylon stockings. Mrs. Truman at the head table was overheard, "That Elizabeth Taylor child has some nerve coming here dressed up like one of those hussies Joan Crawford plays in films. If (my daughter) Margaret ever did that to me, I would take her out to the woodshed and give her a whipping she'd never forget."

Back in Hollywood, Elizabeth found that in spite of her grown-up appearance in Washington, she was still seated at the children's table at the MGM commissary. She was approached by a photographer, who asked her if she'd pose for pictures in a bathing suit.

After checking with Sara, Elizabeth agreed to pose on a Santa Monica beach. She wore a revealing one-piece white bathing suit. The photographer snapped some two-hundred pictures of her, which were widely printed and distributed. At the end of the shoot, he told her, "You are the most beautiful woman I have ever photographed, and I've shot all the top stars—Rita Hayworth, Ava Gardner, Betty Grable, Lana Turner."

The next day, Sara telephoned Hedda Hopper, who repeated the photographer's praise in her column, stating that Elizabeth was "the most beautiful woman in the world." So far as it is known, this was the first time that appellation— soon to be repeated around the globe for

GENERATION GAP:
left photo: **Elizabeth Taylor** kissing **James Lydon** in *Cynthia*

right photo: First Lady **Bess Truman** at the White House:
Dire warnings about what would happen
"If my daughter (Margaret) ever dressed
like that Elizabeth Taylor....."

years to come—first appeared in newsprint.

The next week, Hopper ran another headline—ELIZABETH TAYLOR'S PARENTS REUNITED. Sara had taken ill and had called Francis to come home and take care of her and help her look after Elizabeth. She reminded him that she considered divorce out of the question. He agreed to those terms and would bring her son, Howard, back into the household.

However, during their discussions of a reconciliation, he informed her that he planned to continue his affair with Adrian. He also reserved the right to bring young men in for sleepovers after Elizabeth and Howard had gone to bed.

It was during this time that Michael Curtiz ended his affair with Sara, tossing her aside for the blonde World War II goddess with the peek-a-boo bangs, Veronica Lake.

Upon its release, *Cynthia* became the most popular film shown at U.S. military bases all over the world. During its depiction of Elizabeth's screen kiss, the servicemen often hooted and hollered. As one soldier put it, "Compared to the noise the men made over *Cynthia,* our artillery fire sounded like small firecrackers."

Across America, movie houses organized "Why I deserve to be kissed by Liz" contests. One sailor maintained that he deserved the award because he had an abnormally long tongue that could not be completely concealed when he closed his mouth. "I could reach to the back of her throat," he wrote on his entry form at a movie theater in San Diego, enclosing a picture of himself with his tongue out.

When Howard Strickling, representing MGM's publicity department, jokingly presented this contestant's application and picture to Elizabeth, she said she found it disgusting. She refused to reward any of the contest winners from around the country with a kiss.

She showed the sailor's picture to Roddy McDowall. "I bet he'd be good at cunnilingus and rimming, too." Roddy exclaimed. Then he was forced to explain to Elizabeth what both of those terms meant.

"Then perhaps I'll have to reconsider this long-tongued sailor boy," she told Roddy.

When *Cynthia* was released, Bosley Crowther of *The New York Times* dismissed it, referring to it as "a synthetic morsel right from the Metro candy box." Other, more appreciative critics interpreted it as a cinematic milestone in the depiction of adolescent independence, defining Cynthia as a rebel who opts not to let life defeat her the way it did her parents.

Audiences were treated to a revised public image of Elizabeth—one where she looked "drop-dead gorgeous." For the first time, she appeared with her hair swept up. Around her neck, she wore a heart-shaped locket that had been depicted on the cover of *Life* magazine.

Elizabeth had already seen *Cynthia* at a preview, but she asked Roddy to take her to a regular afternoon screening of the film in Pasadena. She slipped in after the screening began and ducked out right before the final scene, as she didn't want to be recognized.

Afterward, she asked Roddy, "I looked grown-up, didn't I?"

"You looked exactly like Greta Garbo in *Two-Faced Woman,*" he said facetiously.

"From now on, I'm no longer a teenager except in age," she told him. "Let's face it: Both of us like dick and plenty of it. You've already had every actor in Hollywood, and I want to top your record, even though you've got a head start. I'm tired of waiting."

"You're not waiting," he reminded her. "You've already had more affairs than the typical American gal has in a lifetime."

"Just watch me go," she said. "I'm only at the starting gate."

***

The knave of hearts, the greatest rogue of them all, the swashbuckler in countless adventures: At last, Michael Curtiz brought Errol Flynn to the set to introduce him to Elizabeth. He wasn't quite forty when she met him. The talk in Hollywood was that he had prematurely aged because of all his drinking, drugs, and debaucheries.

She found him amazing looking, one of the most handsome men she'd ever met. He was charming and suave and spoke with a slight British-Australian accent. He'd obviously come from a tennis game. She was aware that most players on tennis courts in those days wore only white, but he was dressed in sunflower yellow shorts, a yellow T-shirt, and even yellow tennis shoes and socks.

"Hello, I'm Errol Flynn. You obviously are Elizabeth Taylor."

She'd dreamed about what her first words to him would be. She wanted them to be piquant and memorable. "There's one thing no one told me about you," she said.

"And what might that be, my dear?" he asked.

"You have the male version of Betty Grable's legs,"she said.

"That's not all I have," he said, kissing her on both cheeks.

She was dazzled by his eyes. They were a beautiful brown color but flecked with gold, and they twinkled as he spoke. He took her hand. When he smiled, he flashed pearly white teeth. After kissing her hand, he gently held it.

She wanted to remember this moment so she could report every tiny detail to Dick Hanley and Roddy McDowall. Here was "Robin Hood" and "Captain Blood" in the flesh, perfectly tanned and with perfect manners, except when it came to speaking to Curtiz.

Curtiz and Flynn often exchanged insulting banter, as each man knew the other's most deadly secrets. "You've got to watch this guy," Errol warned Elizabeth. "He's a vicious Hungarian with a tongue like a cobra's."

"I decided on first picture Flynn's a bum," Curtiz said. "Can't act. So what happens? Warner's assign this jerk to me time and time again."

"Which of my pictures did you like the best?" Errol asked Elizabeth.

"I've seen only two," she said. *The Adventures of Robin Hood* and *Captain Blood.*"

"I've got a great idea." Errol said. "Why don't you guys come with me to my farm on Mulholland Drive? I've got a copy of my 1937 film, *The Perfect Specimen.*"

"I was the director," Curtiz said. "Hal B. Wallis told me to cast an actor who's athletic, cultured, smart, very handsome, and charming. I get this idiot."

Two views of superstar **Errol Flynn**
lower photo: In his notorious
"fuck pad"

"In the film I have a boxing scene, Errol said. "I get to show off my Betty Grable legs and my perfect specimen of a chest. "Members of the audience screamed and fainted when I came out half-naked."

"I can't wait to see it," she said. "I'd love to accept your invitation."

"Come on," he said. "Let's hit the road. Curtiz, you take your own car, and Elizabeth can ride with me."

"I know that sitting beside temptation like me, you'll be the perfect gentleman," she told him.

Elizabeth was apprehensive as Flynn pulled into his driveway, but was relieved to see that Curtiz had trailed them in his own car. Built in the "California colonial" style on a mountaintop, 7740 Mulholland Drive, though modest by A-list movie star standards, was the most notorious private residence in Greater Los Angeles.

As he showed her around, she was amazed at the number of French doors. "That means I can throw them open at parties—I'm always giving parties. You must come to them."

Roddy had already told her about

some of these parties and even provided details about the special features of the house—bugging devices, hidden passageways, two-way mirrors, and peeper holes. "One hidden chamber is called "the jerk-off room" although I've never heard that anyone actually masturbates there. They don't have to."

As she returned with Flynn to the living room to join Curtiz, a Mexican maid brought in pink champagne and caviar. "I usually like my liquor brown, but in honor of you, I made it pink champagne tonight," Flynn said.

"Not for me," Curtiz griped. "I'm no god damn fairy. Bring me a whiskey."

As Elizabeth drank gingerly, Flynn pointed out a new glass-fronted cupboard he'd ordered as a display case for his collection of ancient Greek vases, some of which had been excavated by divers off the Aegean coast of the Greek island of Lesbos.

Curtiz, meanwhile, set up the screening for *The Perfect Specimen,* the story of a super-rich character played by Flynn, who is kept sheltered by his grandmother until a vivacious Joan Blondell comes crashing through his fence, launching a whirlwind courtship.

At the film's end, Flynn turned on the lights. Curtiz had disappeared. Flynn with Elizabeth migrated to a panoramic terrace, with its view over Los Angeles.

"At night, everything looks so beautiful," she said. "All the ugliness of Los Angeles is hidden. The moonlight is very forgiving."

"The moon is not needed to enhance your beauty," he told her.

"Thank you for the compliment," he said. "But if you want to see beauty, just check out the image in the mirror when you take a shave in the morning."

"No teenage girl has ever said that to me before," he said. "I love it! More! More!"

Flynn poured more pink champagne, as an incredibly beautiful, blonde-haired young boy who appeared to be no more than fourteen, came onto the terrace. "Mr. Flynn," he said. "Miss Doris Duke is on the phone."

An avid reader of gossip columns, Elizabeth knew who Doris Duke was. The tobacco heiress was the richest woman in the world, and Elizabeth wondered if Flynn was her kept boy. Judging from her pictures and the articles that had appeared about her in the press, Duke was known as a not particularly beautiful woman who had developed a knack for distracting and eventually "purchasing" the men she desired.

When Flynn returned, he said, "That was Miss Duke. She's flown into town from Hawaii and wants to see me."

"I hope you didn't tell her I was here," she said. "I don't want to make such a powerful enemy."

"It would not have mattered," he assured her. "We have an understanding about such things. We're just fuck buddies, nothing more serious than that."

94

As Stephanie Mansfield, author of *The Richest Girl in the World* put it, "Flynn was Doris Duke's kind of man—bisexual, promiscuous, and not above asking Doris for money. His whole life was once described as a trespass against good taste, which appealed to her."

Over dinner, where pheasant was the main course, Flynn entertained Elizabeth with stories of his early life "growing up as a wicked little Tasmanian Devil."

"But I thought you were from Ireland," she said.

"You've been reading my press. Privately, I called my mother 'The Cunt,' and despite her lack of nurturing, I eventually grew, all by myself, into a strapping lad. Every married woman and every homosexual in Australia tried to get into my trousers. I decided to charge them for the privilege. I was a bona fide male whore until I went to New Guinea to search for gold. That didn't pan out, forgive the pun, so I sold natives as slave labor to the miners. One night I killed a man. But he was only a native, so what the hell?"

"You are the most dangerous man I've ever met," she said.

"For saying that, you get a kiss." From his perch on her side of the sofa, he leaned over to kiss her. One kiss led to another. Unlike her experience with Marshall Thompson, she didn't have to teach Flynn to open his mouth when kissing. Before the session ended, each of them had removed most of their clothing, or so she'd relay later to Dick Hanley.

Flynn did a striptease for Elizabeth; his body was that of an athlete. During their time together in bed, she uncovered one of his sexual secrets. He rubbed cocaine on the tip of his penis before intercourse.

"He hurt me," she later told Dick, "but did so in such a thrilling way."

After their lovemaking, during pillow talk, he'd complained that "I'm just a god damn phallic symbol to the world. They say I'm always trying to seduce young girls—statutory rape and all that. Hell, I come home to find the little vixens hiding under my bed. In my dressing room, I just lie there reading the trades while they work me over."

Curtiz called Flynn the next day to see how it had gone. "We're not fated to have a long affair," Flynn told the director. "There's a big drawback to Elizabeth. I'm a leg man, not a breast man. Her legs are too short. Her breasts are terrific, but how do you make love to a breast?"

"Someday when you're older, you fucker, I'll tell you," Curtiz said before hanging up the phone.

To both Roddy and to Dick, Elizabeth breathlessly supplied the details of her one-night stand. "Suddenly, there he was, all six feet two inches of delicious manhood. I was smitten from the first moment he walked in. I know girls have charged him with rape. He didn't have to rape me. To me, Errol Flynn is romance, danger, adventure."

He called Elizabeth shortly after their experience together, telling her, "You are a very special girl, and I worship you." Before ringing off, he asked her to come back to the house on Mulholland Drive the following Saturday afternoon, and she willingly accepted.

When she arrived, the house was very different, not romantic at all. She heard the giggles and screams of children coming from the swimming pool. In the living room, Flynn presented her with a large toy poodle whose fur had been artfully dyed pink. "It's adorable, but how do I explain this when I take it home?"

"Tell Sara it's a gift from a crazed fan, which would be the truth in my case," he told her before kissing her.

He walked with her to the edge of the swimming pool where he pointed out his young son, Sean, who was nine years younger than she was. He was playing in the shallow side of the water with two slightly older girls. Then Flynn directed her to a dressing cabana where he told her she'd find a bathing suit her size. In the cabana, she discovered at least twenty women's swim suits, making her wonder who'd worn these suits before.

Then she joined the kids in the pool, playing games as if she was a child again. She found Sean an extremely beautiful, blonde-haired boy. He provided her with a black inner tube, then struggled to overturn it once she'd settled into it. After being dumped in the water, she chased him from the pool, threatening to rip off his bathing trunks. Comfortably seated in a chaise longue, Flynn seemed to enjoy the scene as he puffed on a Havana cigar.

Two hours later, Elizabeth was in Flynn's bedroom. He'd left the door open, and was bouncing her up and down on a king-size bed large enough for four couples. He'd toss her into the air, catching her as she came down. When she looked up, she spotted Sean at the door.

"She's only a girl," he said, coming into the room. "That's the game you play with me!" It sounded like a protest.

"And you're only a boy, sport," Flynn told his son. "See this girl I'm bouncing up and down? Show some respect. She's going to become your stepmother one day."

Sean stormed out of the room, slamming the door behind him.

Later that evening, Elizabeth told Sara that she'd spent the afternoon at Roddy's house. But in the privacy of her bedroom, she called Roddy to report on the day's events. "I'm going to tell you the biggest secret of my life."

"You're pregnant," he said, only half in jest.

"You wish. No, not that. Errol is going to marry me."

"Did he propose?" Roddy asked.

"Not quite, but he more or less did. He practically swore on a stack of bibles to his son, Sean, that I was going to become his stepmother."

***

Errol Flynn had appeared suddenly into her life, and he disappeared two weeks later with the same suddenness, without telling her of his departure.

"He was 'in like Flynn,' and then out like Flynn," she told Dick Hanley. During his reaction to that observation, Mayer's secretary told her that he thought Flynn had gone on a mysterious trip to Mexico. "He can indulge in debaucheries South of the Border that would get him arrested in the U.S."

As a young girl who was emerging fast but somewhat prematurely into the adult world, Elizabeth suffered from a kind of attention deficit syndrome, even if that term had not yet been made known to her. "Her interest in certain men shifted from week to week," said Dick. "She would continue to visit Flynn from time to time, but when Robert Stack walked into her life, Robin Hood went back to Sherwood Forest."

***

After a spree with Sara in England, Elizabeth was summoned back to Hollywood by Louis B. Mayer, who had hired Richard Thorpe to direct the feel-good film *A Date With Judy* (1948) at MGM.

Its cast included Jane Powell in the title role, Wallace Beery, Selena Royle, and, for laughs, Carmen Miranda and Xavier Cugat. As mentioned before, Robert Stack would play one of the male leads in a frothy, and somewhat flawed, film about the "coming of age" of a character played by Elizabeth.

The best scene in the movie did not include any of the more prominently featured leads, but featured Carmen Miranda suggestively teaching a wealthy patriarch, as played by Wallace Beery, how to dance the rhumba. But everything ends happily by film's end, when it's made obvious that Rosita is destined for a future with her true love, a character played by Xavier Cugat, at the time Hollywood's most successful Latino entertainer.

That same year, 1948, Thorpe had directed Peter Lawford in *On an Island With You,* co-starring Esther Williams.

But despite his many previous successes, Elizabeth was mainly intrigued about why Thorpe had been fired from the directorship of *The Wizard of Oz.* He was very blunt in telling her.

"I directed Judy Garland for only two weeks. Mayer didn't think I had the right air of fantasy about the picture. I gave her a blonde wig and was accused of giving her a cutesy 'baby-doll' makeup, making her look older than the innocent little girl from Kansas they wanted. George Cukor came in temporarily and got rid of the wig, the make-up, and me."

"Well, we won't have this problem on *A Date With Judy,*" Elizabeth responded. "I want to look older and very sexy."

"You certainly have the tits for it, kid," her director told her. She would work with him on future pictures.

A Date With Judy's producer was Joe Pasternak, who, in 1939, had cast Stack in his inaugural film, *First Love,* starring Deanna Durbin. Stack gave Deanna her first screen kiss. But that decade had passed and, as the forties were coming to an end, Deanna was *passé.* When Elizabeth was introduced to Pasternak, she told him, "Robert Stack is not going to give me my first screen kiss. He's much too late for that."

"Don't worry, kid," he told her. "Stack is going to give you your first *adult* screen kiss."

Elizabeth was mesmerized by Carmen Miranda, the "Brazilian Bombshell."

"Why does MGM think I have an accent?" she asked Elizabeth in heavily accented English. "What do they expect from a South American?"

Carmen's banana hats fascinated Elizabeth, and the star loved to drive fast cars. One afternoon, when Sara was ill, Carmen volunteered to drive Elizabeth home. "My God, she went one-hundred miles an hour," Elizabeth later said. "She was arrested for speeding. The cops suspected her of being drunk. I went with her to the police station where she was booked. I got home by eleven that night. Miraculously, I was still alive."

Typical of post-war MGM musicals, *A Date With Judy* was light froth, with all the stars—more or less— required to sing.

Elizabeth recalled bandleader Cugat walking around with a little Chihuahua under his arm. Whenever he passed by Elizabeth, he pinched her butt.

Like his former co-stars, Elizabeth found Wallace Beery obnoxious. The most unlikely superstar of Hollywood's golden era, he had been married to screen vamp Gloria Swanson throughout most of the course (1916-1919) of World War I. He was usually cast as a jowly, lovable lug. Offscreen, he was anything but the image he portrayed. "He never spoke to me, walked right past me, even though out of respect I always addressed him. He was known for his scene stealing and constant mugging, and he was also a thief. Anything that wasn't nailed down, including some of the props, he took home with him."

A Date With Judy represented the first time Elizabeth wore make-up on screen, and the first time she had a leading man who wasn't four-legged. "One minute I was kissing a horse and the next thing I was kissing Bob Stack with tongue. I loved it. I had such a crush on him."

Depicted in luscious Technicolor, Elizabeth was the sultry schoolmate of MGM's singing sensation, Jane Powell, known as "The Girl Next Door." Thanks partly to her startling singing voice, she'd begun performing since the age of two, and had arrived in Hollywood with hopes of becoming the next

Shirley Temple.

In the film, Elizabeth played a rich girl, the rival of Powell. She and Powell were never very close, although they attended MGM's schoolhouse together, and Powell was frequently invited to Roddy McDowall's Sunday afternoon gatherings.

Powell later recalled, "Elizabeth was younger than me, and she got to wear green eyeshadow, show off her figure in a tight sweater, and look sexy. That hurt. I was really a little jealous, not of her, but of that green eyeshadow. Just once, I would love to have appeared as sexy in a movie. Bob Stack also gave me my first screen kiss, but Elizabeth got him at the end of the movie. She was really beautiful, with breasts."

Elizabeth echoed Powell's comment. "I got Stack in more ways than one."

Months later, after seeing the movie's final version, Elizabeth told a reporter, "My silly character never left the first dimension, although I looked gorgeous in those gowns by Helen Rose. I was so impressed with her dresses that I had her design my wedding gown. When I met her, though, she wore a nondescript black dress with food stains on it, and her slip was showing. She'd tied her hair in an unflattering knot. She obviously concentrated on designing clothes for others, not for herself. She made me look very grown up."

A Date With Judy was Elizabeth's first attempt to mold herself into a young *femme fatale* and "not be turned out to pasture" like other child stars, including Margaret O'Brien and Deanna Durbin. "I did not want an awkward period of adolescence to destroy my daughter's screen character," Sara stated. "She became a young woman overnight."

Powell shared a dressing room with Elizabeth and remembered that she complained that she was "mad for Peter Lawford and he doesn't give a shit for me."

Light froth "in luscious Technicolor:"
Elizabeth Taylor and **Jane Powell** in
A Date with Judy

"She was inconsolable and didn't seem able to accept rejection," Powell said.

Bob Stack made her forget about Lawford.

"With Robert Stack in bed beside you, what girl in the world could want anything better?" Elizabeth asked.

***

After three years of military service as a gunnery instructor dur-

99

ing World War II, Robert Stack returned to Hollywood, wanting to be cast in adult action roles. "What did I get? I ended up as the boy next door in love with the girl next door. But it was worth it. That girl happened to be Elizabeth Taylor. Unlike Errol Flynn, I didn't want to be brought up on a statutory rape charge. But everybody on the set kept telling me that Elizabeth wanted to go out with me. Even though I was twenty-nine years old and she wasn't quite sweet sixteen. I knocked on her dressing room door. My good friend, Flynn, had told me that he'd broken her in already, so I didn't have to teach her sex education courses."

She came to the door in her brassiere. "Unlike Flynn, who's a leg man, I'm a breast man. 'I've come to ask you out on a date,' I told her."

"Well, it's about time," she said. "We've already kissed on camera, so we can get over that kiss-on-the-first-date shit and move on to the next stage."

"That's the best offer I've had since I returned to Hollywood," Stack told her. "I gave Deanna Durbin her first kiss, and didn't get anywhere with that one."

"Your luck is about to change," Elizabeth said.

***

On her first date with Stack, he picked her up at her home in Beverly Hills at ten o'clock in the morning. He was not an actor that Elizabeth had to conceal from either Francis or Sara. The Taylors knew Stack's mother, Elizabeth Modini Wood Stack, who had long been a Hollywood socialite—in fact, she'd been part of Rudolph Valentino's wedding party early in the 1920s. Stack's father, James Langford Stack, was a powerful advertising executive who had created the slogan, "The beer that made Milwaukee famous."

Mr. and Mrs. Stack had previously visited Francis' art gallery and had, over the course of two years, purchased three valuable paintings from England. The Taylors had also gone to A-list Hollywood parties at the home of the Stacks.

Before Elizabeth dated Stack, Sara had told her, "Bob might make a good match for you, a fine husband. He comes from good stock. I think young girls should marry older men, as a means of giving them stability in life, instead of running off with some wild young thing."

"In that case, maybe I should marry Errol Flynn," Elizabeth said.

"Oh, my dear," Sara said, her face reflecting a look of horror. "We're not talking about a sexual degenerate."

Stack had planned the day, beginning with a trip to a skeet-shooting range. He told Elizabeth that at the age of seventeen, he'd won an award as the national champion of skeet shooting.

"What in the fuck is that?" she asked, using what had become—and would remain—her favorite expletive.

He explained that trapshooting involved clay targets which are mechanically hurled into the air in a way that simulates the movement of wild birds in flight.

That particular description didn't impress her, as it sounded like something to be practiced in a penny arcade. Later, however, on a target range, she was surprised by his skill. In rapid fire, he hit each of his fifty targets. "So what do you think of the sport now?" he asked.

"I've got to tell you the truth: I can't stand it. I've always abhorred fox hunting and the shooting of birds. I saw men do this on the estate where we lived in England. I always ran into the house screaming. A bird in flight is so beautiful. Who in his right mind would want to take it down?"

"Well, obviously, my skeet shooting didn't awe you," Stack said. "Perhaps if I told you who we are having lunch with at the clubhouse, you'll be awed."

"Who might that be?" she asked.

"Clark Gable," he said. "He's a skeet shooter himself. I taught him everything he knows about the sport."

Seated at table in the clubhouse, Elizabeth spotted Gable at the entrance, making his way to their table. Stack whispered to her, "At the age of thirteen, I fell in love with his wife, Carole Lombard."

Elizabeth didn't need to be introduced, as previously, she had talked very superficially with him at the MGM commissary. She didn't know if she could confide in him that she'd once harbored a schoolgirl crush on him. As she'd later relay to Roddy McDowall, when she gave him a detailed description of the day's event, "I'm glad I didn't bring up the subject of that crush. The man sitting across from me was not the Clark Gable of the early 1940s. He had aged badly over the war. I feared he might soon be playing grandfather roles."

Much of the luncheon talk centered on skeet shooting, of which Gable was a devotee. "He's a pretty good shot—not as good as me, though," Stack claimed.

"Like hell, you say." Gable protested. "I can wipe your eye any day."

"Why would you want to do that?" she asked.

"Wiping your eye means shooting a bird that someone has missed," Stack explained.

At long last, the King of Hollywood, occupying a shaky throne, turned to her. "Little girl, I have some news that might startle you. I talked Thursday with Mayer. He told me you're a pain in his ass, but he still has big plans for you in spite of your insolence. He wants to star you in pictures with some of MGM's leading male stars, although we are far older than you are. Yes, he's actually suggested that you and I play on-screen lovers. I might go for it, but I don't want to appear onscreen looking like I'm chasing jailbait. Therefore, I've suggested that we voluntarily submit to a screen test to see if we can blow up any chemical works. I don't want to be laughed off the screen."

"I'd love to do that test with you, Mr. Gable," she said.

"If we're going to be making love on the screen, you call me Clark. Of course, Spangler Arlington Brugh has also been suggested as your screen lover."

"I don't know him," she said. "Is he new?"

"That's Robert Taylor's real name," Stack said. He then told a joke about going on a hunting trip with Robert Taylor and Andy Devine. "We'd had a lot of beer as we traveled along a backroad in Colorado. With all that beer in us, nature called. Andy and Bob stood next to each other irrigating the wildflowers. Andy checked out Bob's pecker. He said, 'That thing doesn't look like it belongs on the world's greatest lover.' Without missing a beat, Bob shot back, "I know, but don't tell my wife. She thinks they're all the same size.'"

Gable laughed at that, before telling a self-deprecating story about himself. "At Hollywood dinner parties, Carole [Lombard] used to tell guests that if I had once inch less, I'd be known as the Queen of Hollywood."

Elizabeth seemed amazed that Gable was so secure in his manhood that he could reveal such a remark. As she would tell Dick Hanley the next day, "The thought of doing a screen test with Gable—a love scene, no less—scares the hell out of me. I hope I don't faint."

"Give it hell, Elizabeth," he said. "After all, do you want to be the only female star at MGM who hasn't had Gable's tongue down her throat?"

The night had not even begun, and the date with Stack was stretching into one long day. After a morning on the skeet-shooting range, and lunch with Gable and that promise of a screen test, Stack told her, "I'm taking you to the polo grounds. Spencer Tracy will be there."

Dating Judy (and Jane, and Elizabeth)
left to right: **Robert Stack, Jane Powell, Elizabeth Taylor, and Scotty Beckett**

"I've seen him checking me out in the commissary several times," Elizabeth told him.

"Don't be too flattered," he said. "He's always checking me out, too."

"You mean, he's a homosexual?"

"Yes," he said. "Actually, bi."

"What about Katharine Hepburn?" she asked.

"She's into girls," Stack said. "Better give her wide berth. Remember, in Hollywood, image is everything. The fan magazines want the myth, not the truth."

On their way to the polo field, Stack told her that he'd been introduced to Tracy through Gable. "Spence admired my skeet shooting, but when he heard I'd been cast in *First Love* with Deanna Durbin, he said, 'We've lost a good shot and probably gained a lousy actor.'"

Elizabeth patiently watched as Tracy and Stack played polo, and was more fascinated by that sport than skeet shooting because of her love of horses.

Hot and sweaty, Tracy come up to her after the game. "Hey, kiddo, I hear Mayer is going to start casting you with leading male stars. What about it? Want to try me out?"

"Mr. Tracy, you are the greatest actor on the screen," she said. "I wouldn't dare appear in a picture with you. Besides, you've got Katharine Hepburn as a co-star."

In one of those amazing Hollywood coincidences, in 1950, Elizabeth would be offered a co-starring role with Tracy and Hepburn. Elizabeth accepted, and so did Tracy; only Hepburn turned it down. The picture was *Father of the Bride.*

For dinner that night, Stack took her to Chasen's, where she surprised him with her order. She bypassed the elegant French dishes on the menu and asked for *chili con carne*, a dish she'd heard much about in America, but had never tasted. That night marked her life-long passion for *chili con carne.* In the years to come, when she was in such remote locations as alpine Switzerland, she would have Chasen's chili flown to her.

After dinner, as she relayed later to Roddy and Dick, she was mildly surprised when Stack drove her to Errol Flynn's "farm" on Mulholland Drive. "Errol's away, but I have the key. He lets me use his place when I want to."

"How convenient," she said, not disguising the sarcasm in her voice.

While she sat in the living room on the same sofa where she'd made love to Flynn, he disappeared into the kitchen and emerged with a bottle of champagne—not pink this time.

On the sofa, Stack and Elizabeth talked for about an hour about Flynn and about their movie, *A Date with Judy.*

"Errol told me he was a Tasmanian devil," she said. "I didn't want to appear stupid, but what in the fuck is that?"

"It's a carnivorous marsupial known for its extreme ferocity," he said.

"What a learned definition," she said. "I'm impressed."

"Don't be—those words were taught to me by Errol himself. There's no one like him. He got so mad at what your friend, Hedda Hopper, wrote about him that he went over to her house and masturbated on her front door while she hid behind the curtains laughing. It probably excited the old bitch."

As he began to kiss her and fondle her, he said, "Don't be afraid. We don't have an audience tonight. We're in the house alone."

"What do you mean, not have an audience?" she asked.

"See that mirror on the ceiling?" He pointed overhead. "That's a two-way mirror. Any guest in that upstairs bedroom can look down on whatever's happening on the sofa."

"Hell, Errol and I had a heavy session here," she said. "I hope no one was watching. How embarassing."

"I don't think there were too many Peeping Toms that night," he said. "Maybe only Bruce Cabot and David Niven...perhaps Tyrone Power."

"Oh, ONLY THOSE!" she said, heatedly.

"There's more," he said, taking her hand and leading her into the downstairs bedroom. "Errol got the best technician at Warners to install a hidden camera in this room. I'm sure he documented his boudoir performance with you. He likes to show these loops to his party guests on movie night."

"I'm ruined," she said, "Even before I get started in Hollywood. That god damn Tasmanian devil would do that to me! Wait till I get my hands on him and his film!"

"Congratulations," Stack said. "You've made your first blue movie!'

"I can't let this happen," she said. "He tricked me. I'll threaten him again with statutory rape."

"I'll speak to him about it," Stack promised, trying to soothe her. "There are no cameras on tonight. Let's make our own blue movie." He began to smother her with kisses, and she finally succumbed to him, especially when he told her, "I think I'm falling in love with you." She seemed desperate to hear words like that.

When he'd taken off his clothes, she told him, "You have a chest as perfect as Errol's. You can star in the remake of *The Perfect Specimen.*"

Before midnight, they were back in the living room drinking more champagne. She felt very tipsy.

"I've got another surprise for you," he said. "One of my best friends is coming to town. I told him about you. I was shocked when he said he knew you. He met you in 1939."

"I was just a little girl in London then," she said. "Who in hell could he be?"

"He said you had this awful crush on him. He's like a fisherman who catches a fish too small and takes it off the hook and returns it to the lake until it grows bigger."

"Come on," she said. "The suspense is killing me. "Who is this guy?"

"John F. Kennedy. You know...the ambassador's son."

CHAPTER NINE
So Many Men,
SO LITTLE TIME

For Elizabeth's possible screen test with Clark Gable, Louis B. Mayer issued one of his strangest orders: "To make her look older," he told Benjamin Thau, his vice-president, "have make-up paint a Joan Crawford mouth on her."

When Gable heard that, he called Elizabeth and suggested that he should take her over to Crawford's home for some career, dress, and make-up advice. "She's helped many a young actress in the past, and no one knows how to become a star better than Joanie."

"I've always wanted to meet her," she said. "She's the kind of star I'd like to be. I asked Michael Curtiz to arrange an introduction, but he never did. He was too busy fucking my mother."

If Gable were taken aback by a teenager talking this way, he made no comment about it.

Two hours later, Gable called Elizabeth back and told her that Crawford had also invited Adrian, whom Elizabeth already knew, since the designer was her father's lover.

Gable drove Elizabeth to Crawford's home where she was ushered inside by a maid. In all her life, Elizabeth had never seen such an immaculately kept house. Gable said he "had a little business to conduct upstairs with Joanie," and that she'd be down later.

The maid ushered Elizabeth out onto a terrace, where Adrian was waiting with a warm embrace. It appeared that the designer had been drinking heavily with Crawford before her arrival.

The subject of Francis was obviously on both of their minds, but only one comment was made about him. "I'm meeting your father around five for cocktails, so I hope Joan and Clark don't take all day."

"You've known them for a long time, haven't you?" she asked.

"I met them both in 1931, when pictures were still learning to talk. Joan told

William Haines, 'Adrian for gowns, Gable for fucking.'"

While waiting, Adrian amused her with stories of his early days at MGM. "I go back to the Silents, when I designed some wardrobe for Rudolph Valentino," he said.

"At MGM, they still talk about those shoulder pads you designed for Miss Crawford," Elizabeth said.

"There was a reason for that," he said. "Her hips were too broad, so I padded her shoulders to distract from that. It became known as the coat-hanger look. Bette Davis claimed that I made Joan look like Johnny Weissmuller."

"I'm so honored that you're going to design a gown for my screen test with Clark."

"It's my pleasure," he said. "It's important to remember that with you, the face is the most important thing. Therefore, don't wear anything that will compete with your photogenic face. Your dresses should be elegant, tasteful, even sexy, but remember, in your case, it's face, face, face. You'll want to look as mature and sophisticated as possible, which means we should make Clark look younger."

"He's still a handsome man," she said.

"He owes a lot of that to me," Adrian said. "I didn't think much of him at first—decaying teeth, acute halitosis, jug ears, a loutish personality, and large 'Jack the Ripper' hands. But with new teeth and a new wardrobe, he was transformed."

"Any tips you have about transforming me from an awkward teenager to an MGM harlot will be much appreciated," she said. "Of course, I'm joking about the harlot remark."

Two views of **Joan Crawford** in dresses by Adrian. *Inset photo:* **Clark Gable**

"The trick is to emphasize a woman's most attractive feature," he said. "In Joan's case, her large eyes and her showgirl legs are dynamite. With Harlow, I brought out her sensuality; with Norma Shearer, her sedate elegance; and with Garbo, her mystique. If you're properly made up, your face can dominate the screen and actually create a sense of wonder that any woman can be as beautiful as you are. And those eyes! They're really blue to me, but with the right wardrobe, you can make them violet, which is far more dramatic."

When Gable and Crawford descended an hour later, Gable excused himself to go play golf, telling Elizabeth that he'd pick her up later that afternoon.

Crawford kissed Elizabeth briefly and gently on the lips and gave Adrian a passionate hug. She assured Elizabeth that she thought "one day, somewhere in the 1950s, you'll be the Queen of MGM."

Adrian told her he'd brought along a gown he'd designed for her to wear to an upcoming premiere.

"Let me try it on," Crawford said. Right in front of them, she pulled off all her clothes. The panties were the last to go. "All the MGM cows were jealous of me because I wore the smallest panties at the studio," Crawford told Elizabeth.

Elizabeth tried to look away, but was drawn to checking out Crawford's nude body. Without her "Joan Crawford fuck-me high heels," she was a very short woman, standing only five feet, four inches. She looked taller because she was long-waisted. Her legs were perfectly formed, but out of proportion to the rest of her body. Elizabeth noted that her own breasts were much larger than Crawford's.

Adrian had designed a stunning gown in champagne colors for Crawford, and she paraded around the living room in it just like a professional model.

"You've still got it, Joan," Adrian assured her.

"You look stunning, and the gown is spectacular, Miss Crawford," Elizabeth said.

After Crawford had changed back into a dress of cabbage roses, she offered drinks to her guests. She and Adrian preferred vodka, but Elizabeth settled for a soft drink.

Sitting on a sofa whose surface was covered with plastic, Crawford said, "I believe in helping young actresses who are struggling for recognition. Back in the 1920s, no one helped me. Norma Shearer hated me. But I made it, and I know you will, too. I gave Gail Patrick a big push, lending her my make-up man and hairdresser when she tested for a role in *No More Ladies*. I even gave her a gown designed by my lovely friend here."

"Thank you for anything you can do for me," Elizabeth said. "But I'm afraid that the idea of teaming me romantically with Gable is a bit much."

"Not in today's Hollywood," Crawford said. "Clark can make love on the screen with a twenty-year-old, as can Gary Cooper. Male stars over fifty can keep rolling along, but when most actresses reach forty, or even before, they're considered has-beens. The Hollywood Hills are full of them."

Adrian had to leave, but said that within ten days, he'd design the perfect dress for Elizabeth's screen test.

After he was gone, Crawford invited Elizabeth upstairs to her combination bedroom/dressing room. Going inside, Elizabeth noticed the rumpled bed covers so recently vacated by Gable. Crawford had installed a bar in her bedroom and poured herself a hefty vodka, although Elizabeth turned down any beverage.

Ready for business, Crawford suggested that Elizabeth strip so as not to ruin her pretty dress with make-up. Elizabeth pulled off her dress but left on her bra and panties. She sat at a vanity table laden with creams, lotions, powders, beauty accessories, and lipsticks.

As Elizabeth would later tell Dick Hanley, "Crawford painted several faces on me, none of which satisfied her. She even painted a 'Joan Crawford mouth' on me, but it looked ridiculous. Neither of us was satisfied with the results. She had continued to drink and was getting sloppy. Completely without warning, she began fondling my breasts. At first, I was shocked. I just couldn't believe it. This legendary man eater was a part-time lesbian coming on to me. I almost panicked, but kept my self-control."

"How did you escape alive?" Dick asked.

"I got up and quickly slipped on my dress and headed for the door. I told Crawford that I had hardly learned how to sleep with men, much less women. She made an ugly grimace. She told me, 'You obviously don't appreciate what I can do for you.' I left the room. She stood at the door watching me go. I thanked her for everything and asked her to make my apologies to Clark."

"Downstairs, I asked the maid to call me a taxi. I had to wait nervously for fifteen minutes on the front stoop. When the taxi pulled up, I jumped in and headed for home. It would be my last visit to Crawford's house."

If Elizabeth thought she was through with Crawford, she was wrong. The temperamental star would come into her life once again.

***

Dick Hanley came into Elizabeth's dressing room an hour before the scheduled beginning of her screen test with Gable, and was amazed at how MGM technicians had transformed her look. "Holy shit!" he said. "Is that a twenty-four-year-old Hedy Lamarr sitting on that stool?"

Adrian had designed a stylish black dress for her with a plunging *décolletage*. An MGM hairdresser and two make-up experts had painted an alluring and almost sultry face on Elizabeth.

Although she still had trepidations about appearing on screen with Gable, she was thrilled with her new look. "Where is that little girl from *National Velvet?*" she asked her mirror in front of everyone.

After the finishing touches were applied, Dick escorted her to Gable's dressing room. As she came into his room, he revealed to her one of his "beauty secrets," as he jokingly referred to them. "I'm applying hemorrhoid ointment to reduce the size of the bags under my eyes," he told her.

"You don't need to," Dick said in jest. "You look young enough to play Little Lord Fauntleroy."

Under Sara's guidance, Elizabeth had carefully memorized her lines for the test. The script concerned a widower recovering from the death of his loving wife in an airplane accident. The material seemed inspired by the 1942 airplane crash that had taken Gable's third wife, Carole Lombard.

Elizabeth's role was that of a young woman who, since she'd been a girl, had been in love with the character played by Gable. He was her father's best friend. In the loop, she urges Gable to come out of mourning and form a new life with her.

Her most memorable line was, "Love has no respect for age, national border, color, race, or sex." That line was far too provocative to have been included in an A-list movie in the late 1940s, but she nonetheless delivered it with passion and conviction.

After complimenting Elizabeth on her startling new look, Gable gazed intently at his own remade face. "I swear I don't look a day over thirty-nine." He turned to Elizabeth. "They painted you so you look like you've been around for half a century. Many women marry men fifteen years older than they are, so we just might get away with it."

Before they headed out, she apologized to him for not having been there when he returned to pick her up at Joan Crawford's house.

"I understand," he said. "I've known Joanie for years. Now you know her secret. She walks on both sides of the street. But the less said about this, the better."

"My lips are sealed," she promised.

Clark Gable with Elizabeth Taylor in 1948

When a waiter with late morning coffee arrived from the commissary, Gable looked very sternly at Elizabeth. "Listen, kiddo, we have one thing in common. Both of us are depending on this screen test to chart our futures in film. You want to stop playing some little girl attracted to animals, and I want to continue playing romantic leads through the 1950s. But a whole army of young actors in their twenties are beating down doors in Hollywood. Dick was in

Mayer's office when we talked about this. Tell her what we talked about, Dick."

"It was agreed that every decade produces a different type of star, both male and female," Dick said. "Take Clark here. In the 1930s, he represented the Depression Era hero, never better than in *It Happened One Night.* But World War II changed everything. Benjamin Thau—you must meet him—has convinced Mayer of the new type of male star coming up."

"Exactly what kind of guy are you talking about?" she asked dick.

"A John Derek type, someone you know only too well," Dick said. "Pretty boys like Guy Madison. I bet that cocksucker Henry Willson is auditioning three or four of them as we speak. Monty Clift is the new pretty boy in town, but in his case, he can act. I don't know about some of the others."

In the years to come, Elizabeth would not only watch this prediction come true, but in many cases, she'd get involved as a friend or lover of various members of this new beefcake brigade—Tony Curtis, Rock Hudson, Robert Wagner, Tab Hunter, James Dean, Troy Donahue.

"No wonder Clark Gable didn't feel he'd fit into these changing tastes in male stars," she said.

Before leaving his dressing room, Gable said, "Style in actors change like style in clothing and other things. I'll either keep abreast of those changing styles or become a has-been. You've got to change your image too, Elizabeth, or risk becoming a distantly remembered child star of the 40s."

"You're so right, and I begin that today," she told him. "I'm surprised that an established star like you agreed to a screen test."

"It was for my own protection," Gable said. "In *The Hucksters,* when they wanted to cast Deborah Kerr, I asked for a screen test with her so I could determine if we had any chemistry. Ava Gardner was in that picture, too, and I knew Ava and I had screen chemistry. In fact, Mayer has talked about having me try to re-create with Ava what I had going on the screen with Harlow and Crawford during the 30s."

"Maybe I'll become your new screen partner," Elizabeth said.

"That remains to be seen," he told her. "When I appeared with Anne Baxter in *Homecoming,* where she played my young wife, I got a lot of shit thrown at me because of the difference in our ages."

"Let's go see what we can do," she said, taking his hand.

Facing a noon-day camera at MGM studios, Gable and Elizabeth emoted, fervently, their dramatic scene together, ending in a passionate love scene.

She'd later tell Dick, "I really got to him. I could feel it getting hard. I think we'll burn up the screen in that test."

Mayer demanded that Dick, his secretary, show the screen test to him first, asserting, "I will rule on it."

Watching the test with Dick, Mayer was silent, but Dick noticed him fidgeting in his seat.

When the lights came on, Mayer stood up. "Destroy every god damn copy of that fucking test. No one must see it. It's obscene. Gable comes off like a dirty old man robbing the cradle, and Taylor looks like a teenage whore."

The film was destroyed before Elizabeth got to see the screen test. Although she beseeched Dick for details, all he could safely say was that, "Mayer said that Gable looked far too old to be playing love scenes with you. But he thought you looked terrific, and he's making plans to co-star you with Robert Taylor. He was born in 1911 and Gable in 1901. Bob still looks handsome and with him there won't be that great mountain to climb when it comes to age—only a steep hill."

"Bring him on," Elizabeth said. "Any older actor except for that disgusting Wallace Beery. I just want to play a grown-up on the screen."

"Have I got news for you, sweet cheeks," Dick said. "In your next picture, entitled *Julia Misbehaves,* you'll get to co-star with your all time dreamboat, Peter Lawford. Not only that, but you'll elope with him in the film—perhaps you'll run off with him in real life too, if you work it right."

***

At long last, Errol Flynn was back in Hollywood and called Elizabeth. She immediately berated him, accusing him of filming the two of them having sex.

He immediately denied it. "I have done things like that in the past. I admit it. But not with you. Such a film, if it got out, could have me brought up on another statutory rape charge. This time I might not get off. I might go to jail, where I'd have to endure countless rapes. I imagine half the men in any prison would want to fuck Errol Flynn. I may be an idiot, but I'm not that much of one."

She didn't believe him and slammed down the phone.

"A week later, her more compassionate side emerged when Dick Hanley told her that Flynn had been rushed, in critical condition, to a hospital.

He accompanied her to Flynn's room at Los Angeles' Monte Sano Hospital. They found him perspiring heavily, with a temperature of 102° F. "Last night it was 104°," he told them. "I'm also suffering from the world's worst cast of hemorrhoids. The doctors can't operate on me right now because of my temperature. I'm also suffering from a recurrence of malaria."

In his weakened condition, he talked to them about the trouble he was having trying to film *The Adventures of Don Juan.* "That bastard, Jack Warner, sent me a telegram. Because of my hemorrhoids, he's worrying that I can't film a dueling scene."

Two days later, she returned to the hospital where she found Flynn with a temperature of 103° F. He was also in the grip of pneumonia. "My piles grow worse by the day," he said. "If anything else happens to me, I think I'm going to die."

She assured him that he'd recover, although when she returned the following afternoon, she found him newly infected, suffering from chest congestion. "A quack has shot me full of penicillin. Some fucking good it did. Now I have an ear infection that's driving me crazy."

After his release from the hospital, he called her and told her he was going to Phoenix, Arizona for some rest and recuperation. He phoned her again in three days. "I heard from Warner. He assured me, in his words, 'with the sun beating down on your vivid kisser, you'll soon be your normal self again and your twelve inches will be back in operation.' The next day, he sent another telegram. The fucker told me, 'there was an error in my previous telegram. Delete the phrase twelve inches and insert six inches instead.'"

"At least you can laugh at yourself. That's a sign that you're getting better," she said.

He called her when he returned from Arizona. She asked him about the dueling scene. He explained that the fictional setting was the king's palace in Madrid. "As Don Juan, I was to make a seventeen-step leap to duel the Duke of Lorca—Robert Douglas, that is—in a sword fight to the death. They shot the scene with our doubles because Robert had an injured knee. Both of my doubles refused to do it. They got Jock Mahoney [later a famous screen Tarzan] to make that leap. He made the jump all right, but didn't handle his sword the right way. It castrated the other double. That poor stunt man will now have to go through life without his balls—poor guy."

He also asked her about her own career, and she explained that she had been heavily made up to look older for a screen test with Gable.

"Quite the opposite with me," he told her. "I have to go in two hours early to be made up. The old queen who does my face claims it takes him all that time to cover my debauchery. I'm not in my prime these days, dear girl."

Errol also told her that, "I got Nora a cameo in the movie."

That was his first reference to his second wife, Nora Eddington. Elizabeth always wondered where he stashed her while he carried on his adventures and his various amours, brawls, whore-mongerings, drug abuse, and heavy drinking.

One afternoon, when she had no work, Elizabeth went to Warners to join Errol for lunch. Here, he introduced her to the director Vincent Sherman, who had previously made love to such stars as Bette Davis and Joan Crawford.

She arrived in time to hear a fight between Sherman and Flynn over his crotch. Flynn had ordered the wardrobe department to shorten his jackets so that they only partially covered his crotch. Sherman had seen the first take, and he protested that Flynn's "protrusion was too pronounced."

"Jack Warner won't go for it. Perhaps you could handle it more modestly and do what I tell ballet dancers to do when they're bulging out of their leotards: Pull up your thing and put a piece of tape across it. Then put on a tight-fitting jockstrap or codpiece."

"Listen, sport," Flynn said. "I've done many things for Warner's in my day, but I'm damned if I'll tape up my cock for them. Right, Elizabeth? I'm sure she agrees." He then invited her to the commissary to have lunch with him.

Sherman later recalled, "Flynn was Warner's biggest headache. Women and liquor were the devils that tormented him. He could not resist a pretty girl." The director later admitted that he was astonished that a young beauty like Elizabeth would show an interest in Flynn. "He had reached his peak and was rapidly descending, just like his role model, John Barrymore, had done. But I've never understood women, especially if that woman calls herself Bette Davis."

Over lunch, Flynn told Elizabeth that Doris Duke had hooked up again with Porfirio Rubirosa whom she had married in Paris in 1947. "Doris and Porfirio have invited us to dinner: When not involved with their other lovers, they're spending a few days here in L.A."

Both Rubirosa and Duke were tabloid fodder, and Elizabeth was thrilled at the idea of spending time with these media stars. That the tobacco heiress was also the richest woman in the world added an extra excitement.

Elizabeth would later relate in detail the evening she spent with Rubirosa and Duke. "It was my first really grown up evening, and I'm sure a sign of things to come. I was no longer treated as a child, and I was in adult company talking about adult things. The wonderful thing is I felt like I belonged."

For years, she'd read about the adventures of Doris Duke and her many lovers, who had included Cary Grant, Aristotle Onassis, General George C. Patton, and lots of Hawaiian beach boys.

Peter Lawford had described Rubirosa's legendary endowment: "It's at least eleven inches long and thick as a beer can. Doris has a preference for dark meat." The playboy of the Western world was originally from the Dominican Republic and had a very dark complexion.

***

At dinner, Flynn congratulated Duke and Rubi for getting back together again.

"Marriages, divorces, it's just so much paperwork from the state," Rubi said. "Governments should stay out of one's boudoir."

"Rubi and I will continue to come and go from each other's lives and bedrooms as frequently as we choose." Duke said. "Whether we're married or divorced hardly matters. Of course, there will be other men or women in our lives. For people like us, that must always be the rule. We are citizens of the world, not just one country. Errol is like us."

"I can only aspire to be like you. Just the idea of being tied down to one person sounds boring to me," Elizabeth said.

"Hear, hear!" Flynn said. "I, of all rogues, agree with that sentiment."

"When government interferes in one's life, there's always a problem," Duke said. "The State Department tried to confiscate my passport because they came across a picture of me entertaining Hermann Göring before the war. I entertain lots of people, regardless of their politics. If Hitler had invited me to Berlin, I would have gone. Likewise, if the Roosevelts had invited me to the White House, I would also have accepted."

"Just because of who we associate with, J. Edgar Hoover thought Doris and I were Nazi spies," Flynn said,.

"That's bullshit," Rubi said. "They were not Nazi spies. As for me, that's perhaps a story for another day."

Over dinner, Duke called Rubirosa "Rube" instead of the more commonly used "Rubi." "I decided I wanted a real man, so I purchased the best on the market," she said, looking over at him.

"When Doris married me, she thought she owned me," Rubi said. "After all, she'd paid for me. But I'm not a sex slave on an auction block. During the first week of our honeymoon on the French Riviera, I ran off with another woman."

"But I got even," Duke said. "When he came back to my hotel suite after a few days, he caught me in bed with two black musicians that a club in Cannes had imported from New Orleans."

"Doris adores black musicians," Flynn said.

Doris Duke with **Porfirio Rubirosa** in Paris in 1947

"So I see," Elizabeth said. At that point in her life, she was a bit taken aback by biracial liaisons.

"The more I learned about Rube—jewel thief, Nazi sympathizer, rogue, world class liar, whoremonger—the more I adored him" Duke said.

"And the more I learned about Doris, the more intriguing she became," Rubi said. "I especially like hearing that she fills entire vaults within Swiss banks with gold bars in her name."

When all three adults at table

focused on Elizabeth, she told them about her career crisis and her desire to play more mature roles. "I want to be a movie star, maybe not the greatest actress in the world, but more famous than Lana Turner."

"My darling, I think you'll make it," Rubi said. "It's a treacherous town, though. Two studios wanted me. I could play a Latin lover type. But when I applied for a special work visa, I was rejected by some bureaucrat. He claimed my role could be played by any number of American actors."

"I'm sure you would have become a star," Elizabeth said. "Too bad you didn't get a chance."

"But he's still the *big* attraction in boudoirs on two continents," Flynn said. "Even better at it than I am, and of that, I'm certain."

After dessert, Duke rose from the table and took Flynn's hand. She announced that she and Flynn had some business matters to discuss upstairs, and Rubi had to make some important phone calls. "He's in trouble again with various governments, including Spain, France, and the United States. But my lawyers will help him."

"In the meantime, darling, I have an amusement for you," Duke said. "Go into that library. I took out some jewelry. They're all valuable pieces, but I don't keep my world class gems here. Look at them, decide which one you want, and feel free to take it home."

"Miss Duke, surely you don't mean that," Elizabeth said.

"But I do," Duke said.

In the library, Elizabeth picked up each piece of jewelry, each more dazzling than the one that preceded it. She could not decide, as she wanted all of them. She'd later recall, "My world interest in jewelry began that night. It was one of the hardest decisions of my life, but I finally decided on a ruby-and-diamond bracelet."

When she returned to join the others, Flynn and Duke had not yet emerged from upstairs, but she spotted Rubi smoking a cigarette on the terrace. She joined him in the moonlight.

"Nights like this remind me of Santo Domingo," he said. "I'm a funny kind of guy. Wherever I am, I'm dreaming of being someplace else. When I'm sitting under a café canopy in Paris, as the winter rains come down, I'm thinking of sunny California. When I'm dining at Chasen's in Los Angeles, I want to be entering Maxim's in Paris. In New York in a penthouse overlooking Central Park, I'm remembering the fading light over the Colosseum in Rome."

"I want to experience all those places, too," Elizabeth said.

"In time, you'll know them all, I'm sure," he assured her. "You'll even know what it's like to make love to me."

"You certainly have confidence," she said.

"One thousand, perhaps two thousand—I forget—women have made me very confident. Instead of making love to you tonight, I think I'll wait a few years, but not too long. I'll let others break you in for me. Perhaps one night when I hear we're both in Paris, I'll call you."

"I think I'll accept your invitation," she said. "After all, you're known as the world's greatest lover."

At that point, Duke and Flynn joined them on the terrace.

Elizabeth thanked Duke for the evening, and showed her the bracelet she'd chosen.

"A wise choice," Duke said. "You and Errol have been a delight, and I want to invite both of you to join Rubi and me on a flight to Buenos Aires. After the war, I bought a B-25 bomber and had it converted into a private passenger plane. It has a bar and a lavish kitchen, and it seats ten people. Rubi likes to fly to Argentina every now and then to fuck Eva Peron, while I seek other amusement among the tango dancers. He even donates money I give him to Eva's charities."

"When Juan Peron learned of this," Rubi said, "he was quoted as saying, 'It's the first time in recorded history that a pimp ever gave money to a harlot.'"

On the way back home, Elizabeth chastised Flynn. "You told me you're still weak and out of commission, but I noticed you had enough energy to go upstairs to fuck Doris."

"That's not quite true," he said. "I didn't bang her, sport. She likes to masturbate while I voraciously suck her toes."

"Oh, I see," she said. "Little Miss Taylor is learning more about the world every day."

***

On a previous date with Robert Stack, he had informed Elizabeth that John F. Kennedy, newly elected to Congress from Massachusetts, would be at his house at around noon on Saturday. She accepted an invitation for a late luncheon with Stack and his longtime friend.

Before World War II, a mutual friend, Alfredo de la Vega, had introduced JFK to Stack. It was the beginning of a friendship that lasted throughout the course of JFK's life.

Since she'd last seen JFK, he'd become a naval hero, partly because of the publicity generated by his father's media machine in association with his military service during World War II. She'd read that his PT boat had been rammed and sunk by a Japanese destroyer, and that JFK had heroically rescued his men from death in the South Pacific.

Prior to JFK's arrival, Stack relayed stories to her about the young politician's previous visits to Hollywood, and how many doors had been opened to

116

him thanks to his status as son of "the Ambassador," the former movie producer Joseph Kennedy, Sr., himself a legend in Hollywood.

During the early days of his friendship with JFK, Robert occupied a small apartment that lay at the end of a cul-de-sac, Whitley Terrace, between Cahuenga and Highland Boulevards in the Hollywood Hills. One of the apartment's bedrooms had a low ceiling only five feet high. Stack had defined this as "The Flag Room," a "chamber of seduction." On its ceiling, Stack had pinned replicas of the flags of many nations. When he escorted a woman inside, she lay on the bed and was instructed to memorize the position of each of the flags with the understanding that later, after cocktails, she'd be quizzed as to which nation each of them represented. If she flunked the quiz, she had to "pay the piper."

"All the girls flunked," Stack told Elizabeth. "There were too many flags to remember. One beautiful young model, Norma Jeane Baker, flunked four times and had to suffer punishment from both Jack and me."

[Norma Jeane, a short time later, changed her name to Marilyn Monroe.]

In his memoirs, *Straight Shooting,* Stack confessed that it was in this Flag

Room that "I learned about the birds, the bees, the barracudas, and other forms of Hollywood wildlife." He had persuaded his parents to rent the hideaway apartment for him as a retreat where he could pursue his studies. "I studied all right," he said, "female anatomy. As for those flags, I taught Jack to recognize the banners of many countries, and therefore helped prepare him for the geopolitics he needed later in his life."

Stack rearranged the flags every night so that some foxy lady, paying her third or fourth visit, would not be able to memorize their positions and lineup order.

Top photo: Highly sexed bachelors at large: **Robert Stack** with **John F. Kennedy** in the early 1940s
Lower photos: 17-year-old **Elizabeth Taylor** and *(right)* **June Allyson**

He recalled that through his humble portals passed "a guest list that ran the gamut from chorus line cuties to Academy Award winners."

Judy Garland, who dated both JFK and Stack, had been seduced there by both of them, and later asserted that they were "the two most desirable bachelors in Hollywood. All the girls were after them, and some of the boys, too."

"I'd known most Hollywood stars, and JFK could attract more women than anybody." Stack said. "He'd just look at a gal, and she was ready to give him a tumble. To my regret, most of the girls went for Jack instead of me. In my conceited way, I thought I was much prettier than Jack, and certainly a better swordsman."

To his best friend back East, Lem Billings, Jack referred to Stack as "my libidinous buddy. He threw down the red carpet for me on my last visit to Hollywood. Crossing it were beautiful stars, lovely starlets, and so-so wannabes."

In later years, Stack told friends that before his latest arrival, JFK had told him, "I want to fuck every woman in Hollywood...I want to specialize in celebrity poontang."

Before JFK's expected arrival, Elizabeth learned early one morning in make-up at MGM that she wasn't the only woman awaiting the upcoming arrival of the handsome young politician from Massachusetts. She sat next to June Allyson, and learned that she, too, was eager to date JFK after having had an affair with him back in 1946.

The stars lining up every workday for make-up were often amazingly frank in their discussion of men. It was their favorite sport and distraction during an oft-repeated ritual performed by mainly homosexual technicians, who glamorized the actresses' faces and eavesdropped on every conversation.

Allyson was billed as the wholesome-looking "Girl Next Door," but throughout MGM, she was known as a predatory nymphomaniac. She'd invite members of the film crew, including grips, to her dressing room during breaks.

"I know you're dating Bob Stack, and Jack Kennedy will be staying with him," Allyson told her. "Perhaps we'll go out on a double date."

"Perhaps," Elizabeth responded, concealing her jealousy of the older star.

"I fell really big for him a couple of years back," Allyson confessed. "Later, I found out I was competing with Gene Tierney and that overbite of hers. In many ways, Jack reminds me of our mutual friend, Peter Lawford. Both are fun loving and good looking."

"Jack can literally charm the pants off a girl," Allyson continued. "He calls his penis 'the implement.' He wants a girl at both the front and back doors. I'd never had anal sex before. It hurt. He's utterly ingratiating, but not that great in the sack. He's a sort of 'Slam, Bam, Thank You, Ma'am' type of lover. When the dirty deed is done, he wants to move on to his next conquest."

Elizabeth deliberately did not tell Allyson that she'd spent a day with JFK when she was a little girl growing up in pre-war London. She was thrilled with anticipation when Stack picked her up on Saturday and drove her to his house, where JFK had arrived and had been taking a nap when he'd left him. "He told me he's seen only *National Velvet,* so he has no idea of what you look like now."

When they reached his house, Stack directed Elizabeth to his pool, where JFK was waiting. Looking rail-thin, he wore only a pair of white shorts and was resting on a *chaise longue* in the sun. He did not get up to greet her, but put out his hand, capturing hers and holding it for a long time. "Hi, Elizabeth, you are living proof that little girls grow up in delightful ways. You've changed. For the better, I'd say."

"You have, too," she responded.

"In what way," he asked.

"Better looking. More manly. I guess it was the war and the years. I hear you're a big time naval hero."

"Fuck!" he said. "I don't care what you've heard. I won the war single-handedly. Don't let anyone tell you differently." The twinkle in his eyes revealed that he was satirizing his own exploits.

"And now, you're a congressman!" she said.

"If Dad has anything to say about it, I'll be sitting in the White House at least by 1964."

"I hope you'll issue me a presidential pardon," she said.

"Not likely," he smiled. "I'll summon you to the White House for a command performance."

At that point, Stack came out onto the patio calling them to lunch.

As they ate, JFK told Elizabeth and Stack that he'd flown to the West Coast to escape election debts and because he couldn't attend any more *chicken à la king* dinners.

"And you're out here to get your jollies!" Stack interjected.

"There's nothing wrong with that!" JFK said. "Right, Elizabeth?"

"There's nothing wrong if you get them with me!" She shocked even herself at how forward she had become.

JFK laughed. "A promise I'll make you keep."

Even though they indulged in mostly small talk, there was sexual tension in the air. She would later confess to Roddy McDowall that she was waiting for one of them, especially JFK, to make the first move.

Two views of **Robert Stack**

119

After lunch, he got up and pulled off his white shorts in front of them. He was completely casual about his nudity, as his future wife, Jackie Kennedy, would eventually claim.

"Let's all go for a nude swim," he proposed, jumping into the pool.

In front of her, Stack pulled off his shorts and jumped into the water to swim after JFK. As Elizabeth would later relay to Dick Hanley, "I knew it was show time, and I didn't want to disappoint. I pulled off my dress, bra, and panties, and swam in after them."

At that point, the screen goes black. She refused to relay any of the juicy details to Dick, even though he wanted a blow-by-blow description. "I can live vicariously, can't I?"

All she'd confess to was a three-way. "It was my first such experience, but I don't think it will be my last. Bob is the better lover, but Jack has more charm. All I'll tell you is that he's mainly concerned with getting himself off—and not the girl who's lying under him. Bob has better staying power. Jack went first. But he shot off rather quickly. Would you believe that Bob and I were still going at it, and Jack was up beside the bed making a phone call? Then Bob and I finished the dirty deed."

"Are you going to pursue Jack?" Dick asked, "or was that it?"

"No, I'll keep after him," she said. "Not so much because of his love-making, but because of his charm. He has this amazing ability to look at you while you're talking and make you feel that you're saying something so vital that the fate of the whole world depends on it."

During an early-morning make-up session at MGM the following Monday, Elizabeth found herself seated once again side by side with Allyson.

In hushed tones, Allyson whispered to Elizabeth, "You would not believe what happened to me on Sunday. I went over to Bob Stack's house to meet with Jack Kennedy. I found him swimming nude in the pool. Before the afternoon ended, Jack, Bob, and I piled into bed together for a three-way."

"June Allyson, I'm shocked," Elizabeth said. "I would never do anything like that...*ever.*"

"You're such a puritan, girl," Allyson said. "After a few more years in Hollywood, you'll be ripe for the plucking."

"Was that 'plucking' you said or something else?" Elizabeth facetiously asked.

***

For her next picture, a tedious romp entitled *Julia Misbehaves* (1948), Louis B. Mayer decided to team Elizabeth with Greer Garson and Walter Pidgeon, those fabled *Mrs. Miniver* stars of World War II. The popularity of Garson during the darkest years of World War II had transformed her into the unofficial "Queen of MGM." But after the war, her popularity had waned, and Mayer was scheming to reinvent her as a screen *comedienne*, an unwise choice.

Afraid that Garson would steal the picture from her, Elizabeth quipped, "Greer seems to believe that actresses are ageless." Even at the young age of sixteen, Elizabeth had already developed a sharp tongue. As director Jack Conway said, "She was so young, so beautiful, and couldn't say three sentences without at least one curse word."

Conway fascinated Elizabeth, as he was a walking textbook of the history of Hollywood, having started his career as an actor in 1909 in *The Old Soldier's Story*. He had directed Clark Gable in films which included *Boom Town* (1941). Most recently, he'd directed Ava Gardner and Gable in *The Hucksters* (1947). That same year, he also partially directed Garson in one of her all-time disasters, *Desire Me,* yet nonetheless, he was chosen to helm her once again in this newest frothy film. Three other directors had shared in the debacle of *Desire Me,* including Victor Saville, Mervyn LeRoy, and George Cukor. "I hope I have better luck with Greer on this picture," he told Elizabeth. "On *Desire Me,* during the filming of one scene, it took 125 takes for her to just say 'no.'"

When Garson objected to foul language on the set, Elizabeth told her to "go fuck yourself." But Garson was gracious in spite of the insult, even inviting Elizabeth to four o'clock tea. Elizabeth quickly warmed to the star. "Someday in the years to come, you'll be in my same position, trying to hold onto a fading career while fighting wrinkles."

Julia Misbehaves cast Elizabeth as Susan Packett, a rich girl who invites her estranged mother to her wedding, where the complications flow like a river. The young bride's ultimate aim involves orchestrating a reconciliation of her long-divorced parents. Walter Pidgeon, Garson's frequent co-star, was cast as Elizabeth's father.

As Conway said about the ironies associated with his role in directing this film, "Mayer gave me three gay actors—Peter Lawford, Cesar Romero, and Walter Pidgeon."

Other screen stalwarts in the film included veterans Mary Boland, Lucile Watson, and Nigel Bruce. Elizabeth told Conway, "The script parallels my own life. I brought Francis and Sara back together. I'd better qualify that. I mean, they now live once again under the same roof."

Filming began in mid-January of 1948. Elizabeth was delighted to be working with twenty-five-year-old Peter Lawford again. She told Roddy, "I'm still mad about the boy."

"I was, too," Roddy told her, "until he dumped me."

"To me, Peter is the first and last word in sophistication," she said. "He's princely and refined, the kind of man I'm going to marry. Sara wants me to marry him, but he hasn't asked me yet."

At afternoon tea, Elizabeth realized that Garson was a sympathetic soul. She poured out her romantic complications to her. "I fear both Pidgeon and Romero will also be trying to get into Peter's trousers."

"Don't worry," Garson said. "Peter can run faster than either of those men. I had the same problem with Laurence Olivier when we had an affair in London in the 1930s. I had to compete with Noël Coward and an array of other gentlemen for his affections."

Elizabeth later recalled, "Peter was one of the guys I had this tremendous crush on, and he had already made love to me. I thought he was terribly, terribly handsome. He had such an elegant speaking voice. I avoided his mother, Lady May, because she was a bitch from hell. The whole cast of *Julia Misbehaves* knew that I was in love with Peter and teased me about it. The trouble was, he wasn't really in love with me."

During the filming of *Julia Misbehaves,* Elizabeth reached her full height of five feet four and a half inches. Her ideal weight fluctuated between 118 and 120 pounds.

In February of that year, Conway and the cast of *Julia Misbehaves* threw a "Sweet Sixteen" party for Elizabeth, presenting her with jade earrings and a silver choker. Her present from Mayer and MGM was the chic wardrobe she wore in the film. Sara and Francis gave her the greatest gift of all, a solid gold key to a baby blue Cadillac, even though she hadn't learned to drive yet. The bill for the Cadillac came from Elizabeth's own earnings. In addition, she received word from MGM that her weekly salary had been raised to $1,000.

Lawford was enlisted as her escort to her Sweet Sixteen party, but he hadn't shown up. She was very tipsy when the chocolate layer cake was brought in. By the time Lawford did arrive, she had fallen asleep on a nearby sofa, having drunk too much champagne. But she recovered in time for him to take her dancing at the Cocoanut Grove.

That night at the Ambassador Hotel, site at the time of the Cocoanut Grove nightclub, Elizabeth and Lawford double dated with Garson and E.E. ("Buddy") Fogelson, a rich Texas oilman. For Fogelson,

upper photo: **Greer Garson, Peter Lawford,** *and* **Elizabeth Taylor** in *Julia Misbehaves.*

Inset photo: **Greer Garson**

122

it was love at first sight when he met the red-haired beauty. Before the evening ended, he told Garson, "I'm going to marry you." He did. She was at his bedside on December 1, 1987, when he died at the age of eighty-seven.

"Elizabeth welcomed the mobility that a car provided," Roddy recalled. "Carmen Miranda must have been her driving teacher. Elizabeth was hell on wheels. As for parking, she always managed to hit the rear of the car in front of her and the one parked behind her."

One morning she crashed into John Wayne's new, fire-red Thunderbird. He was furious or "boiling mad," as he put it.

After bashing in The Duke's car, Elizabeth became a hit-and-run driver. However, two stagehands witnessed her plowing into Wayne's vehicle.

When confronted with the evidence, she dismissed complaints. "Duke should not have parked there in the first place since it was my spot. Also, he should have left room for me to park. I think the Road Hog got what he deserved."

Wayne never quite forgave her and used future occasions to attack her. When he was having a torrid affair with actress Gail Russell, he said, "Gail is ten times more beautiful than ugly Liz with her thunder thighs will ever be."

His anger continued to bubble over for years. He attacked her for appearing in two screen adaptation of plays by "that queer, Tennessee Williams." He was referring, of course, to the 1959 *Cat on a Hot Tin Roof* and to the 1959 *Suddenly, Last Summer.* The latter picture infuriated Wayne, who called it "garbage from a diseased mind."

"I don't like to see Hollywood's bloodstream polluted with perversion, or immoral and amoral nuances. The film depicts homosexuality, murder, and psychotherapy," Wayne charged. Privately, he told friends that Elizabeth "cursed like a sailor and had a filthy mind." He was also infuriated when she won an Oscar for appearing as a prostitute in *Butterfield 8* (1960). "At least MGM knew that she'd be great playing a whore, a role she knows only too well. I heard she even tried to get Lassie—a male collie, incidentally—to fuck her in her first movie."

John Wayne *(photo above)*: "Playing a whore is a role she (E.T.) knows only too well,"

Elizabeth Taylor *(about John Wayne)*: "These closeted queens have such bitchy tongues."

When she heard about this, she said, "Oh, Wayne, Oh, Johanna Wayne. These closeted queens have such bitchy tongues on them."

Although Mayer had warned Lawford to stay away from Elizabeth and to protect her innocence, he continued to see her secretly. "Louis B. doesn't know that I've already tasted the honey," he told her.

"The less Mayer knows about my private life, the better," she said.

She found dating Lawford unsatisfactory, although Sara told friends that Elizabeth and Lawford planned to marry when she turned seventeen. Even during the peak of their dating, Elizabeth suspected that Lawford was carrying on affairs with both men and women on the side.

As the dean of Hollywood biographers, Lawrence J. Quirk, wrote: "Peter was compelled to make love to a number of women he involved himself with. They expected it, and he needed it, for pleasure and for his image's sake, and to help dispel rumors about his relationships with men—and there were a number of them. These relationships worried him; they were often a sexual release rather than a romance. When he fell in love or entertained romantic feelings toward a man, Peter grew inescapably depressed. This side of his erotic life he found ominous, threatening, baleful, yet he needed it, too."

Amazingly for her age, Elizabeth seemed to understand Lawford's dilemma, a harbinger of the sympathy and support she'd offer during later friendships with Rock Hudson, James Dean, and Montgomery Clift.

Lucille Ryman, chief of talent at MGM, noted that the teenage Elizabeth "seemed to be chasing after anything in pants, and she seemed desperate to find a husband, probably because she'd be able to move out of the house she shared with Francis and Sara."

Lawford didn't believe that Elizabeth's love for him was genuine. He dismissed her "as a girl in love with love."

Sheilah Graham, a rival columnist of both Louella Parsons and Hedda Hopper, was the first journalist to suggest in print that Elizabeth was a sexual predator, even though she was only sixteen years old. Graham drew up a list of what she privately called "the biggest whores in Hollywood."

Photoplay would not print that, of course, and the list's name was changed to "Hollywood's Most Dangerous Women." The list was headed by Lana Turner, Ava Gardner, and Joan Crawford, and also included Jane Wyman, Rita Hayworth, and—as the youngest star on the roster—Elizabeth Taylor.

Some editors at *Photoplay* objected to Graham putting Elizabeth's name on that notorious list, claiming, "But she's only a child."

"Like hell she is!" Graham shot back. "If you're fucking Ronnie Reagan, Peter Lawford, Robert Stack, John Derek, Marshall Thompson, Mickey Rooney, and Errol Flynn, you're a child no more. Admittedly, she's had only a fraction of men, unlike the other whores on my list, but they'd had years to seduce men. At the rate Elizabeth is going, she will have beat out all of them by the time she's forty."

One "fan" letter arrived at MGM from Betsy Blywood in Athens, Georgia. "Elizabeth Taylor may have turned sixteen, but she dresses and acts like the Whore of Babylon. I will pray for her."

A Date with Judy and *Julia Misbehaves* were each released within a week of each other. Most of the reviews sounded similar, using the same vocabulary—"Silly," "trivial," "vacuous," or even "vulgar," although why any critic would have used the term "vulgar" in association with either of these somewhat saccharine screenplays was never fully explained.

Critics claimed that Sidney Guilaroff, one of the leading hairdressers in Hollywood, went too far in "maturing" Elizabeth's screen image. They complained that she was "one of the loveliest girls in movies, but in *Julia Misbehaves,* she was made up and her hair done in such a way as to make her prettiness tiresome and conventional."

In spite of bad reviews, the film had a strong opening at Radio City Music Hall in Manhattan, the *New York Herald Tribune* hailing Elizabeth as "one of cinema's reigning queens." But the movie flopped overall, and did nothing to advance the fading career of Greer Garson.

MGM itself seemed confused as to how to promote Elizabeth's screen image. As author Alexander Walker wrote, "MGM was guilty of giving out confusing signals. Perhaps it, too, was confused. Elizabeth, in a photo spread taken by the fashionable photographer, Valezka, could pass for thirty with her hair drawn back close to her skull. And one picture of her, bosom thrust forward and stretching a tight, off-the-shoulder blouse, while she tilts her head back in a look of unashamed enjoyment of her own sexuality, must rank among the frankest photos MGM permitted an up-and-coming star—and a legal minor, too—to be pictured at that time."

"I'll be god damn if I'm going to be Judy Garland having my breasts strapped down so as to look fourteen," Elizabeth warned MGM.

In spite of this blatant publicity, and despite rumors about her sexual promiscuity, Mayer decided to give Elizabeth "one last chance," at playing an innocent virgin. He cast her as one of the leads in Louisa May Alcott's children's classic, *Little Women,* which had been brought to the screen before, with Katharine Hepburn playing the lead.

Elizabeth's "ripening" as a woman was concealed by a period costume showing nothing. Even her celebrated raven-black hair was concealed with a blonde wig.

She didn't want the role in *Little Women* and privately protested to her friends. "This is my last time appearing in a child's part. I want to heat up the screen like Ava and Lana. God damn it, I will, too, even if I have to go into the executive headquarters at MGM and suck off Benjamin Thau like Nancy Davis [later, Reagan] does every morning."

***

George Cukor had directed Katharine Hepburn, Joan Bennett, Jean Parker, and Frances Dee in *Little Women* way back in 1933. In the 1940s, David O. Selznick planned a remake starring Jennifer Jones and Shirley Temple, but later, he abandoned the project. Then MGM picked up the property and named Mervyn LeRoy to helm this glossy 1949 remake of Alcott's gentle account of teenage girls finding maturity and romance.

The Alcott story was largely autobiographical, the tale of sisters growing up in Concord, Massachusetts, during the 1860s. The little women keep the home fires burning as their preacher father serves in the Union army during the American Civil War.

Under a strawberry blonde wig, Elizabeth was cast as Amy, a character described as "snooty, anxious, nervous, and haughty." Ironically, Amy had been played by Bennett in the 1933 version. Bennett, a few months after the completion of the 1949 version, would play Elizabeth's mother in one her most popular films, *Father of the Bride* (1950).

At the age of thirty-two, June Allyson snagged the lead as Jo in the 1949 version of *Little Women,* playing a fifteen-year-old. Allyson was married to Dick Powell at the time and pregnant with her first child.

Other sisters included Janet Leigh as Meg and Margaret O'Brien as Beth. Cast with Elizabeth once again, Mary Astor played the beloved Marmee, with Peter Lawford in the role of "Laurie." Other members of the cast included Rossano Brazzi, Lucile Watson, Leon Ames, and the old and very grand C. Aubrey Smith, who would die before the picture's release.

Elizabeth despised Astor and resented having to appear in another movie with her. The hatred was mutual. "Elizabeth spoke all the time with this boyfriend stationed in Korea while holding up production. She mercilessly ticked away MGM's money while we waited on the set for her to get off the phone. I had never encountered such a brazen attitude on the part of a child actor. Nobody in the company, including the director, dared utter a word about it to the precious darling, despite the fact that she was holding up the shooting schedule for weeks."

"Elizabeth visited me a lot in my dressing room between takes," Allyson said. "She obviously was thinking about marriage and asked many questions. She wanted to know if a married woman has to submit to sex any time her husband wants it. She also was eager to know if she had the legal right to demand sex from her husband."

"I told her that technically in marriage, a man and a woman should agree on having sex before committing the act. 'Usually, it's a spontaneous act,' I said. 'But men being men often want it when they want it. Of course, you can demand sex from a man, but they have such different plumbing. If they don't want to, you can't get a rise out of those fuckers.'"

126

In addition to Allyson, Elizabeth also bonded with Janet Leigh on the set. In fact, they became such close friends they began to go out on double dates.

"Elizabeth was always looking for some diversion to take her mind off wearing that blonde wig—she detested the thing," Leigh claimed. "The light hair really didn't do justice to her coloring. Our daily exposure allowed me a deeper perception of Elizabeth. I think I had anticipated a different person, because of the early recognition of her incredible beauty and success. I didn't expect the warmth, the humor, the openness, and the regard she extended to her friends."

Despite Leigh's rosy portrait of Elizabeth, her future husband, Tony Curtis, had a different view. "Janet got some good parts in spite of the fact that she was forced to dwell in Elizabeth's shadow. Janet and the girls at MGM didn't have an easy time competing with Elizabeth, who had an incredible allure and got any star role she wanted, which made it very hard on the other young actresses. As for me in 1948, I didn't need Elizabeth Taylor. To hell with the bitch. I was fucking Marilyn Monroe."

Co-starring with Lawford again, Elizabeth maneuvered it so that he would ask her out. One day at work, she said, "Peter, we both love the beach. Why not go together?"

He seemed to have other plans, but agreed to take her to Will Rogers State Beach.

Later, she complained about that date to Roddy McDowall. "To my regret, Peter spent most of the day looking at the bodies of all those gorgeous young men. I noticed that he made frequent trips to the gents' toilet and was gone for a very long time."

"Perhaps he has a weak bladder," Roddy said, jokingly.

"One time, when he came back from the loo, I accused him of not paying me much attention," she said.

As she relayed to Roddy, Lawford became very blunt with her. "Elizabeth, my dear, if you had better legs, I'd be more attentive. You don't have shapely legs. You have pods. Too many hot fudge sundaes at Will Wright's Ice Cream Parlor."

"Of course, it broke my heart to hear him say that," she confessed. "I really have dieted. My waist has gone from twenty inches to eighteen. But all my life I'd never been able to do anything about my pods. I thought swimming would help. At Malibu, I thrashed around in the water so long I got this awful cramp. Fortunately, my brother Howard was on the beach with some of his friends. He jumped in and swam out to rescue me."

Opening at Manhattan's Radio City Music Hall in March of 1949 as an Easter attraction, *Little Women* in its latest incarnation became one of the top-grossing films of that year.

***

Until the summer of 1948, most of Elizabeth's fans assumed she was still a virgin, as erroneous reports circulated that she was guarded, day and night, by Sara. Elizabeth laughed at these fan magazine fantasies. Among the columnists, Sheilah Graham, former lover of novelist F. Scott Fitzgerald, knew that Elizabeth had indulged in a number of affairs, and as such, she printed an occasionally negative blurb. Perhaps Louella Parsons and Hedda Hopper knew it, too, but for the moment, at least, it served their purposes to present Elizabeth as "The Virgin Princess of Hollywood."

The first of her romances to hit the press was largely a creation of the MGM publicity factory. At the time, Glenn Davis, the most famous football player in America, was as well known on the sports pages as Elizabeth was in the movie magazines. He had won the Heisman Trophy in 1946, and the same year, the Associated Press named him "Male Athlete of the Year."

MGM publicists wanted to link Elizabeth romantically with this "dreamboat" athlete as a means of generating publicity, since her last teenage films had not fared as well, commercially, as her earlier films as a child star, especially those Lassie vehicles.

Just prior to the period of his greatest exposure in Hollywood (and to Elizabeth), Davis had completed twenty-two weeks of infantry training at the U.S. Army's Fort Benning. He was scheduled to be in Los Angeles that summer playing football before being shipped off for military duties in Korea, beginning in September.

Davis stood tall and handsome, with auburn hair. His former girl friend, Glenda Neal, said that he was "built like a Greek god, especially where it counts."

A romance between Elizabeth and Davis was promoted by Dorismae Kearns, who worked for Howard Strickling in the publicity department at MGM. Sara invited Dorismae and her husband, Hubie Kearns, to their beach bungalow at

Question: What happens when you mix the two most famous football players in America, the publicity department at MGM, and everybody's favorite emerging new starlet?

left figure: **Doc Blanchard**
right figure: **Glenn Davis**
inset figure: **Elizabeth Taylor**

Malibu one Saturday afternoon. At MGM, Dorismae's duties included overseeing publicity for Elizabeth, which was almost a full-time position.

Hubie was also an athlete, formerly renowned as a track star for the University of Southern California. He had won a bronze medal in the 400-meter event in the 1948 Olympics, and was a good friend of Davis.

Accompanied by Davis, now an army lieutenant, Dorismae and Hubie Kearns walked onto the beach at Malibu to discover Elizabeth engaged in a game of touch football with her brother Howard and his friends from school. Elizabeth's first words to Davis were, "I bet I can play football better than you."

"You think so, squirt?" he said. "You're on." The game became more tackle football than touch football, and both Davis and Elizabeth ended up wrestling together in the sand.

After that, they headed for the nearby Taylor home, where Davis greeted Sara, who would later recall the moment: "When I saw that frank, wonderful face, I thought this is the boy for my girl."

Davis remembered their first dinner together. "Elizabeth and I didn't have much to say to each other. I stared at her, and she stared at me. We seemed to like what we saw."

"I never saw much of Francis Taylor," Davis recalled. "Sara was clearly in charge. Francis was always in his bedroom. I heard he had a drinking problem."

The next morning, Elizabeth called Dick Hanley, who was on a three-day leave from Louis B. Mayer's office. "Glenn is yummy—oh, god, what a guy!"

"We have an expression for that in America," Dick said. "Built like a brick shithouse."

"You Americans can be so unromantic," she responded.

The next day, she showed Glenn the sights of Beverly Hills. She went window shopping with him, passing a jewelry store. A necklace of sixty-nine graduated pearls caught her eye. He asked her to come into the store with him where he purchased the expensive necklace for her.

As the years went by, Elizabeth eventually presented the necklace to her mother. In her will, Sara bequeathed it "to my beloved granddaughter, Liza Todd."

After Elizabeth's weekend with Glenn Davis, their coming together was referred to as "spontaneous combustion" in Hedda Hopper's newspaper column.

Davis invited Sara and Elizabeth to be his guests at an exhibition football game, where the Los Angeles Rams battled the Washington Redskins. Rams fans (who included Elizabeth) shouted, "We want Davis! We want Davis!"

Then Elizabeth turned to her mother. "And god damn, I mean that. I'm gonna have him, too."

"Glenn was in our bungalow at Malibu every minute that Elizabeth was there," Sara claimed. "Those lovebirds sure saw a lot of each other that summer."

During their long talks together, it seemed that Davis maintained ambitions of Hollywood stardom after his scheduled return from Korea. He'd already appeared in one film with Felix ("Doc") Blanchard, *The Spirit of West Point,* about the Army's championship football team.

At MGM, Dorismae Kearns speculated that Davis was using the spotlight focused on the time he was spending with Elizabeth as a means of launching himself as an actor.

The publicist was largely responsible for generating headlines that appeared across the nation: ALL AMERICA HERO DATES MGM'S TEENAGE STAR.

Roddy McDowall claimed that Peter Lawford was jealous of Elizabeth for snaring a stud like Davis. The actor called Davis and invited him for a weekend at a house where he was staying at Laguna Beach. Davis had seen three of Lawford's movies and seemed impressed with the invitation.

But Elizabeth protested vehemently, warning Davis that if he accepted Lawford's invitation, "You might have to sing for your supper."

"You mean he's *that way?"* Davis asked. Elizabeth nodded her head. That night, Davis called Lawford and cancelled their "date."

Officially, Davis later told reporters, "Elizabeth and I didn't drink or smoke, and I never laid a hand on her. We kissed and stuff like that, but we certainly didn't sleep together."

Because he knew otherwise, Roddy mocked Davis' comment, having been delivered a full report from Elizabeth. "Glenn might not have laid a hand on her, but he screwed her royally with his handlebar. He's right about their not sleeping together. When they were in bed, they were too busy fucking to get any sleep. I admire him, though, for being a gentleman and trying to protect Elizabeth's reputation."

Davis told Hubie Kearns, Doc Blanchard (his football-playing comrade), and Dick Hanley, "I scored with Elizabeth on every date. I don't know where she learned all her tricks, but she's a woman of the world, even at her age. In fact, she was the aggressor."

To Davis' shock, Elizabeth announced to the press that she and Davis "were engaged to be engaged."

"That was news to me," Davis later said. "I hardly knew her. We'd never talked about marriage."

Elizabeth told both Dick and Roddy that she was falling in love with Davis and didn't "want him to die in some swamp in Korea from some communist bullet." Then she placed an emotional phone call to Howard Young, her father's rich and aging uncle, and begged him to contact one of this best friends,

General Dwight D. Eisenhower with the intention of arranging an exemption for Davis from military service. Young said he didn't like to do that, but agreed to intervene for "my favorite gal."

He did speak to the general and reported back to Elizabeth a few days later. "Ike saw *National Velvet,* and he thought you were wonderful. But he's always had a strict policy against granting requests such as yours. He thinks a young man must serve his nation in time of peace or war. There is nothing more I can do."

"Oh thank you, Uncle Howard," Elizabeth said before bursting into tears and hanging up.

Davis invited Elizabeth to a dinner with his football playing friend, Felix ("Doc") Blanchard, who had been the first ever junior to win the Heisman Trophy. At the time, he was studying at, and played football for, West Point. He later joined the United States Air Force.

Dick Hanley arranged for Elizabeth to see a film, *The Spirit of West Point,* that had co-starred Davis and Blanchard. Both of the athletes had portrayed themselves in this dramatization of two All-America football players at West Point. Davis hoped that the film might lead to a contract as a romantic lead in Hollywood, but it didn't happen. Blanchard, on the other hand, planned to devote his career to the military.

Years later, Elizabeth wrote that her romance with Davis was "so childish. We were just two sweet children. It was not a big, hot romance."

After he read her memoirs, Davis resented her dismissive tone, reporting to Blanchard and others, "Hell, I was fucking her. We weren't two innocent sweet children. She was crazy for it. By the time I married Terry Moore, I was much wiser about these Hollywood stars. Of course, in both the cases of Elizabeth and Terry, Howard Hughes was waiting to move in for the kill."

On September 8, 1948, Elizabeth captured the attention of America when she kissed Davis good-bye before his departure for military service in Korea. In front of photographers, he gave her his lucky gold football chain, which she wore for a time around her neck. "She told the press, "Just call me a war bride."

Davis' tour of duty lasted seven months, during which period he wrote to her frequently, addressing her as "Mona Lizzie." She answered as many of his letters as she could.

Upon his return, Elizabeth showed up at the Los Angeles airport to welcome him home, embracing him and kissing him for the benefit of the cameras. She even shed "a tear of joy." When a photographer didn't capture this welcome home *tableau,* Elizabeth repeated it.

She didn't want to immediately drop Davis, and for that reason, she invited him to the Academy Awards Ceremony. But he didn't seem to fit into all the glitz and glamour.

MGM, through Howard Strickling, announced to the press that Elizabeth's relationship with Davis was ending because of a conflict of interest in their careers. Privately, Stickland said, "Davis went from the frying pan into the fire. He fell in love with Terry Moore on the rebound, and entered a disastrous marriage to Howard Hughes's girlfriend (or wife) depending on which story you want to believe."

Most biographers were led into believing that Davis just disappeared from Elizabeth's life after their romance came to an end. But that was not what happened. She actually wanted him out of her life, because she was pursuing other men, but Davis kept reappearing. Later, she referred to their final farewell to each other as, "the long goodbye."

***

During the time Glenn Davis spent in Korea and still hadn't proposed, Elizabeth was receiving at least a dozen marriage proposals per week, most of them from young men in American colleges. Her fan mail rose to one-thousand letters a week. Harvard University sent her a Valentine, claiming that its male students had voted her "The Girl We Would Never Lampoon." In later years, Harvard students would not honor that old promise, viciously lampooning her.

On the home front, Sara somehow managed to learn that Davis had only $20,000 in savings. She quickly changed her mind about him as a prospective bridegroom for Elizabeth. She sat her daughter down for a "heart-to-heart" talk.

"Maybe in the future, you'll become the greatest screen vamp of all time," Sara told her. "But whereas man supposes, God disposes. By 1954, you could be a has-been. You know how fickle public taste is. Now is the time you should strike it rich, and entice a man of great wealth into marrying you."

"What are you saying, Mother? Are you trying to pimp me out to some old goat?"

"There's nothing wrong with marrying a rich man," Sara said. "Greer Garson did it and now she's a billionaire in Texas...or is it New Mexico, one of those rattlesnake-infested states."

Davis' friend, Hubie Kearns, claimed that "Elizabeth was desperately in love with Glenn. But that didn't preclude some harmless dating on her part. I set her up with George Murphy—not the movie star—but USC's quarterback. That didn't go anywhere. I also arranged a date for her with Bill Bayliss, a member of the USC track team. He turned out to be a deadhead and didn't have anything to say to her. She called me the next day and denounced me for arranging a date with such a 'dud.'"

In her memoir, *There Really Was a Hollywood,* Janet Leigh wrote about double dating with Elizabeth after they had bonded on the set of *Little Women.*

They agreed to go together to the annual Society of Hollywood Press Photographers Costume Ball, borrowing wardrobes from an MGM storeroom.

"Elizabeth and I went as Spanish *señoritas*—Elizabeth in white and me in black. We looked like we were having a 'Who Can Wear the Lowest-Cut Bodice' contest. The photographers stood on chairs shooting downward for maximum exposure of our *décolletages*. Elizabeth and I were exercising the rule, 'If you've got it, flaunt it.'"

Janet's date was the handsome, San Francisco-born actor, Barry Nelson, who was thirty-two years old. He is known today as the first actor to portray Ian Fleming's secret agent James Bond in *Casino Royale*. Playing the agent as an American named "Jimmy Bond," Nelson appeared in the 1954 TV anthology series *Climax,* preceding Sean Connery's iconic interpretation of *Dr. No* by eight years.

"At the time, no one had ever heard of James Bond," Nelson recalled. "I hadn't read the book or anything like that, because it wasn't well known."

Elizabeth noted that Nelson and Leigh were deeply in love. Or, as Leigh put it, "He released my trapped emotions and freed my slaves. Wisely, tenderly, he opened a fresh depth of feeling in me." Leigh suffered guilt about her rather notorious past, and she credited Nelson with "defusing my fears. He didn't dispel my qualms about my shaky past altogether, but he was responsible for my somewhat healthier attitude."

"Barry's the kind of man I'd like to marry," Elizabeth told Leigh. "A man who you can talk to and share your problems with. All I get are men in awe of me who can say nothing more to me than tell me how beautiful I am."

Leigh eventually dumped Nelson, comparing her feelings to those of Elizabeth. "Right at this point in our lives, no one man can satisfy us" Leigh said. "Both of us have so many more worlds we want to explore. It's like I have this deep well of emotions, and I don't want to stop filling that well. I've talked it over with Elizabeth, and she feels the same way."

During her first double date with Leigh, Elizabeth was accompanied by Tom Breen, the son of the notorious Joseph I. Breen, Hollywood's chief censor and enforcer of "The Code," a strict set of puritanical moral guidelines that Hollywood was forced to follow from, roughly, 1934 to 1954.

Elizabeth, the first A-list actress who would

Who is an actress likely to meet when her boyfriend takes her home to meet his parents?

Joseph I. Breen *(photo above)* Hollywood censor and enforcer of The Code: "E.T. is a limey slut."

use the word "fuck" on the screen, visited Tom at the Breen home, where she was introduced to his father. As his biographer, Thomas Doherty, put it, "Shaped by parochial schools, and guided to maturity by the Jesuits, Joseph Breen embodied the restraint, repression, and rigidity of a personality type known as Victorian Irish. This is characterized neither by Leprechaun charm nor whiskey soaked gloom, but by a sober vigilance over the self and a brisk readiness to perform the same service for others, solicited or not."

Joseph discussed very briefly some key decisions he'd made over the years. His biggest battle, he told her, was his dilemma over allowing Clark Gable, as Rhett Butler in *Gone With the Wind,* to say, "Frankly, my dear, I don't give a damn." He also told her he struggled a great deal about allowing the word "hell" to be used in World War II movies.

After his son, Tom, had a few dates with Elizabeth, Joseph concluded that she was "not fit company for my boy." When he saw her performance as a prostitute in *Butterfield 8,* he condemned her as a "limey slut."

In spite of his father's objection, Tom continued to date Elizabeth. One of their rendezvous was at Malibu Beach, where she learned for the first time that he'd lost one of his legs in Iwo Jima. He had a wooden leg strapped on. Later, she spent a weekend with him in a wooden cabin overlooking Lake Arrowhead near San Bernardino. He had removed his wooden leg and was lying on a sofa as she tossed some logs into the fireplace. "For God's sake," he told her. "Don't burn my wooden leg."

In addition to the massive adulation Elizabeth enjoyed over the years, she would also be subjected to vulgar jokes, and evoked by Joan Rivers during her stewardship of *The Tonight Show* when she frequently ridiculed Elizabeth's weight gain.

When Hollywood discovered that Elizabeth was dating Tom Breen, "the man with the stump," locker room humor incited some people to (tastelessly) assert, "A horse in *National Velvet* wasn't good enough for Liz. Only a man's stump can fill that cavity."

Elizabeth wept bitterly when she heard those obscene putdowns, but as the years went by, she would toughen herself against such outrageous assaults.

Tom Breen faded into Elizabeth's dating history after Bing Crosby introduced her to Ralph Kiner, the former home-run king of the Pittsburgh Pirates, a team which the singer owned at the time. Kiner took her to the premiere of *Twelve O'Clock High* (1949), starring Gregory Peck in a World War II story about U.S. flyers in England.

The next day, Crosby invited Elizabeth and Kiner for lunch at his clubhouse on the golf course. When Kiner went to change into his "whites" for a match on an adjoining tennis court, Crosby propositioned Elizabeth.

As she'd later tell Dick Hanley, "I told him I preferred *older* men, and that was the end of that."

"Don't feel sorry for Bing," Hanley told her. "He's been seen with this gorgeous blonde model from New York, a gal named Grace Kelly."

Sara wanted Elizabeth to date "someone rich," and arrangements were made for Arthur Loew, Jr. to take her out. A wealthy playboy who later became a film producer, Arthur was the offspring of a maternal grandfather, Adolph Zukor, who had founded Paramount Pictures. His paternal grandfather, Marcus Loew, had founded MGM and the Loew's chain of movie theaters. His father, Arthur Loew, Sr., had been president of MGM. Born into wealth and privilege, Arthur was in some ways the harbinger of Elizabeth's first marriage to Nicky Hilton, son of the hotel tycoon.

During these double dates, Leigh had fallen in love with Danny Scholl, who was a Broadway singer and soon to appear in a 1949 hit called *Texas Li'l Darlin'*. During his big number, he swung around on stage and his cock popped out. (He'd forgotten to button his fly.) That night, he received a standing ovation.

Elizabeth and Leigh always enjoyed hearing stories about Scholl, especially in 1966 when he married Corinne Griffith, who was twenty-five years older than he was.

Scholl invited Elizabeth and Janet Leigh to dinner one night at Griffith's luxurious home. In the days of the silent pictures, Griffin had been dubbed "The Orchid Lady of the Screen," and was publicized as "the most beautiful woman ever to appear in movies." With the coming of sound, her career failed because she "talked through her nose."

Both Leigh and Elizabeth were awed by Griffin's wealth, a fortune of $150 million (a staggering sum back then), which she'd accumulated in real estate ventures.

| Arthur Loew, Jr. | Ralph Kiner |

Scholl had been married to Griffin for only a few days. Shortly after that dinner, he contacted Elizabeth and Leigh to tell them that the real estate tycoon was divorcing him.

In court, Griffin claimed that she was not Corrine Griffith, but her younger sister by twenty years. She said she took her sister's place upon her death. Eyewitnesses were called to testify that she was, indeed, the silent screen star. The marriage was annulled.

At a dinner party shortly after Griffith's death in 1979 at the age of eighty, Elizabeth said, "I envied Corrine Griffith, not just for her money and jewelry, but for her having the balls to play a character called 'Pussy,' and that was back in a silent movie made in 1916. My dream is to play in a talkie where I'm called 'Pussy.'"

Elizabeth "adored" Arthur Loew, Jr., but interpreted their relationship as more of a friendship than a love affair. Coincidentally, his future girlfriend, Joan Collins, eventually dumped him, finding their dating "too platonic."

Every Tuesday night, Elizabeth, Leigh, and others, including Farley Granger and Shelley Winters, would convene at Arthur's home because he owned one of the few TV sets in Los Angeles. "We'd watch 'Uncle Miltie' in drag, or the *Texaco Star Theater,*" Elizabeth said. "Although Farley would arrive with Shelley, he'd often leave with one of the cute boys at the party, especially John Dall, his co-star in *Rope*."

Arthur and Elizabeth would remain lifelong friends, and she often enlisted him as a babysitter for her children when she had to travel.

But after only a few dates, she "surrendered" him to Leigh, who was enthralled with him. "He was the most natural, easygoing person," Leigh said. "He was comfortable in all situations and blessed with a superior sense of humor. He introduced me to the grand social life of Hollywood. He had his regular table at such clubs as the Cocoanut Grove, Ciro's, and Mocambo's."

Elizabeth recalled being invited by producer Joe Naar to Arthur's house for his birthday celebration. "Janet was Arthur's date that night, and Peter Lawford was my escort. Before the drunken party ended, I was propositioned by Dean Martin, Jerry Lewis, and Sammy Davis, Jr. I had truly arrived in the adult world. A drunken Sammy told me that I had not experienced life until I'd sampled black dick. Gene Kelly spent most of the evening going after Peter. I'm sure Frank Sinatra would have gone for me, but he was out of town. I called that party a prehistoric gathering of the infamous Rat Pack."

Naar recalled Elizabeth looking gorgeous in yellow chiffon, "a real lemon meringue pie. She was sixteen going on thirty. I saw the guys clustering around her. She turned down Jerry Lewis, but I think she set up something in the future with Martin. I thought she might one day cross that bridge with Sammy, but I don't think she was quite ready for that type of biracial experience yet."

***

Short of cash, Errol Flynn was forced to give up his home on Mulholland Drive, which was being put on the market at a "sheriff's sale." Flynn's business manager, Al Blum, had died, and records revealed that he had embezzled thousands of dollars from the star. Flynn's first wife, Lili Damita, was in hot pursuit of him for back alimony payments.

He had run out of money in Europe producing an independent picture, *William Tell,* and creditors were after him. He'd given a role in that movie to his long-time friend and former roommate, Bruce Cabot, who was also suing him for back pay. Flynn's personal belongings had been seized, including two of his automobiles.

As part of the rituals associated with his departure from his "farm" on Mulholland, Flynn decided to invite A-list Hollywood to a party there. He included the silent screen vamp Gloria Swanson, then shooting *Sunset Blvd.,* Joan Bennett, Ann Miller, Clark Gable, Joan Fontaine, Virginia Mayo, Jack Benny, James Stewart, Dorothy Lamour, George Cukor, Walter Pidgeon, Van Johnson, Jennifer Jones, Greer Garson, Jane Wyman, Loretta Young, Robert Young, and David O. Selznick.

Huge water lilies floated on the pool, and guests dined on roasted pheasant served on silver plates provided by Romanoff's. Entertainment included white mice races and hillbilly skits by Judy Canova. A lookalike transvestite, an exact image of Louella Parsons, went around the room revealing deadly secrets about other Hollywood stars. Alexis Smith was revealed as a closeted lesbian, and Dorothy Lamour was exposed as a former prostitute who used to work for the most notorious madam in New York City, Polly Adler.

Elizabeth was escorted to Flynn's party by Robert Stack, whom she was dating less and less frequently. Janet Leigh arrived at the party escorted by Arthur Loew, Jr, Elizabeth's former *beau.*

At one point, Leigh whispered to Elizabeth, who already knew her way around Flynn's house, "I want to see that famous boudoir."

Elizabeth had just heard that Shirley Temple and "her living doll of a husband," as Elizabeth referred to John Agar, had arrived at the party.

She decided to show off Errol's boudoir to both Leigh and Arthur Loew and, at the same time, "to repair any damage to my make-up before presenting myself to Miss Temple."

Leigh and Arthur were amused by Flynn's bedroom, where the bed rested on an elevated platform like a throne. Mirrors sheathed the walls and ceiling. Leigh wrote in her memoirs, "As the wolf said to Little Red Riding hood, 'The better to see you with, my dear.'"

Elizabeth had played roles on the screen that were considered right for Temple, so there was jealousy there. David O. Selznick had pitched the idea of Temple starring in *Little Women,* as he'd also tried to seduce her, as she related in her memoirs, *Child Star.*

But eventually, the producer dropped the plan, suggesting that she go to

Italy, change her image, and appear as "a film vamp, a sex symbol in an Italian vineyard."

Elizabeth's role in *Life With Father* had also been suggested as a vehicle for Temple, who was trying to hold onto a film career as she matured.

For Elizabeth, there was also the lingering resentment she harbored for Temple "for having taken John Derek from my clutches."

In Flynn's boudoir, Elizabeth excused herself to go into the toilet as Leigh and Arthur Loew returned to another part of the house.

Making herself even more gorgeous than she already was, she heard someone enter the bedroom. She feared it might be Flynn seeking another seduction, and was surprised to see John Agar at the door.

"Forgive me," he said. "I'm Mr. Shirley Temple, desperate to take a leak. I was drinking in the car on the way here. I hope you don't mind."

"A man must answer nature's call," she said, flirtatiously, applying more lipstick.

"You're more gorgeous in person than you are in your movies," Agar said.

"So are you, Big Boy," she said.

At the toilet bowl, he didn't turn his back to her, but stood to its side. Unzipping his pants, he removed his penis, which he clearly exhibited to her before he urinated.

As she would later tell Roddy McDowall, "It was love at first sight."

Shirley Temple *(left and center photo)* gets married!
to **John Agar** *(center and right photo)*

CHAPTER TEN
Sex and the Single Girl

In the wake of the Errol Flynn home eviction party, Elizabeth began a clandestine affair with John Agar, who, after his marriage to Shirley Temple in 1945, had generated a headline: AMERICAN PRINCESS MARRIES PRINCE CHARMING.

Their secret liaison was launched during the waning months of the rapidly deteriorating "storybook" marriage between Agar and Temple. Elizabeth and Agar never dared go out in public together, and only a handful of her closest friends knew she was dating the handsome, young, and athletic former member of both the Naval Air Corps and the Army Air Corps.

Elizabeth's rendezvous with Agar were usually conducted at the home of Roddy McDowall, at the apartment of Dick Hanley, and on occasion in Marion Davies' guest cottage at the Hearst compound in Beverly Hills.

"I find him irresistible," she told Roddy. "That square jaw, those blue eyes, and that handsome face…"

The actor stood six feet, two inches, the son of a meat packer from Chicago. "He packs his own meat," Elizabeth jokingly told Dick.

"If he makes it big in the movies in the 1950s, he'll be another William Holden."

Temple had first met Agar in 1943, as her home was next door to the Agar family's. Joyce Agar became her friend, and one day Shirley invited Joyce's older brother, John, over for a swim. At the time, he was twenty-four, and she was only fifteen, so he didn't pay her much attention. He was not a movie buff and had never seen one of her pictures.

When he left for seven months of basic training in Texas, she wrote him nearly every day. She'd developed a powerful crush on him. He began to take her seriously during his furlough for the Christmas holiday of 1944. The following year, when Temple turned seventeen, they were married.

"Shirley and I had our first fight on the morning I woke up after our honeymoon night," Agar said to Elizabeth. "I accused her of not being a virgin."

During his affair with Elizabeth, Agar found her to be a good listener to his professional and private woes.

"I married a little girl who had been worshipped by millions in the 1930s. To her, it must have seemed like the universe revolved around her. Now that all that attention is fading, our storybook marriage is a joke."

Eleven years older than Elizabeth, Agar was very experienced in the bedroom. "I think he was broken in early in life by a lot of older women, perhaps in Chicago," Elizabeth told Dick. "He's a great lover...at least when he's sober."

Agar had never wanted to be an actor until David O. Selznick, who held Temple's contract, suggested that he might go over big in the movies because of his good looks and charm. His first picture, *Fort Apache* (1948), had starred Temple. John Wayne was the real star, and John Ford was the director. Wayne took up for Agar and befriended him, but Ford attacked him viciously during the making of *Fort Apache,* or so Agar told Elizabeth.

John Wayne, Shirley Temple, Henry Fonda, and **John Agar** in
Fort Apache (1948)

John Agar *(left)* with **John Wayne**
in *Sands of Iwo Jima (1949)*

Ford's biographer, Ronald Davis, wrote: "Psychologists might suggest that Ford feared the feminine side of himself and lashed out at pretty boy types. An even darker interpretation might infer that the director's need for dominance was a form of seduction."

Regrettably for Agar and his marriage, the young actor became a close drinking buddy of Wayne's night after night. The bond became so close that The Duke insisted that Agar appear in five more of his movies: *Sands of Iwo Jima* (1949); *She Wore a Yellow Ribbon* (1949); *The Undefeated* (1969); *Chisum* (1970), and *Big Jake* (1971).

"I think Wayne went for me big time," Agar told Elizabeth. "I ended up spending more time with him than I did with Shirley. I also hung out with Clark Gable and Spencer Tracy. All the closeted homos in Hollywood seem to go for me. A lot of Hollywood's big stars carry dubious sexual reputations from when they were young, unknown actors struggling for recognition."

"As you probably already know, it's called the casting couch," Elizabeth said. "I never had to actually lie down on it, because I became a star when I was only a child. If I'd launched my career at the age of twenty, I might have had had to suck as much cock as that blonde trollop that everyone's talking about, Marilyn Monroe."

Agar admitted he could be a brute, bringing home other women with Temple in the house and even beating her. As Temple herself revealed in her memoirs, she ended up on the floor on several occasions, "a disheveled woman with an aching heart and a crumpled spirit. It was growing ever harder to keep the lamp of love lit."

In spite of knowing the details of these stories, Elizabeth remained defensive of Agar, even in the aftermath of his arrests for drunk driving. "He's always portrayed as such a Bad Boy in the press," she said, "but I have found him to be a young man with good manners, always a gentleman, rather soft spoken, and with tremendous respect for women."

"I'm sure that's how you see him," Roddy said. "In fact, I think you and John Wayne are the only stars in Hollywood in love with Agar."

The only public comment Wayne ever made about Agar was, "John is just too good looking for his own good."

One night, Agar asked Elizabeth if she respected him less because he was not faithful to Temple. "I mean, I live in her shadow. I turn to other women because they make me feel like a man. The Temples have castrated me."

"I don't believe that a man or woman should remain faithful in a marriage," Elizabeth said. "It's a middle class concept. All adventurous people have a roving eye."

On another occasion, Agar told her he'd met a tall, good-looking guy in a bar, an aspirant actor named Rock Hudson. "He's a homo, but said he'd love to meet you because he is your biggest fan."

Ironically, both Agar and Hudson would end up working together in one of Wayne's movies, *The Undefeated* (1969), and Elizabeth, of course, would become one of Hudson's all time best friends.

Years later, Hudson would tell Elizabeth that he was nervous about meeting Wayne, who had a reputation for "faggot bashing."

"I met Duke in his dressing room as he was applying natural lipstick and wearing heels to make himself look taller," Hudson said. "We got along fine and played bridge together. John Agar told me what Wayne had said about me one day. He told Agar, 'Look at that face on Rock Hudson. Too bad it's wasted on a queer. You know what I could have done with a face like that on the screen?'"

When Agar's divorce from Temple was finalized, he'd wanted to marry Elizabeth, but by then, she'd moved on to other lovers. Actually, she told Dick

Hanley the real reason for their breakup: "One drunken night, John told me his dream was to marry a long-legged model."

"But no such luck for me," Agar later recalled. "I ended up marrying Shirley Temple and dating Elizabeth Taylor, two gals with stumps for legs."

***

After *Little Women,* Elizabeth vowed that she'd played her last juvenile teen role. "From now on, I plan to appear on the screen as an adult, playing love scenes with grown men, even though I'm still sixteen," she told Dick Hanley.

"I adored Elizabeth," Hanley said, "but she was a scheming little vixen. She was not willing to prostitute herself to Louis B., whom she still despised, but her attention focused on the Veep, Benjamin Thau, whom we called Benny. He was actually responsible for her contracts and, in the main, for the roles assigned to her."

Instead of passively waiting for roles, Elizabeth decided to lobby for them. She was learning a lot just from listening to the gossip every morning in the make-up department, where she was talking to Ava Gardner, Katharine Hepburn, Lana Turner, and Lucille Ball.

One morning, one of her favorite actresses, Barbara Stanwyck, arrived on the lot for the filming associated with *East Side, West Side* (1949), which also contained roles for Ava Gardner and Nancy Davis. Stanwyck was married at the time to one of the screen world's most talked-about "pretty boys," Robert Taylor.

Stanwyck checked out Elizabeth and told Hepburn, "No woman, if the Taylor dame can be called that, has a right to look that gorgeous at five o'clock in the morning."

In one of the many ironies of Elizabeth's life, she would, within a matter of months, be playing the role of wife, onscreen, to Stanwyck's real-life husband, Robert Taylor.

Sidney Guilaroff, the prominent hairdresser who had styled Elizabeth's hair for *National Velvet,* noticed her checking out Nancy Davis (later, Mrs. Ronald Reagan), who was co-starring with Ava Gardner and Stanwyck in *East Side, West Side.*

When Elizabeth had finished her make-up and was heading for coffee with Guilaroff in the commissary, she wanted to know more about Davis. "She certainly won't challenge Ava or Lana for movie roles," Elizabeth said. "Maybe she could get some minor parts—perhaps a housewifey thing, or the girl next door. And she looks old enough to be my mother."

At this point, Judy Garland joined their table, having overheard their talk.

"Nancy Davis is Benny's new *protégée*," Garland said. "She's a ripe twenty-eight years old, if she's a day, and Metro, as you know, rarely hires gals over twenty-five. Nancy, or so I hear, has a special talent. She visits Benny's office every morning to give him a state-of-the-art blow-job."

Garland's statement can't be lightly dismissed as mere gossip. The famous biographer, Anne Edwards, visited Thau in 1983 when he was dying at the Motion Picture and Television Hospital in Los Angeles. He admitted that Nancy was known during the late 1940s for performing oral sex, her lucky conquests including not only Thau, but Clark Gable and Spencer Tracy. Tracy had been her main sponsor at MGM.

Elizabeth was still dating Peter Lawford, on occasion, and he was also romancing Nancy Davis. He confirmed that "Nancy gives great head, and you know what an oral type I am."

Ironically both Lawford and Davis were also romancing actor Robert Walker, who had been married to Jennifer Jones until producer David O. Selznick made off with her.

Not to be upstaged by Davis, Elizabeth asked Dick to arrange a private meeting between Thau and herself, and the MGM executive welcomed her, because he viewed her as the studio's best prospect for major stardom in the 1950s.

Thau later told Dick, "She really came on strong to me. I believe all I had to do was unzip and she'd go for it. But she was so young, and I'd already been serviced that morning by Nancy. Actually, her little rendezvous with me was completely unnecessary. I was going to contact her that afternoon with some good news. Mayer had agreed to cast her as the wife of Robert Taylor in a movie to be shot in London." It was *Conspirator,* eventually released in 1949.

"I ran into Elizabeth when she'd just come out of Thau's office," Garland recalled. "She was almost hysterical at being assigned her first adult role."

"How was sucking Benny's dick?" Garland asked in her typically blunt fashion. "Did he say you were better than Nancy?"

"Oh, Judy, I didn't have to do that, although I would have. In my next movie, I'm going to star opposite Robert Taylor, and I'll be able to say that I did it based on my talent, and not by just moving from zipper to zipper!"

Starlet **Nancy Davis** before she became Mrs. Ronald Reagan in 1951

***

143

Elizabeth, accompanied by Sara, sailed from New York to England aboard the *Queen Mary* in October of 1948 to begin the filming of *Conspirator*. Because of her age, and because technically, as a seventeen-year-old who hadn't yet graduated from high school, she had to carve out time for lessons with a "schoolmarm"—in this case, the white-haired Birtina Anderson, whom MGM kept on its payroll—to at least maintain the illusion that she was proceeding with the "normal" life of an American teenager.

"Between love scenes with Robert Taylor, I had to meet with Birtina, who thought I was a horrible student in English, algebra, and history."

Because Elizabeth had dual nationality, both American and British, the question of her being granted a work permit did not come up.

An MGM limousine waited at Southampton to drive them to London and their suite at Claridges, where red roses and orchids awaited them.

Back in her hometown of London, Elizabeth was shocked at the devastation wreaked by the bombings of World War II. Entire neighborhoods of the city had been destroyed during the Blitz. But at Claridges, the most prestigious hotel in England, everything was elegance itself, especially the suite assigned to Sara and Elizabeth.

She was introduced to Percy Rogers, a very effeminate version of Roddy McDowall, with a solitary wisp of dyed blonde hair that fell across his forehead. He'd been hired by MGM as an "expediter" specifically assigned to Sara and Elizabeth.

"Miss Taylor, you are my favorite movie star. I've adored all of your films. Anything you want in London, I've been ordered to get it for you."

"How about Prince Philip?" she asked.

"Oh, you sweet darling, you have a wicked sense of humor. Prince Philip is on my list, too. You know, he fucks around, don't you? I want him first, then I'll pass him on to you."

"You're my kind of guy," she said, kissing him on the cheek in front of a rather disdainful Sara.

The next morning, after an English breakfast in Claridges dining room, Sara stayed in the suite while Percy drove Elizabeth to the Taylor family's former home on Wildwood Road near Hampstead. She was shocked to find the house in disrepair. He asked her if she wanted to go inside, informing her that it was now occupied by the Women's Voluntary Services, but she declined. "I'd rather remember it as it was."

Back at Claridges she told Percy, "I want you to escort me everywhere. But don't get your hopes up. I don't put out, at least not for you."

"Oh, my dear, that's something you, with your ghastly plumbing, will never have to worry about."

That weekend, Percy drove Sara and Elizabeth to the estate in Kent associated with the late Victor Cazalet, where they were entertained by his sister, Thelma.

The Taylors were welcomed warmly as part of the family. There was much talk of London before the war and loving memoires of Victor were shared. "I also miss Francis so much," Thelma said. "I wish he could have come."

"He simply can't afford it," Sara said. "Even though Elizabeth is a movie star, she doesn't make *that* much money."

"She will one day," Thelma assured Sara.

On the following Monday at around noon, Percy escorted Elizabeth and Sara to a luncheon at London's Ritz Hotel, where they met the British director Victor Saville, one of the founding fathers of British filmmaking. Having been associated with MGM since 1941, he'd previously directed such classics as *Goodbye, Mr. Chips* (1939), and worked closely with such stars as Greer Garson, Katharine Hepburn, Joan Crawford, Ingrid Bergman, Lana Turner, Errol Flynn, and Hedy Lamarr.

Saville was so supportive of Elizabeth, and so complimentary of her, that she felt she'd have a good working relationship with him.

Thirty minutes late, the star of the picture, Robert Taylor, finally showed up.

Before becoming the pretty boy of MGM in the 1930s, he'd trained as a cellist in Nebraska, where he was known by his birth name, Spangler Arlington Brugh.

Elizabeth knew Robert's image only through two pictures she'd seen—*Camille* (1937), where he'd co-starred with Greta Garbo, and *Johnny Eager* (1942), with Lana Turner. Elizabeth was startled at how his face had changed since World War II. No one would accuse him of being a pretty boy ever again.

As critic David Thomson put it, "Taylor's history is like that of Tyrone Power: of hollow, gorgeous youth dwindling into anxiety. But in Taylor's case, there is something touching in his decline. For he became not plainer, but harsher: Churlish, peeved, disagreeable—no more than that, never enough to make him an absorbing villain."

A villain was what MGM had miscast him as in *Conspirator,* where he played a British officer spying for the Russians and married to an unsuspecting, twenty-one-year-old American, as portrayed by the sixteen-year-old Elizabeth.

"Just think," Elizabeth said to Robert, "You've had girlfriends on the screen who have included Greta Garbo, Katharine Hepburn, Jean Harlow, Vivien Leigh, Joan Fontaine, and Hedy Lamarr—and now you get me."

He looked her over. "And how lucky I am."

Robert regaled his luncheon table with stories about his early days at MGM.

"After several months of studying with MGM's acting coaches, I was told to go back to my family farm in Nebraska. That made me so god damn sore, I stayed on in Hollywood."

"I remember in 1937 when MGM tried to counter your pretty boy image by releasing photographs of you shirtless, revealing hair on your chest to prove your '*He-ness*,' as it was defined at the time," Saville said.

"I'd rather forget that," Robert said.

Before leaving, Robert told her, "We have love scenes coming up in the film, but would you at least give me a peck on the cheek as a preview?"

"Of course I will," Elizabeth said, kissing him on the mouth.

"Aren't there laws about making love to a minor like Elizabeth?" Saville asked.

She smiled at him. "Laws are only made to be broken."

Later, Percy told Elizabeth, "I used to have the hots for Robert Taylor. But in my fantasies, I've moved on to dream about younger men."

Elizabeth eagerly awaited her first kissing scene with Robert. She later said that she closed her eyes and pretended it was Glenn Davis.

"Robert isn't as good a kisser as Glenn is," she told Percy. "But he did give me some advice. He told me to powder down my lips before kissing him. That way, I wouldn't smear his make-up. How unromantic!"

Much MGM publicity was generated by that first kissing scene. The word got out that to conceal Robert's "enormous erection," he'd ordered cameraman Freddie Young to shoot him only from the waist up.

Reportedly, Young mocked those remarks. "Taylor couldn't produce a big hard-on if his life depended on it—call that one 'Princess Tiny Meat.'"

Elizabeth wrote Roddy, complaining about having to do schoolwork while co-starring in a film. "It's hard to concentrate on algebra when Robert Taylor is sticking his tongue down your throat."

Two Taylors (Elizabeth and Robert)
in *Conspirator,*
She was 16, he was 38.

Robert told Saville, "That Elizabeth Taylor is stacked. I didn't realize it until she appeared in one scene in a *négligée*. Good god, she is just a child, but I can't help myself." He later told Saville that he slipped her back to his hotel suite and seduced her.

"How was it?" Saville asked.

"I've had better," Robert said. "I told her that if she didn't shave her legs, I would do it for her."

During the shoot, Elizabeth was asked how she felt about very young actresses appearing on the screen with middle-aged men. "Hollywood thinks nothing of romantically pairing older men with young girls," she said. "But you never see the reverse. Imagine seeing Roddy McDowall on the screen making love to Barbara Stanwyck."

One scene that Saville shot with both Taylors didn't go over with Dore Schary at MGM's home office in Hollywood. Schary ordered that the director reshoot it. "When Elizabeth's robe flies open in a scene where she's struggling with Bob, we see far too many of her God given assets," he wrote. "Please try to keep in mind that this is not a blue movie."

When the rough cut of *Conspirator* was rushed back to MGM, Pandro S. Berman was not impressed with Elizabeth's first venture into an adult movie. "She has the face for it, but doesn't possess the strength of voice to go with it. It was like she was half child, half grown woman. I advised MGM to hold up the picture for a while until her career was more secure."

Ultimately, when the film was released in 1949, the critics agreed with Berman, although many claimed that Elizabeth delivered a fine performance in an otherwise mediocre movie. *Conspirator,* evaluated by the box office as a flop, did nothing to advance the post-war career of Robert Taylor.

Even though the two Taylors failed to excite audiences, it would not be the last time they would be cast together in an MGM film.

During the filming of *Conspirator,* Elizabeth blossomed as a social flower in London, meeting people who would alter her life forever.

***

One noonday, Elizabeth and Percy Rogers were enjoying some fish and chips at the MGM canteen in London, and he was filling her in on all the movie and theatrical gossip of the West End. She obviously could not have known it, but two of her future husbands—Richard Burton and Michael Wilding—would also be having lunch that day in the canteen.

During that era, MGM talent scouts were successfully luring the most talented British stars, both male and female, to Hollywood. Among those solicited, Deborah Kerr was already in California, and such actors as Stewart Granger, Wilding, and Burton would soon be on their way to America, too.

147

Orson Welles, whom Elizabeth had known since the days of filming *Jane Eyre,* had stopped by her dressing room earlier that morning. He was having lunch with Wilding.

In his memoirs, *The Wilding Way,* the British actor recalled the first time he spotted Elizabeth, although he associated the circumstance with the wrong year of 1951. That was when she returned to England to film *Ivanhoe,* once again with Robert Taylor as her co-star. Wilding actually met her when she was filming *Conspirator* in MGM's London commissary in 1948.

"I was aware of her beauty," Wilding wrote. "Instead of asking the waitress for the salt, she sashayed down the whole length of the canteen to pick it up from the counter. All eyes focused on her, and I'm sure that was her intent."

Wilding claimed that Welles, his luncheon partner, raised a satirical eyebrow and quipped, "The girl didn't ought to do that, you know. Upsets the digestion."

Back at her table, Elizabeth asked Percy the identity of the man dining with Welles.

"He's an actor, Michael Wilding, under contract to Henry Wilcox, the producer. I think he's making a picture with Wilcox's wife, Anna Neagle."

"Very handsome, very debonair," she said. "When I walked past his table, he looked at me with devouring eyes."

"That's because he's a notorious breast man, but he's too old for you, my darling. The old sod must be forty if he's a day. Before the war, he met and married this woman named Kay Young because he said her beauty reminded him of Joan Crawford. But his true love, and this has been so since the war, is actually sitting over in the far corner of the room making eyes at your Robert Taylor."

Elizabeth stared long and hard at Robert's luncheon guest. "He's stunningly attractive, too. What's his name?"

"Stewart Granger," Percy said. "He's a real swashbuckler, our British film industry's equivalent of your Errol Flynn. He was madly in love with Deborah Kerr before she went to Hollywood. When he made *Caesar and Cleopatra,* Vivien Leigh fell madly in love with him. But, in spite of all his philandering, his most consistent lover has been Michael Wilding himself. Of course, those two are never faithful to anybody. Stewart right now is obviously making a play for Robert, because he wants to star in pictures for Metro in Hollywood. He knows that Robert can open many doors for him. I have no doubt that those two hot guys will be exploring each other's bums before Big Ben strikes midnight."

Elizabeth spent the rest of her time glancing first at Granger, then at Wilding. "When I think of the two, Granger has the most sex appeal," she said. At the time, of course, it was inconceivable that in a relatively short time, she would be living under the same roof with both men.

"Stewart is in love with Jean Simmons, who is being billed as Britain's answer to Elizabeth Taylor," Percy said.

"I saw her play Ophelia opposite Laurence Olivier in *Hamlet,*" Elizabeth said. "She was very good and very beautiful."

As Elizabeth looked at the entrance, she spotted Laurence Olivier entering the canteen with a handsome young actor. "What is the deal with those two?" she asked.

"Larry is mad about the boy," Percy responded. "That's Richard Burton, an actor from Wales. He's the biggest whore in the business. He's seduced all the stately homos in the British theatre, including Noël Coward and John Gielgud. He's also gone through half the actresses in the theater."

"I adore British actors," she said. "They seem to play musical chairs every night. Everybody is sleeping with everybody else, regardless of gender."

"We're far more sophisticated about such things than you uptight Americans," Percy said.

Olivier nodded as he walked by Elizabeth's table, and she met Burton eye to eye. After he was out of earshot, she said, "I will not become another notch in Mr. Burton's belt."

"I wouldn't be so sure about that," Percy told her. "Richard's got the most seductive voice in the British theater, far more so than Larry. Richard is also generous with his cock. Once in his dressing room, he owed me a favor, so he let me go down on him. Seven and a half inches at full mast, in case you do become interested."

"That is most doubtful," she said. "Give me this Stewart Granger any day, even Michael Wilding."

At that point, she saw Welles, trailed by Wilding, heading toward their table. "Elizabeth, my sweet, dear child, I'd love to drop by your suite tonight to pay my respects to you and Sara. I also am friends with the world's most intriguing personality, who's also staying at Claridges and would adore meeting you."

"I'd be delighted, as always, Orson," Elizabeth said. "not only to see you, but to meet this mystery guest of yours—no doubt, Winston Churchill himself."

Welles looked over at Percy. "No need to introduce me to this one. His reputation has preceded him." Then he turned around to Wilding. "Forgive me, Elizabeth, this is Mr. Michael Wilding."

"Miss Taylor, an honor," Wilding said. "Are you real or merely a painting that Leonardo da Vinci did by dawn's rosy light?"

"I'm just a lonely little chit from Hampstead, wiggling her ass across the canteen, hoping to attract some handsome British gentleman who will invite her out on a fucking date. Is that too much to ask?"

"I'd like to be that gentleman," Wilding said. "However, the first time a waiter asks, 'And Mr. Wilding, what will your daughter order tonight,' I'm out the door."

She laughed heartily. "I'm at Claridges, and most anxious to escape my mother, Sara. Perhaps you can fix her up with Robert Morley. She just loves bushy eyebrows."

"I'll call tomorrow, since Orson here has you booked for tonight," Wilding said. "In fact, I need a date to take to Lord Mountbatten's ball in honor of his daughter. Princess Elizabeth and Prince Philip will be there. I'm sure they'd love to meet a British girl who went to Hollywood and made good. They'll probably entice you back to England to make films here on your native soil."

At that moment, a messenger from MGM stopped at Elizabeth's table, passing a note to Percy. He read it quickly and looked up at Welles and Wilding. "Sorry, gents, but Elizabeth and I have to go. We just got word that two guests have dropped by the set to call on Elizabeth—Patricia Neal and Ronald Reagan."

***

During the cold, bleak winter of 1948 in London, four homesick Americans bonded, waiting for the weeks to pass in the bombed-out city, with its deprivations and food rationing, until they could return to sunny California. During their frequent evening excursions, Patricia Neal was escorted by Ronald Reagan, her co-star in *The Hasty Heart,* and Robert Taylor was Elizabeth's date. Neal was desperately lonely for the arms of Gary Cooper, and Reagan was still in deep mourning over the end of his marriage to Jane Wyman. At that point in her life, Elizabeth hadn't quite ended her love affair with Glenn Davis.

For Robert Taylor, his "lavender marriage" to his bisexual wife, Barbara Stanwyck, was over except for the final divorce proceedings.

On the set of *Conspirator,* Elizabeth had renewed her acquaintance with Reagan and was introduced to Neal. He suggested that Robert Taylor join them that Friday night for a steak dinner at the Savoy Restaurant. In meat-scarce London, Reagan had ordered a dozen steaks flown in from "21" in Manhattan.

In the Savoy Dining Room, Patricia remembered that "Elizabeth was so exquisite, so young, and Robert delighted in teasing her. There seemed some intimacy between them that I could only guess at. I also got the vague suspicion that something had gone on between Ronnie and Elizabeth back in Hollywood, but perhaps I was wrong. He didn't have a reputation as a child molester."

The *maître d'hôtel* arrived with the bad news. The steaks shipped from New York had gone bad, or so he claimed. Reagan suspected that the meat-hungry staff had either consumed or sold them. Nonetheless, he ordered a dozen more, warning the *maître d'*, "When they get here, I don't want you coming into the dining room with blood dripping out the corners of your mouth."

"Over dinner, which consisted of stale mutton chops, Robert amused us with stories of MGM, and Ronnie lobbed complaints about Jane Wyman and their failed marriage," Neal said. "Elizabeth and I listened patiently."

"When I starred with Garbo in *Camille* in '36, she told the director I was 'so beautiful but so dumb,'" Robert said. He also told them that when he signed to make *The Gorgeous Hussy* (1936) with Joan Crawford, Hollywood wags asked, 'To which of them does the title refer?'"

Reagan claimed that he was going to make a deal with Wyman that each of them should not discuss the other to members of the press. "I was really pissed off when she told reporters that I'm as good in bed as I was on the screen."

"I read the other day in the papers that she'd made another crack about me," Reagan said. She told some reporter, 'Don't ask Ronnie what time it is, because he will tell you how a watch is made.'"

When Robert took Elizabeth to another steak dinner at the Savoy, Reagan learned that, according to the *maître d'*, "only six of your steaks went bad this time."

One night, when Robert did not show up for a previously scheduled dinner, Elizabeth contacted Percy, who told them what had happened. Earlier that evening, Robert had been arrested in a room above the Wounded Pelican, a pub with upstairs bedrooms in Soho. It was a hangout for London homosexuals, who could rent "hot beds" for sex. Robert had been caught with a young hustler from Birmingham.

Both Reagan and Neal seemed very concerned, but Elizabeth less so. She was convinced that MGM publicists, operating on orders from Howard Strickling at headquarters in Hollywood, would hush up the scandal.

Patricia Neal in *Hasty Heart* with future U.S. President **Ronald Reagan**
"You know, an actress can learn to hate Elizabeth Taylor."

Elizabeth had had more than her quota of champagne that night. She mischievously goaded Reagan, "Thank God you didn't get arrested with Errol Flynn," she said, "He told me that he went for you big time when you guys made *Santa Fe Trail.*"

"Errol is such a tease," Reagan said, looking embarrassed.

"He could have told you anything—and probably did—but I don't go *that way*. If you ever run into Lana Turner, Betty Grable, or Susan Hayward, they'll establish my credentials. But in your case, Elizabeth, ask yourself."

"I couldn't believe it," Patricia later said. "I took that to be a confession. So, Ronnie had taken our little teen darling, Elizabeth, to bed. I couldn't wait to tell Gary."

Reagan wisely suggested that the next time they had dinner with Robert that each of them make no mention of his arrest, which, as Elizabeth had predicted, was covered up and did not appear in the newspapers.

When reunited as double-dating "couples" again, Neal suggested that Reagan and Robert take Elizabeth and her dancing at a local dance hall in Holborn that she'd heard about, and they agreed.

As Neal remembered the evening, "Elizabeth showed up way overdressed, in a gown designed by Christian Dior. We went to this hall where most of the other patrons were shabbily dressed, still suffering from wartime deprivation. All eyes turned to look at her. The British people still had their wonderful *bravado* about them. Elizabeth was moved when the patrons sang *The White Cliffs of Dover,* the name of that wartime movie she'd made when she was a child."

That weekend, Elizabeth agreed to drive into the English countryside with Robert, Reagan, and Neal, in a large car driven by Hamish Thomson, a young dentist who wanted to show them the Cotswolds. During the slow drive there, Thomson suggested they play a game—"A little quiz I've read about in this London magazine. Everybody has to reveal a secret wish."

Neal claimed that her wish involved Gary Cooper divorcing his wife and marrying her. Robert told them that he hoped Stanwyck would ask for no alimony when she divorced him. Elizabeth shocked the passengers in the car by claiming that her wish involved marrying Michael Wilding. When the game focused on Reagan, he said, "My wish—no, not my wish, my destiny—is to become President of the United States."

One weekend when he wouldn't be needed in the movie studio the following Monday, Robert went with Stewart Granger to the country house of one of his friends. Neal couldn't join Elizabeth and Reagan because she'd eaten a slice of West Country ham that had poisoned her. "I'm spending all my time on the toilet," she told Elizabeth.

Reagan called Elizabeth and asked her to go for dinner and dancing with him at the Ritz Hotel in London, and she accepted, although she would have preferred if Michael Wilding rather than Reagan had invited her.

"That was one very despondent date I had," Elizabeth told Percy the following morning. "The reality of losing Jane Wyman seemed to have finally settled in. We sat in a remote corner of the Ritz Hotel's lobby near a potted palm, and he broke down and cried. I held him in my arms and tried to comfort him."

Reagan later pulled himself together and had dinner with her, but didn't feel up to dancing. She agreed to go back to his suite with him.

"I thought if I threw him a mercy fuck—a term I learned from Roddy McDowall—that would cheer him up. But sex was about the last thing on his mind. He spent the rest of the evening talking about how he was going to run for senator from California."

When Michael Wilding finally called her for a date, Elizabeth quickly dropped Robert, Reagan, and Neal in favor of spending time with this older British actor.

"When I told this trio good-bye, we made some vague promise about getting together in Hollywood," Elizabeth told Percy. "Actually, I had no plans to see either of them again."

In the years ahead, Neal would refer to Elizabeth as "that God damn bitch," blaming her for "stealing the two most coveted roles of my lifetime."

In the summer of 1958, Neal was in London playing Catherine Holly in Tennessee Williams' *Suddenly, Last Summer.* Her performance received rave reviews, and she called it the "most thrilling acting experience of my life."

Producer Sam Spiegel came to see it and was impressed enough to acquire the movie rights, promising Neal that she could repeat her stage performance on the screen.

"Imagine my surprise when I picked up the paper to read that Elizabeth Taylor had signed to do the part with Monty Clift," Neal said. "Losing that role to Taylor was one of the hardest professional blows of my life. I still cannot talk about it without bitterness."

"There was more to come," Neal said. "I was for a time the leading candidate for the role of Martha in Edward Albee's *Who's Afraid of Virginia Woolf?* I was ready to sign the contract. Only Bette Davis stood in my way. Guess what? I picked up the morning paper to read that Miss Elizabeth Taylor, cunt from hell, had signed to do the role with her husband *du jour.*"

Elizabeth herself often discussed the irony of what she called "the second act for Ronnie and me. No Hollywood script, regardless of how far-fetched, would have me playing the housewife of a Republican senator, John Warner, hanging out at the White House with Ronnie, the President of the United States, and Benny Thau's fellatio artist, now installed as First Lady of the Land, a position once occupied by Eleanor Roosevelt."

***

Orson Welles, a larger-than-life creature, once claimed, "I have always had the hots for Elizabeth Taylor." After three postponements, he finally came to visit Sara and Elizabeth at their suite at Claridges.

Settling in for a drink, he lamented how difficult it was for him in post-war Hollywood. "During the war, I could have any woman I wanted. There was no competition. All the men were overseas. Today there are one hundred actors competing for every job. Everybody has a film script to sell. I want to continue making movies, but I have this unfortunate habit of spending all my money on women. No one seems to want to lend me any more dough."

"Perhaps Louella Parsons hasn't forgiven you for *Citizen Kane* and your depiction of her boss, William Randolph Hearst," Elizabeth said.

"I haven't forgiven her for all the rotten stuff she wrote about me during my marriage to Rita [a reference to Love Goddess Rita Hayworth]," Welles said. "Of course, much of the failure of my marriage was my own fault. A beautiful woman comes alone, and I can't resist her. Maria Montez, Judy Garland, Lucille Ball...well, maybe not Lucille."

"You certainly are known for seducing beautiful women," Sara said.

"That is so true, yet during my last visit to Hollywood, Guinn Williams, the one they call 'Big Boy,' attacked me at the Brown Derby restaurant, accusing me of being a queer. I demanded that he apologize. He didn't. Instead, he took a knife and cut off half of my tie."

"Perhaps you should have cut off something of Big Boy's," Elizabeth said.

Welles looked startled for a minute. "You do have a wicked sense of humor, which makes you all the more adorable."

After an hour of exchanging Hollywood gossip, Welles invited Elizabeth, but not Sara, to meet a special guest, who was also staying in a suite at Claridges. Sara seemed miffed that the invitation didn't include her.

A knock on the door of the "special guest's" suite summoned a maid from India, dressed in a sari. Elizabeth and Welles were ushered into the living room of the suite where they had to wait fifteen minutes for their host to appear.

"The suspense is killing me," Elizabeth said, "From the smell of perfume, I gather our host is really a hostess."

Suddenly, Marlene Dietrich emerged from the bedroom, wearing a silvery gown and draped in white furs, ready for an evening at the Café Royal with Welles.

"Oh, the darling girl with the violet eyes," she said to Elizabeth.

"Miss Dietrich," Elizabeth said, standing up. "You are so very lovely."

"It's all an illusion, my dear," Dietrich said. "I'm far too old to still be alive."

Welles came forward to kiss Dietrich. Then he quoted from Shakespeare, "Age cannot wither her, nor custom stale..."

She cut him off. "I know, I know. I'm called the timeless wonder. But time always wins."

She came over to Elizabeth and held her hand. "Orson and I must be leaving soon, but I really wanted to see you in the flesh. It is true: You are without a doubt the most beautiful girl in the world."

"But becoming less of a girl every day," Elizabeth said.

"Don't wish for youth to go by too quickly, or you'll regret it," Dietrich warned. "Oh, to be sixteen again. Didn't you know, my child, that the dream of every red-blooded man involves crawling into bed with a girl of sixteen?"

"If I didn't know that, I'm finding it out now," Elizabeth said.

"I heard that you met with George Bernard Shaw," Welles said before downing the rest of his drink. "How did that meeting of two legends go?"

"Like you, he's a genius," Dietrich said. "You're well aware that when I meet a genius, I kneel in front of him. Once on my knees, I unbuttoned his fly and removed his penis. I made love to it. Of course, I had to do that before we could sit down and talk."

Elizabeth didn't know how to respond to that. "Miss Dietrich, I will treasure meeting you, one of my great honors. You are today's Helen of Troy, the Queen of Sheba, Cleopatra reincarnate."

"You are so very kind," Dietrich said. "But I'm the mere wife of a chicken farmer, my dear Rudy."

That was a reference to her husband, Rudolph Sieber, with whom she no longer lived but never divorced. "We must meet again soon. I will share with you my secret of vinegar and ice water douches. It will prevent pregnancy."

She reached down to kiss Elizabeth. Her lips were very, very wet.

Back in her own suite, Elizabeth told Sara, "I simply adore Marlene. I'm sure she's going to become one of my very best friends."

"Perhaps you'd rather her be your mother instead of me?" Sara said.

"Mother, jealously doesn't become you."

During that evening at Claridges, Elizabeth could hardly have imagined that in a few short years, she and Dietrich would be competing for the love of one man, and that "The Kraut" (as Ernest Hemingway called her) would seduce at least four of her future husbands and many of her lovers.

***

Twenty years her senior, Michael Wilding was still handsome, in an offbeat kind of way. Elegant and polished, he talked, walked, and moved in a manner common to British aristocracy. In many ways, he evoked the decorum of Victor Cazalet, her standard for measuring an English "gent."

During their first outing together, he took her to The Salisbury, a pub and "watering hole" for many actors in London's West End. "The food is ghastly,

155

but so English it will make you homesick." He ordered steak-and-kidney pie for both of them.

After lunch and a walk through Mayfair, he took her to the National Gallery, where he told her that his dream had been to become an artist before "I wandered into acting."

After the museum, he guided her through some of the war-torn neighborhoods of London, a city still recovering from Hitler's last desperate attempt to destroy it. He told her many stories of the bravery and endurance of Londoners during their worst hour. At one point, she was moved to tears.

Back at Claridges, she filled Percy and Sara in on the details of her day. Then, after a brief rest, she put on her most revealing dress, since he'd invited her to dinner downstairs in the hotel's elegant dining room. Over dinner, she said, "I feel like Queen Victoria will walk in the door at any minute."

She urged Wilding to consider migrating to Hollywood, but he dismissed the idea. "I feel there are few roles for cultivated English gentlemen in post-war Hollywood. I think there would have been more parts for me in the 1930s. Someone wrote in *The Times* that I was the poor man's answer to Ronald Colman. I'm not sure there are that many roles for Colman himself these days."

She apologized for never having seen any of Wilding's films.

With a sense of self-mockery, he said, "You mean to tell me you haven't seen *The Courtneys of Curzon Street, Piccadilly Incident, Tilly of Bloomsbury,* or *Spring in Park Lane?* At least my next picture will be a change of pace for me. My producer, Henry Wilcox, told me that my sophisticated wit, if I dare call it that, and my English sensibility would never go over in Tinseltown. David Niven is the best example of that. Americans like Gary Cooper and John Wayne…and, I might add, Elizabeth Taylor."

He told her that Alfred Hitchcock had signed him to film *Under Capricorn* in New Zealand with Ingrid Bergman and Joseph Cotten. "Hitch said to watch out for Ingrid. He claims she'd fuck a tree. Margaret Leighton is going to be in the film, too. I find her talented but rather toffee-nosed. I don't go for her at all." [Ironically, Leighton would eventually become Wilding's fourth and final wife.]

Elizabeth's competitor for the affections of Michael Wilding:
Marlene Dietrich

"I've already met with Cotten," Wilding said. "We sniffed at each other at first—you know, like two suspicious dogs. Now we like each other. He calls the upcoming film *Under Crapicorn."*

Before leaving her that evening, he invited her to accompany him to Broadlands, Lord Mountbatten's country estate, where he was hosting a dinner/dance in honor of Lord John Brabourne, who had married his daughter, Patricia Mountbatten. "Princess Elizabeth and Prince Philip will be there." Wilding said.

But before the ball, Elizabeth was privileged to meet the future Queen of England at a command performance of the film *That Forsythe Woman,* starring her friends, Greer Garson and Errol Flynn.

Standing in a receiving line beside the former screen queen, Myrna Loy, Elizabeth met Queen Elizabeth (the former Elizabeth Bowes-Lyon) and her daughter, the Princess Elizabeth, who in a relatively short time would ascend to the throne after the death of her father, King George VI.

That weekend, in a chauffeured Rolls Royce, Elizabeth was driven to Broadlands with Wilding, Henry Wilcox, and his actress wife, Anna Neagle.

By ten o'clock that night at the ball, arrangements were made for Prince Philip to dance with Elizabeth Taylor. As she'd later reveal to Percy, "I pressed up against him and got the desired response. I think I really excited him, but with his princess in the room, what could he do? I am definitely targeting him as a future conquest."

By midnight, Wilding was drunk on champagne. He was approached by Lord Brabourne, who informed him that it was his turn to dance with Her Royal Highness, Princess Elizabeth. Wilding protested, "I've had too much to drink. I'm afraid I'll step on her royal toes." But His Lordship insisted.

At her table, Princess Elizabeth told Wilding, "I'm reluctant to dance with you, having seen you dance on the screen." Nonetheless, she arose and walked to the dance floor with him as the band struck up a waltz.

"Thank God," she said. "I feared the band was going to play a rhumba. I can never get the hang of those Latin rhythms."

After the dance, he dutifully returned her to her table and said, "I'm relieved that I got through the dance without hitting you."

She gave him a startled look. He'd meant to say, "without kicking you." But he was so embarassed, he thanked the princess and retreated back to Elizabeth (Taylor).

Wilding saved the last dance for her, holding her tightly in his arms. "I'm going to miss you."

"Oh, Michael," she said. "I never want to leave you."

Wilcox and Neagle spent the night in the same room in a nearby hotel, where separate bedrooms had been assigned to Elizabeth and Wilding. When Elizabeth articulated an account of the night's events to Percy, she said, "I kept my door unlocked all night waiting for him, but he never dropped in for a visit. In his affair with Stewart Granger, is Michael strictly a bottom?"

"No, he's both a top and a bottom, Stewart strictly a manly top," Percy claimed.

157

"You precious angel," Elizabeth said. "You do seem to know everything about British actors."

"It's my calling in life," he told her.

Three days later, Percy escorted Sara and Elizabeth to the airport as the first segment of their previously scheduled return to the U.S. Claridges sent a separate London taxi for transport of their luggage.

After exchanging many hugs and kisses with Percy, she disappeared into the VIP lounge at Heathrow. To her surprise, Wilding was waiting there for her. Sara discreetly removed herself to enjoy tea and some movie magazines.

The airplane to New York didn't leave for another hour, and Wilding sat with Elizabeth, holding her hand and talking intensely with her. No one knows what was said, and she avoided revealing anything to her confidants, but it was obvious that an intense bond had been formed between them.

He was seen giving her a deep throat goodbye kiss. A flight attendant overheard his final words to her and reported his words to the press: "Grow up very, very fast and come back to me."

***

Elizabeth had first met and befriended Merv Griffin at one of Roddy McDowall's Sunday afternoon barbecues.

Witty, charming, bisexual, and generically English: **Michael Wilding.** Unknown in America, but big in Britain

From the beginning, the future TV talk show host was impressed with her beauty and her kindness. He told Roddy, "She is the least judgmental person I know. She seems to recognize that all people have needs—and that love takes many forms."

When they were first introduced, she talked to him about the perils of being a child star. "Hedda Hopper told me there is no second act for child stars in movies. 'What awaits a child star?' she asked me. 'A decline in fans. A dwindling bank account. Personal disasters in relationships. Booze. And premature death. Most child stars can't adjust to life when the sound of applause no longer rings in their ears.'"

Back in New York, Elizabeth was on her own, as her mother had flown down to Florida. Elizabeth later claimed that this interlude in her life was "the beginning of my being an adult, with no parent or chaperone around telling me when I could take a crap."

Hearing that Griffin was in town, she called and invited him out on a date, with the understanding that it was a brother-sister type relationship of the sort she had with Roddy.

Merv arrived at her hotel suite with three dozen long-stemmed yellow roses, her favorite.

Escorted by him to the Stork Club, she introduced a "New Elizabeth Taylor" to public view, one clad seductively in a gown with plunging *décolletage.* "Let's dance the night away," she told Griffin.

The occupants of the other tables couldn't stop staring at Elizabeth, who seemed to tune them out. One aspect of her body disturbed Merv. He noticed that her bare arms were peppered with fine black hairs. They were unsightly, detracting from her otherwise stunning beauty.

At two o'clock, they left the club, and he took her back to her hotel, with an invitation for dinner the following night at 21.

The next evening, midway through their meal, Clark Gable walked in with his new wife, Lady Sylvia Ashley, a willowy blonde with a peaches-and-cream complexion and Wedgwood blue eyes. Nancy Davis (later Mrs. Ronald Reagan) had failed to persuade Gable to marry her.

Lady Sylvia pointedly ignored Elizabeth when they were introduced, but Gable leaned over and kissed Elizabeth on the cheek. Then the newlyweds departed quickly for their table.

"What do you think of Lady Sylvia?" Merv asked.

"That gold-digging bitch," Elizabeth said, "I heard she got her start modeling bras and bloomers. You know, she was once a chorus girl in the seediest clubs in London's Soho."

That night, back at her hotel suite, Elizabeth invited Griffin in as a means of continuing their discussion. "I'm thinking about getting married," she told him.

"Well, I'm an available candidate," he said, not at all seriously. "Who's the lucky guy?"

"I have five candidates in mind, and I'm currently conducting auditions. I can't tell you now. You'll read about it in the papers. Now I've got to get my beauty sleep. 'Night, love, and thanks for a darling evening. You're sweet."

***

Later, from New York, Elizabeth flew to Miami, where Francis and Sara met her at the airport and drove her to her Uncle Howard Young's mansion on Star Island. Reunited with her beloved uncle, she learned that he was tossing a big bash to celebrate her seventeenth birthday, to which he'd invited about one-hundred guests, including the power élite of South Florida.

To the party, he invited a handsome, twenty-eight-year-old bachelor, William Pawley, Jr., whose wealthy father had been the U.S. ambassador to both Peru and Brazil. A pilot during the war, Pawley was the president of Miami Transit. Uncle Howard had selected Pawley as a more suitable *beau* for Elizabeth than Glenn Davis.

She later stated that she found him "tall, dark, and handsome, with blue eyes that matched my own." He stood six feet tall, with jet-black hair. Escaping from the party with her, he walked through the Star Island gardens with her, telling her fascinating stories based on his travels in Brazil, Peru, China, and India.

Her discarded *beau*, Glenn Davis, later claimed that the Taylor family "pushed Elizabeth into the arms of this rich guy, a real slick operator who could show her a better time than I could afford and buy jewelry for her."

Davis also claimed that Sara and Francis "didn't have a pot to piss in, and Elizabeth was their meal ticket. Sara was interested in three things—Elizabeth as a money maker, Christian Science, and her blocked bowels. I was later glad I didn't marry Elizabeth Taylor."

After meeting Pawley, he booked her for dances, parties, yachting trips, fishing expeditions, leisurely luncheons overlooking the bay, and romantic lobster-and-caviar dinners.

"Sara wanted Elizabeth to marry a guy who lived in a mansion with servants and a swimming pool, and who owned a yacht," Davis claimed.

In the beginning, Elizabeth seemed dazzled by Pawley, a dashing young man, but problems emerged after only a week. She confided to Francis and Sara that, "He's already acting like a dominating husband. He even tells me what to wear. I think he prefers high-necked dresses—no breasts showing."

The Pawley family exerted a powerful influence over their heir. His parents reportedly told him that Elizabeth Taylor was a very vulgar young woman, and they'd much prefer him to marry a Florida *débutante* from a good family—"not some Hollywood tramp." Apparently, the Pawleys had hired a private detective in Los Angeles, who had uncovered and reported shocking revelations, including the accusation that both of her parents were bisexuals—and gold-diggers as well, living entirely off whatever profits they could make off Elizabeth. It was also alleged that she had attended sex parties at the home of Errol Flynn, and that she'd engaged in nu-

So This is Love?
Merv Griffin,
singer and movie star hopeful,
signing autographs in 1953.

160

merous affairs with actors who had included, among others, both Robert Stack and John Derek, even though it was widely implied in fan magazines that she was still a virgin.

At an upscale party hosted aboard the Pawley family's yacht as it was moored at a dock in Miami's harbor, family members and much of *tout* Miami virtually ignored Elizabeth, even though she was accustomed to being fawned over by the press and public alike.

Ignoring the objections of his family, Pawley proposed to Elizabeth and she accepted.

He presented her with her first "white diamond"—a three-and-a-half carat emerald-cut solitary ring for which he paid $16,000. She described it as a "Nice piece of ice," to the press, uttering that line in an imitation of Mae West.

Once the engagement ring was on her finger, Pawley became even more possessive, claiming that she'd have to give up her career in Hollywood and devote herself full time to being his wife. Amazingly, she agreed, asserting, "I'd rather be making babies than making movies," to the press.

"I have no intention of becoming known as Mr. Elizabeth Taylor," Pawley chimed in.

That news sent shock waves all the way to Louis B. Mayer's office. He immediately dispatched MGM producer Sam Marx, who was in Miami Beach at the time, to visit the Pawley mansion for a showdown with Elizabeth.

At first, Pawley didn't want to let Marx into his home, claiming that he was about to take Elizabeth fishing. But she ran down the stairs and told Pawley that she'd already agreed to meet with Marx, because years before, he had arranged for her first big break in films.

Over tea, Marx told her that he was in Miami supervising the filming of *A Lady Without a Passport,* starring Hedy Lamarr. "Lamarr looked great in those 1940s films, but she's getting a bit long in the tooth. Mayer agrees that you are the only one on the lot who can become the Hedy Lamarr of the 1950s. No one else is that beautiful."

He also told her that *Time* magazine was planning to put her picture on the cover of its August, 1949, issue. The magazine was going to announce that such golden stars of yesterday—Barbara Stanwyck, Marlene Dietrich, Bette Davis, and Joan Crawford—had reached their "sell-by dates."

"*Time* will editorialize that a new type of goddess will soon emerge onto the American landscape—and her name is Elizabeth Taylor," Marx said.

He also told her that MGM was planning its biggest picture of the year, a vehicle where she'd play a bride, the daughter of Spencer Tracy. He went on to say that Mayer wanted to lend her to Paramount for "the female role of the year," appearing opposite Montgomery Clift in a film based on Theodore Dreiser's *An American Tragedy.*

"If you leave the film industry now, you'll be remembered, if at all, as a little girl who rode a horse in *National Velvet,*" Marx said. "*Conspirator* bombed at the box office. If you must eventually leave Hollywood, make these two big pictures and go out in a blast as the world's biggest female box office attraction who abandoned everything for the man she loved. Otherwise, you'll be tossed into the dustbin with Shirley Temple and Margaret O'Brien, two kids who couldn't make it as adults in film. Do you want to become the forgotten bride of some guy down in Miami, or do you want to reign as the Queen of MGM?" Marx asked her.

That question seemed to cinch the deal for Elizabeth, who told Marx she'd return to MGM. However, before she could star in the two blockbusters he described, she had been cast opposite Van Johnson in a movie entitled *The Big Hangover.*

After a tearful farewell with Pawley, and despite his objections, Elizabeth flew back to Hollywood with Sara and Francis. When she got there, she told Roddy McDowall and Dick Hanley, "I'm starved for love. Bill and I have agreed not to do it until our wedding night. In the meantime, spread the word secretly that I'm available for dates."

Pawley telephoned her every day and agreed to fly to Hollywood to escort her to Jane Powell's wedding to Geary Steffen, Jr., scheduled for September 17, 1949. Elizabeth caught the bridal bouquet. Afterward, the wedding party converged on the Mocambo nightclub, where Vic Damone was the headliner.

Elizabeth had long harbored a crush on him, and the singer joined the bridal party between his sets. When Pawley excused himself to go to the men's room,

Elizabeth Taylor with her wealthy Florida beau, **William Pawley, Jr.**.

she slipped Damone her phone number.

That same night, she told Pawley, "I won't abandon my career until I play a monster on the screen, a real hellion, for which I will win an Oscar."

That, of course, was a dream destined to come true.

At that point, Pawley probably realized that Elizabeth was never going to settle down to marry him, but that she planned to continue, hell-bent, on her career. As a means of soothing his frustration and disappointment, he flew to his father's estate in Virginia. There, he read in Hedda Hopper's column that his engagement to Elizabeth had been canceled.

After that, partly because of her role in the collapse of previous engagements to both Glenn

Davis and William Pawley, Elizabeth began experiencing her first bad press. She was portrayed as a heart-breaking *femme fatale,* a very-mature teenager flitting duplicitously from man to man.

The writers and editors at *Photoplay* were particularly incensed with her because of how its October, 1949 issue, meticulously prepared and edited many weeks in advance, had laid out a splashy (and already out-of-date) feature article that showcased Pawley and Elizabeth as two beautiful people madly in love with each other.

The *Sunday Pictorial* in London attacked her "New Look" in fashion. During the filming of *Conspirator,* before returning to the United States from London, she'd flown to Paris and acquired gowns from Christian Dior, then, arguably the most sought-after *couturier* in the world. But despite her *haute* sense of revised glamour, *Sunday Pictorial* stated, "For breaking off her most recent engagement, somebody should administer a series of resounding smacks behind the bustle of Elizabeth Taylor's latest Paris fashion creation. She is a living argument against the employment of children in the studios."

Pawley had some difficulty getting Elizabeth to return his engagement ring, but she finally shipped it back to him. Her predilection for acquiring and hanging on to jewelry came out in another way, too.

At the Diamond Jubilee of the Jewelry Industry Council, where she functioned as one of the figureheads, she was lent, as a prominently showcased accessory, a $22,000 diamond tiara. At the end of the event, she begged council officers to let her keep it. They simply could not do that, but compromised, allowing her to keep it for one week before she had to surrender it.

After writing Pawley some loving and regret-tinged letters, Elizabeth emerged more or less unscathed from her most recent broken engagement. When reporters at the Mocambo asked her about the breakup, she said, "Bill and I went well together under the palm trees; we looked nice on the dance floor; we loved to go boating. But we had nothing in common."

Many decades later, during the spring of 2011, the weekly tabloid, *The Globe,* conducted an interview with the then-elderly Pawley, finding him living in Pembroke Pines, Florida, with relatives. "I loved her with all my heart, and I know she loved me," he told reporters. "I planned to spend the rest of my life with her. Studio officials wrecked our romance, leaving me devastated. I still haven't gotten over her, and I'm ninety years old."

He'd saved her letters, which she had written in purple ink on pink stationery. In one of them, she wrote:

"My heart aches and makes me want to cry when I think of you, and how much I want to be with you and to look in your beautiful blue eyes, and kiss your sweet lips and have your strong arms around me, oh so tight and close

163

to you. I want us to be lovers always—even after we've been married 75 years and have at least a dozen great-great-grandchildren."

Pawley waited until 1974 to get married, a quarter of a century after his engagement to Elizabeth. When his wife died in 2002, Elizabeth, from Hollywood, placed a call to him to extend her sympathies.

Upon Elizabeth's own death, Pawley told the press, "If Elizabeth had married me, she would not have needed all those other husbands."

***

An odd request for Elizabeth came in from Benny Thau at MGM. Mayer had hired Stewart Granger, whom they'd planned to launch into major American stardom after his robust success in British films.

Granger was fresh from the beds of Jean Simmons and Michael Wilding, and a recent affair with Robert Taylor during the making of *Conspirator*. Granger was being seriously considered for the lead role in MGM's big production of *Quo Vadis?*

Thau wanted Elizabeth for a screen test with Granger, with the understanding that as a result, she might be selected as the lead, opposite Granger, in *Quo Vadis?*

She had seen Granger lunching with Robert Taylor at the MGM canteen in London, but they had never been formally introduced.

Granger later recalled, "I found her incredibly beautiful and curvaceous, but was disappointed by her rather squeaky voice. She would have been better in silent pictures. Except for the voice, she had everything else in abundance, and she could speak British to me. In the test, she was my demure slave and I the lecherous Roman conqueror."

John Huston was set to direct the scene.

Granger had learned that Elizabeth was just past her seventeenth birthday. "I was dressed in a skimpy tunic—shades of *Caesar and Cleopatra* that I did with Vivien Leigh—and I had my hair curled, Roman style. Huston said, 'Play the scene like a big buck drunken nigger.'"

"I broke up the crew ogling Elizabeth's assets." He later recalled that Huston, as an experiment and test, also filmed a love scene whose footage was later destroyed, like her screen test with Clark Gable. "She pressed that body against me, and I got overly excited. I was lecherous all right. I didn't know if the bitch was play acting or, perhaps, was desperate to get fucked. I finally concluded that she wanted me to fuck her. Since my precious Jean (Simmons) was away, I made plans to have this hot-to-trot teenager for the night."

When Elizabeth was allowed to see the screen test, she told Dick Hanley,

"Huston wanted to see if Stewart and I had any chemistry between us. We not only had chemistry, we blew up the chemical works."

"I saw the screen test too," Dick later said. "I think Mayer should send a memo to future actors appearing in love scenes with Elizabeth. He should order all of them to wear jock straps."

Originally, Gregory Peck had been offered the lead. He arrived at MGM and dressed in Roman gear, but looked into a full length mirror and decided, "My calves were far too skinny for such a role."

Both Elizabeth and Granger lost the lead roles in *Quo Vadis?* Their parts went instead to Robert Taylor and Deborah Kerr. When Taylor signed for the lead role, he was shown the screen test of Granger and Elizabeth. The director, Mervyn LeRoy, told Taylor to play the part just like Granger did. "If I were so great and just right for the part, why didn't MGM use me?" Granger asked. Instead, he was assigned the lead in *King Solomon's Mines,* which, coincidentally, starred Deborah Kerr. "Deborah and I renewed our love affair," Granger later confessed.

As he'd anticipated, Granger found Elizabeth only too willing to go out with him for the night. He informed her that they couldn't go to any public place where photographers were likely to spot them. "I'm committed to Jean," he said, "but I've always been a naughty lad."

"Please," she responded. "I'm used to back alley romances. You're not my first secret date." She looked provocatively at him, as he remembered. "Are you going to kiss me or not?" she asked.

"Bloody hell," Granger said. "The little minx had just gotten into my rented car. We kissed all right. I felt her up—what breasts!—and she fondled my jewels. She got me so hot we skipped dinner and drove to the apartment where I was staying."

"Instead of dinner, we feasted on each other," Granger told Huston, who spread the gossip around. "Elizabeth confessed to me that she believed in love at first sight. I told her to pull back, that I was in love with Jean, and that we shouldn't see each other any more. I didn't want to break her heart. She was an impressionable seventeen-year-old."

"That morning, when I drove her home, she cried all the way there," Granger recalled.

Years later, he said, "Oh, what tangled lives we actors lead. Other than making films, the second best business in Hollywood is laundering sheets from hot beds."

***

[Ironically, in a strange twist of fate, and despite the murky dramas associated with Granger, her young age, and the fallout associated with their screen test, Elizabeth ended up in *Quo Vadis?* anyway—as an extra.

During her honeymoon in 1950 with hotel heir Nicky Hilton, she flew with him to Rome. After she learned that he'd spent the night in a Roman bordello, the newly married couple had a violent argument and he attacked her.

To escape from him, she called Mervyn LeRoy, the newly appointed director of *Quo Vadis?,* a replacement for John Huston. She begged him to find a place where she could hide from Nicky. When she arrived on the set, he told her that the best place for her to hide was in a crowd scene. He ordered her to go to wardrobe, where she was attired in a toga, and instructed to join the extras. For one entire week, she played the role of a Christian martyr in a replica of the Colosseum.

"I got this fucking job as an extra, while that rat fink, Nicky Hilton, searched all over Rome for me," Elizabeth said.

As a means of accommodating her, LeRoy had to cut short the involvement in the film of Claire Davis, a British starlet. "I begged Taylor not to accept the role, because I was pregnant at the time and needed the job to qualify for health insurance. She refused to listen to me, claiming that LeRoy would give me another part. He didn't, and I lost all around. To me, Elizabeth Taylor was spoiled and heartless."]

***

As a means of coinciding with her new sultry image of herself, Elizabeth decided she wanted to be photographed by Philippe Halsman, who had famously photographed a long-time friend of his family, Albert Einstein, in 1947.

Stewart Granger

Halsman's other subjects would eventually include Pablo Picasso, Winston Churchill, Judy Garland, Alfred Hitchcock, John F. Kennedy, and Marilyn Monroe.

She was intrigued by Halsman's background. A Latvian Jew, he moved to Austria with his family when he was a child. In 1928, he was sentenced to four years in prison for patricide, having allegedly murdered his father during a hill-climbing expedition in the Alps. After appeals to Austrian authorities from both Albert Einstein and Thomas Mann, Halsman was released from prison in 1931 and kicked out of Austria.

In the United States, Elizabeth Arden used his photograph of model Constance Ford against a backdrop of the American flag in an ad campaign for "Victory Red" lipstick. The image became one of the iconic symbols of War War II.

When Elizabeth met Halsman in 1949, he was collaborating with the surrealist artist Salvador Dalí.

Elizabeth had been particularly amused by his 1948 *Dalí Atomicus,* depicting three cats airborne, a bucket of thrown water, and Dalí himself floating in mid-air.

Life magazine arranged for Halsman to photograph Elizabeth in his studio on Manhattan's Upper West Side. In the photograph, Elizabeth's violet eyes appear rather vacant; her figure voluptuous, and three-quarters of her ample breasts are exposed. Her gown was described as "the color of melted money." Edith Head once ordained that green was not a sexy color for a woman, but Halsman disagreed. He'd later enshrine Grace Kelly in green chiffon against Grecian columns.

"You have bosoms," Halsman shouted at her during their photo shoot. "Stick them out!" She followed his instructions.

To protect her husband from this teenage *femme fatale,* Yvonne, Halsman's wife, made it a point to remain in the studio throughout the photo shoot. "I was struck by the sight of her arms. They were covered with what Philippe called 'dark eyelashes,' an abundance of unsightly black hair."

Elizabeth later recalled, "Philippe saw I had a woman's body and insisted I exploit it for the camera. In one day, I learned how to pose provocatively. In short, I developed sex appeal."

On seeing Halsman's portrait before it was published, critic Richard Roud asserted, "Elizabeth Taylor looks like a girl who would really put out and I mean really put out."

Yvonne reported that Elizabeth arrived at the photo shoot alone. When it was over, she said, "I have no date for tonight. All the men seemed to assume I'm heavily booked. But no one has called me, even though the papers have reported I'm in New York. I'm facing a lonely evening."

During her time in New York, Elizabeth made that "lonely girl" remark to a number of people. Somehow, the word got out, because at seven o'clock that night, the phone rang in her hotel suite.

It was from another sultry star, this one male. Actor Steve Cochran, who had thrilled her with his sexiness in *The Best Years of Our Lives* (1946), was on the phone. "What you doing, doll?" he asked.

"Waiting for you to call," she said, inviting him up to her hotel suite at eight that night.

"I can get there even earlier," he told her, "because I'm in your hotel lobby right now."

"Pretty sure of yourself, aren't you?" she asked.

"I've got a lot to be pretty sure about," he told her.

As she'd later confide to Dick Hanley, "I knew I was in for some action. When Steve had appeared with Mae West on the stage in *Diamond Lil,* she'd told half of Hollywood how well endowed he was."

Additional praise for this tough guy, who portrayed hoods and cutthroats in the movies, came from Joan Crawford, with whom he was to co-star in *The Damned Don't Cry* (1950). The stud was not opposed to letting other actors or singers, such as Merv Griffin or Danny Kaye, "service" him, although he preferred teenage girls like Elizabeth, who had long held his attention. After seeing her in *National Velvet,* he told his producer, Samuel Goldwyn, "I'd like to kidnap that little number and rape her ten times a day."

As she'd recall to Dick, "Steve and I never left my suite that night. We called room service when we got hungry. He's really white trash, but glorious white trash. I've never been so down and dirty with a man before. He forces a really decent girl to do filthy things. But he made it fun, really exciting."

She also claimed that Steve wanted "to make it a permanent thing with me, but I turned him down. Every gal should have a few sleazy nights in her life, but not on a regular basis—that's not my style. He's one of Hollywood's really bad boys, and will probably make a lot of police news in his life before he dies young."

"Frankly, I'm afraid of him. But give the devil His due. He's the best sex I've ever had and may ever have again."

***

Millions ultimately saw Philippe Halsman's photograph of Elizabeth in *Life* magazine, but it captured the eye of one man in particular. The aviation hero and movie mogul, Howard Hughes, became fascinated by her, especially her breasts. He was the man who had developed a cantilevered bra for Jane Russell to wear in *The Outlaw* (1943), the most erotic Western ever made at that time.

Hughes told his public relations agent, Johnny Meyer, who was actually his pimp, "I'm going to marry Elizabeth Taylor in spite of the difference in our ages. When a man has money, what does age matter to a woman?"

***

When director Norman Krasna, guided by MGM executives, assigned Elizabeth Taylor to co-star with Van Johnson in *The Big Hangover* (1950)*, both stars knew, after reading the script, that it was a "silly, boring comedy." Johnson was cast as a war veteran and an up-and-coming young lawyer who was in a wine cellar in France during a bomb attack, breaking most of the bottles, almost drowning him in a river of wine. Now everytime he gets a whiff of alcohol, he has hallucinations, acts irrationally, and imagines that his dog is talking to him. Elizabeth was cast as the daughter of his boss, who makes it her mission to save him from his dilemma. She denounced her role as "the stooge part."

Krasna frankly admitted, "I'm a lousy director, But I've got bills to pay." Unlike George Stevens in *A Place in the Sun,* this director's camera paid virtually no attention to what the press referred to as Elizabeth's "burgeoning sexuality."

Johnson and Elizabeth had been correct in predicting that the only thing big about *The Big Hangover* was that it was a big flop at the box office. It opened in May of 1950 at Grauman's Egyptian Theater in Hollywood and at Loew's State Theater in New York, playing mostly to empty houses. Even so, as a means of holding on to Elizabeth, MGM raised her salary to $2,000 a week.

For the most part, the reviews were bad, *The New Yorker* asserting that, "Miss Taylor is beautiful and cannot act. This puts her one up on Mr. Johnson."

Elizabeth had a long-standing crush on Johnson, who in the 1940s had been defined by the studio's PR staff as "The Boy Next Door." In real life, he was anything but that, and led a rather active homosexual lifestyle. Character actor Keenan Wynn was Johnson's lover and best friend. Wynn was married to the former stage actress Evie Lynn Abbott.

When it became apparent that word was rapidly spreading that a hot MGM property like Johnson was gay, Mayer issued a bizarre mandate. He told Wynn that he would not renew his contract if he didn't divorce Evie so that she could enter into an arranged marriage with Johnson.

Although all parties later regretted being forced into such an arrangement,

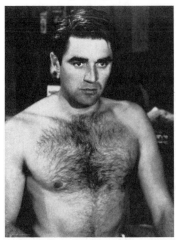

Steve Cochran

they agreed to Mayer's terms. Even after Johnson's marriage to the former Mrs. Keenan Wynn, her former and present husbands continued their love affair with one another, although Johnson had many dalliances on the side.

Johnson and June Allyson in the late 1940as had been billed as "America's Sweethearts." It was Allyson, Elizabeth's friend, who warned her, "Get over your crush. I used to date Van, and he's handsome and charming, but our dates were arranged by MGM for publicity purposes. After a premiere, he would dump me back on my doorstep, and run off with his boyfriend of the moment. Van and I are friends, but we've had our arguments in the past, especially when we both pursued the same man at the same time. We ran into serious conflict when we fought over which of us was going to sleep with Peter Lawford."

"The public believes what it reads in those movie magazines," Elizabeth said. "Thank God our fans don't know what's really going on in Tinseltown."

"Let's hope it stays that way," Allyson said. "Thank God I've got an understanding husband—one who overlooks my indiscretions."

She was referring to her marriage to actor/singer Dick Powell, who had been married to Joan Blondell, who had been married to Mike Todd, who would soon wed Elizabeth herself.

"Let's face it," Allyson said, "many of us in Hollywood change boyfriends as often as we change our panties." At the time she made that pronouncement, she was lusting for the handsome actor Alan Ladd, who was himself a bisexual.

Even though no romance ever developed between Johnson and Elizabeth, they became friends and would co-star in a future movie together. She was only mildly surprised when Roddy McDowall called her and announced that he had fallen madly in love with Johnson, and they were "having a wild affair. "He's got eight inches and gets rock hard," he assured her.

To celebrate their "engagement," Elizabeth invited several of her friends to a beach party, based in the vicinity of the Taylor cottage in Malibu. Everybody had a date except her. Peter Lawford heard about it and called her to ask if he could show up with "the love of my life." He was referring to the handsome young actor, Tom Drake, who had played "the boy next door" opposite Judy Garland in *Meet Me In St. Louis* (1944).

Elizabeth called Roddy and asked him if it would be all right "to invite your ex."

"You mean Peter?" Roddy said. "Of course, we're still friends, even though we no longer bump pussies together."

Dick Hanley was invited as Elizabeth's escort. "It is said that the sexual revolution didn't reach America until the hippie era of the late 1960s," he recalled years later. "But actually, young stars such as Elizabeth and Roddy launched it in Hollywood in the early 1950s. A lot of good-looking guys and gals of all sexual persuasions were thrown together, and everybody was making it with everybody else's boyfriend the following weekend. A typical example was Elizabeth and her friend, Janet Leigh. They double dated a lot in those days and often switched boyfriends from weekend to weekend. Elizabeth, believe it or not, often ended up getting Janet's boyfriends after she'd auditioned them."

"A case in point involved the notorious gangster, Johnny Stompanato, who was Mickey Cohen's right hand henchman," Dick said. "Janet dated him briefly before he took up with Elizabeth. Regrettably, Johnny eventually met Lana

Turner, and they began the most notorious affair in Hollywood history. Too bad Lana fatally stabbed him. In his short, sex-filled life, Johnny made a lot of horny women and a lot of gay guys very happy."

Dick claimed that he was sitting on a beach blanket with Elizabeth the afternoon of her Malibu party when Leigh introduced Johnny to Elizabeth."

"Janet appeared on the beach with a tall, handsome, dark-haired guy with a great build on him," Dick said. "He was wearing a skimpy white bikini that was virtually see-through. It looked like a handlebar, and it was still soft."

Leigh introduced her new boyfriend only as "Johnny," without including a last name.

When Leigh and Johnny went for a swim, Elizabeth turned to Dick. "I think he wants me. He undressed me with his eyes."

"Do you think what he's showing in that bikini is real—or is it padding?" Dick asked.

"I'm sure that sooner than later either you or me—or perhaps both of us—will find out for ourselves," she said. "Janet shouldn't have squatter's rights on Johnny. It looks to me like there's plenty to go around for all of us."

Before the end of the party, Johnny spent some time alone with Sara. Elizabeth heard her mother laughing at his jokes.

After her guests had left, Elizabeth went to take a shower. Her mother was in the kitchen preparing supper. "I hope you don't mind, but I met this charming young man. His name is Johnny. He told me he's a businessman in Los Angeles, and I suspect he's very rich. I gave him your phone number."

"For once in your life, you did something right," Elizabeth said, unfastening her top as she headed for the shower.

***

In the late 1940s and early 50s, actor Farley Granger was known as "the most beautiful male animal in films."

Elizabeth had known him when she'd attended a studio-run schoolhouse for its stars under the age of eighteen. Farley, Peggy Ann Garner, and Roddy, among others, were Elizabeth's fellow schoolmates.

During the making of *The Big Hangover,*

top photo: **Tom Drake**
lower photo: **Van Johnson**

171

Elizabeth was often a guest at parties thrown by Van and his wife, Evie Johnson, who had become one of the most prominent hostesses in Beverly Hills, on a par with Edie Goetz, the daughter of Louis B. Mayer, according to the Ronald L. Davis biography, *Van Johnson: MGM's Golden Boy.*

On two separate occasions, Elizabeth attended these *soirées* with Judy Garland, who invariably would kick off her shoes and entertain guests of the Johnsons. "She always drank too much and got out of control," Elizabeth recalled.

Henry Willson, the most notoriously homosexual talent agent in Hollywood, was a frequent guest at the Johnson parties. On the side, he provided Van with handsome young men eager to have sex with an established star.

One night, Willson brought a young actor he'd recently renamed Rock Hudson. Tall, masculine, and extraordinarily handsome, he was introduced to Elizabeth.

He was so in awe of her, he had almost nothing to say. In time, of course, he would become one of her closest friends and confidants. Later, she'd meet another of Willson's homosexual discoveries and *protégés*, Tab Hunter. The studio would arrange publicity dates between them in her future.

Phyllis Gates, who worked for Willson and later entered into a marriage of convenience with Hudson, told Elizabeth, "My boss is a virtuoso at arranging sexual affairs—heterosexual, homosexual, bisexual, you name it, he's a master."

One night, Dick Hanley escorted Elizabeth to the Johnson home, where she had a talk with Van's wife and charming hostess, Evie.

Both Elizabeth and Evie bonded over their mutual dislike of Louis B. Mayer, Evie referring to him as "a dictator with the ethics and morals of a cockroach."

"Mayer told me that if I didn't divorce Keenan and marry Van, as a means of suppressing rumors about his homosexuality, that he would not renew Keenan's contract," Evie said. "I was young and stupid and let Mayer manipulate me. I'm sorry I ever did that."

"Whatever you do, Elizabeth, don't marry a homosexual or bisexual husband," Evie advised her.

"I'll insist they be straight as an arrow," Elizabeth said.

One night, Farley Granger called and asked if he could escort her to one of the Johnson parties. Elizabeth was aware, through June Allyson, that Farley and Van Johnson were having a torrid affair.

At the party, which lasted until dawn, she and Farley had far too much to drink. Evie asked him to put Elizabeth to bed in one of their guest bedrooms.

As she would relay to Dick Hanley the following Monday, "I woke up nude in bed with Farley Granger. I found him devastatingly attractive."

She told Hanley that "before we made an appearance around noon, we did it—and he's definitely bisexual. A beautiful man and a beautiful lover."

Both Farley and Elizabeth joined Van and Evie beside their swimming pool for lunch that day.

"I left late that afternoon," Elizabeth said, "but Farley stayed on with the Johnsons for two more weeks—how convenient for Van."

"Farley and I dated two or three more times," Elizabeth later recalled. "But one day I got a call from Shelley Winters. She told me to leave Farley alone or else she'd cut off my left tit. Why not the right one? By that time, I'd moved on from Farley and it didn't matter. A few months later, Shelley called me in tears, claiming that Farley had met Ava Gardner and was involved in an intense affair with her."

[In New York in November of 1963, in the aftermath of John F. Kennedy's assassination in Dallas, Farley met his life partner, Robert Calhoun, who remained at the actor's side until Calhoun's death in 2008. Farley himself died in 2011.]

***

In the period preceding her first marriage, Elizabeth seemed to race from one man to another. One reporter asserted, "[Elizabeth] is the Lana Turner of the younger generation, turning into a real man-eater."

One of her final schoolgirl crushes was directed at singer Vic Damone, following his 1947 appearance, at the age of nineteen, on *Arthur Godfrey's Talent Scouts,* where he sang "Prisoner of Love." Impressed both with him and with his voice, Milton Berle secured two nightclub bookings for him, which eventually led to a contract with Mercury Records.

Elizabeth thought he looked adorable, with black, close-cropped curly hair and a slim physique, very Italian-looking to her. She fell in love with his voice—and the image of the man himself—when she heard his first release. One by one, she'd collect recordings of the more than 2,000 songs he recorded over the years, beginning with his "I Have But One Heart."

Throughout the course of 1948, she listened faithfully to his weekly radio show, *Saturday Night Serenade,* and adjusted her own schedule so she wouldn't miss a single broadcast.

She read about him in the fan magazines, learning that he'd been born in Brooklyn, the only boy in a family that otherwise included four

Farley Granger

173

girls, and that he'd started singing lessons at the age of ten.

She began dating him after he appeared at the Mocambo in Los Angeles. In her column, Hedda Hopper wrote, "Fickle Elizabeth Taylor has fallen in love again, this time with the handsome young crooner Vic Damone, who is giving Frank Sinatra's fading career a push toward oblivion."

Elizabeth dated Damone only briefly, finding the man of her fantasy different from reality. He announced that he had no objection to a future wife of his having a career, though in the same breath, he claimed he wanted a household "filled with *bambini.*"

He didn't seem to know how to spend money, telling her, "Everything happened so fast. One day, I was singing for subway fare. The next day, I'm hauling in $5,000 bucks a week."

"Vic was adorable," Elizabeth recalled in later years. "A dear man. But in 1950, he was drafted, and another *beau* came along."

"Vic seemed a very insecure man, in a hurry to get some place," she said. "Even though I stopped seeing him, I always like his music. My favorite recording of his remains 'On the Street Where You Live.' He was a young Sinatra with a touch of Mel Tormé."

In the years to come, Elizabeth read about Damone's five marriages, including one to Pier Angeli whom he "stole" from James Dean. Damone also had a long-term liaison with Diahann Carroll, the African-American singer.

"Those people who draw up lists of movie star lovers always include Vic on the list of men who seduced me," Elizabeth said. "I deny categorically that he ever fucked me—at least I don't think that he did. But who knows? It was a long time ago, and so many men have had the privilege. How can one remember who seduced one and who didn't? Ask Peter Lawford. He'd agree with me."

***

Unknown to Elizabeth one night at the Mocambo, a handsome, rich young man, the heir to a hotel dynasty, sat observing her throughout the evening. He was having drinks with Peter Lawford and Judy Garland, both of whom he'd previously seduced.

"See that girl over there at the far table?" he asked. "That's Elizabeth Taylor. I'm going to marry her whether she likes it or not."

His name was Conrad Hilton, Jr. Everybody called him "Nicky."

Vic Damone

174

CHAPTER ELEVEN
Elizabeth and Monty
SEARCHING FOR *A PLACE IN THE SUN*

As the 1940s faded into the 50s, Elizabeth became embroiled in the biggest soap opera of her life, far more intriguing and a lot more complicated than any of the movie scripts she'd been offered.

For many years, Howard Hughes, the aviation hero and RKO movie mogul, would stalk Elizabeth, hovering in her background and spying on her. He became obsessed with her.

Sometimes, Elizabeth would be directly involved in the dramas whirling around, and usually catalyzed by, Hughes. On other occasions, she voyeuristically watched as the brohahas unfolded from afar—blackmail, bribery, threats of murder, violent beatings, broken hearts, failed marriages, the secret production of sex films, bisexuality, and rampant adultery.

As a young man, Hughes had married Texas socialite Ella Rice, but that union soonafter collapsed. And although he had abandoned hope that Ava Gardner would ever marry him, as he moved deeper into his forties, he once again had marriage on his mind.

Among the bevy of movie stars he considered for conquest and wedded bliss, Elizabeth and Terry Moore topped the chart.

Terry and Elizabeth were friends, though not particularly close. On several occasions, they showed the same taste in men—Glenn Davis, Nicky Hilton, and later, Robert Wagner.

Hughes' pimp, Johnny Meyer, regularly scanned the popular magazines of the day, looking for beauties with large breasts who might tempt his boss. Hughes became fascinated by Terry when he saw her picture in *Look,* and he became even more intrigued when he spotted Elizabeth's photo in both *Time* and *Life* magazines.

As the 1950s dawned, Terry found herself locked in battle with Marilyn Monroe for the title of Hollywood's sexiest starlet. Many fan magazines, however, awarded that title to Elizabeth. Hughes had already seduced Marilyn, even going so far as to hire her as a player in a pornographic film with his heartthrob of the moment, Guy Madison.

Hughes had had affairs with both Madison, whom he called the "handsomest man in movies," and with Monroe. In 1946, he gave each of them $10,000 to make a "blue movie loop," as he described it, for him. As Madison told his gay agent, Henry Willson, "Getting paid $10,000 to fuck Marilyn Monroe is not the worst gig in this town."

The film was shot at 7000 Romaine in Los Angeles, with Hughes assisted in its production by his pimp, Johnny Meyer. "Guy had a gay streak in him, but he didn't show it that night," Meyer said. "Monroe was really turned on by Marilyn. When he stripped off his pants and presented her with a long, straight, thick tool, she squealed with delight and went to work polishing it. I had to practically pull him off Monroe when Howard called 'cut.' I never saw the finished product. Boss man kept it for his own viewing pleasure. He later acquired a blue movie loop of Elizabeth Taylor and this gangster boy. But Elizabeth would be set up for that one, not knowing about a concealed camera in the bedroom."

As Meyer proclaimed, "Boss was always a sucker for some gal with big tits and a schoolgirl face." Terry, Elizabeth, and Marilyn Monroe each fitted that category. According to Meyer, in Hughes' pursuit of these blossoming beauties, Hughes set out to recapture his lost youth.

His pursuit of Terry became particularly aggressive when she went on a twenty-six city tour promoting her film, *The Return of October* (1948), starring Glenn Ford. From Indianapolis to Buffalo, Hughes would suddenly fly there to chase after the starlet.

Before he tried to insinuate himself into the lives of Elizabeth and Terry, proving that power and money talk, Hughes had already compiled one of the longest list of seductions of both actors and actresses in the history of Hollywood.

Over the years, the revolving door to his bedroom had admitted some of the most beautiful and talented men and women in Hollywood—Billie Dove, Tyrone Power, Robert Taylor, Errol Flynn, Clark Gable, Ava Gardner, Ginger Rogers, Robert Stack, Marlene Dietrich, Cary Grant, Randolph Scott, Bette Davis, Paulette Goddard, Veronica Lake, Rita Hayworth, Katharine Hepburn, Faith Domergue, Hedy Lamarr, Kathryn Grayson, Ingrid Bergman , Gene Tierney, Carole Lombard, and Marilyn Monroe.

But whereas Terry had been an easy conquest, Elizabeth had repeatedly eluded the net he'd cast for her.

On Thanksgiving Day, 1949, aboard his yacht, *Hilda,* Hughes married Terry in a ceremony conducted by his captain, Carl Flynn. The yacht was more than five miles off the coast, and the legality of such a marriage would later come into question.

A few days later, Terry called Elizabeth, informing her that although her husband refused to let her release the news officially to the press, she was now Mrs. Howard Hughes. She lived with her new husband in a bungalow within the garden of the Beverly Hills Hotel.

Hughes deserted her for weeks at a time while he pursued other conquests.

***

Terry was one of the luscious bombshells of the 1950s, hailed as having "a schoolgirl face mounted on an atomic chassis." She had attracted Hughes when she was only fifteen years old. Since their "marriage" at sea had little or no legal recognition, Hughes felt free to propose marriage, soon after, to another beautiful actress, Jean Peters, whom he would eventually "officially and legally" marry. On the same day he proposed marriage to Jean, he also proposed marriage to Janet Leigh, who turned him down, as had Elizabeth.

When Terry could no longer tolerate her cheating "husband or non-husband," depending on how you interpret her union with Hughes, she felt free to pursue Glenn Davis, who was virile, handsome, and young, and who had been a highly visible player for the Los Angeles Rams.

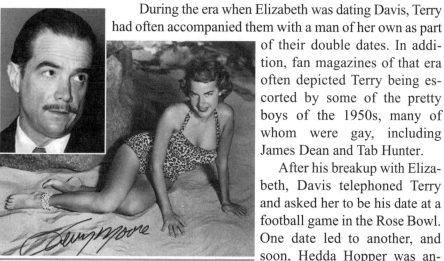

Starlet **Terry Moore**
("the girl with the atomic chassis")
with *(inset photo)*
demented billionaire **Howard Hughes**

During the era when Elizabeth was dating Davis, Terry had often accompanied them with a man of her own as part of their double dates. In addition, fan magazines of that era often depicted Terry being escorted by some of the pretty boys of the 1950s, many of whom were gay, including James Dean and Tab Hunter.

After his breakup with Elizabeth, Davis telephoned Terry and asked her to be his date at a football game in the Rose Bowl. One date led to another, and soon, Hedda Hopper was announcing that Davis "had replaced Elizabeth Taylor in his life with the rising young starlet,

Terry Moore."

In a call to Elizabeth, Terry told her that although Hughes was still in pursuit of her, she'd broken off their relationship, referring to him as "a cheat, a liar, and an adulterer."

The news that Terry had replaced Hughes with Davis disturbed Elizabeth. Although she'd dumped the football hero, she seemed jealous to learn that he was dating a friend of hers.

At the time, the press labeled Davis "the greatest catch in America." Although she'd been invited Elizabeth opted not to attend the Terry Moore/Glenn Davis wedding on February 9, 1951, at a Mormon church in Glendale. "I've been betrayed," Elizabeth told Roddy McDowall. "Those two must have been carrying on behind my back all along."

Davis and Terry soon faded from the radar screen, and Elizabeth learned that she was living with the athlete in a modest apartment with a Murphy bed in Lubbock, Texas. Hughes had not given up on her, however. He'd come across a script for a movie entitled *High Heels* that he felt would be ideal for either Terry, Elizabeth, or Marilyn Monroe.

Using the script as bait, he lured Terry back to Hollywood, with the promise that she would play the lead. Unknown to Terry, Hughes also arranged for Dick Hanley to deliver a copy of the script of *High Heels* to Francis Taylor's art gallery, asserting that Hughes was ready to produce the film at RKO with Elizabeth as the star. It is not known if Elizabeth ever read the script or not, as she was already under contract to MGM, which had assigned her a role in Paramount's *A Place in the Sun,* an adaptation of Theodore Dreiser's *An American Tragedy.* Montgomery Clift had been signed as her co-star, with Shelley Winters in a supporting role.

Glenn Davis

Hughes eventually sold the script of *High Heels* to another studio. It soon became obvious that Terry had been lured back to Hollywood under false pretenses.

Back in Lubbock, Davis was furious at the turn of events and the "theft" of his wife. He, too, flew to Hollywood, where he confronted Hughes one evening at the home of Terry Moore's parents. Hughes was not a fighter, but Davis was.

Roddy McDowall was the first to call Elizabeth after he heard the news: "Your boy Glenn beat the shit out of Hughes. I mean, he's seriously injured. He was flown to a hospital in San Francisco as a means of avoiding the press in L.A." Nonetheless, the story soon broke in *Confidential* magazine.

After he recovered, Hughes came up with yet another scheme. He called Davis and told him, "There are no hard feelings. In fact, you struck me—no pun intended—as a powerful hunk of American beef. I think I can make a movie star out of you. All the girls in America will dream of going to bed with you every night, but only if you're a bachelor—not a married man."

Since his dream had been to become a movie star, Davis telephoned Elizabeth to discuss Hughes' proposition with her. She warned him that Hughes routinely double crossed people, and she suspected that this offer might be a trick to get him to divorce Terry.

Although Davis sought Elizabeth's advice, he didn't follow it. He let Hughes' lawyers arrange his divorce from Terry. But when he went to sign his contract with Hughes, the RKO studio head had vanished. There was no contract, no stardom. Elizabeth had been right. Davis tried to call her again, but she was never available. Davis faded from her life, and she never heard from him again.

It seemed inevitable that Elizabeth, along with her fellow sex goddesses, Marilyn Monroe and Terry, might be considerd for the same roles. Although all three had lost out on Hughes' never-realized film project (*High Heels),* each of these actresses became interested in the publicity surrounding the role of the *ingénue* in the film version of *Come Back, Little Sheba* (1952), whose screenplay was based on William Inge's hit Broadway play. During a visit to New York, Elizabeth had been escorted to the play by Monty Clift. Both of them spent the rest of the night drinking and discussing how she might interpret the role onscreen.

Neither Elizabeth, Terry, or Marilyn ever appeared in any movie entitled *High Heels,* although three foreign film companies used the title for unrelated productions of their own.

***

The producer of *Come Back, Little Sheba* was Hal Wallis, working in collaboration with Paramount. One day, Elizabeth, without the permission of MGM, called him for an interview, which he willingly granted. The two leads, Shirley Booth and Burt Lancaster, had already been cast.

Elizabeth was kept waiting in Wallis' outer office while he interviewed another actress who wanted the role. When the door to his inner office opened, Monroe emerged. Elizabeth had never seen her before.

There was a look of recognition between them, followed by a hardening of each of their faces into expressions of hostility. She walked past Elizabeth without speaking. As she would later tell Dick Hanley, "Monroe looked like some whore working Santa Monica Boulevard."

Wallis was polite during his meeting with Elizabeth, and promised he'd give her serious consideration if it appeared that he could persuade Louis B. Mayer to lend her out from MGM.

To her disappointment, Elizabeth later picked up a copy of *Variety* and read that the role she coveted had been assigned to Terry Moore. Elizabeth was even more disappointed when Terry received an Oscar nomination as Best Supporting Actress of 1952.

Coincidentally, about 18 years later, in 1969, Elizabeth did end up working for Wallis when he produced *Anne of a Thousand Days,* starring Richard Burton. She appeared only briefly, in a cameo.

A trio of men—Nicky Hilton, Montgomery Clift, and Howard Hughes—were about to become semi-permanent fixtures in Elizabeth's life.

But first, there was Johnny Stompanato.

***

Howard Hughes had never seen any of Elizabeth's movies, but he was captivated by her image in fan magazines. When he started to pursue her, he was forty-five years old, and she was a tender seventeen. Hughes had shown a tendency, when an actress was that young, of first wooing her parents before moving on to his real prey.

Looking like an unshaven bum, he appeared one day at Francis' art gallery in Beverly Hills. Before his departure an hour later, he had purchased eight very costly and overpriced paintings as part of the biggest art deal Elizabeth's father had ever made.

After leaving the gallery, Hughes drove to the apartment of some unknown starlet, and spent approximately two hours with her. Careless about locking doors, he had left the doors to his car unlocked as it stood in front of the apartment building. By the time he emerged onto the street again, he discovered that all eight paintings had been stolen. He didn't really seem to care, as he hadn't wanted the art anyway.

Before his departure from the gallery that day, he'd invited Francis and Sara to fly with him to a vacation in Reno, Nevada. As an afterthought, he added, "Oh, and don't forget to bring along your daughter."

Before flying to Reno, Hughes called Louis B. Mayer and attempted to purchase Elizabeth's contract. Then in the waning months of his once-iron-bound grip over MGM, the gruff studio chief informed Hughes that her contract was not for sale. "You'll have to find another way to seduce her, Hughes," Mayer told him before putting down the phone.

When Hughes met Elizabeth for the first time at the airport, he was stunned by her beauty, more compelling than any color magazine photograph could ever convey. "A real looker with tits," he told Johnny Meyer. "I wish I had some way to find out if she's still a virgin."

"Have your doctor examine her," Meyer said.

"Don't be an ass," Hughes snapped at him. "What am I going to do? Call her up and say I've made an appointment for my doctor to examine your hymen to see if it's been pierced?"

At the resort in Reno, Hughes met privately with Sara and Francis, telling them that he was prepared to put up a dowry of one million dollars if they would consent to let Elizabeth marry him. Always ambitious for the advancement of their daughter, Sara promised her cooperation. She didn't seem to be bothered by the difference in their ages.

Francis, however, urged caution. "Elizabeth's a very independent girl these days. She'll have to make up her own mind. But I'd love to have an art patron like Howard Hughes in our family."

Goaded by the encouragement of Sara, Hughes approached Elizabeth later that afternoon. She was clad in a white bathing suit by the hotel pool. Dressed in a rumpled business suit, he came up to her. In the same cardboard box he'd once carried gems for Ava Gardner, he brought a similar unprepossessing package for presentation to Elizabeth.

Opening the box, he dazzled her with rubies, diamonds, and emeralds. He turned over the box and let the stones fall onto her stomach. "C'mon," he said. "I'm taking you to get married. I've had someone make the arrangements. We'll be married tonight. The chapel's already reserved."

Astonished at being on the auction block, she rejected both the stones and the proposal. Jumping up, she scattered the gems onto the pool tiles before racing back to her bedroom.

That night over champagne and *crêpes suzette*, with Sara and Francis listening, Hughes proposed marriage to Elizabeth. Saying nothing, she excused herself and left the table, retreating back to her bedroom.

The next day, Hughes sent Meyer to apologize instead of doing it himself. "Howard gets carried away sometimes," Meyer told her. "He didn't mean to insult you, certainly not rush you into marriage."

"Tell that fucking madman to stay away from me," she shouted at Meyer. "Your boss bores me, flaunting his money. For god's sake, he reminds me of Louis B. Mayer, and I have no intention of marrying that monster. Or *your* monster, either!" Showing him to the door, she slammed it in his face.

Nonetheless, Hughes remained persistent and continued to pursue her, even after he'd flown the Taylors back to Los Angeles. From her home, Elizabeth telephoned Roddy McDowall. "I know what I want, and I don't want Howard Hughes. A man can hit on me if he wants to, but when I'm not interested, the word is no. I don't give a flying fuck who he is…or how much money he has."

"Oh, Elizabeth, tell Howard that I'm available." Roddy said.

Despite her protestations, she reluctantly agreed to go out with Hughes on three more dates. She didn't really want to, but Sara kept urging her, almost launching an aggressive campaign to get her to see Hughes again.

On their first date, he drove her to the Cocoanut Grove night club in the Ambassador Hotel to hear Merv Griffin sing. After the night was over, she avoided a kiss at the door and called Roddy to report on the evening. "Hughes was such an out-and-out bore," she said. "I wouldn't marry him for all his money. He just sat there, staring into space and never answering any of my questions. That's because he's deaf in one ear and won't wear a hearing aid. He smelled like he needed a bath. His trousers were wrinkled and hung on him like a scarecrow. He wore dirty sneakers and no socks. His left toe stuck out of one of his shoes."

For his second date with Elizabeth, Hughes drove her to the airport. She thought the venue included taking her on a night flight over Los Angeles to see the dramatic lights along the coast. Instead, he flew her, against her wishes, to San Francisco.

Once there, he checked himself and her into adjoining suites at the Fairmont and invited her out to a night club, Finocchio's, the most famous club in San Francisco for female impersonators. Previously, on separate occasions, he'd escorted both Errol Flynn and Ava Gardner there to see the show.

The headliner was a performer named Pussy-Katt, who had been born as Steve Clayton in Ohio. Her publicity read: "Pussy-Katt is much too pretty to be a boy—and much, much too pretty to be a mere gal."

Elizabeth laughed hilariously during the show and drank too much champagne. She insisted that Hughes stay around for the second show because she was reluctant to return to the Fairmont alone with him.

Between acts, Pussy-Katt came to their table and engaged in conversation with them. Hughes had to excuse himself to make some phone calls.

Elizabeth found Pussy-Katt very amusing. She was curious to learn how she knew Hughes. Pussy-Katt claimed that Hughes had read a book about eunuchs, including sexual practices in ancient Egypt. It seemed that the most beautiful boys in the land—each highly prized as sexual objects—were subjected to the practice of having their penises, testicles, and scrotums removed.

According to the theory, sodomites of that era claimed that the young boys who survived the surgeries were more sexually satisfying because they had only one way to receive sexual pleasure—and that involved being penetrated rectally.

Pussy-Katt claimed that in years previous, Hughes had persuaded her to fly with him to Mexico City, "where I underwent sexual mutilation. There wasn't that much to cut off anyway, honey," she told Elizabeth. "Besides, for

$50,000, I was willing to surrender anything."

That night, back in one of the two adjacent suites in the Fairmont, Elizabeth refused to open the connecting doors in spite of his persistent knocking.

For her third and final date with Hughes, he ordered Edith Head to design a special gown for Elizabeth—the most expensive she'd ever owned in her life. It was tasteful and elegant, with ample *décolletage*. Before taking her out, he had arranged a special fitting for her with Head, who had selected all black accessories for her. From Tiffany's he leased a stunningly beautiful diamond necklace, which, according to legend, had once belonged to Marie Antoinette.

She was astonished at the elaborate preparations he was undertaking just to take her to some party. He sent two hairdressers and a top make-up team to her home. "What is this?" she asked. "Is Hughes getting me ready for some sort of coronation?" A Rolls-Royce was sent to fetch her, its driver outfitted in shades of olive green. It was understood that Hughes would not be in the vehicle, but that he'd be waiting to welcome her at the entrance to the party.

She was taken to a mansion in Bel Air where, as planned, Hughes met her and escorted her into a massive reception area. To her surprise, each of the guests, some sixteen in all, were middle aged or older men, each attired in a tuxedo. The champagne flowed, and troughs of caviar were served as she was introduced around. She recognized none of these men and doubted very seriously if they were from the film colony. Most appeared to be titans of industry.

During the two-hour reception, Hughes discreetly arranged conversations between Elizabeth and each of the men there. Her upper-class British accent came back from memory. For some reason, she seemed to understand that he wanted her to impress each of these distinguished gentlemen.

After the men left, Hughes revealed that she had been auditioned for the possible real-life role as First Lady of the United States. Each of the men she'd talked to were powerful contributors to the Republican Party, in search of a candidate to run for President of the United States in the (upcoming) 1952 elections. Already, "Hughes for President" clubs had formed across America.

"But I'm too young to be a First Lady," she protested. "First Ladies are Eleanor Roosevelt and Bess Truman."

"Not always," Hughes said. "When Grover Cleveland was president, he married his bride, Francis, who was only twenty-one, about what your age will be when I run for president. The men wanted to see if you had enough poise and charm to function as a possible First Lady, and you passed the test by a country mile."

"I can't marry you, Howard," she said. "I don't love you."

"Forget love," he told her. "We're talking raw power here. Is there no ambition in you? Just think—you'd become the most famous woman on the planet, the envy of the world, the most beautiful and elegant First Lady in American history, more famous and more widely publicized than that other Elizabeth over in England."

"I'll sleep on it," she said. "Please take me home."

Years later, Hughes would attempt one final launch into politics. In the meanwhile, however, he continued, through a surrogate, to pursue Elizabeth.

One night, she received a call from the most handsome and dashing attorney in Los Angeles, Greg Bautzer. He'd been the lover of such stars as Ginger Rogers, Ingrid Bergman, Ava Gardner, and Joan Crawford. He'd been engaged to Lana Turner, Dorothy Lamour, and an unfortunate choice, starlet Barbara Payton, who later fell on hard times and became a prostitute, charging ten dollars a throw.

Although Bautzer was twenty-one years her senior, she was thrilled to date him since he was considered the most desirable bachelor in Hollywood.

She accepted his invitation to fly with him to a villa in Palm Springs. Except for servants, she'd have the villa to herself, as he stayed in a suite at a nearby hotel.

She worked for two hours preparing herself and dressing in her most glamorous outfit for the dinner he'd scheduled with her. Photographers would be waiting.

When the doorbell rang, she opened it only to find Hughes standing on the doorstep, looking his usual bedraggled self.

"I have something to show you," he said, insisting that she walk out to door to his battered old Chevrolet. "It's a surprise."

From the front seat of the car, he retrieved a red bandana like something Aunt Jemima might have worn. He opened it to reveal a queen's ransom in jewelry purchased from Tiffany's. It was larger than the cache of jewelry he'd tossed at her in Reno. "Come with me," he said, "and all of this will be yours."

Racing back into the house, she slammed the door in his face. Packing hurriedly, she fled from Palm Springs and returned to Beverly Hills on her own.

On the phone to Roddy, she asked, "Who does Hughes think I am? One of his bimbo starlets at RKO?"

Before ringing off with Roddy, she said, "Howard Hughes is out of my life forever."

As it happened, she was very wrong about that.

***

A short while after Janet Leigh introduced Elizabeth to "Johnny" (i.e., the gangster, Johnny Stompanato), she told Elizabeth that she'd broken up with him. "He frightens me," was all the explanation that Leigh ever provided.

In the two weeks that followed, flowers and expensive chocolates began to arrive at the Taylor household, carrying no message except for a card signed "Johnny." Elizabeth wasn't sure, but she believed that they were gifts from the mysterious former beau of Leigh's.

One Saturday afternoon, Elizabeth joined her brother Howard on the beach at Malibu. He'd brought along some school friends, all boys, but none of them showed any interest in her. Eventually the boys, including Howard, wandered off in pursuit of some girls farther up the beach.

Within the hour, Johnny appeared on the beach, walking toward her in a white bikini so sheer he might as well have been nude.

Suddenly, this strikingly handsome young man was sitting beside her. In addition to his impressive physique, the Italian American stud had flashing brown eyes, black wavy hair, and a courtly manner. George Raft had referred to him as "the most cunning and cocksure man in Hollywood."

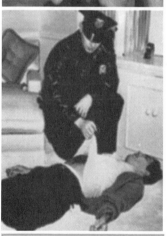

Two views of
Johnny Stompanato
(top photo) with **Lana Turner,**
and *(lower photo)* dead from a
stab wound administered in
Lana's house by the star
herself.

She didn't know at the time that Johnny was the henchman and bodyguard for the notorious gangster, Mickey Cohen.

In Cohen's memoirs, *In My Own Words,* the mobster had written: "Johnny Stompanato was the most handsome man I've ever known that was all man. He was an athlete and a real man, without any queerness about him."

Eric Root, Lana Turner's longtime companion, wrote in his memoirs, *The Private Diary of My Life With Lana Turner:* "Stompanato had a reputation for bilking and beating women. He was a punk—not a big-time gangster. He preyed on weak, lonesome, desperate, wealthy women and some wealthy men. He was a known pimp and hustler."

Elizabeth and Janet Leigh were exceptions to Stompanato's usual dating pattern, which focused on richer, older women. He'd been married three times before, once to Helene Stanley, whose face and figure were copied by artists at Walt Disney Studios to create the images of both Cinderella and Sleeping Beauty.

As Elizabeth would later confide to Roddy McDowall, "Johnny was the most seductive man I've ever met. He exuded charm and masculinity. When he talked to a girl, he gave her his undivided attention. His words were as smooth as velvet. As he held my hand, he kissed my fingertips, I was overcome by him."

Before leaving that day, Johnny Stompanato invited her to go with him to an exclusive party. "I didn't even know your last name," she said.

"It's Steele," he said. "John Steele. I'm a businessman." He failed to say what kind of business he was in.

That Sunday night, he arrived at her Beverly Hills home at around six, driving a brand-new black Cadillac with red upholstery.

After complimenting her on her beauty and her gown, he headed north along the Pacific Coast Highway. At a point near the southern edge of Malibu, he turned right, heading up a steep driveway.

He stopped at a huge iron gate, where two armed guards stood at attention. "Hi, Johnny," one of them called to him, as the other guard opened the gate. The car pulled into a lot filled with other Cadillacs. He escorted her to the main entrance to the house, whose columns evoked Tara in *Gone With the Wind.*

"I'm taking you to a very exclusive private club," he told her. "I'm a member. You'll knock their eyes out."

The door was opened by a stately, gray-haired black butler in tails, who escorted them into the grand hallway, lit by a trio of mammoth crystal chandeliers.

From there, Johnny guided her into a large parlor where well-dressed men, most of them middle-aged, sat drinking at tables with a bevy of expensively gowned women. Peggy Lee was on the small stage, entertaining the guests at this private party.

Eased into their seats, Elizabeth and Johnny were served champagne as they listened to Lee's last three songs. "She's getting paid $10,000 to come here and sing a few numbers," Johnny whispered to Elizabeth.

After the show, Johnny sat quietly with Elizabeth drinking champagne. She learned that he'd joined the U.S. Marines in 1944 and that he'd been part of the U.S. invasion of China the following year. "I wanted to stay in China after the war, and I met this Turkish woman and married her. For a few months, I became a Muslim. My friends nicknamed me 'Oscar.'"

"Why such an odd name?" she asked.

"I don't mean to embarrass you, but it has to do with the length of something I usually keep concealed."

"Oh, I see," she said, flushing red.

She noted what he'd opted to wear that evening, a battleship gray, tailor-made suit with a dark orange silk shirt unbuttoned to the navel. He wore a silver-buckled leather belt and black lizard skin shoes.

She later informed Roddy that, "I found Johnny highly desirable. Janet might have rejected him, but after the second bottle of champagne, I succumbed to his charms. He took me upstairs to one of the bedrooms. He didn't exaggerate about Oscar. He has to be one of the most skilled lovers since Adam."

He dated her three more times, and on each occasion, he took her to the same gated mansion and the same bedroom.

He told her that he'd evolved from being a Muslim to becoming a Catholic again, the way his Sicilian mother had wanted it. "I've got the Madonna under my skin, which means I experience an attack of conscience every now and then."

Confiding in her, he said that he'd once hoped to be an actor but had opted to become a movie executive instead. "Everybody in Hollywood is trying to climb to the top of the mountain. The route there is hazardous, and most poor slobs don't make it. What they don't know once they reach the top is that the route down is even more rugged and hazardous."

"Oh, God," she said. "Is that what I have to look forward to?"

One aspect of his work for Mickey Cohen involved the seduction of famous stars, both male and female, and secretly filming these liaisons. In one of the mansion's bedrooms, unknown to his celebrity partner of the moment, he'd be filmed and/or photographed having sex. These secret films would later be used to blackmail the players.

Cohen knew that Elizabeth was being paid only $2,000 a week, most of it—because she was still a minor—in trust through her parents. Whatever videography was crafted would be held in reserve until she became, as he predicted, one of the biggest stars in Hollywood. Then he planned to blackmail her with the contents of the film.

Howard Hughes, through Johnny Meyer, had arranged for one of his men to trail Elizabeth to the gates of the mansion south of Malibu, and Hughes later learned that Cohen had filmed and was holding a pornographic film featuring Elizabeth. Using Meyer as his go-between, Hughes delivered $50,000 to Cohen for the relinquishment of the secret film. Apparently, Elizabeth never found out about this generous act of intervention by Hughes. If she had, she might have been kinder and more receptive to his advances.

According to Meyer, Hughes played Elizabeth's porno tape repeatedly—almost as frequently as the one he'd previously commissioned with Marilyn Monroe and Guy Madison.

***

Trying to forget about both Hughes and Stompanato, Elizabeth turned her mind to her career. It didn't seem to be moving fast enough, and her pictures weren't doing well enough to please her.

Benny Thau asked Elizabeth to report to make-up for some early costume tests, one of which involved a bridal gown for *Father of the Bride*, even though she'd been scheduled to film *A Place In the Sun* before that.

She encountered Ava Gardner sitting beside her in the make-up department. Gardner had heard that she'd dropped Hughes. "Good going, gal," she said. "I'm glad you said no. You and I are the only cunts in Hollywood who can't be bought. I'm more tantalized by the size of a man's cock than I am by the size of his bank account. Surely you agree?"

"Both, I think, are equally important."

"Right now, I'm running away from both Frank Sinatra and Hughes." Gardner said. "I've got a new boyfriend, and he's great in bed. His name is Johnny Stompanato, although he calls himself 'John Steele.'"

Elizabeth tried to conceal her shock.

She never heard from "Johnny" again.

***

In the immediate aftermath of the night of April 4, 1958, everyone in the world, it seemed, learned the name of Johnny Stompanato. He'd been stabbed to death after a violent quarrel in the home of his last and final lover, Lana Turner.

Angered that Turner had not invited him to escort her to the Oscar ceremony, the gangster had threatened to "carve up" Turner's beautiful face. In a "state of madness," she ran down to the kitchen, where she retrieved an eight-inch knife. Returning to her pink satin bedroom, she stabbed him in the stomach. He lived for another fifteen minutes.

Also in the house that fatal night was fourteen-year-old Cheryl Crane, the daughter she had conceived with her former husband, Stephen Crane.

In typical Hollywood fashion, everyone was called before the police, Among several others, the famed attorney, Jerry Geisler, arrived at the house. He was still famous for having successfully defended Errol Flynn during his trial on a charge of statutory rape.

In five hours, a plan was concocted. To avoid a jail term for Turner, Geisler orchestrated a plan wherein Lana would assert that Cheryl went to the kitchen, got the knife, entered the upstairs bedroom, and stabbed Stompanato in an attempt to defend her mother.

The belief was that Cheryl, as a juvenile, would receive a light sentence, if one at all, whereas a jury might "throw the book" at Lana.

Frank Sinatra also arrived that night at the scene, and the singer agreed that Geisler's plan was the way to go. "Let Cheryl take the fall—she'll get off."

Later, when Elizabeth had an affair with Sinatra, he told her the details associated with the night Stompanato was murdered.

Not only that, he informed her that Hughes had very generously ordered his security forces to guard Turner for the next eight months until fear of mob reprisal from Mickey Cohen died down.

Hughes had been a lover of Turner's, and although he'd long ago ceased to have relations with her, he had remained loyal to her.

Elizabeth told Janet Leigh, "Hughes has no more interest in me, although I hear he still has the hots for you."

She firmly believed that, and was therefore surprised one afternoon when the doorbell rang at the Taylor home in Beverly Hills. Both Sara and Francis were at the art gallery at the time. On the doorstep appeared Hughes, looking like he was auditioning for the role of a tramp.

Hughes no longer pressed his case for marriage. Instead, he presented her with a present—tubes of vaginal jelly, which he claimed might prevent an unwanted pregnancy.

"Use this and you won't get pregnant," he instructed her. "If you do get pregnant, your nipples will turn brown instead of rosy pink, and you'll also get stretch marks. If that ever happens to you, I definitely will not marry you."

Then, without saying anything else, he turned and headed back to his battered old Chevy, which offered no clue that its driver was the richest man in America.

***

When Monty Clift was told by Paramount that he'd be appearing with Elizabeth Taylor and Shelley Winters in *A Place In the Sun,* he said, "I know Shelley from the Actors Studio, but who in hell is Elizabeth Taylor?"

It is inconceivable that he had not heard of her, although he'd never seen one of her films. They knew dozens of the same show business personalities. To discover who she was in 1949, all someone had to do was walk by a newsstand and look at the covers of various magazines, including *Time.*

Elizabeth certainly knew who Monty was, as he'd been the hottest actor in Hollywood since his recent release of his screen debut in *Red River* (1948), followed by *The Search* (also 1948). She claimed, "He is the most beautiful man in films today."

As a means of generating advance publicity for their joint upcoming film appearance, the studio arranged for Monty to escort Elizabeth to the premiere of his latest film, *The Heiress* (1949), in which he'd appeared opposite Olivia de Havilland. *The Heiress* was based on Henry James's novel, *Washington Square.*

When Paramount explained that Elizabeth was a seventeen-year-old child star who had appeared in her first adult role in *Conspirator,* Monty said, "I'm twenty-nine years old, not a child molester. I'm not taking a kid to any premiere." The studio insisted, however, and he finally relented.

The day before Monty escorted Elizabeth to *The Heiress,* he spent the night on death row at San Quentin State Prison as a means of better understanding how to interpret his upcoming role as George Eastman who, during the final reel of *A Place in the Sun,* is sent to the electric chair on a charge of murder.

In the back seat of a long limousine heading for Grauman's Chinese Theater, he quickly learned that Elizabeth was not the "stuck-up, spoiled Hollywood baby doll" he'd anticipated.

Sliding into the car beside him, she'd said, "Hello, Monty. Thanks for taking me out of my god damn house. My mother is such a pain in the ass, at times, I'm tempted to strike a match to her hairy cunt."

Although at first he was shocked by the vocabulary coming from one so young and beautiful, he quickly adjusted to it and was delighted by her blunt talk. "You're my kind of gal, Bessie Mae."

"Where did you come up with this 'Bessie Mae' shit?" she asked.

"All the world calls you Elizabeth Taylor," he said. "I want to call you what no one else does."

For Elizabeth's appearance at *The Heiress's* premiere, Helen Rose had designed something "sexy and sophisticated," in this case, a strapless gown with a snowy Polar Bear fur cape. Monty sat gazing at Elizabeth, fingering his lucky red dice on the way to the premiere of his latest movie.

Hedda Hopper spotted Elizabeth straightening Monty's tie before they entered the zany, pagoda-inspired movie palace. The next day, Hopper printed, "These magnificent lovebirds are very soon going to be married."

Inside, as *The Heiress* flickered across the screen, Monty slid farther and farther into his seat until he was sitting on his coccyx.

Elizabeth had high praise for the movie, constantly reassuring him how great he was.

Leaving the theater, Monty was accosted by an aggressive reporter, who wanted to know what he thought of *The Heiress.* Brushing him aside, Monty said, "I hated the fucking thing. Let me out of here."

After the film, Monty and Elizabeth were driven to the home of William Wyler, who was hosting a party for A-list movie stars. Here, she met one of the film industry's favorite British actors, David Niven. He later said, "Monty and Elizabeth looked like twins. I'm sure Adam and Eve, in the Garden of Eden, looked just like them."

Later, she was seen chatting with Clark Gable, who told her that he was sorry they didn't get to appear together on the screen.

"I heard Tracy is going to play your dad in *Father of the Bride.* I could have played that role."

Gary Cooper came up to her. "I've never dated a gal with lavender eyes before, but I sure would like to," he told her.

Back on her doorstep, Monty escorted her to the stoop and kissed her on the forehead. "I promised Paramount I'd stay sober while escorting you. Now Marlon Brando and I are going to let it rip. Get stinking drunk."

"I'd like to join you guys some night," she said.

"You do so at your own risk," he said. "We might double rape you."

"That would be okay," she said, stepping inside and shutting the door.

***

Built into the deal that Louis B. Mayer had arranged between MGM and Paramount, MGM would receive $35,000 for ten weeks of Elizabeth's services during her loanout for the production of *A Place In the Sun*. On October 2, 1949, Elizabeth and Sara left together for location shooting on Lake Tahoe, high in the Sierra Nevada mountains on the border between California and Nevada. The Sierra Nevada was where the desperate and snowbound Donner party, a century before, had regressed to cannibalism as a means of surviving the winter.

A Place In the Sun was based on Theodore Dreiser's celebrated novel, written in 1925, *An American Tragedy*.

above, left: novelist **Theodore Dreiser**
right: director **Josef von Sternberg**
"explicit condemnations of capitalism and materialism in America."

It was inspired by a notorious criminal case that unfolded in New York State in 1908. Chester Gillette was put on trial and convicted of drowning his girl friend, Grace Brown, although he maintained all the way to the electric chair that he was innocent. The event occurred on Big Moose Lake in New York State's Adirondack mountains.

An earlier version of the film, entitled *An American Tragedy* and released in 1931, had starred Phillips Holmes in Monty's role, Sylvia Sidney in Shelley Winter's part, and Frances Dee as the rich girl (i.e., the role played by Elizabeth). It was directed by Josef von

Players in the real-life version of
American Tragedy
Chester Gillette *(left)* and **Grace Brown**

Sternberg, a German-Austrian director already widely known at the time of his film's release, based on his having helmed Marlene Dietrich in *The Blue Angel,* the film that launched her as an international success.

Dreiser's novel from 1925 and von Sternberg's film from 1931 had each been interpreted as explicit condemnations of capitalism and materialism in America. But as New York author Norman Mailer told Shelley Winters about the 1951 film version, "I hear the script is being watered down so much it's going to taste like warmed over piss."

When Shelley told that to Elizabeth, she went to Stevens, the director of the 1951 version, and asked him, in more diplomatic terms, what he thought about that.

He responded, "I'm not going to blame American society like Dreiser did. I'm turning this movie into a psychological drama. Our hero's downfall is that he has this uncontrollable passion for the most glamorous woman on the screen today—read that Elizabeth Taylor."

But Mailer's charge was to some extent accurate. In Washington, Senator Joseph McCarthy of Wisconsin, aided in no small part by the FBI's director, J. Edgar Hoover, had already launched their notorious commie witch hunts, and much of Hollywood was terrified. Paramount brought pressure on Stevens to ensure that *A Place In the Sun* did not evolve into an anti-capitalist tirade, and that it did not appear to glorify the proletariat working class as portrayed on screen by Monty.

In response, he referred to both McCarthy and Hoover as "two disgusting fags." And when he read the script, he told Elizabeth, "Its message is that sex in America is the way to both rise and ruin."

Sara, in contrast, was thrilled that Elizabeth would be directed by Stevens, one of the hottest directors in Hollywood at the time.

Stevens did not have an impressive beginning in Hollywood, having launched his involvement there as a gagman for Hal Roach and later directing Laurel and Hardy. In the 1930s, he became famous for directing such films as *Alice Adams* (1935), with Katharine Hepburn; and *Swing Time* (1936) with Fred Astaire and Ginger Rogers. He would later direct Elizabeth in both *Giant* (1956), and the disastrous *The Only Game in Town* (1969).

One critic referred to Stevens as "a big, raw-faced man who looked just like a character in one of his westerns, escaping from an Indian about to scalp him."

Actually, Elizabeth didn't learn until later why Stevens had selected her for the film. "I wanted the girl on the candy-box cover, the beautiful girl in the yellow Cadillac that every American boy, some time or other, thinks he can marry."

The staff had been instructed not to swear in front of Elizabeth. But that ban was lifted after the first day, when a stream of foul-mouthed invective flowed from her mouth.

She told Stevens, "I can outcuss, outdrink, outsuck, and outfuck the best of them." He was startled. She was so different from her movie magazine image.

"I realized after the first week that a lot of guys in Hollywood had had that pussy," Stevens told his crew.

As factory girl Alice Tripp, Shelley Winters appeared onscreen in tacky clothes with no makeup, playing a 1950s girl from the wrong side of the tracks. Guys knocked up girls like that but didn't want to marry them, figuring they could do better on the other side of the tracks.

Shelley told Elizabeth, "After this role, I will for the rest of my life play the girl most men would like to murder."

Shelley's role was originally intended for Audrey Totter, but MGM refused to release her. Then Stevens briefly considered Gloria Grahame, but her boss, Howard Hughes at RKO, refused to release her, too. Monty had lobbied for the role of Alice to go to Betsy Blair, who was married at the time to Gene Kelly. Coincidentally, Kelly had, for years, had a crush on Monty.

Stern-faced Anne Revere, a descendent of Paul Revere, the hero of the American Revolution, played the role of Monty's mother. Soon after, she was blacklisted for her liberal politics during the McCarthy era witch hunt. Bowing to studio pressure, Stevens cut most of her scenes from *A Place In the Sun,* and after that, probably because of her political positions, she didn't appear in another movie until 1970.

During the cool October nights of 1950, Elizabeth escaped from the clutches of Sara and hid out with Monty, getting to know him. Like his some-

Elizabeth Taylor with **Montgomery Clift** in
A Place in the Sun

times lover and rival, Marlon Brando, rail-thin Montgomery Clift had been born in Nebraska. When he signed to play Elizabeth's doomed lover in *A Place In the Sun,* he met a woman twelve years younger than himself. Since the age of fifteen, he'd been appearing on Broadway, making his film debut in Howard Hawks' western, *Red River* (1948), in which he played the highly strung adopted son of John Wayne as part of a tense relationship both on and off the screen. Addicted to both alcohol and drugs before he met Elizabeth, Monty was also deeply conflicted about his sexuality. He often said, "I love women, but I prefer to have sex with men." Monty's male lovers came and went.

By breaking into films, he started a migration of young New York actors to Hollywood—Marlon Brando, Paul Newman, James Dean, Steve McQueen, Anthony Perkins, George Peppard, and many others.

Shelley Winters later said, "Elizabeth and I once made a bet about how many of those actors we would eventually seduce. I think she won."

Dustin Hoffman, Robert De Niro, and Al Pacino would follow in Monty's footsteps with this edgy, intense, and mutely eloquent style of acting.

Monty was unlike any man she'd ever met. He appeared on the set wearing a scruffy T-shirt washed last season, and a pair of jeans that had been fresh sometime before World War II. He also sported a ripped leather jacket that looked as if an RAF pilot had worn it during an ejection from his airplane during the Battle of Britain.

Monty uttered enigmatic statements that only she seemed to fully understand. "There is an evil in Hollywood that confronts me at every turn. I am unable to handle it. No one can be taken at face value. Everyone is a liar. I feel I'm climbing a ladder to this giant skyscraper, and I have an overwhelming desire to fall off and drop into space."

Although he didn't plan to embrace her as a lover, Monty was mesmerized by Elizabeth's physical beauty.

"My god," Monty said. "She has black sable eyebrows and eyes so deceptively blue that they appear violet in a certain light." She stood only five feet two inches tall, although she always lied about it, claiming she actually stood five feet, four inches. Amazingly, on screen, she photographed as if she was tall.

"She was indeed the kind of woman a guy like my character, George Eastman, would kill for as a means of reaching his place in the sun." Monty asserted.

Their first scene was set in midsummer, although it was filmed during October. The film crew had to hose away a light snow that had fallen the night before.   The script called for both Elizabeth and Monty to appear in bathing suits beside and in the lake. Monty refused to disrobe because of his insecurities about his willowy, hairy frame, with only Elizabeth appearing in a bathing suit.

"In a bathing suit, I look like a monkey," Monty told Stevens.

[For years, Monty made frequent visits to a skin specialist on West 57th Street in Manhattan for electrolysis, with the intention of removing a thick pelt of hair from his thin chest and narrow shoulders. Elizabeth would also undergo such treatments.]

"You know what really caused Monty and Elizabeth to bond?" a drunken

Roddy asked one night at a party. "All that excess body hair that both of them suffered with."

Stevens was not satisfied with Elizabeth's scene in the lake, and ordered one retake after another until Sara protested, claiming that her daughter was menstruating and was likely to get terrible cramps. Then she made the amazing charge that this sequence in the cold water would prevent Elizabeth from ever having children.

After the filming of the lake scene, Elizabeth spent the next three days in her bedroom, since Sara would not let her return to work. Throughout the two decades that followed, Elizabeth would insist that she would not work when having her period, a stipulation written into every one of her contracts.

Stevens found Elizabeth a temperamental star, difficult to direct. He accused her of "spitting fire at me."

"Does the Princess of MGM have distemper (sic) today?" At one particularly difficult moment, he archly reminded her that the title of the picture was not *Lassie Comes Home* but *A Place In the Sun.*

Ivan Moffat, the film's associate producer, later observed, "In Elizabeth's arms, Monty Clift was enveloped by the mothering tentacles of the world…In some hirsute, androgynous way, they did indeed look alike," Moffat said. "In close-ups, they looked like a brother and sister committing incest."

Stevens told Monty and Shelley, "Elizabeth is a sex time bomb waiting to explode."

"Then what am I?" Shelley asked. "Chopped liver?"

"In this picture, that's exactly what you are," the director responded.

Elizabeth Taylor, fashion icon, in a much-copied gown designed by Edith Head

"At night, Monty coached Elizabeth in her role by becoming Angela Vickers—delivering her lines, complete with facial expressions and gestures. "It was amazing to behold," Elizabeth said. "It was as if he became the essence of femininity that Angela Vickers represented, yet it never bordered on drag queen grotesqueness."

For months after the film's release, copies of Elizabeth's white gown, a design by Edith Head, were replicated and purchased by young women across the globe. The design featured a tight bodice embroidered with white daisies and a skirt of ivory tulle over white silk. The designer later remarked, "Elizabeth in the gown was like sunlight moving over the water of a crystal blue lake."

When Monty saw her in the white gown, he said, "Bessie Mae, your tits are fantastic, just fantastic!"

As Elizabeth told her two closest male confidants, Dick Hanley and Roddy McDowall, "I've fallen in love with Monty. I know it's my own misfortune. At first, I denied to myself that he was homosexual. But when he began showing up on the set with hustlers he'd picked up in a bar, I was forced to face reality."

"We have this incredible bond," she said. "Our relationship will not die. But instead of lover, it must turn into something else—soul mate, sister, mama, confidant."

Their intimacy became so close that she'd invite him into her quarters and would take a bath in front of him. As she'd later tell Roddy, "It never excited Monty."

During the course of the filming, Elizabeth wrote girlish love letters to Monty. Rather callously, he turned them over to his current hustler trick, who saved them and later tried to sell them to a magazine. But there were no takers.

Brenda Maddox, author of *Who's Afraid of Elizabeth Taylor?*, brilliantly described another gown designed by Edith Head that Elizabeth wore on screen:

"As Taylor pulls Clift out onto the balcony, compelled by a passion that will send him to the electric chair, she wears a gown of jet-black velvet with a vestigial shred of white broderie anglaise edging her breasts. In the dark, away from the glare of the party, they do a scene that can only be described as oral sex."

In the flickering light, and almost mirroring their own behind-the-scenes drama, Monty says, "How can I tell you how much I love you? How can I tell you all?"

She responds, "Tell Mama...Tell Mama all!"

Elizabeth had objected to her dialogue. "Who in hell wrote this shit?" she asked Stevens, knowing that he was the one.

Twenty years later, she saw the film again. "Now I understood the line. Stevens wanted to suggest that Monty and I had a relationship so deep it began in the womb."

When Stevens first viewed the close-ups of Monty and Elizabeth, he proclaimed, "I have mated Hollywood's most beautiful screen duo. Not since Greta Garbo emoted with John Gilbert in *Flesh and the Devil* (1926) has the public seen two such perfect faces."

Rarely has a screen couple been photographed so divinely as in the final reel, when Elizabeth visits Monty on death row, where he has been sentenced to the electric chair for the alleged murder of Shelley Winters, his pregnant former girlfriend. In the film, the script called for the character played by Winters to die of accidental drowning, though he made no effort to save her. Aggressive prosecutors convinced the jury it was murder.

In his cell for a farewell, the character played by Elizabeth swears to the condemned man, "I will love you until the day I die."

The depiction of Elizabeth, tremulous and frightened in a little cloche hat, would be flashed on screens around the world and would become one of her most iconic images.

***

Back in Hollywood for the final takes, Sara invited her old friend, Hedda Hopper, onto the set to watch Monty and Elizabeth make love. At the end of the scene, the columnist, wearing a wide-brimmed, shocking pink picture hat, came up to Elizabeth. "Where in hell did you learn to make love like that? All this time, I've been telling my readers you are a virgin. You obviously are not."

When Hopper left the set, Monty denounced her as "an old gobbler."

Hopper called Monty "a pantywaist." She'd long ago learned that Monty was a homosexual when she'd heard that he'd been arrested in New Orleans on a morals charge. In spite of what she already knew, she continued to promote Elizabeth and Monty in her column as "two lovebirds," predicting that wedding bells would soon be ringing for the beautiful couple.

In a cheap publicity trick, Paramount publicists behind Elizabeth's back released to the press the news of their upcoming marriage. Across the country, Americans read over morning coffee—CLIFT AND TAYLOR TO WED.

Elizabeth broke down in tears, shouting "Monty will blame me for this. He'll never speak to me again."

When Winters was later asked if she felt left out when Monty and Elizabeth became so close, she said, "Like hell I was [left out]! I was making love to both Marlon Brando and Burt Lancaster. Monty was the lonely one, in spite of Elizabeth's presence. He was the loneliest man I've ever known and the best actor, too. Don't tell Marlon I said that."

After the shooting of the last scene of *A Place in the Sun*, Elizabeth expected Monty to make plans for the continuation of their relationship. Emotionally drained, he told her he was flying to New York for a drive to Connecticut, where he would be a guest of the notorious Libby Holman at her estate, "Treetops," set on fifty-five acres of grounds between Greenwich and Stamford.

Libby was nearly twice Monty's age. Noël Coward referred to her as a "fag hag," and told anyone who would listen that she'd been a star of Broadway musicals during the late 1920s.

When Holman heard of Monty's growing friendship with Elizabeth, she was very resentful, denouncing Elizabeth as "a teenage limey nympho."

Holman wasn't one to cast aspersions on others. Even though she'd never been officially declared guilty in any court, the torch singer had been implicated in the controversial suicide (or murder?) of her first husband, Zachary Smith Reynolds, the 22-year-old tobacco heir. He was a homosexual, as was her second husband, actor Ralph (pronounced "Rafe") Holmes, twelve years her junior, who also committed suicide or was murdered.

Like everyone else in America at the time, Elizabeth had already read about Holman's notorious life. She warned Monty, "Please be careful of her. She's the Black Widow. You may be the next one murdered."

Actress and stage personality Tallulah Bankhead confessed to being Holman's occasional lesbian lover. Holman and Bankhead frequently shot barbs at each other, Tallulah observing, publicly and frequently, "I entertain Libby only between murders." Holman responded in kind, at one time saying, "Tallulah's voice is a mixture of British and Pickaninny."

As journalist John Parker wrote, "As Monty Clift's personal conflicts over his Hollywood career and his homosexuality intensified, Libby became a willing participant with him in long bouts of experimenting with drugs and strange sexual excursions into strip joints and whorehouses, which went against his apparent leanings, but satisfied her perverted whim. Monty told of wild scenes at Libby's magnificent home, filled with the aromas of erotic eastern perfumes and joss-sticks, topped up with marijuana and pep pills.

When Monty departed from Hollywood after the filming of *A Place In the Sun,* Elizabeth told him, "Look, Monty, I'm always here for you whenever you need me." He said nothing else, but gave her a gentle kiss on the lips and walked away.

She ran from the set in tears and stayed in her dressing room for two hours.

Many years later, Monty made a confession to Frank E. Taylor, the producer of *The Misfits,* in which he was starring with Marilyn Monroe and Clark Gable in the last picture either Monroe or Gable would ever make.

Libby Holman

"I did try to have sex with Elizabeth one time, but couldn't rise to the occasion," Monty said.

Taylor herself claimed, years after Monty's death in 1966, "He also confessed to me that he had a small penis and that that was the secret tragedy of his life." In the first and unexpurgated edition of Kenneth Anger's *Hollywood Babylon*, he referred to Monty as "Princess Tiny Meat."

"Is nothing sacred?" Monty asked when he read that and before he called his lawyer to get the reference removed in the subsequent edition.

Elizabeth asked Paramount to let her attend a special screening of *A Place In the Sun* with Dick

Hanley. At the end, she gave her own movie review to Dick: "Monty is the most sensitive and magnetic actor on the screen today. He's not afraid to be vulnerable. At first, he draws the audience in with his sheer beauty, but it is his barely concealed torment, as reflected on his face and in his body movements that keeps that audience glued to their seats. I plan to make movie after movie with him. I have truly found my lifetime partner on and off the screen."

"We may go to bed together in the future, but it's all too obvious that we'll have to conduct a *ménage à trois* with some trick of his," she told Dick at dinner that night after seeing the movie.

Returning to Metro, Elizabeth bombarded Benny Thau's office and virtually demanded that he lobby for her to get the lead role in *I'll Cry Tomorrow,* the story of a nightclub singer, Lillian Roth, and her lifelong struggle with alcoholism. "I can pull it off," Elizabeth said. "Hell, I'll become a drunk just to get the part."

She was bitterly disappointed when the role went to that fiery redhead, Susan Hayward. "Dame Bitch," became Elizabeth's name for Hayward.

"Deanna Durbin is a fading memory, and Margaret O'Brien grows more obsolete every day," Elizabeth said to Thau. "*A Place In the Sun* will change my movie life. No one will ever call me a child star again, except in a historical reference."

Upon the release of *A Place In the Sun,* Charlie Chaplin hailed it as "the greatest movie ever made about America." Writing in *American Cinema,* Andrew Sarris claimed, "Those gigantic close-ups of Elizabeth Taylor and Monty Clift kissing were unnerving—sybaritic—like gorging on chocolate sundaes."

The critic for *The New York Post* wrote that "As for Miss Taylor, she has only to pass a camera to provide abundant reason for a man to commit murder, or any other crime of violence, in her favor."

Some critics hailed her as "the virgin temptress." It required the passage of two decades before more modern critics could more accurately describe Elizabeth's performance: "She's the ultimate cock-tease," wrote one reviewer in 1970.

For his performance as a loner and misfit in *A Place In the Sun,* Monty was nominated for a Best Actor Oscar, as was Marlon Brando for his memorable role as the brutish Stanley Kowalski in Tennessee Williams' *A Streetcar Named Desire.* But these Actors Studio candidates ultimately lost to Humphrey Bogart for his role in *The African Queen,* arguably his greatest performance.

A Place In the Sun had its release date postponed for a year because Paramount did not want to compete with its epic *Sunset Blvd.* in the Oscar race. That film starred Gloria Swanson as the fading silent screen vamp, Norma Desmond. Monty, ironically, had originally been offered the role of Joe Gillis, but turned it down, the part eventually going to William Holden, launching him into super stardom.

Monty feared that the role would evoke his own real life drama unfolding at that time with the older, richer, Libby Holman.

For the most part, critics had previously condemned Elizabeth's film performances. But after *A Place In the Sun,* she was actually praised for her acting, and not just for her beauty.

The critic for *Boxoffice* wrote, "Miss Elizabeth Taylor deserves the Oscar this year."

Elizabeth observed, with irony, "I wasn't nominated because I'm beautiful. If you look like I do, nobody gives you an Academy Award."

In contrast, Shelley Winters was nominated for an Oscar, but lost it to Vivien Leigh for her memorable portrayal of Blanche DuBois in *A Streetcar Named Desire* by Tennessee Williams.

After her unrequited love affair with Monty, Elizabeth was depressed, but not for long. "She was too full of life to remain in her bedroom moaning over something that could not be," Roddy recalled. He telephoned her there and volunteered to escort her to a party with his friends at Lucey's Restaurant.

At first, she rejected his offer, but he finally prevailed upon her to go. "Forget Monty," he told her. "The world is filled with gorgeous men, and if you and I play it right, we'll be able to have most of them."

"At the restaurant, I'll introduce you to this handsome rich devil who's been pestering me to bring the two of you together," Roddy said. "But there's a drawback."

"He's a serial killer?" she asked.

"Not that," he told her. "But girls—or boys, as the case might be—usually have to go to the hospital to get stitched back together after a night in the hay with him. I'm talking about Nicky Hilton."

A Place in the Sun

CHAPTER TWELVE
So This Is Marriage (Nicky Hilton)
WHAT A PIP!

After circling each other for months, Elizabeth and Nicky finally met. It was an Indian summer afternoon in October of 1949. He was awed by her beauty, and had been ever since he'd seen her at Jane Powell's wedding party at the Mocambo.

He photographed badly, but in person, he was extremely handsome, speaking in a soft Texas drawl. He was tall and broad-shouldered and wore a tailor-made suit from Savile Row in London. He had a reputation as a playboy, and his dark brown eyes suggested mischief and desire at the age of twenty-three.

Even though he looked like he'd just been graduated from college, he was a man of the world, having launched affairs with members of both sexes since he was fourteen years old. He was at ease with people, having spent his teenage years meeting movie stars, industrial tycoons, presidents, senators, and even fading members of the European aristocracy.

Nicky almost never worked, but he held two important positions—one as the vice-president of the Hilton Corporation, and the other as the manager of the swanky Bel Air Hotel, which he referred to as "my fuck pad."

As it happened, it wasn't Roddy McDowall, but Pete Freeman, son of Paramount's chief, Y. Frank Freeman, who introduced Nicky to Elizabeth. He'd invited both Nicky and Elizabeth to a lunch at Lucey's, a Mexican restaurant on Melrose Avenue across from the Paramount lot.

Elizabeth arrived wearing a violet sheath dress which made her eyes appear more violet than blue.

Nicky was half an hour late, a harbinger of chronic tardiness and irresponsibility to come. But in the meanwhile, Gloria Swanson stopped by Elizabeth's table, as she was waiting there with Freeman. Swanson was filming *Sunset*

Blvd. for Paramount. "You have a marvelous face, child," she told Elizabeth. "We had faces during days of the Silents. With your expressive face, you would have made it back when pictures didn't talk. Today, any little high school debutante can be put up on the screen and called a movie star. Norma Shearer even promoted Janet Leigh. Joanne Dru...*please!*...Barbara Hale...oh, dear, I'm getting ill."

Elizabeth told her how honored she was to meet such a great star.

"One final word of advice," Swanson said. "Take lovers, but don't marry them. Marriage is a trap for a big star."

Two days later, Elizabeth ran into Janet Leigh on the Metro lot. She avoided reporting on Swanson's dig at her, but raved about meeting Nicky Hilton. "He exudes masculinity—what a guy!" Elizabeth said. "He seems like a decent, clean-cut, all-American boy, except when those wild eyes of his undress me, symbolically speaking. We come from very different backgrounds, but we have much in common. We both like hamburgers with onions. That's not all. We both adore Enzio Penza."

Penza, a *basso profundo* from Milan's La Scala opera house, was currently appearing in two musicals at MGM. Nicky and Elizabeth played his recording of *Some Enchanted Evening* time and time again.

When he dropped out of Baltimore's Loyola College at the age of nineteen, Nicky joined the Navy, where he had a number of sailor lovers, most of whom fell for him when they saw him in the shower.

At the time he met Elizabeth, Nicky was involved in a torrid affair with his former stepmother, Zsa Zsa Gabor, who had married Conrad Hilton, Sr. in April of 1942. Because of Hilton Sr.'s ownership of his hotel chain, newspapers had dubbed him "the man with the 100,000 beds."

The Hungarian bombshell divorced Nicky's father in 1946, but her affair with Nicky continued. At the Bel Air hotel, she'd make "Dracula Goulash" for

Love and publicity, Hollywood style, in the Atomic Age
Nicky Hilton with **Elizabeth Taylor**

him before bedtime. Zsa Zsa once asserted that her stepson had "a ten-inch penis and the sexual stamina of a racehorse."

After his divorce from Elizabeth, Nicky dated Terry Moore. She told a reporter, "He had absolutely the largest penis—wider than a beer can and much longer—I have ever seen. To make love to him was like fornicating with a horse."

When he wasn't dating Zsa Zsa, Nicky was seen with actresses Denise Darcel and Jeanne Crain, or else with socialites like Kay Spreckles and Hope

Hampton. Ironically, Conrad Hilton, Sr., had previously dated both Spreckles and Hampton.

After returning home from that lunch at Lucey's, Elizabeth found a box with three dozen long-stemmed yellow roses. Nicky had taken the time to learn the species of her favorite flower. The card he enclosed read, "To bring back the sun—Nick."

That night, after repeatedly smelling the yellow roses, Elizabeth called Roddy. "I've met that darling man, Nicky Hilton. The most eligible bachelor in America, as you well know. All the girls are after him."

"And half the boys, too," Roddy chimed in.

"That's understandable," she said. "He's so sexy. I know he wants me. A girl can tell."

"I can see a page from the history books now: Elizabeth Taylor married Nicky Hilton, and the couple lived happily ever after—just like in the movies."

"But, Roddy, some dreams come true," she said.

"And others are meant merely to be dreamed."

Nicky and Elizabeth began to date each other seriously, and she described him in glowing terms to Dick Hanley, who knew him.

"Nicky is Dr. Jekyll and Mr. Hyde," Dick warned her. "You see the side he presents to the world. There's another side to him—a compulsive gambler, woman-beater, alcoholic, closeted heroin addict, sex maniac. It doesn't matter to him if he's with a man or a woman. He believes that all cats are gray at night."

Nicky invited Elizabeth to go riding along Bel Air's bridle paths, and often took her to the beach and to Hollywood parties. He escorted her to lavish dinners, but on occasion, he dined more modestly at the Taylor home on Elm Drive. For his first dinner there, Sara made her specialty, steak-and-kidney pie. With a fork, he isolated the pieces of kidney, but as a Texan, he ate the chunks of steak.

When Nicky's relationship with Elizabeth became serious enough, he felt it was time to introduce her, along with Sara and Francis, to his own father, Conrad Sr.

A Hilton limousine carrying Francis and Sara pulled up for dinner at Conrad Hilton's sixty-four room mansion in Bel Air. "My god," Francis proclaimed when he emerged from the limo. "We've arrived at Shangri-la!"

Inside, tuxedoed servants raced about, and formally dressed butlers in tails offered drinks. Maids in black uniforms with frilly aprons waited to fulfill every request. "Each of them looks like she should be called Fifi," Sara said.

The mansion was like a boutique hotel, with sixteen bedroom suites and twenty-six bathrooms, with fixtures plated with fourteen-karat gold. Along with five kitchens came an equal number of wet bars. Sara was amazed at the dozen marble fireplaces, each in a different pattern or color of marble, ranging from scarlet red to mint green.

As an art dealer, Francis noted the 18ᵗʰ-century panels painted by the French artist, Jean-Baptiste Hult, and he was awed by Hilton's collection of Ming vases.

Nicky showed the Taylors around the house, or at least around a portion of it, promising Elizabeth that he'd take her on a tour of the grounds the following day.

Tap-dancing Ann Miller was Conrad Sr.'s companion for the evening. The dancer-actress had been having an affair with the hotel magnate, although in her memoirs, she claimed "we were just good friends."

"Yeah," said one maid. "Friends who sleep in suites in the same bed together."

Miller recalled that "Connie was a little jealous that his son had acquired a beauty like Elizabeth Taylor. I think he would have preferred to have her for himself."

Acting as chaperones, Y. Frank Freeman and his wife drove Elizabeth and Nicky to the Hilton vacation retreat at Lake Arrowhead. Once there, Freeman, although nominally on vacation, conducted business for Paramount on the phone, while Elizabeth and Nicky were left virtually alone. It was here, beside this beautiful lake, that he first made love to her.

They were assigned adjoining bedrooms with connecting doors. At two o'clock on their first morning there, he opened the doors between their rooms and stood in the dim light, completely nude.

Elizabeth would later confide to Roddy that as a lover, Nicky was tender and gentle with her, never pressuring her or going too far. "He was so very responsive to my needs, yet so very skilled at bringing me pleasure. It's easy to fall in love with a man like that. I have truly found my Prince Charming."

Nicky and Elizabeth would often sneak away to the home of his younger brother, Baron Hilton, who was already married. Later, they'd retreat to a wing of his house where they would not be interrupted.

BE MY GUEST!
Hilton dynasty patriarch **Conrad Hilton** *(left photo)* with *(top right)* **Zsa Zsa Gabor** and *(lower right)* **Ann Miller**

Elizabeth's friends noted that a panic seemed to have consumed her, as her romance with Nicky became more serious. She desperately wanted to flee from the protective womb of Sara, yet on the other hand, feared she might become the closely guarded possession of another man.

Roddy McDowall, meanwhile, had taken a temporary lease on an apartment in The Dakota, the most fabled apartment building in Manhattan. Roddy's contract at Fox had expired, and his lanky teen years had come to an end. He was trying to rejuvenate his career, hoping to find work on the Broadway stage. On an impulse, she'd accepted an invitation to fly to New York to see him. His roommate was their mutual friend, Merv Griffin.

Sara wanted to accompany Elizabeth as chaperone, but Elizabeth defied her, rejecting her offer. When Nicky objected to her trip, she decided to defy him, too, traveling there without him.

In New York, Monty Clift joined Elizabeth, Griffin, and Roddy for nights on the town. They became regulars at Gregory's, Monty's favorite bar on Fifty Fourth Street and Lexington Avenue.

As author Ellis Amburn wrote, "Often joined by a nineteen-year-old, whom Monty was trying to seduce, and Kevin McCarthy, they always huddled in a wooden booth to the right of the bar, chain smoking and drinking. None of the other customers—pimps, winos, a few undergraduates, and middle-aged women nodding over drinks bothered them or even recognized them. One night, Monty flaunted a cute chorus boy in front of Elizabeth."

She had long known that Kevin was Monty's best male friend, and also that he was one of the most talented actors in New York. Before introducing him to Elizabeth, Monty told her that "Kevin is the love of my life." He had married Augusta Dabney in 1941. Monty told Elizabeth that in his loneliness, he often went to the McCarthy apartment at night to sleep between the actor and his wife.

Kevin came from a distinguished family. He was the brother of Mary McCarthy, one of the best known writers in America, and also the cousin of U.S. senator Eugene McCarthy, who ran for President in 1968, challenging Robert Kennedy right before his assassination. Kevin would soon be nominated for the Best Supporting Actor Oscar for his appearance in the film version of Arthur Miller's *Death of a Salesman*.

Elizabeth soon learned that a movie script was arriving almost daily at Monty's apartment, but that he didn't bother reading any of them. He told her, "I'm not doing any more movies for the time being."

Elizabeth, Monty, and their friends often ended the evening at Bickford's an all-night gay cafeteria patronized by hustlers. Sometimes, Monty would approach one of the young men for rent, asking, "Would you like to fuck a movie star?"

She noted sadly that Monty had become a confirmed alcoholic, whereas she was just launching a lifetime of heavy drinking herself.

Monty took them to jazz joints like Condon's, and on one night, Elizabeth went with Kevin and Monty by taxi to Chinatown, later ending the evening walking around the Bowery.

One of their most raucous evenings was at a restaurant in Greenwich Village. Each of them ordered lemon meringue pie for dessert. Monty put his face down on the table and began to lick the meringue off the top. For a laugh, a drunken Griffin pushed Monty's face into the pie. A food fight erupted, with Elizabeth joining in.

Management called the police, but when two studly patrolmen came in and discovered Elizabeth wiping pie off her face, she persuaded them to let them go if she'd give the manager a hundred-dollar bill. He gladly accepted, and the drunken party fled into the night.

Sometimes, neither Monty nor Roddy were available, so Griffin volunteered as Elizabeth's escort at such haunts as the Stork Club and 21, a former speakeasy. Word soon got back to Hollywood that Griffin was dating Elizabeth. Columnist Walter Winchell promoted this *faux* romance in his column, although he obviously knew that the Taylor/Griffin association was platonic. He'd once said, "Merv Griffin is as queer as a three-dollar bill."

Griffin didn't deny the romance, since he led a life in the closet and was always eager to promote publicity that he was heterosexual.

Although he didn't tell Elizabeth, Roddy learned that while she was away, Peter Lawford, their mutual friend, supplied the hotel heir with a steady stream of beautiful starlets eager to break into the movies. "Nicky returns the favor by letting Peter occasionally go down on that tree trunk he carries in his trousers," Roddy told Griffin.

Both Roddy and Griffin, and especially Monty, felt that Elizabeth should break off her romance with Nicky. Yet they didn't want to "bad mouth" Nicky in front of her, based on their fear of offending her.

One night, Roddy and Griffin decided to play matchmakers, hoping to interest Elizabeth in another potential boyfriend.

"I have an idea," Griffin said. "I met this sweet kid at RCA Victor. Eddie Fisher. He's also under contract there. Real cute. Jewish. I bet Elizabeth will go for him. If she doesn't, maybe Eddie will give me a tumble?"

"I hear he doesn't swing that way," Roddy said.

"In my case, he might make an exception," Griffin said.

"Dream on," Roddy said. "Let's invite him. He's sure to be awed by Elizabeth, at least."

***

Merv Griffin arranged tickets to the Broadway Theater where Mae West was appearing in a popularly priced revival of *Diamond Lil*, which she had written herself and had first performed in April of 1928. In his memoirs, Merv remembered the play as *Catherine Was Great*, which Mae had brought to Broadway in 1944. Ironically, the original producer of that play back in 1944 had been the flamboyant showman, Mike Todd, who in years to come would marry Elizabeth.

As Griffin entered with Elizabeth, even though the lights had dimmed and the curtain was about to go up, a murmur was heard from the audience. Word spread quickly that Elizabeth Taylor had entered the theater and was being ushered to her seat. Only the opening of the curtain silenced the crowd.

All thoughts of Elizabeth vanished as a usually *blasé* New York audience greeted Mae's appearances with applause and huzzahs lasting five minutes. In this mixture of comedy and melodrama, Mae seemed to take delight in reviving her "classic," still getting laughs from such now-familiar lines as "I'm one of the finest women who ever walked the streets."

Reviewers still critiqued the play as "pure trash . . . or rather impure trash," but through it all the buxom, blonde Mae prevailed in her Gay Nineties garb. She still maintained her reputation as "the world's wickedest woman." Ironically, in years to come, Elizabeth herself would be dubbed as such in the hate press.

Out of courtesy, Griffin and Elizabeth went backstage to pay their respects to the star of the show. She was engaged in a noisy fight with producer George Brandt, and was furious that some critic had written of the "dromedary dip with which she walks," and she was demanding a retraction. The producer was patiently trying to explain to her that she couldn't force a reviewer to retract something like that.

Seeing Elizabeth, Mae, who had changed into a white satin robe, became all smiles. She was introduced to Griffin, but apparently had never heard of him.

Elizabeth complimented Mae on her wisecracks. "You were wonderful. You are so Americana. You're in the great tradition of Charlie Chaplin, Buster Keaton, W.C. Fields."

"Please!" Mae protested. "Don't mention that old drunkard Fields to me. He once stuck his filthy paw up my dress to see if those stories about me were true. He learned I'm a real woman down there. Not a transvestite!"

The aging sex diva invited them back to her dressing room, which Griffin later asserted had more flowers than the funeral of a head of state. He remembered her "looking like a pagan love goddess, getting ready for the mating season."

After arranging herself, Mae advised Elizabeth to "stick to the movies—don't go on the wicked stage. The damn producers, when they go on the road, will try to book you into an outhouse and try to ruin your play, washing it right down the tur-let." Elizabeth was surprised that she still spoke in pure Brooklynese.

Mae liked to give advice, and she had plenty of it for Elizabeth. "I know everything worth knowing about show business," Mae said. "First, you've got to insist to a director that at least one redheaded actor be hired. Redheads are good omens. I've got one appearing in this play with me. I run my fingers through his red hair every night before going on. Second, you've got to surround yourself with a real swish, maybe two. A woman always looks more feminine when she's got a swish hovering over her, doing her hair, her nails, tightening her dress."

"I'll keep that in mind, Miss West," Elizabeth said.

"Now the important part," Mae confided in a confessional tone. Before facing the camera or going on stage in front of an audience, select the husky of the crew. Demand that he give you an orgasm if he wants to keep his job. When I was doing *Catherine Was Great* for that God damn bricklayer, Mike Todd, I had this *sri*, who not only supervised my yoga lessons, but could give me an orgasm in thirty seconds. Some men can't do that after sweating over a woman's body all night. After orgasm, a woman looks more beautiful, more regal than ever. Don't you agree, Griffin?" She looked him up and down skeptically, as if seeing him for the first time. "On second thought, you're not a man to answer such a question."

Vaudevillian / Love Goddess
Mae West

About fifteen minutes later, Griffin escorted Elizabeth out of Mae's dressing room. The blonde goddess stood at her door. Ignoring him, she gazed into Elizabeth's violet eyes. Mae was no longer impersonating herself but looked like a real woman for the first time that night—not a caricature. She also appeared fifteen years older.

She took Elizabeth's hand. "There was a time, dearie, when I was as beautiful a woman as you are tonight."

* * *

After their exit from Mae's dressing room, Griffin put Elizabeth in a taxi to haul her to the Broadway hangout, Lindy's, whose patrons looked like a cast of characters released from

Guys and Dolls. All the comedians hung out here—even Bob Hope, who dropped in whenever he flew in from California. On any given night you could see Jack E. Leonard trading insults with Jack Carter or Joey Bishop. Milton Berle was a regular.

As Griffin entered Lindy's with his "arm candy," even this rather sophisticated Broadway crowd stopped eating and started rubber-necking. Martha Raye they were used to, not Elizabeth Taylor, the screen goddess. One awe-struck young waiter, an aspiring actor, almost spilled a double order of matzo ball soup onto Mary Martin's table.

Since she'd already eaten a big dinner, Elizabeth had come here for one reason, and that was to sample Lindy's celebrated cheesecake. Frank Sinatra had recommended it as a "must" on her visit to New York, although he claimed his mother could make a better one.

As Elizabeth dug into her cheesecake, Griffin looked up to see "Uncle Miltie" heading for their table. Milton Berle usually ignored Griffin, but tonight greeted him like his best friend. "Baby, I've missed you. We've got to get together. After all, you're my favorite band singer."

Griffin knew that this effusive greeting was just staged so that he would introduce him to Elizabeth. After being introduced to the "King of Comedy," Elizabeth merely smiled before digging back into a large dab of her cheesecake.

Knowing all eyes were on him, Berle sat down in their booth and attempted in vain to engage Elizabeth in conversation. She just wanted to eat the cheesecake and get out the door. Looking disappointed, he finally got up and left, returning to his own table.

"Why did you snub Uncle Miltie?" Merv asked.

"Never heard of him," she said.

"Don't you watch television?" he asked.

"Never," she said. "It bores me."

"But he's one of the most famous entertainers in the business, the King of Comedy."

"Since when did he dethrone Bob Hope?"

Soon after, Griffin excused himself "to go to the little boy's room."

Standing at the urinal, he was surprised to see Berle enter and take a position beside him. He reached in and pulled out what looked like a foot-long cock, one of the biggest Griffin had ever seen.

"What's with that stuck-up little bitch you're dating tonight?" Berle asked. He shook his penis. "She needs for me to stick this whopper up her cunt. I'll

Milton Berle

209

have her screaming all night for more."

Griffin quickly zipped up and headed back to Elizabeth, who was surrounded by fans complimenting her on her fur coat.

As he was shepherding her into a taxi, she said, "Women usually compliment my beauty, not my fur. I'll have to get rid of it. No woman should have her apparel detract from her looks."

As she snuggled into the fur for the ride back to her hotel, she said, "That was the best fucking cheesecake I've ever had in my life."

* * *

When Roddy and Griffin learned that Jane Powell was going to be in New York, they decided to throw a joint party for both Elizabeth and Jane at their sublet at the Dakota. In his memoirs, Griffin claimed that the party took place at his suite at the Hotel Meurice, but Eddie Fisher accurately remembered in his autobiography that the venue was The Dakota.

Perhaps the ever-closeted Griffin did not want his public to know that he was rooming with one of Hollywood's best-known homosexuals, Roddy McDowall. Griffin especially wanted to conceal from the public that they were sometimes lovers.

Ever since he'd met Eddie Fisher at RCA Victor studios, Griffin had wanted to get to know him better. Using Elizabeth as bait, he decided to call Eddie and invite him to the party.

Griffin was jealous of Eddie's success as a singer, and knew that their recording studio was predicting big success for him. Yet he also had a secret crush on Eddie, even though Roddy assured him that "You'll strike out with him. I know Eddie. He's a connoisseur of beautiful women."

"So is Nicky Hilton, and he puts out for men," Griffin said.

"Regardless of what people say, lightning doesn't strike twice," Roddy warned.

When Griffin called Eddie, the singer at first didn't believe that Elizabeth would actually be at the party, but he agreed to come over anyway. Although the invitation was for two o'clock, he arrived at 1:45pm.

"Oh, yeah, right," Eddie said skeptically, once he was inside the apartment. "I'm sure Elizabeth Taylor is going to show up at any minute."

"Actually," Griffin said, "she's already here." He led Eddie into the bedroom which he shared with Roddy. Seated on a padded stool in front of a vanity mirror, she was applying the finishing touches to her makeup. Unlike Milton Berle, she knew who Eddie was. She gracefully turned and smiled at him. At first he didn't know what to say.

He later recalled the moment. "I was awestruck by her extraordinary beauty. I mean, by that point I had been around a lot of beautiful women, but I'd never met anyone like her. I fell in love with her that afternoon. I can still close my eyes and see her sitting there."

Griffin had disappeared to answer the buzzer, as Roddy was busy in the kitchen. It was Monty at the door, another honored guest. For the first time in his life, the actor had arrived somewhere on time.

Rushing back to his bedroom, Griffin announced to Elizabeth, "Monty's here." Taking one final look for reassurance in the mirror, Elizabeth rose and headed for the living room and Monty.

"She brushed right past me and went to the side of her co-star in *A Place In the Sun*," Eddie said. "At that point I might not have existed. I spent most of my time that day talking to Roddy and Jane, but I cast frequent glances at Monty and Elizabeth, who seemed engaged in some epic battle."

Griffin later revealed what was going on between Elizabeth and Monty. "It was her final attempt to get Monty to marry her before he headed back to Hollywood. Even though Monty told me he'd never marry anyone, Elizabeth was persistent."

At the end of the party, Eddie went over to tell Elizabeth good-bye, but she was still engaged in her dispute with Monty. She brushed Eddie aside. He later told Griffin that he saw her back in Hollywood when he was visiting the MGM lot. "She was obviously furious and talking out loud to herself. She walked right past me and didn't even look at me. At that time I could never have believed that one day she'd marry me. You figure."

***

Griffin returned to Hollywood to accept an engagement at the Cocoanut Grove in the Ambassador Hotel. On his first night back, he was tired from the flight and ordered dinner from room service. There was a knock on his door. Thinking it was a waiter, he opened the door to discover a drunk Nicky Hilton standing there. His clothes were rumpled, "and he looked like he'd come to decaptitate me," Griffin later confided to Roddy.

Griffin called Roddy in New York the following day to relay what happened. "Nicky was too drunk to beat up anybody," Griffin claimed. "The night ended when I stripped him of all his clothes—yes, most definitely his underwear, too—and put him to bed. You did not exaggerate. That's some equipment on that stud. I spent the night enjoying it while Nicky snored."

After that, Nicky no longer viewed Griffin as serious competition for Elizabeth's affection. According to Griffin, "As he departed, Nicky told me, 'I'd heard that you might be a fairy. Elizabeth always gravitates to them—take that Monty Clift, for instance.'"

Griffin called Elizabeth, but didn't mention his encounter with Nicky the night before. She tried to explain her reasons for wanting to marry Nicky. At no point did she mention love. "I love jewelry," she said. "Nicky's rich—or at least his father is. Connie Hilton could buy me all the jewelry my little heart desires."

After his singing engagement, Griffin moved into Roddy's house in Los Angeles. Nicky visited on a few more occasions, but only when he was drunk. "When he's sober, which is rare, he's a warm and generous person," Griffin told Roddy. "But on liquor or drugs, he turns violent. He takes heroin, too, you know. He's also a racist, ranting about 'kikes" and 'niggers' all the time. One night he beat the shit out of me. I was black and blue. But the next morning he had no memory of it."

On another night, Nicky arrived at Roddy's house in a shiny new black Cadillac which Conrad Sr., had acquired for him. Griffin had never known him to be that wild before. He carried a loaded .38 revolver. For fun, he began shooting out the lights in Roddy's house until Griffin wrestled the pistol from his drunken hand.

When Roddy returned to Los Angeles, a check was waiting from Conrad, Sr., as reimbursement for the damages. "For god's sake, don't invite him here again," Roddy told Griffin. "Poor Elizabeth. What hell is heading her way? Should we warn her about Nicky?"

"You can't tell a girl like Elizabeth what to do," Griffin said. "When she wants something, she goes after it, and won't listen to anybody. She'll find out for herself. I have a feeling that Nicky will be just the first of several husbands for Elizabeth, and that all of them will be disasters."

***

Late in 1949, Elizabeth returned to Hollywood and to her sizzling romance with Nicky, who had found plenty of companionship during their separation. She'd been scheduled to begin, almost immediately, the filming of her latest MGM picture, *Father of the Bride,* alongside veteran actors Spencer Tracy and Joan Bennett, who'd been cast as her onscreen parents. They had last appeared together in the wisecracking melodrama, *Me and My Gal,* eighteen years earlier.

A blandly handsome actor, Don Taylor, who had served in the Air Force during World War II, was cast as her husband-to-be. After having lunch with him, Elizabeth told director Vincente Minnelli, "About all we have in common is a last name."

She didn't like her role, finding it evocative of those *ingénues* she'd played in MGM films during the late 1940s. Now, in the new decade of the 50s, she wanted meatier, more dramatic parts. "I was tired of playing daughters."

Minnelli had told her that Jack Benny had desperately wanted the role of the penny-pinching father, but was turned down, which the veteran comedian found humiliating. He'd even submitted to a screen test to get the part.

Tracy was perfect for the role, and the script revolved around his trials, tribulations, and the mounting expenses of marrying off his daughter.

After Katharine Hepburn rejected the part, Bennett was selected for the thankless role of the mother because of her coloring, her dark hair, and certain facial features she shared in common with Elizabeth.

After meeting her, Bennett said, "An enduring star like me goes through periods. In the 1930s, I was the winsome blonde *ingénue*. By the forties I was the sullen temptress with raven tresses. Now, for the first time, I'm the chic matron. One day, it will happen to you."

Louis B. Mayer was delighted with Elizabeth's plans to marry Nicky Hilton, and scheduled the release of *Father of the Bride* as a means of taking advantage of the massive publicity which her real-life wedding would generate. As the aging head of MGM, he was about to be replaced by Dore Schary, who told MGM executives that he viewed Elizabeth "as a surefire moneymaker for MGM in the 1950s."

When Elizabeth heard of Mayer's upcoming departure, she said, "I will shed no tears for the disgusting old shithead."

The first day Elizabeth reported to the set of *Father of the Bride,* Schary came out to welcome her and to introduce her to the film's director, Vincente Minnelli, who was married at the time to Judy Garland. The unhappy couple had produced a daughter, Liza.

During the first day of the shoot, Francis dropped by to see his daughter, but ended up spending more time with Minnelli.

"Vincente and Francis really hit it off," Elizabeth later told Dick Hanley.

Elizabeth, however, was genuinely surprised when Francis began showing up on the set every day, not as a means of taking her to lunch, but to spend time, usually alone, with Minnelli in his dressing room.

Elizabeth often ate lunch in the commissary with Dick, who knew everything happening in and around the studio. "What goes here?" she asked her confidant.

"My darling," Dick said. "You're a woman of the world at this point. Francis and Vincente are having an affair. He and Adrian have broken up."

"My father and Minnelli?" she asked in astonishment. "I can't believe that. The man has the head of a lizard. Not only that, but he wears lipstick, probably a tube of it borrowed from Judy."

In later years, Joan Bennett shared her memories of working with Elizabeth. "I was surprised that she was only a teenager, but had taken to downing big highball glasses of Jack Daniels like Frank Sinatra. She seemed very upset about a lot of things."

"Nicky Hilton often visited the set," Bennett said, "and he was nuts. Both Spence and I knew that, but neither of us had the nerve to warn her. Who did? She was hell bent on matrimony at any cost. For her, it was love on the rebound, as Monty had dumped her. Elizabeth didn't have the right equipment between her legs for Monty, if you'll forgive my vulgarity. One day, she offered to introduce Nicky to Spence and me. Spence told her, 'Skip it!'"

Character actor Leo G. Carroll, a cartoonishly serious-looking Brit with an imposing brow, years later, recalled his experience on the film. "Nicky Hilton came by several times, but he seemed hopelessly bored with the making of a film. I had a feeling he wanted to be somewhere else. As for Elizabeth, she was a real princess. Everybody, including Minnelli, catered to her, when he wasn't lusting after her father. The first week, she arrived at MGM in a shiny new black Cadillac, a gift from somebody, probably Conrad Sr. She told me, 'A car is the best mode of escape for a girl who feels that the people around her are smothering her.'"

Schary called her into his office one day and told her that if *Father of the Bride* became the hit he anticipated, he envisioned casting her in a series of newlywed pictures with Don Taylor.

"I hope you don't," she said. "Newlywed pictures sound more like roles for Janet Leigh. Don is a nice guy, but I find him sexless. There is no chemistry between us. I once invited him to my dressing room and changed my dress right in front of him. There I was, stark nude. You know what he did? He turned his head and looked at the fucking door, which I think he wanted to escape through."

Elizabeth's most intriguing visitor on the set was Judy Garland, who on a nearby set was filming *Summer Stock* (1950), the last picture she'd make for MGM before she was fired. At first, Elizabeth was apprehensive, fearing that Garland was going to pick a fight over her husband's romantic liaison with Francis.

Garland carried a flask with her, and appeared tipsy, not drunk. Elizabeth always admired her sharp wit. "Schary told me that Vincente is directing a picture that's a sort of genial jab at the nuptial rites of upper middle class suburbia in America. I also heard somewhere that Mayer wanted it edited into a depiction of a typical American family in that bracket. What a joke!"

"I don't quite understand," Elizabeth said.

"Oh, I'm sure you guys will pull it off brilliantly," Garland said, "but let's hope the American public never discovers what's really going on behind all this happy schmaltziness."

"I'm aware," Garland continued, "that my husband and your father have become the dearest of pals. But there's so much more bubbling away at MGM these days. Take Spence, for example, the man who took my virginity when I was fifteen years old, younger than you. He's a closeted homosexual engaged in a platonic relationship with Hepburn, who's a secret dyke who long ago put the make on me. Your mother-in law in the film, Billie Burke, is another closeted lesbian who, when she was married to Flo Ziegfeld, used to seduce only the most beautiful of showgirls."

Garland continued: "Joan Bennett is an elegant whore. She and Spence first slept together back in 1932, when they made *She Wanted a Millionaire* (1932). She's fucked everybody from Bing Crosby to Errol Flynn. She even fucked John Emery, Tallulah Bankhead's former husband. He's known for having the biggest dick in Hollywood. Bennett gave Myron Selznick—David's brother— blow-jobs, and right now, she's shacked up with Jennings Lang, her agent. And there will be hell to pay if her husband, Walter Wanger, finds out."

[Garland was right about a looming scandal. On December 13, 1951, Wanger did indeed find out, and shot off one of Lang's testicles, for which Wanger received a four-month prison term.]

"What? No scandal about Don Taylor?" Elizabeth asked.

"Not really. Dick Hanley told me that Don is a chronic masturbator, sometimes five times a day. He told Dick that he finds his right hand more satisfying as a sexual outlet than someone else's genitals."

"You left out one of the stars in the picture...namely me," Elizabeth asked, provocatively.

Movie star **Elizabeth Taylor** as a fantasy bride at a fantasy wedding for MGM

"Oh, darling, you are as pure as the drifting snow...emphasis on 'drifting.'"

Tracy later told Bennett, "That Hilton boy will be the first of Elizabeth Taylor's many husbands. I suspect she's the marrying kind."

On the final day of the shoot, Elizabeth told Tracy that, "Every time I walked down the aisle to the altar with you, I was living it. It was like I was rehearsing for my own upcoming marriage. Nicky is going to treat me like an angel and make love to me morning, noon, and night."

"Sounds tiring to me," Tracy quipped. "Never be too romantic, or too unrealistic entering into marriage, or into any relationship for that matter. Remember, someone else, not you, is writing the script."

Oscar night—March 29, 1951—was celebrated at the RKO Pantages Theater in Los Angeles. *Father of the Bride* had been nominated for Best Picture, Best Screenplay and, for the performance of Spencer Tracy, Best Actor.

The film, however, produced no winners, and at least one very sore loser. "That fucking Academy didn't nominate me, and I was the one who made that god damn movie," Elizabeth said.

One reviewer interpreted *Father of the Bride* as "a 1940s comedy released in a humorless decade, the 1950s."

Right before Christmas of 1949, Nicky was ordered by his father, Conrad Sr., to attend a business conference in Houston, Texas. He didn't want to go, but his father insisted. He would return in time for Christmas, which the Hilton family planned to celebrate with the Taylors.

Monty Clift had flown into Los Angeles to discuss a movie deal, and he invited Elizabeth to a party hosted by the author, Norman Mailer. Mailer was celebrating the upcoming cinematic adaptation of his bestseller, *The Naked and the Dead*, originally published in 1948 when the author was twenty-five years old, about the physical and emotional carnage of World War II. Monty was considering starring in the movie version of the novel, which would focus on a screenplay by Lillian Hellman.

Monty suggested that they double date with Shelley Winters and Marlon Brando, and that they arrive at the party as a foursome. Elizabeth agreed, as she was eager to meet Marlon.

In her memoirs, Shelley Winters provided only a limited hangout, not revealing too many of the details associated with that party. But she was on target when she wrote: "Norman invited *everybody* in Hollywood, both left and right, and you didn't do that in 1949. Adolphe Menjou was there, snubbing Charlie Chaplin. Bogart was giving Ginger Rogers the fish eye. Monty, Elizabeth, and Marlon were very uncomfortable."

Elizabeth had absolutely no interest in politics, but she was thrilled to be hanging out with the Hollywood elite, feeling very grown up. She was introduced to such stellar members of the A-list as directors Cecil B. De Mille and John Ford, along with composer Leonard Bernstein. She and Judy Garland had a "kiss-kiss" moment together.

Elizabeth was also introduced to actor Larry Parks, with whom she would soon star in a film. At the time, she didn't know that J. Edgar Hoover was investigating him for alleged communist activities. She spoke briefly with Gene Kelly and his wife, Betsy Blair. Monty's friend, Kevin McCarthy, gave Elizabeth a wet kiss on the mouth.

As proof of her new status as an adult, Elizabeth later claimed, "I was hit upon by several big names, most of whom were drunk."

A drunken Bogie accosted her and said, "Hey kid, when are we going to make a movie together? I'm looking forward to our love scenes. The trouble with you, kid, is that you've never been properly fucked." She moved quickly away from him, only to run into another left-winger, actor John Garfield. He told her that "Jewish dick is the best and the biggest" if she wanted to sample it.

Marlon said to her that the only reason he'd come to the party was to meet Charlie Chaplin. At the star-studded event, Marlon and Chaplin talked for an intense half hour. Regrettably, Marlon got more than he wished for when Chaplin directed him in the disastrous *A Countess from Hong Kong,* co-starring Sophia Loren, in 1967.

Marlon brought Chaplin over to meet Elizabeth, and she had a few minutes alone with him, finding him a braggart.

She later told Marlon, "I found Chaplin disgusting and a bore. I know he's famous for his love of teenage girls, but he insulted me. He told me he's good for at least six bouts a night, and he also claimed that he has a foot-long penis, which he refers to as the 'eighth wonder of the world.'"

"Did you make a date with him to sample it?" Marlon facetiously asked.

"Not bloody likely," she answered.

In one of the bathrooms, one which had been exclusively designated that evening as a ladies' powder room, Elizabeth encountered Shelley and told her about her meeting "with the great Charlie Chaplin."

"Been there, done that," Shelley said. "As you know, I had this torrid affair with Sidney Chaplin. During that time, I also managed to accommodate both Charlie Sr. and Charles Chaplin, Jr. In other words, I fucked all three of them. So did my former roommate, Marilyn Monroe."

"Monroe must make the rounds nightly," Elizabeth said sarcastically.

"She sure does," said Shelley. "One drunken night at our apartment, she even fucked me."

"I'm sure she'll eventually get around to fucking me, too," Elizabeth said, little knowing the degree to which her words were prophetic. "From the way I see it, Monroe is working her way through every listing in the *Player's Directory,* the *Screen Directors Guide,* and the *Producers Guild Book.*"

When Shelley learned that Elizabeth had not met the host of the party—Norman Mailer—she ushered her over to chat with him. Shelley said that she was very grateful to Mailer, who had intervened with George Stevens to get her the role of Alice Tripp in their movie, *A Place in the Sun.* "I returned the favor to Norman and let him fuck me."

Except for Marlon and the host himself, everyone was well dressed at the party. Mailer looked disheveled, wearing a casual print shirt and slacks with socks that nestled down around his ankles. His first words to Elizabeth were, "Welcome to the ugliest city in the world."

As Shelley wandered off to pursue John Garfield, Mailer spoke to Elizabeth about their joint friend, Monty. "I love your boyfriend," he said. "He's a very sensitive artist, not our typical fucked-up movie star. He's not cocky, he's not self-centered, and he plays it low key. He's like one of us, not some thimble brain movie star cashing in on his looks. The trouble with Hollywood is that there are too many god damn movie stars out here."

Mailer went on to assert that "Hollywood is all wrong for Monty. It brings out all sorts of fear and guilt in him about who he is. He should be back in New York."

Then the author went over to a fruit bowl and handed Elizabeth a big fat banana. "Put this in your bloomers to protect yourself."

She looked astonished. "What in the hell for?"

"Fredric March over there is drunk and going around feeling up the young women," he said. "When he reaches between your legs and feels that banana, he'll think you're a man in drag."

On the night of the party, Mailer was living with the French writer, Jean Malaquais, and they were working on a script together, *Lonelyhearts,* for Samuel Goldwyn. All three of them wanted Monty to play the lead in this script based loosely on Nathanael West's novel of the same name. Ultimately, Goldwyn would reject their script, defining it as "un-American."

In 1958, Monty would star in a much different and much weaker film called *Lonelyhearts*, also loosely based on West's novel. Dore Schary wrote the screenplay.

At one point, Shelley approached Elizabeth in panic. "You've got to help me. Burt Lancaster is just arriving, and he's threatened to beat the shit out of me if he ever catches me with Marlon. I'm leaving with him now to avoid bloodshed."

"What shall I tell Marlon?" Elizabeth asked.

"Oh, tell him I've gone to have a miscarriage. *Anything.*"

Shelley hurried off, having stridently informed Lancaster that she needed to be driven to another party immediately. In her haste, she grabbed Elizabeth's beaver coat.

Later, Elizabeth made excuses to Marlon, who agreed to drive Monty and Elizabeth back to their respective homes. Throwing a fit when she discovered that someone had stolen her coat, Elizabeth stood in the pouring rain with Monty while Marlon fumbled, trying to find his keys. By the time he located them, all three of them were dripping wet.

Marlon invited them to his home, where he lit the logs in his fireplace and went to find robes for them until their clothes were dry.

The next day, Shelley called, wanting to find out what happened. Elizabeth explained that someone had stolen her coat and that she'd become soaked, and later caught a cold. "At Marlon's, we pulled off our clothes to dry, and one thing led to another," Elizabeth said.

"What in hell does that mean?" Shelley asked.

"If you must know, we had a three-way," Elizabeth said.

"I can believe that Marlon would fuck anything that moves, but I find it hard to believe that you got plowed by Monty," Shelley said.

"Actually, as it turned out, Marlon fucked both Monty and me," Elizabeth said.

"I don't know if you're making up this story just to upset me...or what."

"Every word is true," Elizabeth said.

Two weeks later, a photo of Shelley was taken as she was being escorted to a movie premiere by actor John Ireland. She was wearing Elizabeth's beaver coat.

***

For the Christmas holidays of 1949, Conrad Hilton, Sr., invited Elizabeth, Sara, and Francis to a hotel he'd recently purchased on Lake Arrowhead.

On Christmas Eve, the Hiltons and the Taylors opened their presents, Elizabeth discovering that Nicky had given her a super expensive set of diamond earrings with dangling white pearls.

On Christmas Day in the hotel's library, Nicky asked Francis for permission to marry Elizabeth, who was still seventeen and had not yet finished high school.

"I'd be delighted if you took Elizabeth as your bride," Francis said. "You can give her so many things."

Elizabeth spent the rest of the night alone with Nicky, who used the occasion to propose marriage to her. She accepted, but cautiously, agreeing to his proposal only after he'd promised to let her continue with her film career.

Nicky was Roman Catholic, and he wanted Elizabeth, even though she had little enthusiasm for it, to join the Catholic church. She did agree to sign a document that she would rear any of their children in the Catholic faith. She also had to sign a document that she would never practice birth control or get a divorce.

Francis wanted his daughter to have a high school diploma, but MGM's little red schoolhouse was not legally qualified to provide one. Howard Strickling, head of MGM publicity, solved the problem by making an arrangement with Los Angeles University High School, where Debbie Reynolds, Elizabeth's future rival in love, was already enrolled as a *bona fide* pupil.

Elizabeth would be allowed to wear a cap and gown and join in the graduation ceremony, thereby receiving a diploma, even though she'd never attended the school.

Dozens of students who had legitimately earned their diplomas crowded around her, asking for her autograph.

Conrad Hilton, Sr., jumped the gun and telephoned Louella Parsons with news of his favorite son's engagement to Elizabeth. The next morning, the entire world seemingly was aware of the news. Because of the worldwide publicity, Conrad Sr. noted a massive increase in bookings throughout the Hilton Hotel chain.

News of Elizabeth's engagement to Nicky soon became the hottest topic of gossip in Hollywood. In her column, Hedda Hopper openly speculated that Elizabeth might not follow through with her plans to marry Nicky. Because she had run out on both Glenn Davis and William Pawley, Hopper had labeled her "Liz the Jilt."

When she next appeared in public, Elizabeth was wearing a five-karat diamond engagement ring.

Her bridal shower was staged by members of the S.L.O.B club, the initials standing for "Single Lonely Obliging Babes." Partly as a publicity device, Elizabeth and Betty Sullivan had established this Hollywood Club for bachelor girls. Betty was the daughter of the famous New York columnist Ed Sullivan, "Mr. Show Business."

Elizabeth officially resigned from her position as the club's president that day because she was on the verge of losing her status as a "single, lonely, and obliging babe." After the shower, she asserted, "I got a hell of a lot of loot."

Before her wedding, she put through a final desperate appeal to Monty. "Will you come and see me after I return from my honeymoon?"

"Somehow, Bessie Mae, I don't think dear Nicky Hilton is my kind of guy. I'll not be calling on the newlyweds."

After a mediocre education, the high school graduate is congratulated by her mother, **Sara.**

"But you promised me that we'd always be friends, that you'd always stand by me regardless of what happened to me," she protested.

He gently put down the phone.

Fifteen MGM seamstresses had worked for two months making Elizabeth's high-necked satin wedding gown, a design by Helen Rose. Like Snow White, she was dazzling. "Her wedding gown didn't show half as much tit as did Princess Elizabeth when she married Prince Philip," Rose claimed.

The gown was decorated with seed pearls and lilies of the valley, with a tight cinch waist to emphasize her slimness.

The bridesmaids wore organdy gowns in

tones of buttercup yellow. In celebration of the season (springtime) they carried clusters of yellow tulips and daffodils.

For her *trousseau*, famed couturier Ceil Chapman had called, volunteering his services and creating a chic wardrobe for her upcoming travels on the Continent.

Acquaintances of Elizabeth, many of whom were not included on the guest list, called Elizabeth and pleaded with her to let them come to her wedding. She agreed to their requests, until she ran out of seating. Patricia Neal called and begged for an invitation. "Okay," Elizabeth told her, "but you must bring a present—and don't be stingy, baby."

Arriving daily at the Taylor household was what Sara defined as "a queen's ransom" that included a staggering array of blue Wedgwood china, Swedish crystal, Wallace sterling silver flatware, and initialed Italian linens (only in pink).

Francis presented his daughter with a Frans Hal painting—the one he had famously acquired between the wars at a flea market in London—and a "Breath of Spring" mink coat. Sara gave her a white mink stole paid for by MGM.

Uncle Howard Young sent a $65,000 pearl ring from New York. To make room for the armada of gifts that had flooded in, Sara was forced to move the furniture out of her living room and even stuff the bedrooms with overflow bounty. It included a forty-five piece sterling silver service from the Gorham Silver Company.

There is a line in *Father of the Bride* when Spencer Tracy tells Elizabeth, who's interpreting the role of his daughter, "You look wonderful, kitten, just like a princess in a fairy tale."

She remembered that line. On her real wedding day, she said, "That is exactly how I felt, a real princess in a fairy tale. I just knew, like Cinderella marrying Prince Charming, that Nicky and I would live happily ever after."

One hour before Elizabeth was scheduled to depart for the church, her doorbell rang. Sara answered it herself, thinking it was another messenger with wedding gifts. She faced an angry William Pawley, Jr., who barged into the house without an invitation. Sara didn't feel she could constrain him.

He headed straight for Elizabeth's bedroom, where he confronted her behind closed doors for about fifteen minutes. Sara heard Elizabeth shouting at him, but dared not enter the room.

When Pawley came storming out, she stood silently by until he'd let himself out. Then she rushed to Elizabeth's bedroom, finding her daughter in tears. "What did he want? Or say?"

"It's none of your god damn business," Elizabeth told her mother. "Now let me get on with this fucking wedding."

Among the onlookers gathered at the church, an alert photographer managed to snap a picture of an angry Pawley among Elizabeth's adoring fans.

The ceremony was held at the Catholic Church of the Good Shepherd in Beverly Hills.

The wedding was scheduled for the afternoon of May 6, 1950. Flanked by a police escort blasting their sirens, she was driven to the church in an MGM limousine. On a bizarre note, an odd choice back in 1950, she demanded that the driver wear a pink uniform.

Some 5,000 fans, the largest gathering in Hollywood since the funeral of Jean Harlow way back in 1937, turned out in the stifling heat, the thermometer registering 104°F. The police and MGM security guards tried to control the mob. There was a fear that after the wedding, the fans would break through the barriers and rip Elizabeth's wedding dress to shreds so they could retain a souvenir of the event.

MGM boasted "more stars than there are in heaven," and many of the biggest names turned up for Elizabeth's wedding. Greta Garbo, the former queen of MGM, a figure who had made her last movie in 1941, was invited too, but she cabled her regrets: "I do not believe in marriage."

A fleet of black limousines carried the MGM hierarchy. They had been more or less commanded by Louis B. Mayer to attend, even if they didn't like Elizabeth. In a touch of press agent irony, honored guests included Spencer Tracy, her screen father, and Joan Bennett, her screen mother, sitting with her real parents, Sara and Francis. Bennett, one local wag observed, seemed almost to be competing with Sara for photo ops.

William Powell summed up the attitude of many MGM stars. "I didn't particularly like Elizabeth Taylor. But Mayer told me to get my ass over there." Mickey Rooney showed up, bragging, "I've already had her.' Whether he had or not is still a matter of some dispute.

Stars came dressed in their finery, including Janet Leigh, Greer Garson, Ginger Rogers, Esther Williams, Walter Pidgeon, Ricardo Montalban, Red Skelton, Peter Lawford, Zsa Zsa Gabor, Margaret O'Brien, Roddy McDowall, Phil Harris, Debbie Reynolds, Gene Kelly, Gloria DeHaven, Fred Astaire, Van Johnson, Arthur Loew, Jr., Rosalind Russell, and Terry Moore, who would later have an affair with Nicky Hilton. Of course, columnists Hedda Hopper, Louella Parsons, and Sheilah Graham were there, too.

Mayer, who detested Elizabeth, occupied the most central and visible pew in the church, dabbing at his eyes with a red silk handkerchief. Upon entering the church, he'd told the press, "I feel I'm losing a daughter."

Mara Reagan also showed up. She would soon marry Howard Taylor, Elizabeth's beautiful brother, which caused sadness among Roddy's homosexual friends, who had hoped that he would join their colony.

After Monsignor Patrick Concannon pronounced Nicky and Elizabeth husband and wife, "Nicky gave the bride the longest kiss in recorded history," according to Ann Miller, who showed up as the "date" of Conrad Hilton, Sr. After the kiss continued to embarrassing lengths, the monsignor intervened, warning the couple to "save it for later."

The wedding ceremony took just twenty minutes. When it was over, Elizabeth's name was changed to Mrs. Conrad Hilton, Jr. "He is my darling," she later told the press. "I shall love no other until my dying day."

After the wedding ceremony, Elizabeth and Nicky stood in the doorway of the church, posing for pictures. She begged Nicky "to kiss me once more." That kiss, too, went on for such a prolonged time that Francis eventually interrupted with the quip, "Get a room, kids."

MGM paid for the lavish reception at the Bel Air Hotel, where Sara noted in horror that her daughter could hardly stop kissing Nicky to shake the hands of some six-hundred guests.

The governor of California, Earl Warren, showed up at the reception to kiss the bride. He was later appointed as Chief Justice of the U.S. Supreme Court.

At the reception, it took Elizabeth and her new husband almost four and a half hours to shake the hands of all their guests. Elizabeth soon tired of "all that kiss-the-bride shit." Nicky was clearly bored.

As she got into a limousine for the northbound trek toward her wedding night, she whispered to Sara, "Oh, Mother, Nick and I are one now…for ever and ever."

On the way to their honeymoon night, Elizabeth snuggled up to Nicky in the back seat of an MGM limousine. "We no longer have to slip around when you want to fuck me. After our so-called 'wedding of weddings,' we're legal now. I'm no longer your bitch, but your wife."

He sat solemnly in his seat, staring at the coastal road ahead. As she'd later confide to friends, "I got the feeling that Nicky was sorry he'd married me."

A lavish suite filled with flowers had been selected for their honeymoon in a Hilton-affiliated resort on Pebble Beach on California's Monterey Peninsula, near Carmel. Before arriving at the resort, Elizabeth told Nicky, "I know that some people call me the most beautiful woman in the world. But they need to change that title. Because of you, I am the happiest woman in the world."

***

The honeymoon was a disaster, hitting Elizabeth like a bolt of lightning and forcing her into a new reality about her husband.

It began when a bellhop referred to Nicky as "Mr. Taylor." Nicky slapped the young man, but later gave the manager a hundred dollar bill to give to the bellhop with an apology for his violence.

In the back of the limousine during the ride to Carmel, he'd been drinking heavily and was already drunk upon his arrival.

After dinner, Elizabeth retired to the bridal suite, which for some reason contained three bedrooms. She dressed in her specially designed *négligée,* and waited and waited for Nicky's return. She spent most of the night sitting alone on the terrace that overlooked the Pacific. She went to bed at 2am and fell asleep.

Sometime around four in the morning, Nicky came back into the suite and woke her up. She'd never seen him so drunk. He looked half dressed, having come from a room he'd rented for himself and two hookers whom he had patronized before during one of his previous visits to the hotel. Perhaps the prostitutes wondered why he was seducing them on his honeymoon night, in the immediate wake of his widely publicized marriage to "the world's most beautiful woman."

Nicky and Elizabeth indulged in their first of many fights. Finally, he told her to "go to hell" and retreated into one of the suite's bedrooms, where he slept until noon.

When he awakened, showered, and dressed, he went down to the lobby, where he found Elizabeth making purchases in the overpriced, on-site boutiques and charging the expenses to their room.

He apologized for his behavior the previous night, and she forgave him, telling him that she understood that he had "the jitters."

That night, the resort's chef prepared a special seven-course celebratory banquet for them. Nicky drank more than he ate, and Elizabeth had little appetite. Like he'd done the previous night, Nicky did not return to the bridal suite until dawn. He was in a particularly foul mood because he'd lost $100,000 the previous evening when he'd been driven to a private residence where an illegal gambling casino was operated by the mob.

When she confronted him and started making accusations, he struck her, sending her sprawling onto the floor. As she sobbed, he retreated into one of the bedrooms.

Zsa Zsa Gabor, who was still Nicky's lover, later said, "He was truly his father's son. Connie pursued the most glamorous women on the planet, including *moi,* but he had no talent for actually living with them once he'd won them over."

Once again, on the morning of the third day of his marriage, Nicky apologized for his behavior, and once again she forgave him. Earlier that morning, she'd called Sara, asking her if she should leave Nicky. "Do so and you'll be mocked and ridiculed in the press. You've made your bed. Now sleep in it. I've made my own marriage work, in spite of the fact that I married a homosexual."

"Over lunch that afternoon, Nicky told her that when he drank, his mood shifted, and he was filled with rage and anger. She pleaded with him to give up drinking. "Without that crutch, I couldn't get through life," he confessed.

That night, after dinner and after three more bottles of champagne in the bar, he returned with her to the bridal suite.

He was no longer the skilled seducer he'd been before. As Elizabeth's biographer, Alexander Walker, put it, "He didn't waste time letting girls know what he wanted, and how. He'd already been involved in one unpleasant episode with the daughter of a family friend, which had been hushed up."

Walker must have been referring to a weekend in Palm Springs when Hilton had brutally sodomized a seventeen-year-old and sent her to the hospital for stitches. His father, Conrad Sr., paid off the girl's family with a $10,000 check, and the episode was hushed up.

Even to her closest confidants, Elizabeth relayed very little of what happened during her three-night honeymoon in Carmel. She did admit to Dick Hanley that "Nicky wanted me to perform unspeakable acts on him. He told me that when he goes to bed with a woman, he is not satisfied until he has plugged all three holes. His idea of passion involves spitting into a woman's mouth—disgusting, revolting. Before our marriage, he had been such a gentle, considerate lover. On my honeymoon, I learned that I had married Mr. Hyde."

Dick later said, "During that time in Carmel, Nicky and Elizabeth realized for the first time that they lived in completely different worlds. He had no interest in the movie business, and she had even less interest in the hotel business. They didn't really have anything to talk about. He was a playboy used to his freedom. He liked variety in his sex life with young men and young women. He often said he liked sexual partners 'who will do anything I ask.' He didn't want to feel owned by any woman. 'I want to be as free as a bird ready to take flight at any minute,' he told me."

"Nicky viewed a movie contract as tantamount to slavery. Both he and Elizabeth were spoiled brats. They'd been catered to all their lives. Elizabeth's world had always revolved around her, her wants and her needs. From the day he was born, Connie Hilton had given his son anything he wanted—the world's most expensive hookers, an airplane, a new Cadillac every time he wanted one, and a banker who always paid off his gambling debts."

Back in Los Angeles for Mother's Day, Elizabeth told Sara, "All the world knows Elizabeth Taylor as movie star, not Elizabeth Taylor, housewife. It's a role I can't play."

"You'd better learn," Sara told her. "When you get back from your honeymoon, Mayer wants you to play an expectant mother in *Father's Little Dividend,* the sequel to *Father of the Bride.* Tracy and Bennett will be your parents again, Don Taylor your husband."

"The idea sounds like a crock of shit to me!" Elizabeth said.

***

From Los Angeles, the newlyweds journeyed to New York via Chicago, to sail on the *Queen Mary* from the Port of New York for a three-month holiday in Europe, paid for by Conrad, Sr.

In New York, Elizabeth registered at the Waldorf-Astoria, a Hilton-owned property since 1949, as Nicky was called into the manager's office for an emergency call of some sort from Conrad, Sr. Of course, he treated the hotel like his New York home, which it was.

The desk clerk handed her an envelope from Conrad Sr., containing some shares of Waldorf-Astoria stock. "You're part owner now," he wrote on a card. "So feel perfectly at home here."

She later bragged to friends, "In New York, I stayed at *my* hotel, the Waldorf."

The presidential suite was glorious and filled with flowers. Before dinner, Nicky attacked her. He preferred his sexual encounters with his wife to be tantamount to rape. As Elizabeth later told Janet Leigh, "If Nicky doesn't cause you pain and make you scream, then he feels he's failed as a man."

After she cleaned up and made herself presentable after a bubble bath, Nicky informed her that they were having dinner at the hotel with his best friend, the Texas oil magnate Glen McCarthy. Ironically, the James Dean character in *Giant,* a movie that loomed in Elizabeth's future, would be based on McCarthy.

Over dinner, Elizabeth found the Texan *gauche,* especially when he'd had a lot to drink. Like her husband, McCarthy was a racist, denouncing "niggers." He also was virulently anti-Semitic. Yet when he went to the toilet, Nicky told her that he often took Jewish or black women as his mistresses, although he abused them horribly, and, in some cases, sent them to the hospital.

At the end of the meal, McCarthy announced that he was going "on a rampage to find me the hottest poontang in New York City." He invited Nicky to accompany him, and Nicky accepted, leaving Elizabeth alone at the dining table.

She ordered another bottle of champagne, and sat there drinking it alone until she was approached by the hotel manager.

"Mrs. Hilton," he said, "I hate to intrude on your privacy. But Mr. Hoover has heard that you and Mr. Hilton are on your honeymoon at the hotel, and he wishes that you'd drop by his suite for a celebratory drink."

"You must be talking about Herbert Hoover, since J. Edgar Hoover is not the marrying kind," she said.

"Exactly," he told her.

"I'm free now, if you'd like to escort me to his suite, she said. "Regrettably, Mr. Hilton is engaged in a business conference tonight."

The next morning, very early, Elizabeth, from the Waldorf, awakened Sara in Beverly Hills. Nicky had returned to the suite at around 7am, and he was in the suite's second bedroom, sleeping it off.

She told Sara that she had spent the first night of her honeymoon in New York alone "except I stayed up until midnight talking with Herbert Hoover. He seemed pleasant enough for an old goat, and he feels he should not be blamed for the Great Depression. He also told me he misses his wife, who died five years ago."

"What did you say to him?" Sara asked.

"I advised him to get a new wife, one who's a bit younger and healthier."

"I'm sure he appreciated that, dear. Very sound advice."

"I told him that I had just gotten married and already my husband was running out at night," Elizabeth said.

"What sort of presidential advice did he give you to handle a situation like that?"

I think President Hoover blamed me for Nicky's straying. He told me, 'When a man strays, it's usually because he's not getting what he needs in the boudoir.'"

***

Elizabeth brought so many steamer trunks aboard *The Queen Mary* that Nicky complained bitterly about paying the freight surcharges. Even though he was a rich man who ran up enormous gambling debts, he could be very stingy with money, especially when it had to do with Elizabeth's vast wardrobe.

"You'll also be buying out every fashion house in Paris, so why in the fuck do you need all these clothes with you?"

He became even more enraged when he learned that he and his new bride would not be occupying the ocean liner's bridal suite. It has been presented *gratis* by Cunard to the Duke and Duchess of Windsor, as part of Cunard's life-long commitment to the ex-Royals for free travel aboard any Cunard ocean liner.

In the Hilton's suite, an invitation was waiting for the following night from the Duke and Duchess, who wanted to have dinner with them. Nicky seemed to have little interest in the royal couple, but Elizabeth, partly because of her English heritage, was awed by the invitation, and could not wait to relay details of the evening to Francis and Sara.

Elizabeth didn't know at the time that the Duchess was impressed with anyone rich and famous, regardless of their pedigree.

She was dazzled by Wallis' jewelry—so awed, in fact, that she would, decades later, at the estate sale of the jewelry that had belonged to the (by then deceased) Duchess, pay $577,000 for a diamond-and-platinum brooch patterned in the shape of the "Prince of Wales feather." For that piece of jewelry, Elizabeth would outbid Prince Charles.

Both the Duke and Duchess were pillars of fashion, always attired immaculately in the latest *haute* styles. Elizabeth hoped that the former king would relay some pointers about dress to her new husband, partly because Nicky preferred ties adorned with illustrations, including some patterned with bathing beauties.

Elizabeth had not fully developed her own sense of fashion yet. She and the Duchess talked about jewelry and Paris *couture*, while Nicky seemed bored and the Duke actually fell asleep at table before the end of the dinner.

The following day, Elizabeth and the Duchess bonded again in the play room, discovering that they both had a fondness for canasta. They met every day of the transatlantic crossing for card games, while the Duke preferred to play bridge in another area of the ship.

During the late afternoon, the Duke and Nicky often went together to the ship's steam room, reserving it just for themselves. One night, shortly before dinner, Nicky returned to the quarters he shared with Elizabeth and said, "Guess what? The Duke of Windsor gave me a fabulous blow-job in the steam room. Forget all that press shit about the love affair of the century. He's a fucking cocksucker, one of the best, and I should know. A real sword-swallower."

"You allowed him to do that to you?"

"Hell, yes!" he said. "What was I supposed to do? Turn him down? After all, he was once the King of England and the Emperor of India."

Later that night, Nicky staggered to the casino after drinking far too much at dinner. Once again, he dropped $100,000, the same amount he'd lost at that mob-operated gambling house in Carmel.

Returning to their suite at four o'clock the following morning, he woke Elizabeth up primarily to fight with her. By dawn, she was seen wandering the decks of the *Queen Mary* alone. He'd beaten her very badly, taking out his rage at losing all that money on gambling.

During her first day out in the sun aboard ship, when Elizabeth appeared in her play clothes, revealing a lot of skin, Nicky was heard yelling at her, "Hey, monkey, come over here."

WELCOME TO HELL
Wallis Warfield Simpson
(The Duchess of Windsor)
and the former King Edward VIII
(aka, **Edward, the Duke of Windsor**)

The hypertrichosis of her childhood had reappeared. She tried to seek a treatment within the *Queen Mary's* beauty salon, complaining, "My husband calls me 'The Hairy Ape.'"

The steward noted how Nicky bossed her around. "Go find me a waiter and tell him to bring me a drink." Or else he'd tell her loudly, "C'mon, hon, we're going to watch a Robert Mitchum movie."

She'd shout back at him, "I've seen *Holiday Affair* twice—and that's enough."

A staff member reported that Nicky then grabbed her and pushed her against a bulkhead. "Listen, bitch, you'll do what I say or else I'll smash your face in. Take your fucking choice."

During the long voyage, a lifelong friendship was formed between the Duchess and Elizabeth. Partly because of her lesbian streak, the Duchess was powerfully attracted to the beautiful young star, although Elizabeth shocked her by wearing blue jeans during the day. In 1950, that apparel had not yet become fashionable.

Also sailing to Europe aboard the *Queen Mary* was Elsa Maxwell, who informed the Duchess, "I've got to meet the Hiltons, have dinner with them, and get to know them."

The Duchess agreed to set up an onboard dinner for their final night afloat, but warned, "They act like a couple at the end of a marriage instead of a young man and wife on a honeymoon. But they're rich and important."

Maxwell, at mid-century, was known as "The Hostess with the Mostest." As she said of herself, "Not bad for a short, fat, homely piano player from Keokuk, Iowa, with no money or background." She was traveling aboard the *Queen Mary* with her longtime lover, the Scottish socialite and singer, Dorothy Fellowes-Gordon, whom Maxwell lovingly referred to as "Dickie."

The hostess organized parties for prominent social figures. She was also a sort of international pimp, introducing A-list men to celebrated women. She claimed that she had introduced Prince Aly Khan to movie goddess Rita Hayworth and Aristotle Onassis to opera diva Maria Callas.

At dinner that night, Maxwell dominated the evening, delivering one *bon mot* after another. "Someone said that life is a party. You join in after it's started, and leave before it's finished." She also said, "Under pressure, people admit to murder, setting fire to the village church, or robbing a bank, but never to being a bore."

Was she talking about both Nicky and the Duke of Windsor?

Back in their suite, Nicky told Elizabeth that he found the evening disgusting. "There you were sitting between the two most internationally famous dykes in the world—the Duchess of Windsor and Elsa Maxwell."

Before disembarking from the *Queen Mary,* Maxwell promised Elizabeth and Nicky that she would throw a lavish party for them at Maxim's in Paris. She didn't plan to pay for it herself, but would charge the guests $1,000 per couple to enter.

"I know everybody in Paris, my dear," Maxwell said to Elizabeth. "Who would you like to attend your party?"

Put on the spot, Elizabeth could think of only one French personality. She blurted out, "Maurice Chevalier."

"A dear old friend," Maxwell said. "Of course, he'll be there along with everybody else worth knowing. If they are not at your party, that means they are not important and aren't worth your time."

Most Parisians saw Nicky Hilton's picture for the first time when he checked into the swanky George V, where photographers had been waiting for his arrival with Elizabeth.

Paris Match wrote, "He was chewing a large wad of gum, how very American, and he spoke in monosyllabic tones. He is the heir to a vast fortune but wore an ill-fitting suit, far too baggy. He also has the smile of a ferret."

In their suite at the George V, Nicky told Elizabeth that he was going downstairs to the bar to have a drink. The hotel bar was known for attracting the most expensive prostitutes in Europe at the time. He didn't return to the suite until five o'clock that morning. A violent argument ensued in which she called him a "whoremonger," for which she was severely beaten.

Both Elizabeth and Nicky pulled themselves together to be the guests of honor at Elsa Maxwell's gala staged for them at Maxim's. As the press noted, Elizabeth had never looked lovelier than in a spectacularly stylish gown designed for the occasion by Christian Dior.

In addition to celebrities, Maxwell rounded up a gaggle of mostly deposed

Professional Hostess to the postwar glitterati: **Elsa Maxwell**

aristocracy of the lost kingdoms of Europe, including counts and their countesses, dukes and their duchesses, some ex-kings, and several couples who had attached a Marquis or a Marquise in front of their names.

Among the latter were included Henri and Emmita de la Falaise (a.k.a. Le Marquis et La Marquise de La Coudraye). In the 1930s, he had been married to screen vamp Gloria Swanson. He invited Nicky and Elizabeth to lunch and to attend the *Prix de Paris* horse races with them in the Paris suburb of Longchamps.

Nicky accepted for them. Before she'd leave Paris, the Marquis would place a personal call to Elizabeth, telling her that if she ever decided to divorce Nicky, that he could arrange for her to marry a titled "*personage*," for a fee, of course.

Maxwell's self-anointed duties that evening involved presenting Nicky and Elizabeth to the VIP guests, although they didn't understand why their first introduction was to a rather dull-looking man who seemed as if he might fit the role of an insurance salesman to chicken farmers in the hinterlands of central France. Vincent Auriol stood before them, chatting, asking Nicky if Conrad Sr. planned to open Hilton hotels in Paris and in Cannes.

Nicky was noncommittal, uttering a "maybe." Then he excused himself to go to the bar, and Auriol spoke for another ten minutes to Elizabeth, who signaled Maxwell to come and rescue her. When Auriol had departed, Elizabeth asked Maxwell, "Who in hell was that? An out-of-work actor looking for character roles?"

"Vince, my dear, is the President of the Fourth French Republic. He's a socialist, and I don't care much for that type, but he called me and asked me to invite him. You don't want to turn down a request from the President of France."

"Oh, I see," she said. "He's the equivalent of our President Truman."

"Exactly," Maxwell said. "But I did receive another call about you. It was from Mohammed V, the Sultan (later, King) of Morocco. He is willing to deposit five million dollars in gold bars in a bank of your choice in Zurich if you will divorce Nicky and marry him."

"I'll get back to you on that," Elizabeth said. "Howard Hughes, the cheap bastard, offered me only one million dollars."

For Elizabeth, the star attraction of the party became Gérard Philipe, a devastatingly handsome French actor. As he was being escorted by Maxwell to meet her, Elizabeth whispered to the Duchess of Windsor. "I'd give up Nicky for that one. He's gorgeous."

In accented English, Philipe murmured pleasantries and kissed Elizabeth's hand, and then said, "It is true. You are the world's most beautiful woman."

"Where have you been hiding all my life?" she asked him. "You are, without a doubt, the world's most beautiful man."

"I fear film critics usually reserve that title for my rival, Louis Jourdan," he said.

"I hope that in the future, I can make films with you—and not with Jourdan," she said.

[Ironically, she would one day, with Richard Burton, make *The V.I.P.s* (1963) with Jourdan. Regrettably, like Marilyn Monroe, Philipe was slated to die at the age of thirty-six.]

At long last, Elizabeth met Maurice Chevalier, the only guest she'd made a point, specifically, to invite. The veteran French showman spoke with her for about fifteen minutes, whispering to her: "Marlene Dietrich, whom I adore, is always spreading this rumor that I'm impotent. But since you wanted to meet me, I'd like to arrange a rendezvous at my apartment to prove to you that her mischievous lie is not true."

Before Elizabeth could bow out from that proposal, she faced the legendary French cabaret and film entertainer, Mistinguett, who planted a long, wet kiss on Chevalier's lips. Chevalier then introduced Mistinguett to Elizabeth, who—despite the fact that Mistinguett was a legend throughout the French-speaking world—had never before heard of her.

"Mistinguett and I have been appearing together since 1919, making love on and off the stage, and watching the sun rise over the Seine on many a morning," said Chevalier.

Mistinguett kissed Elizabeth on both cheeks and said that Maxwell had asked her to mount the stage at Maxim's in about thirty minutes and sing her signature *"Mon Homme."*

She fulfilled her promise. The moment she went on stage, an almost reverent hush fell over the chattering guests. Mistinguett, as always, gave a beautiful rendition of her ode to undying love: *"Sur cette terre, ma seule joie, mon seul bonheur."*

From his position beside Elizabeth, Chevalier translated the words, whispering in her ear: "On earth, my only joy and happiness, is my man."

During the song, a very short woman in a simple black dress approached and stood beside Elizabeth. When Mistinguett finished her number, the woman stood on her tiptoes and whispered, "I could have sung it better than that bitch." When the lights brightened, Elizabeth recognized her as Edith Piaf, one of the genuinely famous singers, internationally, of the postwar era.

Then an overfed Orson Welles came up to Elizabeth and gave her a lustful

The overdressed
French cabaret entertainer
Mistinguett

kiss before introducing her to the Maharajah of Kapurthala. Then Welles spun around and brought the French author and artist, Jean Cocteau, into her presence. This was the first time she'd ever seen a man wear a black cape lined with chartreuse-colored silk.

Elizabeth was not aware of Cocteau's reputation, but was amazed at his appearance, a fakir-thin body with legs so willowy they evoked broomsticks. He extended a frail hand that looked as if it would be crushed if squeezed too tightly. She would later tell Maxwell, "He had a certain fish-eyed look and the saddest eyes I have ever seen."

You and I, *ma chère,* are going to spend eternity together," Cocteau told her. "I don't think I understand," she said.

"You see, we are standing at the doorway to hell. I will be there before you, but you'll be on the way one day to join me. Together, we'll live forever, experiencing the tortures of the damned."

"I certainly hope not," she said, turning to meet the next guest Maxwell was presenting to her.

Maxwell had carefully instructed Nicky to stand in line with Elizabeth, greeting all the guests in the same way he'd done during his wedding reception in Bel Air. But he kept wandering off. Elizabeth spotted him returning to her receiving line with Maxwell and another young man, who was talking with great animation to Nicky.

Maxwell introduced Jimmy Donahue to Elizabeth, describing him as, "You know, the heir to all those Woolworth five-and-dime stores."

He paid her scant attention, continuing to be mesmerized by Nicky.

Donahue's biographer, Christopher Wilson, in *Dancing With the Devil,* summed up his subject:

> *"Blonde and slender, Jimmy Donahue was the archetypal postwar playboy. He could fly a plane, speak several languages, play the piano, and tell marvelous jokes. People loved him for his wit, charm, and personality. The grandson of millionaire Frank W. Woolworth, he was the cousin of Barbara Hutton, one of the richest women in the world....Gay at a time when the homosexual act was unmentionable, Jimmy was notorious within America's upper class and loved to shock...At the time Elizabeth met him, Donahue was about to embark on a long affair with both the Duke and Duchess of Windsor."*

Jean Cocteau to E.T. "Together, we'll live forever, experiencing the tortures of the damned."

After a few minutes of idle chat with Elizabeth, Donahue wandered off with her husband, getting lost amid the splendor of the restaurant's *belle époque* décor. Maxwell had also disappeared.

Barreling in on her next was Porfirio Rubirosa. "We meet again, beautiful angel, without Doris Duke and Errol Flynn. Perhaps the two of us can forget them if we have each other."

Debauched Woolworth heir **Jimmy Donahue**

"Rubi!" she said. "What a delight."

"Welcome to Paris," he said. "I noticed that your new husband often deserts you, which is a dangerous thing to do in a room filled with the most deadly of international sharks."

"Maybe he needed something from Woolworth's five-cent store," she said.

"I know Jimmy very well, as I am planning to marry Barbara Hutton, his kissing cousin." Rubirosa said. "Any man who wanders off with that Jimmy won't be seen again at least until morning. Please, let me be your escort through the rest of this evening as a means of guiding you safely through Elsa's international riffraff."

"It's a deal, big boy," she said. "I'm just a hopelessly lost little teenage girl far away from home and her mama."

"I am the maiden's prayer," he said, taking her arm.

"So I've heard," she said with a smirk.

After endless chitchatting and endless goodbyes, with promises of future lunches and future parties before her departure from Paris, Rubi guided Elizabeth out of Maxim's and into a waiting taxicab. He ordered the driver to stop four blocks from the George V so that they could walk through the nearly deserted streets of Paris.

"I bet I'm not the first girl you've rescued on her honeymoon," she said to him.

"Not the first," he answered, "Nor the last, I'm sure. But when I'm with the world's most beautiful woman, I can't think of yesterday or tomorrow…only tonight."

***

Elsa Maxwell was the first person who called Elizabeth the next day at the George V, to find out what had happened with Rubirosa. "My dear, you don't have to go into all the clinical details. From Doris Duke, Joan Crawford, Tina Onassis, Zsa Zsa Gabor, Dolores del Rio, Evita Peron, and even from Manouche, I've heard about that sex organ of his—eleven inches long and thick as a beer can. I also know Rubi can go all night."

"You said it all," Elizabeth told her. "There is nothing else for me to add to your wonderful description. At least I know why he's dubbed 'Rubber Hosa.'"

"What you did last night is called 'a revenge fuck,'" Maxwell said. "A very common occurrence in high society marriages. Husband runs off with somebody else. Wife takes on another lover in his absence. I heard that Nicky is attending a three-day party with Jimmy at this château in the Île de France. Don't expect to see Nicky again until sometime on Wednesday. I'll have to speak to that Jimmy and tell him what a low-down cad he is to make off with a woman's husband on her honeymoon. For him, it wouldn't be the first time."

"I want Nicky to come back to me," Elizabeth said, "I love him so. I can't believe how insensitive he is."

"Let me give you some advice," Maxwell said. "Let him go away whenever he wants. But collect those diamonds; stock up on Hilton stock; and shop the fashion houses of Paris, but buy only the most expensive gowns. And take up with any hot lover your heart desires. I've got a long list of desirable men who want to date you. I might even fix you up with a king here or there, one who has lost his throne to the communists, but made off with the state treasury."

"It's not the kind of life I envisioned for myself," Elizabeth said.

"It's rare for a person to write the scenario of his own life," Maxwell said. "God...or more likely The Devil...does it for us. Happy times to you on the Côte d'Azur."

Nicky did return on Wednesday and spent his time in the bar of the George V. Elizabeth came down to join him and encountered Chevalier there, enjoying cocktails with Mistinguett.

Elizabeth courteously acknowledged Chevalier, but ignored Mistinguett. She had a reason for her rudeness.

Someone on the hotel staff had translated a comment the French performer had made to the Parisian press about Elizabeth the day after their meeting at Maxim's. Mistinguett had not been impressed: "Elizabeth Taylor can't act; her voice sets your teeth on edge, and all she does is flash diamonds and show *décolletage*. I guess she'll go far."

"One of the saddest sights I ever saw was Elizabeth sitting in the bar of the George V begging her young husband to come upstairs and go to bed with her," said Chevalier. He later told Elsa Maxwell, "Every man in Paris wanted her, and she was having to beg for sex from her husband. I spoke about it to Marlene Dietrich. She found the story appalling. 'I would never beg for sex,' Marlene told me. 'And I predict that MGM will never be able to turn Taylor into a *femme fatale* like me.'"

On June 12, 1950, Elizabeth and Nicky flew to England to attend the London premiere of *Father of the Bride.* Nicky stood inside the lobby of the theater, fuming, as Elizabeth signed autographs for some 2,000 of her British fans.

Nicky told the theater manager, "I don't think I can stand another day of being Mr. Elizabeth Taylor. You won't believe this, but in America, I'm much more important than she is—and a hell of a lot richer."

Nicky always found London boring, and he was anxious to fly to the French Riviera, with its gambling casinos, where they had scheduled stopovers in both Monte Carlo and Cannes. Their first stopover was in Cannes where Nicky had booked the bridal suite at the Carlton. Here, they joined Europe's *haut monde.*

Alerted to their arrival, French photographers practically mobbed them, and soon after, Nicky punched one of them in the face. After his camera fell to the pavement, Nicky stomped on it before rushing into the relative safety of the hotel. Elizabeth understood enough French to realize that a lawsuit would be pending.

During his first night in Cannes, Nicky deserted her and headed for the casino. He could not take her along, because she was not old enough to satisfy the age requirements of French law. When fans tried to crowd into the hotel lobby to get a look at her, Nicky angrily told the manager, "I didn't marry a girl, I married an institution."

One night, he ran off with two French hookers and drove with them in a rented car to St-Tropez. He remained absent for two nights. Elizabeth was in the lobby gift shop of the Carlton when she saw him return, picking up his messages at the front desk. An argument immediately ensued. He knocked her down onto the lobby's marble floor, calling her "a dirty little whore." He also claimed that, "While I was away, you must have fucked every beach boy in Cannes."

The fall injured her already weak back, and the manager summoned an ambulance, which hauled her off to the local hospital. There, she was ordered to rest for three days. At no point did Nicky come to visit her.

Two *gendarmes,* however, came to visit her, suggesting that she press charges, but she refused. She did, however, decide that she wanted to leave Europe. An immigration officer journeyed all the way from Nice to discuss her options. Under normal circumstances, she would have had to visit his office, but he wanted to meet her. He explained that she and Nicky were traveling on a joint passport, which could not be used for her single return. Besides, Nicky had possession of the passport. She'd have to apply to the U.S. consulate for an individual passport, which was bound to involve her new husband. When all the red tape became too much for her, she abandoned her whim.

***

Elizabeth may have been away from Hollywood, but the town had not forgotten her. Louella Parsons' spies reported that the Hilton/Taylor marriage was in trouble. In her column, Parsons wrote: "Their fights get nastier and nastier. The biggest blow-up came in the south of France. Nicky leaves his bride alone night after night in favor of the gambling tables. This is a new and unbearable situation for her. No man has ever ignored her before. In Hollywood, she was always the center of attention, like Shirley Temple before her star flickered out."

Sam Marx at MGM told the press, "Elizabeth is going into this marriage sexually unawakened."

When she read that, she was furious. "Tell Sam he can stick a fourteen-inch dildo up his ass. How does he know if I'm sexually asleep or awake? Was he following me around all this time with a god damn camera?"

***

When the unhappy couple checked out of the Carlton Hotel in Cannes, Elizabeth and Nicky were driven by limousine to Monte Carlo. A hotel van followed them with all her luggage. Reservations had been made at the very upscale Hotel de Paris, close to the casino.

During her so-called honeymoon in Monte Carlo, Elizabeth expected to spend her nights alone while Nicky patronized the Monte Carlo casino. Indeed, on his first night there, he exited from the hotel's very grand entrance and strolled down the street to the casino. A monument to opulence, it, along with the Opera in Paris, had been designed by Charles Garnier, and had welcomed luminaries who had included Sarah Bernhardt, Mata Hari, King Farouk of Egypt, and Prince Aly Khan.

Through the intervention of her new friend, Elsa Maxwell, invitations to gala events in Monte Carlo arrived the following morning. Two that particularly appealed to Elizabeth included invitations from the shipping tycoon, Aristotle Onassis, for supper aboard his yacht; and one from Prince Rainier III for a dinner at his palace. Both men had included Nicky in the invitation, but he rejected both offers, asserting that his luck at long last had changed, and that he was on the verge of a winning streak at the casino.

Elizabeth decided to accept the invitations and to go alone. Her rebellious streak was reinforced because of Maxwell's support.

When she informed Nicky that she would attend the dinners without him, he told her she could not. "Send them your regrets."

"I will not!" she said defiantly.

He slapped her face. "You're such a god damn whore," he yelled at her before storming out. "Don't you leave this hotel suite."

The more immediate of the two invitations had come from Onassis. Elizabeth, following his instructions, arrived aboard his yacht, *Olympic Winner,* while it was anchored in the Port of Monte Carlo.

With the appearance of a man in his early 40s, he elaborately welcomed her aboard. He wore tinted glasses under hair the color of squid ink. He was smoking a cigar and did not have a pretty face, but his strong personality was charismatic and made up for other failings.

By now, she was familiar with older men making the usual compliments about her beauty. Onassis had a different twist, however, referring to her as "a modern day Aphrodite."

Over vintage champagne, she settled in to get to know Onassis. She asked about his wife, Athina ("Tina") Livanos Onassis, whom he'd married in 1946 when she was seventeen.

"She's resting at our château near Antibes, and we are expecting a child around December."

Tina had been quoted in the paper as having said, "Celebrities are important to Ari. All of his fantasies are connected with them."

He told her that beautiful women like his wife cannot be moderate. "They need an inexhaustible supply of excess. That's why I rented this beautiful villa for her. It has forty-two rooms with a staff not quite as large as that of Buckingham Palace. The Duke and Duchess of Windsor used to live there. You must come and stay with us this weekend."

"That sounds divine," she said.

"Tina likes me to provide her with a lot of places to live—a home on Sutton Square." (He failed to name the city.) "A permanent suite at the Plaza in Buenos Aires, and a villa in Montevideo. An apartment on the Avenue Foch in Paris, a seaside villa outside Athens."

Over a dinner of Iranian caviar and lobster, he told her fascinating stories of the sea. She was shocked to realize he believed that mermaids were real, claiming to have seen three in his lifetime.

"A millionaire should always live a bit above his means," he told her.

"I don't think you need to tell my new husband that," she said. "He already knows it, throwing away vast fortunes in gambling casinos."

"That's what keeps Monte Carlo rolling," he said. "That damn casino brings in enough money so the locals don't have to pay income taxes."

She told him that she found him so easy to talk to he could become her Father Confessor.

"I'd rather you think of me as a potential lover, but Father Confessor will do," he said.

She poured out a litany of complaints about Nicky, making reference not only to his gambling, but his desertions, his womanizing, and his brutality.

"He must be Greek," Onassis said. "I tell you, all Greek men, without exception, beat their wives. It's good for them."

"I can see that we will not always agree on everything," she said. "Nicky also withholds sex from me. He makes me beg for it."

"Now that is unforgivable," he said. "I can't imagine any man not giving you sex morning, noon, and night."

Waiters kept filling her tulip-shaped glass with champagne, and provided Onassis with glass after glass of his favorite drink, ouzu.

After he'd heard her complaints, he recommended that she get an annulment. "You tell me he's Catholic. If the marriage is annulled, he can marry his second wife in the church. Your marriage will never have existed, and you'll be completely free to marry again, too. Call me a matchmaker. I may have your new husband already selected for you. He's the man you're having dinner with tomorrow night at his palace."

"Prince Rainier!" she said. "I hope he's young and handsome."

"He's young and reasonably handsome, and he's looking for a wife. If he does not produce a male heir, this principality will revert to France. That means locals will pay French taxes for the first time, probably at a rate that's higher , much higher, than what they're paying to Monaco now."

I'm not sure the prince would want to marry an American film star," she said. "It might be too shocking."

"Quite the contrary. If he married a film beauty, it would attract international publicity and bring thousands of high rollers to Monaco to lose their fortunes in the casino. Marriage to Rainier would make your marriage to the Hilton boy look like a minor side show at a roadside carnival."

"Would I have to give up my career?" she asked.

"Of course, my dear. After all, the Prince can't marry a working woman. But becoming a fairytale princess would mean more than being a movie star. You'd be known as Princess Elizabeth."

"There's already a Princess Elizabeth," she said.

"Yes, but not for long. In London, I was told that her father is slowly dying. She'll soon be known as Queen Elizabeth."

"Well, we'll see what chemistry there is between us tomorrow night," she said. "He might not find me appealing."

"That, I doubt."

Before the night ended, she accepted his invitation for a weekend at his château.

"My wife will be there, but I'd prefer it if you didn't bring your husband. I can't tell you why at this point."

At the gangplank, he gave her a sloppy kiss.

During a transatlantic call to her mother the following morning, she raved about Onassis.

"The only drawback is that at the end of one of his dinner parties, he gives you a liver-lipped wet kiss, but that is a small thing to endure for the pleasure of his company. The next time you hear from me, you may have to address me as the Princess of Monaco."

Before Sara could probe any deeper, Elizabeth had hung up the phone.

***

The following morning over a late breakfast, Nicky was in a foul mood, which had become customary for him. His winning streak at the casino had turned into a losing streak, and he vowed that he would return to the casino over the upcoming weekend "to win back the bundle I lost—and a hell of a lot more than that, too."

She told him she hoped he wouldn't object to her spending the weekend "with Mr. and Mrs. Onassis at their château."

"Frankly, my dear, as Rhett Butler told Scarlett O'Hara, 'I don't give a damn.'"

Then he wandered off for the rest of the afternoon as she spent the rest of the day beautifying herself and reading about the Grimaldis before her dinner that night with the prince at his palace.

From reading the popular magazines, she knew that he was a sports-loving outdoors man addicted to fast boats, fast cars, and fast women, with deep-sea diving thrown in as a hobby.

She also learned more about his pedigree, including that the Grimaldis came from the oldest ruling family in Europe. There was much speculation as to when he would marry and produce a male heir. Seemingly none of the Monegasques wanted their little country to return to French control…and French taxes.

As for the Prince, his blood did not run as blue as it seemed. Elizabeth learned that his mother had been born to a woman out of wedlock, and that his grandmother had been a cabaret dancer. Her mother (i.e., Prince Rainier's great-grandmother) took in laundry for a living.

That night, as Nicky headed for the casino again, the palace sent one of its limousines to retrieve Elizabeth and transport her to her royal dinner.

Inside the palace, she stood for fifteen minutes in a grand reception chamber, waiting for Rainier. As she recalled, "My biggest fear was that I had not worn the proper hat, though my Dior gown was perfect."

Almost without warning, the Prince appeared, walking toward her. He was better looking than his pictures, with a cleft chin, hair, like Onassis, the color of squid ink, sapphire blue eyes, and a perfectly trimmed mustache that reminded her of Clark Gable's. He stood only five feet, six inches, and was dressed in a well-tailored navy blue yachting outfit, as he'd been at sea all day.

She curtsied before him, as she had for Princess Elizabeth in London. "Your Highness," she said.

"How do you do?" he asked her in perfect English, with no French accent, as he'd attended schools in England.

"I am very well," she said, "and honored to be here."

"Forgive me for arriving late," he said. "We had trouble at sea, and it left me no time to change for dinner."

He showed her around the palace and led her into his private gardens, spotlit at night. He told her he wanted to install a zoo here. "The gardens are at their most beautiful this time of year. Look at those plumes of bougainvillea climbing up the palace walls."

"I didn't know that roses came in so many colors," she said, as she wandered past those flowers to take in the snapdragons, tulips, and carnations.

From the terrace, he showed her his kingdom, beautifully lit at night. He explained that it was divided into four districts, with the capital, Old Monaco, which he called "*Monaco Ville*," sitting atop *Le Rocher* ("The Rock").

Perhaps because of his military background, he seemed very formal with her, a bit stiff, really. The talk was idle, although he did tell her that he wanted to visit the United States for the first time.

"Please let me be your guide," she volunteered. She felt nervous around him, afraid of committing some *faux pas*. In the years ahead, she would dine and even sleep with royalty, but at this point, as a late teenager, she was insecure in such an august presence.

At the end of their evening together, he escorted her to the entrance of the palace, where he personally opened the door to a limousine and guided her inside. Before departing, he said, "Please give my regards to your husband. Perhaps his father would consider opening a Hilton in Monaco one day."

As the car drove her back to the Hotel de Paris and an empty bridal suite, she feared she had not made a good impression on Prince Rainier. After all, according to his reputation, he was used to seducing the most sophisticated and beautiful women in France, including the gamine-faced French actress, Gisèle Pascal.

The next morning, she telephoned Onassis aboard his yacht to arrange the details of her upcoming weekend visit. "I don't think I broke through to Prince Charming," she said. "I tried to storm the walls of the Grimaldi Palace, but it was too steep for 'lil ol' me."

"I wouldn't be so sure of that," he told her. "Over the centuries, European royals have learned to conceal personal emotions."

After an early morning "rape" from Nicky, she was driven by Onassis' driver to the Château de la Croe in Cap d'Antibes. Set on 14 acres of prime ocean fronting land in one of the Riviera's most expensive municipilties, it had been built in 1927 by a British newspaper magnate and later owned by the Duke and Duchess of Windsor. A vision in magenta, she stepped out of the limousine, and was greeted by Onassis and his young wife, Tina. In contrast to Elizabeth's dress, Tina wore a simple white silk blouse and black slacks with leather sandals.

Accustomed to greeting royalty and the titans of industry, Tina was a gracious hostess and an amusing storyteller. Over late morning tea, she sat alone with Elizabeth. "Before I met Ari, I was dating a man closer to my own age. But I found Ari so charming and so romantic that I fell for him."

"With such a wealthy father, you must have lived a life far more luxurious than a mere princess," Elizabeth said.

"My father, Stavros Livanos, owns a great shipping empire, but he's tight-fisted with money. He pays his Greek sailors one British pound a month. When they complain, he reminds them that if they work a thousand months, they will have saved a thousand pounds. Of course, he doesn't take into consideration what they might live on in the meantime. His idea of being extravagant involves bringing us a paper bag filled with chestnuts for roasting. He walks five miles to avoid paying a taxi fare."

"When Ari started dating me, I was so young, my father accused him of being a child molester," Tina said. She told Elizabeth that her family came from the eastern Aegean island of Chios (aka Hios or Khios), the legendary birthplace of Homer.

Tina was only three years older than Elizabeth, and the two women bonded, discovering that each of them had a love of horses. Tina promised to take Elizabeth riding in the morning along the Riviera's coastline.

After a lavish Greek dinner, Tina and Onassis were ready to retire, but after Tina left, Onassis called Elizabeth aside. "I have a very important guest arriving at around eleven o'clock, a person most anxious to see you. Would you wait in the library and greet this special guest?"

"Of course," she said. "Since you are friends with everybody, it might be anybody from Winston Churchill to Greta Garbo."

At around eleven, the butler knocked on the door and admitted the mysterious guest. It was Prince Rainier.

She curtsied before him. "Your Highness, we meet again."

"A double pleasure in so short a time," he said, taking her hand and kissing it tenderly.

She realized at once that the Prince had come for what her future friend, Michael Jackson, would define as "a sleepover."

Athina Mary "Tina" Livanos Niarchos (1926-1974) with her first husband, **Aristotle Onassis**

The next morning, Onassis took the Prince and Elizabeth on a tour of his grounds, pointing out the gazelles, a gift from the King of Saudi Arabia.

After she returned to the United States, Elizabeth was very close-mouthed about her midnight tryst with the Prince of Monaco, even supplying her best friend, Roddy McDowall, with few details.

She did admit, however, that she'd had her first "waterbourne fuck."

"What does that mean?" he asked.

"On Sunday morning, we had a bubble bath in this huge gold-plated, swan-shaped tub with gold-plated fixtures shaped like fish," she said. "It once was in the suite of the Ritz Hotel in Paris and before its reinstallment in the Château de la Croe, it was used by the corpulent Edward VII—you know, Queen Victoria's son. He got stuck in one of the smaller tubs, so the Ritz had this big tub specially designed for the King. Rainier and I put it to good use."

Roddy pressed her for more details, but she told him, "case closed."

"Please tell me more," he said. "You know I'm a size queen. I want to know how many princely inches, girl."

"Okay, but that's all I'm telling you," she said. "A princely six, and not a centimeter more."

After her departure from Monaco, Elizabeth continued her on-again, off-again affair with Prince Rainier, even though, in 1956, he married the blonde goddess Grace Kelly.

On several occasions, Elizabeth was seen entering the Prince's private address in Paris. One reason she was so secretive about their affair was that she wanted to maintain at least a surface friendship with Grace Kelly. Had Kelly remained in Hollywood and continued with her movie career, she would almost surely have clashed with Elizabeth, as they'd have competed for the same roles.

"Let's face it," Clark Gable once said, "By the mid-1950s, there were only three goddesses left in Hollywood—Elizabeth Taylor, Marilyn Monroe, and Grace Kelly. The others were getting a bit long in the tooth—forgive me, Ava." [Ava Gardner, though still a beautiful woman in spite of her constant heavy drinking, was ten years older than Elizabeth.]

Originally, the lead female role in *Giant* had been offered to Kelly, with her lover, William Holden, as her co-star. But eventually, the parts, of course, went to Elizabeth and Rock Hudson. Kelly was also offered the lead role as Maggie the Cat in Tennessee Williams' *Cat on a Hot Tin Roof.* When Elizabeth took it over, a reporter asked her if she minded "taking over Grace Kelly's sloppy seconds."

"I've spent a lifetime taking the sloppy seconds of other women," Elizabeth quipped. In the tamer 1950s, such a comment was not printed.

Historically speaking, however, it was Kelly who took Elizabeth's sloppy seconds, since Elizabeth had seduced Prince Rainier first.

[As the years passed, the Rainiers were often seen with Elizabeth at galas and charity events, including the 1974 premiere of her film, *Identikit* (a.k.a. *The Driver's Seat),* based on a 1970 novella by Muriel Spark. Its premiere was staged as part of a benefit for the Red Cross in Monaco.

In the film, Elizabeth played a psychotic German housewife who flies to Rome in search of the ideal lover, but finds the perfect murderer instead.

Critics, including Elizabeth herself, have denounced *The Driver's Seat* as the worst movie she ever made. Andy Warhol had a cameo role within it. In later years, his estate would make millions off his lithographs of Elizabeth.

The Taylor/Rainier passion for each other was still flaming as late as 1981, when the Prince and Princess Grace attended the Broadway opening of *The Little Foxes,* a revival of a play by Lillian Hellman, in which Tallulah Bankhead had enjoyed a triumph in 1939.

In C. David Heymann's book, entitled *Liz,* he quoted Felice Quinto, the backstage photographer for the Broadway run of *The Little Foxes*. Quinto claimed that both of the Rainiers came backstage to congratulate Elizabeth for her performance.

"Somehow, he left Grace behind for a private talk with Elizabeth," Quinto claimed. "Rainier was worse than John F. Kennedy. He dragged Elizabeth into a dark corner, and they kissed—more than just kissing in a friendly manner—for three or four minutes. They were literally all over each other."]

***

In Rome, the honeymooning Nicky Hilton had compiled a list of the six most deluxe bordellos in the city, with the intention of visiting many of them, without telling Elizabeth where he'd be going.

Fortunately for her, Monty Clift was in town to attend the Roman premiere of *The Heiress*. At their reunion dinner in a hard-to-find restaurant off the beaten track near the Colosseum, he told her he'd just attended the London premiere of his film. On that occasion, he'd also been presented to Queen Elizabeth.

"After the presentation, I was invited to dinner at the Café Royal by Laurence Olivier, Monty said. "He called me 'darling boy' and propositioned me."

"I won't ask you if you accepted his invitation," Elizabeth said. "I don't really want to know."

"The next night I had supper with Noël Coward, who told me I was the world's most beautiful man."

"I'm sure Coward also called you 'darling boy,' too," she said.

The next night, Monty and Elizabeth dined with Tennessee Williams and his Sicilian-American lover, Frank Merlo. Monty told the playwright and his companion that in Rome, he was indulging in "a fuckathon with gorgeous Italian hustlers. I could live in this Eternal City eternally," he said.

Williams later claimed that he got "the spark of an idea" for his novel about Italian gigolos, *The Roman Spring of Mrs. Stone,* from listening to Monty talk about the hustling scene in Rome.

At his home in Key West years later, shortly after Monty and Elizabeth had co-starred in the film version of his drama, *Suddenly, Last Summer,* Williams recalled that long-ago evening in Rome.

"Here I was, dining with what the press called the most beautiful man and the most beautiful woman in the world. If only their fans could see them in real life: Monty ordered raw ground beef, really bloody, which he proceeded to eat with his fingers. Blood ran down his lips. Elizabeth ordered two big pasta dishes. My dear Frank here has a foul mouth, but Elizabeth topped him. Fortunately, we dined in a trattoria in Trastevere, and in those days, no one spoke English, so they didn't know what she was saying."

"Monty was a farter. It was awful. He said it was a medical condition, some bug he had picked up in Mexico. At the end of each course, Elizabeth let out a loud belch. Frankie and I at that meal had to endure a poison gas attack that evoked the trenches of World War I."

Monty had to cut short his Roman adventure to rush back to New York. His close friend and mentor, Libby Holman, had called him to tell him that her seventeen-year-old son, Christopher Reynolds, had died in a climbing accident during his ascent of Mount Whitney.

At one point, Elizabeth ran away from Nicky and hid out while working as an extra on MGM's ancient Roman epic, *Quo Vadis?*. Nicky had become enraged and smashed a room filled with 16th-century antiques at their rented villa. Conrad Sr. spent thousands of dollars in replacement costs.

Nicky spent his last night in Rome with Elizabeth, during which she was brutally raped by her new young husband.

The next morning, she flew with him to Berlin to christen the newly constructed Berlin Hilton. She was horrified to find much of the city still in ruins. She told Nicky that the city evoked that romantic Marlene Dietrich movie, *A Foreign Affair* (1948). "Was Marlene a former girlfriend, or is she a current girlfriend, for all I know?" Elizabeth asked him.

"A gentleman from Texas never kisses and tells unless he's a politician braggart like that guy my father knows, Lyndon Baines Johnson."

At the end of their stay in Berlin, Nicky and Elizabeth flew to Paris once again. Both had been invited to a lavish Paris ball, the social event of the season. For her farewell to Europe, she wanted to make a dazzling appearance. She spent a small fortune, the equivalent of about $60,000 in today's coinage, for her appearance in a Balmain gown. She also made an arrangement with a Parisian jeweler on the Place Vendôme to wear $150,000 worth of diamonds.

After only an hour at the ball, Nicky told her he was going out gambling, as he'd heard of this town house in the 17th arrondissement where gambling flourished. She pleaded with him not to leave her stranded at the ball.

He raised his voice to her, and she shouted back at him, introducing some of the ballroom guests to English-language expletives they'd never heard before. Photographers were there from the Paris newspapers, and their pictures were snapped, appearing the next day on the frontpages of the morning tabloids.

It could be said that the Hilton/Taylor honeymoon ended in a knockout punch when he struck her in front of many witnesses, sending her sprawling to the marble floor.

After Nicky stormed out of the building, Elizabeth looked up to stare into the handsome face of Gérard Philipe, the charismatic young actor she'd met through Elsa Maxwell.

"We meet again," he said, gallantly. "If your leg isn't broken, would you dance with me? After that, we'll watch the sun come up over Paris."

"You're on," she said. "My father told me that if you get knocked down in life, pick yourself up and start again."

"And so we shall," he said, as she was lifted from the floor into his muscular arms.

***

In September of 1950, a grim-faced Nicky was photographed at Cherbourg boarding the *Queen Elizabeth* for his trip back to the port of New York. Elizabeth had purchased a French poodle, naming him "Bianco." She held him tenderly in her arms.

Elsa Maxwell was on the return voyage, too. She noticed that Elizabeth looked haggard, having lost twelve pounds. She'd also taken up chain smoking and was drinking more heavily than before.

In her memoir, *Elizabeth Takes Off,* she wrote: "By the end of the voyage,

it was clear that my husband was having great difficulty in reconciling himself to me, as well as to my celebrity. He became sullen, angry and abusive, physically and mentally. He began drinking. He taunted me in public."

In New York, from her hotel suite, the first person she called was Roddy McDowall, who occupied that rented apartment in The Dakota with Merv Griffin. Roddy was still looking for work.

He asked about the honeymoon, as he'd heard terrible stories about it from the Continent.

French romantic heartthrob
Gérard Philipe

"At this point," she said, "all that is needed in the melodrama starring Elizabeth Taylor and Nicky Hilton is for THE END to flash up on the screen."

CHAPTER THIRTEEN
Wild About Wilding
LOVE IS NOT NECESSARILY BETTER
THE SECOND TIME AROUND

Back in New York, Elizabeth seemed overjoyed to be on America's shores once again. But her happiness would not last long.

She faced an aggressive press which asked her if a divorce was imminent. "Nicky and I have resolved our problems—call it a period of adjustment. Most couples go through that. I'm going back to Hollywood, where I'll be a proper wife to him, even at the sacrifice of my career. I'll even learn to cook. Right now, I'm trying to master the art of frying an egg, and I'm also going to learn the right temperature at which to boil water."

That was her public front. What was going on behind the scenes was a different matter. Nicky had booked a two-bedroom suite at the Plaza Hotel. His first night with her was romantic, a cozy candlelit dinner followed by "hot sex," as she'd describe later to Roddy McDowall.

She was mildly disturbed that Nicky had placed a loaded pistol on his nightstand beside their bed. Around it, he'd wrapped a rosary. One of his future lovers, Joan Collins, recalled his having such a rosary-wrapped weapon. He told Elizabeth that he wanted the pistol close at hand, as he feared reprisals from some sexual partners he'd mistreated who might seek revenge.

Roddy met with Elizabeth for dinner the following night. He was appalled at both her mental and physical condition, fearing she was on the verge of a nervous breakdown. "She was smoking two packages of cigarettes a day and looked gaunt."

He told her that he was in the process of reinventing himself after child stardom. "Of all of us movie kids, you've been the only one who glided seamlessly from child star parts into adult roles." She had heard that many times before.

She told him that she was having dinner the following night with Monty Clift. Roddy warned her that he was a complete mess. "He drinks everybody under the table. He never meets a pill he doesn't pop or a drug he doesn't take. One night, he brought three hustlers back to his apartment and had sex with each of them. Before they left, they beat the shit out of him, and robbed him of all his valuables, even his watch and that ring you gave him."

Twenty-four hours later, Elizabeth was spotted dining with Monty at his favorite Italian restaurant, Camillos. She noticed that he was shaking, and she even had to light his cigarettes. "I'm losing it," he told her. "I feel a cold black night is descending on me, and I have no clothes to protect me from the elements."

A call to her from Kevin McCarthy the following morning informed her that he'd had to rush to Bloomingdale's Department Store to rescue Monty. "I found him there, prostrate and half naked." Apparently, he'd gone to buy some casual clothes, but faced with crowds of autograph seekers, he experienced a meltdown. Bloomingdale's management was relieved to see him rescued and removed from their premises without undue publicity.

The next afternoon, she visited Monty at Regent Hospital, where McCarthy had checked him in the night before. He was going through "cold turkey" withdrawals from all pills, drugs, and booze. He was shaking all over and sweating profusely. She held him in her arms. "Oh, Bessie Mae," he said, "I think I'm going to die young...very young."

She offered him all the comfort she could muster and promised to stand by his side her entire life, regardless of what happened. "I'll never desert you...*never!*"

After she returned from the hospital to her lodgings at the Plaza, Elizabeth faced her own life, which was in turmoil. David Brett, in his biography, *Elizabeth Taylor: The Lady, The Lover, The Legend,* wrote that Nicky, after his return to New York from his honeymoon, embarked on another sex-and-gambling spree, this time with a well-known actor."

The actor, in fact, was more than well known: He was the internationally famous Tyrone Power. The matinee idol had begun an on-again, off-again affair with Nicky, the Hilton heir, during the post-war years.

The following evening, after visiting Monty in the hospital, Elizabeth returned to the Plaza in a state of uncertainty about where Nicky was. She hadn't heard from him all day.

As she entered the suite's living room, she found Nicky in his briefs, drinking with Power, who had his trousers on, but wore only an undershirt. He had always been on the list of men she considered the most handsome in Hollywood, but because Power worked for 20th Century Fox, and because she was employed by MGM, their paths had not crossed. She had, of course, followed his romantic escapades in the fan magazines, most of which had occurred when he was married to the French actress, known only as Annabelle, his co-star in

Suez (1938). He'd been romantically linked to Joan Crawford, Judy Garland, Betty Grable, Rita Hayworth, Sonja Henie, and Loretta Young, among others. He'd had a tumultuous and widely publicized affair with Lana Turner before he'd dumped her.

Very few of his fans knew about his bisexuality at the time, but he'd had a history of being one of the "kept boys," of Howard Hughes, and he'd also had affairs with Laurence Olivier, Noël Coward, Robert Taylor, Errol Flynn, and the film director Edmund Goulding. Powers was also widely known in the Hollywood *demi-monde* for seducing his best friend, César Romero, and George Sanders, the bisexual husband of Zsa Zsa Gabor, Nicky's former mother-in-law. He'd also had an affair with the Argentine dictator, Eva Peron.

Elizabeth found Power mesmerizing as she chatted pleasantly with him over glasses of champagne. Perhaps fearing that her presence was unwanted, she excused herself and retreated to her bedroom, locking the door behind her.

About an hour later, a drunken Nicky pounded on that door when he realized it was locked. Reluctantly, she opened it, finding him standing there completely nude and drunk. "I'd like to talk to you," he said.

"What in hell about?" she asked.

"Ty wants a three-way with us," he said. "He's had three-ways with Lana Turner and Howard Hughes, and really enjoys them. How about it? I know you want him. *Everybody does.*"

"NO! Forget it!" she said, slamming the door in his face and locking it again. He went away and didn't bother her for the rest of the night.

After a troubling pre-dawn, she fell asleep at seven that morning and slept until noon, when the hotel maid woke her up.

Stumbling into the living room, she found the other bedroom empty. Power and Nicky were nowhere to be seen. On the coffee table, she picked up a hastily scribbled and unsigned message written in pencil—FLYING TO LOS ANGELES.

Over coffee, she read Dorothy Kilgallen's column, which informed the world that Lana Turner had arrived in New York and had checked into the Plaza Hotel. On a few occasions, Elizabeth had sat with Turner during early morning make-up sessions at MGM.

On an impulse, she called Turner, who agreed to meet downstairs for afternoon tea. A few hours later, Turner made a grand entrance into the Palm Court, dressed in an olive green suit with pink accessories.

After some shared gossip about Louis B. Mayer's upcoming departure from MGM, Turner got to the point: "I heard Ty visited you and Nicky in your suite last night. That must have been fun. I'm still in love with him, you know."

"I didn't know that," Elizabeth said.

"He was my only lover who took the time to find out what I was as a human being—not just a pretty face with a shapely body. I call him 'the man who got away.' Imagine turning me down for that international trollop, Linda Christian."

Publicly, Turner always denied that she ever saw any evidence of homosexuality in Power. Privately, she seemed well aware of his sexual proclivities. "Let's face it, Elizabeth. I fell in love with a bisexual –and so did you with Nicky Hilton. And in a flash, almost within the hour, Ty could switch from being a hetero to a homosexual. He left me without a word because he can't stand confrontations. Perhaps Nicky will do the same to you."

"I suspect that I will be the one who abandons ship," Elizabeth said.

"For your sake, I hope so," Turner said. "Ty is incapable of making a commitment to another man. He turns to men for physical love, but prefers emotional bonds with women, if that makes sense."

"You could well be describing my friend, Monty Clift," Elizabeth responded. "It makes perfect sense. I think Nicky is the same way."

"Ty was the most sensitive and gentle man I've ever known," Turner said. "I don't think I'll find anyone like him again."

"Nicky is the most violent and destructive man I've ever known," she said.

"Then you must leave him," Lana said. "Otherwise, he might do something that will permanently mar your face. It's not worth it. Put your career first, not some man. I know that makes me sound like a heartless vamp—and I'm not. I would never get involved with a person who might threaten me or even kill me."

Ironically, when Turner said that, the gangster Johnny Stompanato lay in her future.

Elizabeth's competition:
Lana Turner depicted above in August,1946

Before leaving, Turner said, "I've always thought of you as a child star. But I can see you're very grown-up. I fear that in the future, you and I may have conflicts over certain men and over certain film contracts. I just learned that MGM is considering making a movie called *The Queen of Sheba*. Guess who is being considered for the female lead? Lana Turner, Elizabeth Taylor, and this upstart whore, Marilyn Monroe, who is sucking every cock in Hollywood that's unzipped for her. It's one way to get ahead in the film business, I guess."

Then, as an afterthought, Lana said, "By the way, in the future, let's both deny that Mickey Rooney ever fucked us."

***

To avoid the press, MGM used one of its New York publicists to arrange the transport of Elizabeth and her massive quantities of luggage back to California. It was falsely announced that she'd be flying directly to Los Angeles. Instead, she boarded an airplane headed to L.A. with a scheduled layover in Chicago.

To her surprise, Nicky had learned of her ploy, and was waiting for her at the Chicago airport. In the back of a limousine hauling them to the Blackstone Hotel, he begged for her forgiveness of his past indiscretions, and pleaded with her to give him another chance. Before they reached the hotel, she was madly kissing him back. As the driver later reported to the *Chicago Tribune*, "Elizabeth Taylor was all over Mr. Hilton."

A day or two later, along with her trunks filled with designer clothing, she flew onward, with Nicky, to Los Angeles, where they checked into a five-room suite at the Bel Air Hotel. At the time, he owned forty-one percent of the stock of this supremely prestigious hotel.

Two nights later, Jane Powell hosted a welcome home party for Elizabeth and Nicky, inviting young friends who included Dick Hanley.

"Nicky was clearly bored," Dick recalled. "With sarcasm, he even attacked Jane for serving a buffet supper where the guests were expected to sit on the floor. He told me that even in Texas, Jane's party would be viewed as pure cornpone."

In the aftermath of that party, Nicky fled to Las Vegas for three nights, hitting the casinos and running up gambling debts. Seemingly, he had forgotten everything he'd said to Elizabeth in Chicago, about "I can't go on without you."

Years later, she learned what actually happened during his trip to Vegas. He'd flown there with Marilyn Monroe and installed her in a sprawling suite, giving her a pair of diamond earrings. Between September and December of 1950, he would spend three more off-the-record weekends with Monroe in Palm Springs.

Back in Hollywood at MGM, Elizabeth was filming *Father's Little Dividend,* the sequel to *Father of the Bride.* The sequel followed a predictable pattern within young marriages: Petty quarrels and reconciliations preceding the eventual hysteria surrounding the arrival of a first-born in the house.

Don Taylor once again was her less than dynamic screen husband, and for the second time, Spencer Tracy and Joan Bennett played her screen parents.

Producer Pandro S. Berman recalled visiting Elizabeth on the set of *Father's Little Dividend.* "She looked weary and forlorn. I remembered her for having a sharp tongue and a keen sense of humor. But she no longer thought anything was funny. She didn't laugh. She complained of pains in her stomach.

251

Because she was drinking and chain smoking, she had lost the fresh-faced beauty she'd shown in *Father of the Bride.*"

As the filming neared its end, Elizabeth discovered that she was pregnant in real life and not just on the screen. Privately, she revealed to both Dick and Roddy that she didn't know if Nicky was the father. "Perhaps it was Rubirosa's. If the kid comes out of me with the longest baby dick in the world, I'll know it belongs to Rubi. If it pops out of my womb speaking French, then it belongs to Gérard Philipe. I had unprotected sex with both of them."

One Monday, after one of his weekend disappearances in Palm Springs with Monroe, Nicky came home angry and drunk. Elizabeth might have been acclaimed for having the most beautiful face in the world, but he told her, "I'm god damn tired of looking at that face of yours." He called her "a fucking bore," and told her that he'd changed his mind. "I want a divorce after all."

Their fight occurred at the Pacific Palisades home he'd rented. He admitted that he'd been having an affair with Monroe and that she wanted to marry him. "She's a real woman, not a hairy ape like you. The only hair on her body is on her pussy, where it belongs."

Elizabeth struck him in the face, and he responded by knocking her down onto the floor. Then he kicked her several times in the stomach.

As she'd later claim, "He literally kicked my baby out of me." Then he rushed out the door, ignoring her screams of pain. Crawling to the nearest phone in agony, she called Sara, who summoned an ambulance.

Elizabeth was rushed to the Cedars-Sinai Hospital where the doctor confirmed that she'd had a miscarriage. She rested for two days, but was not physically harmed in any other significant way.

Later, she told Sara, Francis, and her friends, "I realized at this point that there could be no reconciliation between Nicky and me. It was not like those silly screen spats Don Taylor and I were having when we filmed *Father's Little Dividend.*"

When Dore Schary at MGM heard of the impending divorce, he said, "Perhaps we should follow *Father's Little Dividend* with yet another sequel entitled *Father's Darling Divorcée.*"

At around midnight, she received an urgent call from Conrad Sr. in Houston. He refused to describe the reason for his urgency, but insisted that he had to speak to his son—"a matter of life or death."

She telephoned the Bel Air Hotel and learned that Nicky was in his suite, but that he was not answering the phone or the urgent knocks on his door.

Getting dressed, Elizabeth drove to the hotel, fearing that Nicky might be incapacitated and perhaps needed to be rushed to a hospital.

Letting herself into the suite with her own key, she entered the darkened living room. There was a light shining from the bedroom. She heard voices, one of them a woman giggling. She stopped at the door and looked in horror at Nicky and Monroe fornicating. She yelled at him. "Your father wants you to call him at once. Why not tell the blonde trollop you'll fuck her later?" Then she turned and headed back to the suite's entrance. He did not pursue her.

Monroe, however, with a towel wrapped around her otherwise nude body, came after Elizabeth, following her into the living room. "I'm sorry, Miss Taylor, for taking your husband away from you. He prefers me to you. You're beautiful and I'm sure you'll find another man. Somewhere, someone out there must find you desirable."

"Get out of my sight, you brazen little tart," Elizabeth shouted at her. "You can have Nicky Hilton."

As Elizabeth headed into the hall, Monroe stood at the door, calling to her. "Miss Taylor, I loved seeing you in the movies when I was a little girl."

In fury, Elizabeth stood before the elevator doors. Actually, Monroe was six years older than she was, which made that parting remark from her all the more infuriating.

Leaving the hotel, Elizabeth drove to Beverly Hills to spend the night with her parents. Only Sara was home. In addition to Elizabeth's mental anguish—or perhaps because of it—she was suffering from another bout of colitis and another ulcer. Her mother put her on a diet of Gerber's Baby Food.

The next day, Sara, with two hired assistants, drove two vans to the Hilton's rented home in Pacific Palisades and removed all of her daughter's possessions.

After seven months of orchestrating publicity about a "made in heaven" marriage, MGM released a statement to the press, presumably from Elizabeth, although it had been written by Howard Strickling in MGM's publicity department.

"I am sorry that Nick and I are unable to adjust our differences, and that we have come to a final parting of the ways. We both regret that decision, but after personal discussion, we realize that there is no possibility for a reconciliation."

Stunned by the finality of the announcement, Nicky impulsively decided he wanted her back after all. She refused to see him or accept his urgent phone calls. He bombarded her with yellow roses.

In a telegram, she notified him that, "All the long-stemmed yellow roses in the world will make no difference. You and I are through."

He telegraphed her back, "The thing between MM and me is over. I found out the tramp is seeing at least eight other men. She must schedule

Hitting on a Hilton:
Marilyn Monroe

one every hour. Come back to me. I promise to be a good boy from now on, a real family man."

She wired back, "Your promises have the market value of rat's piss."

***

Elizabeth's lawyers proceeded with her divorce. Two nights before her appearance in court, she met with Janet Leigh, telling her, "My fairytale marriage didn't even make it past the honeymoon night before the harsh reality set in. I never knew the real Nicky Hilton. He was on his best behavior until he married me. I think he's psychotic."

She also told Leigh that Sara wanted her to move back home. "I'm not going to. I've rented my own apartment. At the age of eighteen, I'm experiencing a nervous breakdown, probably the first of many I'll suffer in my life. But going ahead with the divorce is the first grown-up decision I ever made by myself."

Nicky did not appear at the divorce hearing, although he was represented by two high-priced attorneys. On January 29, 1951, in a Santa Monica court, Elizabeth testified before a judge.

Until the last hour, Sara maintained that the marriage could be saved. She did not want to see Elizabeth "walk away from the Hilton millions." Elizabeth steadfastly refused to listen, and Sara and Francis opted not to go with her to court.

In a barely audible voice, she told the court that "Mr. Hilton was indifferent to me and used abusive language."

Since it quickly became clear that she was having great difficulty speaking, her attorney (also her agent), Jules Goldstone, decided to limit his questions to interrogations that would require only an affirmation.

"Mrs. Hilton, starting from the beginning of your marriage, your husband was very argumentative for no apparent reason and would become very violent. That recurred repeatedly during your marriage. In addition, he spent most of his time away from you."

She uttered a weak "yes."

"You have a substantial income from your work as a motion picture actress, and I understand you wish to waive any alimony."

Again, she uttered a weak "yes." Later, she explained her decision, claiming, "I do not want to be rewarded for failure."

"And you seek the return of your maiden name?" Goldstone asked. "Henceforth, you want to be known as Elizabeth Taylor, not Elizabeth Hilton?"

Again, another soft "yes."

On the stand, she could have related a litany of horrors she'd suffered with

Nicky, including rape, beatings, and the attack where he kicked her in the stomach and caused a miscarriage. But she chose not to, admitting only the weakest grounds for divorce, claiming he insulted her mother and was rude to her in front of her friends. She didn't want to cause Nicky any disgrace or to hurt him, she told her friends. "I really don't like playing the role of the wronged woman." The judge, Thurmond Clarke, granted the divorce on grounds of mental cruelty, not physical abuse.

Her answers of "yes" became a "no" when Nicky's lawyers petitioned the court to have the marriage annulled, so that he would be free one day to re-marry in the Catholic church. Defiantly, she refused his request, and the judge denied Nicky's request.

She covered her face with her white-gloved hands and sobbed. The kindly judge invited her into his chambers to give her a cigarette before facing an aggressive cabal of photographers and reporters gathered outside.

Her marriage to the man she had promised to love "until my dying day" had ended after just seven months and twenty-four days.

Before she left the courthouse, the judge gave her some advice. "Perhaps you should seek a husband who is older and more mature the next go-around."

Outside the courtyard, as reporters rushed her, Elizabeth turned and faced them defiantly. "I never want to hear anyone mention the name of Nicky Hilton to me again." Then, with Goldstone, she got into the limousine that MGM had sent to rescue her.

MGM's final reaction to Elizabeth's divorce was to demand the return of her $3,500 wedding gown.

In Texas, Conrad Sr. told the press, "My son was not prepared to be married to a movie star, and Elizabeth refused to give up her film career. Nicky could not stand the crowds of adoring fans who demanded autographs while he stood helplessly by. The reporters and photographers followed him wherever he went, and he had not privacy. Nick was resentful, hot tempered, and acted badly under all the pressure. Sometimes his temper really flared, and he stalked out."

"They never had a chance," Conrad Sr. continued. "Beauty was the prime cause of the breakup. Elizabeth is a princess who isn't allowed to lead a normal life, and those near her are affected, too. If she had been a shade less beautiful, if she had been a counter girl at Macy's instead of a movie star, if Nicky had been older, wiser, less headstrong...who knows?"

In the aftermath of the divorce, Nicky was furious at Elizabeth and at those around her. He told a reporter, "Marriage to her was like life in a goldfish bowl. One time a battery of reporters and photographers invaded our suite—it happened all the time—and one of the buzzards said to me, 'Hey, Mac, get out of the way. I want to snap a picture of Elizabeth Taylor.'"

Although Elizabeth had waived alimony, Goldstone fought Hilton lawyers for several months over a property settlement. Finally, she won the right to retain all the stock her father-in-law had offered her. She was also granted complete ownership of all the presents given to the couple at their wedding. In today's market value, an economist estimated that all that loot would be worth two million dollars.

In the next few weeks, the newspapers were full of speculation about who Elizabeth would marry next. The public had begun its life-long fascination with her love life.

Possible candidates included Peter Lawford. It was even suggested that she might marry "the handsome blonde god, Tab Hunter." At that time, the American public did not know he was a homosexual.

The most speculation centered on a possible marriage to Monty Clift. "They were meant for each other," Louella Parsons proclaimed over the air, although she surely knew better than that.

Howard Hughes, never one to give up easily, once again came knocking on Elizabeth's door with the offer of jewelry and, this time, two million dollars— double the amount he'd offered before.

He also made an offer that almost no star in Hollywood would have refused. Knowing that she was reaching the end of her MGM contract, and that the contract was paying her $2,000 a week, he proposed setting up Elizabeth Taylor Productions and agreed to finance her first six films whether they made money or not. She rejected even such a seductive proposal.

On a less frenzied note, the press continued to follow the romances of Nicky Hilton. They included affairs with Joan Collins, Terry Moore, and the blonde starlet Barbara Payton, who later became a drug addict and a hooker. For a while, it was rumored that he was going to marry nineteen-year-old Betsy von Furstenberg, a German countess who wanted to become a film star.

The British temptress, Joan Collins, asserted that Nicky was "a sexual athlete. Between his brother Baron, his father, and himself, those boys possess a yard of cock."

As Elizabeth watched Nicky date such women as Mamie Van Doren and Jayne Mansfield, Nicky read in magazines about her interactions with a string of men who included Ted Briskin, ex- husband of Betty Hutton; George Stevens, Jr., son of the director of *A Place in the Sun;* producer Ivan Moffat; and once again her ever faithful Arthur Loew, Jr.

Nicky said, "Every man should have the opportunity of sleeping with Elizabeth Taylor, and at the rate she's going, every man will."

He would wait seventeen years after his divorce before he married again, this time to another teenage bride, oil heiress Patricia McClintock. The year was 1958.

Many observers have written that Elizabeth never saw Nicky again, but privately Roddy knew better. In the years after their break-up, Elizabeth and Nicky arranged to spend several weekends together. Twice they met at the Connecticut estate of her rich uncle, Howard Young. Also, on occasion, they arranged a secret rendezvous at the Thunderbird Hotel in Palm Springs where she traveled incognito, registering herself as "Rebecca Jones."

As she told Roddy, "A girl has a hard time finding a love machine like Nicky. I did see him on occasion whenever I needed a really good fuck. At a time when many uptight American housewives didn't even know women were supposed to have orgasms, Nicky invented multiple orgasms."

After a life of dissipation, Nicky died at age forty-two in 1969. The press noted that Elizabeth did not attend the funeral, nor did she send flowers.

However, on the first anniversary of his death, Dick Hanley made arrangements for her to pay a midnight visit to the Holy Cross Cemetery in Culver City, California. Accompanied by two security guards, she placed a wreath of yellow roses on his grave.

She told Janet Leigh, "We married much too young. I'm so sorry I hurt him. I think in his own way he did love me very much."

It was up to Richard Burton to deliver a latter day epitaph to the hotel heir. "Nicky's life could not have been totally unhappy. After all, he did get to live with Elizabeth for a while."

***

In the wake of her divorce, Elizabeth moved into a two-story apartment complex covered with ferns at 10600 Wilshire Boulevard. She lived upstairs over newlyweds Janet Leigh and Tony Curtis, who were often referred to in the press as "America's Sweethearts."

As Leigh recalled in her memoirs, "The building was a hot property, and it was infested with photographers and reporters once it was discovered. No possibility of clandestine operations here. One false move and you would be on the front page."

The beautiful young MGM star must have been dealing in hyperbole, or else she didn't have a clue as to what was going on in her apartment building, especially with her sex-crazed bisexual husband.

"I visited Elizabeth Taylor often in her bachelor quarters," said Dick Hanley. "There was a lot of hanky-panky going on there, mostly from Tony Curtis, who started cheating on Janet even during the first month of their marriage, the first week, perhaps."

Before his marriage to Leigh, Curtis had double dated on five occasions with Elizabeth and her *beau* of the moment. She found this "Kid from the Bronx" amusing and enjoyed his frankness. "I spent my first months in Hollywood going around with a lump in my pants chasing after girls," Tony confessed to Elizabeth.

The inevitable happened: Leigh had to fly to San Francisco for four days, and Elizabeth invited Curtis up for dinner during her absence. Since she had not mastered the art of cooking, she ordered Chinese take-out.

"I was still despondent over my divorce from Nicky and my self-respect was at a low ebb," she later confessed to Roddy. "For the first time in my life, I was drinking excessively. I know I sound like I'm making excuses, but Tony and I did it. He can be very persuasive when he turns on that charm. It wasn't my greatest lay, but he was sincere."

Later, when Curtis was on assignment and away from the apartment complex, Leigh invited Elizabeth downstairs for lunch one early afternoon. In those days, she had compiled a "picture wall" of photographs of herself in the company of various Hollywood personalities. One of the photos depicted Leigh with Lex Barker outfitted as Tarzan. This New York born actor was the first to replace Johnny Weissmuller on the screen as Tarzan the Ape Man.

Half naked and outfitted in a loin cloth, he had visited Leigh when she was filming *Holiday Affair* (1949) with Robert Mitchum. That afternoon, he'd asked her out on a date, and they went together for about three weeks.

Elizabeth informed Leigh that Barker was her dream man, and she'd love to go out with him. "I can call Lex up. I'm sure he'd like to go out with you. You see, he likes his girls very young."

Elizabeth said she'd be thrilled. Three days later, Barker called her. When she opened the door, she encountered a handsome giant of a man, standing six feet, four inches. He was dressed in a black suit, and offered to escort her to the Cocoanut Grove night club at the Ambassador Hotel.

"He was no Ape Man," she told Roddy the next day. "I found that he was well educated, debonair, and sophisticated. It's a bit of a stretch for him to play Jungle Boy."

He took her out on a number of dates, once inviting her to Malibu to enjoy the beach life, stopping off at his favorite hangout, Malibu Cottage, for drinks.

"I've got to keep my emotions in check," Elizabeth told Roddy. "I could go ape shit—no pun intended—for a guy like Lex. He's a school girl's dream fantasy. He is a great lover, not the King of the Jungle, but the Emperor of the Boudoir. He's never given me the slightest clue that our relationship is anything but physical. But if he proposed

Lex Barker in *Tarzan's Magic Fountain* (1949)

258

marriage tomorrow, I'd go for it."

Three days later, Roddy called Elizabeth, asking her how her affair with Body Beautiful was going. "He hasn't called me in several days," she said. "I fear he's dropped me. You know, every time a cockroach crosses Hollywood Boulevard. What's going on here?"

"I didn't want to tell you this, but Lex has been seeing a lot of Marilyn Monroe."

She exploded in fury. "That blonde bitch! Every time I turn around, that whore is crossing my path. She'd better watch out. One night she might get her tit caught in a wringer, if she fools with me anymore."

**

One rainy Sunday afternoon, a bored Elizabeth sat in her modest living room, going over a scrapbook Sara had accumulated of her film career so far. Reviewing her past work, she felt, "I have a long way to go," as she'd told Tony Curtis.

He, too, believed that his greatest work lay ahead of him "once Universal gets me out of these god damn Arabian Nights pantaloons."

The silence was broken by the ringing of her phone. It was an unexpected call from Tyrone Power. He apologized "for that last damn mix-up in New York. I'm afraid I did not put my best foot forward with you." He asked her if he could drop by if she weren't doing anything.

Remembering how attractive he was, she asked him to come over that afternoon. Within an hour, he arrived dripping wet but with a cluster of yellow roses. Nicky must have told him that those were her favorite flower.

Over a late afternoon drink, he made no mention of his affair with her former husband, and she avoided the subject as well. When recounting the evening's events with Leigh. Elizabeth said, "Some subjects are just too embarrassing to bring up."

Power's only reference to Nicky was vague. "The best way to get over a former love affair is with someone new."

Over dinner, he almost set the agenda of their relationship before it had even begun. "I always warn people not to fall in love with me, because I'm moody and unpredictable. Sometimes I invite people over for drinks and dinner, but tire of them before the evening is over. I retreat to my bedroom until they are gone."

"At that rate, you'll never compete with Elsa Maxwell as the world's greatest host...or hostess."

Joan Blondell was one of the few stars in Hollywood who learned that Power was dating Elizabeth. She'd had an affair with him when they appeared together in *Nightmare Alley* in 1947.

She told the author of this book, "Ty just oozed so much charm there should have been a law against it. He virtually seduced every man and woman he went after. His tastes evoked a smörgåsbord. Poor Lana. She never knew what hit her. He was suddenly in her life, making her the happiest woman alive. Then, like a bird in flight, he was gone with the wind."

"Ty and I had a brief affair when he made that geeky movie," Blondell recalled. "It didn't last very long. In a few months or so, I heard he was dating Liz Taylor, although I'm sure both of them were seeing other people at the time. Liz, by the way, ended up getting my third and final husband, Mike Todd."

"If it were 1937," Blondell continued, "Miss Taylor would not have taken either of those guys from me. After all, George C. Scott said I was the sexiest woman ever to appear on the screen."

For some reason, Power never invited Elizabeth out to a public restaurant. Sometimes they shared dinners downstairs with Leigh and Curtis. They also took walks along the beach in the early twilight at Malibu and sometimes went on long drives up the Pacific Coast. One weekend, they drove to Big Sur.

"It was the most idyllic weekend of my life," she told Leigh and Curtis when she came back. "I've never been that comfortable with any man before, certainly not with Nicky, who could ignite into a firestorm at any minute. Ty and I spent hours together reading or listening to music on the radio. We could go for hours without speaking, but there seemed to be this bond between us."

"Together, they were the most beautiful couple I've ever seen, except for Janet and me," Curtis said. "But somehow, I didn't hear church bells ringing. Not at all."

One of the three or four most handsome men in Hollywood: **Tyrone Power**

Leigh said, "Elizabeth told me she wanted the relationship to go on and on, never to end. She told me, 'Ty is so stunningly handsome and such a sweet, endearing personality—so unlike Nicky.'"

One drunken night, overcome with nostalgia about the family units that might have been, the delicate subject of their respective "lost children" came up. Power confessed that Lana Turner had aborted a child that he had fathered, and Elizabeth tearfully confessed that Nicky had assaulted her in ways that led to a miscarriage when "he performed an Indian War Dance on my stomach."

Power then made a wild proposal to her. "Let's make our own baby. With you as his mother—or *her* mother—and me the father, it will be the world's most beautiful baby. It'll probably grow up to become the biggest star in the world. It can become that whether it's a boy or a girl."

As Elizabeth later confided to Leigh, "Ty and I made several attempts, but I never got pregnant. I had a wonderful time trying."

After Power went with Elizabeth for a screening of *A Place in the Sun,* he seemed jealous of her scenes with Monty. "Critics are referring to you guys as the most beautiful couple on the screen. I want you to appear in a movie with me called *Forever.* It's by my favorite author, Mildred Cram."

He explained to her that many of Cram's novels had been made into films, including his favorite, *Love Story* (1939), starring Charles Boyer and Irene Dunne.

Forever, the sixty-page novella by Cram, had been kicking around Hollywood studios for years, and was once considered as a vehicle for either Norma Shearer or Janet Gaynor.

Unknown to Elizabeth, Power had suggested appearing in the film with Judy Garland when he was dating her. "I practically memorized it [the novella] word for word," Garland claimed.

Later, Power, in a Machiavellian flip-flop after he began dating Lana Turner, suggested it as a co-starring vehicle for Lana and himself.

The romance between Elizabeth and Power that began one rainy afternoon seemed to disappear in the glare of the sun. As Elizabeth told Roddy, "I didn't see the end coming. In spite of his protestations, I thought I could change him. Like Lana, I was in such a state of jubilation that I didn't see the train wreck ahead. Suddenly, days would go by and he wouldn't call. Then he'd show up with no explanation as to where he'd been. There were nights he could not sleep and would pace the floor until dawn." She suspected he was deeply conflicted over his sexuality.

"I remember, once when I brought up a future plan involving the two of us, he responded in anger," she revealed to Roddy. "He told me that he didn't want to think about tomorrow, only today. Then he started kissing me, and it went on forever. I, too, forgot about tomorrow. We got so carried away, we completely forgot that we'd accepted a dinner invitation from Janet and Tony."

Power later told his gay friend, actor Cesar Romero, that "Elizabeth and I might have continued dating a little longer but, like Lana, she was becoming too possessive. She was so very insecure that it became unbearable to live with her at times. She worried that in a few years, she'd be washed up because she claimed that she was hired by MGM only because of her face and breasts. Once I came back to her apartment and caught her painting wrinkles on this studio blowup of herself so she'd have an idea of what she'd look like when she was old."

Intuitively, Curtis seemed to know that Elizabeth's affair with Power was over before she did. In Key West during the making of *Operation Petticoat* (1950), Curtis recalled that he let Power into Elizabeth's upstairs apartment one afternoon when she was delayed at the studio.

"We had a few drinks," he said to Cary Grant and some gay friends working on the movie. "It was very hot in the apartment, and Ty suggested we strip down a bit. I guess one thing led to another. We balled each other. Or, more to the point, I balled him. He was a great bottom. By the time Elizabeth got home, Ty had fled. He'd already had his fun for the day."

Somehow, Hedda Hopper got wind of the Taylor/Power liaison and called her to inquire about it. Elizabeth refused to confirm or deny the romance which by then had already ended. She did, however, issue an enigmatic statement to Hopper which was never printed.

"Tyrone Power is a closed chapter in a book never read."

***

Back in Hollywood early in 1951, Elizabeth learned that Harvard University's *Lampoon* had named her "one of the most objectionable movie *children* of the year," claiming that in *Conspirator* she gave "the worst performance of the decade." She was also cited for being "objectionably ingénue." The *Lampoon* said that she persists in her career "despite a total inability to act." She also was the recipient of Harvard's first Roscoe ("Oscar" spelled "sideways"), an award for bad acting.

Her reaction to those Harvard students was graphic. "Every one of those fuckers can stick a fourteen-inch dildo up their dingleberry-coated assholes."

Dore Schary at MGM became so alarmed at some of her foul language that he asked her co-stars, Sara, and even some of her friends if they could "clean out her beautiful mouth. We expect words of love and compassion coming from it, and we get talk a whore would find offensive."

At a time when it was dropping stars, MGM wanted to hold onto Elizabeth, seeing great potential in her as a future moneymaker and a potent incentive to lure Americans away from their television sets.

Finally her agent/lawyer, Jules Goldstone, and MGM came to an agreement on a new contract for Elizabeth. It would remain in force from 1952 through 1958, with an escalating salary beginning at $5,000 a week. Although that sounded adequate for the early 1950s, it was hardly lavish, as the tax bite in effect at the time took ninety percent of the upper tier of her salary.

For her next MGM movie, *Love Is Better Than Ever,* Elizabeth would be cast opposite Larry Parks and helmed by a young director, Stanley Donen.

She was cast as a dancing teacher, Anastasia, who falls in love with a smart theater agent, Jud, as played by Parks.

His name was billed above Elizabeth's because he'd become a major star in *The Jolson Story* (1946) and in its sequel, *Jolson Sings Again* (1949). He was among the first Hollywood personalities to admit that he had been a member of the Communist Party during testimony before the House Un-American Activities Committee. As a result, MGM postponed the release of the film until February 23, 1952. After his testimony, Parks' promising screen career went up in flames, and the film became one of Elizabeth's lightweight, less publicized efforts.

During the filming of *Love Is Better Than Ever,* Elizabeth asked her director, Donen, to prove the validity of its title with a performance in bed. He obliged and a torrid affair began, brief in its intensity but scandalous because Donen was already married.

Once, she tried to explain her attraction to Donen, which did not sound all that physical. "He is witty and wise and sympathetic to my problems. I know he's always there for me if I need to cry on his shoulder."

Sara, who had been secretly anti-Semitic throughout most of her life, was not impressed with the short, swarthy, twenty-seven year old director. He wasn't rich, and he was also a Jew. When she heard he'd worked with gay actor Gene Kelly and had been a chorus boy on Broadway, she assumed he was a homosexual with no supporting evidence that he was. She called Hedda Hopper and made that accusation, but Hopper wouldn't print it. Sara also told the columnist that "Donen should be run out of town."

MGM hired Marjorie Dillon as Elizabeth's stand-in because of their facial resemblance, height, and body structure. She was also assigned the task of looking after Elizabeth, who was sometimes breaking down into hysterical fits of uncontrollable weeping during the filming of *Love Is Better Than Ever.* "Hours would go by, and she seemed all right and in control," Dillon claimed. "But the least little thing could set her off, and she'd flee from the set and run back to her dressing room, where she sobbed until her eyes were too red to face the camera."

Director **Stanley Donen** with **Elizabeth Taylor**

Elizabeth warned Dillon to keep Sara off the set. "If she sets one foot in here, tell Dore Schary I'm leaving and not coming back." Elizabeth threatened.

Barred from MGM, Sara frequently called Dillon and pumped her for information about her daughter, especially for details about her ongoing affair with Donen. Sara claimed that "under no circumstances will my daughter ever marry a Jew."

Sara also asked Dillon, "Is it true that Donen

is divorcing his wife? Where did Elizabeth go last night? Is he sleeping over at her apartment?"

"I didn't tell her anything," Dillon said. "But everybody on the set knew that Donen had become Elizabeth's lover."

Donen and Elizabeth formed a social group, "The Fox and Lox Club." Curtis and Leigh were among the charter members, as were actors Barry Sullivan, Diana Lynn, and Colleen Gray, each a B-list star. "We got together for house parties and Sunday brunches," said Marty Ragaway, a comedy writer and member of the group. "I saw Donen and Elizabeth together on many an occasion. I'd call it a transitional romance for her, love on the rebound."

Each member of Fox and Lox was assigned the task, on one Sunday or another, of hosting the other members. When Donen and Elizabeth were designated as co-hosts for a luncheon gathering of the club within her apartment, screenwriter Stanley Roberts was assigned the task of delivering the silver, cutlery, and porcelain. Elizabeth became seriously annoyed when Roberts was an hour late to a party which was quickly, without cutlery or porcelain, beginning to unravel. On the table was a big chocolate cake with peppermint frosting. As Roberts entered her apartment, she picked up that cake and smashed it in his face. Her guests were shocked and quickly made excuses to leave.

That was the last meeting of the Fox and Lox Club.

Even though Donen was still married, Elizabeth decided to get confessional and go public with her affair. She created a media-feeding frenzy when she showed up with him at the Academy Awards in March of 1951, where members of the press opted to define him as an escort and not as a serious lover.

However, on April 5, 1951, she made an appearance with Donen at the premiere of *Father's Little Dividend* at the Egyptian Theater. In the wake of their joint appearance, rumors spread the couple was secretly planning a wedding. Photographers ignored the other stars in a frenzy of snapping pictures of Donen with Elizabeth.

Four days after the premiere, Donen's estranged wife, Jeanne, filed for divorce, citing alienation of affection for "another woman." Elizabeth was not named, but the whole world seemingly knew the identity of the "other woman" who had stolen her husband's love.

For the first time, Elizabeth was labeled a homewrecker in the press, a charge that would be frequently leveled at her in the future. When a reporter asked her the name of her next film, she sarcastically said it would be *The Other Woman.*

After receiving so much bad press, she faced reporters and tried to defend herself. "I know I've been spoiled, but I think people are unfairly severe. I'm just a normal girl with the average faults and virtues, but being a movie actress, I wasn't allowed to develop along normal lines. I've been able to wear a plunging neckline since I was fourteen years old, and ever since, then, people expected me to act as old as I look. All my troubles started because I have a woman's body and a child's emotions."

Larry Parks remembered Elizabeth frequently breaking down in tears on the set: "On occasion, she was unable to perform, and Donen offered her much comfort. Her personal life was in shatters, and her mother no longer seemed of much help."

At one point during the filming, she collapsed on the set and was rushed to the Cedars of Lebanon Hospital. Registering under the name "Rebecca Jones," she was diagnosed as suffering from nervous exhaustion.

After she was released from the hospital, she flew on a short visit to New York to see Monty and Roddy. She checked into the Hilton-affiliated Plaza Hotel, assuming her visit would be *gratis.*

Monty and Elizabeth behaved like lovers, but apparently it was a platonic relationship even though they often slept in the same bed together, cuddling each other against the night.   She admitted to her new friend, Truman Capote, that, "I've slept with Monty but we never fucked."

Later, Capote reported that assertion to Tennessee Williams. "It's just as well she didn't fuck Monty," Capote said. "Elizabeth would have been disappointed. I went to bed with him only once. He didn't actually have a cock, just foreskin that looked like a puny piece of dried okra."

Shortly before she was scheduled to check out of the Plaza, the manager presented her with a $2,500 bill, telling her, "Miss Taylor, we are so sorry that you are no longer a part of the wonderful Hilton family."

Before her departure, and in revenge, she invited Roddy and Monty to her suite, where she ordered three pitchers of martinis for them before they went on a rampage. They removed the stuffing from pillows and crammed them down the toilet. They cut up the draperies and the sheets.

Fans had sent her lots of flowers. They tossed them about the room and emptied wastepaper baskets onto the carpet. As a final gesture, she packed one of her suitcases with Plaza monogrammed towels.

***

After the breakup of the Fox and Lox Club, Elizabeth accepted invitations to Hollywood parties. One of them originated with that dashing swashbuckler Stewart Granger, who had moved to Hollywood. He carried special greetings from Michael Wilding in London.

Both Wilding and Elizabeth had written letters to each other since getting to know each other during her filming of *Conspirator.*

Granger told Elizabeth that Richard Burton had arrived in Hollywood after vowing for years that he'd never do that. "He's my house guest, and he's here now. He'd like to see you. When he's finished showering, I'll send him out."

"After a few more defections of actors from the Britain, the press will start calling it 'The London Invasion,'" she said.

"Dick is unique," Granger said. "You'll like him or hate him. I met him at a small theater in Hammersmith when I went backstage to congratulate him on a performance. He opened the door to his dressing room, wearing a jock strap, with a can of beer in his hand. He said to me, 'Oh god, a bloody film star.' For us, it was love at first sight. We've been friends ever since."

Within fifteen minutes, Burton, wearing an almost see-through white bathing suit, headed toward Elizabeth, who was lying on a *chaise longue*. He was immediately attracted to her and wanted to talk. He would later recall the historic event, likening it to when Romeo first spotted Juliet

"She was the most astonishing, self-contained, pulchritudinous, remote, re-moved, inaccessible woman I had ever seen," Burton said. "Her face was di-vine, but her breasts were nothing short of apocalyptic. They would topple empires before they withered. Indeed, her body was a miracle of construction."

"She was so perfect she made me aware of my own imperfections," Bur-ton said. "Every pockmark on my face became a crater on the dark side of the moon. I lifted my hand to cover my cheek. As I did so, it occurred to me that she probably would find my hand as ugly as my face. I lowered it to my side and kept on staring."

She wished him well in his Hollywood career, but warned him "to watch your ass in this town unless you want to get it fucked. Everybody's a god damn phony and a liar. Stars like Crawford and Stanwyck were former whores. There are one hundred pederasts per square mile. Some directors will hire you just to sniff your panties, preferably with skid marks. It's one big parade of hustlers, pimps, dope fiends, alcoholics—you name it. If they're not assholes, they're shitheads. If not that, they're fucking embezzlers who'll rob you blind. Every time you let out a fart in this town, some jerk will try to sue you. Hollywood is nothing but a swarm of greedy locusts."

She was feeling particularly bitter that day, and she seemed to realize that her words shocked him. "Don't they use words like that at the Old Vic?" she asked.

"Yes, in Bloody Olde England they curse like fishmongers, but not neces-sarily on stage." Then he wished her good day and walked away. Later, he told Granger, "That Elizabeth Taylor talks like a drunken lorry driver."

Elizabeth wanted to know what was going on between Burton and Granger. Out by the pool, when Granger's houseman, an elderly gray-haired African-American, served her a drink, she offered him a twenty-dollar bill to tell her de-tails about what went on in Granger's house at night. Jean Simmons had not yet arrived in town.

"Miss Taylor," the old man told her, "I'm ashamed for my poor old eyes to have seen it. But these two Englishmen walk around jaybird naked, flaunting their junk and getting drunk as skunks. They go at it every night like two jackrabbits in heat. It's against God's will. Our Lord did not create Adam and Adam."

***

Dore Schary at MGM did not approve of Elizabeth's relationship with Donen and shipped her off to England to film *Ivanhoe* (1952), a costume period drama starring her former flame, Robert Taylor.

On her final night in bed with Donen, Elizabeth promised him that, "I will belong to you forever. I'll be gone only a short time. And don't worry, I won't be fucking Robert Taylor. Been there, done that—not memorable."

After she got to London, however, letters and phone calls to and from Donen gradually ebbed until there were none at all.

Months later, looking back on the interlude of her life that included Donen, Elizabeth told Granger, "Promises are made to be broken. It's the way life works."

For Elizabeth, Donen became "emotionally obsolete" with the arrival of Michael Wilding in her life. But first, there was a major hurdle to overcome, and it was formidable: Marlene Dietrich.

***

One of the motivations that prompted MGM to cast Elizabeth in *Ivanhoe* (1952), a medieval drama co-starring Robert Taylor, involved getting her out of the country and separating her from the potentiality of scandal associated with her affair with Donen.

She had frequently tuned in to Tallulah Bankhead's *The Big Show*, a ninety-minute radio program that would eventually lure some of the A-list stars in the entertainment business, including Marlene Dietrich and Ethel Merman.

Elizabeth had steadfastly refused to go on the show, but Tallulah referred to her anyway. "Elizabeth, you know, my darlings, married one of the *biggest* men in the hotel trade, Nicky Hilton." She was referring to Nicky's endowment, which she'd sampled only the week before. "What else could I do?" she asked her friend, TV producer, Stanley Mills Haggart. "I met Nicky at Sardi's and invited him home for a drink. He raped me, and darling, I struggled valiantly. The next morning, when we both woke up at eleven o'clock, I insisted he rape me again...and be even more forceful if I resisted."

Long before she converted to the Jewish religion, Elizabeth was cast in *Ivanhoe* as Rebecca of York, "the Jewish infidel."

She had protested to Schary that she did not like the script, and that she did not want to appear in *Ivanhoe,* and he retaliated by threatening her with suspension. Eventually, she acquiesced, but lobbied, unsuccessfully, for the role of Rowena, the film's female love interest. But Schary had already contracted with Joan Fontaine to play that part. Elizabeth was therefore forced into the lesser role of Rebecca.

The film was one-fourth shot when she confronted its director, Richard Thorpe, claiming she had been miscast as Rebecca and was pulling out of the role. Briefly, there was talk of replacing her with Deborah Kerr, who had recently co-starred with Robert Taylor in *Quo Vadis?* But when Schary heard of this, he threatened Elizabeth with "hell and damnation," and she reluctantly resumed her role as Rebecca.

The plot was so loosely adapted from Sir Walter Scott's epic novel that the original author might have denounced it if he'd still been around. George Sanders, one of the film's co-stars, referred to it as "historical hokum," and Elizabeth described it as "a piece of *cachou.*"

Even Robert Taylor objected to it, claiming, "I prefer to do Westerns." During the shoot, he told Thorpe, "I'm getting mighty tired of walking around in an iron jockstrap."

Returning from the Crusades in the Holy Land, Ivanhoe (as played by Taylor) learns that (the good) King Richard the Lionheart is imprisoned and being held for ransom in Austria. Ivanhoe's demand that the ransom be paid is ignored when the evil Prince John and his corrupted cronies refuse to relinquish their prestige and power. Joining forces with Robin Hood, whose appearance in the movie is very brief, Ivanhoe selflessly, and for the good of England, rustles up the money to release King Richard, simultaneously re-establishing a relationship with his father, who disowned him years previously.

In the film, Elizabeth was tried publicly as an infidel witch and a seductress who has taken advantage of Ivanhoe, a Christian knight. One critic noted that "Elizabeth Taylor is seen going to the stake with the expression of a girl who has been stood up on a date. So much for martyrdom. Cast her next as Joan of Arc."

When Robert met Elizabeth on the set, he told her he was furious at the terms of his divorce from Barbara Stanwyck. "The bitch got our mansion and all that was in it except for my underwear. Not only that, the dyke was awarded fifteen percent of all my earnings unless she remarries. Believe you me, *that one* will never remarry. She'll suck my balls dry until I die."

Thorpe, the director, privately told his friends in London that MGM had hired two heterosexual leading ladies, Elizabeth Taylor and Joan Fontaine; three bisexual co-stars—Robert Taylor, Robert Douglas, and George Sanders—and one homosexual Welshman, Emlyn Williams.

I was never invited, but Bob Taylor threw some wild parties with Douglas, Sanders, and Williams," Thorpe said. "A lot of handsome young Englishmen worked either as extras or as page boys, and they often attended these homosexual orgies. We were always worried that word would reach the tabloids in London. Many guys in the cast and crew, who were basically straight shooters, were willing to hang out with these big name stars, perhaps hoping to advance their careers. They ended up getting sucked dry by my male stars, not the female ones."

Thorpe had directed Elizabeth before in *A Date With Judy* and had found her fairly easy to work with, an actress who took directions. But he encountered a very different Elizabeth on the set of *Ivanhoe*. She looked ghostly thin, complaining of an ulcer. She didn't give a performance, but sleepwalked through her role, using a voice that was hardly audible. "Her line reads were so incomprehensible we later had to have them dubbed back in Hollywood," Thorpe said. "We had to hire a voice coach for her."

At MGM, the word was that her drama coach, Lillian Burns Sidney, dragged Elizabeth "kicking and screaming through the entire *Ivanhoe* script until she got it right."

Opening in the summer of 1952, *Ivanhoe* eventually grossed $6.2 million, making it MGM's biggest earner for that year. Its premiere in New York set a box office record for the studio. *Ivanhoe* was nominated for an Oscar as Best Picture of 1952.

Both Elizabeth and Michael Wilding were filming at Borehamwood (aka Elstree) Studio outside London. Wilding was starring in *Trent's Last Case* with Orson Welles, who had known Elizabeth intimately.

In *Ivanhoe,* Elizabeth as Rebecca falls in love with the knight, as played by Robert Taylor. Off screen, another actor whom she mistakenly interpreted as her "knight in shining armor," Wilding, became the star attraction in her life.

***

After filming began on *Ivanhoe,* Thorpe recalled that Wilding dropped in every afternoon for tea with Elizabeth. "At first, he seemed reluctant to start dating a girl so young," Thorpe said. "I was there when she got the ball game launched."

"I wish you'd stop treating me as if I had a child's mind inside a woman's body," she said to Wilding. "Why don't you invite me out to dinner tonight?"

The next morning, Thorpe asked Elizabeth how her date with Wilding went.

"He has the day off, and he's sleeping it off at my suite at the Savoy," she told him. "He hit the spot last night."

"It was all too obvious to me that he'd seduced her," Thorpe said. "The gleam in Elizabeth's eyes reminded me of Vivien Leigh in that scene as Scarlett O'Hara where she wakes up the morning after Rhett Butler has plowed her royally."

From London, Elizabeth wrote Janet Leigh. In her letter, Elizabeth described Wilding as "a man with sand-colored hair, a broad forehead, and a narrow chin—a cross between Bing Crosby and King George VI." In many ways, he reminded her of her childhood idol, Victor Cazalet.

At the time she became involved with him, Wilding, in England at least, was at the peak of his matinee idol charm.

After about a week had passed since the debut of their mutual seductions, Elizabeth joined in the praise of Wilding as a great lover. Wilding's expertise was discussed one night at a party in the Manhattan apartment of Tallulah Bankhead when Bankhead was gossiping, publicly, with Paulette Goddard: "Michael Wilding, unlike Charlie Chaplin, gives endless satisfaction to a woman in bed," Goddard claimed. "Even though he's pushing forty, he has marvelous stamina in the sack."

"Lucky Liz," Tallulah said. "The bitch always seems to catch those two-handers, or three-handers, like Nicky Hilton."

***

Before his involvement with Elizabeth Taylor, and before his box office disaster in Alfred Hitchcock's *Under Capricorn* (1949), opposite Ingrid Bergman, Wilding had shot *Stage Fright* (1950) with Marlene Dietrich and Jane Wyman, who had recently divorced Ronald Reagan.

As Dietrich's biographer, Steven Bach, described Wilding at the time, "he was tall, thin, and elegant as a whip from Asprey's. He had charm and a dashing way with the ladies. Marlene took one look at Wilding and the laziest gal in town got busy." In direct competition for the British actor, Dietrich trounced Wyman.

Now, Dietrich faced far more formidable competition in the form of Elizabeth. When not before the cameras, Wilding was dividing his time between visits to Dietrich's suite at Claridges and Elizabeth's suite at the Savoy.

It took two or three weeks before nineteen-year-old Elizabeth realized she was competing with forty-nine-year old Marlene Dietrich.

Although Elizabeth had youth and beauty on her side, Dietrich, in her capacity as one of the most formidable *femmes fatales* of the 20th century, had an allure that had attracted suitors who had included, among many others, Gary Cooper, Howard Hughes, Barbara Stanwyck, Frank Sinatra, Ernest Hemingway, and U.S. Army Lieutenant General James Gavin.

To members of the press, Wilding appeared reluctant to get too involved with anyone. "I have serious doubts about marrying another actress."

Actually, Wilding was using the fact that he was already married as an excuse to avoid emotional entanglements. It was believed in London that he had not seen his wife, actress Kay Young, since 1945.

Partly as a means of making Wilding jealous, Elizabeth went out on two dates with the blonde heartthrob Tab Hunter, who was in England at the time filming *Island of Desire* with Linda Darnell. These dates, of course, weren't any particular threat, as Elizabeth knew that Hunter's heart belonged to a fellow actor, Anthony Perkins.

The Hunter ploy worked, however. Wilding finally got up the courage to ask Young for a divorce, and eventually booked Elizabeth every night. He'd arrive on time at her suite at the Savoy, but she was never ready. "Punctuality was not her *forte*," he said. Often, she'd invite him into her dressing room, where she sat in front of her vanity mirror coquettishly applying heavy coats of make-up. He felt she was using far too much make-up for one so young and beautiful. "I understand why Marlene applies so much make-up," he told Elizabeth. "She's trying to erase the ravages of time. But you...."

"I'm trying to make myself look older so you might finally get around to asking me to marry you."

When it became obvious to her that Wilding was stalling, Elizabeth jumped into one of London's taxicabs and asked to be driven to a jewelry store in Mayfair which had been recommended to her. Once inside, she purchased a large sapphire ring encircled with diamonds. Placing it on the fourth finger of her left hand, she announced that afternoon to the press, "I am engaged to Michael Wilding. Look at the lovely ring he placed on my finger."

Her aggressive scheme goaded him into proposing to her. "Of course, I'll have to wait for my divorce to become finalized."

Friends of both Elizabeth and Dietrich, including Stewart Granger, were amazed that they had linked up as a couple. "Michael always preferred the woman as a dominant partner, and Marlene fitted that role perfectly," Granger said. "On the other hand, Elizabeth was searching for a father figure, a man who could dominate her. Personally, I didn't give their relationship much chance, although Michael had a big one, I didn't think that a mere cock would be enough to maintain a marriage."

Maria Riva, Dietrich's daughter, wrote a biography of her mother, in which she maintained that she "preferred fellatio so she could better control the situation." An entry in Dietrich's diary was also published: "Michael is inventive in coitus," she wrote, and I was staining as a result of his steeple chasing and always had to insert a firecracker the minute he dismounted."

271

Such an entry requires translation: "Staining" is a reference to bleeding, and "steeple chasing" refers to sexual intercourse. A "firecracker" was her nickname for a tampon.

When queried about Dietrich, Wilding was polite, "I kept asking myself, how could such a goddess find the ideal companion in me?"

Wilding had never before seen one of Elizabeth's movies, and she made arrangements for him to view *National Velvet.* She later said, "What a strong-willed and determined girl she was even back then. She says she wants a strong man in her life, but I don't know who'd wear the trousers. I suspect that in a marriage, she would be passive/aggressive."

At the studio, he arranged for her to see his 1949 film, *Maytime in Mayfair,* in which he co-starred with Anna Neagle. Over dinner, after watching the film, he asked, "Well, what do you think of me as an actor?"

She didn't directly answer the question, but told him, "When you're up close and looking down at Anna, you evoke a British gent trying to conceal a hard-on."

As Wilding's romance with Elizabeth deepened, he made it a point to have dinner with his longtime producer, Henry Wilcox, and his frequent co-star, Anna Neagle, who was married to Wilcox. They had long been his confidants.

"He was very honest with us," Wilcox later recalled. "He admitted that he didn't love Elizabeth, but was powerfully attracted to her. Michael was very ambitious in that he wanted to become an international star. He didn't want to be limited to making films only in England. He knew that by marrying Elizabeth, he would become a household name in America. He looked at me with those piercing eyes of his and said, 'Forgive me, Herbert, but you can't make me an international star, and Elizabeth can.'"

Wilcox told him, "If you marry Marlene, you'll be accused of wedding your grandmother. If you marry Elizabeth, you'll be labeled a cradle-snatcher."

Wilding told Neagle, "I'm running after Elizabeth, and she's desperate to catch me."

Wilding confided to Wilcox, "I can't make up my mind. I want both Marlene *and* Elizabeth."

"I can hardly feel sympathy for you," Wilcox said, "having to choose between two of the most desirable and famous women on God's good earth."

At a party in London, Elizabeth learned that Dietrich was also having an affair with the terse and acerbic theater critic, Kenneth Tynan, who told Elizabeth, "The secret of Marlene's mysterious appeal lies in the fact that she has sex without gender."

When Elizabeth met Wilcox at the same party in Mayfair, she told him that, "Michael can give me security, maturity, and tranquility. That's what I'm looking for in a relationship." She would later retract that in a memoir. "I found out that unfortunately, you can't get those things just by touching someone else."

Wilding later wrote that, "I dreaded hurting Marlene," yet he chose an awkward way to announce to her that he he'd rejected her in favor of Elizabeth. He invited her to Dietrich's one-woman show in London at the *Café de Paris,* where Noël Coward introduced her every night, asserting onstage that "God has a talent for creating exceptional women."

Wilding took Elizabeth backstage to Dietrich's dressing room. In her diary, Dietrich later wrote, "Michael was there last night with Liz Taylor, with Michael sitting rather stiffly in a corner and looking at me quite steadily and sadly. I thought that that could not happen to me, seeing him with another woman. I felt quite sick."

"Dietrich got that stupid song all wrong—something about 'Whatever Lola wants, Lola gets,'" Elizabeth later said. "It should be rewritten as 'Whatever Elizabeth wants, Elizabeth gets.'"

During her evaluation of Dietrich's performance, Elizabeth told Wilding, "She's got a throaty kind of glamour, rather old-fashioned for the 50s. But as I understand it, she attracted Hitler and Goebbels. With that perfectly chiseled face, she seems to have discovered the secret of perpetual middle age."

"Even if I couldn't compete on the level of youth and beauty with Taylor, I could always upstage her in glamour," Dietrich told James Stewart, when she was filming *No Highway in the Sky* with him in England. "Sexual allure is all about glamour and illusion anyway, and I'm the mistress of the genre."

When Dietrich had filmed *Destry Rides Again* (1939) with Stewart, these two co-stars had launched an affair, eventually leading to Dietrich getting an abortion.

She claimed that Wilding was the British version of James Stewart—"He mumbles like Jimmy, and is ever so shy. But when Michael is unleashed, he becomes a tornado, his passion suddenly appearing without warning."

As Dietrich reported to Stewart, "I have to hand it to that Liz creature. Her breasts are bigger than mine, but she has short, stumpy legs. As you well know, I'm celebrated around the world for the shape of my legs. What I don't often hear about Liz is that she has hair on her arms, lots of black hair. I'm certain that centuries ago, her distant ancestors mated with the Neanderthal."

During pillow talk with Elizabeth, Wilding expressed his desire to produce a family. "I can bear your children," Elizabeth told him. "Dietrich is far too old. Besides, she's already married to some chicken farmer." She was referring to Rudolph Sieber, whom Dietrich had wed in Berlin in 1924, and had never divorced.

Actually, Elizabeth was not exactly candid with Wilding, since two doctors—one in Los Angeles, another in New York—had told her in the wake of her violent miscarriage, that it was doubtful she would ever have children again.

One night after dinner, when they were talking and drinking, Michael told her he wanted to confess his darkest secret. She apparently felt that he was going to Out himself to her as a bisexual, exposing his years-on affair with Stewart Granger and others. But it was something else.

"I suffer from epilepsy, and at times I have seizures that cloud my consciousness."

In the early 1950s, there was a great social stigma attached to epilepsy. Wilding feared that producers would not hire him if word of his disease got out.

"I will love you regardless," she promised him.

After being dumped by Wilding in favor of Elizabeth, Dietrich flew back to New York when her part of the filming of *No Highway in the Sky* was finished.

As it happened, because of business commitments, Wilcox was also in Manhattan at the time. Dietrich met with him for lunch, mainly to ask the producer questions about Wilding. "What's Taylor got that I haven't?"

Wilcox later recalled, "I was far too gallant to mention the 'Y' word." He was referring, of course, to "youth."

Not getting a satisfactory answer from Wilcox, Dietrich came up with her own. "Michael tells me he cannot live without me, and then he goes and fucks Elizabeth Taylor. It must be her bovine tits. In bed, Michael likes breasts dangled in his face."

Then she relayed to Wilcox that one night, she mentioned Wilding's breast fetish to Noël Coward. "Noël responded that Michael also prefers another and very different appendage dangled in his face."

***

After finishing *Ivanhoe* in early September, Elizabeth stayed in London until October 6, 1952, when both Tab Hunter and Wilding escorted her to the airport. She gave Hunter a kiss on the cheek but tongue-kissed Wilding before taking off for New York. "Goodbye, Mr. Shilly-Shally," she told him. "Let's forget we ever met."

In a week, he sent her a cable. AM CATCHING THE NEXT PLANE TO HOLLYWOOD. SIGNED, MR. SHILLY-SHALLY.

***

In New York, Elizabeth and Monty Clift basked in their rave reviews for *A Place in the Sun*. With Elizabeth picking up the tab, they were spotted at "21"

Club, Voisin, and Le Pavillon.

But Monty much preferred escorting her to seedy dives such as Gregory's, where he'd taken her so many times before, and which was still his favorite. One drunken night at the tavern, Monty had consumed too many Nembutals and had drunk a quart of Scotch.

In the men's toilet, Monty propositioned a drunken sailor, who slugged him viciously, breaking his nose and knocking him to the floor where he stomped on his shoulder, dislocating it. Calling an ambulance, Elizabeth hovered protectively over him and stayed at his apartment until he could look after himself.

Through the MGM office in New York, she arranged two private screenings of Michael Wilding films, since Monty had never seen him act. He sat impatiently through the double feature.

At the end of the screenings, he grabbed her arm. "Let's get the hell out of here." Over drinks, he warned her against marrying Wilding. "If he's not better as a husband than he is as an actor, he'll be rotten. His acting is very dated, a kind of romantic leading man style left over from one of the English parlor dramas the Brits made in the 1930s."

After flying back to Hollywood, Elizabeth spent many evenings with Stewart Granger and his young wife, Jean Simmons, who was sometimes referred to as "the British Elizabeth Taylor." The British couple, trying to make it in Hollywood, had married in Texas in 1950, with Wilding designated as Granger's best man.

As a trio, Granger, Simmons, and Elizabeth drove to the Burbank airport to welcome Wilding to Hollywood. Elizabeth and Wilding were invited to stay in the guest room at the Granger home in the Hollywood Hills.

For a while during the winter of 1951, Granger, Simmons, Wilding, and Elizabeth lived under the same roof. "I took a child bride," Granger said, "and now Michael plans to follow my example."

In the nights to come, the friendly couples would be seen dining and dancing together at the Mocambo, at Chasen's, and at Romanoff's. At the latter, the "watering hole" for Humphrey Bogart, Bogie wet kissed both the bride (Simmons) and the bride-to-be (Elizabeth).

Even after Simmons had signed with 20th Century Fox and Elizabeth had renewed her contract at MGM, Howard Hughes still had dreams of buying out their contracts. Although he was increasingly resentful of Hughes, Granger invited him over to dinner, a provocative move.

"Hughes was met by two of the most beautiful girls in the world," Granger wrote in his memoirs, referring to Elizabeth and to his wife. "His pale blue eyes bugged out of his head, and he literally drooled as he stood looking down at them sitting demurely side by side on a couch. He practically overbalanced himself by trying to look down at their cleavage, both of them being well-endowed in that department. I'd heard a rumor that Hughes was a tit man."

"Which one of them would you prefer, Howard?" Granger asked.

"God damn, I can't make up my mind," he replied, watering at the mouth.

"Well, hard cheese, old boy," Granger said. "You're not going to get either of them, so up yours."

"Howard turned and looked at us," Granger recalled. "We thought we were teasing a nut. But we were teasing a cobra."

Columnist Hedda Hopper was outraged when she heard of Elizabeth's living arrangement, and she summoned her, along with Wilding, to her home in Beverly Hills. During her dialogue, she referred to Granger and Wilding as "two dirty old men taking advantage of those teenagers, the limey bastards."

Within her living room, Hopper spoke to Elizabeth as if Wilding were not in the room. "Do you know, my dear child, that Mr. Wilding is a homosexual and has engaged in a decades-long affair with Stewart Granger?"

Wilding sat in stunned silence, and Elizabeth made no attempt to defend her husband-to-be. He was visibly shaken, knowing that if Hopper printed such charges, his Hollywood career might be over before it had even begun.

Back in the Hollywood Hills, Wilding told Granger what had happened.

"Oh, Mikey, don't worry about what she said," Elizabeth told him. "It doesn't matter to me."

Granger challenged Elizabeth for not defending Wilding. "You silly bitch, you just sat there and didn't take up for him? Well, she'll hear from me."

He went into his study and placed a call to Hopper, calling her "a monumental bitch. How dare you accuse a friend of mine of being queer, you raddled, dried-up, frustrated old cunt!"

Obviously shaken by such a call, Hopper would stick the needle into Granger in any future column where his name came up.

The following morning at six o'clock, Bogart called Wilding "Have you read Hedda's column?"

"Hell, no," Wilding said. "I'm trying to get some sleep." But after putting down the phone, he went downstairs and retrieved the morning paper. In it, Hopper had run a picture of Wilding and Granger on a yacht during one of their shared vacations along the French Riviera, clearly suggesting that the two handsome actors "were more than just mere friends."

Wilding asked Granger if he'd join them in a joint libel suit against Hopper.

The English Abroad:
Stewart Granger with his wife
Jean Simmons

"Suing Hopper is like suing God," Granger told him. "remind me the next time we go out on a boat together not to hold your hand."

Granger ultimately got his revenge on Hopper by "outing" her actor son, William Hopper, who was a homosexual. Granger spread the word at Hollywood parties. William would later become a household name on television, playing Perry Mason's assistant, Paul Drake. The star of the show, Raymond Burr, playing Perry Mason, was also gay and in love—for a while at least—with Hopper's son.

Louella Parsons encountered Hopper at a party. "What makes you so sure that Wilding is a homo?" she asked.

"He's mad for Judy Garland," Hopper responded. "Have you ever met a homo who's not mad for Judy Garland?"

"Can't say that I have," Parsons said. "My objection is that Wilding is too old for Liz. As for that homo thing, all Hollywood husbands are queer at some point in their lives. Speaking of that, what is your adorable son doing tonight?"

At the same party, Elsa Maxwell was asked if she was concerned about Elizabeth marrying a potentially homosexual husband. "My dear, when you travel in international society, you learn that all men, on some rainy night or another, become cocksuckers."

A fellow Brit, David Niven, rushed to the defense of Wilding and Granger. "On that Riviera trip in the South of France, they nailed so many coquettes that the population there doubled overnight." Of course, that was gross, vulgar hyperbole. When Marlene Dietrich read his comment, she said, "Poor David is just covering up his own bisexuality, including his affair with Errol Flynn when they lived together."

In her 1962 memoir, *The Whole Truth and Nothing But,* Hopper restated her charge that Wilding and Granger were homosexual lovers. Reacting quickly, Wilding filed a libel suit, and she settled out of court for $100,000. He also forced her to claim that she had made the charge "in a malicious and wanton fashion with complete disregard for the plaintiff's feelings."

The irony of that legal challenge was that Hopper actually had her facts right. "I was forced to pay for telling the truth," she told friends.

Elizabeth didn't need Hopper to tell her that her future husband was bisexual. She already knew it. She had firsthand evidence when she came home early from the studio one afternoon, and heard Wilding and Granger showering to-

William Hopper
(aka Paul Drake in the *Perry Mason* series)

gether and bragging about which of them was the real top. She went back into the garden for about half an hour before entering the house again, where she found them sitting on a couch with towels wrapped around their midsections.

The next day, she'd relay the entire episode to Roddy McDowall, who had already warned her to expect such encounters if she married a bisexual with a known reputation for philandering.

MGM announced the engagement of Elizabeth to Wilding. She told the press, "It's leap year, and I leaped."

To marry Elizabeth and move to Hollywood meant that Wilding would have to break his twenty-year contract with producer Henry Wilcox. At first, the British producer was furious. He told his wife, Anna Neagle, Wilding's frequent co-star, "But why sue him? He's got nothing."

Neagle pleaded with her husband "not to stand in the way of Michael's happiness." Wilcox did warn Wilding that he would not go over in Hollywood, a prophecy that turned out to be true.

While Elizabeth was at MGM, Wilding stayed at the Granger home, spending lots of his time reading movie magazines and trying to learn more about Hollywood. Elizabeth's favorite reading material were articles about herself. On a coffee table at the Granger house rested eighteen magazines with her picture gracing the covers.

Shortly after his arrival in America, Wilding came across an item that particularly intrigued him. A reporter, David Randolph, asked: "Do you prefer Luscious Liz or Mammillary Marilyn? The race is on to see who will reign as the next sex goddess of Hollywood, following in the footsteps of Jean Harlow, Lana Turner, and Rita Hayworth."

Apparently, another star read that same item. One afternoon before Elizabeth returned home from work, Wilding picked up the receiver to hear Marilyn Monroe on the phone.

"Hello, Mikey, this is Marilyn…you know, Marilyn Monroe. I guess you read what Mr. Randolph wrote in the paper."

"Indeed I did, Miss Monroe."

"Well, I wanted to let you know that a man like yourself doesn't have to settle for just strawberry or banana ice cream at Will Wright's ice cream parlor. You can have a scoop of banana, with a scoop of strawberry on top."

"If I read you correctly, I think you're telling me that I'm not forced to stick exclusively to Elizabeth, but can have Marilyn as a delectable topping."

"You read that right, you sexy Brit!" she answered.

"It's a cool day, as you know, in Los Angeles, it being autumn and everything. But I bet if you came over this afternoon, you could keep me warm. Elizabeth doesn't have to know. I'm very discreet."

"Miss Monroe, it's an honor to talk to you, but let me get back to you on that offer," he said. He couldn't wait to tell Granger about the invitation he'd received.

As it happened, the prospect of a roll in the hay with Monroe excited Granger. "Go for it," he urged Wilding. "I hear the bitch does three-ways. Call her back and ask her if I can come along."

Granger later told friends of the offer Monroe had made to Wilding, leaving out the part about his own proposal of a three-way.

Jeanne Carmen, another blonde goddess and Monroe's *confidante*, revealed the outcome of the *ménage à trois*. Hired for a modeling job by producers Rodgers Brackett and Stanley Mills Haggart, Carmen said, "Marilyn told me that Wilding and Granger had her in the same bed at the same time."

The occasion was the night that Howard Hughes threw a party at the Beverly Hills Hotel, where he rented a bungalow. The party was in honor of Elizabeth and Simmons, and he did not invite Granger or Wilding. The two men were "seriously pissed off when our womenfolk wandered into the Hughes lair," according to Granger.

The errant actors used that occasion to slip away and see Monroe. As she later told Carmen, "I knew Michael would come over, and I welcomed Stewart too. I thought they were both very handsome, although a bit old. Michael is hung better than Stewart, but neither of them would be turned down in a gay bar."

Monroe would enter Wilding's life on one more occasion, and this incident would be revealed in his memoirs, though he gave a very "limited hangout" in reference to what actually happened between them.

Jeanne Carmen
A refreshing, outspoken witness to the naughtiness of La-La Land.

By now, it was obvious that seducing the husband of her arch rival, Elizabeth, was the most compelling of Marilyn's motivations.

The venue for Hughes' party was the Beverly Hills Hotel. As part of the game Hughes was playing, he did not show up himself, but sent a surrogate, Pat DiCicco. Stated bluntly, DiCicco was a male hustler selling his services to men or women. He'd been famously married to the heiress Gloria Vanderbilt before she got wise and divorced him.

DiCicco was assigned by his employer, Hughes, as Elizabeth's escort. Over glass after glass of champagne, he pitched the glories of his client—that is, Hughes—to Elizabeth. "He could give you anything in the world you want—all the jewelry, all the money," DiCicco claimed. "He could make you the biggest star in Hollywood."

"I'm already the biggest star in Hollywood, with no

help from Hughes. I prefer to do it on my own."

Still committed to bribing her into marriage, Hughes had never abandoned his pursuit of Elizabeth, having learned that she was seriously strapped for cash "and on the verge of marrying a limey pauper."

With the intention of arranging his affairs in England, Wilding left Hollywood on February 17, 1952, with the understanding that Elizabeth would join him there later.

When the time came for her own transit to London, Elizabeth was startled to have DiCicco booked into the airliner's seat immediately next to hers, a ploy that had obviously been influenced by Hughes. All across the Atlantic, DiCicco pleaded with her not to marry Wilding, asserting that it was well known that he was a homosexual. "He's had an ongoing affair with Stewart Granger," DiCicco said. "Now get this: He even had a hot affair with Errol Flynn in England, which Howard knows will continue once he settles into Hollywood. When Wilding doesn't come home to you, you'll know where he is—getting fucked by Flynn."

After they'd landed in the U.K., while clearing customs with DiCicco, Elizabeth told him, "Tell Mr. Hughes he can dream on and present all the evidence he wants against Michael. I'm still going to marry him. If he also has affairs with Stewart and Errol, then I must compliment his good taste. They are two of the most desirable and sought after men on the planet. I'm sure there are thousands of stars in Hollywood who would jump at Mr. Hughes' offer. Tell your tomcat boss to chase after one of those pussycats."

***

Met by Wilding at the airport in London, Elizabeth was put into a taxicab for transport to her suite at the Berkeley Hotel. Another large taxi was rented for her luggage. En route to the hotel, Wilding kissed her passionately.

Marlene Dietrich was furious after hearing the news of Elizabeth's upcoming marriage, denouncing her young rival as "an English tart."

The forty-eight-year-old Anna Neagle had agreed to be Elizabeth's maid of honor, with her husband, Henry Wilcox, functioning as Wilding's best man. Wilcox was still angry at his star for breaking their twenty-year contract, but he generously agreed to pay for their wedding reception at Claridges.

Neagle helped Elizabeth apply the finishing touches to her wedding dress, which once again had been designed by Helen Rose. This time, it was fashioned in tones of battleship gray instead of "first wedding" white. Her "getaway garb" was a wool suit with a three-tiered organdy collar and cuffs, and she wore a pillbox hat adorned with white flowers.

From Beverly Hills, Sara and Francis Taylor cabled their regrets, claiming that they would not be able to attend. Sara wrote, "I hope the second time around for you won't be the disaster your first marriage was."

Elizabeth became Mrs. Michael Wilding on February 21, 1952, twenty days after the finalization of her divorce from Nicky Hilton. Some five thousand on-lookers gathered outside Claxton Hall in London where the ten-minute ceremony took place. Hundreds of her fans, in mourning because of the recent death of King George VI, wore black armbands. Another woman named Elizabeth had already been designated as the future queen.

Elizabeth (a.k.a. Mrs. Wilding) was mobbed by crazed fans when she left the hall. One woman ripped off her pillbox hat. Efforts were made to tear off other pieces of her clothing, even locks of her hair. Bobbies literally had to hoist her up in the air to carry her to the waiting limousine that transported her, along with Wilding, Neagle, and Wilcox, to the reception at Claridges.

Once there, she told London reporters that "this is the happiest day of my life, repeating the line she'd said when she married Nicky Hilton. To a reporter from the *Daily Express,* she said that "My career is of little importance. Being a good wife to Michael is my ultimate goal. Most of all, I'm glad to be British once again."

That same reporter also noted that "Wilding looked weary and bored—he did not smile once."

Because of Britain's post-war currency restrictions, Wilding was able to take only sixty British pounds out of the U.K. for their honeymoon in the French Alps. That meant that it was up to Elizabeth to pay for their modest eight-day honeymoon.

A waiter told *Paris-Match,* "For Miss Taylor's twentieth birthday, Mr. Wilding put a little candle in a cup of *crème caramel* and sang ten choruses of 'Happy Birthday' to her. There was no cake, but he did order champagne."

Back from their honeymoon, Elizabeth and her new husband lived briefly in London at his *maisonette* at 2 Bruton Street in the exclusive district of Mayfair. In a 1951 issue of *Photoplay* magazine, he'd already read an article by Sara in which she proclaimed that Elizabeth was virtually helpless around the house. "What Sara didn't say is that Elizabeth didn't believe in walking her dog," Wilding said. "The mutt went anywhere he wanted to. You had to watch where you stepped."

Before his departure for Hollywood, Wilding was presented with a bill from Inland Revenue for about £40,000, an amount that converted into around $100,000 worth of 1952 dollars. That was virtually every shilling he had. The bill represented the taxes due on the income he had earned on his previous two pictures.

He cabled Granger in Hollywood. "I'll be landing in Hollywood with about twenty dollars in my purse. I've got to be supported by a girl who was only a teenager yesterday—or else it's the soup kitchen for me."

On the morning before she was scheduled to depart for London's airport for a flight headed back to New York, Elizabeth received an envelope slipped under the door of Wilding's flat. She tore it open. It ominously read: YOU WILL NOT LEAVE LONDON ALIVE UNLESS YOU TURN OVER 50,000 POUNDS TO ME. AWAIT FURTHER INSTRUCTIONS.

Wilding immediately called Scotland Yard, which put investigators on the case.

Chain smoking and visibly shaken, Elizabeth, with Wilding, headed to the airport.

When she finally reached Hollywood, she confessed to Janet Leigh, "I felt at any moment that I would be assassinated—or else the plane would be bombed."

Scotland Yard never tracked down the author of the threat. But for Elizabeth, it was the beginning of her paying the price for fame and notoriety.

Throughout the rest of her life, she'd be stalked, blackmailed, or threatened with death.

CHAPTER FOURTEEN
Love Amid the Rubbish
(OF ELIZABETH'S ALMOST-FORGOTTEN FILMS)

In Hollywood, Elizabeth barged into Benny Thau's office at MGM and virtually blackmailed him. Even though she'd signed a contract for seven years, she demanded that he also sign Michael Wilding as a contract player, at least for three years, even though the studio was letting others of its contract players go. "If you don't, I'll settle in England with him—and make no more movies for MGM."

"Do I have to remind you that I have just let Clark Gable, Spencer Tracy, Greer Garson, and Mickey Rooney go—to name only a few?" Thau said.

Nevertheless, Wilding was granted a three-year contract at $3,000 a week, plus a two-year option for $4,000 a week if MGM decided to retain him.

Wilding told Louella Parsons that, "My greatest ambition in life involves being very, very rich, but not work too hard for the money."

When Elizabeth and her new husband spent the weekend with her parents, Sara made what she called "a horrible discovery—he's wearing a damn *toupée*. Not only that, he has a weak chin, but everybody can plainly see that. I wonder if we can get a plastic surgeon to give him a chin like Kirk Douglas, complete with dimple."

***

Once again, Richard Thorpe, to his horror, was assigned to direct Elizabeth in *The Girl Who Had Everything* (1953)*, even though he still nursed bitter memories from his experience with her during the shooting of *Ivanhoe* (1952).

Based on columnist Adela Rogers St. Johns' memoir of her father, *A Free Soul*, originally published in 1927, the 1931 film with the same name had brought early stardom to Clark Gable when he appeared opposite Norma Shearer and Lionel Barrymore. Barrymore had won an Oscar playing a lawyer who defends gangster Gable, only to find that his free-spirited daughter, as played by Shearer, has fallen in love with his street-savvy client.

In the 1953 remake, the film's title was changed to *The Girl Who Had Everything*. Elizabeth was assigned the Shearer role, the role of the charismatic gangster went to Fernando Lamas, and the role of the father assigned to William Powell. Powell would be playing Elizabeth's father for the second time. He'd last portrayed her daddy onscreen *Life With Father* (1947).

In the movie, Elizabeth gives up her dull but amiable boyfriend, Vance Court (Gig Young), and falls for a rakish and dangerous gangster, Victor Ramondi (Fernando Lamas). The heartthrob from Argentina was known as "Hollywood's leading Latin Lover." In Buenos Aires he'd had a heated affair with dictator Eva Peron.

The producer of the film, Armand Deutsch, read the script and told Thau, "Don't waste a big name star like Elizabeth Taylor in this silly little melodrama. Give it to Gloria DeHaven or Janet Leigh. It's a B-picture, and we're not using Elizabeth properly."

But Thau claimed that since Elizabeth was pregnant, he had to cast her in a vehicle very quickly that could be shot in a short time. Deutsch's original judgment had been right. Critics attacked the picture, and it bombed at the box office.

On the set, Elizabeth knew not to speak too early on any given day to Thorpe, who tended to be very cranky every morning. When she first greeted him with a "good morning," he yelled at her, "What's fucking good about it? I've got to get this picture made before your belly grows too big. Couldn't you have refrained from getting deep-dicked? Did you know there's a way to prevent pregnancy? Frankly, if you want me to, I can arrange an abortion."

Sobbing, she ran to her dressing room.

Elizabeth told Dick Hanley about her first meeting with Lamas on the MGM lot. "What a knockout! I later learned he'd used the same word to describe me. He is tall, handsome, and the color of bronze. When he smiled at me, flashing those pearly whites, I swooned. He wore a sky blue blazer and a buttercup yellow silk scarf. But pink slacks! Yes, pink! A man can be beaten up for wearing pink. Perhaps that outfit is fashionable on the streets of Buenos Aires. His trousers were so tight they made everything obvious. Believe me, there was meat there for the poor."

During the shoot, the cantankerous director and his hot-tempered Latin star, Lamas, often became enraged at each other. Dick remembered visiting Elizabeth one afternoon in her dressing room. "I found Lamas wearing only his briefs, lying on her sofa in a fetal position. She was cuddling him in her arms. A fight with Thorpe had led to one of his terrible migraines. I was told that he often developed these splitting headaches when he got angry."

"Seeing them in this position, I realized for the first time that Elizabeth was more than a mere sexpot," Dick claimed. "She was a very loving and nurturing mother, the way she was with her pets. I thought she'd make a great mother when her baby was born. As a side attraction, I was impressed by the mound on display in Lamas' jockey shorts. Back before it was fashionable, he had his tailor make pants for him that were very tight in the crotch. As he once told me, 'If you've got it, flaunt it. It turns on the horny women and the gay boys.'"

In the movie, rich girl Elizabeth and her crooked lawyer father (Powell) are watching a telecast of a Capitol Hill crime commission investigating the illegal rackets of gangster Lamas.

"What's he like?" Elizabeth's character asked her screen father, who plays the gangster's lawyer. "Is he married?"

He answers that the gangster, Victor Ramondi, "is an animal." This doesn't turn off Elizabeth, but piques her sexual curiosity. The stage is set for the debut of a dangerous romance.

At one point, Lamas grabs her on screen and kisses her passionately. "You're no gentleman," she says to him. But it's obvious that she's excited by the kiss.

When Thorpe saw the rushes, he knew that to make the film go over at the box office, he needed to direct (within reason) scenes of passionate lovemaking onscreen between Lamas and Elizabeth.

Thorpe decided to write a scene himself at night, giving his stars their scripts in the morning. For their first passionate love scene, Lamas knocked on Elizabeth's dressing room door to rehearse with her. She brazenly answered the door in her bra and panties.

As she would later relay to Dick Hanley, "Fernando practically devoured me when we were pretending to rehearse. Call it gaucho charisma. When he turns on the charm, the sexual dynamic is irresistible. What is a poor little British girl like me to do with the guy's tongue down my throat and his skilled fingers reaching into my panties? He's a sex machine. Even a strong-

"THE GIRL WHO HAD EVERYTHING"

Two views of **Fernando Lamas**
lower photo: Foreplay with **Liz**

285

willed woman like Evita Peron could not hold him at bay."

Thorpe was so pleased with their love scene, he wrote three more. "Their chemistry exploded on the screen. I predicted that they would become the screen's new love team—Garbo and Gilbert, Gable and Harlow."

The movie was doubly explosive for its time in that Powell treats Elizabeth like his girlfriend instead of like his daughter.

"Lamas had a keen sense of humor," Thorpe said. "On the set, he and Liz were always joking around and whispering secrets to each other, acting like two school kids. I was very serious about bringing this movie in on time before she dumped that baby on the set."

"The way they were carrying on really pissed me off," he said. "After all, I wasn't getting in on the action. They could at least have let me watch, or perhaps film it for my later viewing pleasure."

The film was wrapped on August 4, 1952, and Elizabeth went home to await the birth of her baby.

After editing Elizabeth's scenes with Lamas, Thorpe at a private screening showed them to Thau. When the lights went on, Thau rose in fury and denounced his director. "What in fuck is wrong with you? You've made a blue movie. All these scenes have to be cut."

Thorpe was furious, but had no choice. That's why the film today is only seventy minutes long.

The third male lead in *The Girl Who Had Everything* went to Gig Young, who never achieved the major stardom he so longed for, in spite of his good looks and charm. He was known mainly for second leads and supporting roles.

Thorpe claimed that even though Young was married at the time, "He fell big time for Liz. I think he walked around the set with a perpetual erection."

"I lost out to Lamas both on the screen and in real life," Young recalled. "She flirted with me and was the ultimate prick teaser. Even so, we became friends."

When Elizabeth met Young, he had divorced his second wife, Sophie Rosenstein, in 1952, and had not remarried. In 1956, he wed Elizabeth Montgomery. "I was a bachelor-at-large and raring to go when Elizabeth walked onto the set," he recalled. "We had four 'official' dates but not a lot came from it. We were just out for fun, nothing too serious."

"I'm not going to say if we did it or not, as it's nobody's god damn business. She always had a boyfriend and a husband stashed away somewhere. She warned me about my excessive drinking, but then, she wasn't one to point fingers."

"Our relationship finally devolved into phone calls, but she was also supportive and encouraged me," Young said. "She gave me a little party when I won the Oscar."

In 1969, Young appeared in *They Shoot Horses, Don't They?*, starring Jane Fonda. His Academy Award was for Best Supporting Actor in that film.

[Elizabeth was horrified to learn of her co-star's death in 1978. His career was in decline because of his alcoholism. That same year, he'd married a 21-year-old German woman, Kim Schmidt. On October 19, three weeks into his marriage, the police found the newly married couple dead in their Manhattan apartment. Young had shot his wife and then shot himself in a murder/suicide. The motive for the killings has never been made clear.

Elizabeth had her own speculation. "Gig had a dark side to him, and that is one of the reasons I never got too involved with him. One night in my car—he was too drunk to drive—we were heading up the coast to Malibu with me at the wheel. He kept urging me to go faster, and I refused. At one point, he pressed down on my foot with his big left foot. The accelerator was pressed against the floor. I screamed that I was losing control of the car since I was not the world' greatest driver. I almost crashed head-on into an oncoming truck. At that speed we would have been killed instantly. At the last minute, he took his foot off mine, and I brought the car under control. I never went out with him again."

Elizabeth told Roddy McDowall that the last time she'd talked to Young, he complained bitterly that he'd become impotent. He cited that as the reason for his wanting to marry a girl the age Elizabeth was when he first worked with her.

"He was very despondent, and he seemed to have plunged deeper and deeper into the bottle," Elizabeth said. "Obviously, the marriage to that girl didn't work out as he planned. He had a lot of pride. Maybe she said things to him and mocked him as a man. We'll never know."]

***

Gig Young, in happier times

Elizabeth was pregnant throughout most of the shoot, and her weight really ballooned at the very end, going from 112 pounds to 155 pounds before term. She was no longer capable, with any believable continuity, of facing the camera, and MGM put her on a limited suspension, lowering her salary back to $2,000 a week until she could face the cameras once again after childbirth.

When she was placed on suspension, Elizabeth had some choice words for Thau and Dore Schary—"Shitassed motherfucking faggot cocksuckers." At least that is what her friend, author

Truman Capote, later attributed to her.

Setting out on a house hunt, Elizabeth announced, "I need a nest in which to hatch the egg."

Her friend, George MacLean, was a talented architect, and he designed a home in Beverly Hills especially for her. It was surrounded by a wall and had a locked gate which was electronically controlled from inside the house as a means of blocking out overeager fans.

"The architecture and landscape were perfectly integrated," she later wrote. "Both house and garden seemed enchanted, like a scene from a fairy tale. Michael and I scraped the money together and bought the place."

Elizabeth also got Thau to advance her $50,000 as the down payment on her dream house. To make the full nut, she withdrew all the money set aside for her in bonds under the Jackie Coogan law for child stars. The bonds she cashed brought in $47,000. Any money left over went for the payment of pediatric bills.

In the spring of 1952, the Wildings bought the house at 1771 Summitridge in Beverly Hills. Even though she'd been married twice, Elizabeth had enough clout to get Thau to grant her mother a contract paying $300 a week, designating Sara as her "chaperone," a position usually reserved for child stars.

Elizabeth and Michael moved into the house before it was fully furnished. He wanted to ship over some of his English antiques, which had been in storage in London, but she demanded that everything be modern.

In their new kitchen, she explained the new diet that would be in effect if he expected her to cook. "I can pop corn, make fudge, and cook bacon and eggs. Sometimes I burn the bacon, though. But my specialty, a never-fail dish, is sliced tomatoes and capers fried in bacon grease."

During Elizabeth's pregnancy, Wilding decided he much preferred the life of a painter instead of that of an actor. He practiced his painting by drawing faces on her distended stomach. She'd bought a dozen maternity blouses in rainbow-hued colors, and at parties she'd lift the garment to show off, not only her belly, but Wilding's latest artistic endeavors.

A pregnant Elizabeth and Wilding were asleep in their bedroom when they heard an urgent ringing of their doorbell. Someone had obviously circumvented their locked gated. "Who in hell is it at this hour?" a drowsy Elizabeth asked.

"I'll see," he said, before going downstairs. She heard voices in the hallway. Wilding seemed to be talking to some hysterical woman. In about ten minutes, he called up the stairs for Elizabeth: "It's Lana!," he shouted at her. "Come on down."

In the living room, Elizabeth encountered Lana Turner sitting on her sofa, nervously smoking a cigarette and belting down a glass of vodka.

A turban crowned her head, and her bruised face was not made up. On seeing Elizabeth, she burst into tears. Elizabeth sat beside her on the sofa and embraced her; "What is it, darling?"

"It's too horrible," Turner said.

At first, Elizabeth was horrified, thinking that somehow Turner had learned about her studio romance with her boyfriend, Lamas, on the set of *The Girl Who Had Everything,* and that she'd come to raise hell about it. But that was not the case.

Wilding was already well acquainted with Lamas, since he'd starred with Greer Garson and him in *The Law and the Lady* (1951). He filled Elizabeth in on what had occurred the night before, telling her what Turner had just confided to him.

Turner and her live-in lover, Lamas, had been a guest at a party thrown by Marion Davies in Santa Monica. The mistress of William Randolph Hearst was known for her fabulous parties.

When Lex Barker, the screen's Tarzan, came into the party, Turner did not suppress her immense attraction to the handsome hulk. Unknown to Turner, Elizabeth had already sampled the wares of this astonishingly attractive male, and she couldn't blame Turner for her response to his immense sex appeal.

"Apparently, Lamas went into a jealous rage when Lana here was dancing too close to Barker," Wilding said. "They had a public row. Shouting, threats, face slapping—the works."

"We fought all the way back to my house," Turner said, regaining her composure. "Once we got inside my hallway, Lamas attacked me. I fell on the floor, and he kicked me in the ribs. He pounded my face, threatening to destroy my beauty. I screamed and tried to protect my face from the blows of this hot-tempered jerk. I threatened to call the police and I ordered him out of my house...*forever.*"

Elizabeth was well aware that Wilding was set to appear in his first MGM film, *Latin Lovers,* with Turner and Lamas.

"I can't work with the bastard now," Turner said. "I need Michael's support. I want him to take me to Benny Thau's office this morning. *Latin Lovers* is about to go before the cameras, and I refuse to do the picture with Lamas."

"Michael, get dressed, and I'll get Lana some coffee," Elizabeth said. Then she turned to Lana. "You look in bad shape. You can't face the cameras today."

Over coffee, Elizabeth told Turner that Wilding had serious reservations about his own role in *Latin Lovers.* He'd been cast as the second male lead. "Your meeting with Thau will give Michael a chance to air his own grievances."

"There's an obvious replacement for Lamas," Turner told her. "Ricardo Montalban."

"There's irony here," Elizabeth said. "The Argentine beefsteak was imported to Hollywood to replace Ricardo. But if Thau goes for it, Ricardo could indeed replace Lamas."

"Lamas told me that the difference between Latin and Anglo-Saxon men is that a Latin will give you a little more of everything—more headaches, more temper, more tenderness." Turner said, ruefully. "I got the temper and the headaches."

An hour after Wilding left to drive Turner to MGM, Lamas placed a call to Elizabeth. She reported to him what had just transpired in her living room.

"The bitch blames me for our breakup," Lamas said. "But when Jungle Boy came into the room, Lana threw herself at him. She danced with him, rubbing her body up against him. When I could stand it no more, I jumped up and confronted her on the dance floor. I told Barker, 'Why don't you just take her out into the bushes and fuck her?'"

"She slapped my face," Lamas said, "and I called her a fucking cunt. Back at her house, the reason I got violent was because she kicked me in the *cojones.*"

Elizabeth warned him that Turner was in Thau's office, trying to get him replaced by Montalban.

"That fucking spick," Lamas said. "If I get fired from that picture, I want you to promise me one thing. As soon as you dump Wilding's kid, will you insist that I be your leading man in your next movie, whatever it is?

"I faithfully promise I'll do that," she said.

"And Liz," he said, "as soon as the baby comes, and you're ready for action South of the Border style, you know who to call."

"I'll keep that in mind," she said.

Lamas and Elizabeth never mated again, as Arlene Dahl and Esther Williams were waiting to snatch him.

When Wilding came home that afternoon from MGM, he looked downcast. "I was put on suspension," he said. Then he sat down with Elizabeth in the living room to tell her what had happened that day in Thau's office.

"Lana got her wish," he said, "but I'm on suspension. Without Pay."

"What in hell are you talking about?" she demanded.

"After Lana's problem was solved, I told Thau how disappointed I was with the shitty role he was offering me in *Latin Lovers*. I attacked my role, and told him it wasn't suitable for an actor of my stature. That's when he hit the ceiling."

"Mikey, you shouldn't have said that," she said.

"I know that now," he said. "He described my status as something as low as a piss ant. He told me that the only reason I was hired in the first place was because I was married to Elizabeth Taylor—and for no other reason. My paycheck won't resume until *Latin Lovers* is wrapped."

"You arrogant prick!" she shouted at him. "We desperately need the money, and I'm already on suspension. I practically had to get down on bended nylon and give Thau a Nancy Davis-style blow-job to get the loan for this house!"

Elizabeth became so furious that Wilding had to flee from the house, driving over to the home of Stewart Granger, where he'd first lived when he came to Hollywood. Granger was still his best friend and part-time lover, and he always turned to him during moments of crisis.

"As you know, I'm a mild-mannered man, and Elizabeth almost had me fearing for my life, especially when she started throwing things," Wilding said. "She became a wildcat, intent on devouring a pound of human flesh."

"It was our first big fight," Wilding told Granger. Although he and Elizabeth had moved out of the Granger house into their own home, he later moved back in again for a week. When Elizabeth rages, I'm no match for her."

The only way Wilding was accepted back into the house with Elizabeth was when he promised to call Thau and accept the role in *Latin Lovers.*

"Too late, you limey prick!" Thau shouted at him. "Yesterday, I contracted with John Lund to play the role." Then he slammed down the phone.

Elizabeth warned Wilding to take the next role he was offered by MGM after he went off suspension—"Even if you're forced to dress in drag."

***

Before the birth of his son, and with no film work, Wilding had plenty of time to spare when Elizabeth was away during the day at work. His bisexual friend, Robert Taylor, who had starred with Elizabeth in *Ivanhoe,* had divorced Barbara Stanwyck and was free once again to engage in indiscriminate sex, the way he'd done in the 1930s when he was hailed as "Hollywood's Pretty Boy."

Ever since they'd met in England, Robert Taylor and Michael Wilding had had a strong physical attraction for each other. In October and November of 1952, Taylor invited Wilding on two different hunting trips to Idaho. Taylor liked to hunt and Wilding didn't, but Elizabeth's husband did appreciate, however, the wilds of America's Northwest and he enjoyed exploring it with a companion as charming and handsome as Taylor.

Beside a campfire one night, Taylor confessed to Wilding that he'd proposed to Elizabeth during the filming of *Conspirator,* even though she'd been only seventeen at the time.

"I was a little drunk and I was half joking, but I shared with her a letter I'd received from a rich woman in Texas who was worth millions. She wrote that Elizabeth and I had the same coloring, that both of us had jet black hair, blue eyes, and were fabulous looking. She wanted us to have a kid together for which she would pay each of us a million dollars. At first, I thought it was a joke, but then I called the woman and talked to her for an hour. She not only had those millions—and a lot more—she was willing to post the money in bond. Along with my marriage proposal to Liz, I told her about the offer. She took it seriously, and maybe I was serious, too. At any rate, she rejected my proposal. I know that you and Liz are strapped for cash. Maybe you can talk her into selling your first born. It would certainly alleviate your financial burden."

"You know, I'm British, and we're a cynical people, cold hearted," Wilding said. "We love our dogs more than our children. Frankly, if that woman is still around, and if that offer still holds, I'd go for it. But it's hopeless. Elizabeth would file for divorce immediately. I know her too well."

Ironically, Elizabeth in her future would end up buying a baby instead of selling one.

In addition to Robert Taylor, Wilding was also well-acquainted with another of Hollywood's fading heartthrobs, Errol Flynn.

Wilding had been introduced to Flynn at two parties. But their actual friendship began at Le Touquet on the English Channel on the northern coast of France, when Wilding's boat, which he had named *Folie de Grandeur* had moored alongside Flynn's yacht, *The Medina*.

Wilding owned the boat jointly with Stewart Granger. Although Wilding hardly knew Flynn at the time, he called out to him, "Hiya, Mike, come aboard."

Wilding recalled his inaugural meeting with Flynn in his memoirs, *The Wilding Way*. "Errol invited me down below to see his all-black bathroom, a first for me, including a black bidet."

The two actors spent the rest of the day drinking champagne aboard *The Medina*. At any rate, an intimate friendship was formed between these two playboys.

Once he moved to Hollywood, Wilding was eager to resume his friendship with Flynn, and the swashbuckler seemed more than eager to hook up with him again, too.

At the time of Wilding's reunion with him, Flynn still owned his hilltop home on Mulholland Drive before his creditors took it away from him. Wilding arrived at twilight, since Elizabeth had announced her intention of spending the evening with Sara. He recalled Flynn taking him into the garden, where he could see the twinkling lights of Hollywood. "From this vantage point, I can piss down on Warners," Flynn told him.

Wilding was also invited into Flynn's private den, its walls covered with photographs of naked women. "I took each of these pictures myself," Flynn boasted.

What Wilding left out of his memoirs was that Flynn, shortly before midnight, showed him a "blue movie loop" of him making love to a very young Elizabeth.

Instead of being outraged, Wilding, as he'd later relay to Granger, was "indulgent" with Flynn, and actually got turned on by the pornographic film.

Flynn later told actor Bruce Cabot and others, "Where Michael Wilding and Elizabeth Taylor are concerned, I was like Julius Caesar—that is, a husband to every wife and a wife to every husband."

During his status as an out-of-work actor in Hollywood, Wilding had a number of other encounters with some of the top stars of Hollywood. He was seen at one point leaving Judy Garland's suite at the Beverly Hills Hotel.

"The only break in my lonely day was a lunchtime visit to Elizabeth at the studio. There, I was surrounded by famous names all in make-up doing a day's work, while I tagged along as Elizabeth's side like a tame poodle."

One of his most memorable encounters, which he relayed in a highly edited version in his memoirs, involved yet another encounter with Marilyn Monroe. He recalled that he was in the garden of his home on Summitridge painting one afternoon when he heard the doorbell ring. When he opened the door, he was startled to find Monroe standing there.

In a breathless voice, she told him that her photographer was taking publicity stills of her and wanted to use Elizabeth Taylor's home as a picturesque background.

"I need a place to change my outfits," she told him.

"Say no more," Wilding replied. "Welcome to Chez Wilding." Ushering her inside, he told her that Elizabeth was at the studio and that she could use their bedroom.

Throughout the rest of the afternoon, Marilyn was running in and out of the house, changing costumes. When the photo shoot was over, he offered her a glass of champagne.

She smiled at him, "Do you mind if I take my shoes off?"

"Take off *anything* you like," he told her.

Although he left his readers dangling at this point in his memoirs, apparently Monroe pulled off everything and stood before him. "Please make me feel like a pulled-together woman and not like a cracked egg. That is, my face all coming apart—you know, my eyes pointing in two directions and two noses like a Picasso painting."

From his later reports to Granger, it was determined that Wilding, "Like the staunch Englishman I am, I did my duty for Queen and Country."

In a few short years, he mourned the early deaths of his friends, Flynn and Robert Taylor, and also the demise of Monroe, asserting, "She died so tragically young."

***

Back in Hollywood, Monty called Elizabeth to tell he that he was making pictures again. "I want to see you, of course, but my main reason for doing so is to feel your belly. I want to know how big it is."

She agreed to meet him at his favorite dive in Malibu, *Mary's*, which was popular with gay couples. Cozy and intimate, it had only eight tables and was run by a friend of Monty's, Betsy Jane Elkin, recently from Georgia. She operated the place entirely by herself, including doing the cooking and waiting on tables. Sometimes Monty was behind the bar, mixing drinks for her customers.

Monty told Elizabeth that he was attracted to Betsy Jane because she managed all the chores with a wooden leg.

Within the cozy bistro, Elizabeth gorged herself, ordering two bowls of pasta (lasagna and tortellini). Monty had never seen her this fat. "I'm eating for two people," she said.

At table, with Betsy Jane providing the food and friendly service, Elizabeth and Monty talked and talked...and then talked some more. "It was one of our marathon gabfests," she later recalled.

Regarding her disastrous marriage to Nicky Hilton, he wanted to known, "How is *Life With Father?*" He was referring to both her 1947 film and also to her new life with Wilding.

"There are problems," she said. "He doesn't like being Mr. Elizabeth Taylor. In London, he was a big deal in films. Here, he's on suspension. Mostly he's a housewife—somebody's got to do it. You know me, the biggest slob in the world."

"When is the baby due?" he asked.

"In January," she said. "I was thinking of making you the godfather."

"Oh, Bessie Mae, I can't even look after myself, much less take care of your child, if you and Michael were killed in an accident."

It was three o'clock in the morning when Betsy Jane served their last round of drinks. Closing time was usually at midnight. "I've got to paint this little bistro of mine before I open tomorrow night, and I've got to start now."

Elizabeth later asserted that she and Monty joined in. "It was a lot of fun. We painted the walls until eight o'clock that morning. Betsy Jane and Monty got up on a ladder. Because of my condition, I painted the lower part."

When she finally got home, it was nine o'clock in the morning. Wilding was in a nervous state, fearing something had happened to her since she had not bothered to phone. When he discovered that she'd been out all night with Monty, he became enraged. "So you've been out fucking the man you're really in love with and wanted to marry."

"Like hell, I have!" she said. "You stand a better chance of fucking Monty than I do. I'm going to bed and don't wake me until two o'clock this afternoon. Then I'll want breakfast in bed."

She saw Monty on three other occasions before he had to fly to Rome for the filming of *Terminal Station* (1953) for David O. Selznick. It was later retitled *Indiscretion of an American Housewife.* Selznick had cast his wife, Jennifer Jones, in the lead role of this picture directed by Vittorio de Sica.

Elizabeth later learned that Jones fell madly in love with Monty during the filming. When she discovered that he was a homosexual, she became hysterical and had to be sedated.

When Monty returned to Hollywood, Elizabeth noted that he'd lost weight, which he could not afford to do. "You can borrow some extra pounds from me," she volunteered.

On his first night back, they dined at Mary's again, admiring the new paint job. He told her that he'd signed to play one of the key roles in the filming of the James Jones bestseller, *From Here to Eternity,* set on the eve of the Japanese attack on Pearl harbor. The other stars included Burt Lancaster and Deborah Kerr, with Frank Sinatra in a supporting role.

Before her dinner with Monty, Elizabeth had received an urgent phone call from "my first flame," John Derek. He told her that Harry Cohn, the head of Columbia Pictures, wanted him to play the role of the renegade boxer, Prewitt, in the film, but that the director, Fred Zinnemann, was holding out for Monty.

"Oh, John, I'd love to help you, but I have no say in casting at Columbia. Hell, I don't even have any influence over who's cast in my own pictures."

"Monty listens to you, and if you try really hard, you can get him to drop out—I know you can," Derek asserted. "Don't you see, my career is going nowhere. This is going to be a big picture. I could win an Oscar, be taken seriously as an actor. It would be a new beginning."

"The only thing I can promise is that I'll talk it over with Monty," she said.

"Elizabeth…" He hesitated, as if reluctant to say what he was going to. "You know I'm called the best looking guy in Hollywood, and I don't have to tell you I've got a big dick. It can all be yours again if you'll do this for me."

She was insulted by such an offer, but, according to Dick Hanley, Elizabeth confessed that she "covered up my feelings and promised John that I'd get back to him." Of course, she never did, and Monty kept the role in spite of Cohn's objections.

After dinner at Mary's, Elizabeth and Monty retreated to the Beverly Hills home of Oscar Levant. There, the pianist played Cole Porter tunes for them, as they sat on his sofa, holding hands and occasionally kissing. Sometimes, he'd feel her baby bump, telling her that one day he hoped to become a father himself.

She remembered the night at Levant's as "one of the most tranquil and relaxing of my life. It's what could have been between Monty and me."

Elizabeth remained out of touch with Monty, still her best friend, during his shooting of scenes for *From Here to Eternity* in Hawaii.

After the filming was over in Hawaii, director Zinnemann ordered the cast and crew back to Hollywood, where the final interiors would be shot at Columbia. For a brief time, Monty, along with Frank Sinatra and Merv Griffin, were staying at the Roosevelt Hotel. For many months, Monty had been a roommate of Griffin's.

Before seeing either Sinatra or Monty, Elizabeth was invited to lunch with Griffin at the Brown Derby. He warned her that Sinatra and Monty had been in such bad shape that it was a miracle they'd gotten through the picture at all. "Monty paid for me to fly down there," Griffin said. "I had nothing to do but be the nursemaid for those guys. They didn't just drink. Both of them poured it down their throats. It was frightening. They seemed to want to drink themselves into oblivion."

"Monty has his usual demons," Griffin told her. "And although Frank is at the nadir of his career and owes $150,000 in back taxes, Harry Cohn at Columbia is paying him only $8,000 for his role in the film. That hardly covers Frank's bar tab."

She told him that she was scheduled to see Monty for dinner that night.

"He's in real bad shape," Griffin said. "Sometimes, at three o'clock in the morning, he hangs dangerously out of the hotel window, tooting his bugle. The manager is threatening to kick us out."

"Frank is in even worse shape," Griffin told her. "His vocal cords have hemorrhaged, MCA [his theatrical agent] has dropped him. There are no more movie deals. And Ava is off fucking other guys."

"The other night, I woke up early in the morning and discovered Frank nude on the bathroom floor, an empty bottle of sleeping pills beside him," Griffin said. "He appeared to be dead. But we called an ambulance and got him to the hospital on time. He told me he'd learned that Ava had flown to London to have their baby aborted."

That night at dinner, Elizabeth saw firsthand that Griffin had not exaggerated. Monty had lost weight, was chain smoking and drinking excessively, and at times, was seized by a condition where his entire body trembled nervously.

She tried to reassure him, telling him that she'd heart reports from Zinnemann that his role in *From Here to Eternity* was going to win him an Oscar.

"Big fucking deal," he said. "I'll use the bare-assed statue for a doorstop."

A week later, Elizabeth received an urgent phone call from Griffin, pleading with her to come to their suite at the Roosevelt Hotel.

Once there, she found that Monty had been severely beaten. Like a nurturing mother, she held him in her arms and comforted him.

From Griffin, she learned what had happened: Since Hawaii, Sinatra and Monty had been sleeping nude in the same bed together after more than one of their drunken nights. But apparently, Monty had finally confessed to Sinatra that he was in love with him. Up to then, theirs had not been a sexual relationship, but was what in later years might be described as a "bromance."

Outside the bedroom, Griffin told Elizabeth, "I think a declaration of love from Monty was more than Frank could take. He wasn't going to go from the arms of Ava Gardner into the arms of Monty Clift. No way! Not Frank!"

He also told her, "I'm checking out of here. Frank has already packed his bags. Please look after Monty and take care of him."

That morning, Elizabeth drove Monty to her doctor, who found he had no broken bones, but was in a critical condition. Her doctor warned her, "He's got to stop drinking or he'll die."

In the days ahead, she went by every evening to nurse him back to health. One night, she arrived and found strangers living in his suite. The manager informed her that Monty had checked out that morning.

The next day she reached him at his apartment in New York. "I just had to leave Hollywood," he said. "I was smothering to death. I'm not going to appear in another movie unless it's with you."

***

During the closing days of 1952, Michael and Elizabeth were invited to a New Year's Eve party at the home of their recent hosts, Stewart Granger and Jean Simmons. Currently, the London-based guests living with them temporarily were Richard Burton and his wife, Sybil Williams, an actress.

In later years, Granger would claim, "Burton was a clever actor, but a shit, an absolute shit."

In contrast, when he first came to Hollywood, the bisexual Granger had been powerfully attracted to Burton, although not avoiding dalliances with Wilding as well. Elizabeth was aware of Granger's sexual interest in Burton, but she learned far more about her future husband's sexual adventures when she attended the Granger party.

As she headed for the kitchen, Burton was telling Granger and James Mason, fellow British actors, about his recent sexual fling with Marilyn Monroe. Elizabeth dallied at the entrance, wanting to hear what he was saying without making Burton aware of her presence. She would remember virtually every word and write it down in her diary, which one night in her future, she'd read to him.

"Unlike many of the guys she's slept with, I can't offer her shit," Burton claimed. "We're doing it just for fun. She's incredibly beautiful and very sexy, but she's a studio plaything at Fox. Yet she is the loneliest lady I've ever met. She's like a lost little girl wandering around a crowded room, even if surrounded by hot-to-trot blokes. She told me she loves my voice, and I told her I love her body. After coitus, I recited poetry to her, and she actually cried. I am reciting, and she kisses my pimply neck. Call it poetic love. We're still going at it. It's blinding hot passion, but I don't dare fall in love with her. I'm getting put off by hearing so much about her promiscuity. In a way, I don't want to go where so many other men have gone before me. She's really a prostitute."

"Don't you think you're being a bit harsh, old boy?" Granger asked.

"What in the fuck do you call a woman who offers sex in return for career advancement? I also went after Miss Olivia de Havilland, while we've been filming *My Cousin Rachel,* but I don't think Miss de Havilland is succumbing to my charms. She told someone, 'Burton is a course-grained man with a coarse-grained charm and a talent not completely developed.' She may be right. I don't know what in hell I'm doing in front of a camera."

At that point, Elizabeth decided it would be discreet to enter the room.

Seeing her, Burton said, "Let's get Mrs. Wilding's opinion on the subject. Elizabeth, do you think Marilyn Monroe is as sexy as they say?"

Knowing that the actors were not aware that she'd eavesdropped, she snapped, "Not at all! I hear she's frigid and no man has ever given her an orgasm. Now get out of my way, gents. Who do you have to fuck around here to get a drink?"

Until midnight, Burton, as Elizabeth observed, spent the entire night dancing with Jean Simmons. He held her lasciviously close, rubbing his body up against her. A television set was blaring about the countdown to midnight, and what the world might expect from the New Year.

Elizabeth was stunned when Burton began kissing Simmons. He continued to kiss her as the old year faded and the new year began. Elizabeth was rewarded with a "hen peck" on her lips from Wilding, followed by a "deep throat" kiss from Granger.

When she broke away from Granger, she noted that he, too, was aware of how Burton was kissing his beautiful young wife, but laughed it off. As Elizabeth later said, "What could Stewart say? React with jealousy? Like hell. Burton was plowing Stewart's ass as well as Jean's. It was obvious."

She noticed Sybil standing in a corner of the room, looking on in anger at her husband as he was kissing another man's wife. Finally, when Sybil could take it no more, she walked over and slapped Burton across the face.

From that point on, the New Year revelers lapsed into a stony silence.

Pamela, the wife of James Mason, later asserted that "Sybil's slap resounded across the room like a bomb blasting off."

Sybil rushed sobbing to her bedroom, as Burton chased after her. Granger, at long last, stepped in front of his own wife and belatedly extended the tongue so recently sampled by Elizabeth.

Elizabeth tugged at Wilding's sleeve. "Let's get the hell out of here."

The next day, Elizabeth called Granger. He treated the whole event rather matter-of-factly. "Sybil became a bit bored with Jean and me. She moved out this morning. Burton left with her. They are going to be living with James and Pamela Mason. Sybil will have no problem with James going after her. But she'd better watch him with Burton. James told me that for the past three years, he's had the hots for Burton."

***

After an examination, Elizabeth's doctor, M.E. Anberg, showed her some alarming X-rays of her fetus. Her umbilical cord had shifted its position. "It now runs the risk of being wrapped around the baby's neck and could choke him. You must have a Caesarian."

Birthed by Caesarian section on January 6, 1953, Elizabeth's first baby entered the world as Michael Howard Wilding, Jr. Weighing seven pounds and three ounces, the baby shocked her doctor and the attending nurses. As it came out of the womb, it already had a thick crop of black hair, evoking the birth of Elizabeth in London in 1932.

Coincidentally, Elizabeth's first baby was delivered in the same Santa Monica hospital room where Shirley Temple had been born. Elizabeth predicted that Michael Jr. would grow up to become a child star like Temple had. The fan magazines reported that Elizabeth was "deliriously happy and madly in love."

After the birth of her boy, Benny Thau at MGM ordered that Elizabeth report to him every two weeks so he could monitor her weight. Almost exhibitionistically, she had her strip down to her bra and panties for an intimate inspection.

While on a crash diet, she lost two film roles, the first, *Young Bess* (1953), which went to Jean Simmons, who appeared opposite her husband, Stewart Granger. "Elizabeth threw a jealous fit," according to Wilding, but managed to restrain herself around Simmons.

She also lost a leading role in another movie, *All the Brothers Were Valiant* (1953). Director Richard Thorpe, who didn't want to work with Elizabeth again, assigned her part to Ann Blyth. As such, Elizabeth lost the chance to work with her friends, the film's male leads, Robert Taylor and Stewart Granger. Granger called her, "Listen, fatty, when are you going to slim down so we can make a picture together?"

She turned down *Roman Holiday* (1953), and regretted it for the rest of her life, as it made a major star out of Audrey Hepburn. A former ballet dancer who fled Nazi-occupied Holland, Hepburn would be launched into major stardom playing a princess opposite Gregory Peck in *Roman Holiday*.

299

Throughout the rest of her life, Elizabeth would be compared unfavorably to Hepburn, who represented style and elegance on the screen. Each actress would also vie for the title of "The World's Most Beautiful Woman."

In 1953, Elizabeth went to Benny Thau's office and virtually begged him to lobby for her to win the role of *The Barefoot Contessa* (1954), a script based loosely on the tumultuous life of Rita Hayworth. "Please, please, please, Benny," she beseeched him.

When Thau called the picture's director, Joseph L. Mankiewicz, he said, "No way. Ava Gardner has already been cast. She's fucking Joseph Schenck." He was the head of United Artists, which was financing *The Barefoot Contessa.*

Elizabeth also turned down the lead female role in *Elephant Walk* (1954), a picture scheduled for filming in Ceylon. The coveted role went eventually to Vivien Leigh instead.

Since Elizabeth was growing increasingly bored with Wilding, she often staged suppers which she would have her local delicatessen prepare for her, since she didn't know how to cook. Their guests were strictly from the A-list. Monty was invited to every gathering, as were Stewart Granger, Jean Simmons, Roddy McDowall, Dick Hanley, Spencer Tracy, Katharine Hepburn (but only sometimes), Errol Flynn, and Humphrey Bogart. On many a night, Judy Garland sang for the supper guests.

At the party, Richard Burton showed up without his wife, Sybil. He'd been on three straight nights of prodigal drinking and what he preferred to call "rampant wenching." He sat with Garland and Elizabeth, as his hand traveled up Garland's dress. She did not resist, as she was known for unzipping her dance partners on the floor and checking out the merchandise.

Burton told Elizabeth and Garland, "I'll never divorce Sybil, and she'll never divorce me, because she loves me and understands me. Not only that, she, above all, knows I'm a genius."

After Burton departed, Elizabeth said, "There goes 1952's Toast of Hollywood—a man likely to continue as the town's toast throughout 1953 as well."

Then, sarcastically, she glanced over at Wilding and said about him, "And there stands a man who in Hollywood is just toast."

"Then he's welcome to join my club," Garland said. "We can call my clan of has-beens 'the Post-Toasties Club.'"

Later that night, Elizabeth became much too drunk and denounced Wilding in front of their guests as if she were already rehearsing her role in *Who's Afraid of Virginia Woolf?* (1966). "I want a man made out of flesh and blood, not some well-mannered wax dummy from Madame Tussauds."

Dick Hanley, who still seemed to know everything going on in the film world, even in remote parts of the globe, kept her informed of the scandals whirling around the making of *Elephant Walk* in Ceylon.

Hanley told her that Vivien Leigh's mental and physical condition was deteriorating rapidly, and that feelers would be going out in February of 1953 to see if Elizabeth was willing to reclaim the role, originally intended for her.

Time magazine did not approve the casting of Elizabeth in *Elephant Walk:* "Elizabeth Taylor, though very beautiful, is too young and inexperienced an actress to fill a role designed for Vivien Leigh."

The final scenes of *Elephant Walk* were to be shot in Hollywood. From Ceylon, Leigh arrived in California, but her mental condition had deteriorated so rapidly that Paramount had to fire her.

With Leigh out of the picture, Paramount negotiated with MGM for a loan-out because of Elizabeth's physical resemblance to Leigh. Because of their similarities, many of the long distance shots of Leigh filmed in Ceylon could be retained for the final cut.

After learning that MGM had signed a contract to lend her out to Paramount for $150,000, Elizabeth stormed into Benny Thau's office and demanded a raise.

"You're getting ten times my full salary," she shouted at Thau.

"Tell me something I don't already know," he said sarcastically. "A contract is a contract. You signed it!"

"So you won't give me a raise, even if I come by every morning and suck you off?" she asked.

"No raise. Now get out. You're such a whore."

Bitchily commenting on Elizabeth's weight gain during the birth of her first son, Hedda Hopper wrote "The title of *Elephant Walk* fits Elizabeth Taylor perfectly, considering the new ballooning figure she shows off to the world."

At the moment she read that, Elizabeth was "living mainly on ice cubes and fruit juices."

As a heavily tranquilized Leigh was put on an airplane from Los Angeles headed back to London, Elizabeth began shooting interior scenes for *Elephant Walk,* having regained her full pay and her former figure. She resumed work on March 19, 1953.

Elizabeth was only twenty-one when she shouldered the burden of the movie role that Leigh had abandoned, and submitted to the direction of William Dieterle.

"When a reporter asked Elizabeth if she liked Leigh as an actress, Elizabeth asserted that she did. "She has an innocence bordering on decadence."

On the first day of shooting, she told Dieterle. "My character of Ruth Wiley is rather underwritten. This appears to be a rather weak fable of men and pachyderms, with me brought in for female relief from all this macho shit."

She continued with Dieterle: "I know that you just directed Rita Hayworth in *Salome;* you've directed Bette Davis, and even gave Charles Laughton his hunchback, but now you're faced with Elizabeth Taylor. I want to look fucking gorgeous in this piece of crap. Got that?"

The director's final summation of Elizabeth on screen—"Beautiful but dull. In private, however, she's beautiful but hardly dull. She's a regular little harridan. I wish my leading men, Mr. Finch and Mr. Andrews, had put more energy into their roles instead of satisfying Miss Taylor's insatiable lusts. Michael Wilding could never satisfy that maneater."

Actually, Laurence Olivier, Leigh's husband, was originally slated to play the role that went to Peter Finch. In the story, the owner (John Wiley, as played by Finch) of a tea plantation in Ceylon courts Elizabeth in England, then marries this "lovely English rose" and takes her back to Ceylon. The sprawling manor house (identified coyly in the script as "a bungalow") was built directly astride the pathway used for centuries by migrating elephants. On site, facing a preoccupied and indifferent husband, the character played by Elizabeth develops a passion for Dick Carver (as played by Dana Andrews), the plantation's manager.

Elizabeth referred to *Elephant Walk* as "the Ceylonese version of *Rebecca.*" Dieterle asserted that Elizabeth had been "fatally miscast. Who in hell would believe that Finch would prefer to hang out with his buddies instead of going upstairs and fucking his wife...unless, of course, he preferred sex with his mates? That would be the only reasonable explanation as to why Finch would ignore the sexual needs of a wife like Taylor."

Because of complications, *Elephant Walk* ended up costing $3 million, the most expensive Paramount Picture ever made up until that time.

Elizabeth slipped into Leigh's scenes with professional ease until few movie-goers could detect which actress was which, especially in long shots (nearly all of which focused on Leigh) or when the character of Ruth Wiley shows her back to the camera in certain scenes. Of course, all of Leigh's close-ups ended on the cutting room floor and had to be reshot with Elizabeth.

Upon its release, *Elephant Walk* was savaged by the critics, Leonard Maltin claiming that the "pachyderm stampede climax comes none too soon."

Brunettes menaced by elephants:
Vivien Leigh *(left)* and **Elizabeth Taylor**

***

Liberated (at least temporarily) from her increasingly boring husband, Elizabeth fitted in perfectly with her two hellraising co-stars in *Elephant Walk,* Peter Finch and Dana Andrews.

Both of them could close down any bar in the world. "Immediately after meeting her, we knew she was one of us," Andrews said. "We invited her to become a charter member of our exclusive fraternity, the 'Fuck You Club.'"

"For a member to join our club, she has to have a foul mouth—I don't mean an occasional 'fuck you,' but a stream of profanity that would shock a fifty-year-old Barcelona whore," Andrews said. "Not only that, a new member has to have the most awful table manners—I'm talking Henry VIII with all the belching and farting that that implies. From what I heard later on, we taught Elizabeth well. For the rest of her life, she became known for breaking wind at the most formal of dinners, including at the homes of those billionaires, Doris Duke and Malcolm Forbes."

"I wish I had been old enough to star opposite you in *Laura,*" Elizabeth told Andrews. "The part would have been so much better with me and without Gene Tierney's buck teeth. I heard you were once arrested for assault with a deadly weapon," she continued. "Am I to become the next victim of that deadly weapon?"

The next day, she showed him an item a columnist had written about them. "As the stars of *Elephant Walk,* Dana Andrews and Elizabeth Taylor are perfectly matched. Overall, they are reliable actors, rather uninspired, who on occasion are capable of doing something impressive on the screen, but both of them are rather wooden. They've been accused of sleepwalking through their performances. I hope they're both awake to get out of the pathway of those rampaging elephants at the end of the movie."

Andrews visited her in her dressing room late one afternoon after both of them had finished their scenes for the day. "Peter told me he's fucking you, and, as a charter member of the Fuck You Club, I should be pounding you too. But I fear I'm too drunk to get it up."

"Oh, Dana," she said, "you're such a dear. Perhaps you'll do the honors during our lunch break tomorrow?"

When Dick Hanley came over to Paramount to visit Elizabeth, she told him that she found Finch "most compelling. His blue eyes can penetrate right through you. He's very alert, very intelligent, and has ruggedly masculine features."

"It sounds as if Milady is in love," Dick told her. Later, he recalled, after his introduction to Finch, "He stands so close to you, you can smell his breath."

Born in London in 1916, Finch had a buoyant, devil-may-care kind of rugged individualism. The illegitimate son of a Scotsman, he had endured a tumbleweed childhood traveling from England to France and on to India before settling in Australia.

Finch had been "discovered" by the Oliviers, Laurence and Vivien, during their triumphant sweep through Australia. In 1948, as part of an arrangement with the Old Vic, the Oliviers set out to bring a trio of plays to Down Under—*School for Scandal, Richard III,* and *The Skin of Our Teeth,* the latter a huge success for Tallulah Bankhead on Broadway.

Bored to some degree with each other, and jaded at this point about promiscuous adventures outside of their marriage, both actors were immensely attracted to Finch. Before long, on location in Australia, Finch launched secretive affairs with each of them.

Aged thirty-six, the bisexual Finch was "compulsively unfaithful" to his wife. "Finchey never met a hot young woman or a nice piece of boy-ass he didn't want to fuck," said Stewart Granger.

"I may be wrong," said Dick Hanley in later years, "but I think Finch prepared Elizabeth for the entrance of Richard Burton into her life. Talk about hell-raisers. If Finch had stayed on in Hollywood, I believe that Elizabeth would have divorced Wilding and married Finch. He was more her kind of guy. Or, as Finch phrased it himself, 'Elizabeth loved my sense of obstreperous camaraderie.'"

After meeting her, Finch said, "On screen, I play your caddish spouse, but off screen, I'm prepared to be your ardent lover."

"Check with me later," she said, heading for her dressing room.

Confronted with her rapidly retreating back side, he called to her, "You've got a great ass on you, kid."

She turned around and almost shocked him. "I can forget about your rear. It is what's up front that counts in a man."

Finch told Elizabeth that in Ceylon, Vivien Leigh had been completely out of control, drinking heavily straight out of the bottle, tearing off her clothes, and running naked through the streets until apprehended by the police. "She would toss dangerous objects at her friends and through the windows, even throw things to hit people in passing cars."

Finch also told Elizabeth that when Leigh arrived in Hollywood, she'd thrown this big party for him, to which she even invited Clark Gable to talk about their making of *Gone With the Wind.* Stewart Granger, Jean Simmons, and David Niven were among the guests.

"Vivien disappeared upstairs and came down about half an hour later," Finch said. "She held a pair of scissors in her hand like a character in some *Psycho* movie. She rushed down the stairs and raced toward Tamara, my wife. I managed to subdue her before she plunged those scissors into Tamara's heart."

Elizabeth was horrified to hear these stories, feeling sympathy for Leigh's condition. "I pray I don't end up in some psycho ward."

Finch told Elizabeth that the Hollywood of 1953 was such a disappointment to him, not at all like his fantasies of "where blonde cuties would cling to my arms and sexy chorus girls in black velvet shorts and white satin blouses would seductively tap-dance around me."

Instead, he discovered that the boom years had ended, and Hollywood was still suffering from the commie witch hunt launched by Senator Joseph McCarthy. It was also battling that new horror that threatened everyone's livelihood—television.

On many a night, she left Wilding at home with the baby while she and "Finchey" pursued one of their favorite pastimes—chewing popcorn during the screening of horror movies, followed later by "a roll in the haystack," as Elizabeth claimed to Dick Hanley. She also claimed, "I made him forget all about Vivien Leigh...at least for a while."

After *Elephant Walk* was wrapped, Paramount offered Finch a seven-year contract which he rejected. "Bloody hell, they wanted me to star with Jane Russell in *The French Line*. Maybe we could have done a striptease together. I could flash my dick and she could flash her big tits. Why cast me as a Spanish gigolo? Why don't they get Fernando Lamas?"

"On the other hand, I'm not so eager to return to London," Finch told her. "Call me an escapologist. In England, I have to face the joint explosions of Larry and Vivien. As you know, both of them demand that I fuck them constantly."

Finch would resurface in her life when she was told that he'd been cast as Julius Caesar in her upcoming 1963 film, *Cleopatra.*

After *Elephant Walk* was wrapped, the studio wanted publicity pictures. Elizabeth agreed to pose in a Jeep. The photographer wanted to depict them in a wind storm in Ceylon. A wind machine was brought in.

During the photo shoot, the giant fan blew a steel splinter into Elizabeth's eye and it became deeply lodged. She was rushed to the hospital, where delicate surgery removed the splinter. Because the surgical technique required that she respond to the instructions issued by the surgeon, she had to remain awake during the eye surgery. She later remembered the sounds of the instruments cutting into her eye, which she compared to the sound of "eating a slice of watermelon."

Released from the hospital, Elizabeth returned home to Wilding and her infant son. On the first night back, during playtime with her son, he inadvertently delivered what she later defined as "a knock-out punch." Within days, her already-injured eye became ulcerated and she was forced to re-enter the hospital to face eye surgery once again, this time as part of a procedure more dangerous than the first.

In the wake of the operation, both of her eyes were blindfolded, and she had to live in darkness for three weeks during the healing process, as neither of her eyes could tolerate light.

Of all her friends, Roddy McDowall offered the most comfort, visiting her every day to keep her abreast of what was going on in Hollywood.

At least she was spared reading a Los Angeles headline: LIZ TAYLOR GOING BLIND.

During her time in the hospital, she received some shocking news, although later she didn't appear to be all that disturbed by it. In her absence, Monty had moved into her household, "assuming my role. My housekeeper told me he slept in bed with my husband. I guess Michael was fucking Monty. It appeared that Monty was getting more of a rise out of him than I ever could."

Wilding always spoke lovingly of Clift. "I would cry on his shoulder all day, and he would feed Elizabeth soup in bed at night, light her cigarettes, re-fill her liquor glasses, and hear what a cold, insensitive bastard I was."

The gossip in Hollywood involved stories about how Monty, Wilding, and Elizabeth were members of a *ménage à trois* after she was released from the hospital. But whereas that tale might have been true to some degree in the emotional sense of the word, it was not apparently true in the sexual, or physical sense.

When she'd first met Richard Burton, she'd thought he was "too bloody much," and she would return to express that opinion many times in her future. But she was deeply touched when he had come to her hospital bed and recited passages from Shakespeare as a means of easing her long, blindfolded days.

She considered him an actor of "unquestionable charm—and that voice. Of course, he also makes good out of a routine he's got down pat—you know, the poor Welsh coalminer's son among the Hollywood hedonists."

At the end of her hospital stay, her doctor removed the bandages and pronounced her eyes in good condition. "Glory to hell," she said, "I can face the camera again. My new film is called *Rhapsody* (1954). My co-star will be that Welsh actor, Richard Burton. I'm sure that charming bastard will rate at least a chapter in any memoir I write."

***

Before the collapse of their marriage, Wilding recalled it as "the happiest time of my life, living in this kind of cloud-cuckoo-land, needing money but spending it like drunken sailors."

Louella Parsons was the first to rush into print about the dying embers of Elizabeth's marriage. She wrote: "When they go out to parties, the Wildings have eyes for everyone but each other." Hedda Hopper claimed, "The Wildings fight like cat and dog."

Humphrey Bogart, of all rogues, warned Wilding, "You're always surrounded by the most beautiful babes at one end of the room, while Liz holds court with all the most attractive males at the other. Married folk didn't ought to act that way."

To accommodate their expanding family, Elizabeth once again obtained a loan from MGM to purchase a more luxurious home designed by her friend, architect George MacLean. Selling for $150,000, it had a dramatic sheer glass wall that opened onto a view of the valley below.

She also moved in her barnyard of three cats, two poodles, and two tame ducks, none of which was housebroken. Her chief form of décor, according to Wilding, involved the placement of magazines with her picture on the cover in every room of the house. These were supplemented with a huge stack of them beside her toilet bowl.

Meanwhile, Michael Wilding—"in a fit of madness," Elizabeth said— turned down the role of Professor Henry Higgins in a nationwide tour of the Broadway version of *My Fair Lady*. "He earned my eternal gratitude," said Rex Harrison, who went on to make the role famous.

Wilding also turned down the role of the Pharaoh in *The Egyptian* (1954). Ironically, Marlon Brando had also rejected a role in this film. Because of financial pressures, Wilding was forced to reconsider and ended up contracting to star in *The Egyptian* in what he called "a stuffy nightshirt role," because of the pharaonic costume he was forced to wear. He dreaded the day shooting began.

Most of the time Wilding was unemployed, hanging out during the day at Barney's Beanery on Santa Monica Boulevard, a joint which attracted a lot of other out-of-work actors. Sometimes, he made some sexual conquests there in spite of the sign the owner had posted: FAGOTS (sic) KEEP OUT!

In addition to his homosexual affairs, Wilding also engaged in sexual liaisons with two famous female movie stars of the 1940s. The queen of Cinematic Camp, Maria Montez, born in the Dominican Republic, lives today on the late show as *Cobra Woman*. Her accent was thick, her acting a joke, but Wilding found her a "hot tamale in bed. I'm one of her kitsch fanciers," he confessed to Stewart Granger and Jean Simmons. "She claimed I was better in bed than her husband, Jean-Pierre Aumont, whom Vivien Leigh told me 'hit the spot as a lover,'"

Montez was not the only adulterous conquest Wilding launched with a movie star sex symbol. He also became involved in a torrid liaison with the buxom starlet Marie McDonald, who was nicknamed "The Body" because of her shapely curves.

In the years to come, McDonald enraged Elizabeth with her "brazen" public comments about her affairs with Elizabeth's husbands.

"Michael swore on a stack of Bibles that I was better in bed than Elizabeth," The Body proclaimed.

As one of Hollywood's most popular pin-up girls of World War II, Mc-Donald also admitted to having a one-night stand with Elizabeth's future husband, Mike Todd.

Another future husband of Elizabeth's, Eddie Fisher, revealed in his memoirs that he had a sexual fling with McDonald in Paris at the end of one of Bob Hope's Christmas tours to military bases.

Elizabeth made only one comment about McDonald, in 1966. "I heard she once escaped from a mental hospital in Austria. She was married to a former husband of Debbie Reynolds [a reference to Harry Karl]...She even claimed she was kidnapped by six men and repeatedly raped. Her off-screen life sounded a hell of a lot more intriguing than anything she did on the screen. Too bad she died of a drug overdose in 1965. One shouldn't speak bad of the dead...so *good*."

***

Richard Burton could not wait for Elizabeth to recover from her eye surgery. His role as a musician in *Rhapsody* was reassigned to the Italian actor, Vittorio Gassman.

Instead of filming *Rhapsody,* Burton starred in *The Robe,* based on the best-selling novel by Lloyd C. Douglas. *The Robe* was an episodic costume drama about a Roman centurion (Burton), who presides over Christ's crucifixion. Jean Simmons was cast in the female lead. Burton won an Oscar nomination, although his performance seems stiff and superficial today. Victor Mature was cast as his slave Demetrius. *The Robe* became the first movie ever shot in CinemaScope.

Elizabeth told Dick Hanley, "Working with Jean will make it easier for Burton to fuck her every day in her dressing room. Thank God Stewart Granger is taking care of the sexual needs of my husband since Mikey and I are now doing it only once a month, if that. I can also thank God Peter Finch came into my life. Before he left, that devil wanted it morning, noon, and night. No wonder Vivien Leigh had that nervous breakdown."

One night, when Wilding complained of having a migraine, he stayed home and tended to their baby while Elizabeth accepted a dinner invitation from Jean Sim-

Guess who's sleeping with Michael Wilding? **Marie ("The Body") McDonald**

mons and Stewart Granger. Still uncertain of her eye condition, she took a taxi to the Granger's hilltop home.

She'd long admired Mature, and had been thrilled by his muscular screen presence in the 1949 *Samson and Delilah,* in which he'd co-starred with Hedy Lamarr for Cecil B. DeMille.

For years, she'd read that he was king of the boudoir, and fan magazines had covered his list of conquests that included Alice Faye, Betty Grable, June Haver, Rita Hayworth, Betty Hutton, Veronica Lake, Carole Landis, Anne Shirley, Gene Tierney, and Lana Turner.

At dinner, Elizabeth found him to be charismatic and even better looking and more dynamic than he was on screen. He amused the Grangers and Elizabeth, telling them he'd pressed the imprint of his bare buttocks into a slab of concrete and had it placed outside his dressing room as a symbol of his annoyance at not being invited to place the more conventional imprints of his hands and feet into the concrete in front of Grauman's Chinese Theater.

Elizabeth was uncertain of his marital status, remembering that in 1948, he'd wed a divorcée, Dorothy Stanford Berry, but the couple had had so many breakups and reconciliations that she had virtually lost count. As Elizabeth later relayed to Dick Hanley, "I didn't plan to marry Vic, only to fuck him."

"The press likes to label you 'Luscious Liz' and me as a 'Lush Lothario,'" but that's all crap, of course," Mature said.

"Just the other day I read that you're also called the 'Technicolor Tarzan' and an 'Overripe Romeo,'" she said.

"Cool it with that 'overripe' shit," he said. "I'm ripe for plucking, not 'overripe.'"

"Plucking, how amusing," Granger said. "Rhymes with…"

Mature entertained them with stories of his early days, claiming that after he'd arrived in Hollywood he had only eleven cents left after paying his eight dollar weekly rent. "I wired Dad and asked for money. He wired back that when

Victor Mature

he had arrived in America from Austria, that was six cents more than he had—and furthermore, he couldn't speak English, and I could."

"That's what's called 'tough love,'" Elizabeth said.

He told the Grangers and Elizabeth that "in spite of my three marriages, Rita Hayworth is the only girl I ever felt I truly loved. Apparently, the way to Rita's heart is to saw her in half."

He was referring to Orson Welles'

magic act in which Hayworth appeared on stage with him and was "sawed in half," or so it appeared to astonished members of the audience.

"Every reporter has to write about my muscles, and I'd like to be so much more," Mature said.

"It's better to be written about than ignored," Elizabeth said.

"I've long ago come to that conclusion," he said. "But I get tired of being a male striptease. But fuck it all…I make money and have a blast and screw any woman I want. So life is good."

At the end of dinner and several more rounds of drinks, Elizabeth announced that she was heading back home. "Jean, would you call me a taxi?"

"Hell with that!" Mature said. "I'll drive you home."

After everybody kissed everybody else, she got into the car with Mature. On the way back, she warned him, "Better keep your eyes on the road, buster, instead of looking at me."

"Don't blame me because you look so fucking gorgeous men can't take their eyes off you. I want to see more. Why not stop in at my place for a drink?"

"You're on, big boy."

She spent five hours at his apartment, and later told Dick Hanley, "Not since Nicky have I had such a deep dicking. Vic is welcome to put his shoes under my bed any time in the future. What a hunk of beef. He is living proof that God did not create all men equal."

When the gay author, Gore Vidal, saw a (now famous) nude photo of Mature lying in a bunk during his World War II service in the Coast Guard, he wrote, "If the Germans had seen that picture, they would have surrendered months before 1945."

The sun was up when Elizabeth arrived back at her house. Wilding was in the kitchen preparing breakfast for himself and their baby. "Where in hell have you been?"

"I was afraid to drive at night so I slept over with Jean and Stewart," she said.

"That's odd, because I called Stewart," he said. "He told me that Victor Mature drove you home."

She stared at him. "Why don't you go fuck yourself?"

Then she stormed into their bedroom, locking the door behind her.

***

Elizabeth herself defined the pictures she made between 1952 and 1956 as "rubbish movies." Even so, much of the press hailed her as "the Queen of Hollywood," or at the very least, "The Queen of MGM." Grace Kelly, speaking off the record, said, "Elizabeth Taylor was not the Queen of Hollywood since 1952. I was. All of my films made more than $5 million, and Taylor went from one disaster to another. Her movies were so bad I could not sit through them."

Elizabeth may not have been the reigning queen, but according to the *Picture Post* in Britain in 1954, she was at the very least, a monarch. "If imitation is the sincerest form of flattery, Elizabeth Taylor is the most flattered girl in the world—apart from being the most beautiful. Not since the war, when every girl one saw was Veronica Lake, have the girls of this country striven so hard to look like Taylor."

According to Britain's *Picture Post* in 1954, she was the one Hollywood star that young girls, from secretaries to sales clerks, from nurses to telephone operators, wanted to look like.

For a 1954 release, almost at the same time as *Elephant Walk,* MGM hired Charles Vidor to direct Elizabeth in *Rhapsody,* where she played a rich young woman, Louise Durant, in love with two different musicians—Vittorio Gassman cast as Paul Brontë and John Ericson in the role of James Guest. Veteran actor Louis Calhern, who had seduced Marilyn Monroe on and off screen, and who had previously appeared with her in *The Asphalt Jungle* (1950), was cast as Elizabeth's father, Nicolas Durant.

Against a musical background of Tchaikowsky, Liszt, Debussy, Mendelssohn, and Rachmaninoff, Elizabeth drifts between these two handsome musicians, who seem to love music more than her in a film which by today's standards looks like a blend between a soap opera and a made-for-TV film.

When Shelley Winters learned that Elizabeth would be appearing in the movie with her husband, Vittorio Gassman, she placed a telephone call to her. "Don't fall for the son of a bitch," Winters said. "He'll charm the pants off you. When he gets what he wants, he'll leave you for some sixteen-year-old Roman wench. Both of us love pasta. You'll mourn his leaving and you'll gorge on pasta. You'll get fat and won't be able to face a camera. Listen to your mother here. I know what a maneater you are, but keep your mangy paws off Vittorio. He belongs to me."

Elizabeth knew almost nothing of her two leading men, Gassman and Ericson. Actually, she'd been looking forward to starring in the film with Burton. At first she was resentful of the two actors ultimately cast.

She found Ericson "very good looking, but rather Germanic and cold. The silly boy still seems to be in love with the girl he'd just married, Milly Coury," she said. "How very un-Hollywood."

There was some talk about how Ericson was going to "become the next big male movie star," but that dream would never be realized. His film career gradually flickered out, and he became better known on television. His peak fame came in the 1965-66 season when he co-starred as the partner of Anne

Francis in the ABC detective series, *Honey West,* about a female private eye.

To Elizabeth, Gassman was a far more intriguing specimen. He was born in Genoa to a German father and a Pisan-Jewish mother. In Rome, he'd played Stanley Kowalski in Tennessee Williams' *Un tram che si chiama desiderio (a.k.a. A Streetcar Named Desire).*

In 1952, Gassman had married Winters, but at the time, Elizabeth met him, that short marriage was nearing its end. Gassman had a roving eye for beautiful women.

Ten years older than Elizabeth, Gassman in his twenties could have played Romeo. Tall, with black curly hair, he appeared in a perfectly tailored, beige-colored suit from Rome. Although he was intelligent looking, he had not perfected his English yet.

She had been warned by Director Vidor that Gassman didn't like anything American, especially American girls. But for a man who detested American girls, he was gracious, charming, and solicitous to Elizabeth.

He kissed her had, saying, *"Lei e una grande artiste. Ho visto Un Posto del Sole."* She gathered that he was praising her performance in *A Place in the Sun,* the only movie of hers he'd ever seen. She'd never seen one of his movies, not even the celebrated *Bitter Rice* (1950) *(a.k.a. Riso Amaro; 1949),* a film which had been condemned by the Catholic League of Decency.

The next morning, when she entered her dressing room, she found it filled with yellow roses he had sent. He had obviously learned what her favorite flower was.

Gassman had written a note (in English), perhaps with some assistance. "These roses must suffice until I can present my heart to you tonight. Shelley does not have to know. Yours forever, Vittorio."

After reading that note, Elizabeth told Vidor, "I'm in love. I crave romance. I don't want to come home any more to that that dull, boring British gentleman stashed there."

As Elizabeth would later tell Roddy McDowall, "On my first date with Vittorio, we drove to Malibu and spent the night in some tacky motel room. Let's face it: Those god damn nosy reporters would never think of looking for a world class movie star like Elizabeth Taylor in a hotbed motel."

"He's a great lover," she claimed. "During lovemaking, he yells out all sorts of things in Italian. They sound so endearing. I don't know what he's saying. For all I know, it's 'Take this, you bitch,' but it sounds like Romeo wooing Juliet."

"I laugh at his linguistic mistakes, and I'm teaching him all the dirty words in English I know," she said. "What's wrong with Shelley? Didn't she teach him the English word for fuck?"

"His nickname for me is *Primavera,"* she said. "I already know that means

312

Spring. He told me he wants for me to divorce Wilding and go live with him in Rome."

"He promises to teach me Italian. I can't exactly see myself starring in some great epic in Rome, but who knows?"

Gassman may have had a more accurate sense of her future than she did, except that when *Cleopatra* was made, he was nowhere around.

"During the filming of *Rhapsody,* "Vittorio made love to me at least twice a day—sometimes in my dressing room, sometimes in that seedy Malibu motel room which, if I remember, was painted purple," Elizabeth told Vidor. "The towels were thin and threadbare, so I bought luxurious red ones."

"I found we came from different cultures," she said. "Michael went away with Bob Taylor for the weekend, and I invited Vittorio over for dinner. He adored my son. I just assumed he liked pasta, being Italian. I had orderd lasagna from some local eatery, with a pizza on the side. I'd put the food in the refrigerator and planned to warm it up for dinner. When he saw me removing the food from the refrigerator, he went ballistic. He told me that 'electricity kills food.' He claimed that fresh produce has to be bought every day and never refrigerated. Instead of the lasagna, he cooked some spaghetti for me and flavored it with just olive oil and fresh garlic. It was divine."

Later that night, before he retired to her bedroom, he played a record he'd brought to the house. It was a Neapolitan love song titled "Scalinetta," whose name, roughly translated, meant "Little Steps Leading to Love."

"He began to discuss our upcoming marriage—presumably the marriage that would take place after some messy divorce details were handled. He said he wanted to take me to Portofino for our honeymoon."

Elizabeth shared details about her involvement with Gassman with very few of her friends, but included Roddy McDowall and Dick Hanley among those in whom she confided. She also revealed what was going on to her director, Charles Vidor, "because he would be a total fool not to see what was happening right in front of him."

As the shooting ended, Gassman confided to Elizabeth that he wanted to take her away to Palm Springs for the weekend. As a cover-up, Elizabeth mendaciously told Wilding that she was going to go off with Roddy and some of his gay friends.

To Roddy, she remembered that weekend as "one of the most passionate of my life. By the time Vittorio made love to me that final Monday morning, I was hopelessly, madly, crazily in love with him. For the first time in my life, I learned that a

Vittorio Gassman

313

man's armpits taste like ambrosia."

"Oh, baby," Roddy said. "I could have told you that a long time ago."

During their drive back to Los Angeles, from whose airport he was scheduled to fly back to Rome, she said, "We did nothing but talk about our future. He even speculated about what our *bambini* would look like."

She still had a week's work at MGM. "I didn't go in until Tuesday. I found a note with one yellow rose. I was from Vittorio. Someone may have helped him with his English."

"My darling Elizabeth,
On my dying day the last memory for me before I depart this earth will be the beauty of your face in the rosy glow of a California dawn. It was surely the light that inspired Leonardo da Vinci to paint the Mona Lisa. Some things are not meant to be. But the glorious memory of you will linger on forever and ever until we meet again on some distant shore. There we will live and love together through eternity, but for the moment in this mad cesspool called earth, we must follow our separate paths until the road one day leads back to each other.
Your amante through the ages.
Vittorio"

Shelley Winters divorced Gassman in 1954, the same year *Rhapsody* was released. It is not known if Winters became aware of her husband's adulterous affair with Elizabeth. She certainly suspected and one night confronted Elizabeth about it at a party.

Elizabeth staunchly denied it, falsely claiming that she'd fallen in love with the film's second male lead, John Ericson. "If John's new wife finds out, that marriage will be over before it begins."

Winters could not complain too bitterly about Gassman's seductions outside marriage, since she was still carrying on with three bisexual actors—Marlon Brando, Farley Granger, and Burt Lancaster.

In reviewing *Rhapsody,* a critic for *The New York Herald Tribune* wrote, "Elizabeth Taylor's animation is only the animation of the doll with the strings being pulled behind the scenes. Even her evident and genuine beauty seems at times to be fake."

In marked contrast, Bosley Crowther, in an uncharacteristically supportive review in *The New York Times* got carried away in his overview of *Rhapsody:* "Her wind-blown hair frames her features like an ebony aureole and her large eyes and red lips glisten warmly in close-ups on the softly lighted screen. Any gent who would go for music with this radiant—and rich—Miss Taylor at hand is not a red-blooded American."

***

At long last, MGM took Michael Wilding off suspension, and he was told to report to Benny Thau's office to discuss a new film project.

Before he departed for his meeting, Elizabeth warned her husband, "Take my advice, don't commit yourself until you've seen the script. He'll talk you into some second-rate picture and make you think it's *Gone With the Wind.*" This contradicted her previouis advice in which she had told him to "take anything thrown at you."

At MGM, after a long wait, he was finally ushered into Thau's office. "Have I got a deal for you. Robert Taylor begged me to give him the role, but I turned the queer down. I said this part is for Michael Wilding. You'll play a blind pianist opposite Joan Crawford in a script called *Torch Song.* I predict that it will be the hit of the year."

Fired by Harry Cohn from *From Here to Eternity* because of a dispute over wardrobe, Crawford was eager to do *Torch Song* (1953), after Benny Thau sent her the script. She signed a contract and agreed to return to MGM, after a decade-long absence, in her first full-length color film. [Because of some technical issue, her hair appeared in the final print as tangerine-colored.]

In the film, Crawford played the role of Jenny Stewart, a part defined as a "witchy," self-involved Broadway diva, who clashes with her blind pianist Tye Graham (as played by Wilding).

She told Thau, "It's a good part for a woman who no longer is a spring chicken."

Wilding didn't want the role, but couldn't risk going on suspension again. As a blind pianist, he accompanies Crawford, who was cast as a hard-as-nails Broadway musical star who chews up people for lunch.

Crawford would later refer to *Torch Song* as "one of my best bad movies.:" At this stage in her career, she was forty-eight years old and hadn't danced in fourteen years, even though her body was in remarkable shape. Fearing that her breasts had sagged as she neared the half-century mark, she insisted that wardrobe fit her with a "bullet brassiere." Her singing voice, never very good even at its best, had to be dubbed by the relatively forgotten singer, India Adams, who sounded something like a pale and watered-down version of Marilyn Monroe.

The director of the movie was Charles Walters, whose previous successes with Judy Garland included both *Meet Me in St. Louis* (1944), and *Easter Parade* (1948).

There had been speculation that Crawford would try to seduce Wilding, but actually it was Director Walters who went after Elizabeth's husband, although apparently he did not win the prize.

This hilariously clichéd melodrama is viewed today chiefly by camp followers, often aging gays, who watch it just for the musical number where Crawford appears on the screen in blackface *à la* Al Jolson. Gig Young, whom Elizabeth had dated briefly, stars as the second male lead.

Crawford sings "Two-Faced Woman" in blackface, although many of her loyal fans, embarrassed by her use of blackface, assert that she's only wearing "tan-colored make-up" as a means of transforming herself into "merely the suggestion" of an Ebony Venus.

During the 1930s, Crawford had fancied herself as "The Queen of MGM," despite the fact that her chief rival, Norma Shearer, married at the time to studio boss Irving Thalberg, also claimed that title.

On the occasion of her return to MGM, Crawford was given a royal welcome from stars past and present. As Director Walters said, "There were so many flowers, it looked like the funeral of a sitting U.S. president." Ann Blyth, who had played Crawford's daughter in *Mildred Pierce* (1945), sent beautiful orchids. Fred Astaire sent red roses. And Clark Gable, Crawford's longtime lover, presented a basket of chocolate delicacies from Rome.

Crawford refused to speak to Wilding other than a terse "Good morning," followed at the end of the day by a staccato "Good evening."

Walters could not understand the source of Crawford's enmity, since Wilding had never been anything but gracious to her. "I finally concluded that Wilding's mistake was being Mr. Elizabeth Taylor."

Wilding's first day on the set required him to kiss Crawford passionately as part of a love scene. He later told the press, "Kissing Crawford was like kissing Hitler." That same line would be used by Tony Curtis, as it applied to Marilyn Monroe during the shooting of *Some Like It Hot* (1959).

After she was thoroughly kissed, Crawford broke from him and marched over for a conference with Walters. She then retreated to her dressing room. Walters then approached Wilding, telling him that, "Miss Crawford says the scene will have to be reshot. Your right shoulder blocked her profile."

Crawford and Elizabeth, on occasion, would sleep with the same men, notably John F. Kennedy, Steve Cochran, Rock Hudson, and Tyrone Power. But Elizabeth did not have the slightest fear that the aging screen diva would move in on Wilding.

When Walters visited Crawford in her dressing room, she opened the door completely nude, but was unable to seduce him, as Walters was more interested in the hot male lover he kept at home.

Consequently, Crawford never seduced either Wilding or Walters, but turned her attentions instead to Gig Young, whom she found "extremely sexy." She'd erroneously heard that Elizabeth had had a torrid affair with him, and she set out to conquer Elizabeth's former boyfriend and not her husband. She invited Young on several occasions to her dressing room for a drink, but he kept rejecting her amorous advances. She reacted with fury, and he shot quickly upward on her "hate list." As a means of retaliating against him, she arranged for the film's director to cut his scenes to the minimum. "Since I didn't produce a hard-on for her," Young later said, "she castrated me."

The one star who didn't slavishly toady to Crawford on the set was Elizabeth herself, who fancied herself as the new reigning queen of MGM. Elizabeth hadn't spoken to Crawford since that time she'd visited her home, as arranged by Clark Gable, for "fashion advice" and had rejected her sexual advances.

On four different occasions, Elizabeth visited Wilding for lunch, since she was shooting *Rhapsody* on a set located only a short distance away. Unlike the other stars paying elaborate homage to Crawford, Elizabeth ignored her. At one point, she walked right past her without speaking. Or, in Crawford's words, "Princess Brat came swanning onto my set."

Crawford was furious, venting her rage to Walters and demanding that he "bar this little tramp from my set."

As a means of preserving peace, Walters talked with both Wilding and Elizabeth, pleading with her not to come onto the set of *Torch Song* again.

"If you want to have lunch with Mike, meet him in the commissary," Walters said. "Your presence on the set is a painful reminder that the Queen of MGM has been dethroned."

"Dietrich hates me because I stole Mike from her, and Barbara Stanwyck detests me because Bob Taylor fucked me. The only bigtime screen diva who has not feuded with me is Bette Davis. But I'm sure that dispute lies in my future."

As regards that statement in particular, Elizabeth turned out to be a prophet.

In later years, Crawford claimed, "Miss Taylor is a spoiled, indulgent child—a blemish on public decency."

***

Before its reincarnation in the mid-50s, *Beau Brummell* (1954) had previously been released as a silent film in 1924 starring John Barrymore. In the 1950s version, Stewart Granger played the fashion-conscious dandy, an adviser to an 18th-century Prince of Wales, as interpreted by Peter Ustinov. Elizabeth, in a wig and period costume, plays Lady Patricia, the female lead and Granger's love interest. The costume epic was filmed in England during the summer of 1953.

On the set, Granger said to his co-stars, "Here comes my friend, Elizabeth Taylor. She's voluptuous in every way—big tits, big ass, big violet eyes, and a tiny rosebud mouth ideal for sucking dick. Just look at those bosoms— WHOOOA!"

Back in Hollywood, Jean Simmons had to endure a four-month separation from Granger, who was still her husband at the time. Along with Michael Wilding, Victor Mature, Gene Tierney, and Peter Ustinov, she, too, had been cast in *The Egyptian* (1954), by director Michael Curtiz.

In the same year, Ustinov appeared in both *Beau Brummell* and *The Egyptian.*

Elizabeth asked Dick Hanley to visit the Los Angeles set of *The Egyptian* and relay all the gossip back to her during her involvement with *Beau Brummell* in England. Like a dutiful servant, he obeyed her. "Here's the latest. Mature is fucking Gene Tierney—lucky gal. I heard that Stewart Granger is banging you in England, so it's only fair that Jean is screwing your ever-so-stiff-and-formal husband, Michael Wilding. Don't you just love Hollywood?"

On the set of *Beau Brummell,* both Elizabeth and Granger detested their German director, Curtis Bernhardt. Elizabeth showed her contempt by yawning in his face whenever he gave her direction. Granger almost attacked him one day when he kept poking him with the stick he always carried around. After one poke too many, Granger, in front of Elizabeth, grabbed the stick from the director's hand and broke it in two.

The Granger/Taylor affair ended almost before it began. In England, Granger came down with intestinal flu, an infection which led to colitis. Elizabeth accompanied him to a hospital for "colonic irrigations," which were so messy, and so horrible, that they destroyed Granger forever as a dashing and romantic ideal in her life.

Months later, in Hollywood, Granger, perhaps during pillow talk, confessed to Wilding, his long-time lover, that he'd been intimate with Elizabeth during the London filming of *Beau Brummell.*

When Wilding asked Elizabeth about this, she said, "He fucks you. Why not me? Besides, darling, it is no secret. I always fall a little in love with my leading men, and I expect I always will. So live with it!"

What had really destroyed the last vestiges of romantic feeling Elizabeth had for Granger centered around events associated with the filming of *Green Fire* (1954).

During the making of *Beau Brummell,* Granger had received an advance screenplay of *Green Fire,* some South America-based hokum about love and conflict between an emerald prospector (Granger) and a coffee-plantation owner (Grace Kelly). As Elizabeth later discussed with Wilding, "All Stewart did was talk about his upcoming love scenes with that stuck-up bitch, Grace Kelly. He's heard the rumors—and they're true, I'm sure—about how she fucks all her leading men. He was worried to death about halitosis. He was afraid that his nervousness about kissing her would cause an upset stomach which would lead to his having bad breath."

During Granger's location shooting for *Green Fire* in South America, Elizabeth invited Jean Simmons to come over to her house for dinner. "Are you afraid to have Grace Kelly alone in the jungles with your Stewart?"

"Not really," Simmons replied. "As you know, I'm playing one of Napoléon's mistresses in *Desirée*. Instead of Stewart, Marlon Brando is doing the honors."

In his memoirs, Granger admitted that "Jean liked Brando a lot, but I found him fairly insufferable."

Granger later wrote, "Grace had one phobia—her behind. For me, it was the most delicious thing imaginable, but it did stick out a bit, and she was very self-conscious about it. Our last scene was played in a torrential downpour and when the final kiss came, we were both soaking wet, which accentuated that fabulous behind. To save her embarrassment, I covered it with both hands. If you look closely at the kiss, you'll see Grace give a start as those two eager hands take hold."

When shooting was finished on *Beau Brummell*, MGM generously financed six weeks of travel on the Continent for Elizabeth and Michael. There was talk that this second honeymoon might save their marriage, but the couple often got into epic battle in their hotel suites.

***

Almost immediately after Elizabeth completed filming on *Beau Brummell*, and the European holiday that followed it, she was rushed into the filming of *The Last Time I Saw Paris* (1954), her fourth film in less than a year. It was based on a short story by F. Scott Fitzgerald, *Babylon Revisited*. In addition to Van Johnson, her co-stars included Walter Pidgeon, Donna Reed, and Eva Gabor.

The crew noted that on the set, Elizabeth fought virtually every day with the film's director, Richard Brooks. When he called her "a bloody cunt," she told him "to go stick a dildo up your dingleberry-coated asshole, you dirty son of a bitch. You should have been smothered at birth."

Elizabeth had been excited when she received the script. "I'm to play Zelda and Monty is going to be F. Scott Fitzgerald."

But when Monty read the script, he rejected it. Soonafter, Michael Wilding, then in the final throes of his marriage to Elizabeth, made it clear that he'd accept the role if it was offered to him. Brooks, however, at the last minute, made a bad casting decision and offered the role to Van Johnson, with whom Elizabeth had previously worked on that disaster entitled *The Big Hangover* (1950).

Although Wilding had wanted to appear opposite his wife, he rejected the chance to star opposite Grace Kelly in *The Swan*. Whereas his best friend, Granger, had been eager to appear with Kelly, Wilding had never been that impressed with her. *The Swan* had been filmed as a silent in 1925 and as a talkie in 1930, when it was retitled *One Romantic Night*. In this fluffy melodramatic comedy, Louis Jourdan was cast as Kelly's suitor, but she's promised to a prince. Wilding was to play the stuffy prince, but the role eventually went to another English actor, Alec Guinness.

The Last Time I Saw Paris marked the acting debut of Eva Gabor, who told Elizabeth that, "We are distantly related. After all, Zsa Zsa married your former father-in-law, Conrad Hilton."

Wilding wanted to go to the premiere of *The Last Time I Saw Paris,* but Elizabeth rejected his offer, attending the event with Monty as her escort instead.

"My greatest fantasy," she told Stewart Granger, "was for Monty to have Michael's dick transplanted onto him—and for him to be straight."

On three different occasions, Monty brought Rock Hudson to Elizabeth's house for dinner. "I'm madly in love with him," Monty told Elizabeth. "He's the top. I'm the bottom. Unlike me, he's got this monster cock and knows how to use it. I can't get enough of him. Jane Wyman's after him, too."

Dick Hanley, years later, recalled being invited to dinner one night at the home of Stewart Granger. "Jean Simmons, of course, was the hostess. Guests included Monty, who was there with Rock Hudson. Michael brought Elizabeth, but those two former lovebirds sang to each other no more. Victor Mature, who had seduced both Elizabeth and Jean, showed up solo. Richard Burton arrived with the glamorous Lana Turner as his date. Each of them had signed to star in a film entitled *The Rains of Ranchipur* (1955), a remake of the 1939 *The Rains Came,* which had starred Myrna Loy and Tyrone Power in equivalent roles."

"What a strange evening for my beloved Elizabeth," Dick said. "She was

Elizabeth Taylor with her onscreen beau, **Stewart Granger**

there with her present husband, Michael, and her future husband, Burton. Not only that, but she was there with her lover, Mature, and Monty, if he could be called a lover, and also a future lover, Rock. And she'd also fucked Stewart, the host. It must have been a lot of fun having all of them together."

In the summer of 1954, Elizabeth and Wilding moved into another, larger home, at 1375 Beverly Estate Drive, high above Benedict Canyon Drive in

Beverly Hills. It was a high-tech house, built of steel and adobe. Elizabeth immediately took to swimming nude in the pool, even if she had guests. She told Dick, "Most of my male guests have already fucked me, so what the hell?"

Joan Bennett, who had played her screen mother in *Father of the Bride* and *Father's Little Dividend,* did not have her phone number and just showed up at Elizabeth's door one day. Wilding opened it and went to tell Elizabeth of her arrival. Lounging beside her pool, Elizabeth said to Wilding, "Tell Joan to go fuck herself."

Bennett had always befriended Elizabeth, and the two actresses had gotten along together for both "The Bride" and "The Dividend" pictures. But Elizabeth later told Wilding, "Who in hell does she think she is? Showing up on my doorstep without an invitation. Bennett has to realize I'm a star now and that I deserve some respect."

Four dogs, including two poodles, along with five cats and two ducks, roamed through the house. None of them was housebroken. Her dog, "Gee Gee," was allowed to lick her newborn child, a policy that horrified Sara. Elizabeth told her that "a dog's saliva is the purest thing in the world, a true disinfectant."

By the time of Elizabeth's second pregnancy, she and Wilding were hardly speaking. He slept on a large lavender-colored divan in the living room, and she occupied the master bedroom by herself or whatever animal wandered in. She later admitted that, "This was one of the most miserable times of my life— I was dead old at twenty-four. It was just smog and no sunshine."

With the debut of her second pregnancy, Elizabeth in her own words was "living hand to mouth." Instead of undergoing another cut in salary as before, she agreed that MGM could extend her contract by an extra year, a decision she'd later regret.

"The best way I know to celebrate my twenty-third birthday is to give birth."

Between films, Elizabeth gave birth to her second child, again by Caesarean. On the day he was born, February 17, 1955, she named him Christopher Edward Wilding. Edward was the first name of Monty.

Jules Goldstone told her that having her two sons had cost her a million dollars because of the MGM suspensions the births had necessitated. "My boys are worth it," she shot back.

Even though she'd just given birth, she told Janet Leigh, "My marriage is over. Mike and I are now brother and sister."

Monty was at the Wilding home nearly every night. He nicknamed her older son "Britches," and seemed to dote on him so much that rumors spread that the second baby was actually Monty's child.

Right after the birth, an invitation arrived from the Academy Awards officials, asking her to appear at the March, 1955 ceremonies at the RKO Pantages Theater in Los Angeles to present the Oscar for Best Documentary.

Still overweight, she immediately went on a diet of fresh fruit juices and ice cubes "to get back to my fighting weight."

Reviewed by the international press, her appearance was stunning. There were gasps from the audience when she came out onto the stage wearing a white fur stole over a gown of white silk, organza, and satin, with stiletto high hells, a bouffant hairdo, and a fortune in diamonds around her neck and dangling from her ears.

Backstage, she said, "Tell all my fucking critics that Elizabeth Taylor is back and ready for a long reign as the Queen of Hollywood."

***

At two o'clock in the morning, an urgent phone call was placed to the home of Roddy McDowall. He was in bed that night with an unidentified partner, perhaps Tab Hunter, or perhaps another of agent Henry Willson's "pretty boys."

"What in hell's going on?" Roddy asked her. "Are you okay?"

"I feel great!" she said. "I want you to be the first to know. I've been royally fucked."

"I didn't know Prince Philip was in Hollywood," he said.

"Cut the shit!" she said. "I've been fucked by a handsome Irishman from Dublin. For the past three hours, he's deep-dicked me twice. God knows he'll want it again before dawn breaks over Malibu."

"Who is this divine creature, and does he make house calls?" Roddy asked.

"His name is Kevin McClory," she said. "It rhymes with glory, and is he ever glorious. Great body, great everything."

"Never heard of him," he said.

"He's a production assistant to that loud-mouthed jerk, Mike Todd," she said. "Sooner than later, I'll be writing my name as Elizabeth Taylor Hilton Wilding McClory.

"How did you meet him?" he asked.

"Shirley MacLaine introduced me," she said.

"God, I hope that Kevin hasn't invaded her too."

322

CHAPTER FIFTEEN
Giants

To Elizabeth, the new man in her life, Kevin McClory, was a dashing figure. He'd descended from two of her favorite authors, those literary sisters, Emily and Charlotte Brontë. Both of his parents had been actors in Dublin.

He told her tragic stories of his service in the British Merchant Navy during World War II. At one point, his ship was torpedoed in the North Atlantic. Most of the crew drowned, but he drifted for more than 700 miles in a lifeboat in freezing conditions before he was picked up off the coast of Ireland with four other survivors.

He became friends with famous writers and directors, including John Huston, who defined him as "a man's man like Bogie." Huston hired him to work on *The African Queen* (1951), with Humphrey Bogart and Katharine Hepburn.

McClory was also a close friend of writer Ian Fleming, and he was one of the first to realize the cinematic potential of his James Bond character. "Your secret agent would be ideal in a dynamite series of movies," he told Fleming.

right photo: **Kevin McClory**
upper left photo: **Sean Connery** as 007
in the much-disputed *Thunderball*

Long after the ending of his affair with Elizabeth, McClory would become famously associated with the James Bond character. He became a player in a series of legal battles asserting that Fleming had plagiarized his script, *Thunderball*. Eventually, after prolonged wrangling in and out of courts, McClory prevailed and was cut into the profits generated by the film, *Thunderball* (1965) and in its remake entitled *Never Say Never Again* (1983).

In later years, McClory spoke several times to journalists about his affair with Elizabeth. "I did not break up her marriage," he asserted. "When I fell in love with Elizabeth, she had long ago fallen out of love with Wilding. It was all over except for the divorce. I was crazy for her, and she was in love with me—and we planned to get married after she divorced Wilding. Of course, I warned her that I was a man of modest means and could not give her the trappings of a wealthy film producer."

"It doesn't matter," she told him. "I'd live in a log cabin with no jewelry, scrub your floors, and cook Irish stew for you every night and serve it with cold beer if you'd make me your wife."

"Do you really mean that, my darling girl?" he asked her.

"I mean it as much as a man does when he tells a woman he'll put in only the first two or three inches," she said.

***

"Kevin has brought me more joy and happiness than I've known in years," Elizabeth confessed to Dick Hanley, "still and always" one of her best friends.

But Dick was in a despondent mood. After eleven years of devoted service to Louis B. Mayer, he asked if he could take his first vacation, volunteering to do so without pay.

"You are most deserving of a *long* vacation," Mayer said. "A very long vacation. Don't bother coming back to MGM. You're fired!"

Dick revealed this news about his job loss to Elizabeth at a dinner with McClory. "I never loved Kevin more," Elizabeth said, "than when he showed me what a take-charge kind of man he was." Within two days, he had secured a job for Dick with his own boss, Mike Todd.

All of them were working on Todd's upcoming blockbuster, *Around the World in 80 Days* (1956). "Todd wanted me to do a cameo in his big movie, but MGM said no," Elizabeth said.

After the first week of working with Todd, Dick began learning secrets, the way he had at MGM when he'd been employed by Mayer.

"What's the biggest scandal you've learned so far?" Elizabeth asked him.

She knew nothing of Mike Todd's background. Dick told her Todd had a fondness for big-breasted women and that he defined himself as a self-made man. The son of a Polish *émigré* rabbi, he had hawked newspapers on the streets of Brooklyn and shined the shoes of Wall Street brokers before breaking into show business as a gag writer.

"Mike's having an affair with Marlene Dietrich but shacked up with Evelyn Keyes full time. Not only that, he sees Marilyn Monroe now and then, ever since he got her to ride that pink elephant at some big event at Madison Square Garden."

"Busy man," was Elizabeth's only comment, since at that time, she didn't

324

have the slightest interest in pursuing a relationship with Todd, viewing him as both brash and vulgar.

"Mike's best friend is Eddie Fisher," Dick said. "They spend a lot of intimate time together. I don't know if this is true or not, but the whole staff, including your boyfriend Kevin, believes that Todd on occasion pounds Eddie's ass."

"C'mon," she said. "This is Hollywood. That isn't so hard to believe. Fisher has told the press on many occasions that he's not gay, even when nobody asks him. I think he brags too much about all the beautiful women he fucks."

"Maybe he doth protest too much," Dick said. "I'll make a pass at him and will let you know if he accepts. Right now, he shares Dietrich with Mike. I also knew John Garfield. He told me that one night at Grossinger's resort in the Catskills, Eddie followed him around like a lovesick puppy. Garfield told me he gave him a mercy fuck."

"There must be more—tell me more," Elizabeth said. "You're making Fisher sound more intriguing than ever."

"Well, he's fucking Pier Angeli, who is supposed to be in love with Kirk

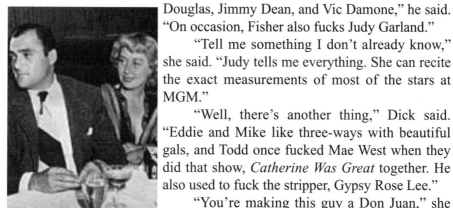

Douglas, Jimmy Dean, and Vic Damone," he said. "On occasion, Fisher also fucks Judy Garland."

"Tell me something I don't already know," she said. "Judy tells me everything. She can recite the exact measurements of most of the stars at MGM."

"Well, there's another thing," Dick said. "Eddie and Mike like three-ways with beautiful gals, and Todd once fucked Mae West when they did that show, *Catherine Was Great* together. He also used to fuck the stripper, Gypsy Rose Lee."

"You're making this guy a Don Juan," she said. "I never thought of him that way before. All you and Kevin do is talk about your boss. Forget about Judy, Mae West, and Gypsy. Tell me some shit that even *Confidential* won't print."

"Okay, but you asked for it. On occasion, Todd even pounds one of your best friends, dear sweet and demure Jean Simmons."

"The way Stewart Granger cheats on her, he deserves to be married to a fellow whore," she said.

Two views of **Joan Blondell** *top photo:* with her then-husband, **Mike Todd**

"Are Stewart and your husband Michael still an item?" Dick asked.

"Until death do them part," she answered.

"Mike Todd has a really violent streak," Dick said. "Even worse than Nicky Hilton, who beat the shit out of you. In a way, Mike murdered his first wife. He lied about his age and got married when he was fifteen to a student, Bertha Freshman. One night they got into a violent argument, and he grabbed a kitchen knife and slashed her hand, practically cutting it off from her arm. She was rushed into surgery at some New York hospital and died on the operating table."

"How ghastly!"

"At the time, Mike was having an affair with Joan Blondell, whom he was stealing from her husband at the time, Dick Powell," Dick said. "He got Joan to lie to the police, and she claimed that he was with her all night during the butcher knife incident. Mike bribed someone and the autopsy report then asserted that the Freshman girl died of a heart attack."

"There's more," Dick told Elizabeth. "With the Freshman girl dead, Mike married Blondell after she got a divorce from Powell. It was a stormy, very violent marriage. During the first months of their marriage, he spent all her money, and she'd made a million films and found herself without a penny. They were staying at the Waldorf-Astoria in Manhattan in a room fifteen floors above street level. The argument became so violent, he ripped off her clothes. At one point, he grabbed her and dangled her body out the window, holding onto her by her ankles. She nearly died of fright, but ended up with just a broken arm— at least not dead like Freshman."

"Remind me not to take Todd as a husband," Elizabeth said.

"That will never happen," he said. "The other day, Mike told Kevin and me that after Blondell, he'll never marry an actress again. 'To live with a star, you gotta worry about her fucking hair,' he said. 'You gotta worry about when her bosom starts to drop. And when that first wrinkle comes, you get all her bills from a headshrinker.'"

***

After spending a long night with McClory before departing for Texas, Elizabeth promised him faithfully that she'd rush back into his arms as soon as the exterior scenes for *Giant* were completed.

In the meantime, Mike Todd "has me hysterically running around the world trying to complete *Around the World in 80 Days* with insufficient funds," he told her. "I'll probably get arrested for bad debts in Thailand, or some such place."

He was delighted, however, that Todd was going to list him as one of the film's three producers—Todd himself, of course, William Cameron Menzies, and McClory.

As a parting gesture, McClory told her, "Mike is using 112 locations in 13 countries. The whole thing is going to cost at least six million."

"My god, I should have done that cameo in it—or taken Shirley MacLaine's role. This film is going to be bigger than *Gone With the Wind.*"

***

Long before Edna Ferber's generational saga, *Giant* (1956), went into production, Jennifer Jones lobbied George Stevens, after he'd been designated as the film's director, for the juicy female lead, a character named Leslie. More than a decade before, she'd won an Oscar for *The Song of Bernadette,* and she promised the director that in the part of Leslie Benedict, she would win one again.

But Stevens had his mind set on Audrey Hepburn. Sometime around July of 1954, he visited the petite actress in New York, where she was appearing on Broadway in *Ondine.* Almost from the beginning, Hepburn and Stevens disagreed over the interpretation of *Giant's* character of Leslie, and soon, Hepburn was no longer in the running.

Then, beginning in January of 1955, Stevens zeroed in on Eva Marie Saint, only to learn that she was pregnant with a baby due in April.

Stevens then began to focus on Grace Kelly as a candidate for the role. A potential conflict arose, however, with MGM, which had slated her for some other film. Complicating the issue further was Prince Rainier of Monaco, who had other plans for Kelly.

Then a colleague of Stevens, producer Henry Ginsberg, recommended Marlene Dietrich for the role. "Are you out of your mind?" Stevens asked. "She could play the grandmother part, but for any of the younger parts, she's too old, too Teutonic."

During several tense weeks, Elizabeth knew that the role she coveted, that of Leslie in *Giant,* was almost beyond her reach. George Stevens, who had directed her so brilliantly in *A Place in the Sun,* "seemed to want every other actress in Hollywood, but considered me chopped liver, I guess," Elizabeth told Wilding. "But I want that part, and I'm going to go for it. Imagine, I go from being a beautiful young bride to a grandmother. Oscar, you've got Elizabeth Taylor's name written on your ass."

When it became clear that Grace Kelly would not be available, Elizabeth jumped with joy and headed for Benny Thau's office to beg him to have MGM lend her services to Warner Brothers.

There was still one problem. MGM didn't want to lend her to Warner Brothers. "I had to go on a sitdown strike…well, almost," she said. "Dare I say blackmail in certain quarters? No, don't print that…it wasn't exactly blackmail."

Then, she engaged in a big brawl with Thau. "I think he wanted me to play

Lassie's mother—or some such shit—in a sequel." She finally won out, "but my bruises were black. I got no extra money. MGM took it all for the loan-out."

Finally, convinced that Elizabeth was the right actress for the part, Warner Brothers offered $250,000 for Elizabeth's services, although she was making only $100,000 a year from MGM at the time.

During his selection of candidates for the male lead, the character of Bick Benedict, Stevens was bombarded with phone calls from William Holden, Gary Cooper, and Clark Gable. At least a dozen other Hollywood males also made their voices heard.

Lying on different massage boards at their gym, John Wayne told Forrest Tucker, "I'm gonna play Bick Benedict."

"Like hell you are," Tucker responded, lying nude on his board. "The role calls for a big dick." Then he ripped the towel off Wayne. "As you can plainly see, my Moby Dick is six times the size of yours."

Sterling Hayden said: "Forrest Tucker is too drunk to play the part. I'm the right size to play Benedict…in all departments."

Robert Mitchum said: "I've practically got the role of Bick Benedict sewn up! Stevens has always had a hard-on for me. I can just see billboards across America: ROBERT MITCHUM AND ELIZABETH TAYLOR STARRING IN GIANT WITH JAMES DEAN."

Late one afternoon, a call came in from Ross Hunter, the producer of *Magnificent Obsession,* starring Rock Hudson and Jane Wyman. "I want you to consider Rock for this part. He's going to become the biggest macho male star since Gable."

Universal, however, didn't want to lend Hudson, rushing him instead into another soapy tearjerker with Wyman, *All That Heaven Allows.* But when it became clear that Hudson could fulfill his obligations to both films, he persuaded Warners to let him star in *Giant.* "I had to let a lot of guys at Universal suck my cock to get the role of Bick," he later told Elizabeth.

Before deciding on Hudson, Stevens had more or less made up his mind that the role of Bick Benedict should go to William Holden. Hudson later recalled that on the day the announcement was made that he would be the male star of *Giant,* he entered the studio sauna nude, only to discover an equally nude Holden sitting on a slab of marble.

Hudson would describe the incident's irony to Elizabeth: "Here I was, the new star of Hollywood, confronting an aging star with my better body, a bigger dick, and a more awesome presence. I felt embarrassed for Holden."

After Elizabeth won the role of Leslie, Stevens called her to announce that he was thinking of casting Richard Burton as the second male lead, the role of Jett Rink, the hell-raising wildcatter, who is secretly in love with Bick Benedict's wife, Leslie, as played by Elizabeth.

"I know Burton," she said. "He's a good actor and for him to play a hell raiser would certainly be type casting. But wouldn't there be a problem with Burton's voice? He's Welsh, you know. Maybe you could get Howard Hughes—he's Texan, you know—to dub his lines?"

After rejecting Burton for the role, Stevens offered it to Alan Ladd, who was almost suicidally despondent at the time, and drinking heavily. He feared facing the camera, and was undergoing a lot of personal hell, including fear of a blackmail attempt from one of his hustler lovers, who was threatening to tell all to *Confidential* unless he surrendered $10,000 in cash.

Finally, after sitting mesmerized through Elia Kazan's then-recent release, *East of Eden* (1955), Stevens offered the role to that film's star, James Dean. Stevens then hurriedly but thoughtfully cast *Giant's* supporting roles, with choice parts going to Mercedes McCambridge, Chill Wills, Nick Adams, Carroll Baker, Jane Withers, Dennis Hopper, Rod Taylor, Earl Holliman, and Sal Mineo. Mineo told his gay friends, "With Hudson and Dean in the cast, I expect to get my ass pounded A LOT."

Then, Warners convened a press conference to present the stars of *Giant* to the world. Elizabeth met Dean for the first time. For his appearance, he wore a pair of "shit kicker" jeans, a threadbare red flannel shirt, tattered boots, and a cowboy hat he claimed had belonged to Gary Cooper. He hid his eyes behind a pair of dark sunglasses, and a cigarette dangled out of the corner of his mouth.

When he was introduced, Dean was deliberately rude to Elizabeth. Stevens had indiscreetly relayed to Dean that, "Elizabeth doesn't want you in our film. Up until the last minute, she pushed Monty Clift for the role. But those guys who insure films at Warners refused to insure Monty because of all his drinking and his drugs."

Right before flying to the film's location in Marfa, Texas, a drought-stricken whistle-stop of 3,600 inhabitants in the high desert of West Texas, where daytime temperatures sometimes rose to 120° F., Dean had been featured in a black-and-white TV commercial promoting safe driving. In the clip with him was Gig Young, who'd had a very brief fling with Elizabeth. At the end of the commercial, Dean says, "Drive safely because the life you save may be my own."

The filming of *Giant* had been delayed because of Elizabeth's pregnancy, which gave Dean the chance to shoot *Rebel Without a Cause* (1955), and gave Hudson the chance to complete his film with Jane Wyman.

In *Giant,* Elizabeth was cast as a young woman (Leslie) from Maryland's blue grass country, who marries a wealthy Texan, Bick Benedict (Rock Hudson) and becomes the mistress of his Reata Ranch. Dean was cast as a surly ranch hand who inherits what appears to be worthless desert. However, he discovers oil in a footprint left by Leslie on his property. He drills for oil and hits his first gusher. In the years before World War II, Jett (Dean) starts an oil-drilling company that makes him enormously wealthy.

During the course of *Giant's* approximately 200 minutes, it moves through the rise and failing fortunes of Texans, with side detours into moral dissipation, racism, miscegenation, the oppression of women, oil well conflicts, and the changing social scenario of Texas itself. The movie's subplot involves the war between the longtime Texas aristocracy and the *nouveau riche* wildcatters whose oil well have "come in big." Budgeted at $2 million, *Giant* would end up costing $5 million, an almost-unheard-of price at the time.

For Elizabeth, after suffering through all those "rubbish" movies at MGM, *Giant* became a milestone in her life. Other than being saddled with a husband she didn't want, her biggest problem involved having to postpone her flourishing romance with Kevin McClory.

***

Elizabeth recalled, "In Texas, Rock and I hit it off right away. The heat, humidity, and dust in Marfa were so thoroughly oppressive we had to bolster our spirits any way we could. So we stayed out drinking all night and luckily were young enough and resilient enough to go straight to the set in the morning with fresh complexions and with no bags under our eyes. During our toots, we concocted the best drink I've ever tasted—a chocolate martini made with vodka, Hershey's syrup, and Kahlua. How we survived, I'll never know."

"Rock and Elizabeth were like kids again," claimed Stevens. "They indulged in a kind of baby talk, and they liked to play pranks on each other, tossing water at each other from our rapidly dwindling supply."

She told Dick Hanley, "Rock has become my second best friend—no one will replace Monty as Number One."

Because of the severe housing shortage in such a small town, Elizabeth was the only member of the cast and crew assigned to a private house of her own. Local residents moved into tents so they could rent rooms in their houses to the actors, staff, and crew who had descended on their town for the filming. Hudson and Dean were assigned a shared room with twin beds in a small house whose adjoining single room was occupied by the character actor, Chill Wills.

"With Dean and Hudson in the room adjoining mine, they were like two pigs rolling in shit for the first few nights," Wills later claimed. "The walls were shaking, and I heard the sound of creaky bedsprings until two or three in the morning. Then the fights set in. By then, I knew the honeymoon was over for these two queer boys."

Dean complained to Elizabeth, "Every night, Rock is trying to queer me and make him his bitch. My ass is sore. I'm moving out of that house."

When Hudson got to know Elizabeth more intimately, he confessed to her, "I want sex, real man-on-man sex, but I don't go in for this kinky stuff. Dean wants to get into that claw-footed, old timey bathtub we have, and then he begs me to piss on him. He also likes me to burn his ass with my cigarette butt—shit like that. I'm not into all this sicko crap."

In Texas, Hudson and Elizabeth discovered nachos, devouring them along with a massive consumption of alcohol. "Then they staged belch-and-fart contests," Dennis Hooper said.

On the set of *Giant,* Elizabeth had to battle her weight problem. All those chocolate martinis she consumed with Hudson were obviously fattening. But Stevens complained that she compounded the problem with her midnight snacks, which consisted of homemade vanilla ice cream drenched in fudge and peanut butter, preceded by a series of mayonnaise sandwiches, "which I just adore."

For about ten nights, Hudson seduced Elizabeth. Actually, she was the aggressor. She'd later tell Roddy McDowall something he already knew. "Rock is really endowed, and I mean *really.* As a lover, he's very efficient and eager to get on with it. For me, it's over before it begins. We've decided to be great friends, not lovers. No woman will ever succeed in igniting his enthusiasm in bed, and of that, I'm certain."

Dean ended up claiming that Hudson acted "like a lump of wood," and Hudson called Dean "that little scruff." On other occasions, when he was particularly angry at Dean, he referred to him as a "dick-crazed schizoid."

Dean was very blunt around Stevens. "Before I met Rock, I've had my cock sucked by four of the biggest names in Hollywood. After meeting Rock, I can now make that five big names."

One hot afternoon between set-ups, Dean confided one of his sexual fantasies to Stevens: "In World War II, I heard women wore a lipstick called Victory Red, or some shit like that. My greatest sexual turn-on would be to have three women paint their mouths with this lipstick and give me a blow-job—Elizabeth Taylor, Tallulah Bankhead, and Edith Piaf."

Giants killing time with one another in the high deserts of West Texas
Rock Hudson with **Elizabeth Taylor**

"George always had to have a patsy to pick on throughout every one of his films," Elizabeth claimed. "On *Giant,* it was both Jimmy and me. Actually, Rock and I speculated that George secretly had the hots for Jimmy. Whenever he thought Jimmy wasn't looking, he was always eying him like a lovesick schoolgirl. One scalding hot afternoon, when Jimmy didn't show up for work, George told Rock and me, 'I should punish the little bastard and make him suck my dick.'"

"George and I staged some epic battles under that hot sun," Elizabeth said. "Our biggest fight was when he wanted me to wear those thick brogue shoes and a long grandma-in-the-wilderness skirt, plus a man's battered old cowboy hat. I attacked him for trying to force this ludicrous getup on me. I told him, 'What are you trying to do? Make me look like a lesbian in drag? I'm Elizabeth Taylor, in case you forgot it.'"

At first, Dean and Carroll Baker sat together whispering conspiratorially. "Our main diversion was making fun of Rock and Elizabeth," Baker later said. "We were cruel and cutting."

During the first two weeks, Elizabeth and Hudson spent every night together. Dean was frequently seen bonding with Baker, whom he'd known from the Actors Studio in New York.

Carroll Baker

Hudson constantly complained to Elizabeth about Stevens. "He gives Dean all the close-ups, and I'm left out in the cold," Hudson claimed.

Elizabeth and Hudson feared that Dean was stealing the picture. Both actors set out to woo Baker into their cabal. In that, they succeeded, and subsequently, Dean stopped speaking to her, feeling betrayed.

"Dean got the ultimate revenge," Baker said. "He succeeded in stealing Elizabeth from Rock and me. The dirty rat wanted Elizabeth for himself, and I went into a state of mourning. Elizabeth went off every evening with Jimmy, ignoring Rock and me. The tables had turned."

During the final three weeks of the shoot, Elizabeth temporarily deserted both Hudson and Baker. Her friendship with Hudson would be recharged after Dean's untimely death.

The film's cast and crew were shown the daily rushes in an battered old movie theater that had closed down with the coming of television.

Elizabeth (a penitent Madonna worshipping at a crucifixion?) with **James Dean** in *Giant*

Most of the participants preferred to sit on the theater's ground floor, but Elizabeth and Dean usually retreated to the balcony where they were alone. Elizabeth brought popcorn from her house to share with Dean.

"They were like two lovebirds," Wills said. "I never could figure out these switch-hitters. One night they're taking it up the ass, and on another night, they're pounding pussy. You figure."

Throughout the shooting of *Giant,* Elizabeth was plagued with various illnesses, some of which required hospitalization. The first of her health emergencies began in July of 1955, when she developed a severe sore throat and could not deliver her lines. That was almost immediately followed by a bladder infection and thrombophlebitis, a blood clot in a vein of her left leg. She blamed its flare-up on Stevens for "making me wear those tight breeches."

Dr. John Davis examined her and asserted that she suffered from "a congenital anomaly of the spine." To alleviate the pain in her lower back caused by a dysfunctional sciatic nerve, she took heavy doses of Novocaine.

One scene in *Giant* called for Elizabeth "to do a lot of jumping and twisting on a bed." Her always-sensitive back exploded in pain again, as she suffered a ruptured intervertebral disc. She was shot with Novocaine and Hydrocortisone and also given Demerol and Meticorten. "I was a god damn walking pharmacy," she claimed.

Stevens didn't believe in any of her illnesses, calling them "psychosomatic." On August 12, she returned to the set on crutches.

***

Stevens called Dean's first shot with Elizabeth on June 3, 1955, "a day that will live in infamy in the annals of cinema history." It was filmed on an open set at the Worth Evans Ranch, which Stevens had temporarily rented. It was the site of the famous scene where Dean was depicted with a rifle hoisted over his shoulders—he called it "my crucifixion pose."

Time and time again, he flubbed his lines. Watching the proceedings, Dennis Hopper said, "That was one nervous queen. He was fucking up big time with another queen (i.e., Elizabeth) of Hollywood."

In front of at least 250 onlookers, Dean ruined take after take by freezing up. A total of sixteen shots failed. Suddenly, he broke from the set and walked over to a wire fence in front of the assembled population of Marfa, some of whom had skipped school to attend this first ceremonial film shoot. As everyone looked on, Dean unzipped his jeans and hauled out his penis. Hopper claimed it looked about four inches soft. Shock waves were heard from the crowd as Dean took what he called "a horse piss."

He later told Hopper, "I knew if I could piss in front of some two thousand *(sic)* people, I could do anything. I'm a Method actor." He returned to the set and did the scene perfectly in one take. Leaving the set, he turned to Elizabeth, "I'm cool, man. It's cool."

Elizabeth later told Dick Hanley, "Jimmy and I in Texas were at first very suspicious of each other. We circled each other like two animals of prey. To him, I was just another Hollywood star, all bosom and no brains. To me, he was a would-be intellectual New York Method actor. We were not prepared to dig each other at all."

"But after a while, we found we were just two human beings, and we became intimate friends that involved tender, loving sex in the beginning, none of that kinky shit that Rock talked about. But, as in the case with Rock, we decided that we could hold each other, protect each other from the cold winds, but as friends, not as lovers."

Evoking Rock's relationship with Elizabeth, Dean engaged in playful games with her. "Two kids on the playground," Stevens called their intimacy.

However, during moments of manic giddiness, Dean had a tendency to go too far. One day, he grabbed Elizabeth, picked her up off her feet, and turned her upside down so that her skirt fell over her head, exposing her "unmentionable" regions to photographers.

As she later told Stevens, "Fortunately, unlike Marilyn Monroe on most occasions, I wore my panties that day, or else my twat would be hanging on every bathroom wall in every man's toilet in America."

To Elizabeth, Dean always remained a mystery, but she came to love him. "Sometimes, Jimmy and I would sit up until three in the morning, talking, and he would tell me about his past life, his conflicts, and some of his loves and tragedies. And the next day it was almost as if he didn't want to recognize me, or to remember that he had revealed so much of himself the night before. And so he would pass me and ignore me, or just give me a cursory nod of the head. And then it took him a day or two to become my friend again. I found all that hard to understand."

He told Elizabeth, "I would have been shot down by some yellow boy in Korea, but I escaped the draft—blame my flat feet, bad eyesight, and butt-fucking."

Shortly before his death, Dean was said to have confided his most painful secrets to Elizabeth, sordid details of his life he shared with no other. One of those secrets was revealed after Elizabeth's death in 2011 by writer Keven Sessums in *The Daily Beast*. Elizabeth had granted Sessums an interview in 1997.

"I'm going to tell you something, but it's off the record until I die," she told Sessums. "When Jimmy was eleven, he began to be molested by his minister. I think that haunted him the rest of his life. In fact, I know it did."

Dean biographers have long suspected there was a sexual relationship with the Rev. James DeWeerd, a Wesleyan pastor in Fairmount, Indiana, who had a penchant for young boys.

The secret that Elizabeth never shared, perhaps because it would portray Dean in a harsh light, was that as he aged, he became a child molester himself.

When Hudson learned that Elizabeth was having an affair with Dean, he jokingly asked her, "Did he piss on you, or did you piss on him?"

"Let's just call it a tinkle-winkle," she said.

For sex, after his break with Hudson, Dean turned to local cowboys who worked on the film. The cowboys Dean befriended taught him rope tricks and invited him to shoot rabbits with them, followed by some male-on-male bonding. He confided to Elizabeth, "Not all Texas men have big dicks."

Dean had told Stevens, "Sal Mineo has the look of the angels" and would be perfect to play Angel Obregon II, the son of poor Mexican immigrants. The director had agreed with Dean's assessment of Mineo's talent and cast him in a small but key role in *Giant.*

Mineo had no scenes with Dean in *Giant.* They became lovers on the set of *Rebel Without a Cause* (1955). Mineo even bought a rebuilt Mercury like the car Dean had driven in *Rebel.*

Mineo later said, "I didn't really become friends with Elizabeth until Roddy McDowall and I appeared together in *The Greatest Story Ever Told* (1965), a big-screen retelling of the epic of Jesus, from his birth through a cinematic reworking of the Resurrection. It was directed by George Stevens, who'd directed me in *Giant.* Then I became close to Elizabeth. Roddy told me many stories about her. He'd even taken nude photographs of her. He also told me that Richard Burton in Rome during the making of *Cleopatra* was fucking him before he discovered that banging Elizabeth was more fun."

Stevens had offered Elizabeth a cameo role playing Mary Magdalene in *The Greatest Story Ever Told.* "Wasn't she that whore who seduced Christ? Hell, I'd be laughed off the screen. Get someone else to play your whore. I read you've cast John Wayne as a Roman centurion who oversees the crucifixion of Christ. George, are you on something?"

***

On the set of *Giant* in Texas, a studio underling rushed Elizabeth the latest edition of *Confidential* magazine, which ran the headline: WHEN LIZ TAYLOR'S AWAY, MIKE WILL PLAY. It detailed the night Michael Wilding picked up two fe-

Sal Mineo

335

male strippers at a club in Hollywood and brought them back to the home he shared with Elizabeth in Beverly Hills. In the scandal's aftermath, Elizabeth told Stevens, "Whether it's true or not, a woman can't let an indiscretion break up a marriage."

Of course, considering her affairs, she was in no position to chastise Wilding.

Flying to Texas with their two sons to check up on Elizabeth, Wilding was greeted with a blaring headline—MICHAEL WORRIED ABOUT LIZ AND ROCK.

When Wilding with his two sons arrived in Marfa, he went to find Elizabeth, perhaps to remind her she was a wife and mother. Not finding her, he was told that she was last seen driving off with a young man.

"Where in hell do you drive to in this one-horse town?" he asked.

Instead of Elizabeth and Hudson, Wilding encountered Dean. "I have to be very frank with you," Dean told Wilding. "I've fallen in love with your wife. She's going to divorce you—and marry me. But, remember, you had your chance. My turn now."

He was so shocked that he told Stewart Granger back in Hollywood, "I could only conclude that Dean was poking me in the ribs. He could not have been serious. Elizabeth will no more marry Dean than I'll take the Queen Mother for my next bride."

On his first night in Marfa, Wilding was allowed to stay at Elizabeth's rented home, but she didn't return that night.

Nick Adams, Dean's longtime lover, had arrived in Marfa, and Stevens spread the rumor that Dean had fixed Elizabeth up with Adams. "He's living proof that big things come in small packages," Dean told Elizabeth.

Knowing that Wilding would be alone that evening for dinner, Dean brought over some West Texas chili and cold beer.

Over the chili, Wilding pointedly asked Dean, "Your plans to marry Elizabeth shocked me. I was told you were strictly homo."

"I don't want to go through life with one hand tied behind my back," Dean replied. "Depending on how much rain falls on any given night, I can go either way—male or female. What does it really matter, come to think of it? Sometimes I reward people who do favors for me with sex. I recently flew to Key West to fuck Tennessee Williams. I virtually made him sign a blood oath that he

A rebellious three-way:
Taylor, Hudson, and **Dean** in *Giant*

336

would lobby to get me to play the male lead in all the future adaptations of his plays."

"Smart career move, dear boy," Wilding told him.

At the end of their chili supper, Dean said, "Elizabeth is likely to be engaged for the rest of the evening. In that case, would you like to go back to my place and fuck me instead?"

"A tempting offer, but I'm the babysitter tonight," Wilding said. "Give me a rain check."

Wilding claimed that he was still in love with Elizabeth, "but I found the daily tremors of living with such a volcanic creature more and more difficult. After my failure to make it as a star in Hollywood, I felt like James Mason in that role of a has-been in *A Star Is Born* with Judy Garland."

Elizabeth and Wilding quarreled every day they were in Marfa, and he soon flew from El Paso back to Los Angeles, taking their two sons with him.

"I knew it was over at that time," he said. "All that remained was bringing down the final curtain."

***

Back in Hollywood, Elizabeth continued her friendship with Dean, and also "recharged the batteries in my love for Rock, who was going through a troubling time and needed me."

As influenced by his gay agent, Henry Willson, Hudson agreed to marry Phyllis Gates, his lesbian secretary. Willson feared exposure of Hudson's homosexuality in an upcoming article in *Confidential* magazine.

Sham intimacy within a sham marriage

Phyllis Gates with **Rock Hudson**

During his disastrous marriage to Gates, Elizabeth and Wilding often entertained them at dinner. Gates recalled that Hudson spent most of those evening talking to Elizabeth, while she tried to amuse and entertain Wilding. She claimed that at one dinner in her kitchen, Wilding whispered in her ear, "You know, Phyllis, I wish I had met somebody like you. You're the person I should have married." He emphasized that by giving her a pat on the ass.

Gates later wrote a sham memoir entitled *My Husband, Rock Hudson.* In it, she describes scenes of Hudson's "passionate" love making. But Hudson report-

337

edly told Elizabeth one night that the marriage had never been consummated.

"When I returned to Hollywood, Michael and I visited Jimmy at least three times at his little house in San Fernando Valley, and he came to see us," Elizabeth said. "He seemed engulfed in loneliness The first time he invited us for dinner, he heated up two cans of beans—and that was that. We sat and talked and listened to his music. A few nights later, he came over to our house. He loved our Siamese cats. I knew he wanted something that belonged to me, and I gave him one of the cats. He loved that cat from the very beginning and named it Marcus."

On another night, Dean invited Elizabeth for a ride in the pride of his life, a new Porsche Spyder nicknamed "Little Bastard," that had cost him $5,000, the most money he'd ever spent on anything in his life.

He took her for a spin through Beverly Hills and rode up and down Sunset Boulevard past The Strip. He turned left onto Hollywood Boulevard, passing Grauman's Chinese Theater. When they passed the theater with its cement casts of the hands and feet of the stars, Dean told her he was considering having a cast of his erect cock made in the cement instead.

The next day, Dean dropped in at Elizabeth's home to tell her goodbye, claiming that he was driving his Porsche, accompanied with a friend, to the road race at Salinas. The date was September 30, 1955.

"Whatever you do, Jimmy, be safe—just be safe," she cautioned him.

At Warner Brothers in Burbank, Stevens had invited some of his stars, including Elizabeth, Hudson, and Baker, to watch the rushes for *Giant*. At one point, there was an urgent ringing of the telephone. Stevens got up to answer it. Then the cast heard him say, "No, my god. When? Are you sure?"

As Baker remembered it, "The picture froze. The lights shot up. We turned and looked at George. The phone dangled in his hand. He was white and motionless. Death was present in that room. 'There's been a car crash,' he said. 'Jimmy Dean has been killed.'"

An hour later, Elizabeth learned the painful details.

At 5:45pm, Dean and his passenger, Rulf Wütherich, a German immigrant who knew members of the Porsche family, were speeding Dean's Porsche Spyder during their approach to an intersection of Highways 41 and 466, one mile east of Cholame in San Luis Obispo County.

Some reports claimed that Dean was going 120 miles an hour when he saw a black-and-white Ford sedan making a leisurely left turn onto the highway. It was too late for him to stop to avoid a collision with Donald Turnupseed, a student at California Polytechnic.

The student escaped with a broken nose. Dean's passenger, Wütherich, was thrown clean out of the car. He suffered a broken jaw and other injuries, but, unlike Dean, he survived.

In contrast, Dean's head was almost severed from his body. He was DOA at Paso Robles War Memorial Hospital. The doctor who signed his death certificate had called Warner Brothers in Burbank.

In the aftermath of Dean's death, Wilding sat up until dawn with Elizabeth, "who sobbed the night away." Not respecting her grief, Stevens demanded that she show up for work the next day to shoot a final scene.

"That sod!" she shouted at Wilding. "The heartless sod!"

Although she could barely manage it, Elizabeth showed up as instructed on the set. She was still given to crying fits, but she stumbled through the scene as best she could, with a lot of help from her make-up artist. At the end of the day, she turned to Stevens. "This is the last time I'll ever work for a god damn ghoul like you!"

The next day she collapsed, complaining of abdominal pains. An ambulance was rushed to the set and, with dome lights flashing, took her to the hospital. She stubbornly remained there for two weeks, delaying some retakes and holding up production, which faced mounting costs because of her absence.

Before his death, during the filming of Dean's final scenes, he had mumbled and in some cases had been virtually incoherent. Stevens called back Nick Adams, Dean's former lover, who could do a perfect imitation of his voice, for dubbing the sound track, where appropriate, of Dean's voice.

One night at three o'clock in the morning, when Elizabeth returned home, she received an urgent phone call from Monty Clift, who was in Los Angeles at the time. He sounded drunk and drugged. Through his slurred words, she understood him to say, "With Jimmy gone, I see no reason to go on living."

His words shocked her. At that point she was unaware that Monty had had such a strong bond with Dean.

"Monty! Monty!" she shouted at him. "Live for me. Live for your Bessie Mae. Have you taken sleeping pills? I'll be right over."

When she arrived at Monty's apartment, she discovered that he had not taken pills or cut his wrists. But he was drugged and had thrown up on his red satin sheets. She spent the night with him, often cuddling him in her arms like a protective mother, even though he was twelve years older than she was.

Late the following morning, he confessed to her something he'd never told her before. "Like so many others, I was in love with Jimmy."

**

Leaving George Stevens with almost a million feet of film to edit into an appropriate running time for a movie, Elizabeth flew to Europe and on to Morocco. Michael Wilding had been cast as the second male lead in *Zarak* (1956), an action-adventure film co-starring Victor Mature (the Afghan outlaw who saves the life of a British officer at the cost of his own) and the Swedish bomb-shell, the big-busted Anita Ekberg.

There was speculation as to why Elizabeth went to Morocco. Ostensibly, it was viewed as perhaps a last-ditch attempt to save her marriage. Dick Hanley took a more cynical view. "The marriage at this point could not be saved. If she wanted to save anything, it was to save Victor Mature from the clutches of Anita Ekberg. At that time in her life, Elizabeth had a deep crush on Vic. But then who wouldn't go for him?"

Before her departure for Morocco, Elizabeth had visited MGM to discuss her next assignment. There, she ran into the 1940s swimming star Esther Williams, who had taught her how to swim when she was fourteen years old. Williams said, "I don't know if Victor Mature is having an affair with that Ekberg woman or not. But I've known Victor. Sex with him is like a force of nature."

Elizabeth later relayed that quote to Dick Hanley: "Telling me that is like preaching to the choir. What Esther doesn't know, presumably, is that I have also sampled the love-making techniques of Fernando Lamas. The very mention of his name seems to send a thrill through her." (As it happened, Williams later married Fernando Lamas).

From the day of her arrival in Morocco, Elizabeth quarreled with Wilding. She also detested the country, calling it "a horrible, filthy, and smelly place with sewage running through the streets." She was followed by street boys wherever she went, and later compared her experience there with "all those young boys pursuing Sebastian in *Suddenly, Last Summer*" (1959).

In a society where women wore veils and covered their bodies, Elizabeth shocked locals by wearing tight sweaters, revealing her large breasts, and short skirts without stockings. She purchased silk caftans but never wore them. "You look like some god damn bitch in heat," Wilding told her.

"If I have the name, why not play the game?" she shot back at him.

The Wildings occupied suite 106 in the Dersa Hotel, some forty miles from the seedy French and Spanish-colonial Mediterranean port of Tétouan. One afternoon, Wilding came home two hours early and found Mature in bed with Elizabeth.

Victor Mature with **Anita Ekberg** in *Zarak*

But what was happening in room 106 with Elizabeth Taylor was hotter than what was happening on screen.

Elizabeth emerged from her involvement with all that beefcake to yell at her husband, "Get the hell out of my room. I'm getting fucked by a *real* man."

That night, Wilding moved into a separate room two doors down, and Mature occupied Elizabeth's suite.

After *Zarak* was wrapped, Elizabeth flew back to Los Angeles, and Wilding headed for London, where he stayed with Stewart Granger, who was filming interior scenes for *Bhowani Junction* (1956), and having an affair with Ava Gardner.

Wilding told him about Elizabeth's affair with Mature.

"I know Mature," Granger recalled. "He is a big, craven lump of lard with a dick that is like a sledgehammer, or so I've heard."

Since Mature, too, was in London at the time, Granger sought him out and asked him to apologize to Wilding. "Mature was a massive fellow but a chickenshit at heart," Granger said. "He agreed to apologize. I told him if he'd fucked Jean Simmons, I would have broken his fucking jaw."

One night, Wilding came home and told Granger how Mature had apologized. "The most extraordinary part of it was that while he was apologizing, he sort of bent his knees."

Granger picked up on that immediately. "Okay, Michael, he apologized by giving you a blow-job—that's okay. In addition to being the greatest stud in Hollywood, Mature is also a cocksucker. Everyone in the business knows that."

"I didn't," Wilding said, "but I do now."

When Wilding returned to Hollywood, he discovered that Elizabeth had taken up with Frank Sinatra.

News about the Taylor/Mature affair broke in *Confidential* magazine under the heading of WHEN MIKE WILDING CAUGHT LIZ TAYLOR AND VIC MATURE IN ROOM 106. The exposé ran in July of 1956.

Instead of what Elizabeth actually said to Wilding, *Confidential,* in print, asserted its version of what she told him: "Remember how silly you looked at 6am, dancing around with those stripteasers you'd brought home to our house wearing nothing but a G-string on your head? Well, snookums, you look just as silly now. So close the door before mama catches cold."

***

"Like those crazed bobbysoxers of the 1940s, Elizabeth had this thing for Frank Sinatra," claimed Roddy McDowall. "Like Marilyn Monroe, she played his records all the time in her dressing room and at home—and was wild about him. She once told me, 'I wanted Frank to take my virginity, but, alas, Peter Lawford beat him to it.' It took a little time, but Elizabeth finally got her man, Frankie. But like all our fantasies, it didn't exactly work out the way she'd dreamed."

Nearly all of Elizabeth's biographers seemed unaware of her affair with Sinatra, which occurred during the final months of her marriage to Wilding. It began after Elizabeth returned from Texas and resumed when she returned from Morocco, where Wilding was filming *Zarak*. While he remained in Morocco (and later during his time in England), Sinatra and Elizabeth were seeing each other virtually every night.

The source of details about the Taylor/Sinatra affair was Peter Lawford, after he was "banished" from the Rat Pack. Ironically, Lawford was the subject of a biography called *The Man Who Kept the Secrets* by James Spada. Over the years, the keeper of the secrets spilled many of them.

It was Lawford who first told Sinatra that Elizabeth's marriage to Wilding was all but over except for the divorce. "They sleep in different rooms and go for days without speaking to each other," Lawford claimed. "You always said you wanted her. Here's your chance to move in."

Before Wilding went to Morocco, Elizabeth accepted an invitation to visit Sinatra in Palm Springs. Her husband had gone off to San Francisco with Stewart Granger for the weekend. At first, she seemed reluctant to accept Sinatra's invitation, but he was very persuasive. He told her he'd send a limousine to Beverly Hills to pick her up and drive her to the desert.

Arriving in Palm Springs, she was greeted at the door by Sinatra, who wore an orange (his favorite color) shirt and white shorts.

"As you know, I'm sure, I just adore Monty Clift," she told him. "You guys were terrific in that *Eternity* picture. But he warned me not to fall in love with you, because he is already in love with you himself."

"Monty's loss will be your gain," he told her, kissing her on the lips.

Later, Lawford pressed Sinatra for details of the torrid weekend. He would in time learn a lot more from Sinatra, but for the moment, the singer merely said, "I taught her how to drink Jack Daniels."

Lawford learned that Elizabeth and Sinatra had sex "more than once." A lot of the time was spent with him listening to complaints about her loveless marriage to Wilding. During his recitations about his own tales of woe, he told her about how much in love with Ava Gardner he'd been—"and still am." But he added a postscript: "She's a woman not to be trusted. If you took Ava on a honeymoon, you'd surely catch her at some point going into the bushes with one of the busboys."

Elizabeth admitted that Wilding had been a father figure to her, and, as such, he was doomed to outlive his usefulness when she matured. "I escaped to find peace and tranquility with Michael, which was better than getting the shit beat out of me every night by Nicky Hilton."

The British actor confessed, "In the beginning, I tried to guide her and influence her, but after a few months, when I opened my mouth, she told me to shut up. In contrast, Marlene Dietrich listened to me for hours, or at least pretended to."

As her marriage to Wilding entered its death throes, Elizabeth secretly dated Sinatra with Lawford serving as "the beard." One night, a waiter at a dive in San Fernando Valley must have tipped off a photographer from a newspaper. The photographer arrived at a restaurant where Elizabeth was dining with both Lawford and Sinatra. The manager alerted Sinatra, who exited through the kitchen. Lawford left through the front door, telling the photographer, "Dining alone tonight."

When Elizabeth got serious about her affair with Sinatra, he more or less deflected it, since it was obvious that she wanted to marry him after she divorced Wilding.

Both of them were lounging nude by his pool at Palm Springs one Sunday afternoon when she asked him, "What is your philosophy of life?"

"You gotta love living. Dying's a pain in the ass."

As the days went by, Elizabeth grew more and more dependent on Sinatra, although he was not really in love with her. He'd told Lawford, "I've had Ava, the most desirable woman in the world. But I lost her. Right now, I'm screwing the second most desirable woman on the planet, Elizabeth Taylor. Not bad for a skinny little kid from Hoboken."

One night, she arrived at his home in Beverly Hills without an invitation, showing up unannounced on his doorstep. Fortunately, he was alone that evening, as he'd been dating other women during the course of his affair with Elizabeth.

Alarmed by her physical appearance, he invited her in, demanding to know what had happened. Resting on the sofa in his living room, she revealed that she'd told Wilding, "I'm in love with Frank Sinatra and I want a divorce. He's not a violent person, but he slapped my face. I fell back over a coffee table, and my back is in agony."

"The son of a bitch," Sinatra muttered. "I could get him for that. In the meantime, I'm going to get help for you."

He called his doctor, who got her admitted to the Cedars of Lebanon Hospital for five days. She lingered there under an assumed name.

When Wilding showed up at Sinatra's house, demanding to know where his wife was, Sinatra slugged him.

Wilding wasn't the only one to experience Sinatra's notorious temper. Three weeks after Elizabeth's release from the hospital, he was dining with her at one of his favorite restaurants in Palm Springs. The manager knew to keep fans away from Sinatra's table, because he was aware of how much the singer hated autograph seekers.

However, on that night, the manager failed to alert a new waiter. It was the star-struck waiter who asked both Elizabeth and Sinatra for their respective autographs. But whereas Sinatra refused, Elizabeth graciously complied. She turned to Sinatra, "I'll sign for both of us." Then, in large letters so that he could read what she'd written, she wrote "ELIZABETH SINATRA."

That was too much for him to take. Right in the middle of the dinner, he told her, "We're going back to the house."

"I want to finish my meal," she protested.

"Then take a god damn taxi home," he shouted at her, barging out of the restaurant.

In a drunken state, she arrived about an hour and a half later at his desert villa. A servant let her in. "Where is that Italian bastard?" she shouted.

"He told me to tell you he's driving back to Los Angeles tonight," the servant said. "You can stay on and use the house if you wish to."

She left the following morning. Back in Beverly Hills, her calls to Sinatra went unanswered. When she phoned Lawford, he told her, "Frank flew to New York."

She wanted Sinatra to abandon all other romantic entanglements and marry her, but he adamantly refused.

In desperation, she called Lawford and told him the bad news. "I'm pregnant. A doctor just informed me of this lovely tidbit. Maybe Frank will come to his senses. Having a kid out of wedlock doesn't go over big in Hollywood."

When he heard the news, Sinatra bluntly told her, "I'm not going to marry you. We'll have to see that that kid in the oven doesn't become fully baked."

Elizabeth had told Wilding that during her last bout in the hospital, she'd instructed her doctor "to do whatever is necessary, but see that I don't get pregnant again." Obviously whatever surgical procedure she'd hinted at had never happened.

He arranged for the abortion. Details are lacking, and Lawford was not forthcoming with what happened next. It is believed that Sinatra's close friend, gangster Mickey Cohen, played a role. Somehow, Cohen could pull off these things.

One night at a Hollywood party, Elizabeth encountered Ava Gardner, and those two beautiful actresses, after a couple of drinks, became confidential with one another. Elizabeth admitted to Ava that Sinatra had insisted that she abort their child, even though Elizabeth had wanted to have his baby.

"I'm an old hand at aborting Frank's babies," Ava told her.

In the aftermath of the abortion, Elizabeth was very bitter toward Sinatra and wanted nothing to do with him. But in time, she forgave him and resumed her friendship with him.

During her first marriage to Burton, Sinatra's manservant remembered serving drinks to Sinatra, Burton, and Elizabeth, each star lying nude by the pool at his villa in Palm Springs. "I just assumed Mr. Sinatra and Miss Taylor had let bygones be bygones."

***

When Kevin McClory returned from his international travels for Mike Todd and for tasks associated with the release of *Around the World in 80 Days,* Elizabeth was waiting for him. Apparently, he had not learned of her affair with Frank Sinatra.

He was, however, almost certainly aware of her adulterous affair with Victor Mature, because *Confidential,* in one of its more accurate articles, had published insider details, obviously from some anonymous source who was privy to very "confidential" tidbits of their sexfest.

"Love had nothing to do with my fling with Vic," Elizabeth told Janet Leigh. "It was about his dick. Every woman in Hollywood should sample it—and many of them do."

Wilding was left with the care and feeding of their sons, as Elizabeth spent her romantic Saturday and Sunday nights with McClory in her Malibu beach house. Often the "two lovebirds," as Shirley MacLaine defined them, had dinners with the red-haired actress and her husband, Steve Parker, who eventually became a film producer in Japan.

In later years, MacLaine told Elizabeth the secret of a happy marriage. "I live in America, Steve lives in Japan, a perfect arrangement." She also confessed, "I have one vice—fucking, even if it means with three different men in one day."

Ava Gardner with **Frank Sinatra**

Ava to Elizabeth Taylor: "I'm an old hand at aborting Frank's babies"

McClory later asserted, "Elizabeth was a very difficult person not to love. At that time, I was having a real struggle visualizing myself getting married to a star like Elizabeth with my meager finances."

"One night, we dined with Shirley and Steve, who had a boxer, a marvelous animal. We got back to the house and the dog had been sick and messed all over the floor. Without any hesitation, Elizabeth, who was wearing a lovely frock, got down and scrubbed up the mess. Right then and there I said, 'This is the woman for me.' I knew then she was the girl I was going to marry."

One evening, Elizabeth was dining at

345

Chasen's with McClory when a call came in at around nine o'clock from MGM's Benny Thau, who was working late. He'd tracked her down. "Please come to my office tomorrow at ten o'clock," he told her. "You'll love what I have to tell you."

The following morning, Thau greeted her warmly. "My darling," he said. "We at MGM know you're going to be our next big star. Okay, there were some rotten pictures, but beginning with your next film, you're going to become big, I mean big, right up there with Marilyn Monroe, Susan Hayward, and Jane Wyman, each of whom is box office. Do you know when you're a star? When I was in Japan, I noticed that the face of Susan Hayward was imprinted on the package of every condom. Now *that's* bigtime."

"What is this delicious surprise for me?" she asked. "You're going to re-make *Little Women*...yet again?" She didn't disguise the sarcasm in her voice.

"We're going to film the Yankee version of *Gone With the Wind*. It's going to be the picture of the decade. It's called *Raintree County,* and as its star, you're going to win an Oscar, the first of many, I'm sure. And we're casting Montgomery Clift as your co-star."

***

While *Around the World in 80 Days* was being edited, Mike Todd called Kevin McClory into his office. McClory later recalled the conversation:

TODD: "Everyone knows who you're dating, and I don't think it's right."
McCLORY: "What do you mean?"
TODD: "You know what I mean. Elizabeth Taylor, that's who."
McCLORY: "Her marriage to Wilding is on the rocks. We are in love with each other and plan to marry as soon as her divorce comes through. I will work for you around the clock, but my private life, Mike, is my own personal business."
TODD: "What you're doing is a sin."

In the wake of that conversation, McClory thought about Todd. "Hello Kettle, meet Pot."

Three days later, as he continued editing his film, Todd told McClory, "You know, I'd like to meet the Wildings. I might use them to publicize our film. We could all go out on that big boat I've rented, *The Hyding."* It was a 117-foot yacht.

"If that would please you, I'm sure they'd be delighted," McClory said, planning to extend the invitation that night for a trip to begin on June 29, 1956.

346

Todd had a mixed motive. He'd long wanted to meet Elizabeth, but he also planned to film a Japanese training vessel in the Santa Barbara harbor for use in his movie.

With McClory and Dick Hanley, Todd's new secretary, as fellow passengers aboard the yacht, Wilding and Elizabeth came aboard, but immediately separated once on deck.

All eyes focused on Elizabeth in her tight-fitting flamingo pink pants that outlined her crotch and her violet-cashmere sweater that accentuated the color of her eyes. She delivered her familiar refrain: "Who do you have to fuck to get a drink around here?"

Mike Todd came to the rescue with a chilled bottle of champagne. "Not since Cleopatra set her gilded foot onto her barge has such a dazzling queen taken to the sea."

"Flattery will get you anything," she said. "And I'm not bullshitting."

Todd ordered one of his handsome waiters to keep Elizabeth's ruby-colored champagne glass full throughout the rest of the trip.

Evelyn Keyes, "Scarlett O'Hara's Younger Sister" from *Gone With the Wind,* more or less volunteered as Elizabeth's "chaperone" for the duration of the cruise.

She'd been previously married to directors Charles Vidor and John Huston. Although not married, Keyes and Todd had been living together like man and wife for the previous three years.

Three views of **Evelyn Keyes**
Upper right: as Scarlett O'Hara's
little sister in *Gone With the Wind*

Keyes was "preening proud" of an engagement ring Todd had presented to her the night before. It was a 29.4 carat diamond engagement sparkler for which he'd paid almost $100,000, a stunning price back then for a piece of jewelry.

"I just know that any day now, he's going to propose to me," Keyes told Elizabeth. "I've got to be careful I don't lose it. It's too big for my finger, and Mike is going to take it back and get it resized."

The next time Keyes saw that diamond sparkler was months later on the finger of Elizabeth Taylor when she was married to Todd. Elizabeth often cited that ring as the beginning of her love affair with very large and very expensive diamonds.

[In 2002, Elizabeth would write a book entitled *My Love Affair With Jewelry* in which she stated: "I don't believe I own the pieces. I believe I am their custodian, here to enjoy them, to give them the best treatment in the world, to watch after their safety, and to love them.]

Keyes later claimed that Todd paid scant attention to Elizabeth during their two-day yachting trip aboard *The Hyding*. "I did not suspect a thing. Elizabeth and I amused each other with stories about our experiences in Tinseltown, and we talked about previous boyfriends. She asked me what it was like to fuck Kirk Douglas, David Niven, Dick Powell, and Anthony Quinn, and I gave her all the details. 'Since Niven is aboard, you might want to sample it for yourself.' I suggested to her."

"She was showing a lot of bosom, and I told her that I'd often wondered what would have happened to me if I had needed a size 38 bra instead of a modest 34," Keyes said.

"Let's face it," Elizabeth said. "We live in a tit culture."

She amused Keyes with stories about her struggles with Louis B. Mayer, and Keyes told her about working for Harry Cohn at Columbia. "He shoved his hand between my legs and rubbed my vagina," Keyes claimed. "He said, 'Save some of that for me, 'cause I'm gonna marry you.'"

"It never crossed my mind that Mike was checking out Elizabeth," Keyes later said. "She was everything he professed to dislike, the epitome of a movie star in dress, attitude, and demands. She never stopped drinking champagne from the moment she came aboard, and Mike didn't like women who drank. And she had a husband aboard."

Technically, the yachting party was in honor of Niven, who had interpreted the role of the eponymous hero, Phineas Fogg, in *Around the World in 80 Days*. Niven had been the former roommate and lover of Errol Flynn, and he was obviously aware of Flynn's fling with the then-underage Elizabeth.

Although bisexual, Niven was mostly known for his affairs with the A-list stars of Hollywood, an impressive range that had included Grace Kelly ("my finest lay"), Ava

upper photo: **David Niven** as Phineas Fogg in *Around the World in 80 Days*

lower photo: a detail from the illustrations associated with that film. Some critics say that the artwork was more consistently charming than the movie itself.

Gardner, Paulette Goddard, Hedy Lamarr, Carole Lombard, Norma Shearer, Loretta Young, Mae West, Ann Sheridan, Ginger Rogers, Ida Lupino, Deborah Kerr, Rita Hayworth, and Merle Oberon. Both Flynn and Niven had been bedtime companions of tobacco heiress Doris Duke. Before she became Todd's current mistress, Keyes and Niven had been lovers. She had high praise for his "beer can penis."

Niven told Flynn, "I always meant to get around to Elizabeth Taylor, but the poor girl so far has been denied the pleasure."

Todd wasn't the only one concealing his attraction for Elizabeth. Since Wilding had been invited, McClory did not pay as much attention to Elizabeth as he wanted to, and he was denied the privilege of sleeping with her.

After their first night at sea, she told McClory, "Mr. Wilding slept with me, but didn't get to enjoy the honeypot. I'm saving that for you, baby."

In spite of what she promised, McClory, months later, said, "Do you remember that old song 'Tennessee Waltz,' a big hit? Well, like the woman singing that song, I lost Elizabeth, my little darling, the night we sailed on *The Hyding*. The prize went to Mike Todd."

After their trip at sea, Wilding drove Elizabeth back to their crow's nest home. He'd later tell Stewart Granger, "I think three men are after Elizabeth— at least one of them is…perhaps all of them. David Niven, Kevin McClory, and, a remote shot, Mike Todd."

Driving up the treacherous road to their home, Wilding asked her, "What do you think of Mike Todd?"

"A real high roller," she said. "He reminds me of that Damon Runyon character in *Guys and Dolls,* Sky Masterson. A bit too pushy, a bit too vulgar, and a bit too brash. He should go over big in Hollywood."

In the weeks ahead, Todd decided to throw a spectacular A-list party at his rented Beverly Hills mansion. The occasion was in honor of the newscaster, Edward R. Murrow, who had narrated the introduction of *Around the World in 80 Days.* Todd admired Murrow for having stood up against Senator Joseph McCarthy during his "witch hunt" for communists in the movie colony.

Tanked up on champagne, Elizabeth was escorted by Todd to meet the celebrated news anchor. After a few polite interchanges, she provocatively said to him, "Tallulah Bankhead spreads the word at every party that you're the best lay in New York."

Not missing a beat, he shot back, "Why don't you climb the mountain and find out for yourself? Tallulah's is not a reliable news source. Like all true Southern women, she likes to embellish to make a good story even better."

At one point at the party, Elizabeth encountered the "bitchy-and-oh-so-terribly-witty" Noël Coward, who had completed a cameo for Todd's *Around the World in 80 Days.* "My dear." he said. "Wonderful to see you again. I noticed that your latest boyfriend, Kevin McClory, has a stutter. To mock him, Todd refers to him as 'Klevin.' How do you find him?"

"I find him very campy," she said, using a word that had not yet come into general usage.

"Talk about camp, darling," he said, "you're gazing upon the master. I spoke to Kevin or Klevin about you. He told me he found you 'totally pornographic.'"

"It pays to advertise," she said.

"Perhaps we'll star together in a picture," Coward said.

"That, dear Noël, I'd bet my left tit will never happen."

She was wrong. In a 1967 release for Universal, Elizabeth, along with Coward and Richard Burton, co-starred in *Boom!*. It was based on a Tennessee Williams play, *The Milk Train Doesn't Stop Here Anymore,* which Tallulah Bankhead had appeared in on Broadway with Elizabeth's former escort, Tab Hunter. It had been hailed as Broadway's "odd couple casting of the century."

Another guest of honor at the Todd gala, David Niven, followed Elizabeth out on the moonlit terrace, perhaps planning to make good on his stated attempt to seduce her. He openly flirted with her, but she seemed distracted. At one point, although usually the perfect gentleman, he took her delicate hand and placed it firmly on his ample crotch. "That is what is in store for you."

"I've had bigger," she snapped, sarcastically. Retrieving her hand, she headed across the terrace and back into the party, where Todd suddenly appeared with a fresh glass of champagne for her.

She later said, "It was fun being with Mike Todd. I was attracted to him, but not overly. I loved hearing him talk about Todd-AO. When I saw *Oklahoma!,* I thought it was the best big screen system ever devised, when he showed it to me."

As the party wound down, Elizabeth decided to find Wilding to take her home, but saw him talking in a secluded corner to Marlene Dietrich and Edith Piaf. She'd heard from Dick Hanley that Dietrich and "The Little Sparrow" in her simple black dress from Chanel were having a lesbian fling. Within the hour, Piaf would sing a dozen love songs in French before the august assemblage of Hollywood flesh.

Unknown to Elizabeth at the time, Wilding had resumed his affair with Dietrich, who had also shacked up with Todd during her appearance in *Around the World in 80 Days.*

Dietrich had told her daughter, Maria Riva, "Michael is a new man now that he's dumping that awful girl who made his life so miserable for so long. Now, we have to get his children away from the little harlot."

Riva would recall visits of Wilding to her mother. "They broke the springs in a double bed," she claimed.

The following Sunday afternoon, Todd once again invited Wilding and Elizabeth, this time for a swim party at his Beverly Hills mansion. Included in the guest list of about thirty were Eddie Fisher and Debbie Reynolds, hailed as America's Sweethearts. Locked in a loveless marriage, the Fishers were anything but.

Rumors were rampant that Fisher was actually in love with Todd and that Reynolds was a closeted lesbian, which she has vehemently and frequently denied.

Todd and Elizabeth spent most of the afternoon lying on one pink and one chartreuse air mattress, floating only a few inches apart on the surface of the pool.

Standing with his wife, Fisher kept his eyes focused on them. He told Reynolds, "Elizabeth has skinny legs. I could never go for a dame like that!"

She later said, "When your husband says that about a woman, she's the one to watch out for."

***

Two days later, Elizabeth received a phone call from Todd, asking her to visit him at his office that morning at MGM, where he'd rented space in the Irving Thalberg Building.

She drove to MGM, thinking that he might want to star her in his next picture after the release of *Around the World in 80 Days,* and after she finished shooting *Raintree County* with Monty.

As she relayed in one of her memoirs, "I was sitting in his outer office with my feet up on a table, drinking a Coke, and he rushed in and picked me up by my arm. Without a word, he practically dragged me out of the office and down a corridor. He shoved me into an elevator, still not speaking, just marching along breaking my arm. He took me into this deserted office. He sort of plunked me down on a couch and pulled a chair up to me. He started in on this spiel that lasted about a half hour without a break."

"He told me he loved me and that there was no question about that. 'We're going to be married,' he said. I looked at him the same way I imagine a rabbit looks at a mongoose. All kinds of things went through my mind. I thought he was stark, raving mad. I had to get away from this lunatic."

"Then he joined me on the sofa and took me in his arms. He tongue kissed me for at least five minutes. When he broke away for air, he told me very forcefully, 'From now on, I'm the only man you're gonna fuck!'"

Rock Hudson

La Liz

GIANT REASONS TO HATE
ROCK HUDSON & ELIZABETH TAYLOR

Actors who wanted the role of Bick Benedict

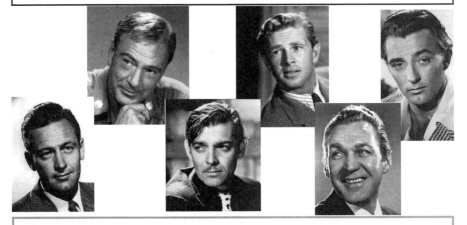

Image-wise, any of these guys might have been a studly Texas rancher: *left to right, above:* **William Holden, Gary Cooper, Clark Gable, Sterling Hayden, Forrest Tucker,** and **Robert Mitchum**

Actresses who wanted the role of Leslie Benedict

But could any of these actresses convincingly play a West Texas rancher's wife? *left to right* **Grace Kelly, Audrey Hepburn, Jennifer Jones, Marlene Dietrich**

CHAPTER SIXTEEN
Around the World with
MIKE TODD

With Mike Todd threatening to wed her, the still-married Elizabeth began work at MGM on *Raintree County* in April of 1956, one of the most troubled and painful years of her life.

Before filming, she had to undergo a series of intricate costume fittings to dress like a rich Southern belle in the months leading up to the election of President Abraham Lincoln and the Civil War.

MGM hired a dialect coach, Marguerite Littman, to teach her the finer points of Southern dialect. In that endeavor, Littman did not succeed. Elizabeth's Southern speech was attacked by many critics, "as the worst in the history of cinema."

Both Elizabeth and Monty agreed that "the script stinks," but each of them, needing the money, decided to give it their best.

When friends called, Elizabeth told them, "I filled in for Vivien Leigh, Miss Scarlett herself, in *Elephant Walk,* and now I've got another *fiddle-dee-dee* character to play—a completely bonkers Scarlett O'Hara type. I'm deranged. I've got to commit suicide in a murky swamp in penance for carrying the 'infection' of Negro blood—or some shit like that. I haven't gotten that far into the script yet."

The Civil War saga was based on Ross Lockridge's epic 1,100-page novel, *Raintree County,* with filming set to begin with a budget of $5 million from MGM, the most money ever spent up to that time on any movie shot entirely in the U.S.

The novelist was a thirty-three year old English teacher from Bloomington, Indiana. He wrote his first and last novel, and sold it to MGM for $150,000, but its production would be delayed for years. He never lived to see it on the screen—"just as well," said Elizabeth—as he committed suicide in March of 1948. The reclusive novelist could not deal with the pressures of fame, or so it was said. There may have been other, more private, reasons.

When Monty was cast as the lead, he was at the peak of his stardom and had a say in the choice of directors. Right from the beginning, that became a problem for MGM, as the actor turned down each of their original choices to helm this massive production.

Monty rejected Richard Brooks, who had scored a triumph with *Blackboard Jungle* (1955) starring Glenn Ford. Brooks had previously directed Elizabeth in *The Last Time I Saw Paris*. Monty also rejected William Wyler, fresh from helming Gary Cooper in *Friendly Persuasion* (1956). Monty agreed, however, to accept the controversial Edward Dmytryk as the project's director.

One of the most famous directors of Hollywood, Canadian-born Dmytryk was known for directing films such as *Back to Bataan* (1945), starring super patriot John Wayne, whom J. Edgar Hoover always maintained "took it up the ass" when he was known as Marion Morrison in the 1920s.

At the time he got sucked into the Red Menace vortex, Dmytryk had directed *Crossfire* (1947), starring three actors named Robert—Mitchum, Ryan, and Young. This *film noir* involved a victim of anti-Semitism and was handled with taste and intelligence. The novel on which it was based cast the victim as a homosexual, but that was viewed as too hot to handle for post-war American audiences. Dmytryk made the victim a Jew instead.

Summoned to appear before HUAC in 1947, he refused to testify and was sent to prison. After a few months, he felt he was going insane while "caged like a wild animal." On April 25, 1951, he asked to appear a second time before HUAC. This time, "the canary sang" [his words].

Under oath, Dmytryk admitted to a brief membership in the Communist Party in 1945 and named twenty-six former members of left-wing groups. He ratted on Adrian Scott, Albert Maltz, and John Howard Lawson, fellow members of the Hollywood Ten. He testified that all of them had pressured him to include communist propaganda in his films.

Regrettably, his testimony damaged pending court cases where these men were trying to exonerate themselves. In a revealing 1996 book, *Odd Man Out: A Memoir of the Hollywood Ten*, Dmytryk recounted his horrible ordeal.

Unlike the others, his directorial career wasn't wrecked. He would go on to helm one of Humphrey Bogart's greatest films, *The Caine Mutiny* (1954). He would also direct Bette Davis, Marlon Brando, Montgomery Clift, Sean Connery, Clark Gable, Spencer Tracy, Richard Burton, Richard Widmark, Henry Fonda, and Barbara Stanwyck, typecast as a lesbian, in *Walk on the Wild Side* (1962).

Although he had nothing to do with determining salaries, Dmytryk had to listen to numerous complaints from Elizabeth about the money she was drawing. "It's unfair," she said to him. "I'm getting $125,000 to make this god damn fucker, and Monty is drawing $300,000."

"Hang in there, kid," Dmytryk told her, "I predict that one day, with your star power, you'll get $500,000 per picture."

Throughout the entire film, Monty rehearsed with Elizabeth in his role as John Wickliff Shawnessy and her part as Susanna Drake. Using Lockridge's novel as a guide, he constantly tried to rewrite Millard Kaufman's screenplay.

Dore Schary had assembled an impressive supporting cast, including Eva Marie Saint (playing Elizabeth's rival in love), Lee Marvin, Rod Taylor, and Nigel Patrick. Others in the cast included Agnes Moorehead, who had long been rumored to be the lesbian lover of Debbie Reynolds. Elizabeth provocatively asked her if that rumor were true. Even though Elizabeth was a big star and Moorehead only a supporting player, the older actress slapped her face. "Maybe I deserved that," Elizabeth said to Monty.

She spent some time with another member of the cast, Tom Drake, talking about their early days at MGM when both of them were in love with Peter Lawford.

Before signing for *Raintree County,* Monty had shown very poor judgment in turning down other scripts. He'd rejected *High Noon* (1952), which became one of Gary Cooper's biggest successes, and he even turned down *East of Eden* (1955), which virtually immortalized James Dean.

His public behavior had also become increasingly erratic. In 1955, he attended the premiere of *Guys and Dolls,* starring "those sworn enemies," Marlon Brando and Frank Sinatra, both of whom had made love to Elizabeth. He had no comment on the performance of Sinatra, whom he'd befriended on the set of *From Here to Eternity* and had lived with temporarily. But in the middle of the screening of *Guys and Dolls,* Monty had stood up. In his loudest voice, he'd screamed that *Guys and Dolls* was "vomitable—this god damn picture stinks!"

Outside in the lobby, he punched his fist into a glass cabinet containing pictures of the stars and severely lacerated his arm. While waiting for an ambulance, he urinated on the street in front of passers-by.

Even before filming of *Raintree County* began, Monty had increasingly been displaying erratic behavior. His doctor said that one day, he discovered "every pill known to mankind," in the actor's medicine cabinet.

For a birthday gift, Elizabeth had presented Monty with a green alligator vanity case, and he carried it at his side wherever he went. It was reported to contain more pills than Bayer had aspirins.

***

On MGM's lot during the filming of *Raintree County,* Elizabeth still had a British husband at home, whom she had yet to divorce; a boyfriend (Kevin McClory) on a leash; and a new man in her life, Mike Todd.

"But in spite of that array," the director Dmytryk said, "she still had a roving eye for male flesh. Many of the more innocent members of the crew thought she was having an affair with Monty Clift, who followed her around like a lovelorn dog. Perhaps he was in love with her, but I doubt if they ever made it in the haystack. He did tell me one day, 'It's no good trying to hide my feelings. I can't get over it—Elizabeth is the only woman I have ever met who turns me on. She feels like the other half of me.' He did say that, but I'd bet two inches off my dick that she wasn't getting anything from Monty but embraces."

She was also seen on several occasions dining with Tom Drake in the MGM commissary. "They make a handsome couple," Dmytryk said, "but they talk about their boyfriends over club sandwiches."

On her second day on the set, Dmytryk introduced her to actor Lee Marvin, a former Marine born in New York. He had a lean and mean appearance, as well as a commandingly deep voice and a menacing aura. In *film noir,* he'd entered the pantheon of screen sadists when he tossed hot coffee into Gloria Grahame's face in the 1953 film *The Big Heat.*

"No one liked him on the set," Dmytryk said. "He was rude and drunk most of the time. He and Marlon Brando had actually attacked each other when they appeared together in *The Wild One* in 1953. I feared Marvin would make trouble on the set."

When introduced to Elizabeth, Marvin said, "I'm a rip-snorter."

"Perhaps one night you can show me the difference between a rip-snorter and a hellraiser," she said.

"I'm your man."

Within two days, Elizabeth came up to Marvin and said, "I hope you don't  consider me forward, but I'd like to go to bed with you."

"Marvin didn't consider her forward at all," Dmytryk claimed "When he got drunk and needed to fuck, he'd chase a jackrabbit into the hills. I couldn't believe it. Against all odds, Marvin and Elizabeth became an item for a few nights."

Drake, however, had trouble believing that Elizabeth would be attracted to Marvin. One afternoon in the MGM commissary, he asked Marvin if the rumors were true about intimacies between Elizabeth and him.

Down and dirty:
Lee Marvin

"The beautiful bitch likes it dirty and deep, which rules you out, gay boy," Marvin shot back.

According to Dmytryk, "I had no idea how the mating game would play out after I shipped this motley crew to the Deep South. But when the interior shots were completed on the MGM lot in Los Angeles, it was time to fly cast and crew to Kentucky for exterior shots. Then tragedy struck."

***

It was a hot afternoon on May 12, 1956, when Elizabeth decided privately to throw her last dinner party—take-out food only—as the wife of Michael Wilding. He had been lying on the sofa all afternoon complaining of lower back pain. "Listen," she said, "in this marriage, I'm the one who gets the back pains."

She proceeded with the organization of the dinner party she'd scheduled for that evening, unaware that it would become one of the most notorious in the history of Hollywood. Wanting to know her director better, she invited Edward Dmytryk and his wife Jean. "J. Edgar Hoover will probably have us arrested as commies for hanging out with the Dmytryks," she told Wilding.

She also decided to invite Rock Hudson, hoping to renew their friendship after she'd more or less deserted him on the set of *Giant* to hang out instead with James Dean. "Of course, we'll have to ask that lesbian Henry Willson forced him to marry—what's the name of the bitch? Oh, yes…Phyllis Gates."

Mostly she wanted to invite Monty, and she had a special reason for doing so. At a party she'd met this handsome gay priest, Father George Long, who told her he'd more or less fallen in love with Monty after watching him play a priest in the 1953 film, *I Confess.* She called Monty, urging him to come. "You've got to meet this priest. He's one hunk. He thinks you're gorgeous, and his favorite word is 'fuck'"

Monty turned her down. MGM had hired a chauffeur for him for the duration of his involvement with *Raintree County*. At MGM, Dore Schary had told Benny Thau, "I don't want Monty to become another Jimmy Dean-style auto casualty, so we'd better get a full-time driver for our druggie star."

On the evening of Elizabeth's dinner party, however, Monty had already released the driver from his duties that night, since he had planned to retire early to bed.

Elizabeth begged and begged for Monty to make an appearance at her party, but Monty would not relent. At four o'clock, she called yet another time, beseeching him to attend. Again, he pleaded that he was too tired, claiming that the road to her house was too dangerous for him to drive at night.

At five o'clock, she called a third time, and still he was determined not to come. He also told her he'd taken sleeping pills, which would make it hazardous to be on any road.

But tenaciously, she asked Wilding to call Monty at around six, and it was through him that Elizabeth finally wangled Monty's agreement to come.

"I can't stay long," he warned.

To entice Monty, Wilding had told him that Elizabeth had invited his best friend, Kevin McCarthy, who was currently filming *Invasion of the Body Snatchers* (1956). Monty had ridiculed him for appearing in this sci-fi horror flick, little knowing that it would become a film classic still being shown during the 21st century.

At the party, Monty sipped "piss-warm, pussy pink rosé" and heard Elizabeth talk about how beautiful both of them looked in the early rushes she'd seen by Robert Surtees, the cinematographer of *Raintree County.*

That gay priest did not show up at the party, so Monty turned his amorous attention instead to one of his all-time favorite lovers, Rock Hudson, who had little passion for him. "Monty doesn't give me much to work with," Hudson had previously confided to Elizabeth.

After Monty went into the bathroom and took some downers, he emerged more hostile to Hudson. The macho star was filming the 1956 *Written on the Wind* with Lauren Bacall, Robert Stack, and Dorothy Malone.

Elizabeth knew that Hudson was having an affair with the very handsome Stack. "But I beat you to him," Elizabeth chided Hudson.

Monty may have been jealous of Stack, and at the party, he told Hudson he was "seriously pissed off at him," but he never said why.

Then, announcing that he was "dead tired," Monty was the first to leave. McCarthy followed him out the door, having stated to the party guests that he had an early morning plane to catch. Outside the Wilding home, Monty asked Kevin if he'd lead the way down the "murderous cork-twisted road" that eventually funneled into Sunset Boulevard.

"If you don't go ahead and drive in front of me off this god damn mountain, I'll be driving in circles all night," Monty claimed. McCarthy agreed, but warned him not to follow "too closely on my tail."

McCarthy recalled that fateful night. "I looked in my rearview mirror, and I saw Monty's car approaching too close to my vehicle. I thought he was playing chicken with me. I put my foot on the gas and went faster when his own car seemed almost on top of me. We both made the first turn, but the next one was treacherous. We were careening, swerving, and screeching. There were no streetlights. I saw his car lights weave from one side of the road to the other. Then I heard this terrible crash. A cloud of dust appeared in my rear-view mirror."

Braking and then parking off to the side, McCarthy got out of his car and rushed to the scene of the accident. Monty's Chevrolet was now "an accordion-pleated mess." He peered into the dark car whose motor was still running. Reaching through a broken window, he managed to turn off the ignition, but he didn't see Monty. Unknown to McCarthy, Monty had fallen into a fetus-like position under the wheel.

McCarthy suspected that his body had been thrown from the car, but he didn't see him anywhere on the nearby grounds. The car had collided into a telephone pole jutting upward from the edge of the cliff and, in the dark, seemed to hang precariously above the ravine. McCarthy was afraid that it might burst into flames.

He desperately needed to get to a phone, but he had noticed on the way down that all the neighboring houses were under construction. He raced up the hill, panting for breath. Passing through the garden gate and into the Wilding home, he pounded on the door, screaming for Elizabeth.

It was Wilding who answered the urgent pounding, and at first he seemed to think that McCarthy was playing some terrible sick joke. "Go home, Kevin!" he said. "The party's over."

"My god," McCarthy shouted into the living room, loud enough for the remaining guests to hear. "Come at once. Monty's dead!"

A screech came from within the house. It was Elizabeth.

***

Her screams of agony pierced the night air as her household, except for Wilding and his painful back, raced to the site of the accident. Hudson had been urged by McCarthy to bring a flashlight.

"My only thought was that Monty was somewhere in that car, perhaps on the floorboard," Elizabeth later recalled. "When we got there, we found the doors jammed shut. Rock shone his flashlight into the front seat. Monty was there and moving. His head looked like it has been smashed into the steering wheel. The windshield was broken, the dashboard smashed. He was bleeding profusely—so much so that it looked like his face had been halved."

"There are various printed stories about how I broke into the car," she said. "In all honesty, I don't remember. I know that I came through the rear because I vaguely remember crawling over

At the scene of
Montgomery Clift's car accident

359

the front seat to get to him. How I did it remains a mystery to me to this day. Everyone at the scene was so involved he told contradictory stories. Rock was the strongest of the lot, and he eventually got the smashed-in front door open."

"I know I had on this pink scarf," she said. "I remember ripping it off and using it to try to help stop the flow of blood. I wore this white dress. It turned scarlet. All my previous revulsion about blood left me. I held his head and he sort of came to. He became almost lucid. Of course, he was suffering from shock. A tooth was hanging on his lip by a few shreds of flesh, and he asked me to pull it off because it was cutting his tongue."

"Suddenly, he was gasping for breath. He motioned that one—maybe more—of his teeth had broken away and had lodged in his throat. I reached in with my hand and removed two teeth so he could breathe. It was perhaps the most ghastly night of my life—yes, the most ghastly."

"The damn ambulance got lost and was about an hour late," she recalled. "But his doctor arrived. Monty, with virtually no head, actually formally introduced us."

Before the ambulance got there, photographers and reporters descended on the scene. Elizabeth yelled at Hudson and McCarthy to form a shield to protect Monty's face from their view. At one point she placed her scarf over his face so they could not photograph "that bloody pulp."

She yelled at the photographers, "You sons of bitches, take one picture of him, and I'll kick you in the nuts. I'll have you barred from every studio in Hollywood, you fucking leeches."

"Finally, that asshole of an ambulance arrived," she said. "Monty could have been dead, the van went via Idaho to get to us."

In back of the ambulance, Monty had passed out. She sat close by his side, holding his hand and telling him how much she loved him. "By that point, his face had swollen until it was almost the size of his shoulders," she said. "That beautiful face of his looked like a giant red soccer ball."

"I wanted to die, and Monty almost did. Guilt overcame me. I knew if I had not insisted he come to my house, he'd be asleep in his own bed right that very moment. That night would haunt me. For years, I'd have nightmares. I'd ruined the life of my best friend…perhaps for always."

***

When news that Elizabeth had insisted that an exhausted Monty make a tortuous drive up and down a mountain, she came in for a lot of press criticism. *The Girl Who Had Everything* wants it her way—or the highway," charged one reporter.

The stongest criticism leveled against her came from Monty's other two close women friends, the notorious Libby Holman and Mira Rostova, his acting coach.

Rostova attacked Elizabeth to Paul Newman, who was a leading contender for the male lead in Tennessee Williams' *Cat on a Hot Tin Roof.*

"It's all the fault of that beautiful witch," Rostova charged. "Monty had repeatedly told her that he was too tired to drive up that dangerous mountain. He never likes to drive at night, and he knew that the access road was treacherous. He should have gone to bed instead. She preferred him to risk his life for her—and for what? Another one of her stupid little parties."

After Elizabeth was allowed at last to see Monty, she said, "In his hospital room at Cedars of Lebanon, it was all I could do not to let out a scream. His head was as big as the biggest pumpkin at Hallowe'en—and far more grotesque. His jaws were wired. He would have to have a series of operations to reconstruct his once beautiful face and teeth. He had a broken nose and a cracked upper cheekbone. There was a gaping split in his upper lip and cuts and bruises all over his face. He was in traction for whiplash injuries."

One Saturday afternoon, Elizabeth arrived to find Libby Holman sitting by his bedside. A fight erupted between these two jealous women. The Broadway Diva denounced Elizabeth, calling her "sensual and silly...a god damn heifer in heat."

"Screw off!" Elizabeth shouted back at Holman. As she was storming out the door, Elizabeth called back to Monty, "I'll return when you've gotten rid of this dyke murderess."

Later that afternoon, Elizabeth became even more furious at Holman when she learned that the fabulously wealthy singer had been smuggling martinis in to Monty, who had to sip them through a straw. His doctors had warned him that drinking alcohol might sabotage plans for the plastic surgery needed to reconstruct a new face on him.

When Holman left, Elizabeth returned to Monty's room. His hand reached out for her. "Oh, Bessie Mae, don't be mad at Libby. I need all the friends I can get right now."

"I want you to live," she said. "That is my only concern."

"Bessie Mae, my Bessie Mae. At one time you and I were hailed as the most beautiful man and woman on the planet. Now you'll have to carry that beauty banner yourself."

Before every hospital visit, Elizabeth stopped at the Farmers Market in Los Angeles to purchase mushy foods such as guacamole and overripe bananas. She could spoon feed him, even though it caused him pain to swallow.

"I nearly cried seeing him struggle just to get some baby food in him," she recalled. "I begged him not to return to work on *Raintree County*. Rock Hudson told me he'd like to take over the role, but I didn't tell Monty that. Paul Newman also seemed willing to take over, the way he'd taken over for Jimmy Dean in two movies."

"I've got to go back to work for you, Bessie Mae," Monty said. "I owe it to you, damaged face or not."

"You owe me nothing," she said. "It is I who will forever be in your debt. At times, I've thought about divorcing Michael just to marry you and take care of you for the rest of my life."

Monty's recovery and reconstruction work went much faster than anyone, including his doctors, had predicted. She was with him when he was released from the hospital. He was driven to his dingy little rented house on Dawn Ride Road. "At least it has a pool," she said.

She called on him every afternoon, finding him drinking heavily, against doctors' orders, and taking morphine-based painkillers.

She once told Wilding, "I can't stand to look him squarely in the face. I do, of course. But I don't find Monty there anymore. His once lustrous eyes are now dead like a fish on ice at the Farmers Market."

"I know my beauty will never be restored," he told her one hot afternoon. "From now on, if I ever work again, I'll be cast in horror movies."

Once or twice, he took his fingers and ran them up and down her face. "Do you remember when I once was as young and beautiful as you are today?" he asked her, expecting no answer.

Both Dore Schary from MGM, accompanied by the *Raintree* director, Dmytryk, made weekly visits to check on Monty and his face. Finally, after a nine-week delay in production, Schary announced that he thought Monty was ready to face the camera again. But both Schary and Dmytryk knew that the early close-ups of Monty's face would not match those in his post-accident scenes.

As author Ellis Amburn wrote, "When he recovered, he was scarcely recognizable as Montgomery Clift, appearing pinched and withered. The famous gullwing eyebrows were now shaggy thickets, the left side of his face was almost paralyzed, the once heroic jawline was soft and mushy. His eyes looked dead, no doubt due to pain, bewilderment, and massive doses of barbiturates."

Dmytryk, after a few tests at the studio, decided that Monty should be filmed whenever possible from the right side of his face. "The left side of his face was immobile and not capable of conveying any emotion. One half of what was once the screen's most expressive face had died."

Dmytryk called Elizabeth and told her to prepare to leave for location shooting in the Deep South, beginning in Danville, Kentucky.

"I loathe going down there with all those bigots," she told him. "Poor Monty and I will be treated like freaks."

***

In July, with her luggage packed, Elizabeth walked out of her home after kissing her sons goodbye. Her only words to Michael Wilding were not of love, but of instructions in child care.

She had not broken with Kevin McClory, her secret lover, but fortunately, he was out of town working for Mike Todd. If any close friend asked, she said, "Kevin and I are madly in love." By now, all of Hollywood, and most of her fans, knew that her marriage to Wilding was heading for the divorce court.

No sooner had she arrived in Danville, Kentucky, to resume her role as the deranged Susanna Drake, than there was a knock on her door. A teenage boy appeared with a telegram from Mike Todd.

"I LOVE YOU," it read.

Within the hour, the manager of the hotel arrived with a bonded and insured present from Todd. It was an emerald bracelet from Cartier. He'd already ordered exotic flowers for her suite. That night he called her, talking for nearly four hours, vowing eternal love and outlining how exciting their life would be together.

The next day, Elizabeth moved into a house that had been rented for her in Danville. Nearby, Monty was moved into an equivalent rented house.

Reporters rushed to Kentucky to follow her after MGM issued a press release on July 19, 1956:

"Much careful thought has been given to the step we are taking. It is being done so that we will have an opportunity to thoroughly work out our personal situation. We are in complete accord in making this amicable decision."

Although not stating exactly what this "amicable decision" was, it was an obvious notice that Elizabeth was planning to file for a divorce from Wilding. MGM publicity agents failed miserably at spelling out the details.

She telephoned Wilding that night, claiming, "I still love you—don't think I don't. You are the father of our children. But as Sinatra told me, when a relationship has lost its *ring-a-ding-ding*, it's time to move on."

Hearing that McClory was back in Los Angeles, Elizabeth telephoned him that same night.

"I was absolutely astonished at the way she broke off our romance," McClory recalled years later. "One day, she told me I was the love of her life, and the next night she's telling me that Mike Todd has taken over and is going to marry her. The Princess was his? How in a matter of days could she fall out of love with me and in love with him? It didn't make any sense at all. I guess I didn't know her at all, even though I'd repeatedly made love to her. I was in a doubly awful position because Todd was also my boss."

The following week, Elizabeth's lawyers contacted Wilding, informing him that she was filing for divorce on the ground of incompatibility. He was to be granted reasonable access to their two sons, and she would waive all rights to alimony except $250 a month in child support. That was a relief to Wilding, since he had less than two hundred dollars in the bank at the time.

When Dmytryk heard of the divorce, he spoke privately to the cast and crew. "It's hard to have much sympathy for Wilding. He was married to Elizabeth but still maintained his steady love affair with Stewart Granger. Monty told me that Wilding fucked him on many an occasion. He was also screwing everybody from Marie McDonald to Marlene Dietrich with a little 'in like Flynn' on the side." Of course, he was referring to Wilding's close pal, Errol Flynn.

When Granger heard the news of the impending divorce, he said, "In essence, Miss Lizzie cut off my mate's balls. Call her the nutcracker."

Wilding and McClory were not the only people who had to be dumped.

Todd had sent his mistress, Evelyn Keyes, on a trip to South America, scheduling stopovers for her en route in London and Paris. Ostensibly, the purpose of her trip was to find screens large enough to show *Around the World in 80 Days* in Todd-AO.

She was staying in Elizabeth's former haunt, the Lancaster Hotel in Paris, when she received what she later labeled as "the call." It was from Todd. "I have to tell you, I've fallen in love with Elizabeth."

"Elizabeth who?" she asked, thinking he was joking.

It was no joke. Finally, he convinced her that he was not going to marry her, but would wed Elizabeth as soon as her divorce came through.

"When I hung up," she recalled, "I realized I had been taken by this beautiful bitch. Mike had delivered the knockout punch. Marlene Dietrich and Marilyn Monroe had been passing fancies of his. I feared Elizabeth would stick around for a while."

Later, Todd contacted Keyes, hoping to keep her as a mistress on the side after his marriage to Elizabeth. "He was furious when I moved to Paris and married Artie Shaw in 1957," Keyes said. The band leader had been previously married to both Lana Turner and Ava Gardner.

In 1959, Keyes encountered her rival, Elizabeth, at a Hollywood party after Todd had died. "Maybe it was a good thing that he dumped me," Keyes told her. "The advantage of his dumping me was that I would no longer have to smell the stench of his cigar. I would no longer be kept awake all night while he and his buddies played gin rummy. Unlike you, I might not have gotten the flu and would have taken that final flight with him. In that case, I would no longer be inhabiting this earth. So, in essence, by running off with my boyfriend, you may have inadvertently saved my life."

Years later, a more bitter Keyes emerged when a reporter asked her, "Who do you think was the love of Elizabeth Taylor's life—Richard Burton or Mike Todd?"

"Neither of the above," said Keyes. "The love of her life is Elizabeth Taylor."

***

Late every Friday afternoon, a chartered plane landed in Danville, Kentucky, to fly Elizabeth to New York, where she stayed in the Park Avenue penthouse of Todd. He told his friends, "Lemme tell ya, any minute that little dame spends out of bed is totally wasted."

Every day on the set back in Danville, batches of yellow roses arrived. Todd called her at least five times every day, and, at night, would often talk for hours, much to the delight of the Danville phone operators who listened in. They later spread stories to their neighbors and often to the press. "It was sex over the phone," one of the local operators said. "I didn't know a man and a woman did such perverted things to each other. It was totally disgusting. Mr. Todd and Miss Taylor had better get right with Jesus—or else they'll burn in hell's fire."

In a neighboring house, Monty's emotional state seemed to grow worse every day. On two different occasions, Danville police arrested him for indecent exposure, as he was picked up walking nude from his house to Elizabeth's.

On most nights, she would take him inside her house and would try to sober him up in the shower. Later, she'd towel him dry and put him to bed, hoping that sleep would come to this troubled soul.

On some nights, and infrequently, she was too intoxicated herself to deal with him. When that happened, he would stand outside the house, pounding on her door, evoking the final scene in his hit movie, *The Heiress,* with Olivia de Havilland.

Everybody thought Monty and Elizabeth were having this torrid affair," said Dmytryk. "I didn't think so. Like I really cared. All I wanted was to pull off MGM's first film in Panavision and not bankrupt the studio with their antics, accidents, and drunkenness. Any day, I expected Elizabeth to have some health emergency."

"My fears came true," the director said. "In the oppressive summer heat of Kentucky, and all that humidity, and in those heavily corseted costumes she had to wear, my star collapsed."

A doctor was rushed to Elizabeth's side when she fainted on the set, suffering from hyperventilation [*faster than normal, or labored, breathing*] complicated by tachycardia [*a heart rate whose speed exceeds the parameters of "normal."*] For a week, she lay in a hospital bed in Danville, having been tranquilized with sodium amytal. Todd flew to her side and stayed with her every day until she was released and could resume filming.

MONTGOMERY CLIFT   ELIZABETH TAYLOR   EVA MARIE SAINT

M·G·M PRESENTS IN M·G·M CAMERA 65 "WINDOW OF THE WORLD"

RAINTREE COUNTY

IN THE GREAT TRADITION OF CIVIL WAR ROMANCE

Sex, insanity, and romance in the Deep South: In this scene from *Raintree County*, **Elizabeth Taylor** emulates Vivien Leigh in *Gone With the Wind*--except that here, unlike any scene in GWTW, the belle's hoop skirts are translucent.

When Elizabeth vacated her rented house to move to other premises, the landlord threatened MGM with a lawsuit. An MGM employee, Steve Miller, inspected the premises of what he called "the world's biggest slob. Bacon grease covered the kitchen walls. Her make-up was all over the bedroom sheets. She even ruined the draperies. Windows were broken. The springs in the sofa were also broken. Doors were missing knobs. Her two toilets overflowed. Liquor bottles were everywhere; the rugs were filthy, the crystal and china in bits and pieces."

On her next location in Natchez, Mississippi, hundreds of locals, including a large armada of black farm workers, turned out to witness Elizabeth's arrival. Although she had been scheduled for scenes against an evocative background of antebellum ruins, it soon became obvious that that schedule would have to be revised.

Nervous and upset over her confused life, she had had too much to drink on the plane. Three men carried her down the runway and into a waiting limousine, where she was driven to her hotel suite and put to bed to sleep it off.

On her first night in Natchez, Monty visited her. Throughout the day and early evening, he'd taken too many barbiturates, tranquilizers, and amphetamines. After finishing off three bottles of champagne, she fell asleep on her bed. He had collapsed onto the floor beside her.

366

Before dawn, she discovered that he'd fallen into a coma with a cigarette between his fingers. Both fingers were burned to the bone, and he had to be rushed to the emergency room of the local hospital.

She somehow managed to get through the next few weeks, with the help of Todd's loving support. Finally, she called him to come for her, "The god damn film is over, and it's taken ten years off my life. It's been a nightmare."

Months later, in Los Angeles, Elizabeth sat in a darkened projection room holding Monty's damaged hand as they watched the final cut of *Raintree County.*

As Monty's biographer, Patricia Bosworth noted, "There were many spliced-together sequences which used both his old and new face; thus one sees close-ups of him before his car crash where the camera has caught his erotic promise, his sense of energy and risk; then in the very next shot he'll be on the screen in his postcrash face—in the same costume, same position, but looking zombie like."

After the showing, Monty denounced the film as a "colossal bore—a soap opera with elephantiasis." Over dinner that night, he asserted, "I'm horrific, wooden, frozen. In my beard I look like Jesus Christ in a Union cap."

He also criticized Elizabeth's performance, telling her, "Bessie Mae, in those mad scenes, you went over the top." Most film critics agreed with Monty's assessment, one reporter labeling her voice as "whining and screeching."

"She was more obnoxious than insane," wrote another critic. "She dies in that swamp none too soon."

Despite the bad press, Elizabeth was nominated for an Academy Award as the Best Actress of the year. She faced formidable competition from Deborah Kerr in *Heaven Knows, Mr. Allison;* from Anna Magnani in *Wild in the Wind,* and from her longtime rival, Lana Turner in *Peyton Place.* The Oscar went to a twenty-three-year-old Georgia-born blonde, Joanne Woodward, for her portrayal of the psychotic heroine in *The Three Faces of Eve.*

"I knew I wouldn't win," Elizabeth said. "The Academy thought Woodward was better at being crazy than I was."

As she moved deeper and deeper into Todd's orbit, Elizabeth and Monty began to drift apart. Before flying back to New York,

A cult *tragedienne* with a hangover: **Elizabeth Taylor** with **Montgomery Clift** in *Raintree County*

Monty told her, "I have two objects in mind. The first is never to step in front of a movie camera again. The second is to try and find what has so far eluded me—a reason to live. What reason do you have to live, Bessie Mae?"

"To marry Mike Todd," she said. "My life with a dead fish Brit is over."

"Sharks can be a lot of fun," he warned her. "But, as you know, they can also be deadly."

***

After a Labor Day weekend spent in Atlantic City during September of 1956, Elizabeth arrived in New York flashing a twenty-carat diamond ring. "I'm engaged to Mike Todd," she announced to the press.

Then she stunned MGM and half the world by suggesting that she was going to retire. "I may never work again," she said. "I want to be a woman to Mike Todd's man. A home, a husband, a real family mean more to me. I'm far more interested in being Mrs. Mike Todd than in being an actress. I'm trading a real life instead of a life of play-acting at make-believe."

Sara was horrified that Elizabeth might retire, knowing she'd lose her weekly check from MGM. Francis Taylor had closed his art gallery and gone into early retirement, hoping to live off his wife and Elizabeth.

At first, Sara approved of Todd, thinking he was a rich Italian. She was horrified when she learned he was a Jew named Avrom Hirsch Goldbogen.

Elizabeth told Todd, "My mother is the most prejudiced woman in the universe."

When Todd was invited for his first dinner with Elizabeth's parents, Sara became even more outraged. Todd put his hand inside Elizabeth's dress and said, "Boy these little Jewish girls sure have big tits."

At other dinner parties, Todd referred to Elizabeth as "my little Jewish broad, Lizzie Schwartzkopf," which translates from the German and Yiddish as "Blackhead."

Even though Todd was older than Wilding, he referred to the British actor as "that boring elderly husband Liz is married to. I doubt if she can get a rise out of him."

The cute, sweet actress Diana Lynn, who often dated homosexuals who needed a girl for the night to escort to a premiere, observed Elizabeth one night at one of Todd's parties. "She had this almost iridescent sensuality. Her eyes, lips, and breasts gleamed. She was so damn sexy and flirtatious. I stood by and watched her work the room. She made every man want to unzip his fly and stick it into her."

Back in Los Angeles, on September 26, 1956, Elizabeth, along with director George Stevens and Rock Hudson, pressed their hands and footprints into freshly poured cement in the forecourt of Grauman's Chinese Theater.

The premiere of *Giant* was announced for this same theater on October 7. Before arriving, Todd and Elizabeth had drinks with Debbie Reynolds and Eddie Fisher. Todd looked across the table at Elizabeth as the first bottle of champagne was served. "As soon as this premiere is over tonight, I'm gonna fuck you."

Todd escorted Elizabeth to the Los Angeles premiere, with Rock Hudson arriving with his new wife, Phyllis Gates. They were followed by Clark Gable escorting Joan Crawford and Tab Hunter with Natalie Wood on his arm.

In late October, Todd and Elizabeth flew to New York for the respective premieres of both *Giant* and *Around the World in 80 Days*.

By the time of the New York premiere of *Giant*, a weird cult had formed around the image of the late James Dean. Thousands of his fanatical fans believed that he had not died, but that he was going to make an appearance at the New York premiere of a movie that had helped make him famous.

Before that premiere, George Stevens hosted a reception for the film's cast. The director warned that there might be a problem associated with security at the premiere. The New York Police Department had assigned extra men to the premises, and wooden barriers had been erected to restrain the throngs. Fears involved the possibility of a riot because of the hysteria engulfing the fans, mostly those who had come to worship the memory of James Dean.

Hudson was among the first to arrive. The identity of his date for the evening—Tallulah Bankhead—came as a surprise. She had gone to bed with him the night before. Hudson called such seductions of older female stars "mercy fucks."

She told a reporter from NBC, "I'm here tonight, darling, because of this divine young man, Rock Hudson, who is a *giant* in every conceivable way."

For the premiere at New York City's Roxy Theater, Todd had presented Elizabeth with a pair of ten-thousand-dollar diamond earrings. The crowd outside the theater grew and grew until it stretched for several blocks. As Elizabeth and Todd emerged from their long black limousine, a roar went up as fans pushed against the police barricades.

Carroll Baker and her husband, director Jack Garfein—a Holocaust survivor for whom she had converted to Judaism—walked directly behind Elizabeth and Todd. As Baker remembered it, "The fanatic Dean cult were nearest the red-carpet aisle leading into the entrance. Those closest to us were thrashing against the barriers, letting out menacing, eerie cries; they had red, distorted, lunatic-like faces. The sight of them filled me with revulsion a moment before the premonition of danger gripped me."

In front of them, Todd, too, was aware of the danger, and he was shoving photographers and reporters aside to make a pathway to safety for Elizabeth. It was as if he was trying to create a tunnel for her to escape.

Baker then described the pandemonium that followed. "There was an explosion of human bodies across the barricades and a stampede of howling maniacs trampling each other and rushing the actors."

Photographers were knocked down along with their cameras. Some of the fans even knocked over police officers, whose caps often went flying through the air. Jane Withers was nearly trampled to death.

The fans tore at Elizabeth, grabbing her hair and trying to rip off pieces of her gown. Todd yelled at them, "Stand back."

A screech went up. "My earring," shouted Elizabeth. "I've lost one of my earrings."

"Forget the god damn earrings." Todd shouted at her. "I'll buy you another pair."

The manager of the Roxy appeared, and ushered Elizabeth and Todd into his office, where he offered them a brandy to steady their nerves. Bankhead had retreated to the women's room, and Hudson joined Elizabeth. His shirt was in shreds, and his jacket had disappeared, along with his wallet.

Giant became the highest grossing film in the history of Warners until the 1978 release of *Superman.*

When the Academy Award nominations were announced, Elizabeth's name was not on the list. Her fellow actors—Rock Hudson, James Dean, and Mercedes McCambridge—were nominated, although only George Stevens as Best Director carried home an Oscar.

Giant earned Dean his second and last Oscar nomination, but, of course, he never lived to see the film's release.

***

Right before *80 Days* opened at the Rivoli Theater in New York, Todd shocked Elizabeth by telling her that he was flat broke. "I've spent every penny I have and I'm deep in debt."

To pay the rent at the theater, Eddie Fisher presented him with a certified check for $25,000. The premiere would go forth as scheduled.

The Los Angeles Times Corporation heard about Todd's financial dilemma and offered him $25 million for the outright purchase of *80 Days.* Elizabeth urged him not to take it. Within months, the picture had earned more than $30 million on a $6 million investment.

The October, 1956 premiere of *80 Days* was a sensation, the movie garnering a standing ovation. *The New York Daily News* called it, "Titanic, titillating, and thrilling."

The next day, pictures of Elizabeth with Todd ran on frontpages around the world.

Todd's film, like *Giant,* was a worldwide smash. After the ovation for *80 Days* in New York, Todd grabbed Elizabeth. "Lizzie, baby, we're the King and Queen of the World."

***

Since Todd and Elizabeth were virtually living as man and wife, there remained the issue of her divorce from Michael Wilding.

On November 14, 1956, Elizabeth's lawyers filed papers in California asking for a divorce. The charge was extreme mental cruelty. He would have to pay no alimony and would get fifty percent of the proceeds from the sale of their home, which was worth around $200,000 on the market at that time.

"For Elizabeth, getting involved with Mike Todd, my boss, also meant getting into Eddie Fisher's crotch," Dick Hanley recalled. "The two men were glued at the hip. Unknown to the public then, or even now, was that Fisher had been sexually involved with Elizabeth even before she married Mike Todd."

"Wilding had first-hand evidence of this affair, and I think Debbie Reynolds at some point came to suspect it," Dick claimed. "Actually, I always viewed the Todd/Taylor/Fisher liaison as a *ménage à trois.* And I was never certain who on any given day was fucking whom."

At two o'clock one morning, Todd and his gin rummy cronies planned to play until dawn, as stakes were the highest ever for this beer-swigging, cigar-smoking lot.

Elizabeth grew bored, and Todd ordered Fisher to drop out of the game and take her back home, where Wilding was still occupying the guest room.

"They talked until around four o'clock in the morning," Wilding later told Stewart Granger and Jean Simmons. "I heard them. Finally, I went to sleep. At around eleven o'clock the following morning, a call came in from Benny Thau. He said it was urgent that he speak to Elizabeth. When I knocked on the door of the master bedroom, Eddie answered it. His face was covered with shaving cream, but nothing else covered him."

Embarrassed, Wilding called to Elizabeth, "It's Thau on the phone. Some emergency at MGM."

"Okay," shouted Elizabeth. "Tell the fucker I'm coming. First, I've got to take a piss. And shut the god damn door."

When Fisher brought Elizabeth back to Todd's Beverly Hills mansion for a late luncheon the next day, Todd said, "I hope you two lovebirds had a good time."

The singer later said that after lunch, Todd practically dragged Elizabeth off to his upstairs bedroom. "If you want to get fucked, let a *real* man do it," he told her in front of Fisher.

Before Elizabeth's marriage to Todd, there were other intimate sightings of Elizabeth with Fisher. A waiter at the Beverly Hills Hotel later said he delivered a room service dinner to them late one night in a suite that Fisher had booked.

"Fisher was in the nude in the living room listening to his own records, and I could see Taylor in the bed since the door was open," the waiter claimed.

That day, Fisher had had a domestic quarrel with Debbie Reynolds and had temporarily moved out.

After her dalliances with Victor Mature and Eddie Fisher, Wilding could take no more humiliation. After Fisher left his home with Elizabeth, Wilding packed his luggage and moved out, leaving his two sons in the care of their nanny.

He moved into the guestroom at the home of Joseph Cotten. The two actors had bonded during their filming of Alfred Hitchcock's *Under Capricorn* (1949) with Ingrid Bergman.

He had completed his last film for MGM. Entitled *The Scarlet Coat* (1955), it was a tedious and unconvincing historical drama set against a backdrop of the American Revolutionary War. In it, Wilding played a stiff and formal British military officer.

The "rebel" in the film was the handsome bisexual actor, Cornel Wilde, a sort of poor man's Errol Flynn, who was always revealing his body-beautiful chest. Wilde had had a fling with Laurence Olivier when he'd toured America playing Tybalt, Juliet's hot-tempered cousin and the rival to Romeo as portrayed by Olivier. Known for his portrayals of swashbucklers, Wilde piqued Wilding's sexual interest. The crew seemed well aware of their mutual "dressing room seduction," and word on the set was "Wilde is wild about Wilding." Their brief fling barely survived the completion of the picture, however.

Cornel Wilde
"Wilde is wild about Wilding"

In the midst of their divorce proceedings, Wilding moved into a modest two-room apartment on Sunset Boulevard, claiming "that a bottle of vodka is my only companion."

Another blow came when he was summoned to Benny Thau's office at MGM. This time, he was not offered another picture. "Let's face it, Wilding," Thau told him. "You're no longer Mr. Elizabeth Taylor.

Your contract is up. You're out the door. Now leave. I've got more important business to attend to, like what to do with Debbie Reynolds."

Despondent, almost suicidal, Wilding was rescued by Hollywood agent Jerry Hogan, who brought him into his business organization as a partner. Wilding was miscast in his job as an agent, but Elizabeth graciously agreed to become his client for a while, and she'd later bring him in on some film contracts signed by Richard Burton.

Eventually, Wilding returned to his native England, which he'd left as a big star to marry Elizabeth. "My return was bleak," he said. "Although I had left Hollywood as a black-listed actor, I returned to England as a forgotten one."

In time, Wilding would marry the British socialite Susan Nell, but that marriage failed. Perhaps he found his true and compatible mate the final time around, when he wed the very talented, elegant, and almost aristocratic actress, Margaret Leighton. She encouraged his desire to be a painter. He married her in 1963 and was at her side and still married to her when she died in 1976.

Having grown up in the British theater, which was peopled by homosexuals or bisexuals, Leighton was very understanding of the same-sex impulse in men. Wilding did not conceal from her the fact that he on occasion patronized "rent boys" in London's Soho district.

Leighton's primary embarrassment came when a gay underground rag published an interview with a teenaged hustler who stated, "Michael Wilding swore on a stack of Bibles that he preferred fucking my bum to mounting that overworked, abused, and tired-out twat of that has-been actress, Elizabeth Taylor, who is fat as a sow right before slaughter time."

***

After those hectic premieres, Todd made an ill-fated decision to take Elizabeth on a vacation. Both of them flew to Nassau in The Bahamas, where the British press baron, Lord Beaverbrook, invited them on a yachting trip.

Before she embarked, Elizabeth told a Bahamian reporter, "This is the happiest day of my life," a line she would often repeat. But her happiness would have the life span of a sickly butterfly.

During the initial stage of the cruise, she'd been drinking heavily, downing champagne beginning at ten o'clock in the morning.

She decided to go below deck and sleep it

Margaret Leighton

off. As she was going down the yacht's steps, the boat lurched. "I fell six steps on my fat ass," she'd later recall. She was overcome with excruciating pain and screamed for help.

Todd carried her into a stateroom and placed her on the bed. She was at this point sobbing in pain.

He didn't trust any of the local hospitals, and he chartered a plane in Fort Lauderdale that flew them on to New York. Elizabeth had to be carried on and off the plane. She was checked into the Harkness Pavilion of the Columbia-Presbyterian Hospital.

After a series of tests, Dr. John Lattimer, one of New York's leading orthopedic surgeons, told Todd that his wife-to-be would require a delicate operation. Several of her spinal disks had been crushed. Her left leg was numb and had started to atrophy. There was grave danger of paralysis and, possibly, amputation.

During a four-hour operation on December 8, 1956, the doctor had to remove dead bone right down to the spinal cord's nerve center. He then surgically removed bone from her hip and pelvis, out of which he fashioned "little matchsticks" that he assembled into a cluster that later calcified into a unified whole. After two months of recovery, this mass of bone fragments had fused into a six-inch "hybrid" component within her spinal column, allowing her to walk again.

The pain was so great that at times that she would pass out. She required care around the clock. Friends such as Monty came to visit, and she expressed one of her greatest fears: "I'm going to spend the rest of my life in a wheelchair."

Todd treated every event in his life as a publicity circus. Renting the room immediately adjacent to hers in the hospital, he issued hourly press briefings.

The doctor also told Todd that Elizabeth was pregnant. That bit of news—that Todd's twenty-four-year-old bride-to-be was expecting a child out of wedlock—did not get inserted into any of Todd's briefings to the press.

To Monty, to whom she still confided her most personal secrets, she admitted, "I don't know. I think it is Mike's child…"

"Mike Wilding's?"

"No, Mike Todd's. But maybe Eddie Fisher, maybe even Victor Mature. If he grows up to be Samson, we'll know it's Vic's kid."

Horrified at the prospect of bad publicity over a child arriving too early, Todd, through his lawyers, arranged for Elizabeth's quickie Mexican divorce, which Wilding agreed to.

To expedite the divorce, Wilding was flown to Mexico. As he told Todd, "I'm a pauper." Todd offered him $200,000 for his cooperation. "As you know, my baby is growing every day in Elizabeth, and you are aware of how provincial the Americans are about such things."

To further entice cooperation from Wilding, Elizabeth offered him all the proceeds from the sale of the Benedict Canyon house—and not a fifty-fifty split.

In a touch of irony, the first buyer who came to inspect the Taylor/Wilding home was Ingrid Bergman. Her Hollywood career had been temporarily put "into the deep freeze" after she had a baby fathered by Roberto Rossellini during the course of her marriage to the Swedish doctor Petter Lindstrom. Bergman was not impressed with the unhappy abode and rejected the idea of buying the house. "It is not suitable," she said, before rushing out the door.

Leaving her hospital bed within the Columbia-Presbyterian Hospital's Harkness Pavilion on January 21, 1957, Elizabeth flew with Todd to Mexico City. Both of them dined with Wilding that night. As Elizabeth recalled, "He could not have been more gracious. After all, money talks."

To their deep regret, the local judge refused their divorce petitions at first. Todd met privately with him and threatened to kill "the god damn fucking wetback son of a bitch." The judge finally agreed to the divorce. Dick Hanley said, "Pesos, a lot of pesos, exchanged hands."

In Mexico City, the divorce came through. Todd announced to the world that he would marry Elizabeth on February 2, 1957 in the Mexican village of Puerto Marquez, near Acapulco.

Joseph Cotten called Wilding and told him about the upcoming marriage which he had heard about on the TV news. Wilding asked Cotten, "Don't you think Elizabeth might have had the consideration to wait until the funeral meats grew cold?"

For the wedding, Todd must have imagined that he was producing another epic like *Around the World in 80 Days*. He ordered one hundred bushels of white orchids flown in, along with 15,000 yellow gladioli. He stocked fifty cases of champagne, and for the wedding feast, imported barrels of baby lobsters, cracked crabs, and tureens of Iranian caviar.

Jazz musicians were imported from New York, and local mariachi bands were booked, for which bandstands had to be constructed.

Local chefs were hired to prepare an array of Mexican specialties such as roast chicken in chocolate sauce. Each of the wedding guests was given a sports shirt to wear: Female guests received versions sporting the initials E.T.T., male guests received versions with the initials M.T.

Kerosene torches were installed to light the night. Hundreds of coconuts were cut in half, later to be filled with champagne.

Since Elizabeth was Protestant, no rabbi they knew at the time would perform a religious ceremony. Todd therefore prevailed upon the mayor of Acapulco, Mario Lepotoguí, to officiate at a civil service.

Eddie Fisher flew in as the ceremony's Best Man, and his increasingly estranged wife, Debbie Reynolds, was designated as Elizabeth's Matron of Honor.

Once again, Elizabeth's favorite designer, Helen Rose, was hauled in to design a stunning wedding gown fashioned from hydrangea blue chiffon. "This is getting to be a habit with me," Rose said.

Sara and Francis Taylor flew in, as did Elizabeth's brother, Howard, and his wife, Mara. Michael Todd, Jr., the son Todd had produced with his first wife, Bertha Freshman, also went to Mexico with his wife, Sarah.

The bridegroom presented Elizabeth with an $80,000 diamond bracelet as a wedding present. For entertainment, Todd already had as his best friend one of the most popular singers in America, Fisher himself, who gave his vocal rendition of the "Mexican Wedding Song."

"Elizabeth had downed two bottles of champagne and was drunk," Dick Hanley said. "She didn't walk down the aisle, she had to be carried down. After they were pronounced man and wife, she had to be hauled out of the wedding ceremony by two beefy security guards. That baby she was carrying probably was going to be an alcoholic before it was born."

Rose later recalled the reception. "Here was this crippled and pregnant lady feasting on roast suckling pig and baby lobsters and all those tamales and enchiladas. She drank champagne until midnight when she came down with stomach cramps, which she blamed on the cracked crabs."

The next morning at around eleven, Fisher was called to their bridal suite, where he found Todd and Elizabeth drinking more champagne. Each of them, with Elizabeth looking especially voluptuous, was lying nude atop pink sheets.

Reynolds later recalled, "Eddie loved it, and I knew he did even though I wasn't invited. It made him part of the marriage. It was what he wanted that he didn't have with me."

Fisher later reported that Elizabeth and Todd fought every day for weeks on end."The gal's been looking for trouble all her life, but everyone was too timid to fight back," Todd said. "They kept her on a milktoast diet. With me, I fed her red meat. When she flies into a tantrum, I fly into a bigger one. We fight because we love it. When she's mad, she looks so beautiful, I take her in my arms and smother her with kisses. Naturally, that leads to other things."

Fisher later said, "I think Elizabeth likes to be hit. I know that sounds crazy. But she and Mike had a violent relationship. Call it foreplay."

One reporter came to interview Todd in Los Angeles, and found him sitting around the swimming pool naked. Halfway through the interview, Elizabeth opened the second-floor window and called down to Todd. "Get your ass back in this bedroom," she shouted at him. "I want you to fuck me this minute!"

Elizabeth later wrote, "What sweet craziness it was to be married to Mike Todd. He translated the impossible life I had been living on the screen to reality. He had a great gift of showmanship and a great heart as well. On the surface, he seemed to be rough, tough, and gruff, but it was an act. He was gentle and honest, with a deeply ingrained integrity that belied his flamboyant exterior. Every woman should have a Mike Todd in her life."

What she didn't know when she said that was that it would be a short marriage, lasting only eighteen months.

"Each of them burned the candle at both ends, and it was destined to flicker out," said Dick. "Such intensity, such fire, could not last forever."

***

For a year, Elizabeth did not appear on the screen in the wake of her hit movie, *Giant.* Her new role was that of a globe-trotting bride, who was secretly pregnant and ensnared within the orbit of a cigar-chomping entrepreneur, that extravagant showman, Mike Todd.

Even though she wasn't making movies, Todd turned her into a media event unlike anything she'd experienced before. Wherever they went in the world—America, Europe, Asia, Australia—he alerted the paparazzi and newspaper reporters. It was a rare day when Mr. and Mrs. Mike Todd didn't appear on the frontpages of newspapers somewhere in the world.

"Elizabeth was turned into a media circus," said Dick Hanley, Todd's new secretary. "For the next twelve years, even beyond, she would be the most written about female personality on the planet, challenged only by Jackie Kennedy when she moved into the White House. Elizabeth and Jackie vied for who would grace magazine covers, and Elizabeth didn't endear herself to the First Lady when she kept telling friends, 'I got to Jack long before Jackie ever got her mangy paws into him.'"

Everything Elizabeth said or did, however trivial, was deemed worthy of a headline. When there was no story about her, some journalist made one up. She appeared on the covers of enough magazines to fill a warehouse.

What had been originally conceived as an extended honeymoon evolved into a world tour to promote *Around the World in 80 Days* in cities as diverse as Rome, London, Paris, Tokyo, and Moscow.

Biographer Brenda Maddox wrote about Elizabeth's new media *persona.* "Todd changed Taylor from a dull movie beauty into an international celebrity whose sybaritic life and loves became a running news story, and into the archetypical star goddess who takes her public with her to the very brink of death. He woke Taylor up sexually, professionally, and financially."

With their honeymoon in Mexico behind them, Todd didn't like that he and Elizabeth would have to depend on commercial airliners to get around the country.

Before leaving Los Angeles, Todd purchased a private Lockheed Lodestar, an aircraft he christened *The Lucky Liz*. The Lodestar was the same type of aircraft that another of Elizabeth's suitors, Howard Hughes, had used to fly around the world in 1939.

In an extravagant gesture, Todd spent $25,000 on the airplane's bedroom, boasting that "it is the only plane in the world with a double bed. Yet he was very penny-pinching when he was confronted with safety features, spending only $2,000 for an overhaul of the antiquated anti-icing system, which would prove to be a fatal mistake.

As a private joke to reporters, he said, "I plan to begin the penetration the moment we're airborne over California, reaching my climax at Idlewild in New York. As *The Lucky Liz* hits the runway for that final bump, bump, it will help me reach the ultimate depth."

Of course, although many reporters laughed at the innuendos, no newspaper at the time would print such a remark.

En route to New York in *The Lucky Liz,* the Todds landed in Chicago in February of 1957, where he presented Elizabeth with another wedding present, "His and Her theaters—yes, her own movie house, which would become a good source of revenue for her in the years ahead.

Then it was on to New York. Once there, they were seen in all the top restaurants, such as "21," and in many of the chic nightclubs. The couple was also spotted in jewelry stores along Fifth Avenue. "A girl can never own too many rubies, diamonds, and emeralds," Elizabeth told the press.

After the whirlwind activities of New York, Elizabeth and Todd landed in Palm Springs. Her longtime friend, Marion Davies, had given the Todds the use of her desert villa for a month. On several occasions, Frank Sinatra entertained the battling couple. "You remind me of the fights Ava and I used to have," the singer said.

Todd invited best friend Eddie Fisher and his increasingly alienated wife, Debbie Reynolds, to visit them in Palm Springs. Fisher was used to witnessing physical violence between Elizabeth and her new husband. But one Saturday night, Reynolds was shocked at what she saw: "Mike knocked her to the floor, really clobbered her. I mean, he *really* hit her. She screamed but rose to her feet and walloped him right back, He dragged her by the hair as she screamed at him and kicked him. He succeeded in dragging her across the room. I went running after him, jumping on his back to help her. The two of them were slapping each other. My heart was pounding. The next thing I knew, they were wrestling on the floor, kissing and making up. Suddenly, I'm like the cop on the beat in a wife-beating case where the cop gets it. They both got mad at me for interfering. Elizabeth telling me, 'Debbie, you're such a little Girl Scout. Grow up!'"

Leaving their desert lair, Mike and Elizabeth returned to Hollywood for the 1957 Oscar presentations. "I'm a royal princess," she announced to reporters, wearing a $25,000 diamond tiara he'd pressed to her.

That night, she was preening proud when Todd walked off with an Oscar for Best Picture for his *Around the World in 80 Days.* Her husband's picture was in a neck-to-neck contest with *Giant,* her own star picture from Warner Brothers. But against her own career interests, she was rooting for *80 Days.* Ironically it would be Todd's picture that would bring her millions to spend—and lots and lots of jewelry.

Her discarded beau, Kevin McClory, was at the presentation, He went backstage to congratulate Todd and Elizabeth. She turned her back on him, no doubt having heard the vulgar remarks he'd been making about their former love affair.

McClory had spoken indiscreetly about their boudoir antics, even telling reporters, who could not print his comments, but were voyeuristically interested nonetheless.

"Elizabeth is great between the sheets," McClory asserted to reporter James Bacon. "She knows how to manipulate a male penis unlike any bitch I've ever known. She has the world's most skilled fingers and, wow, that succulent mouth of hers. She's wonderful in bed. She'll do anything, fulfill any fantasy. Some acts she'll perform you can't get a hardened whore to do."

After clearing up business matters in Los Angeles, and making arrangements for her children, Elizabeth flew with Todd to New York. Once there, she boarded the *Queen Elizabeth* with him and headed for Europe.

As they disembarked at Cherbourg in France, and swathed in champagne-colored mink, she met with reporters. Awaiting her at the pier was a $100,000 Rolls-Royce Silver Cloud for touring France. Todd had already familiarized himself with the names and locations of many of the country's five-star resorts and restaurants for stopovers en route to the French Riviera. The car would later be shipped to Los Angeles.

He'd taken a three-month lease on Lady Kenmare's super deluxe Villa Fiorentina, paying $20,000 a month. The villa was positioned in a panoramic spot on the Côte d'Azur in one of its most chic and expensive towns, St.-Jean-Cap-Ferrat. Decades later, at the end of the 20th Century, billionaire Bill Gates would purchase the villa for $100 million.

Ironically, the first guest Todd invited was Elizabeth's divorced husband, Michael Wilding. There seemed to be no jealousy between her former and present husbands—in fact, Elizabeth and Wilding had comfortably settled into their brother-and-sister relationship and bonded together as parents of two growing sons.

Todd liked to invite guests, and he went for the big names, inviting three world-famous actors with links to Grace Kelly who, as Princess of Monaco, lived nearby.

David Niven arrived first. His friendship with Grace had survived their torrid love affair. His visit was followed by the arrival of Gary Cooper. He told Todd, "Grace looks like she's a cold dish with a man until you get her pants down, and then she explodes."

Finally, yet a third love from Grace Kelly's past arrived, William Holden, upon whom Elizabeth had once had a crush. He told both Todd and Elizabeth that Grace had planned to marry him until she learned that he'd had a vasectomy.

Eddie Fisher and Debbie Reynolds flew in on May 7, 1957 for the European premiere of *Around the World in 80 Days* at the Cannes Film Festival.

Arriving at the premiere, Todd bounded from the limousine but Elizabeth, in his opinion, was moving too slowly. In front of all the reporters and paparazzi, he yelled at her, "Come on, fatty, move that pachyderm ass of yours."

She immediately raised a finger to give him the "fuck you" sign.

In Cannes, he rented the Winter Casino on La Croisette, with all its Edwardian-era elegance. There, he staged a sumptuous banquet for a thousand international journalists from all continents of the world. The supper guests devoured "tons" of Beluga caviar, smoked sturgeon, and a sea of Riviera lobsters. A Cannes reporter called it "glitz and gluttony." While all of this was going on, a mammoth hot air balloon floated over Cannes to evoke his movie.

In Cannes, the world learned that Elizabeth was pregnant. At some point, she seemed to tire of the premiere and retreated to the bar of the Carlton Hotel to drink by herself. British journalist Leonard Mosley encountered her there. She made an astonishing statement: "I'm only twenty-five years old and already tired of life."

The next night, Todd rented a limousine to drive him over to the casino at Monte Carlo, where he'd also been invited to have drinks with Grace Kelly at the palace. "I guess he plans to fuck her Royal Highness, and doesn't want me along," Elizabeth told Dick Hanley, who was accompanying Todd on the excursion. Fisher had also been invited to the palace, but because he had agreed to sing three songs in the casino, he couldn't go.

Before Dick departed with Todd, Elizabeth handed him a sealed envelope to give to Todd when he reached Monte Carlo. When Todd opened the note two hours later, he passed it to Dick to read:

"Dear Mike,
Stay as long as you want in Grace's boudoir, and don't worry about me.
I have Eddie here to fuck me tonight.
Love,
Your devoted wife

Within a few days, Elizabeth had snapped out of her depression. She told *Paris-Match* "With Mike Todd, I feel we could one day own the world. He will make all of my dreams come true." She declined to answer exactly what those dreams were.

After Cannes, Todd and Elizabeth, with Dick, drove to Paris in the Silver Rolls. The producer had booked them into the Presidential Suite at the Ritz Hotel overlooking the majestic symmetry of the Place Vendôme. On his first day in Paris, Todd went to see Alexandre de Paris, the most celebrated coiffeur in France, who gave him a crewcut. Elizabeth liked it so much that she, too, visited Alexandre, who became a friend and would design many coiffures for her in the years to come.

The *haut monde* of Paris fêted the famous couple. Marie-Hélène de Rothschild staged a gala for them, introducing them to the flotsam and jetsam of international society, as Elsa Maxwell had done during her marriage to Nicky Hilton.

Mostly, Elizabeth attended the houses of the famous *couturiers* of Paris, including expensive visits to the showrooms of Yves St.-Laurent, Givenchy, Balenciaga, and Marc Bohan of Christian Dior. She arranged for Bohan to design a ruby-red chiffon gown for her to wear to the Paris premiere of *Around the World in 80 Days.*

Ruby earrings dangled from her ears, and she wore a matching ruby diadem. Bohan told the press, "Let's be honest. Miss Taylor does not have a mannequin figure. But she has a fabulous face—simply fab—and those shattering violet eyes, made even more so with all that ruby flash."

Haute fashion czarina
Diana Vreeland

Elizabeth's fascination with the House of Dior did not always meet with acclaim among fashion critics. A London-based fashion writer, Herb Dorsay, wrote, "She looks dreadful in Dior, like a call girl trying to impersonate a princess. Nothing seems to fit her right."

Diana Vreeland, America's reigning fashion diva, earned Elizabeth's lifelong animosity when she referred to her as "the worst-dressed actress in America since Mae West. Taylor lacks taste,

James Galanos *(right figure, above)*, an authority on E.T.'s "avoirdupois"

which you either have or don't have." James Galanos, a Los Angeles fashion designer, claimed, "Her *avoirdupois* has always been a problem," a grand way of referring to her weight.

In addition to paying for her wardrobe, Todd continued to spend all the money from royalties from *80 Days* as fast as it came in.

While she was in Paris, he purchased three paintings for her—a Degas, a Vuillard, and a Utrillo—for a combined price of $75,000, from the Prince Aly Khan.

He also flew Wilding in from London to stay with them at their three-bedroom suite at the Ritz. "In Paris, that raised only a few eyebrows," Dick said. "The French naturally suspected a *ménage à trois* and let it go at that. After all, these were the people who invented the term."

***

"We took our road show to England in July of 1957," Elizabeth recalled. "In London, Mike seemed to generate more publicity than the coronation of Queen Elizabeth."

"I wanted the world to know that there is another famous woman occupying the planet named Elizabeth," said Todd. "She may not be Queen Elizabeth, but I'm sure that one day, she'll at least be Dame Elizabeth."

How right he was in his forecast.

***

In London, Elizabth was told by John Gielgud that there was only one woman in England "who could equal your beauty—Princess Alexandra (aka The Honourable Lady Ogilvie), the cousin of Queen Elizabeth."

Elizabeth told Todd "I want to meet this alleged beauty." Consequently, he threw a lavish reception at Claridges for Princess Alexandra, who arrived with her mother, the Duchess of Kent (aka Princess Marina of Greece and Denmark).

As Elizabeth chatted with Princess Alexandra, she did indeed realize that she was a stunning beauty. But she could hardly have imagined that one day she would be engaged in a battle with that princess for the charms of Richard Burton.

Standing beside the princess, Marina, the Duchess of Kent, asked Elizabeth, "Are you expecting a boy or a girl?"

"A girl," Elizabeth answered. "The world is not ready for another Mike Todd."

***

When Tony Curtis was in London with Janet Leigh, Todd threw yet another party, this time honoring the wedding anniversary of a couple which had previously been widely recognized as "America's Sweethearts." America's more recent "sweethearts, Eddie Fisher and Debbie Reynolds, also showed up for the event. Fisher was also in London at the time for the opening of his act at the London Palladium.

At the time, Curtis sported a beard as one of the accessories associated with his role in *The Vikings* with Kirk Douglas, who also appeared bearded at the party. When he spotted Curtis, Noël Coward, in front of Elizabeth, rushed up to him. "Come to me, you bearded beauty."

As Elizabeth looked on, Coward kissed Curtis passionately…with tongue.

Coward later huddled with Elizabeth, telling her he wanted her to attend the opening of Wilding in his stage production of *Nude With Violin*. "I'm rehearsing him now," Coward said. "He stumbles and stammers and gets into an increasing frizz at rehearsals. But then he throws me a good fuck at the end of the night and all is forgiven. I know why you were attracted to him."

"Oh, such a sweet memory to share with me," Elizabeth said. "You're such a darling." She walked away from him and sought out Wilding.

"I must introduce you to this charming lady," Elizabeth told her former husband. She took his arm and walked with him across the room and introduced him to the heiress Susan Nell, a prominent London socialite.

"Liz almost had me married by proxy," Wilding recalled. "She raved about what a wonderful personality Susan was, so much charm, so affectionate, the perfect mate for a lonely divorced man such as myself. Liz also told me that Miss Nell 'was a millionairess in her own right.'"

After meeting Nell, Wilding began dating and eventually married her. "For a while she made me the *maître d'* of a seafood restaurant she owned in Brighton, but she soon tired of me," Wilding claimed. "We got a divorce."

At that same party, Elizabeth got a dose of Gallic charm when Louis Jourdan, once voted "the world's most handsome man," appeared. When Todd ducked out to check his stockpile of champagne, Elizabeth kissed the French actor. "One day, we'll do love scenes in a movie together," she promised him.

And so it came to be. Jourdan played the role of her lover in MGM's 1963 film *The V.I.P.s,* with Richard Burton as their co-star.

On July 2, 1957, Todd staged "a night of jubilation," to celebrate the London premiere of *Around the World in 80 Days*. He rented Battersea Gardens, a Thames-bordering park with a small-scale games arcade and amusement park.

As a means of attracting maximum press coverage, he staged the event as a charity for the Newspaper Fund, inviting some 1,500 guests, including jour-

383

nalists and some of the top names of *tout* London. Guests, including the Duchess of Argyll, were ferried across the Thames to its less-frequented, less stylish riverbank in ferryboats. Todd invited Queen Elizabeth and Prince Philip, but the monarch cabled her regrets.

Elizabeth was the belle of the ball, appearing at Battersea in a red velvet Dior gown with a plunging *décolletage* and a ruby necklace from Van Cleef & Arpels. Todd had paid $350,000 for the necklace. "It would have been the envy of Marie Antoinette had she been able to afford it," Elizabeth claimed.

As the evening deepened, and as more and more of the Fleet Street reporters became intoxicated, a journalist from the *Daily Mail* stepped on Elizabeth's gown, causing it to rip. Todd bodily picked up the reporter and tossed him into the Thames. Fortunately, the reporter wasn't too drunk to swim.

Prince Aly Khan showed up with his French mistress, a model known as "Bettina." Laurence Olivier and Vivien Leigh were seen at the event riding pink and purple circus horses. Debbie Reynolds danced the rhumba with Baron Shawcross. Shawcross had led the British team of lawyers at the Nürnberg trials for Nazi war criminals.

At one point during the evening, Dick Hanley brought Aly Khan over for "an audience" with Elizabeth. He whispered in her ear, "I should have married you instead of Rita Hayworth."

As entertainment, Todd had hired six bands and dressed the cigarette girls as can-can dancers from the Moulin Rouge in Paris.

Guests consumed some 500 "Methuselah-sized" magnums of champagne. The producer also provided gold-painted buckets stuffed with florins and shillings for guests to play the slot machines he'd imported onto the site.

Elizabeth received a proposition that evening from Douglas Fairbanks, Jr., who promised her, "I can show you what drove Joan Crawford up the wall if you'll call on me later in my suite at the Dorchester."

Lord Dalkeith was seen swinging on one of the swings designed for kindergarten children, and Mrs. Gerald Legge proved to be the Annie Oakley of the night, an all-time sharpshooter winner in the park's amusement arcades.

A reporter for *The Times* approached Elizabeth. "Please say something I can print in a family newspaper."

Slightly tipsy from too much champagne, she looked up at him. "You can tell your readers that Mike Todd is my greatest lover…perhaps the greatest lover of all time. The first time he made love to me, my heart almost stopped beating."

To feed the roiling masses assembled at Battersea, bear meat was flown in from Colorado; huge prawns from Hong Kong; chocolate-covered giant ants from Africa; curried dishes from India; homemade pastas in thirty varieties from Italy; sweet potatoes from North Carolina; egg rolls from China, and strawberries and Devonshire cream from England itself.

A dozen bars were granted one-night liquor licenses. Amazingly, many Londoners from the press ignored the champagne and guzzled pint after pint of lager, which was dispensed until dawn. *Time* magazine later wrote, "Mike Todd would pass out salted nuts at his own hanging if he owned the beer concession."

The next day, the press raved about the food. Todd had arranged with the fishmongers of Billingsgate for an array of fish and chips served in replica copies of *The Times,* dated 1893, the year the character of Phineas Fogg in *80 Days* had embarked on his trip around the world. For those who didn't want such ordinary fare, Todd had arranged a mammoth display of the most succulent oysters, lobsters, shrimp, and crab. "Elizabeth, revealing what a low-class English girl she was, went for the whelks," Todd claimed.

That morning, Elizabeth announced to Todd that she'd lost their passports. In an amazing feat, he got the American Embassy to open up on a holiday, July 4, and issue them temporary replacements. "You know I'm a big man in New York, a big man in Hollywood," he told her. "Now, after that Battersea event, I'm a big man in London. I bet the Queen wishes she'd attended."

With Dick Hanley opening the doors for them, Todd and Elizabeth were last seen departing London in their Silver Rolls, heading for Southampton and home.

***

On July 4, 1957, Todd and a pregnant Elizabeth set sail aboard the *SS Liberté,* heading for the port of New York. On their first night aboard, over caviar and champagne, he spoke of all the big plans he had for them "over the next forty years." Of course, he had no way of knowing he had only eight months to live.

During his long days at sea, Todd planned his next big film production, telling her he was going to produce and film an epic, Cervantes' *Don Quixote.*

"The fucker was a lousy novelist, but we can hire rewrite men," he told her. "Also, I'm telling the press that I plan to rent all of Spain for my production. I'll hire this artist—what's his face?—Picasso! to do the concept drawing for the advertising."

He wanted her to star as the scruffy, shrewish Dulcinea. Without reading the book, she agreed to the role.

He envisioned Cantinflas, one of the stars of *80 Days,* as Sancho Panza with Fernandel playing the role of Don Quixote. Later, he changed his mind, preferring John Huston in the title role, with the part of the bumbling Sancho Panza going to Mickey Rooney.

"Like Don Quixote pursuing the impossible dream and chasing windmills across the plains of La Mancha, nothing came of the project," said Dick Hanley.

At midpoint across the North Atlantic, all thoughts of film production ended as Elizabeth was rushed into the emergency room of the *Liberté*. She was seized with the pains of premature labor, and she shouted at the ship's two doctors, "My baby's not cooked yet! It can't come out!"

The doctors anesthetized her, thereby preventing her from giving premature birth.

Todd brought up the possibility of a Caesarean birth, but neither of the doctors felt capable of performing such a life-threatening operation. As one of them told Todd, "I don't want to go down in history as the man who killed Elizabeth Taylor and her child."

When rendered unconscious by drugs, Elizabeth's contractions stopped. Even when she disembarked from the *Liberté* in New York and was rushed to the hospital, she appeared in no immediate danger of giving birth.

She was thoroughly examined and tested by more skilled doctors, one of whom warned Todd that if his wife brought the fetus to term, it might cause her to have a permanently curved spine. An abortion was suggested, but he refused. "Not on your nelly!" he said.

In her hospital bed, a metal brace was placed on Elizabeth's always fragile back. Because of that back support, her uterus with her future baby girl had been pushed upward to a precarious position under her ribcage.

She was administered doses of digitalis (foxglove), with the intention of stimulating her heartbeat, but it became obvious that the drug was dangerously affecting the baby's heartbeat too. Todd was warned that his young wife might die unless she submitted to a dangerously premature Caesarean.

The operation was performed on October 6, 1957. In its aftermath, Elizabeth Frances (Liza) Todd entered the world, weighing four pounds, fourteen ounces. She was pronounced a stillborn. However, a resuscitationist, Dr. Virginia Apgar, rushed the baby to a resuscitator, and within fourteen minutes, she drew her first breath, although she had to be confined to an oxygen tent after that for two months.

Her doctor told Todd that because any future pregnancy might kill her, Elizabeth should have her fallopian tubes tied. As he took her hand to tell her the news, he said, "You're no Ma Kettle, baby."

Announcing the birth of his baby girl, Todd boasted to the press. "She is so beautiful, she makes her mother look like the Bride of Frankenstein. My Liz is a brave girl, and I'm currently negotiating with India to purchase a present for her: The Taj Mahal."

During her confinement to the hospital, Todd visited Howard Young, her art dealer uncle, and purchased three paintings from him—a Renoir, a Monet, and a Pissarro. However, after Todd's death, Young had to sue the estate. Todd had never paid for the valuable art he'd taken.

When Liza Todd was released from the hospital, Todd and Elizabeth in their Silver Rolls-Royce, took her to a twenty-three room mansion at Westport, Connecticut, which he'd rented for the summer. The little infant seemed to be suffering no bad effects from her premature birth.

Author Truman Capote came to visit, and he brought Elizabeth up on news about Monty Clift. "He's starting to pick up rough trade. These guys beat the shit out of him," Capote claimed. "Monty seems to enjoy it, and he's still crazy for those pills."

Before Capote left, he told her he was leaving the script of a play sent to her in his care by Tennessee Williams, with a note. "It's in your study."

In the whirlwind that encircled the Todds in the months ahead, she didn't open the script right away—in fact, she postponed it for months.

***

Returning to the Los Angeles area in September of 1957, Todd rented a Mediterranean style, twelve-room white stucco house on Schuyler Road, high up in Coldwater Canyon, overlooking Beverly Hills. Elizabeth didn't like the house, calling it "spooky and gloomy—all the fucking place needs is a resident ghost that looks like Elsa Lanchester in a Frankenstein fright wig."

When Dick Hanley came to visit, Elizabeth showed him the master bedroom. "The only thing I like about this *Sunset Blvd.* mansion is this gigantic baby blue and gold rococo bed where Killer bangs the hell out of me every night." She turned to him. "And who might be banging you these days?"

"A cute blonde Henry Willson trapped for me," Dick said. "Bland, but a real looker. Troy Donahue. Henry says he's going to be a big star. I say, when pigs fly. He's something to warm the bed at night. Not much in the breadbasket, though."

Sometimes Todd paced the floors at night, pondering their finances, or lack thereof. He'd spent all the millions generated so far from *80 Days* and hadn't saved anything. Since he was out of money, he was eager for her to return to MGM to make the two final pictures she owed the studio.

The royalties were still coming in, however, and in a few weeks, his son, Michael Todd, Jr., sent him a check for two million dollars. Todd wanted to spend it right away. "He never could hold onto money," Elizabeth later recalled. He decided to invest these newly arrived royalties on a big publicity blast at Madison Square Garden in Manhattan and on another around-the-world tour, hoping to generate even more millions abroad.

She had hardly settled into her new quarters before Todd announced they were going on the road again. Somewhat reluctantly, she agreed and stashed her children with nannies. On October 17, 1957, Elizabeth and Todd were back in New York to celebrate the first anniversary of the release of *Around the World in 80 Days.* For the occasion, Todd rented New York City's Madison Square Garden for a private party, the same venue where he'd once hired Marilyn Monroe to make a spectacular appearance riding on top of a pink elephant.

On the morning of the party, Todd announced to the press, "This will be the biggest god damn birthday bash the world has ever seen." In contrast, he also told reporters, "I'm throwing an intimate party for a few chums." In all, including gatecrashers, the party would attract 18,000 people.

For the event, Elizabeth in her own words, "tried to make myself look like the Empress Josephine," wearing a designer red velvet gown with a diamond tiara. "Call me Napoléon's midnight delight," she jokingly told the press.

Instead of Monroe, Todd coaxed the distinguished British actor, Sir Cedric Hardwicke, to ride into the arena on an elephant, although he nearly fell off and broke his neck. Fernandel, the famous French comedian and actor, was the headliner on the evening's cabaret bill. Todd also announced that Fernandel had been selected as the star who'd play Don Quixote in his next film epic.

Todd didn't want to spend any of his money if he could get other companies, especially those selling food and drink, to supply a staggering amount of freebies for the throngs pouring into the garden. To help defray other costs, he contracted with CBS to pay him $300,000 to film the event, which would be narrated by the newscaster Walter Cronkite. "It was the nadir of my career," Cronkite later recalled.

After seeing the Garden and its decorations, a journalist from Minnesota wrote: "Mike Todd and Elizabeth Taylor are the leading vulgarians of America."

At one end of the garden stood a forty-foot tall replica of "Oscar," crafted with a sheathing of gold chrysanthemums, evoking Todd's (and *80 Days'*) Academy Award for Best Picture of the Year. Over the heads of the revelers floated a mammoth hot air balloon.

To mingle with the *hoi polloi,* Todd also invited A-list guests. Amazingly, both Ginger Rogers and Janet Gaynor accepted invitations to the *mélée.* The master party giver herself, Elsa Maxwell, joined the list of guests that inevitably included the nosy Hedda Hopper. Beatrice Lillie showed up with her girlfriend Ethel Merman. Walter Winchell, Shelley Winters, and Tony Curtis were among the thousands of guests. Others included Steve Allen, Jayne Meadows, and Bert Lahr.

To join them, Todd cajoled the King of Siam to donate forty exotic cats in cages. Circus animals, including lions, tigers, and elephants were also placed around the Garden in cages. The uproar caused the elephants to panic. "Oh, my god," Elizabeth shouted. "Are we still filming *Elephant Walk?* "

Dozens of prizes were awarded, including four new Oldsmobiles and forty mink stoles. The grand prize was a Cessna two-seater private plane. Valuable pieces of jewelry were also among the coveted prizes of the evening.

George Jessel, "Toastmaster of America," was the emcee that night, appearing before thirty-five million TV viewers. He was followed by the famous clown, Emmett Kelly

Elizabeth was placed next to Senator Hubert Humphrey, who had been hired to make a speech at the event. The day before, Humphrey had rehearsed the final version of his speech before Todd and Elizabeth in their hotel suite. Not knowing who he was, she interrupted him. "Your speech is shit. It's so fucking corny."

Todd called her into the bedroom. "For god's sake, woman, cool it. This man is going to become President of the United States. With him in the Oval Office, we'll have a permanent suite at the White House."

The highlight of the evening was the arrival of a birthday cake, symbolizing the movie's first anniversary, weighing one ton. Todd had ordered the icing to be pale blue in color—"better for the TV cameras." The fourteen-tier cake had consumed 2,000 eggs and $15,000 worth of batter.

Elizabeth, because of her bad back, had to climb a ladder to cut the first piece. She almost lost her footing and nearly fell into this mammoth glob. Those who managed to get a slice of the cake pronounced it inedible.

The cake cutting signaled the debut of a food fight on the floor, where waiters had been selling what was supposed to be free champagne at ten dollars a glass. Chic women in designer gowns ended up fighting sanitation workers for hot dogs with mustard. Melted ice cream cones in the aisle caused slippery floors and several slides. Pizzas were rammed into the faces of guests, and a bonbon war broke out. Guests were pelted; garments ripped and torn.

Duke Ellington and his band tried to play for dancing, but there was not room on the floor. Thus, in lieu of dance tunes, Todd ordered him to play "The Star Spangled Banner."

TV's John Crosby claimed, "While Todd fiddles, New York burns." On stage, baton twirlers from Dallas went wild. Instead of catching their batons, they became missiles when the girls in red, white, and blue costumes threw them high overhead and into the audience.

The following morning, the manager of

Elizabeth Taylor to presidential hopeful (*photo above*) **Hubert Humphrey,** not realizing who he was: "Your speech is shit...it's so f...cking corny!"

Madison Square Garden presented Todd with a clean-up bill which witnesses defined as "massive."

What was to have been Todd's greatest public relations triumph ended in disaster. The press mocked both Todd and Elizabeth.

Not to be intimidated, he announced to her, "Fuck New York, we'll take our show on a world tour where we are more appreciated."

***

After the debacle at Madison Square Garden, Todd and Elizabeth set out on another world tour in November of 1957. Before she left New York, she fell in the bathtub, slipping on a bar of soap, injuring her back once again. She had to be carried aboard an Air France jet before its takeoff from New York's Laguardia airport.

That night, they flew to France to begin a trip that would take them to Stockholm, Oslo, Sydney, Hong Kong, Tokyo, London, and the most controversial stop of all, Moscow.

In Paris, Todd announced, "Napoléon and Hitler didn't succeed in conquering Russia, but I will. In fact, I may bring an end to the Cold War with this goodwill tour. My secret weapon is Elizabeth Taylor."

Before they flew out of New York, Secretary of State John Foster Dulles sent Todd an urgent telegram, pleading with him not to go to Moscow. The Secretary felt that the Todds were such explosive personalities that they might cause damage to already tense U.S./Soviet relations   .

J. Edgar Hoover at the FBI had previously sent Dulles an urgent letter, in which he claimed that Todd was a secret Communist. "He is planning to use Elizabeth Taylor as a propaganda tool against the West."

Todd had written to the Soviet Minister of Culture, urging a private meeting between Nikita Khrushchev and Elizabeth and himself. The Minister gave him the brush-off and did not respond.

Leaving Paris, Todd told the press, "Elizabeth and I lead the simple life. She pours her own Dom Perignon, and I make my own Beluga caviar sandwiches."

After a tour of many countries, including "Down Under," Elizabeth and Todd flew into Prague on January 26, 1958. She told the communist press that she had specifically written to Khrushchev, "demanding that he see Mike and me."

As the plane landed in Moscow, Todd, with Elizabeth at his side, announced that his next big epic was going to be a film version of Tolstoy's *War and Peace,* which would star Elizabeth. Then he denounced director King Vidor's 1956 version of *War and Peace* that had starred Audrey Hepburn and Henry Fonda.

"I will make the authentic version."

Since the Soviet Union did not allow her American films to be shown, Elizabeth found that she was virtually unknown in Russia, even though she dressed like a movie star in ermine, diamonds, and red boots. One fan at the airport asked for her autograph, thinking she must be Marilyn Monroe.

With no private meeting with Khrushchev in the offing, Todd managed to bribe their way into a reception hosted by the Embassy of India, where Khrushchev would be an honored guest.

Dripping in diamonds, Elizabeth arrived at the event in a black cocktail dress sparkling with sequins and with a broadtail fur trim.

She and Todd received a brief handshake from the Soviet dictator, but no particular recognition. A journalist from Sweden wrote that, "Khrushchev must have thought that one of the Romanov princesses had returned from their mass grave."

Elizabeth managed to get her fill of black caviar and chicken Kiev before retreating back to their hotel.

After Moscow, Elizabeth and Todd flew into Belgrade, Yugoslavia, where they had begun to see themselves as traveling American ambassadors of good will. Todd had run into trouble with plans to move ahead with *War and Peace,* so he announced to the press that he was going to remake *Anna Karenina,* one of Greta Garbo's best films. Of course, Elizabeth would star as Anna.

At Belgrade's airport, she asked for a Scotch and soda, finding that she had to settle instead for a fiery *slivotz* which "caused me nearly to choke to death."

She celebrated when her plane flew into Nice. Back on the French Riviera again, she proclaimed it as "a return to civilization."

She told the press, "I don't want to be a movie star anymore. Acting was just a hobby for me."

At long last, by December 17, 1957, she was in Palm Springs, where she entered the hospital to have her appendix removed.

Todd was depressed, telling reporters, "I'm nothing more than a god damn nurse. Life with Elizabeth is a series of hospital visits."

She was furious when this comment was published, but the Todds made up, as they usually did, and by March of 1958, they were settled into Los Angeles once again.

Director Josh Logan visited them, discussing with both of them the possibility of Elizabeth playing Nellie Forbush in the movie version of the Broadway hit, *South Pacific.* Todd urged Elizabeth to go for it.

The next day, she appeared before composer Richard Rodgers for an audition. "She didn't sing," he later said. "She croaked. I'd rather give the role of Nellie to Marjorie Main."

As they were leaving the studio, Todd and Elizabeth encountered Doris

Day.

"Why are you here?" Todd demanded to know.

"To test for the role of Nellie," Day said.

She, too, was rejected for the part, as were both Jane Powell and Janet Blair. The role of Nellie in the film version eventually went to Mitzi Gaynor.

Recovering from her back pain in her study, Elizabeth finally got around to opening the script Truman Capote had left at the Westport rental home.

"Get well, Elizabeth," Tennessee Williams had scribbled. "The role of Maggie the Cat is waiting for you. Sharpen those claws of yours."

Boudoir games and dynastic politics: **Paul Newman** with **Elizabeth Taylor** in
Cat on a Hot Tin Roof

CHAPTER SEVENTEEN
Eddie Fisher
MATING GAMES WITH THE JEWISH SINATRA

Hollywood gossip columnists buzzed with excitement at the teaming of Elizabeth with Paul Newman in the film version of a hot play by America's leading playwright.

"When the man with the glacial blue eyes meets the girl with the eyes of a spring violet, the great movie romance of the century will surely unfold," one columnist wrote. "How can two such sex symbols resist the magnetism of each other?"

Many stars had wanted to star in the film version of *Cat on a Hot Tin Roof.* George Cukor had agreed to direct. At one point, he interpreted the adaptation of the Tennessee Williams drama as an ideal vehicle for Vivien Leigh (though she was too old) opposite Montgomery Clift. Paul Newman and Elvis Presley were among those considered for the male lead of Brick.

After purchasing the film rights for *Cat on a Hot Tin Roof,* MGM feared problems with the homoerotic subtext of its script. The explosive drama about a neurotic Southern plantation family had enthralled Broadway, but MGM felt it needed to "launder" this Pulitzer Prize-winning drama and remove any suspicion that Brick was a closeted homosexual still in love with his dead buddy, Skipper.

Cukor had angered officials at MGM when he announced to the press that the movie adaptation would have to deal up front with the issue of homosexuality. The battle heated up between Cukor and the studio, and the director eventually withdrew, asserting that he could not maintain the integrity of the Williams play because of the censorship imposed. In his place, Richard Brooks was designated as the film's more compliant director.

With Cukor off the picture, so went the focus on casting Leigh as Maggie the Cat. Just as she'd done in *Elephant Walk,* Elizabeth replaced Leigh as the female lead.

Shooting on *Cat* began on March 12, 1958, when Elizabeth showed up on the set to meet the other members of the cast. Coming together with Newman, she said, "You're more beautiful in person than on the screen, if such a thing is possible."

"You took the words out of my mouth," he said. "Surely, you are the most beautiful woman in the world, maybe in the universe for all I know."

"Your flattery will get you everywhere," she said. "If I were naming a perfume after you, I'd call it *Temptation.*"

"If I were naming a perfume after you, I'd call it *Enchantment.*"

"Come on, kids, break it up," said the film's new director, Richard Brooks, who was observing this interchange at the time. Elizabeth felt comfortable working with him. He'd helmed her through *The Last Time I Saw Paris* in 1954, and he'd later marry one of her best friends, Jean Simmons.

Before introducing Elizabeth to the rest of the cast, Brooks invited Newman and her to lunch in the MGM commissary. Over a club sandwich, Elizabeth asked Brooks, "Did Lana Turner really want to play Maggie?"

"She did indeed," the director said. "She's seriously pissed off at both you and me."

"It seems I'm always taking something from Lana," she said. "Usually a man."

"Had Monty accepted the role of Brick, he would be eating lunch with you today instead of me," Newman said.

"Had Grace Kelly not run off and married a prince, Maggie the Cat would be blonde—and not me," she said.

In the words of Brooks, Elizabeth "behaved like a queen when she was introduced to her fellow cast members."

Burl Ives was cast as "Big Daddy," the very Southern patriarch of the Pollitt family. As the film opens, he's the only member of his clan who hasn't been told he's dying of cancer. His dysfunctional family gathers around him for last rites.

Ironically, Ives was only one year older than the actor who had been cast as his son in the movie, Jack Carson, who interpreted the role of Gooper. The brilliant lesbian actress, Judith Anderson, tackled the role of Big Momma, with Madeleine Sherwood playing Gooper's social-climbing, child-bearing wife, May. Gooper and May want Big Daddy's millions and the plantation, too. Their quintet of children (identified early in the script as "no-neck monsters") run amok amid the antiques and fine carpets of the Pollitt mansion.

Over lunch, Brooks delivered disappointing news to his stars. MGM had rejected the first, very provocative, draft of the script. In that original version, Brick confesses his homosexuality and his undying love for Skipper to his wife.

"You've got to understand my dilemma," Brooks said. "The Production Code doesn't even allow us to mention the word 'homosexual' on the screen."

At this point, they were joined at table by James Poe, a writer who was working with Brooks to craft a more acceptable version of the Williams play.

Elizabeth knew Poe because he'd worked with Mike Todd on the script of *Around the World in 80 Days*. Both Poe and Brooks later became sources of information about the relationship between Elizabeth and Newman during the filming of *Cat on a Hot Tin Roof*.

In many scenes during the early part of the film, the script called for Newman to appear topless, wearing only the bottom of his pajamas. He'd have to hobble around on a crutch, having broken his leg one gung-ho drunken night while running the hurdle at his old *alma mater*. He was trying to recapture the days of football glory he had shared with his deceased friend Skipper, for whom he is still in deep mourning, trying to drown his sorrows with liquor.

In the filmed, watered-down version of *Cat*, Maggie lies to the family, especially to Big Daddy, asserting (falsely) that she is pregnant. In the final stages of the script, Brick, as played by Newman, backs her up in her lie. He is seen throwing his pillow into a position beside Maggie's on the bed. The movie comes to an end as they are about to have a "horizontal reconciliation," with the implication that he will penetrate her and that they will actually make that baby whose birth has already been publicly announced by Maggie. As part of the film's happy ending, previous wrongdoings and misunderstandings fade away.

As lunch in the commissary came to an end, Newman turned to Brooks and Poe, saying, "I'll leave it up to you guys, as the writers, to show this shit to Tennessee."

Brooks tried to salvage the mood at the end of the luncheon with some good news: Whereas MGM had originally opted to shoot the picture, budgeted at two million dollars, in black and white, Brooks and Mike Todd had persuaded the studio to shoot it in Technicolor, if for no other reason than to show off the beautiful eyes of the two leading stars.

Film director
Richard Brooks

***

The early rapport established between Newman and Elizabeth did not last through the film's early rehearsals. "She's totally lifeless working with me,"

Newman told Brooks. "We have no chemistry at all. She's holding back."

When the actual filming began, and after Newman had seen the rushes, he revised his opinion of Elizabeth. "The moment the camera is turned on her, she becomes radiant," he said. "She's a much better actress than I ever imagined. I've never seen anything like it. She's a true film actress, not appropriate for the stage."

From the very beginning, Brooks was pleased with Newman's work on the screen. "Even though we were forced to remove a lot of the motivation from Paul's character, he pulled it off with his cool detachment cast opposite the hot-to-trot Maggie. In spite of the weakness of the script, Paul would succeed in making Brick a creditable character, if not always properly motivated."

Mike Todd showed up on the set one day, introducing himself to Newman. He, too, had seen the rushes and thought Elizabeth "has never been better." He made no comment on Newman's performance.

"I completely changed my mind about her," Todd told Newman. "I didn't want her to play Maggie the Cat. I even flew her to London to see Kim Stanley when she was appearing as Maggie in the West End. I took Elizabeth backstage and tried to get Kim to convince her that the role was not for her."

"And why not?" Newman asked. "She's great as Maggie."

"I know that now," Todd said, "but originally I had one serious objection. I said, 'No one's gonna believe that any man—even if gay—would turn down the chance to fuck Elizabeth Taylor.'"

After only a few days of shooting, Elizabeth developed a severe head cold. She was running a dangerous fever and had to be sent home in a limousine. Brooks and Newman learned the next day that her illness had evolved into pneumonia.

Executives at MGM were anxious for Elizabeth to complete *Cat*, for which she was being paid $125,000, according to the terms of her contract. But that contract was running out and slated to expire on June 1, 1958. After that, it was speculated that Elizabeth could command far more money on her next picture—at least $350,000, perhaps a lot more.

Newman was still being paid the small salary in force as part of his original contract. Warners had asked MGM for only $25,000 for lending him out as the star of *Cat*. In contrast, Tennessee Williams was getting $450,000 for the screen rights to his play.

Brooks was the first to inform Newman that he'd have to shoot around Elizabeth until she recovered enough to come back onto the set. "I know her," he said. "She's very fragile, a woman of delicate health. I feared something like this might happen. A head cold was bad enough, but pneumonia could threaten her life. I've just come from a meeting at MGM. They're so worried that Elizabeth won't be able to finish *Cat* that they've called Carroll Baker's agent to see if she could be made available."

"I don't think it'll come to that," Newman said in astonishment.

"Let's face it: Elizabeth could die," Brooks said. "I've always had this intuition. I can smell death in the air."

***

On February 28, 1958, Todd had given a small birthday party for Elizabeth and included just a few friends. She didn't want some big event for the celebration of this, her twenty-sixth year. Eddie Fisher was invited, as were David Niven and his wife, Hjordis. Art Cohn showed up and Todd uncorked a bottle of champagne to celebrate Cohn's completion of his biography, *The Nine Lives of Mike Todd.*

The producer dominated the evening's conversations, talking about how wonderful Elizabeth was in the role of Maggie the Cat, "A sure-fire Oscar bet," Todd predicted. He was filled with life and plans for the future, including the filming of his upcoming epic, *Don Quixote.*

He told his guests that he and Elizabeth were going to board *The Lucky Liz* and fly to New York the following month. "I've painted the bedroom aboard our plane violet to match my little darling's beautiful eyes." Some 1,200 guests were scheduled to attend a Friars' Club dinner at the Waldorf-Astoria in Manhattan, honoring him as "Showman of the Year." The guest list was impressive. It included New York State Governor Averell Harriman, U.S. Attorney General Herbert Brownell, and distinguished stage and film stars such as Sir Laurence Olivier.

But just before departure, Elizabeth was too sick to make the trip. Not wanting to go alone, Todd invited Kirk Douglas, Eddie Fisher, director Joseph Mankiewicz, and comedian Joe E. Lewis to accompany him. He even asked Richard Brooks to take the weekend off from directing *Cat on a Hot Tin Roof.* But each of the men he invited had another commitment.

AP reporter James Bacon originally accepted the invitation to go to New York, but an hour before departure, he called Todd and turned it down. "I urged him not to go," said Bacon. "It was the worst night I could ever remember in Los Angeles, with torrential rain, thunder, and 'second coming' lightning."

Cohn, Todd's biographer, whom he defined as "my second best pal

Elizabeth Taylor and **Mike Todd** aboard her dangerous namesake

after Eddie," told him that he was free to fly to New York with him.

Todd had also dragooned Dick Hanley into flying with him. However, at the airport, Todd changed his mind and instructed Dick, "Go back to my beautiful broad. She's sick and might need you."

Before takeoff, Todd placed a final call to Elizabeth. "I love you, Lizzie Schwartzkopf. You're beautiful, doll. Remember, save those sugartits for your loving man."

Elizabeth later told Dick, "Mike may have had a fear that something dreadful might happen. He came back into my bedroom and kissed me goodbye five different times before leaving."

She pleaded with her husband to postpone his late-night departure until dawn, but he assured her he'd be safe.

"The night was very Macbethian," she recalled. "He didn't want to leave me. He said, 'I'm too happy. When a man is as happy as I am, something goes wrong.' I tried to go with him, but my doctor, Rex Kennamer, absolutely forbade it. When Mike left, my fever shot up dangerously."

Embarking on the final flight of his life, Todd flew out of Burbank Airport at 10:11pm on March 21, 1958.

He had promised Elizabeth that he would telephone her from Albuquerque, New Mexico, where his pilot planned to stop for refueling. It was a call that never came in. He also promised to call from Kansas City, where he planned to pick up Jack Benny for the ongoing segment of the flight to New York. Throughout the eastbound route, the pilot and passengers encountered heavy thunderstorms, lightning, and strong headwinds.

A report of what happened next was made available on April 17, 1959, nearly a year later, by the Civil Aeronautics Board (CAB). An urgent message was received from *The Lucky Liz* by the night air traffic controller at Winslow, Arizona. The pilot, William S. Verner, requested clearance to climb to an altitude of 13,000 feet. The *Liz* was flying at 11,000 feet, and its wings were icing. The controller granted the request.

The next time it was heard from, *The Liz* sent a radio message to the air controller at Zuni, New Mexico, reporting that it had climbed to 13,000 feet, that it had been caught in a violent storm, and that its wings were still icing. It was the last radio transmission from the doomed aircraft.

At Grants Airport control tower in Grants, New Mexico, an air controller reported seeing a brilliant illumination of the March sky. At first, he thought it was a spectacular flash of lighting. However, an Air Force pilot, flying a B-36 through the same night sky, sent an air-to-ground communication, notifying the control tower that a plane had exploded. As revealed in the delayed CAB report, the time of the explosion was 2:40am.

Spiraling out of control after the shutdown of its single engine, *The Lucky*

Liz had plunged to earth through a thick fog and burst into flames.

A CAB agent concluded, "The right master engine rod had failed in flight and the right propeller was feathered. Complete loss of control of the aircraft followed and the plane then struck the ground in a steep angle of descent."

The pilot lost control of the overloaded private plane. It had a weight limit of 18,605 pounds, but was actually carrying 20,757 pounds at takeoff. The extra tonnage contributed to the failure of the flight. The single engine failed, a situation aggravated by surface ice accretion. The anti-icing system was inadequate.

Todd's plane went down in the Zuni Mountains of New Mexico some twelve miles southwest of Grants. The bodies were scattered over a two-hundred yard, snow-covered crash site.

At daybreak, a search party in New Mexico discovered the plane wreckage, which had turned into a funeral pyre for Todd, Cohn, and both pilots, Verner and co-pilot Thomas Barclay.

Although the bodies had been charred beyond recognition, Todd's corpse was initially identified because his skeleton was still "accessorized" with the gold wedding ring he'd worn since his marriage to Elizabeth.

Later, when his ring was returned to Elizabeth, she had it melted down and reshaped for her finger. "I wore it every day until someone else who loved me told me to take it off. I have had two great loves in my life. Mike Todd was the first."

***

The AP reporter, James Bacon, may have been the first person in Los Angeles alerted to Todd's death. An AP stringer in Grants, New Mexico, called Bacon to check up on him. "Your name was on the passenger list. I wanted to make sure you were still alive."

Shocked, Bacon explained that he had cancelled at the last minute. After getting details, he immediately called the Los Angeles Bureau of the Associated Press. Within fifteen minutes, news of the crash was flashed around the world.

Morning programs on the U.S.'s East Coast and in London were interrupted to broadcast the breaking news.

Even though millions of people around the world already knew about Todd's death, Elizabeth did not. At around 5am, after a restless night, she'd fallen into a deep coma after taking sleeping pills.

MGM was notified and immediately, Benny Thau phoned Dick Hanley, asking him to break the news to Elizabeth before the wire services started ringing her. He called Dr. Kennamer and asked him to drive to her home with him. When the men arrived, a maid told them that Elizabeth was still asleep upstairs.

Dr. Kennamer suggested that he and Dick wake her up and tell her the news.

She would later recall the moment the doctor and her friend walked into her bedroom as "one of the most traumatic moments of my life." She had just awakened when the men came into her room. "When Dr. Kennamer and Dick came in, I screamed, 'No, he's *not!*' even before they spoke."

Debbie Reynolds had been at her dressing table that morning taking out her rollers when the call came in that Todd had died. She called her husband, Eddie Fisher, in New York. He'd flown there on a scheduled commercial flight, with the intention of singing at Todd's upcoming Friars' Club gala.

Fisher ordered Reynolds not to go to Elizabeth. It seemed he didn't want to share the tragedy of Todd's death with his wife. Defying him, she got dressed and drove to the Todd home to volunteer to look after Elizabeth's children until she recovered.

Just as Reynolds walked into the house, Elizabeth appeared at the top of the staircase, screaming, "*No! No! It's not true! It's not true!*"

"I'll never forget her look of terror and anguish," Reynolds recalled. "I'll also never forget that face—ashen, her violet eyes desperately sad, hair askew and wild—yet still incredibly beautiful, even in tragedy. And that piercing scream of agony after she called out Mike's name."

In 2003, on the *Larry King Show,* Elizabeth recalled that night and how, consumed with grief, she ran out into the street. "I was Tennessee Williams' *Baby Doll,* you know, with the little panties? I fell onto my knees in the street shouting, '*No, not Mike. Not Mike. Dear God, please not Mike!*' I was almost run over by a car. My doctor, Rex Kennamer, and Dick Hanley picked me up and carried me back to my bedroom. Rex shot me with a hypodermic needle."

At Elizabeth's home on Schuyler Drive, Dick put through a call to *Cat on a Hot Tin Roof's* director, Richard Brooks. "Todd's dead. His plane crashed in New Mexico."

The director claimed he heard "this terrible shrieking noise in the background. I knew at once it was Elizabeth."

The first people to arrive at the Todd home were from MGM: Eddie Mannix and Benny Thau. She screamed at them, cursing them. "You don't give a shit about Mike. All you want to know is can I finish your god damn swampy picture."

Later, when Brooks came by, she denounced him as a "bastard. You've just come to see if I'm able to go back to work. Well, screw you and your Southern Gothic horror tale. I'm *never* coming back. Go fuck yourself!"

Because of the crowds gathering outside her house, the Beverly Hills police erected barricades and stationed patrolmen to guard the property. Before gaining entrance to the house, everyone had to pass through a security checkpoint . After being questioned, Sara and Francis Taylor were allowed inside, as was Michael Wilding. Her favorite hairdresser, Sidney Guilaroff, arrived to tend to her personal needs, including grooming.

Condolences poured in from around the world, including from the White House. One wire read: "The President and I extend our deepest sympathy. Mamie Eisenhower."

Another from Clark Gable, who had lost his great love, Carole Lombard, in a plane crash sixteen years previously, read: "I know what it's like to lose someone you love."

Toastmaster and entertainer, George Jessel, summed up Todd's life. "He went from being a sideshow barker at the Chicago World's Fair to the man who could tell Picasso, 'Wrap up those pictures. They'll make a nice present for Elizabeth.'"

The Todd home was bedlam, as photographers even climbed up onto the building's roof. Looters broke into the garage where Todd stored his liquor and made off with cases of Scotch and champagne.

Dick was out of a job after Todd's death. Subsequently, he took over Elizabeth's household and began to handle her personal and business affairs, even scooping up dog poop.

Phone calls were coming in from *tout* Hollywood and from reporters the world over. Dick handled each call graciously and efficiently, although denying all requests for photographs, interviews, and personal visits.

From New York, Fisher called Dick, claiming that he was "deeply concerned about her, afraid she would try to commit suicide or lose her mind completely."

On his first night alone with her, Dick read her letters from all over the world—"from the famous and the unknown."

In the middle of Elizabeth's depression, Dick told her that Lana Turner's daughter, Cheryl Crane, was said to have fatally stabbed her mother's lover, Johnny Stompanato.

"I bet Lana did it," Elizabeth said. "Johnny was once my lover. I'll always remember him. Lana didn't have to kill him. She could have kicked him out instead."

Dick routed very few of the incoming calls through to Elizabeth. However, she'd instructed him, "When Eddie calls, and I know he will, put his call through to me right away."

From New York, Fisher talked to Dick, telling him he was leaving the following day to fly to Elizabeth's side. He had to conclude some business before he could fly away.

The call from Fisher was directed to Elizabeth's bedroom. At times, Dick heard her screaming in agony into the phone, a call that he estimated took almost two hours.

When it ended, Dick entered the room. "I was contemplating suicide with sleeping pills," she told him. "But Eddie has given me reason to live. He told me he's always been in love with me. He also told me that he never loved Debbie and could never figure out why he'd married her. With him by my side, I know I can get through the night."

***

For many reasons, both professional and personal, Paul Newman was deeply concerned about Elizabeth's condition. He'd gone to her home as soon as he heard the news over the radio. But it was two days before he was able to clear security and was allowed inside.

Amazingly, one of the first persons he encountered in the crowd downstairs was Greta Garbo, who had just descended from Elizabeth's bedroom upstairs. She recognized him immediately. "Go upstairs and offer her comfort. I did what I could," Garbo told him.

Mounting the stairs, Newman knocked on her door. There was no answer. As he turned, he spotted a photographer trying to conceal himself behind the open door of an adjoining bedroom. He confronted the photographer and demanded that he leave. As her security help later learned, the photographer had planned to barge into Elizabeth's bedroom and snap a picture of the grief-stricken widow, which no doubt would have appeared on the front covers of tabloids across the country.

After the photographer was evicted from the premises, Newman returned to the door of Elizabeth's bedroom and knocked again. This time Elizabeth herself opened the door. She stood before him in a sheer nightgown. When she saw him, she fell into his arms, and he guided her back into the room, where he gently returned her to her bed, covering up her nudity.

Without make-up and with no sleep for the previous two nights, she looked at him, her violet eyes bloodshot. In spite of her pain, she remained beautiful. She reached for him. "Don't ever let me go," she said, her voice barely a whisper.

Through tear-streaked eyes, she told him that "Mike had a premonition about that flight."

Elizabeth and Newman talked for about an hour, a session he later shared with Brooks. Fearing that she wouldn't be able to return to the film set of *Cat*, he had desperately wanted to assess the emotional condition of his co-star.

"I was always the strong one in any relationship I ever had," she confessed to him. "Even with my parents, and certainly through my marriages. But when Mike came along, I surrendered myself to him. He made the decisions. He was my shield against the world. I was his vassal. He solved all my problems. He loved me as no man has ever loved me. I was his. Without him, I have nothing."

Spontaneously, Newman blurted out, "You have me." Later, he would tell Brooks that he didn't really know why he'd said that. "The words just came out."

"Stay with me tonight," she whispered in his ear. "I can't stand to be alone. Mike slept here by my side. Last night I kept reaching out for him, finding nothing. No one."

"I'll be here for you," he promised.

If Brooks is to be believed, Newman told him that he made love to Elizabeth that night. "It was not a love of passion but a love of comfort," Newman allegedly told his director. "She needed me. My human warmth."

He also told Brooks that "I came to my senses the moment I left her house. I couldn't replace Todd in her life. I have a life of my own. A wife. Kids. I feared I'd horribly misled her. I can't be the next Mr. Elizabeth Taylor. I just can't."

Brooks assured him that he should feel no guilt for what he had done. "You were just tending to a desperate woman's needs."

The next day Elizabeth placed three frantic calls to Newman on the set, but he didn't return those desperate pleas to speak to her.

***

Still harboring his longstanding crush on Elizabeth, her aviator suitor of yesterday, Howard Hughes, finally connected with Elizabeth on the phone. Very generously, he offered her the use of one of his TWA jets to fly her to Todd's funeral in Chicago and then back to Los Angeles. She willingly accepted his offer and thanked him profusely.

During the flight to Chicago, the crew remembered Elizabeth clinging desperately to Fisher, and cuddling up protectively in his arms. The pilot later said, "Those two clung to each other like long lost lovers."

Ashen and veiled, Elizabeth disembarked from Hughes' TWA plane in Chicago. On the ramp, she was supported by her brother, Howard, and her doctor, Rex Kennamer. Dick Hanley followed them, carrying her two large purses.

Her arrival at Chicago's airport was greeted by some 2,000 fans, screaming her name and clamoring for an autograph, which she would not have given under any circumstances. A limousine whisked her to the Drake Hotel in Chicago, where a suite had been prepared for her. It was filled with flowers from friends and from fans expressing their sympathy.

Michael Todd, Jr., with his wife, Sarah, had met Elizabeth at the Chicago airport. He had gone ahead to make the funeral arrangements.

The next day, police estimated that some 20,000 frenzied fans lined the funeral route to Todd's grave site. It was believed that this was the largest turnout since Bugs Moran gang members were buried in the wake of the 1929 St. Valentine's Day Massacre.

Some of the more crazed fans showed up along the funeral route not to gape at Elizabeth but to scream and shout for Fisher. They were the more dedicated members of his Chicago fan club. Many of them brought their record albums for him to autograph. Of course, in these circumstances, he could not grant such requests.

Designer Helen Rose flew to Chicago with Elizabeth's "widow's weeds"— a black mink wrap, black leather gloves, a black suit trimmed with broadtail fur, a black velvet cloche hat, and a black veil that left her scarlet-painted lips visible.

Elizabeth specifically had not invited Monty, knowing that he found Todd distasteful. Ignoring her wishes, he showed up anyway. She spotted his face in the milling crowds.

Monty was horrified by the crowd. "It was noisy and vengeful. I saw envy in their faces, hatred, and bleakness."

Mike Todd's brother, David Goldbogen, had originally wanted a nine-foot tall replica of an Oscar statuette to function as Todd's tombstone. But the Academy of Motion Pictures Arts and Sciences threatened to sue, and the plan was abandoned.

Defined during its aftermath by Dick Hanley as "a Todd extravaganza," the funeral of Michael Todd took place on March 25, 1958 at the Jewish Waldheim Cemetery in Zurich, Illinois, outside Chicago.

Fans ate potato chips and popcorn, trashing the cemetery with their garbage. Untamed children crawled over the Jewish tombstones. Hot dog vendors peddled snacks and drinks to the mob.

At Todd's grave site, covered with a black tent, Elizabeth bowed before the bronze casket containing his charred remains. "I love you, Mike," she said, sobbing. "I will love you for eternity. There will never be another."

As Rabbi Abraham Rose conducted the Orthodox service, his voice was drowned out by fans shouting, *"LIZ! LIZ! LIZ!"*

A photograph of the young weeping widow, supported by Eddie Fisher, was flashed around the world. In Dick's words, "Eddie had become a surrogate for Mike. Michael, Jr. was yet another surrogate. Elizabeth had two men in her life, both of whom were in love with her."

Fisher later referred to the funeral as "an agonizing ordeal—I didn't think I'd get through it." Like the widow, he knelt before the casket and sobbed. "I've lost the only real friend I ever had."

Dick stood nearby, mesmerized by the scene of the weeping Elizabeth with Fisher. "Eddie was behaving more like a widow instead of as a best friend," he later said. "I had heard only rumors about the intimacy of Eddie and Mike. It was not a traditional male/male friendship. They were asshole buddies in more ways than one, or so I heard."

As the police tried to clear a pathway for Elizabeth back to her waiting limousine, unruly spectators tried to break through the cordon of police, hoping to tear off pieces of Elizabeth's clothing. One woman with a camera ripped off Elizabeth's veil, saying, "Listen, bitch, I want a picture of your tear-soaked face."

Fisher managed to push Elizabeth inside the limousine, whereupon they discovered that the driver was missing—lost in the crowd. The mob surrounded the car. Some of the young men began to rock the vehicle, trying to force her to come out and to pose for pictures. She screamed, fearing the limousine would be toppled over. It took eight policemen to force the crowd to stand back from the limo. The driver finally appeared.

As Elizabeth recalled, "Hordes of people swarmed like insects all over the limo so we couldn't see out the window."

It took an hour for the police to clear a pathway for the limousine to leave the cemetery and take Elizabeth back to the Drake. Once there, she met privately with Monty. The confrontation did not go well, as she had not wanted him to come to Chicago. He was seen storming out of the Drake, where he hailed a taxi to take him to the airport and onto a flight back to New York.

Then Elizabeth and Fisher, along with their special guests, were driven to the airport for the flight aboard Hughes' plane back to Los Angeles in the wake of that grotesque funeral.

Throughout most of the flight, Elizabeth, in front of everyone, huddled with Fisher, his arms protectively around her. He shared a memory of Todd with her:

"Mike told me that most young boys in America grow up wanting to become President of the United States. But Mike told me his life-long wish was to marry Elizabeth Taylor."

***

One of the strangest events occurred at the Todd household in Los Angeles after Elizabeth returned from Chicago. Roddy McDowall came over for a sleepover to look after Elizabeth because Fisher had a singing engagement that night.

Nicky Hilton showed up at the door demanding to see Elizabeth. He didn't wait for an invitation, but stormed up the steps and barged into her bedroom.

Roddy heard a drugged Elizabeth say, "Nicky, oh Nicky, you've come back!"

Roddy was asleep on the sofa when a disheveled Hilton, tucking in his shirttails, came downstairs at around 5am the next morning.

Roddy, who had known Hilton for years, was anxious to learn what had happened.

"I fucked her all night and I mean that literally," Hilton said. "Well, maybe I took a cigarette break here and there. I thought I could fuck her into a reconciliation, but she turned me down at 4am. I won't be back. I'll drop in and see you, kid, the next time I want a great blow-job."

Roddy stood on the Todd family's porch watching Hilton drive away to his next adventure.

By 10am that same morning, Michael Todd, Jr., arrived to see the sultry beauty who was technically still his stepmother. She had seen him only on carefully choreographed occasions during the course of her marriage to his father. Sometimes, he had been with his wife, Sarah, whom he'd married in 1953.

Todd Jr. admitted in his memoirs that he and Elizabeth "never left the house" following his father's funeral. He recalled that on several occasions "she relapsed into a state of near hysteria. She was crying and fighting against the fact of his death. When she'd pull herself together, she would say, 'Mike can't be dead. I don't believe it.'"

In the wake of Todd Sr.'s death, Elizabeth confided to his son, "I dream of Mike almost every night, dream that he is still alive. In the dream, I'm in his apartment on Park Avenue. Suddenly, he comes into the room. 'You silly nigger,' he says to me. 'You thought I was dead, didn't you? But I was just lying low till I got things straightened out.'"

"It wasn't the dream that shocked me as much as Elizabeth dreaming that Dad had called her a silly nigger," Todd, Jr. said. "That made no sense at all. I never heard Dad call anybody a nigger, especially his goddess wife."

Mike Todd Sr. and **Jr.** in 1952

In his hours-long talks with Elizabeth in her bedroom, Todd Jr. shared many stories about her late husband that she had not heard before. Some of these tales amused her; others made her jealous, especially if a woman was involved.

Todd Jr. claimed that Marilyn Monroe had desperately wanted to appear in a cameo in *Around the World in 80 Days,* portraying the saloon singer in San Francisco, a role that had gone to Marlene Dietrich.

"Monroe arrived at Dad's apartment on Park Avenue," Todd Jr. said. "He took her to his bedroom and auditioned her privately there. While I watched a Roy Rogers movie on TV, Dad and Monroe were in there for at least three hours. I heard a lot of giggling. It must have been some audition. Finally, Monroe emerged and wet-kissed me goodbye. In spite of her efforts, she didn't get the part. I never understood why not. Monroe would have brought more publicity to the film that Dietrich."

When the story was repeated to Fisher the next day, he said, "I also auditioned for Mike. He had me sing the same lyric all afternoon, but decided to give my part to Sinatra. He told me that Sinatra would bring him a lot more publicity. For his stint in the film, Sinatra was given a brand-new Thunderbird."

"Dad didn't believe in following the rules," Todd Jr. told Elizabeth, "and you know that's true. When I was eight years old, he told me you don't ask a policeman if you can spit in the subway. 'If you gotta spit, you spit, but you don't ask if you're allowed to.'"

Todd, Jr. said that he once visited his father in Palm Springs, where he and Elizabeth were resting from their world tour. One afternoon, Todd Sr. left to play golf and then to engage in some heavy drinking with Frank Sinatra.

"Elizabeth and I were alone around the pool," Todd Jr. said. "She had on this tight-fitting swim suit with a leopard print. At some point, she casually pulled it off and lay nude in front of me. She didn't come on to me, but she closed her eyes, knowing that I was taking in her beautiful body and big tits. I got an erection and I couldn't get it to go down for a while. If I'd fucked her then, and Dad had caught me, he would have held my head underwater until I drowned. Elizabeth was very provocative to do that. After all, I was her stepson."

"On some nights, we talked about reviving Mike's plan to film *Don Quixote* in Spain," Todd Jr. recalled. "Dad had talked about casting various actors over the years. But Elizabeth came up with a weird suggestion for casting the lean, lanky Don Quixote. 'Gary Cooper could be great in the title role,' she said. Maybe he would. The idea wasn't as crazy as it sounded at first."

"Elizabeth decided, at least for two or three weeks, that I was the only man on earth who could replace my Dad in her life," Todd Jr. claimed. "She went for me—I mean, came on really strong—and I caved in. She told me I was like a younger version of my father—and that thrilled her. She said she'd never gotten to know him as a young man, since he was already in late middle age when they met. She and I were contemporaries, and she said that by loving me, she was getting to experience what young love with Dad could have been. I knew that didn't make any real sense, but it was a conceit she harbored for quite a while, even though it was completely unrealistic."

Eventually, *Cat's* director, Richard Brooks, visited Elizabeth in her bedroom and later observed:

"I feared that a scandal was brewing because of Elizabeth spending so much time with that Fisher boy," Brooks said. "I confronted her. I don't want to sound greedy, but I was afraid fans would stay away in droves if news got out that Eddie had become the surrogate Mike Todd in her life—yes, including the fulfillment of marital duties."

The next day, Brooks shared Elizabeth's response with Paul Newman. It was a shocker, and we have only Brooks' word for this.

"I've known for months that Eddie is in love with me," Elizabeth allegedly told Brooks. "Even Mike knew that, but he dismissed it as a harmless flirtation. 'What red-blooded man on the planet wouldn't fall for Elizabeth Taylor?' he used to say. But I fear I've developed an attachment far more scandalous than Eddie Fisher. I think I'm falling in love with Mike Todd, Jr."

Often, Elizabeth and Todd, Jr. discussed how the death of Todd Sr. could have been prevented. "I urged him to get rid of that fucking plane," Todd Jr. said. "I just knew it wasn't safe. I even gave him an F.A.A. survey to show him that a plane like that was dangerous unless a lot of money was spent on it to bring it up to standards. He wouldn't listen. 'I'm too tough to die,' he told me. 'I plan to be fucking Elizabeth when I'm eighty-five.'"

"One night she asked me to pull off my clothes and get into bed with her," Todd Jr. said. "She couldn't sleep, but I fell asleep since I was exhausted. Sometime in the early morning hours, I woke up with this sensation. She was giving me this fantastic blow-job. I knew it was wrong, but I was too far gone. I had to go for it, and I did. I felt guilty afterward, though."

"It was a bizarre time in my life," Todd Jr. told Dick Hanley. "Elizabeth put my Dad's pajamas under her pillow. She refused to change the sheets where he'd spent his last night with her. She said she wanted to keep them as long as she could, and as long as his odor remained."

After a few weeks, Elizabeth was seen with Arthur Loew, Jr. Roddy Mc-Dowall, who visited Elizabeth frequently at the time, told friends, "Elizabeth was not romantically interested in Arthur. She was trying to throw the blood-hounds off the scent, which was of Mike Todd, Jr."

Elizabeth's agent, Kurt Frings, said, "She went after Eddie Fisher, all right. No question about it. She tried Mike Todd, Jr., first, but his wife Sarah finally said no and put a stop to it before it could develop too far. She got young Mike out of town fast before Elizabeth could move in on him any more than she had already."

"I was a fool at the time," Fisher recalled. "One night in the living room, I saw Arthur Loew, Jr. pull off Elizabeth's shoes and sensually massage her feet. She always said, 'Art and I are just friends.' There are all kinds of friends. Like an idiot, I urged her to spend less time with Loew and more time with Mike's son. That was like sending an innocent lamb to bed down with a she-wolf. What I didn't know at the time was that I was in love with Elizabeth but wasn't ready to admit it to myself."

In later years, Todd Jr. expressed no regret for his brief, rather tumultuous involvement with Elizabeth. "Basically, she was and is a warmhearted, thoughtful, and loving person," he said. "But because of her background as a child star, she can also be spoiled and self-centered. She has the courage, nerve, and ability to get what she wants and sooner or later to overcome any obstacles to her happiness."

It was his wife, Sarah, who rescued Todd Jr. from Elizabeth's clutches. Todd Jr. admitted, "I was very uncomfortable and thought my presence was no longer helping her to reconcile herself to my father's death, nor was it improving my state of mind."

In April, Todd's will was filed for probate. His estate was said to be worth $5 million, but most of that would be consumed by debt. The estate was divided between Elizabeth and Todd Jr., with him receiving his inheritance outright. Her share was placed in trust, an arrangement which had originally been conceived as a means of providing her with an income for life.

Many casual observers thought Todd had left her a rich widow. But as Todd Jr. discovered, her late husband and his father had left a tangled estate. It would take dozens of lawsuits and years to settle. She faced immediate problems with the Internal Revenue Service, as Todd owed thousands in back taxes. Todd Jr. joined with her in filing a $5 million lawsuit against the airplane company which had leased Todd the doomed plane. Negligence was charged. It took five years to settle the claim. In the end, $27,000 was awarded directly to Liza Todd.

Even after they separated as lovers, Todd Jr. and Elizabeth continued a friendship and a business involvement as heirs to Todd Sr.'s estate. Their chief asset was *Around the World in 80 Days,* which by 1960 had begun to show its age, belonging, artistically at least, to the transient fads of the 1950s.

Todd Sr. had already managed to squander most of the gross from the film on his worldwide promotion tours and other stunts. Elizabeth and Todd Jr. were lured into believing that the film would eventually earn $85 to $100 million, but the profit fell far below that. Domestically, it earned only $23 million.

In 1968, with Elizabeth's approval, *80 Days* was re-released, but brought in less than a million dollars. In 1971, Todd Jr. sold it as a telecast on CBS-TV for $2 million, although Todd Sr. had always vowed it would never be shown on TV.

Back taxes on the Todd estate were not settled until 1971. "After everything was paid off, there wasn't a lot in the kitty," Dick said. Todd Sr.'s once vast estate was reduced to just $13,000.

Even though, presumably, Todd Jr. was no longer sleeping with Elizabeth, he still tried to take over her career, something his father had done. At one point, Todd Jr. called a press conference, announcing plans for another roadshow extravaganza evocative of the most lavish of the events associated with *80 Days*. "It's called *Busman's Holiday,* and it's going to be spectacular. Elizabeth will be the star."

When Todd Jr. was producing the first and last Smell-O-Vision film, *Scent of Mystery* (later retitled *Holiday in Spain),* Elizabeth agreed to appear in an unbilled cameo. The film, a so-called mystery, starred Peter Lorre, Paul Lukas, and Denholm Elliott.

Fans of Elizabeth had to wait till near the end of the film for her brief appearance as "The Real Sally Kennedy." Her moment on the screen was greeted with gusts of perfume pumped through the air-conditioning system. Many of her fans coughed and choked.

The movie had opened with images of a butterfly flitting through a sweet-smelling peach grove. Later on, a barrel of wine fell off a cart and rolled down a hill, smashing at the bottom, again to an accompanying odor.

In the advertising campaigns associated with his breakthrough in film technology, Todd Jr. announced "First they moved (1895)! Then they talked (1927)! Now they smell (1960)!"

After sitting through the movie, Fisher told Elizabeth, "The scent emanating from that flick wasn't Chanel No. 5. It stunk like shit."

Initially, the film was shown only in Chicago, New York, and Los Angeles.

"If Todd had lived, I think she would have divorced him by the time she shot *Cleopatra* in Rome," said Dick. "The affair would have burned out by then because it was too intense. Also, he would have driven her into bankruptcy the way he did with his second wife, Joan Blondell."

Todd Jr. also doubted whether the marriage might have lasted forever. "The marriage might have lasted only if Dad never had a financial downturn. What if *Don Quixote* had flopped? Todd-AO faded with the fads of the 1950s. I suspect Elizabeth would have gone on to other lovers, especially Richard Burton, who would have lured her away from my Dad instead of taking her from Eddie Fisher."

Elizabeth said she could no longer stand living in the Schuyler Road house. She left her children with Loew and moved into a bungalow on the grounds of the Beverly Hills Hotel.

Her former beau, Loew was always there for Elizabeth, always willing to take care of her children and solve their many problems while she rushed off to her next adventure in New York or Europe. "I adore Elizabeth," he said, "and am only too glad to take care of her kids."

***

Quite by chance, the author of this biography, in Ireland in the mid-1970s with travel writer Stanley Haggart, once encountered Todd Jr. in a Dublin pub. He'd come in for a glass of gin and ended up having quite a few.

Todd Jr., spoke frankly about his failed dreams of becoming a big-time showman like his father. During the course of the evening, and after his sixth gin, he admitted that he had once fallen in love with Elizabeth. "I was the one who pulled away," he admitted, "because I knew our marriage—which would have been possible only after I divorced my-then wife Sarah—would have destroyed Elizabeth's career. Look what happened to another Oscar winner, Gloria Grahame, when she married her stepson, the son of Nicholas Ray."

Todd Jr., after suffering for years from diabetes—he even had one leg amputated—eventually died on May 5, 2002 in Ireland, the victim of lung cancer.

***

Faced with a mounting pile of bills arriving daily from episodes associated with Todd's promotions and travel worldwide, Elizabeth was also left with three children to rear—two sons from Michael Wilding and the little girl, Liza, from Todd himself.

Elizabeth returned to work on April 14, 1958, at the MGM lot in Culver City. Emerging from a month of seclusion, she had been driven to MGM by Dick. She had not even bothered to phone Richard Brooks. In the back of her limousine, she waited for him to come out of a sound stage and greet her. Dick had gone inside to search for him.

After he got into the limo with her, Brooks studied her face carefully. Her eyes were still red, but she claimed that she was able to go to work. "Mike loved me in the picture, at least what he saw of the rushes, and I want to finish *Cat* for him. Besides, it's a hell of a good role, and a gal doesn't get a lot of those in one lifetime."

He escorted her to her dressing room, which the crew the next day filled with violets to match the color of her eyes.

On her first day back, Paul Newman emerged from his dressing room to greet her. She kissed him gently on the lips. "Thanks for being there for me when I needed you," she said.

"She seemed very practical," Newman recalled. "She

Michael Todd, Jr.

had to get back to work. She needed the money."

Newman was the gallant gentleman, and it was obvious to him that she did not want to continue their relationship after her one-night stand with him. She'd reached out for him in loneliness and desperation. As he told her, "If you need me, I'm here for you. Call me and I'll come running."

Throughout the remainder of the filming of *Cat on a Hot Tin Roof*, Newman provided Elizabeth with strong moral—but not physical—support. Their moment of intimacy, conceived and executed at perhaps the worst moment of her life, seemed to have been relegated to a far and distant memory within both of their brains.

In later years, Elizabeth expressed gratitude to him for his good manners during the conclusion of the shooting of *Cat*. "He was most courtly to me," she told friends, "a real gentleman. If I were about to have a nervous breakdown, he was by my side, guiding me through a scene."

"I think Elizabeth gave her greatest performance in *Cat*," he later claimed. "She turned out to be a real trouper."

That was his public position. Privately, he told Brooks, "I really wish I was a free man. In all my life, I never wanted anything as much. To be the man lying in bed with Elizabeth when she woke up in the morning. Those violet eyes gazing into my baby blues."

Newman remembered with horror the day he sat in a viewing room with Elizabeth, Brooks, and Tennessee Williams. The playwright cringed throughout the screening, and Newman kept shifting nervously in his seat. When the screening was over and the lights came up, Tennessee rose to his feet.

He looked first at Newman. "You looked fabulous without your shirt," Tennessee said. "One tasty morsel. And Elizabeth, you looked so sexy, no gay man could turn you down." Then he turned to Brooks. "You emasculated my play. You bastard! I'm going to urge the public to stay away from it." Then he stormed out of the studio.

On September 20, 1958, when *Cat on a Hot Tin Roof* opened in theaters around the country, Elizabeth was sternly being denounced as "the other woman." Tabloid fodder for the press, she was accused of breaking up the marriage of America's so-called sweethearts, Debbie Reynolds and Eddie Fisher.

But instead of *seguéing* "notorious Liz," as she was called, into box office poison, publicity generated by the illicit romance had movie-goers lining up around the country to gaze upon "this Jezebel."

Cat was nominated for Best Picture, Best Adapted Screenplay (in spite of Tennessee's assault), Best Director, Best Actor (Newman himself), and Best Actress (in spite of the negative press out there on Elizabeth).

At the Academy Awards, Newman faced stiff competition from Sidney Poitier in *The Defiant Ones* and Tony Curtis, also in *The Defiant Ones*. It can be assumed that two nominees for the same picture cancel each other out. Therefore, Newman had to measure up against David Niven in *Separate Tables* and Spencer Tracy in *The Old Man and the Sea*.

Eventually, Niven, playing a bogus war hero and child molester, walked off with the Oscar. Newman modestly admitted to friends, "I didn't deserve the win this time. Maybe next time."

Ironically, Elizabeth lost to Susan Hayward for *I Want to Live*, a script that Newman had urged Hayward to make. That was not because he really wanted her to interpret the role, but because he hoped she'd reject *The Three Faces of Eve* so that Joanne Woodward could get the role.

Cat on a Hot Tin Roof was MGM's biggest hit of the year, and polls in the autumn named Elizabeth as the number one star in Hollywood. "In this case," she said, "notoriety works in my favor. Apparently, the public wants to go into a darkened movie house and gaze upon the scarlet woman."

With the film wrapped, she flew to New York to make up with Monty, but spent far more time with Fisher, who was fulfilling contractual engagements on the East Coast.

She told Dick Hanley and Monty, "I'm starting my life all over again. God knows where the path will lead me this time."

***

Contrary to denials, Elizabeth had been sexually intimate with Eddie Fisher before the blossoming of their love affair into full bloom in Manhattan. He booked a site at Essex House, on Central Park South, and she booked an even more luxurious suite at the Plaza Hotel.

Partly because of such subterfuges, their romance initially escaped the attention of the press, although there were reports about how they were from time to time sighted together. Since Fisher was widely recognized as Mike Todd's best friend, it was assumed that he was merely offering comfort to the Widow Todd. But as it turned out, he was offering far more than comfort.

At the Plaza, after a night of love-making with Fisher, Elizabeth received her first call of the day. It was from Cary Grant. The bisexual actor had always had a crush on her, and he invited her to share an LSD trip with him. She turned him down.

She'd heard from friends that Grant's popularity at the box office had waned as he moved deeper into middle age. Privately, Louella Parsons told her confidants that "Cary wants to marry Elizabeth as a means of beefing up his heterosexual credentials."

Elizabeth said to friends, "Cary came on to me several times, but I never gave him a tumble. Everybody from Noël Coward to Doris Duke told me he's not very well endowed."

In her dates with Fisher in New York, she often used Dick Hanley as her "beard." He warned her, "You don't need Eddie right now. You really don't. Save your reputation and let me take care of his sexual needs."

"Oh, Dick," she said, "You really are so precious. What would I do without you?"

But instead of accepting Dick's advice, she spent the next four days and nights alone with Fisher in the bedroom of her suite. "Talk about getting to know someone," she later told Dick, "I feel more like a woman than I've felt since Mike died."

On Fisher's thirtieth birthday, Elizabeth presented him with Todd's money clip, which read:

BEING POOR IS A STATE OF MIND.
I'VE BEEN BROKE LOTS OF TIMES
BUT I'VE NEVER BEEN POOR.

He recalled, "I can't ever forget how her eyes burned into my heart that day: I felt her need for me from the depths of my soul. My feelings were identical to hers."

Todd had been an older man—forty-nine years old at the time of his death—but Fisher was young, thirty, and passionate. "We made love three, four, five times a day," he said of the weeks of their love affair. "We made love in the swimming pool, on Mexican beaches, under waterfalls, and in the back seat of a limousine on the way home from a party. There is nothing more erotic than Elizabeth Taylor and a moonlit beach. We fit together as perfect sexually as we did mentally."

A domestic drama that reverberated around the world: **Elizabeth Taylor, Eddie Fisher,** and **Debbie Reynolds**

Born in Philadelphia in 1928, Fisher was descended from Russian Jewish immigrants. He referred to his father as "a nasty, abusive man, a tyrant. And they say I'm no actor," Fisher said. "Imagine me having to sing '*Oh! My Pa-Pa!*' and look adoringly at the man I hated smiling back at me from ringside."

Sometimes referred to as "The Jewish Sinatra," Fisher was four years older than Elizabeth. A popular teenage idol, he was good looking and boyish, although Mike Todd, Jr., claimed, "He didn't have much upstairs. His talents lay much farther south…and I'm talking Deep South!"

"Eddie was not just Mike Todd's best friend," said Dick Hanley. "He worshipped the man and tried to emulate him. Mike would order first in a restaurant, and Eddie would order the same. They drank the same liquor and fucked the same women. In time, they'd even marry the same woman."

The press called him, "the golden *boychik* of mainstream pop" or the "dimpled troubadour from Philadelphia." He rose to the top tier of America's entertainment industry between 1950 and 1954, a period which some social historians define as the most tepid and conformist five years in the history of 20th century music. Nineteen of his songs reached the Top Ten. When he was drafted into the Army during the Korean War, President Harry S Truman defined him as, "my favorite PFC."

Many biographers have claimed that Elizabeth's "big" attraction for Fisher was the result of his being hung like a horse. Yet in startling contrast, many of his former bedmates, including Las Vegas showgirls, referred to him as "Princess Tiny Meat." On the Oprah Winfrey Show, Debbie Reynolds, in reference to her former husband and his endowment, once pointedly performed a gesture with her hands, indicating that her former husband measured no more than four inches erect.

During his lifetime, Fisher, or so it is estimated, seduced some 1,000 men and women, mostly women. One would think that all these objects of his seduction could agree on the size of his penis. But such is not the case. Marlene Dietrich told Orson Welles, "Eddie is parlor sized." Her statement was enigmatic. Did Dietrich mean that he was hung appropriately for the parlor—but not for the bedroom?

Jane Ellen Wayne, a Hollywood biographer, worked in public relations at NBC during the period when Fisher was televising his musical show for Coca-Cola. She talked to two or three starlets whom Fisher had dated at NBC. "They would talk about how well-endowed he was, and how skilled a lover he was, ranking right up there with Gary Cooper and Frank Sinatra. If anyone had an interest in good sex—and Elizabeth Taylor is said to have been ardent about it—Eddie Fisher was somebody who would have impressed her."

In addition to maybe one thousand hookers, Fisher also seduced numerous stars over the years. They included Edie Adams, Pier Angeli, Ann-Margret, Nathalie Delon (wife of Alain), Marlene Dietrich, Mia Farrow (to Sinatra's fury), Judy Garland, Hope Lange, singer Jane Morgan, Merle Oberon, Stephanie Powers, Kim Novak, Carol Lynley, Juliet Prowse (to Sinatra's fury), Angie Dickinson (of JFK fame), Maria Schell, and Mamie Van Doren. Exotic conquests included Judith Campbell Exner (mistress of both John F. Kennedy and mobster Sam Giancana), Pamela Turnure (press secretary to Jackie Kennedy), and Virginia Warren, daughter of Chief Justice Earl Warren.

He was also rumored to be a closeted bisexual, and may have had a few discreet affairs with young men, including waiters in Las Vegas. He has gone on record denying almost a hundred times that he was a homosexual.

"Oh, Eddie," Elizabeth said, "you protest too much. Why don't you shut up about it?"

After marrying perky Debbie Reynolds, Fisher's popularity soared, and he had a number of hit records, eventually commanding $250,000 for his appearance at a single recording session.

Even Hedda Hopper approved of the Reynolds/Fisher marriage. "Never have I seen a more patriotic match than these two clean-cut, clean-living youngsters. When I think of them, I see flags flying and hear bands playing." Hopper would soon change her definition of what she saluted and what music she heard.

A popular New York columnist of his day, Earl Wilson, was among the first newspapermen to learn about the Taylor/Fisher love affair. On August 29, 1958, Wilson wrote: "Elizabeth Taylor and Eddie Fisher were dancing it up at the Harwyn Night Club this morning. Eddie having been Mike Todd's close friend is now sort of an escort service for Liz."

"After Wilson's column was published, all hell broke loose," Fisher claimed.

Wilson followed with almost nightly sightings throughout New York ranging from the Quo Vadis restaurant to the Embers Night Club.

What Wilson had to say about Reynolds could not be printed. "To put it bluntly, Debbie has more balls than any five guys I've ever known. She pretends to be sweet and demure, but at heart she's Hard-Hearted Hannah."

When Hedda Hopper read Wilson's column, she shouted, referring to Elizabeth, "That bitch! That slut!"

The Soviets had launched Sputnik, Alaska had voted for statehood, and Dr. Martin Luther King had been arrested in Alabama, but newspapers were obsessed with the unfolding saga of "Liz & Eddie."

On September 8, 1958, *The Los Angeles Herald Express* headlined a story—EDDIE FISHER IS DATING LIZ TAYLOR. That revelation got more play than Khrushchev threatening atomic retaliation against the United States if it attacked Red China.

In Manhattan for the taping of his television show for Coca-Cola, Fisher invited Elizabeth to spend Labor Day weekend with him at Grossinger's, the most famous resort in New York State's Catskill Mountains. Grossinger's was where he had launched his career in 1949. It had also been the setting for his wedding ceremony to Reynolds in 1955, when he had been the number one singing star in America. ("Eat your heart out, Frankie," he said.)

Thousands of Elizabeth's fans, nationwide, were outraged that she did not spend "at least a year in mourning," in the wake of Todd's untimely death.

In Hollywood, Reynolds could take it no more. At 2am on the morning of September 6, she telephoned Fisher's suite at the Essex House in Manhattan. There was no answer. She knew that Elizabeth was staying in a suite at the Plaza Hotel. Through a ruse, she called the Plaza's switchboard, claiming that she was a telephone operator in California and that Dean Martin was on the line, waiting to speak to Fisher.

Fisher came to the phone, "Deano, what in hell are you calling me for at this hour?"

"It's Debbie. Why don't you roll over in bed and give Elizabeth the phone?"

After five minutes of violent arguing, Fisher finally admitted the truth. "I'm in love with Elizabeth. I never loved you. I want a divorce."

"If you marry her, she'll dump you within eighteen months," Reynolds shouted back at him. She later asserted, "And Elizabeth did get rid of him, just as I had warned him."

On reflection, Reynolds claimed, "Eddie wanted to be a movie star. He married one. Then he left me for someone even bigger. Looking back, I can see that Eddie wasn't that interested in me. I was not a woman of the world, or a passionate woman like Elizabeth. He was way overmatched with her, but he didn't know that, and she didn't realize it at the time, probably because she was in such despair."

The New York Daily News claimed, "The storybook marriage of Eddie Fisher and Debbie Reynolds skidded on a series of curves yesterday—Liz Taylor's." *Life* magazine chortled, "Hollywood was caught with its make-believe down."

Elizabeth's former friend, party giver Elsa Maxwell, wrote: "The facts seem to me to prove she has been aggressive in her romances, ruthless in her disregard for the feelings of those who have stood in her path, and indifferent to the wreckage she has left behind her."

At the time this attack appeared, an MGM publicity picture of Elizabeth, sensually dressed in a white silk slip and satin pumps, was plastered across America. *Cat on a Hot Tin Roof* was soon to be released.

All the sympathy Elizabeth had generated after the loss of her husband faded as soon as news broke that she was involved in an affair with Eddie Fisher. In Stockholm, a newspaper headlined the story as BLOOD THIRSTY LIZ VAMPIRES EDDIE.

"Harlot" and "Jezebel" were some of the kinder words used to describe her after that. She was called "a viper," "a cannibal," "a barbarian," and "a man-eater."

Fan magazines such as *Photoplay* urged the public to boycott her films. She was denounced in newspaper editorials, and a minister in Los Angeles had his congregation burn her in effigy.

Max Lerner, a writer for *The New York Post,* for a brief time would become Elizabeth's lover. He defended her marriage to Fisher. "I like the fact that they are quite frank about their feelings for each other. This is a case where a joyous candor is far better than a hypocritical show of virtue."

She liked the column so much, she invited Lerner to visit Fisher and her in her suite. "I fell in love with her," Lerner said. "She told me how stimulating Eddie had been in bed the night before. 'Three and a half times, Mr. Max.'"

The following week, Elizabeth, still in love with Fisher, bizarrely launched a sexual affair with the chubby fifty-seven-year-old political columnist. Their on-again, off-again fling continued until 1961.

She met Lerner at times in secluded pubs in London, eventually inviting him back to her suite at the Dorchester when Fisher was away at a singing engagement. In time, she would tell Lerner, "I thought I could keep Mike's memory alive that way, but I have only his ghost in Eddie."

Until she got involved with Fisher, Elizabeth played Sinatra songs, but she switched to "Wish You Were Here," "I'm Walking Behind You," "I Need You Now," and "Oh! My Pa-Pa."

The adverse publicity whirling around his romance caused NBC to cancel *The Eddie Fisher Show.*

Elizabeth tried to defend herself from attacks. "Mike is dead. I'm alive. Maggie the Cat is alive." She very accurately told the press, "No one woman breaks up a happy marriage."

Reference to the scandal would last in the public mind for years. Even the widowed Jacqueline Kennedy, in analyzing the depth of her popularity in America, commented sardonically on her own situation years later: "Anyone who is against me will look like a rat—unless I run off with Eddie Fisher."

"I never suspected that Elizabeth was going to entice my husband away," Reynolds said. "I might not have been as surprised were it anyone else. But how it all happened was rather scandalous in that they didn't take more care to avoid hurting me. I understand when I look back on it. Who would pass on Elizabeth? No woman living was a beautiful as her. And Eddie had even tried to act like Mike Todd, smoking big cigars."

"I was the last to find out about the affair," Reynolds continued. "There had been hints in the papers, and I had noticed that when I turned up at a party, my own friends were whispering. Although I didn't want to find out the truth, I had to face up to it. Even so, it was a great shock to find them together. It left me shattered. The shock of discovering the affair was the day I lost my innocence. I was a virgin when I married Eddie. I was very religious, so I didn't believe in divorce. But they laid guilt on me that I was keeping them and true love apart. So, I finally let Eddie off the hook. I told him to go."

In later years, Reynolds said, "I should have married my first love, Robert Wagner. All we did was kiss. But Elizabeth, not me, bedded Bob. She knew him as Bathsheba knew David."

Over the years, Fisher made increasingly bitter remarks about Reynolds. "Debbie Reynolds was indeed the girl next door. But only if you lived next door to a self-centered, totally driven, insecure, untruthful phony."

"My trouble with Debbie began on my honeymoon night," Fisher told Elizabeth, "when I left her alone to join Frank Sinatra, Peter Lawford, and Sammy Davis, Jr., in a poker game. That, sweet cheeks, won't happen in my marriage to you."

***

Flying back to Los Angeles on an airplane separate from that used by Fisher, Elizabeth rented an elegant Bel-Air home where Tyrone Power, one of her former lovers, had lived previously with Linda Christian.

On November 15, 1958, Elizabeth was resting in the bedroom that Power had occupied within the house. It was from within the premises of that room that she took a call from Dick Hanley, who told her that Power had died of a heart attack during the filming of a dueling scene in Spain. The movie he was working on at the time was *Solomon and Sheba,* a biblical epic co-starring Gina Lollobrigida. [Power was replaced at that point onward in the film by Yul Brynner.]

Newspaper editors were desperate for stories about "Liz and Eddie." Sometimes copy was falsely created. News stories surfaced that she'd had a nervous breakdown and was committed to the Menninger Clinic in Topeka, Kansas, where she was said to have been forced into a straitjacket.

The day that false story appeared, she made a spectacular entrance into Chasen's in Los Angeles on the arm of Eddie Fisher. From other tables, some celebrities got up and walked across the dining room to greet her, including Gregory Peck, who kissed her on the mouth. "Sorry you didn't make *Roman Holiday* with me," he said. Bette Davis and Myrna Loy also greeted her. However, Joan Crawford, accompanied by a handsome young man, made it a point to parade by her table and pointedly ignore her.

Many of Elizabeth's other friends no longer received her, even refusing to accept her phone calls. She was greatly hurt by their rejections.

Fisher gave a small party for her, inviting those few friends who still were on good terms with her. Perhaps surprisingly, two of her most loyal supporters were Ronald and Nancy Reagan. Others who showed up at the party included the ever-faithful Rock Hudson and directors Richard Brooks and Joe Pasternak. Janet Leigh and Tony Curtis remained faithful, as did Peter Lawford and George Burns and Gracie Allen.

Toward the end of the party, Elizabeth learned that Lawford had given Hudson a blow-job in her bathroom.

During this period of her life, it wasn't all party time, dinners, and love-making with Fisher. Illness of some sort had always hovered over Elizabeth. This time, it was her daughter, not herself, who nearly died of double pneumonia.

Ignoring the press attacks on her, and perhaps as a means of helping her cope with them, Elizabeth devoted all her attention to Liza. "She was sort of blue gray in color." Elizabeth said. "They punctured her lumbars and had great big pipes going into her veins, and her little arms were strapped onto boards taped to the bed. Her chances were very slim. But with hope and a lot of prayer, the poor little thing came through. I don't think I could have borne it if Mike's daughter, my child, had died."

The near death of fifteen-month-old Liza didn't garner any sympathy for Elizabeth in the press. Instead, Elizabeth during this crisis received some of her worst hate mail. Several death threats came in from the Ku Klux Klan in the Deep South. One member referred to her as "The Jew Cunt in need of circumcision."

Elizabeth and Fisher were getting nothing but attacks and threats. In contrast, good and glowing press reports were devoted to Reynolds. She brilliantly played the role of the abandoned wife, appearing before photographers in pigtails with no make-up. For dramatic effect, she had diaper pins fastened to the corner of her blouse. "I am still very much in love with Eddie," she told the press.

When Dick and Elizabeth heard that, they mocked her. "Yeah, right," said Elizabeth. "That fucking bitch! That fucking liar! Twice, she practically hauled him into the divorce courts. The only reason she didn't divorce him the last time around was because she found out she was pregnant."

"I have to tell my children that Daddy's not around any more," Reynolds told the press in her best "Tammy" voice.

Fisher dismissed Reynolds' antics, calling them "a charade for the media. She did not enjoy sex with me. I called her Mount Virgin. It was a real challenge to get to the summit."

As Reynolds glowed in America's approval, Elizabeth made another controversial move.

Before marrying Fisher, she converted to Judaism, a move she'd been considering while still married to Todd. The Arab League immediately banned her films. "I'm proud to be a Jew," she said. "Eddie and I have so much in common now. I love him dearly and plan to be Mrs. Eddie Fisher forever."

"My darling Elizabeth enters into every marriage thinking it is forever," said Roddy McDowall in Hollywood.

"Even as a little girl, I wanted to be Jewish," Elizabeth said. "In *Ivanhoe*, I was, although I was almost burned at the stake. Blame it on eating all those bowls of Louis B. Mayer's chicken soup in the MGM commissary. I identify with the sufferings of the Jews. Being Jewish brings me closer to Mike Todd. I even have a new name—Elisheba Rachel. I also just purchased $100,000 worth of bonds for Israel."

In front of her parents, Elizabeth converted to Reform Judaism at Temple Israel in Hollywood. Sara equated the event as something equivalent "to attending a witches' Sabbath."

Mike Todd might have approved, but Fisher, not that keen on religion in any form, didn't seem to care. He told columnist Rona Barrett, "Jewish girls are no good for fucking. They seem to feel they're doing you a favor."

During Elizabeth's marriage to Fisher, the couple attended a synagogue only once, to observe the high holidays, and she never gave up wearing a gold cross.

In Hollywood, Sara, an anti-Semite, told her friends, "I hated Jews all my life, and now I have one for a daughter."

Fisher now called Elizabeth "My *Yiddena*" ("my little Jewish woman").

After her conversion, one small town newspaper in Alabama wrote that, "Elizabeth, the traitor, had denied Jesus Christ and will burn in hell's fire." Another claimed, "She has now joined the pagans—Marilyn Monroe, Sammy Davis, Jr., and Carroll Baker."

Lesser lights such as singer Polly Bergen and the British bombshell, Diana Dors, had also recently converted to Judaism.

When a slightly tipsy Elizabeth at Romanoff's was asked, "What do you see in all these Jewish husbands," she had an answer: "The only difference is a small piece of skin."

***

The Reynolds divorce from Fisher came through as an interlocutory decree in February of 1959. The final dissolution of the ill-fated marriage would require another year's wait.

Elizabeth announced to the press that she had rented quarters for herself and her children at the Hidden Well Ranch in Pleasant Valley, Nevada, five miles from Las Vegas, as a means of being near Fisher, who had signed for an engagement there at The Tropicana.

Even at the time of the Reynolds/Fisher wedding in 1955, Fisher was already hooked on cocaine and methamphetamines, as he candidly admitted in his memoirs. Since 1953, he'd been receiving injections from the notorious "Dr. Feelgood" (Max Jacobson), who was also injecting Jack and Jackie Kennedy. As Fisher said, "Jack Kennedy and I shared drugs and women."

"I have often been asked what I learned from marriage," Fisher said. "That's simple: Don't marry Debbie Reynolds. Sexually, Elizabeth was every man's dream. She had the face of an angel and the morals of a truck driver."

In divorce court, Reynolds claimed that her husband was interested in another woman, but did not name her. The judge granted her a divorce and the custody of her two children, Carrie and Todd Fisher. She also made off with two houses in Hollywood and a rumored million dollar settlement, plus an alimony of $40,000 a year, with the understanding that the alimony would cease if and when she remarried.

Later, she became horrified when it was reported to her that Fisher was writing an autobiography which alleged that she had had a lesbian relationship with actress Agnes Moorehead. Reynolds publicly denied such a liaison and threatened her former husband with a multi-million dollar lawsuit. Forced to back down, Fisher asserted that he would write about her as "the perfect girl next door."

So that Fisher and Elizabeth would not have to wait a year for his divorce to become final, Reynolds agreed to recognize his brief residency in Nevada. Perhaps she opted to be cooperative because of the generous terms of her divorce settlement.

On the night of April 2, 1959, Fisher opened his act at the Tropicana in Las Vegas, having just learned that his contract for Fisher's *Coke Time* TV series had been canceled because of the public disapproval associated with his *L'Affaire Liz.*

He had desperately needed the six-week engagement. The cost of his divorce, which had included lawyer fees and the million dollar settlement on Reynolds, had drained his savings.

Elizabeth was driven to the Tropicana from her hideaway at the Hidden Well Ranch. As she walked into the club, she was greeted with scowling faces, picket lines, and signs saying "LIZ GO HOME!"

When Fisher received news that his divorce had been finalized months ahead of schedule, he was still singing at the Tropicana. He then directed his lyrics specifically at Elizabeth, who was sitting at ringside: "Another bride, another June, another sunny honeymoon."

After his show, he thanked the owners of the Tropicana for "giving me a job. I needed it."

Like Todd, Fisher bestowed jewelry on Elizabeth, including an evening bag studded with twenty-seven diamonds, one for every year of her life.

But despite his largesse (or perhaps because of it), Fisher had run out of money, supplying presents to Elizabeth he could ill afford—a $270,000 diamond bracelet, $150,000 for that evening bag, and a $500,000 emerald necklace from Bulgari. In the 1950s, these sums were staggering. "To keep Elizabeth happy," he said, "you have to give her a diamond every morning before breakfast."

During Fisher's remaining performances at the Tropicana, Elizabeth made her appearance in the audience at 11:48pm, a few minutes before the beginning of Fisher's midnight show. As the spotlight focused on her in a different gown each evening, she would rise and blow him a kiss. Then he'd sing a love song to her.

While living in Las Vegas, Elizabeth told reporters, "When I began to grow fond of Eddie as a man, I wondered whether it was because I was seeing him as Mike. But I knew you couldn't create someone in someone else. It would be disastrous. I will always love Mike, but that's something different and separate. Eddie does have a lot of Mike's qualities, but finally, I was sure I was not trying to marry an image. I knew I was truly and deeply in love with Eddie."

Vernon Scott, from United Press International, had written many unflattering stories about her. When he approached her, she said, "Why don't you go screw yourself, Vernon?"

On May 12, 1959, during Fisher's court appearance that had been scheduled in the wake of having satisfied Nevada's residence requirement, Fisher spent only two minutes before District Judge David Zenoff before his divorce was approved.

"The Widow Todd," in a civil ceremony, married Eddie Fisher only a few hours after his divorce became final. In attendance were Sara and Francis Taylor, watching their twenty-eight-year-old daughter wed for the fourth time.

Outside, angry ex-fans picketed the wedding. Mike Todd, Jr., Elizabeth's most recent lover, was the Best Man, even though he had never been that close to Fisher.

Mara Taylor, Elizabeth's sister-in-law, functioned as her matron of honor. "I decided not to use Debbie Reynolds this time," Elizabeth said jokingly.

At the wedding, she made a stunning appearance in a magnificent Jean-Louis spring green chiffon dress. On hearing of her choice of color, Marlene Dietrich said, "Brides should never wear green. It brings them only bad luck. But surely no one deserves bad luck more that Liz Taylor, that London tramp."

The bride and groom stood underneath a *chuppah,* which had been decorated with white gardenias that gave off an intoxicating aroma, and a few hundred white and pink carnations.

It was a traditional Jewish wedding with Fisher sporting a yarmulke and stomping on a wineglass. Dick Hanley was there, along with hairdresser Sidney Guilaroff; her agent Kurt Frings; Eddie Cantor (who had launched Fisher's career); Dr. Rex Kennamer, and MGM's Benny Thau. Also present was a hip and handsome young actor, Robert Evans, who would later become the president of Paramount.

In time, Fisher and Evans would pursue the same Renata Boeck, whom both men hailed "as the most beautiful woman in the world." Presumably, they placed Elizabeth as number two in that category.

In the midst of all this turmoil, MGM decided to release *Cat On a Hot Tin Roof,* even though there were certain elements demanding a boycott of the film. In spite of dire predictions, it became a huge box office success for MGM.

Far from being condemned, Elizabeth drew some rave reviews. *The New York Herald Tribune* claimed, "If there is any doubt about the ability of Miss Taylor to express complex and devious emotions and to deliver a flexible and deep performance, this film ought to remove them. *The Los Angeles Examiner* cited her beauty and passion which makes her "the most commanding young actress of the screen." *The Saturday Review* raved, "Hers is unquestionably one of the finest performances of any year."

***

As Mrs. Eddie Fisher, Elizabeth left Las Vegas, flying with her new husband to New York, where she would change planes and head to Europe for her honeymoon, for a new film (*Suddenly, Last Summer*), and for a new life.

"I'm the happiest I've ever been," she told reporters in New York, repeating the line she'd used with her three previous husbands.

"This time around, I've got it right in my choice of a man," Elizabeth told reporters when she landed in London. "Eddie and I will grow old together."

CHAPTER EIGHTEEN
A Honeymoon with Liz and Eddie

"I have never been happier in my life. Eddie and I will be on our honeymoon for thirty or forty years."

—Elizabeth Taylor, at her wedding to Eddie Fisher, May 12, 1959

As Elizabeth embarked on her honeymoon with Eddie Fisher in Spain, she said, "From now on, I want to devote my time to being a good wife and a mother. After all, a career makes a poor bedfellow on a cold night."

The suggestion was that she planned to retire and be supported by Fisher. The trouble with that plan was that Fisher had no singing gigs. She was the breadwinner in the family, and was arguably the most sought-after actress in the world. Some offer of some sort came in every day. In fact, even on her honeymoon, she had work commitments, including shooting exterior scenes for *Suddenly, Last Summer* in Spain. She also had to make a cameo appearance in Michael Todd, Jr.'s ill-fated Smell-O-Vision film entitled *Scent of Mystery,* or *Holiday in Spain* (1960).

Producer Sam Spiegel lent Elizabeth and Fisher his 120-foot yacht, the *Orinoco,* for a cruise of the Mediterranean. *Orinoco* was a converted two-hundred ton minesweeper staffed by six servants and a French maid. But it was the Belgian chef that caused Elizabeth to overeat.

Their stateroom with its four-poster bed was a replica of Christopher Columbus' cabin aboard the *Santa Maria.* Their bed was built into the bow of the ship, and consequently was tossed and agitated more than if it had been positioned in its center. "It was horrible," Fisher recalled. "I hated that bed. We had a hard time making love in it."

At the still fledging resort of Torremolinos, along the Spanish Mediterranean coast, Elizabeth was joined by her children. That Sunday, she and Fisher drove the kids to see their first bullfight at the ring in nearby Málaga.

Once during the bullfight there was a call for volunteers to face off against a deadly bull. Fisher volunteered in spite of a warning from Elizabeth, "If you do, I'll break your fucking head."

Drunk and drugged at the time, he claimed that, "The bull was more attracted to a skinny Jewish singer than he was to red capes. As he came toward me, I was totally paralyzed with fear. I think Elizabeth saw her entire sex life about to disappear as the ferocious bull went for the family jewels." After making a successful pass, Fisher eluded the bull and ran for safety as skilled Spanish matadors re-directed the path of the charging animal.

After Spain, the *Orinoco* sailed east toward the Côte d'Azur, with stopovers along the gilded ports of the French Riviera. At every port at which they anchored, especially St-Tropez, mobs turned out to gape at them. When she went on a shopping expedition, Provençal women from the hills journeyed down to the port to offer their freshly scrubbed babies for sale to Elizabeth.

Coming into port at Cannes, Elizabeth spent five nights at the villa of Prince Aly Khan. At dinners he staged for them, she was also seen with Gianni Agnelli and Aristotle Onassis, each of whom invited her for day trips aboard their own lavish yachts.

On her first night in Cannes, Elizabeth became furious when a newspaper in Paris broke the story that she and Fisher had been intimate even before and during her marriage to Todd. She wanted to sue, but Fisher advised against it. "Since their information is true," he told her, "we might be exposed as liars and even more embarrassed."

With Onassis at her side, a champagne-fueled Elizabeth appeared at the casino at Cannes and won $5,000 for her trouble.

Elizabeth was vastly intrigued with Prince Aly Khan, whom she'd met twice before. She told her secretary-companion, Dick Hanley, "I wonder if it's true that he's the greatest lover of our times. I should have asked Rita Hayworth. After all, she was married to him. Rita and I have shared other lovers— take Victor Mature, for instance."

"You wouldn't dare," he said. "You're on your honeymoon with Eddie."

"Hell with honeymoons," she said. "On the first night of my honeymoon with Nicky Hilton, he balled two prostitutes—and not me."

The Prince was the son of Aga Khan III, who claimed direct descent from the Prophet Mohammed's daughter, Fátima. The Aga Khan III, who had functioned as President of the League of Nations in 1937-38 and who had been instrumental in the formation of the modern nation of Pakistan, was the *Imam* (supreme spiritual leader, a sort of pope) to some fifteen million followers in

Asia and Africa. They were known as Ismaili Muslims.

At the time Elizabeth was the Aly Khan's guest, he was a media event, worshipped by millions as "the son of God." An international playboy, he was not only a religious leader, but a multi-millionaire, bon vivant, sybarite, Casanova, gentleman jockey, horse breeder, hunter, pilot, auto racer, daredevil, solider, United Nations diplomat, and globe trotter.

In spite of that, he was snubbed by certain elements of international society. But he had a comeback: "They called me a bloody nigger, and I paid them back by taking their women."

The number of women in Khan's life can never be known, but it can be assumed he reached the legendary Don Juan figure of "a thousand and three."

Over a drink with Onassis, the Greek billionaire told Elizabeth that "a woman is really *déclassée* if she hasn't been to bed with Aly at least once. When he first meets you, he'll give you a gold cigarette case with a large emerald embedded in it. After he fucks you, he'll give you a diamond bracelet."

Throughout his contacts in the film industry as Louis B. Mayer's secretary, Dick had learned many of the secrets of Khan's success with women. Among a bevy of beauties from all walks of life, he had seduced such actresses as Kim Novak, who claimed, "Aly just loved women too much." Rita Hayworth, who

FAMILIES WHO FEUD
left figure, above: **The Aga Khan III**, *imam* to the Ismaili Muslims, with his Europeanized son (*right*), **Prince Aly Khan**, in Milan in 1936

married and divorced him in 1949 and 1953, respectively, had said, "He went to bed with Gilda and woke up the next morning with me."

Aly's other seductions included Merle Oberon, Irene Pappas, Gene Tierney, Zsa Zsa Gabor, Yvonne De Carlo, Joan Fontaine, and the French chanteuse, Juliette Greco.

When Elizabeth arrived in Cannes to be Khan's house guest, he was in residence with the international model known as "Bettina," whose real name was Simone Bodin.

Dick told Elizabeth, "Aly is known for his 'staying power.' He can have intercourse for hours and hours. In Cairo, he was trained in an ancient Arabic sexual technique. They call it *Imsák*. He keeps a bucket of ice by the side of his bed. When is about to climax, he plunges his arms into the bucket of ice and starts all over again."

"Oleg Cassini learned one of Aly's secrets from Gene Tierney," Elizabeth said. "I hear that Aly is one of the world's leading cunnilinguists. Supposedly, he performs his specialty on any woman he's involved with at least three times a day."

After her first dinner with the Prince, Elizabeth later said she found "Aly's company very seductive. As for Eddie, he seemed to have eyes only for Bettina. At dinner, he didn't look at me once."

On the following night, Fisher was invited to go with Onassis to the casino at Monte Carlo. Elizabeth falsely claimed she had a headache, and Khan said he had a vital business meeting at the Carlton Hotel in Cannes. Bettina agreed to go with Fisher to the casino, followed by a visit to a night club in the same complex.

Within an hour of Fisher's departure for Monaco, Khan, as she'd later confess to Dick, "appeared at my bedroom door. He was completely nude and what a sight it was. I had some music playing and I was wearing a sheer black *négligée.* He took my hand and guided me to the floor, where he danced with me until this foot-long protrusion separated us."

"He was a thrilling lover," she claimed. "He told me, 'I only think of the woman's pleasure when I am in love, and I am in love with you from the day we first met. I want to marry you."

Fortunately, at a party in Paris, Elsa Maxwell had warned Elizabeth, "When Aly falls for a woman, it is madly and deeply. The only problem is that it might last for only one night."

"All the rumors about Aly's sexual success are true," Elizabeth told Dick the next day. "If I hadn't married Eddie, I would have accepted his proposal of marriage, even if it weren't all that sincere. I adore this man. No man ever took me to the plateau he did. Imagine being seduced by a man skilled in the sexual secrets of the ancient Egyptians. If Cleopatra were still around, she would surely have dumped Marc Antony for Aly."

"You look so very sad, and you seemed so happy," Dick said. "I noticed Aly didn't leave your room until four o'clock in the morning. Bettina and Eddie got back at six o'clock from Monaco. So I hope two hours was time enough to recover."

"If I'm looking sad, it's because I know that I have experienced the greatest lovemaking of my life. It will all be downhill from here."

Two views of **Prince Aly Khan:**
top photo: with **Bettina**
lower photo: with **Rita Hayworth**

She and Khan didn't connect again, and he kissed her goodbye before her return to Spiegel's yacht. In front of Dick, she whispered in Khan's ear, "Any time, any place, just give me a call. Let me put it this way: You are the world's greatest host."

"And you are the century's love goddess," he told her.

"Don't let Rita hear you say that."

***

After her not-always idyllic honeymoon with Fisher on the Continent, Elizabeth and Fisher flew into her familiar London, where Sam Spiegel turned over to them a fifteen-room estate next door to Windsor Castle. The property was surrounded with a high wall which had been topped with barbed wire. An ominous sign read: WITHOUT AN APPOINTMENT, STAY OUT!

Tout London ignored her, and she felt isolated at Windsor. Consequently, she demanded (and prevailed) that Spiegel rent the two best suites at the Dorchester for Fisher and herself.

One night at the bar of the very elegant Dorchester, Elizabeth joined Dick and her agent, Kurt Frings, who was actually running her career. She told very unflattering stories about Eddie. "He struggled and struggled last night, but he couldn't give me an orgasm," she admitted to them. "He claims I'm castrating him." Then, when she saw him walking across the bar to join them, she said in a whisper, "Who needs Eddie Fisher?"

Ostensibly, Elizabeth was in London for the exterior shots of *Suddenly, Last Summer* being filmed at the Shepperton Studios in the London suburbs.

Director Joseph Mankiewicz had encountered Elizabeth's divorced husband, Michael Wilding, at a party in Mayfair. "I plan to both direct and fuck your ex-wife," he told Wilding.

"Good luck, ol' boy," Wilding responded.

Although he was one of the most acclaimed singing stars in America, Fisher was unhappily settling into the role of Mr. Elizabeth Taylor. "My real job was keeping her happy," he wrote. "My own career was disappearing. My singing, which had once been the thing I lived for, was becoming more of a well-paid hobby."

Both Fisher and Elizabeth seemed hellbent on spending their every last cent, often on presents for one another. While in London, he flew her to Paris to shop at the House of Dior, where he purchased for her a dozen designer gowns and dresses by Yves Saint-Laurent.

She returned the favor by buying him a Jaguar. He bought a thirteen-room brick mansion for her in Purchase, New York, set on five acres, and also a $350,000 chalet in Gstaad, Switzerland. In addition to the Jaguar, on another oc-

429

casion, she gave him an emerald-green Rolls-Royce convertible.

Imitating Mike Todd, Fisher forged ahead to set up independent film companies such as Pisces Productions and MCL films as a means of starring Elizabeth in such features as Pearl Buck's *Imperial Woman* or Tolstoy's *Anna Karenina*. Neither of these projects was ever filmed.

"What really turned her against Fisher was what he was doing to use her as a future bread ticket," Dick said. "In addition to other film companies, he set up the Fisher Corporation and announced that it would produce all Elizabeth Taylor films in the future. But he was getting nothing off the ground. He was a total failure as a producer. At least Mike Todd had launched *80 Days*. Perhaps the *coup de grâce* occurred when she found out that all those diamonds he was giving her were actually being charged to their joint account."

When Max Lerner came to London, Elizabeth resumed her affair with him. The columnist later admitted, "We got so serious there for a while, we talked of marriage. When my fellow journalists learned of our affair, they called it 'The Beauty and The Brain.' A similar reference had been used to describe the marriage of Marilyn Monroe to Arthur Miller. Elizabeth must have been attracted to my brain. It sure wasn't my body."

Dick wasn't surprised that Elizabeth took up with other men after having been married to Fisher for such a brief time "She was terribly attracted to Eddie in the beginning. They couldn't get enough of each other. But she soon tired of him. She lost respect for him when he lost his career, though she may have been responsible for that. He'd gone out and spent all his money and now he was forced into the position of being her kept boy. She didn't like that. So she started treating him like a slave, demanding he obey her every wish."

She was not only bossing Fisher around, but increasingly, she was using her new found clout with producers and directors. Consequently, Elizabeth insisted that Monty Clift be included in the cast of *Suddenly, Last Summer.*

Unfortunately, in his previous film, *Lonelyhearts* (1958), Monty had virtually ruined his reputation among the power elite of Hollywood during his portrayal as an "agony uncle" [an "Advice to the Lovelorn" columnist]. Because of his drinking and drug abuse, he'd had a rough time getting through the production. Word spread from studio to studio, and, as a result, he became an uninsurable risk. Elizabeth was nonetheless adamant that he be cast in *Suddenly, Last Summer.* Otherwise, she threatened to bolt from the picture herself.

Since no company would insure Monty, Joseph Mankiewicz was placed in the frightening position of having to direct the film with one of its three principal players uninsured.

Mankiewicz had good reason to be worried: In London, Monty came to visit Elizabeth and Fisher in their respective suites at "The Dorch." At one point during the evening, he went out and balanced himself precariously on the iron balustrade of their terrace, "wobbling a few inches from his death," in Fisher's words.

When Fisher lured a drunken and drugged Monty back into the suite, Elizabeth told Monty that many friends, including Janet Leigh, had told her not to accept the role in *Suddenly, Last Summer*. According to Elizabeth, as transmitted by Fisher, "Janet said, 'It will ruin what's left of your reputation.' She said 'The gay stuff is barely acceptable to the general public, but the cannibalism is just too damn much.'"

For the first day of shooting, Elizabeth and Fisher were driven outside London to Skepperton Studios. In her hand, she clutched a hastily marked-up copy of the script of *Suddenly, Last Summer*, which was based on a one-act play by Tennessee Williams. The screenplay had been written by Tennessee's friend, rival, and fellow gay author, Gore Vidal. Since she'd had such success with Williams' material in *Cat on a Hot Tin Roof*, she was hoping to score another win with *Suddenly*.

She was being paid half a million dollars for her participation in *Suddenly*, which made her the highest paid salaried actress in the world.

Showing up for work, she had the hint of a double chin. As Sam Kashner wrote in *Furious Love*, "It seems hard to believe that someone whose reputation and livelihood depended on flawless beauty would risk it all by sheer overindulgence. Yet it's possible that Elizabeth had a love-hate relationship with her beauty. It was her beauty that had stolen her childhood and imprisoned her in an unreal life. She was a freak of nature, constantly being gawked at, lusted after, envied, and subjected to extreme scrutiny. It's not surprising that a part of her would want to destroy it. So she would eat and eat and eat."

The director wanted Elizabeth to take publicity stills of herself in a white swimsuit, which would be flashed across the world. When she first tried on the suit in her dressing room, with Mankiewicz present, he instructed her to "tighten those muscles. It looks like you've got bags of dead mice under your arms."

On hearing this, Elizabeth lunged at him, threatening to "tear out your fucking eyeballs." Dick pulled her off the director.

Just prior to and during the filming, she would go on a crash diet, which restored her youthful beauty. By the end of filming, she claimed, "Hell, I look like I'm seventeen again—and a virgin."

Even though they fought each other, there was an obvious physical attraction between Elizabeth and her director, and this was all too obvious to the cast and crew.

While professing undying love for Fisher, Elizabeth launched a summer (1959) affair with Mankiewicz, who had recently suffered through the ordeal of his wife committing suicide. Elizabeth told Monty, "Joe is my kind of man, like Mike Todd in many ways—bombastic, strong, determined, powerful. He combines strength with vulnerability, a combination I have always found irresistible."

"Dad had a habit of bedding his leading ladies, such as Joan Crawford and Gene Tierney," claimed his son, Chris Mankiewicz. His other son, Tom Mankiewicz, agreed with his brother, "In *All About Eve,* Dad passed on Bette Davis, but not on Eve herself [a reference to Anne Baxter]."

Fisher heard that Elizabeth was having an affair. Perhaps to save his pride, he denied it. When pressed, he said, "Joe is in love with Jean Simmons one day, Judy Garland the next day, and now Elizabeth. There is no affair."

Mankiewicz more or less admitted to the affair in 1962 when he was directing Elizabeth in Rome during the filming of *Cleopatra.* A reporter from a Roman newspaper asked him if he were "having an affair with Cleopatra."

"Fuck, no!" the director shouted at him. "That was during our last picture together!" a reference, of course, to *Suddenly, Last Summer.*

The film was promoted with Elizabeth in that swimsuit, with the caption: "*Suddenly, Last Summer, Cathy* (the character played by Elizabeth) *was being used for evil.*"

The "evil" referred to her being used to attract men that her cousin, Sebastian, would then seduce. Previously, Sebastian had used his mother, Violet Venable (as played by Katharine Hepburn) for procuring, but she had grown too old. The assumption, of course, was farfetched.

Sebastian had been killed in a traumatic episode of cannibalism, and Violet orders Dr. John Cukrowiz (as played by Clift) to perform a lobotomy on the episode's only witness, Cathy (Taylor).

In the film, the details of Sebastian's grisly death are not clearly depicted, but the plot calls for Sebastian to be chased, bludgeoned, and stripped by a group of angry, vengeful young men and pieces of his flesh eaten. After seeing the filmed version of the scene, Tennessee Williams said, "That is the ultimate parody of a blow-job."

Joseph Mankiewicz

Mankiewicz at first had been courteous and respectful of Monty. But when he invited him to dinner, he was appalled. Monty reached for food on the plates of others, and even tossed pieces of meat into the faces of his fellow guests. He ate with his hands and made outrageous remarks. "Let's go around the table," he said. "I want to know the size of every man's penis. As for the women, I want to know the largest object you've ever inserted into your vagina."

Facing Monty before the camera, Elizabeth realized just how much his mental and physical condition had deteriorated. Monty simply could not remember his lines, which incited almost violent attacks from Mankiewicz. At one point, the director wanted to shut down the picture and cast another actor in the role.

Zombie like, Monty walked through the film, giving a strangulated and neurasthenic performance. He spends a great deal of time on screen repeating the words of others, reformulating them in the form of a question.

Elizabeth exploded and denounced Sam Spiegel when she learned that he was negotiating with Peter O'Toole to take over Monty's role. She threatened to walk off the picture.

The character of Violet Venable (Hepburn) was based on Tennessee's mother, Edwina, who permitted (some say encouraged) doctors to perform a lobotomy on his sexually frustrated sister, Rose Isabel Williams.

Several biographies have suggested that until she made *Suddenly, Last Summer*, Hepburn was not aware of what homosexual men did in bed together and that Gore Vidal had to explain it to her. That, of course, is a laughable assertion about a woman who had spent decades in Hollywood among homosexuals. As a lesbian herself, she was deeply involved in a platonic relationship with another closeted homosexual actor, Spencer Tracy. Her best friend was George Cukor, the gay director, and her best female friend and lover was Laura Harding, the American Express heiress.

On the set one sultry afternoon, when London was experiencing a rare heat wave, a jittery Hepburn confronted Vidal and Elizabeth, who were sitting in directors' chairs, discussing the next scene.

"Mr. Vidal, I talked it over with Spence last night, and he and I decided I can't go on with this film. Your script is just too vile. Give the role to that poor, wretched Mildred Dunnock. She'll play any part, no matter how demented. With all its flesh-eaters, lesbian nurses, sadistic nuns, it's all so *Grand Guignol*,"

Discussing the nuances of perversion
Katharine Hepburn *(left)* as Violet Venable
and **Gore Vidal** *(right)*

Hepburn said. "No movie-goer will sit through this muck. The characters you and Mr. Williams have created are perverted. I do not understand perversion— never have, never will. I'm far too mentally healthy to be appearing in such demented trash."

"Miss Hepburn," Vidal said with *gravitas*. "You understand perversion to your toenails. You'll give one of the most electrifying performances of your life. Forget Dunnock. Do you want us to give the role to Bette Davis? You'll probably get nominated for an Oscar."

"Perhaps you're right," Hepburn said before walking away.

She went ahead and finished the film as Vidal had written it. In fact, she worked even harder to improve the demented and perverted quality of Violet Venable's character.

Vidal's prediction about Hepburn being nominated for an Oscar turned out to be accurate.

That same day, a reporter encountered Elizabeth and asked her what she thought about appearing in such a controversial film. "I've always wanted to appear on screen with Venus's-flytraps," she said. That was a reference to the re-

Suddenly, Last Summer
"A world of degenerates obsessed with rape, incest, homosexuality, and cannibalism."

photo above:
Clift and **E.T.**

photo above:
Hepburn, Clift, and **E.T.**

photo above, left to right:
Sebastian (in white suit), **Cathy** (as played by **E.T.**) and the outstretched arms of "all the young cannibals"

photo above:
Tennessee Williams

creation of a carnivorous garden as a set within the movie.

As a kind of gag, Fisher appeared uncredited as a street urchin begging Elizabeth for food. Frank Merlo, the lover of Tennessee Williams, also made an uncredited appearance, as did Gore Vidal. He and Merlo can be seen among the audience in a wraparound balcony observing Monty in his role as a surgeon performing an operation in a "surgical theater" below.

Mercedes McCambridge, cast as Elizabeth's greedy mother, recalled what an unhappy time filming *Suddenly* was for everybody: "Monty was coming apart right on the set, but Elizabeth could not provide her usual help because of her own misery. I read constantly in the papers about how much she loved Eddie Fisher. London was an inferno that summer. She and I walked off the sound stage to get some fresh air. Outside, she was in tears. 'My life is a shambles,' she admitted. 'I made a horrible mistake. I married Eddie and I don't love him. At times, I can't even stand him.' I could not believe my ears. Once we went inside, Eddie was there. She made a spectacle of showing her affection for him."

"Whereas working with Joan Crawford is a nightmare, working with Elizabeth Taylor is merely a disturbing experience. On the set she sounded like a fishwife, calling people 'assholes' or 'schmuck.' I thought she was completely outrageous. She was tender to Monty, but by the end of the shoot, she wasn't speaking to Hepburn. Elizabeth told me that Hepburn came on to her in her dressing room one afternoon—and she was rejected. That's why Hepburn was so bitter. A lot of those old dragon stars of the 1930s were dykes—not just Hepburn, but Garbo and Dietrich, too. Might I have the honor of adding Joan Crawford to that list—I should know!"

Tennessee arrived on the set and spent time with Elizabeth. He told her, "I was with Monty last night. He's washing down his codeine pills with brandy. But who am I to cast stones? He told me that after the accident, he has become impotent and the only way he can achieve sexual satisfaction is to peform fellatio on a man or else be penetrated by one."

"Thank you, Tennessee, you're a darling, but I really don't know what I can do with this personal data about Monty," Elizabeth said.

When Truman Capote saw the movie, he claimed that Elizabeth's final dramatic monologue was "the best scene she'd ever performed before or likely ever again. She should win the Oscar."

Mankiewicz defined her long, concluding monologue as "an aria from a tragic opera of madness and death."

After she shot that scene, Elizabeth became hysterical and couldn't stop crying for hours.

***

435

Throughout the filming, Katharine Hepburn had been consistently furious with Mankiewicz for his brutal treatment of the tormented Monty. She was also furious at him for his treatment of herself as well, interpreting his behavior as condescending.

On the last day of Hepburn's appearance before the camera, the tension between Mankiewicz and Hepburn was obvious to the entire crew. By ten o'clock, she and the director were screaming at each other. But once the camera was turned on her, the star became her carefully controlled, professional self, giving an awesome interpretation of her particular manifestation of evil.

By five o'clock that afternoon, Mankiewicz defined the experience as a wrap. Then Hepburn walked over to him. "Are you absolutely sure that that is all you'll need from me on this film?"

"I am absolutely sure," he told her. "You're free to go."

"Fine, she said. Then in front of everybody, including Elizabeth, she spat in his face, turned her back to him, and stormed off the set.

Wiping the spit off his face, Mankiewicz, in front of Elizabeth said, "Miss Hepburn is the most experienced amateur actress in the world. Her performances, though remarkably effective, are fake."

In contrast, Capote found that "Hepburn is the Queen of High Camp as she stands in that fantasy New Orleans garden filled with insectivorous growths. Monty looks as if he is going to expire at any minute. Although I detest the film's scriptwriter, Gore Vidal, I have to admit *Suddenly, Last Summer* marks the end of the 1950s. The public is obviously eager for a more candid expression of sex."

The Catholic Legion of Decency forced the studio to edit much of the dialogue so that the homosexual theme is only implied, and that the actual gay character has neither a face nor a voice in the film.

"Homosexuality is truly the love that dare not speak its name—or show its face," Tennessee said. When he was presented with a screening of the film's final cut, he sat silently through it. At the end, he rose from his chair. "It made me want to throw up. Elizabeth Taylor was totally miscast."

In spite of their difficulties during the shoot, Mankiewicz later said, "Her role as Cathy was the best performance Elizabeth ever gave on the screen."

Time claimed that watching *Suddenly* was like being crushed in the "clammy coils of a giant snake." The critic for *Variety* made the claim that, "It's the most bizarre film ever made by a major studio."

Inadvertently, film critic Bosley Crowther increased attendance in droves when he wrote that the movie was about "the world of degenerates obsessed with rape, incest, homosexuality, and cannibalism." By "degenerates," he was referring, of course, to Vidal and Williams.

436

"We could not have asked for better advertising," Vidal said, in response.

"It stretched my credulity to believe such a 'hip' doll as our Liz wouldn't know at once in the film that she was 'being used for something evil,'" Tennessee said.

In contrast to Tennessee's objections to Elizabeth and her performance, he referred to Hepburn as "a playwright's dream. She makes my dialogue sound better than it is. She invests every scene with the intuition of an artist born to act."

The *New York Times* shrieked that *Suddenly, Last Summer* "was a celebration of sodomy, incest, cannibalism, and Elizabeth Taylor at her most voluptuous."

Ultimately, she came to prefer *Suddenly* as her favorite film—"emotionally draining, but also emotionally stimulating."

In spite of the critics, and in spite of the doom-predicting Hedda Hopper, *Suddenly* became the fourth highest grossing movie of 1960, earning nearly $6 million in domestic ticket sales alone.

Far from emerging as a flop, as some in Hollywood had predicted, *Suddenly* catapulted Elizabeth into the ranks of Hollywood's Top Ten box office stars, a list that was dominated at the time by Rock Hudson and Doris Day in the wake of their highly successful *Pillow Talk* (1959).

She went to that year's Academy Award ceremony assured that "I will win. They're sure to give it to me for Maggie the Cat."

Dick Hanley warned her, "Don't get your hopes up. Katharine Hepburn is nominated for the same movie. Academy members who like *Suddenly, Last Summer* will split their vote. Hepburn should have run for Best Supporting Actress, but the old dyke wouldn't listen to reason."

As the Oscar winner was announced at the Academy Awards, Elizabeth had her hopes crushed. She and Hepburn came in at second and third place, respectively. The Oscar winner for the year's Best Actress was Simone Signoret for her role in *Room at the Top*.

***

After London, where she'd filmed the interiors of *Suddenly, Last Summer,* Elizabeth's next picture was to be shot in Hollywood. Accompanied by Eddie Fisher, she returned to her old stamping grounds at MGM. According to the terms of her contract, she owed them one final picture, a film that would be entitled *Butterfield 8*.

On September 9, 1959, she and Fisher moved into two rented bungalows on the grounds of the Beverly Hills Hotel. She also moved in her three children, along with their nannies.

She had not yet turned thirty, and already she'd reached a crossroads in her life. Like many stars in the late 1950s, including James Stewart, she was going independent and freeing herself from the influence of Louis B. Mayer and MGM, which had been a stern parent to her since she was a little girl and had first come to work for them.

She'd always detested Louis B. Mayer, but he was now dead (1957). Now that he no longer controlled her professional life, she attacked him as a "bigoted vulgarian." To certain of her friends, such as Shelley Winters and Janet Leigh, she claimed that Mayer had tried to molest her when she was a little girl. There is evidence that she made up this charge after Mayer was gone. During her experiences with him, she'd never leveled such a claim. Neither had she told Sara or Francis. Her accusations appear to be untrue. It seemed to be a way of presenting herself as a victim of the studio which had held such power over her.

When she did arrive at MGM to make her final film, she gave Mayer a backhanded compliment. "If Louis B. were still alive, I wouldn't be playing a whore in *Butterfield 8.*"

***

In one of the bungalows, Elizabeth and Fisher entertained Michael Wilding and his current wife, the British socialite, Susan Nell. As part of what would turn out to be a very rare occasion, Debbie Reynolds, the following night, dropped off Fisher's two young children, Carrie and Todd, as a means of helping to form friendships within their "reorganized" family circle.

Elizabeth had been back in Los Angeles for less than a week when an invitation arrived to join four-hundred of the top stars in Hollywood to greet Nikita Khrushchev, who was paying a visit to 20th Century Fox where *Can-Can* was being shot with Frank Sinatra and Shirley MacLaine.

Elizabeth and Fisher watched as "Richard Burton made an ass of himself" when he threatened to rush to the head table and attack the Soviet dictator for "his malicious attack on capitalism."

The following day, a surprise offer arrived for her to appear in an epic even before she'd begun serious talks about her final film at MGM.

Word had spread across Hollywood that Elizabeth was making her last film for MGM and would be free after that to accept offers from other studios. Nearly every major studio had a movie that might have been suitable for her, but the biggest offer had come in from 20th Century Fox.

Producer Walter Wanger and Spyros Skouras, the head of 20th Century Fox, had been in production on their upcoming movie *Cleopatra* for two years. Originally, they had envisioned a fairly inexpensive movie, even using some of the sets featured in the 1917 version of *Cleopatra*, a film that had starred the silent screen vamp, Theda Bara.

Joan Collins was at the head of the list of possible stars who might bring Cleopatra to life again. Two Italian beauties, Sophia Loren and Gina Lollobrigida, were also in the running. Before settling on Elizabeth as the lead, Fox had also suggested Audrey Hepburn and later, Marilyn Monroe. Skouras, however, thought Elizabeth should play Cleopatra.

Months later, when Pandro S. Berman at MGM learned about the stars being considered for *Cleopatra,* he said, "Audrey Hepburn and Marilyn, presumably in a dark wig, would be the worst casting mistakes in the history of Hollywood. Even Elizabeth Taylor is a bit of a stretch."

Dick Hanley went by Fox and picked up a copy of the original script. In bed with a headache, Elizabeth asked him to read it to her. Drinking champagne, she sat patiently through the entire reading, only commenting at the end.

"That is pure, unadulterated shit," she told Dick. "I hear they want Peter Finch to play Julius Caesar. He's a hot number. Who do they want to play Marc Antony?"

"That good-looking hunk, Stephen Boyd," he said.

"Boyd is gay, Michael Wilding told me, so you'll get to cash in on that," she said.

"What do you want me to tell Skouras?" he asked.

"I don't want to see a headline—LIZ TAYLOR NIXES CLEO—so tell him I'll make the fucking stinker, but only for a million dollars."

He whistled at the amount, as it was considered a staggering sum at the time.

When Dick delivered her demand the following day, Skouras bellowed so loud he could almost be heard across the Fox lot. He told his staff, "Any hundred dollar a week call girl can play that whore, Cleopatra."

However, in a huddle with Wanger, he suddenly changed his mind. "We'll increase the budget to three million and use Hollywood's favorite whore, Miss Taylor herself. Should we keep in the scene where Cleo got fucked by forty-two of her male servants in just one long night?"

Elizabeth needed money and her Austrian agent, Kurt Frings, promised to get it for her once she finished one more picture at MGM, according to the terms of her contract.

His clients included Audrey Hepburn, sex kitten Brigitte Bardot, and Lucille Ball, who was the queen of 1950s television. Elizabeth envied Hepburn for taking home $350,000 for her appearance in *War and Peace* in 1957.

Simultaneous with the details associated with the *Cleopatra* project, Frings began to negotiate a deal for Elizabeth to star in *Two for the Seesaw,* a play that had brought fame to Anne Bancroft on Broadway. There was talk of paying Elizabeth half a million dollars, the largest salary a movie actress had ever received.

Producer Samuel Marx urged her not to accept the part she'd been offered: That of a little Jewish girl from New York who can't get a date and falls in love with a traveling salesman who goes back to his wife.

"Who in hell would believe Elizabeth Taylor can't get a date?" he said.

Eventually, for many reasons, Elizabeth's link with the *Seesaw* deal collapsed, and Shirley MacLaine took the role opposite Robert Mitchum, with whom she eventually had an affair.

With *Seesaw* gone, Elizabeth turned to her two more pressing films. She wanted to appear as Cleopatra at Fox and then, when her work there was completed, return to MGM to film her last movie at that studio. "I want that million dollars from Fox, and MGM will pay me only $125,000 for *Butterfield 8.*"

Lawyers at MGM refused her proposal, telling her that she had to complete her contractual obligations for MGM before she could film *Cleopatra* at Fox. Their motivation derived partly from wanting to capitalize off the notoriety of *l'affaire Fisher* in their selection of her as the hooker in *Butterfield 8*.

John O'Hara, author of the novel which had inspired the movie, had based his character on a prostitute named Starr Faithful, who had been found dead in Palm Beach on June 8, 1931.

When MGM had first sent Elizabeth the script of *Butterfield 8.* she had turned it down, defining it as pornographic. She told her immediate staff, "MGM wants me to play a non-charging hooker. It's their revenge on me for not renewing my contract."

When he heard of her refusal, her longtime friend at the studio, Pandro S. Berman, came to Elizabeth and warned her that, "It's a new day at MGM. Stars are not handled delicately any more. Our lawyers can make it rough on you. Legally, they can hang on to you for another two years and prevent you from working at another studio. You've got to get MGM off your back. Make the fucking movie and then go on as an independent to demand a million dollars for every picture you make in the future."

His argument, after about a two-hour discussion, finally prevailed. "Okay, I'll be MGM's whore. They've fucked me before. Why not one final blast-off?"

What Berman failed to tell her was the he personally owned a huge share of the movie rights to *Butterfield 8*.

Years later, Berman expressed nothing but contempt for Elizabeth. "I went through hell with her. Sure, she had a lot of crummy parts, but all contract players do. I came to despise her. She let herself get fat as a pig. I've been a woman chaser all my life, and I never found her sexually attractive. Katharine Hepburn either. *Those two!"*

Immediately, Elizabeth seized upon the chance to demand that MGM cast Eddie Fisher in a role within *Butterfield 8*. MGM had no respect for Fisher as an actor, considering his utter failure in the 1956 *Bundle of Joy* with Debbie Reynolds. But because of such continuing worldwide press about "Liz and Eddie," it was decided that the pair might jointly generate another $2 million at the box office.

She needed the money and won the concession to have Fisher cast in the movie as her song-writing platonic friend, the second male lead. David Janssen was set to play the role, but at the last minute, he was dropped.

Benny Thau didn't want to use Fisher, but told Berman, "She has us by the nuts. At least with Fisher on the set, he might control the cunt. The kid's a bum, a drug addict, and, to top off matters, a fucking lousy actor. Cast him!"

Tired of all the conflict raging around her in Hollywood, Elizabeth also demanded that the film be shot in New York. MGM also agreed to that.

Fisher had spent more than a year without a singing engagement before he was offered a two-week gig at the Desert Inn in Las Vegas. He received that contract only because Elizabeth agreed to appear at ringside every night cheering him on.

Before Fisher was scheduled to participate in the filming of *Butterfield 8,* he had time to accept an offer for a gig at the prestigious Empire Room at the Waldorf Astoria Hotel in Manhattan. His success at the Desert Inn in Las Vegas had prompted the offer. The hotel was also excited by the prospect of Elizabeth, who had agreed to appear ringside every night he was performing in the Empire Room.

On Fisher's opening night, she was seated at the head table with Prince Aly Khan, who was visiting New York at the time. Other guests included the world's heavyweight boxing champion, Swedish-born Ingemar Johansson, and Dick Hanley.

As Khan listened to Fisher sing love songs to his wife, he secretly ran his hand up her dress, meeting no objections. Dick noted that she also seemed "absolutely enthralled with Johansson. "I was, too, but Elizabeth had more to offer the champ than I did. Aly had another engagement that night, but after Eddie's first performance, we disappeared upstairs with Ingemar. I was the guardian waiting in the living room while all the action took place in the bedroom."

The handsome, solidly built Swede became one of Elizabeth' least known affairs. Nicknamed "The Hammer of Thor," Johansson in 1959, the year Elizabeth met him and seduced him, defeated Floyd Patterson by a TKO in the third round.

She told Dick that Johansson was "an absolute powerhouse in bed. I felt like three pounds of Swedish sausage was pounding inside me. He fucks a woman like he intends to deliver a knockout punch—and he does. He scores a KO. What a guy. No wonder he's called Hammer."

Unlike boxers who were supposed to be in training, Johansson liked the nightclubs of New York. When Fisher was performing, Elizabeth often sneaked off with him. Sometimes, the boxer and the star used Monty's apartment for their sexual trysts.

"I can't get enough of him, and he can't get enough of me," she told Dick. She made arrangements for him to train at the Catskill resort of Grossinger's, Fisher's favorite place and the site of his earlier, long-ago wedding to Debbie Reynolds. Johansson also told Elizabeth he wanted to be a movie star. She was instrumental in getting him cast as a Marine in the Korean War film, *All the Young Men* (1960).

A nude picture snapped of him in a gym shower in 1960 was reprinted on a postcard-sized replica and became one of the best-selling celebrity nudes in the world. Kiosks along the Seine in Paris hawked it to American tourists.

Long after their affair flickered out, Elizabeth occasionally spoke on the phone to Johansson. It was a tragic sorrow for her to learn that beginning in the mid-1960s, the former champion suffered from Alzheimer's disease and dementia. At the age of 76, he died on January 30, 2009 from complications following pneumonia. At the time, he was living in a nursing home in Sweden as his health deteriorated. For years, he kept an autographed picture of Elizabeth by his bedside.

When he died, Elizabeth recalled, "He was a real champ in so many ways. After knowing him, I came to realize why Mae West was so hung up on boxers."

Elizabeth's nightclubbing came to an abrupt end on October 26, 1959 when she collapsed on Fifth Avenue during a shipping expedition with Dick. "I can't breathe," she called to him, gasping for air.

He rushed to the nearest phone and called an ambulance as onlookers crowded around her. En route to New York's Presbyterian Hospital, "she still had her wits about her," Dick said. "She asked me to put lip gloss on her."

Within a few hours, she was diagnosed as suffering from viral pneumonia, complicated by a bad case of influenza.

Bulletins were issued for almost a week. Confined to an oxygen tent, she was in critical condition. While in the hospital, she made a "reckless decision." She ordered her doctors to reverse an operation in which she had previously had her fallopian tubes tied.

Thinking she might solidify her marriage to Fisher by having a son or daughter with him, she wanted to be able to get pregnant again, even though previously, doc-

Ingemar Johansson

442

tors had warned her that bearing another child might threaten her life. She was determined, however, to submit to the surgery.

For reasons not entirely clear, her fallopian tubes could not be untied.

***

While Elizabeth was undergoing exploratory surgery and told she could have no more children, rumors surfaced about one of the unsolved mysteries of her life. Stories spread that she'd had a "love child" in the early 1950s. But details of the rumored birth would not be revealed in print until after her death when stories about it were published in such newspapers as London's *Daily Mail.*

Celebrity psychic John Cohan was a friend and confidant to Elizabeth for many years, in addition to being her psychic. During one of their sessions, she had revealed to him one of her darkest and most painful secrets. She told him that she'd once given birth, out of wedlock, to a baby girl named Norah.

According to rumors, since such a birth would have destroyed any actress's career during the more uptight 1950s, she was forced, based partly on the urging of both Benny Thau and her mother, Sara, to give the baby away.

"Money changed hands," Elizabeth told Cohan. "Norah was adopted by a family in Ireland."

The child, now a mature woman, of course, knows that Elizabeth was her mother, but is said to resent her for abandoning her. She was once quoted as saying, "I want nothing to do with Elizabeth Taylor."

Cohan's revelations were published by Cindy Adams, a columnist for *The New York Post.* Adams admitted that she could not confirm either the accuracy of the story or the existence of the daughter, "but I'm reporting it because one can't ignore the story in case there's some truth."

Elizabeth admitted to Cohan that at the time of the birth, she was involved with three different men and therefore could not be certain who the father was.

"I am still guilt ridden about having to abandon my child, even to this day." Elizabeth said to Cohan. She also extracted from Cohan the promise that he was to "say nothing about Norah until I'm gone."

The celebrity seer also had other shocking revelations. He said that he and Elizabeth were mutually involved in a short affair "between her marriages to Richard Burton. She told me I was a much sweeter and darling lover than Richard ever was. 'He was too rough at times,' she claimed."

She also admitted that Mike Todd had been "the love of my life, my soulmate—and not Richard."

As a final bombshell, she claimed, according to Cohan, that she believed that Burton had died from some AIDS-related disease.

Cohan has been a celebrity psychic to the stars for more than three decades. During much of that time, he has supplied Cindy Adams with his yearly predictions, which have turned out to be surprisingly accurate.

More revelations about the stars can be found in Cohan's memoir, *Catch a Falling Star: The Untold Story of Celebrity Secrets,* published in 2008.

In his book, he has much to reveal about Natalie Wood, Merv Griffin, River Phoenix, John F. Kennedy, Jr., and Elvis Presley. He even writes about what Mick Jagger and Rudolf Nureyev were caught doing at the Flesh Palace Disco in Manhattan. He also writes about his dear friend, Nicole Brown Simpson, as well as "the love of my life," Sandra Dee.

***

"On one day, Elizabeth would become obsessed with fear that she was losing Eddie," said Dick Hanley. "On yet another day, she would be plotting ways to get a divorce that would cause the minimum of bad headlines for her. I never told her, but Eddie was going out with showgirls while she was confined to a hospital bed. He also had some homosexual involvements. During her absence, he even invited me to a small orgy he staged in her suite at the Waldorf with three handsome gay waiters. He assumed that I'd be discreet and enjoy myself, but because of my loyalty to Elizabeth, I didn't go."

When she returned from the hospital to her suite at the Waldorf, and was in bed recovering, Fisher brought Dr. Feelgood (Max Jacobson) for a "medical consultation" in their rooms. The "speed" he injected into her veins caused her to experience sleepless nights, nervous exhaustion, fits of depression, and a dangerously rapid heartbeat.

"She would go to incredible highs and then plunge to the pits," Dick claimed. "She would be walking on some mile-high trapeze during the day, then she'd demand sleeping pills to plunge her back to earth. Sometimes, she fell into a coma-like sleep. Once, she slept for an entire day and night."

To prepare him for his upcoming role in *Butterfield 8,* Elizabeth decided that Fisher should take acting lessons from Monty. When Monty arrived at their suite at the Waldorf, and after he'd paid his respects to Elizabeth, he began to review the script with Fisher.

"I was in no great shape myself to take acting lessons," Fisher later recalled, "and Monty was in even worse shape. As he sat on the sofa with me, he tried to feel my jewels. At the time, I was living on am-

John Cohan
Celebrity Seer

444

phetamines from Dr. Feelgood. I went to get Monty another drink. By the time I got back, he'd fallen asleep with a lit cigarette and had set the script on fire. To complicate matters, Elizabeth was taking three or four hot baths a day. In the middle of my lesson, she called me for a waterborne fuck."

In a weakened condition in the wake of her recent hospitalization, Elizabeth reported to work in January of 1960 to begin the filming of *Butterfield 8.*

The film was heavily censored in the cinematic creation of Elizabeth's character of Gloria Wandrous. Even so, the script still contained references to how Gloria had been sexually abused as a child—and that she had actually enjoyed the experience.

Exterior shots of Elizabeth were filmed in the vicinity of Sixth Avenue and West 10th Street in Manhattan's Greenwich Village.

On her way to the filming, swathed in fur and laden with emeralds, Elizabeth passed by the nearby house of Detention for Women. As she did, she heard all sorts of catcalls—everything from "LET ME SUCK YOUR PUSSY, BITCH!" to "YOU CHEAP WHORE."

The film's director, Daniel Mann, said that when Elizabeth arrived for work, she looked unattractive. "She was overweight and had dark circles under her eyes. Her clothes had to be constantly refitted, and special undergarments and corsets were employed to hold her body in shape. She had lost the firmness of youth and looked matronly before her time. I also determined that she couldn't see a thing without contact lenses; she was myopic."

Brooklyn-born Mann, a stage actor since childhood, had directed the film versions of *Come Back, Little Sheba* (1952) and *The Rose Tattoo* (1955). He had very little flair for visual dynamics, but an excellent ear for dialogue.

The line Elizabeth delivers to Mildred Dunnock, who played her mother in the film, was the one Elizabeth most objected to: "Face it, Mama: I was the slut of all time!" Mann insisted that she utter that line.

With his frequent references to the Method acting technique, Mann did not impress Elizabeth. One afternoon, during the filming of a bathtub scene, he told her, with complete seriousness, "Make believe you're fucking the faucet. That's the expression I want."

After that remark, she gave him the finger and stormed off the set, refusing to work for the rest of the day.

The title of *Butterfield 8* referred to a telephone exchange in Manhattan's "Silk Stocking" district of the Upper East Side.

"I will be the screen's first female Casanova," she said of her role as Gloria Wandrous.

Of course, after leading such a tawdry life, Elizabeth's character in the film had to pay a price. At the end of the movie, her character of Gloria is killed in a car accident. Screenwriter John Michael Hayes concluded, "We can't let a whore like that live. Even her enemies will flock to the movie to see Elizabeth Taylor die, die, die."

On the set of *Butterfield 8*, Elizabeth met the English movie star, Laurence Harvey.

At first, he detested her, referring to her as "The Bitch" or "Fat Ass." But after a few days, he was drawn to her and they became friends, a relationship that lasted until his untimely death in 1973.

It was ironic, but Harvey and Michael Wilding would each wed the same woman, actress Margaret Leighton.

After an onscreen night with the character played by Harvey in his bedroom while his wife is away, Elizabeth, as Gloria, awakens after he leaves the apartment the following morning. She is seen putting on a slip and then "borrowing" a mink coat from his wife's closet. "I'm Venus in furs," Elizabeth (as Gloria) says before heading out to face the day.

The actress playing the very rich owner of that mink coat and the wife of the character played by Harvey was the very rich (in real life) Dina Merrill, the only child of Post Cereals' heiress Marjorie Merriweather Post and her second husband, Wall Street stockbroker Edward Francis Hutton.

Elizabeth found Harvey "very campy and very gay."

"I can keep my panties on around Harvey," she said with a sneer to Fisher. "He'll welcome blow-jobs from you, though."

He told her that "I fuck women on that odd Saturday, but don't get your hopes up. You're not my type, I have this Oedipus complex in that I'm attracted to older women, even that battle axe Hermione Baddeley."

In reference to his own homosexuality, Harvey told her, "When I see a man I like, I go after him, never worrying about rejection. "I think Sean Connery is the hottest man in England. He told me I was such a bitch I could play Hedda Gabler."

"John Gielgud called me Florence of Lithuania," he told Elizabeth. "I was born there. I like to do outrageous things," he said, "especially with a few drinks in me. When I first met that ugly little toad, Peter Lorre, I grabbed him and kissed him, ramming my tongue down his throat. At this party for Princess Margaret, I sat next to Lord Snowdon, her husband of the moment. I placed my hand at his crotch and felt every inch. I told him, 'I just wanted to find out what turns on Her Royal Highness. I'm not a princess, more a queen.'"

"You're my kind of guy, Larry," Elizabeth said. "I adore you."

She also had many serious talks with Harvey, especially about her role in *Butterfield 8*, which, deep into the shoot, she still detested. She later thanked him for giving her "some sound advice."

"Darling," he said, "I should have been cast as the whore. As heaven knows, I am one myself."

During a writer's strike at MGM, Elizabeth wanted some of the dialogue associated with her character sharpened and extra scenes added. She especially wanted changes in the script to include love scenes between Fisher and her. Prior to her involvement, her character had pursued an onscreen relationship with him that was strictly platonic.

She approached her friends, Tennessee Williams and Truman Capote. Williams was rather reluctant to get involved, but agreed to work on some of the dialogue. On the other hand, Capote was delighted. When he came to visit her, she said, "I have to work. I have no money. Eddie has no money. Debbie Reynolds took it all...every last cent."

She and Capote conceived of a torrid love scene "under the sheets" between Fisher and herself. Capote came up with a scenario that Daniel Mann claimed was perhaps too hot to film, yet his curiosity was voyeuristically intrigued, and he arranged for the scene to be shot, despite his sense of caution.

On the set, on the day of the actual filming, both Fisher and Elizabeth stripped completely nude and crawled together under the sheets.

As Fisher later claimed, "Having the camera on Elizabeth and me and with that faggot, Capote, drooling at the mouth, turned me on. I had sex with Elizabeth. We really went at it. She liked it rough, and I delivered."

Later, in his memoirs, he denied that he had a climax, but Elizabeth, in dialogues with Capote, said that he did.

"It was evident that Fisher was blasting off inside Elizabeth," Capote said. "From the look on her face, she was also experiencing an orgasm. She was not good enough an actress to fake it."

Later, their scene was judged as too hot for the screen, and it ended up on the cutting room floor.

Liz *(center figure)* as a tramp and homewrecker coming between **Dina Merrill** *(left figure)* and **Laurence Harvey** *(right figure)*

Any future rewriting that had to be done was given back to John Michael Hayes, who'd been responsible for getting *Peyton Place* past the censors.

After watching a screening of the final cut of *Butterfield 8,* Elizabeth hurled her glass of bourbon at the screen. Storming out of the screening room, she went to Pandro S. Berman's office door, which was partially crafted from a sheet of translucent glass. On the glass, in lipstick, she scrawled NO SALE! She was re-creating a scene from the movie in which her character of Gloria writes NO SALE! on the living room mirror after spending a night having sex with the character played by Harvey.

Dick Hanley had sat with her during the screening of *Butterfield 8*. "Actually, I liked the picture," he said. "I thought that tossing bourbon and writing in lipstick was a very erratic and childish way to conclude her long years of association with MGM. After all, it was MGM which made her a star, and *Butterfield 8* would bring her an Oscar. I wished she had found a more graceful exit from the studio, but no one tells Elizabeth Taylor how to exit a building."

"My final insult from MGM came when I had my last meal in the commissary," Elizabeth said. "The chef had already renamed the Elizabeth Taylor salad 'the Lana Turner salad.'"

After the release of *Butterfield 8,* one critic wrote, "The innocent little girl from *National Velvet* is now a full blown whore."

[On the night of the Academy Awards presentations, Shirley MacLaine, a friend of Elizabeth's, went to the ceremony hoping to win for her brilliant acting job in *The Apartment.* She applauded, but appeared heartbroken when she didn't win, the Oscar going instead to Elizabeth. Later, MacLaine cracked, "I lost to a tracheotomy."

MacLaine was referring to Elizabeth's life-threatening surgery in a London hospital during the early weeks of the shooting of *Cleopatra.*]

***

In Hollywood, Fisher and Elizabeth made plans to go abroad while still living in a bungalow at the Beverly Hills Hotel. Their next door neighbors were Yul Brynner and his second wife, Doris Kleiner, a fashion house executive.

Elizabeth had first met Brynner at a Hollywood party when William Holden had introduced them. After Brynner walked on his way, Holden said, "He's one of the biggest shits I've come across in show business. He is just a pig."

But Brynner had always intrigued her. Like so many actors she knew, Brynner was known in Hollywood circles as a notorious womanizer and part-time homosexual. In Paris, he'd been known for smoking opium and carrying on an affair with the French author, Jean Cocteau.

Sal Mineo had told her that Brynner had pounded him nightly when he was a young boy appearing on stage with him in the Broadway production of *The King and I.* He was also known to be in love with Frank Sinatra, one of his best friends. But mostly he was celebrated for his seductions of actresses, including Tallulah Bankhead, Anne Baxter, Joan Crawford, Claire Bloom, Ingrid Begman, Yvonne De Carlo, Judy Garland, Marilyn Monroe, and Maria Schell. He was infamously linked to Nancy Davis before she married Ronald Reagan. He had also had a long, torrid affair with Marlene Dietrich before he dumped her.

Fisher had become quite close to Brynner during their residency at the Beverly Hills Hotel, and often Fisher was next door with Brynner when Max Jacobson, their Dr. Feelgood, came to visit.

Both men, as well as Elizabeth herself, had become dependent on the doctor's injections of speed.

James Bacon, the columnist, heard some gossip he could not print in the newspaper, but which he later recounted in his memoirs, although his editor cut it. Nonetheless, the story made the rounds at Hollywood parties.

According to the tale, Dr. Jacobson had sent a delivery boy, Horace Bryant, with a shipment of drugs and paraphernalia addressed to Eddie Fisher, to Elizabeth's bungalow.

Bryant had been told that Fisher was not at home, but that Elizabeth, if he knocked on the bungalow's door at four o'clock, would accept the delivery.

Timing his arrival for exactly four o'clock, Bryant knocked on the bungalow's door. It took a long time before the door was finally opened by Elizabeth, who appeared in a see-through pink *peignoir.*

"I could see all the way to Honolulu," Bryant claimed.

"She invited me inside, as she was suspicious that someone might be watching. She went over to her purse and removed a hundred dollar bill. I couldn't believe it was so much, but I was very grateful. From the bedroom emerged Mr. Brynner with a big erection. It had a hood on it, something a Jewish boy like Fisher didn't have, I'm sure," Bryant told Bacon.

"Thanks, kid, for the delivery," Brynner said to him. "As you can see, I'm busy and three's a crowd."

"Excuse me, sir," Bryant said before rushing out of the bungalow with his hundred-dollar bill.

***

On June 20, 1960, Elizabeth and Fisher were flying to New York again. She had been given ringside seats for the heavyweight boxing rematch between Ingemar Johansson and Floyd Patterson.

In her book, *Growing Up at Grossinger's,* Tania Grossinger remembered the bout. She sat three rows behind Fisher and Elizabeth.

"She wore a revealing low-cut blouse that left nothing to the imagination," Grossinger wrote. "Suddenly, out of nowhere, this man walked over, plucked a breast out of her top, held it up for all to see, and shouted: 'Ladies and gentlemen, I ask you. Isn't this a beautiful sight?' Elizabeth was completely nonplussed, and majestically put her tit back where it belonged." [In her memoir,

Grossinger did not identify the man by name.]

Patterson won in a fifth round knockout. As Elizabeth was leaving with Fisher, she was hissed and booed by the crowd. Several boxing fans shouted "whore" at her.

Turning to face the mob, she made a clenched fist, a total "Fuck you!" to her detractors.

The next day, Fisher and Elizabeth sailed from New York to Rome on the maiden voyage of the *Leonardo da Vinci*. In Rome, they attended the 1960 Olympic Games.

The writer, Art Buchwald, traveled with them. He later wrote, "As Elizabeth came into the stadium, a lot of young men crowded around her, more than Fisher could keep at bay. I could not believe my eyes. These guys were feeling her up, grabbing her breasts and the cheeks of her ass. Several greedy little hands reached inside to feel her vagina. Finally, the police arrived to free her. I thought about the cannibal scene in *Suddenly, Last Summer*. She was being devoured. Elizabeth was no longer an international movie star. She was a living legend, but one unlike Hollywood had ever seen before and may never see again."

After their time in Rome, Elizabeth and Fisher flew to London and were installed in suites back at "The Dorch" on Park Lane.

At long last, production had begun on the much-postponed *Cleopatra* at Pinewood Studios outside London.

On their first night in London, Elizabeth invited Peter Finch (cast as Julius Caesar) and Stephen Boyd (playing Marc Antony) for dinner.

Dick Hanley was among the guests, but "I felt like the odd man out. Boyd flirted with Eddie all night, and it was obvious that Finch was going to renew his conjugal rights with Elizabeth, an affair that had heated the sheets during the filming of *Elephant Walk* in 1954."

"Before the evening ended, I realized why Elizabeth always insisted on two suites at The Dorch," Hanley said. "After I left, Finch stayed on for a night cap with Elizabeth, and Fisher accepted Boyd's invitation to visit a hot little club in Soho. The next morning, when I came into Elizabeth's suite at ten o'clock, Finch was still there, moving around in his jockey shorts. I knew where to find Eddie and Boyd. I was certain they were in the suite next door."

"If I thought that was the most outrageous scandal that would happen during the making of *Cleopatra*, I was dead wrong," Dick said. "Before that god damn film was wrapped, Elizabeth would scandalize the world."

CHAPTER NINETEEN
Cleopatra
FALLS IN LOVE WITH MARC ANTONY

CLEOPATRA: *"Without you, this is not a world I want to live in."*
MARC ANTONY: *"Everything that I want to hold or love or have or*
                be is here with me now."

En route to London in 1960, Elizabeth heard that the *Motion Picture Herald* had named her the number one box office attraction of America, followed by Rock Hudson, Doris Day, John Wayne, Cary Grant, Sandra Dee, Jerry Lewis, William Holden, Tony Curtis, and Elvis Presley.

No sooner had she settled into her suite at The Dorchester Hotel on Park Lane in London than Elizabeth picked up the tabloids and read: "It is rumored that Elizabeth Taylor, in London to shoot *Cleopatra* at Pinewood Studios, is already rehearsing love scenes with the handsome hunk, Stephen Boyd, who plays Marc Antony to her Cleopatra."

Seemingly, the London tabloids did not know that Boyd was gay. Perhaps they did, but didn't want that fact to get in the way of his faux romance with Elizabeth.

"If Boyd was screwing around with either of the Fishers, it was definitely with Eddie, not Elizabeth," said Dick Hanley, who'd accompanied her to London.

"Eddie had his own suite next to Elizabeth's at The Dorchester, and I saw Boyd coming and going on several occasions—that is, when Freddie was working out or had a boxing match outside London."

The reference was to Freddie Mills, a famous British boxer, with whom Boyd had a long affair.

Shelley Winters, in London filming *Lolita*, visited the Fishers since she also was staying at The Dorchester. "Elizabeth was spending every evening with Peter Finch while Eddie was drowning in martinis. At one point, Elizabeth got into a screaming match with Eddie, accusing him of trying to run over a drunken Peter with his Rolls-Royce."

In a private talk with Winters, Fisher admitted, "I'm trying my hand at producing. I tried to get *Irma La Douce* for Elizabeth, but it went to Shirley MacLaine. My other job is making love to Elizabeth. I have to have my monster ready any hour of the day or night she wants to get plugged."

"If you ever have a dry spell, stroll down to my room," Winters told him.

The columnist Max Lerner flew into London, and Elizabeth discreetly renewed her affair with him. When Peter Lawford dropped in to visit her at The Dorchester, she told her old friend, "I'm just crazy about Max because he reminds me of Albert Einstein."

When Winters heard of the affair with Lerner, she said, "I always make it a point not to go to bed with men who have bigger boobs than me. Max could pose for a *Playboy* centerfold with those huge tits of his."

Elizabeth eventually ended her affair with Lerner when he published a column comparing her to Marilyn Monroe, after Monroe's death in 1962. In it, he asserted that whereas Elizabeth was a living legend, Monroe was a myth. Elizabeth called him the next day. "How in bloody hell is Marilyn a myth and I'm just a fucking legend?"

"She's a myth because she's dead."

"I don't give a god damn about that. She couldn't hold a candle to me when the bitch was alive."

One Sunday afternoon, Winters met with Elizabeth for a private lunch where they could catch up on all the gossip about Hollywood and New York.

Camelot
Richard Burton *(left)* and
Roddy McDowall on Broadway
in 1963

Winters said that before she left New York, she'd seen their mutual friend Roddy McDowall performing in *Camelot* on Broadway with Richard Burton and Robert Goulet.

"I went backstage to kiss Roddy and to visit with Burton," she said. "When I came into Burton's dressing room, he locked the door and invited me for a drink. After he'd had a couple, he put his hand up my dress and played with my pussy."

"How quaint!" Elizabeth said. "His antics don't amuse me. In Manhattan some time ago, Tyrone Power invited me to his apartment. I went with Roddy. Burton was there."

"Roddy asked me if I knew that Burton was fucking Ty," Elizabeth said. "I told him I wasn't jealous because I'd already had Ty. My affair with Ty didn't work out because I lacked the right sexual equipment. Burton was such a show-off. He amused us by giving these devastating impressions of John Gielgud and Laurence Olivier. As I was leaving, he was singing bawdy songs while Oscar Levant accompanied him on the piano."

The producer of *Cleopatra*, Walter Wanger, visited Elizabeth at The Dorchester, telling her that Fox was having its doubts about casting Peter Finch as Julius Caesar and Stephen Boyd as Marc Antony. "Personally, I think Laurence Olivier would make the best Caesar, and Richard Burton would be perfect as Antony."

"Of course, Larry would be great in the role, but I have my doubts about Mr. Burton," she said.

He also informed her that the casting department at Fox wanted Cary Grant as Julius Caesar and Burt Lancaster as Antony." What Wanger didn't tell her was that the people at casting wanted either Susan Hayward or Jennifer Jones to play Cleopatra.

Actually, Mankiewicz secretly preferred Marlon Brando in the role of Antony. "He had been so good as Antony in *Julius Caesar* in 1951, but he was all tied up making *Mutiny on the Bounty.*"

For a brief period, the director of Cleopatra, Rouben Mamoulian, had promoted the unorthodox casting of the African-American actress, Dorothy Dandridge, in the lead role. "This idea caused heart attacks at Fox," said Wanger. "Remember, this was 1960."

It was the last day of August when Elizabeth in London began work on the ill-fated *Cleopatra*. She suddenly got into a battle with the unionized hair-

WHAT MIGHT HAVE BEEN...
Peter Finch *(left photo)* as Julius Caesar, **Dorothy Dandridge** as Cleopatra, and **Stephen Boyd** *(right)* as Marc Antony

dressers of Britain when she demanded that her favorite hairdresser, Sidney Guilaroff, be employed.

That was not the only problem caused by Elizabeth. Right from the beginning, she came down with a virus infection and a high fever, accelerated by the unseasonably cold and bitter weather in London that September. Near the end of October, Fox was already out two million dollars for a picture that had originally been budgeted at that exact amount.

On the night of November 13, 1960, Elizabeth's condition worsened, and Lord Evans, the personal physician of Queen Elizabeth, was called to The Dorchester. After a brief examination, he phoned an ambulance and had Elizabeth delivered to the privately run London Clinic. There, she was examined by Dr. Carl Goldman, who spoke to Dr. Rex Kennamer, her private doctor in Los Angeles. He immediately flew to London to be by her side.

She suffered from meningitis, an inflammation of the protective membranes covering the brain and spinal cord.

She recovered in a week, but so far had not done one day's work on *Cleopatra* in three entire months. Lloyds of London, which held the insurance policies on Cleopatra, asked Fox to replace her with Kim Novak, Marilyn Monroe, or Shirley MacLaine. Why Lloyds would select Monroe remains a mystery, as she was known for holding up production more than any other actress in Hollywood.

Upon Elizabeth's release from the clinic, she and Fisher flew back to California, where she underwent a period of rest and recuperation at Palm Springs.

In the wake of Elizabeth's illness, during her recuperation, Fox shut down production at Pinewood.

Under threat of getting fired, Mamoulian, from London, placed an urgent call to Elizabeth in California. During that dialogue and in the aftermath that followed, she double-crossed him by advising him to resign "until the heat blows over." She then made a commitment that she would refuse to work on the picture unless Fox re-hired him as its director. Mamoulian subsequently resigned.

| Rouben Mamoulian | Spyros Skouras |

But the very next day, Elizabeth called Spyros Skouras at Fox and told him that unless he hired Joseph L. Mankiewicz, she wouldn't make the picture. Mamoulian never forgave her for her betrayal.

454

Skouras phoned Mankiewicz in The Bahamas, where he was staying with Hume Cronyn and Jessica Tandy.

Mankiewicz came to Fox demanding (and getting) hard terms. In addition to his other compensations, the studio had to pay three million dollars to buy him out of a previous commitment he'd made to direct Lawrence Durrell's *Justine* for Figaro Films.

Elizabeth and Fisher were back in London at The Dorchester in time to attend Walter Wanger's New Year's bash at the elegant Caprice Restaurant, where they welcomed in 1961.

She wore a Dior gown that was the color of her eyes. She showed so much *décolletage* that a Peeping Tom waiter accidentally spilled hot coffee on her, eliciting a scream.

During the first week of January, 1961, Mankiewicz arrived at Pinewood to take over the direction of *Cleopatra*. Once in London to direct Elizabeth again, as he had done in *Suddenly, Last Summer*, he learned that only ten minutes of completed film had been shot "and all of it is unusable. The sets are a disaster, and the fucking script is unshootable."

Mankiewicz wanted Finch and Boyd replaced and a new production launched "from scratch," as he said.

He called Elizabeth with his grand scheme. "I want to make two motion pictures, one starring you and Rex Harrison in *Caesar and Cleopatra*, and the other starring Richard Burton and you in *Antony and Cleopatra*."

***

Rex Harrison was free and willing to sign on for the role of Julius Caesar. Getting Burton to play Marc Antony would be far more difficult and costly.

Burton was pleased with the casting of his friend, Harrison, in the role. "Larry [a reference to Laurence Olivier] would have hammed it up too much."

Spyros personally disliked Burton—"I can't understand Welsh," he said. "Not a word he says."

When Burton heard that, he said, "Anything that comes out of Spyros' mouth is Greek to me."

At the time, Burton was appearing on Broadway in *Camelot*, co-starring with Julie Andrews, Roddy McDowall, and Robert Goulet.

Wanger and Mankiewicz persuaded Burton to sign for $250,000. Fox also paid $50,000 to buy Burton out of the Broadway production of *Camelot*. The understanding at the time was that he would be paid that initial fee for what was to have been three months of work on *Cleopatra*. But, in his own words, "I would make a fortune in overtime when *Cleo* ran months behind in production."

455

Burton had one condition that he insisted upon. He wanted his current lover, Roddy McDowall, to be cast in *Cleopatra* in the role of Octavian. That meant that Roddy would also have to leave the Broadway production of *Camelot*. Even before flying to Rome, Roddy and Burton agreed that he would play Octavian as "campy and sexually ambiguous."

Dick Hanley told Elizabeth that "Marc Antony, so I hear, is pounding the ass of your boy Roddy every night."

"You're just jealous, you bitch," she responded, mocking him. "I bet you wish Burton was pounding you."

"You got me there," Dick said.

During the run of *Camelot*, "Richard was more Lancelot that Arthur toward women," said co-star Robert Goulet. "As a bisexual, he had double the choices than the rest of us regular guys."

His dressing room at Broadway's Majestic Theater, where *Camelot* was playing, became known as "Burton's Bar," drawing the likes of Mike Nichols, who would later direct him in *Who's Afraid of Virginia Woolf?* along with Tammy Grimes, Jason Robards, Jr., Robert Preston, Alec Guinness, Lauren Bacall, and Burton's co-star in *Camelot*, Julie Andrews.

When he arrived in Rome, he would "reopen" Burton's Bar in his dressing room near the sound stages of *Cleopatra*.

He was known for romancing his leading ladies, including Susan Strasberg, Jean Simmons, and Claire Bloom, but he told Roddy, "Elizabeth Taylor leaves me cold, like yesterday's poached egg."

When he spoke to Goulet, Burton had a different point of view. "I'll have Taylor within two days of my arrival in Rome. That's guaranteed."

In New York, between telling his entourage Rabelaisian tales, he revealed that he'd met "the fat little tart" before, at Stewart Granger's house in Hollywood. He added, "that was before she married that busboy," a reference, of course, to Eddie Fisher.

Sometimes, when select members of the *Camelot* audience came backstage, Burton entertained them with a perfect mimicry of Elizabeth's voice. When he impersonated her, his speech was riddled with obscenities.

Roddy warned him, "You just might fall for her."

"No, she's too dark for me," he said. "I also heard she has to shave all that black hair that covers her body. On my women, I like hair on her head and in only one other place."

In New York, preparing for his departure for Rome, Burton told a reporter, "I guess I've got to don my breastplate once more, this time to play opposite Miss Tits."

Before accepting the role of Antony, he had been trying to establish himself as a serious actor, winning the 1961 Tony for Best Actor on Broadway for his role as King Arthur in *Camelot*. He was tired of being labeled as "Britain's Brando" or "the Poor Man's Laurence Olivier."

He'd married a Welsh actress, Sybil Williams, in 1949, but was never faithful to her. He often preferred sex with actresses, his list of seductions including everyone from Lana Turner and Zsa Zsa Gabor to Barbra Streisand.

Even though married to Sybil for more than twelve years, on Broadway, Burton was also romancing Pat Tunder, a beautiful blonde chorus girl who was only twenty-two.

Joan Collins, who had been his co-star in *Sea Wife* (1956), a British drama shot in Jamaica about the survivors from a torpedoed British refugee ship during World War II, found Burton's greenish-blue eyes "piercingly hypnotic." But she was turned off by other aspects of his physicality. "His back and shoulders were deeply pitted and rutted with pimples, blackheads, and what looked like small craters.'

From 1944 to 1947, he had served in the Royal Air Force as a Navigator. "Near the end of the closing months of the war, soldiers fucked each other a lot," Burton said. "Blokes who might die tomorrow didn't care where they put it."

Biographer Melvyn Bragg asserted that Burton had sex with many men in the RAF [Royal Air Force] during World War II, "when hundreds of thousands of men fumbled for comfort and release in the male warrior bondings of the war."

Before meeting Burton to work with him, Elizabeth read a profile of him by Barbara Gelb in *The New York Times*: "A tug of war began in him at the age of two after the loss of his mother, and the two sides of his nature have never been reconciled. He appears to be at once self-possessed and uneasy with himself, unsure where the caustic Welsh clay stops and the silken veneer begins. He is simultaneously the dark and self-destructive Celt and the glossy ideal of classical actor, circumspect and disciplined. In his bemusement over which of these selves to champion, he often takes refuge in a third and safer self—the little boy lost."

Both Burton and Roddy were well aware the night then-Senator from Massachusetts John F. Kennedy and his beautiful and elegant wife, Jackie, came to see *Camelot*. Backstage, the Kennedys greeted Burton and congratulated him, although he later heard that the future president found the music boring. Jackie, however, found the legend of Camelot fascinating. The world would realize the

Richard Burton and his wife **Sybil Williams Burton** in 1962

degree to which she was intrigued after the assassination of her husband in Dallas in 1963.

Whereas Senator Kennedy planned an immediate return to Washington, Jackie planned to remain in New York for two days of shopping.

"I asked her if I could call on her at the Carlyle and discuss the legend of Camelot with her," Burton later confided to Roddy. "To my amazement, she agreed."

The following night, Roddy was eager to learn all the details of Burton's visit to the suite of the future First Lady. "Over drinks, we spent an hour talking about Camelot," Burton said. "We had more than one drink. She's a fabulous dame, really fabulous. If I had a dame like Jackie full time, I swear I'd never have to cheat on her."

"I know, I know," said an impatient Roddy. "The question is, did you score?"

"A bull's eye," he bragged. "She's prim and proper, but once you get her panties off, she's a tigress.'

***

In February of 1961, while Mankiewicz was working almost around the clock to complete the script of *Cleopatra*, Elizabeth and Fisher flew to Paris, where they boarded the Orient Express to Munich.

She wanted to experience Munich's version of *Fasching*, an annual pre-Lenten carnival, with its masked balls, one of which she planned to attend dressed as Marie Antoinette. But instead of impersonating Louis XVI, Fisher, wearing silk breeches, was to be attired as her footman.

Very Famous People who become fascinated with Other Very Famous People:
Richard Burton and **Jacqueline Kennedy**

Once in her hotel suite, she seemed to be relying to an increasing degree on pain killers which were far more potent than her usual sedatives. Partly as a means of understanding her condition better, and perhaps partly as a

458

recreational experiment, Fisher swallowed one of her capsules. As he remembered it, "In a few minutes, the entire suite was moving in front of my eyes, the furniture doing a naughty jitterbug. I collapsed on the sofa in the living room and woke up at noon the following day. I didn't know how she could take such strong medicine."

Later that day, he tried to talk to her. "I was giving up my life for the thankless task of standing by watching the woman I loved self-destruct," he recalled.

Challenged by him, she fought back, and their fight escalated. She hurled vases at him, one glass object hitting him in the forehead, causing him to bleed.

"I made a terrible mistake," he recalled afterward. "I threatened to fly back to New York in the morning, abandoning her to her own survival not only in Munich but in London."

She looked at him in disbelief. She appeared in a state of shock, as if she had not heard him correctly. "Okay, Buster," she said in a voice that would emerge from a future film, *Who's Afraid of Virginia Woolf?*. "You might be leaving in the morning, but I'm departing from the world right now." Then she ran into the bathroom and locked the door.

He knew what she was doing. He called hotel security guards to break down the door and summoned the house doctor, an elderly but efficient Berliner who may have been Jewish, having survived Hitler's gas chambers. "I don't know exactly what he did in her bedroom," Fisher said. "But two interns came with equipment. Perhaps her stomach was pumped. I know I heard the sound of vomiting. The doctor sedated her."

Hoping the press wouldn't find out, Fisher gave the doctor the equivalent of two thousand dollars in Deutschmarks.

When Elizabeth woke up the following morning, she called for him, "Oh, Eddie, darling, come to me. Don't ever say you'll leave me again. I'd die if you ever left me!"

By the time he got her back to London, he noticed that she was suffering from exhaustion. He checked her into a hospital. Then he did a strange thing. Needing a rest himself, he also checked himself into a hospital, pretending he was suffering from appendicitis. Actually, he wasn't. He allowed his appendix to be removed, even though it was a healthy organ.

"I had to get away," he later said, "I had to have someone take care of me and wait on me for a change."

On March 4, 1961, illness struck again, as Elizabeth came down with a severe case of Asian flu.

Fisher wanted the best care for her, and summoned Lord Evans, the personal physician of Queen Elizabeth. He ordered an oxygen tent for her. Not only that, but he sent over a portable toilet, the same one used by Her Majesty when she traveled to remote corners of the Commonwealth.

Fisher also ordered around-the-clock nurses for her. In the early morning hours, a night nurse noticed that Elizabeth's face was turning blue, and she was gasping for breath. She called the desk and shouted for them to get a doctor quick.

In a touch of irony, some doctors were having a late-night reception at The Dorchester. Among them was Dr. J. Middleton Price, one of the best anesthesiologists in the British Isles. He was rushed to Elizabeth's suite. "She had turned blue as the sea," he said, "and was unconscious. I estimated that if I had not gotten there, she would have died in fifteen minutes."

The doctor picked her up by the heels and tried to make her lose some of the congestion in her chest. That did not succeed. Next, he stuck his finger down her throat, hoping to make her gag and breathe again. Still, nothing happened. He then pounded her chest,

"So the doctor started gouging at my eyes," Elizabeth related in her memoirs. "He gouged like mad and I opened my eyes...I took a deep breath, which kept me alive."

Dr. Price determined that only a tracheotomy would save her life. But the operation had to be performed in a hospital, although it was very risky to move the patient. He decided, however, that it was worth the chance, and an ambulance was summoned to The Dorchester.

With dome lights flashing and sirens wailing, she was rushed to the private London Clinic where Dr. Terence Cawthorne awaited her. He performed the life-saving tracheotomy by drawing a scalpel across the soft part of her throat right above her breastbone. Here, he made an incision allowing him to insert a breathing tube connected to a respirator.

His diagnosis was acute *staphylococcus* pneumonia, which is most often fatal. She would retain a small scar at her throat for the rest of her life, although she would in most instances cover it with a piece of jewelry.

Still desperately ill, she was put in an iron lung as a means of controlling the rate of her respiration and linking it to just the right amount of oxygen.

Seven doctors, including Lord Evans, were at her bedside. Dr. Evans even gave Queen Elizabeth a daily bulletin on his famous patient. It was Dr. Evans who also discovered that she was suffering from anemia, and he ordered blood transfusions, intravenous feedings, and doses of antibiotics. He also prescribed a rare drug, staphylococcal bacteriophage lystate, which Milton Blackstone, Fisher's agent, personally carried with him aboard a hastily scheduled flight to London.

While in the hospital in London, Elizabeth had been fed intravenously through her ankle. Regrettably, that caused an infection in her lower leg. As she admitted in her memoirs, "I almost lost my leg...I just let the disease take me. I had been hoping to be happy," she said. "I was just pretending to be happy.

But I was consumed by self-pity."

Early on the morning of March 6, 1961, a radio station in Pensacola, Florida, broadcast the news: "Elizabeth Taylor is dead. Doctors in London fought to save her, but it was hopeless. The little girl who won our hearts in *National Velvet* died a living legend."

The news was picked up and broadcast on other stations before a bulletin was issued from London: "Elizabeth Taylor is not dead. She is the hospital in a fight for her life, but is still very much with us."

London tabloids began preparing "Second Coming" headlines.

A few newspapers published her obituary, and Elizabeth got to read a summation of her life. She later commented, "These were the best reviews I ever received, but I had to die to get these tributes."

On March 10, the first optimistic bulletin was released, claiming she had made "a very rare recovery."

Later, she defined the experience as "absolutely horrifying. When I would regain consciousness, I wanted to ask my doctors if I was going to die. But I couldn't make myself heard. Inside my head, I heard myself screaming to God for help. I was frightened. I was angry. I was fierce. I didn't want to die. I stopped breathing four times. I died four times. It was like falling into this horrible black pit. Dr. Evans later told me I lived because I fought so hard to live."

Also residing at The Dorchester, author Truman Capote was one of the first guests allowed to visit her after her operation. He recalled it as a "media event, with the streets clogged with fans and the idle curious." At her request, he slipped in a magnum of Dom Pérignon and some books to read, mostly his own.

"I visited her in London in the hospital when she had that tracheotomy. She had what looked like a silver dollar in her throat. I couldn't figure out what held it in place, and it surprised me she wasn't bleeding or oozing. A few nights later, I went out with Eddie Fisher. The next afternoon, Elizabeth told me that Eddie thought I was trying to make a pass at him. At that moment, she played a trick on me and yanked at the plug in her throat, spurting out champagne—I'd brought her a magnum of Dom Pérignon—all over the hospital room. I thought I was going to pass out."

Fans on every continent mourned her, even though she was still clinging to life, but just barely. Mobs of people descended on the London Clinic for around-the-clock vigils.

Each day, her condition improved until it was finally judged safe for her to leave the hospital, though in a vastly weakened condition.

On March 27, 1961, Elizabeth, in a wheelchair, made one of the most spectacular departures in England's history. Wrapped in sable, with a white scarf covering her neck and in preparation for her flight to New York, she was handled with the care of a porcelain doll as London bobbies held back the threatening hordes and a mob of paparazzi. Airport security nestled her into a kind of canvas sling, and lifted her into the waiting plane.

With *Cleopatra* delayed once again, Elizabeth was coming home. She predicted to Fisher that "Cleopatra will never sail down the Nile on that barge of hers."

Skouras at Fox sued Lloyds of London for three million dollars, but settled for two million, as compensation for the production delays on their attempt to film *Cleopatra* at Pinewood.

In a huddle, Wanger and Skouras decided that England was no place to film an exotic epic like *Cleopatra*. They agreed to scrap $600,000 worth of sets at Pinewood and relaunch the film in Rome in September of 1961, allowing Elizabeth time to recuperate.

***

By April 18, 1961, she was back in Hollywood to receive her Oscar for *Butterfield 8*, telling the press, "I nearly had to die to wrest this prize." She'd later write in her memoirs, "I was filled with profound gratitude at being considered by the industry as an actress and not as a movie star. I knew my performance had not deserved it, and that it was a sympathy award."

One June 7, 1961, Elizabeth accepted an invitation to fly with Eddie Fisher to Las Vegas for a lavish party at the Sands in honor of Dean Martin's forty-fourth birthday. She almost turned down the invitation when she learned that Sinatra had also invited Marilyn Monroe, with whom he was having an affair. Fisher talked her into going, claiming that "Frankie will be awfully hurt if we don't show up. He might get even with us. He takes these rejections personally."

Finally, Peter Lawford assured Elizabeth that her contact with Monroe would deliberately be kept very brief. "At ringside, I'll see that the headwaiter seats you at the far end of the table from Marilyn."

But at the Sands, Elizabeth was annoyed when Monroe greeted Fisher with a sloppy wet kiss. She was curious as to what, if any, relationship with Monroe that her husband had had to invite such intimacy. When Monroe shook Elizabeth's hand, she did not even fake a smile. She was still furious that executives at Fox had considered firing her as Cleopatra and turning the role over to Monroe.

Later that night, when he was drinking with Rat Packers Martin and Lawford, Fisher admitted he'd "pumped" Monroe on more than one occasion. "What red-blooded male like me would turn her down?"

"One time when Elizabeth was in the hospital, I had to get it from some-body," Fisher said. "Or at least that's what Marilyn told me when she called me for a date. I took the bait. Before the mailman arrived, I'd had the blonde vixen three times."

"Our farewell wasn't all that romantic," Fisher claimed. "Marilyn told me, 'Thanks, Eddie. It's important for me to be reminded of what turns Elizabeth on.'"

At the Sands, the *maître 'd* followed Lawford's instructions and seated Elizabeth and Monroe at opposite ends of the ringside table, very close to the stage where Sinatra would be singing. Seated with Elizabeth were Dean Martin, the guest of honor, and his wife, Jeanne.

Elizabeth noted that Monroe was already drunk before the party had really begun. She was talking loud enough to be overheard by everyone at the table. She told Fisher, "I'll always love Frankie, but I know I can never tie him down. If it were possible, I'd be married to both Joe (DiMaggio) and Frankie at the same time. This is supposed to be a free country, yet bigamy isn't allowed. It should be legal."

Elizabeth whispered to Martin, "I can agree with Marilyn on that bigamy thing. I always seem to be in love with at least three men at once."

As the evening progressed, Elizabeth watched in horror as Monroe made a spectacle of herself, even slobbering on herself.

Fisher took note of this, too, later asserting, "Marilyn is a beautiful woman, but on that night, she looked like a broken-down and washed-up Vegas hooker. But what did I care? I was married to Elizabeth, the most beautiful woman in the world."

At one point, Monroe staggered off to the women's toilet, returning to seat herself between Patricia Kennedy Lawford (JFK's sister) and Patricia's husband, Peter. Then she reached out to fondle Lawford's crotch. "For old time's sake," she said, loud enough for Elizabeth to hear. The other guests also overheard what Monroe then said, as what might have been interpreted either as an insult or as a bemused tease: "What happened to your peter, Peter? It seems to have shrunk."

As Sinatra came out onto the stage, Elizabeth didn't know where to look. Her choices included a view of Sinatra, onstage and singing, or a view of Marilyn, whose ample breasts were literally falling out of her low-cut pink satin dress.

After the show, Fisher escorted Elizabeth backstage to greet Sinatra. Monroe beat them to it. In full view of Elizabeth, Monroe gushed about Sinatra's performance and planted wet kisses on his face. Elizabeth noticed that Sinatra was looking at Monroe with disgust. He'd once told Elizabeth, "If there is one thing I can't stand, it's a drunken broad."

"Then the unspeakable occurred," Elizabeth recalled. "Monroe was so drunk, she threw up on Frank's tuxedo." He ordered a security guard to take her back to his suite. A photographer was standing nearby and attempted to take a candid snapshot, but Sinatra knocked his camera to the floor, stomping on it. He then fled to his dressing room to change into a fresh tuxedo."

With Fisher at her side, Elizabeth stood next to the photographer. "Monroe is a mess, isn't she? How she holds onto her beauty, I'll never know. She drinks far too much, and obviously can't hold her liquor. Now, me, I'm a girl who knows how to handle booze."

Far more intriguing that Monroe's drunken debacle at Sinatra's opening was what occurred the following afternoon when Fisher left the Fisher/Taylor suite to meet with executives from the Desert Inn for a discussion about a possible singing engagement.

Elizabeth was startled when she picked up the receiver and heard Monroe's voice apologizing "for my outrageous behavior last night." After repeated urgings, Elizabeth finally agreed to let Monroe visit her in her suite.

On that hot Las Vegas afternoon, what transpired between Elizabeth and Monroe is still a hotly debated topic. Years later, in their edition of April 11, 2011, *The Globe* revealed that the two women engaged in a shared lesbian tryst.

In her diary, Elizabeth wrote that she was entranced by the way Monroe moved. "She was the sexiest woman I ever met, and her touch was electric," Elizabeth claimed.

She later confided to Roddy McDowall, "I wanted to see how far the bitch would go. But she had to do all the work. I felt empowered somehow, like I was the grand diva and she a lowly slave, if that makes any sense."

Unless there is something not yet discovered, it's likely that Elizabeth never

What happens in Vegas, stays in Vegas—or does it?
The Globe, April 11, 2011

had an encounter like that before. If she did, she carefully concealed it. Unlike Monroe, who "could work both sides of the waterfront" (a phrase from Tennessee Williams), Elizabeth was a woman who reserved her charms for men—and a lot of them.

A short time later at the Beverly Hilton Hotel, Monroe entered the bar accompanied by her masseur, Ralph Roberts. Roddy, Fisher, and Elizabeth were in the bar that night, emptying a few champagne bottles. Elizabeth was overheard telling both Fisher and Roddy, "Keep that dyke away from me tonight."

***

On July 9, 1961, Elizabeth, in plunging décolletage, sat next to Attorney General Robert F. Kennedy at a fund-raising dinner for the Cedars of Lebanon Hospital in Los Angeles. Behind them sat Rat Packers Joey Bishop, Dean Martin, Frank Sinatra, and Peter Lawford. A view of RFK was snapped by photographers gazing down at Elizabeth's amply displayed breasts.

When the attorney general finally diverted his gaze, Elizabeth delivered a short speech written by Joseph Mankiewicz:

"Dying, as I remember, is many things. But most of all, it is wanting to live. Throughout many critical hours in the operating theater, it was as if every nerve, every muscle, as if my whole physical being were being strained to the last ounce of my strength, to the last gasp of breath. I remember I had focused desperately on the hospital light hanging directly above me. It had become the vision of life itself. Slowly, it faded and dimmed like a well-done theatrical effect to blackness.

I died.

It was like being in a long dark tunnel with no light at the end. I kept looking for the light. I heard voices urging me to come back into life, to live. The experience was both painful and beautiful, like child birth itself."

Elizabeth donated $100,000 to the charity, and her fellow guests, including RFK, contributed a massive total of $7 million that night. After the dinner, Kennedy invited her for a drive with him along the coast. She suggested that they stop at her cottage in Malibu for a midnight swim. No one knows where Eddie Fisher was that night.

As she was to tell Dick Hanley. "It was one of the most memorable nights of my life."

She also recorded the events of that night in her diary, and would allow

465

both Dick and Roddy McDowall to read it. She had described her experience in such graphic detail that Roddy was a bit shocked. He said, "Elizabeth, my dear, you should have been a pornographer."

As her two memoirs revealed, no one could write more boringly about her own life that Elizabeth. In two of her autobiographical memoirs, she gave almost no details of some of the most infamous events of her life.

In her diary, however, while relaying her encounter with Robert Kennedy, she may have been more explicit because Peter Lawford had told her that Marilyn Monroe had recorded "steamy passages" in her red diary about her sexual encounters with both President Kennedy and his brother, Robert. "Elizabeth obviously did not want to be bested by Monroe," Roddy said.

"I can write with passion, too," she told Roddy. "After all, I read *Forever Amber*." She was referring to the best selling romance written by Kathleen Winsor, who at one time was married to bandleader Artie Shaw after his divorce from Ava Gardner.

"Bobby and I spent about two hours on the beach in the moonlight," Elizabeth told her gay friends. "Our bathing suits became too restraining. Bobby finally got to enjoy those breasts he'd been staring at all night."

"You've got it bad, girl," Roddy said.

"When it was over, he kissed me several times and told me I was a goddess," she relayed, as reported by Roddy and Dick. "Other men have told me that, but coming from Bobby, I really could delude myself into believing it. That night, with Bobby on the beach, I was a goddess. But when I drove home, I found Eddie there and we got into a big brawl. The goddess, I fear, became a harridan."

Later, in her diary, she wrote: "It is a shame that when a man and a woman want to be together, they often have to leave each other while they pay homage to people in their lives they'd rather not deal with. Men and women should be free. Even though I've been married four times, it was four times too many. I will never marry again—and that's a promise I've made to myself that I will never break."

Breast gazing: **Elizabeth Taylor** with **Robert Kennedy** in 1961

In the months leading up to his assassination, RFK, at least according to Dick Hanley, seduced Elizabeth on three different occasions. On one of these occasions, he left the bed of Jackie Kennedy in New York in 1966, flew to Los Angeles, and woke up in Elizabeth's bed in Beverly Hills the following morning."

As she told Dick, "I have known more perfect bodies, but Bobby's physique thrilled me. He was long and lean, no bulging beefcake. But he moved with such grace…undeniable masculinity. A strong chest, a thin waist, and a cock that was not the biggest I'd ever seen, but one that was gorgeous and knew all the right strokes."

***

It was a busy summer in 1961. The U.S. State Department asked Elizabeth and Fisher to represent the United States at the Moscow Film Festival, beginning on July 11.

Decked out in a white chiffon cocktail dress from Dior, Elizabeth made a spectacular entrance. But she almost screamed when she spotted Gina Lollobrigida wearing an identical outfit. As a publicity stunt, Lollobrigida had learned what outfit Elizabeth planned to wear and had instructed her dressmaker to duplicate it.

To make up to Elizabeth, the House of Dior offered her any gown she wanted from their inventory in Paris. She selected an embroidered number, the most expensive Dior had, one that would otherwise have been priced at $10,000.

Once inside their hotel suite in Moscow, Elizabeth and Eddie, assisted by

---

MOSCOW NIGHTS WITH ELIZABETH AND EDDIE (FUN AND GAMES IN RUSSIA)

Nikita Khrushchev *(left photo)* and his mistress, the Soviet Union's dreaded Minister of Culture, **Yekatarina Furtseve** *(center photo)*

,,,and a fashion catfight with **Gina Lollobrigida**

Dick Hanley, searched every inch of it, looking for hidden microphones and cameras. "Eddie was convinced that the Soviets had wanted to secretly film them making love, probably for Khruschev's evening entertainment," Dick said. "Later, there was a rumor that such a film was actually made, and that it was viewed within the Kremlin. When Elizabeth heard this, she said to me, 'My first porno.'"

When Khrushchev had visited Hollywood in September of 1956, as part of an event hosted by Twentieth Century Fox and spearheaded by Frank Sinatra, he'd had a "private" session in his hotel suite with Marilyn Monroe, but had merely shaken hands with Elizabeth.

Now, at the time of her Moscow visit in 1961, he requested a private session with her. She went alone, thinking it might lead to a sexual tryst "with Nikita and all his hairy warts."

When she arrived at the Kremlin, she found the Soviet premier sitting with Yekatarina Furtseve, his Minister of Culture. She was also his mistress. The meeting lasted only fifteen minutes. Later, Elizabeth said, "Obviously, he prefers Monroe to me."

***

JACKIE: *"I hate Elizabeth Taylor."*
ELIZABETH: *"Jackie Kennedy is a gold-digging bitch."*

When her husband was running for President, and even when he occupied the Oval Office, Jackie Kennedy had to face competition not only from Marilyn Monroe and so many others, but from Elizabeth Taylor, too.

Revelations about the Taylor/JFK affair came to light after the death of Dame Elizabeth in 2011. Details were leaked to the press from her private diaries which may, in time, be edited and published.

Of course, Hollywood insiders like actor Robert Stack knew that JFK had seduced a much too young Elizabeth after his service in the Navy during World War II.

Elizabeth had first met JFK in England in 1939 when his father was the United States' Ambassador to the Court of St. James's.

It appears that Robert Kennedy himself arranged several liaisons between Elizabeth and the President in 1961, as well as enjoying her considerable charms himself.

But long before the affair with JFK came to light, Jackie knew about it. Her informant was Peter Lawford, who often functioned as a "double agent," feeding Jack information about Jackie, and supplying Jackie with secret data about her husband.

Reportedly, Elizabeth was mesmerized by both the Kennedy brothers. (Apparently, Teddy never got around to her.)

During JFK's 1960 campaign for president, she had visited him on occasion in a bungalow at the Beverly Hilton Hotel. She also had perhaps three sexual trysts with him in Beverly Hills during the summer of 1961, when she'd had her first fling with Bobby.

Except for Marilyn Monroe, none of the affairs JFK had were with women as famous as Elizabeth.

"Kennedy did more than fundraising when he came to California," Eddie Fisher later said. "Kennedy was widely known for fucking Elizabeth look-alikes like Judith Campbell Exner. I guess on occasion he wanted the real thing—not merely the mock. I had Judy myself. She made herself up to look as much like Elizabeth as she could."

"Elizabeth swore to me that her relationship with Jack never went beyond friendship," Fisher said. "But I never believed her. I'm sure she never believed me when I told her that I was 'just friends' with some of the women I was bedding. When Jackie heard of the affair, she said some really vicious things about Elizabeth, so I was told. And you should have heard what my potty-mouthed wife said about Jackie. It was a real catfight waged on two different coasts."

The tabloids eventually picked up on the Elizabeth/Jackie rivalry, and sometimes the two "Queens of America" made the front pages of many a magazine, appearing in separate photographs blended together.

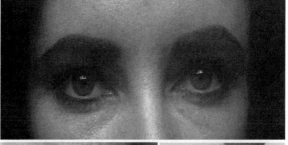

Jackie's rivalry with Elizabeth really broke out in 1968 when the former First Lady married the Greek shipping tycoon, Aristotle Onassis. Word leaked out of Greece that "Ari" had originally wanted to marry Elizabeth when he heard that she was breaking up with Richard Burton. "I can give you even bigger diamonds that Richard Burton because I have more money," Onas-

Elizabeth Taylor *(top photo)*, on the lookout for **John F. Kennedy** and her implacable enemy, **Jacqueline Kennedy**

sis told Elizabeth one night when he was sailing with her aboard his yacht, the *Christina*.

When Johnny Meyer, pimp for Onassis, the same position he'd held with Howard Hughes, told him that Jackie might be available to marry him, Onassis decided to make a play for her. "After all, Jackie is an even bigger prize than Elizabeth," Onassis said.

When Elizabeth heard about the upcoming marriage of Jackie and Onassis, she told *Modern Screen*, "It will be the strangest marriage of the century. Mrs. Kennedy is now reduced to taking my rejects."

Her comment was never printed.

Later, Jackie turned down an invitation to sail on another cruise aboard the *Christina* before her marriage. Word reached her that Elizabeth, who went on the voyage, flirted with Onassis every night over dinner.

When Jackie confronted the shipping magnate about it, she told him, "It's either the Taylor bitch or me. Your friendship with this international tramp has to end—NOW!"

Movie Mirror picked up on this feud, crafting headlines that yelled: WHAT REALLY HAPPENED THE NIGHT LIZ TRIED TO CUT JACKIE OUT!

[After the death of Onassis in 1975 and Elizabeth's second divorce from Richard Burton in 1974, *Motion Picture* magazine began labeling Elizabeth and Jackie as AMERICA'S TWO FALLEN QUEENS.

The only face-to-face meeting between Jackie and Elizabeth occurred on June 20, 1976, when both of them attended a performance by the legendary British ballerina Margot Fonteyn at Manhattan's Uris Theater. Backstage, Elizabeth and Jackie awkwardly encountered one another on the way to Fonteyn's dressing room. Each woman smiled politely at the other. What did the two fabled divas say to each other? Someone who stood behind them revealed, "They said absolutely nothing—not a word."

After that, coverage of the two divas in the tabloids became less shrill and less frequent. In the November, 1976 issue of *Photoplay*, reportage on the exploits of Elizabeth vs. Jackie had been reduced to the last words on the cover, without even a picture, and even that ran beneath the larger headline: THE SALLY STRUTHERS NOBODY KNOWS.

Ironically, after her marriage to Senator John Warner of Virginia in December of 1976, Elizabeth assumed the same official role that Jackie had once held—that of a U.S. Senator's spouse.

Elizabeth told reporters that "John [Warner] is the best lover I've ever had. I want to spend the rest of my life with him, and I want to be buried with him."

After her divorce from Warner, Elizabeth took a final husband, construction worker Larry Fortensky, whom she'd met in rehab. She married this unlikely candidate on October 5, 1991 at a lavish $1.5 million wedding paid for by

Michael Jackson at his Neverland Ranch. Elizabeth said, "At last in Larry I've found the kind of rugged individual I've been seeking all my life. He'll still be with me when it's time to bury me."]

***

Back in Los Angeles in the summer of 1961, Elizabeth underwent plastic surgery at the Cedars of Lebanon to remove most of her tracheotomy scar. The operation was not successful.

Fisher returned to his stamping ground, the Cocoanut Grove, at Hollywood's Ambassador Hotel for a singing engagement which had been offered to him partly, according to local cynics, because of his Elizabeth-related notoriety.

His act was sabotaged when the Rat Pack took over. Frank Sinatra, Dean Martin, and Sammy Davis, Jr. yelled at him from the audience, interrupting his songs. Fisher became nervous and botched three numbers. "If I were you, I wouldn't be singing," Martin called out. "I'd be home fucking my wife."

Finally, the Rat Packers mounted the stage, telling filthy jokes about Fisher. Sinatra did a bad impression of Fisher's singing. Finally, when the three musketeers, who were falling down drunk, left the stage, Fisher was allowed to finish his act.

"There are those, including Elizabeth, who say that that night marked the end of the Rat Pack," Fisher wrote in his memoirs. "They were booed off the stage. Each of them, and that includes Sinatra, made an ass of themselves."

***

By August of 1961, with Fisher's singing engagement over, he and Elizabeth flew to Rome to begin filming "*Cleopatra Segundo*" as they called it, even though no film of any consequence ever evolved from the time and money wasted in London on "*Cleopatra Primero.*"

Before their work was scheduled to begin in Rome, they had time for a brief cruise of the Greek Islands in that same yacht that Spyros Skouras had lent them for a tour of the French and Spanish Mediterranean ports during their honeymoon.

"This was our second honeymoon," Fisher proclaimed.

On his private island, Skorpios, Aristotle Onassis was their host for two days and nights.

Whether true or not, Onassis told friends who included Maria Callas, who repeated it to friends of hers, that both Fisher and Elizabeth, on separate occasions, took sexual advantage of Kostas Cafarakis, the strikingly handsome First

471

Mate aboard the *Christina*.

"Many of my women guests—and some of the men, too—went for Kostas," Onassis said. "He was built like a Greek god, a true son of Zeus."

When the story surfaced in a newspaper in Athens, Fisher vehemently denied it and threatened to sue for libel.

Onassis told him not to bother. "Tomorrow, fishwives will be wrapping the day's catch in it."

"It was the calm before the storm," Fisher later recalled about their flight from Athens to Rome. At the airport, Dick Hanley was on hand to greet them and drive them to their villa, which would become the scene of great drama.

***

At her temporary home, Elizabeth wandered around the fifteen-room Roman mansion, Villa Pappa (sometimes spelled "Villa Papa"), which was faced with pink marble. It stood on the ancient Appian Way, surrounded by gardens and accessorized with an Olympic-size swimming pool and a tennis court.

To Rome, she'd brought her entourage and her children, even her doctor, Rex Kennamer, who was paid a fee of $25,000 for a six-week visit. A staff of twenty had been hired, even a chauffeur to drive Fisher around Rome in the Rolls-Royce she had purchased for him.

Before Elizabeth showed up on the set, Hermes Pan, the famous dance director, was already rehearsing the dancing girls for Cleopatra's triumphant entrance into ancient Rome.

When Dick checked out the studio at Cinecittà, he told her that wardrobe was planning some seventy costumes for her alone, plus thousands of other costumes for members of a black ballet troupe, swordsmen, chariot drivers, and all the other attendants who, collectively, would recreate the splendor of the ancient world. Irene Sharaff had been brought in to oversee Elizabeth's vast wardrobe. Her most spectacular costume would be a fifteen-pound ceremonial dress of gold which Cleopatra wears during her entrance into Rome before the mobs.

Before *Cleopatra* was wrapped, Elizabeth would not be speaking to Sharaff after the designer had suggested that Elizabeth "was putting on a few pounds."

A private beach had been rented from Prince Borghese at Anzio, where American forces had landed in January of 1944 before their march to Rome during World War II, and which, to Fox's horror, had to be swept clear of any remaining land mines, thereby adding another $22,000 to the budget.

At her luxurious Villa Pappa, filled with servants, Elizabeth entertained in a grand manner during her first days. "She really thought she was Cleopatra," said Dick. "She ordered her Italian butlers to color-coordinate everything to match her gown for the evening, and that included candles, napkins, tablecloths, flowers, even cigarette holders and matches."

Dick Hanley made all the arrangements for their first luncheon at Villa Pappa, inviting Audrey Hepburn, Elizabeth's sometimes rival, and her husband, Mel Ferrer, to a Roman meal beside the swimming pool. Most of the talk centered around Hepburn winning the coveted role of Eliza Doolittle in the film version of *My Fair Lady*, a role which Julie Andrews, who had played the character for years on Broadway, had coveted. Audrey told Elizabeth that she would be co-starring with Rex Harrison and planned to meet him while he was in Rome appearing as Julius Caesar in *Cleopatra*.

Elizabeth was most gracious to Hepburn—in Dick's words, "Overly polite, masking her jealousy."

At the end of the luncheon, after everyone had kissed each other, pretending affection not felt, Elizabeth went over to the bar and poured herself a stiff drink. With barely concealed rage, she confronted Fisher. "Listen, Mr. Bigtime Producer. You get me that role of Lisa (*sic*) Doolittle—or else!"

"I can't do that," Fisher protested. "As you plainly heard, Audrey's got it sewn up."

"You little asshole," she yelled at Fisher. "GET ME THAT PART! I'm warning you!"

"Please, I can't do it, but I swear I'll try," Fisher said. "I'll try. I'll meet with Walter Wanger tonight and see what connections he has."

Of course, he failed to get her the part.

Dick said, "Elizabeth never forgave Eddie. Night after night she taunted him for not getting her the role.

"If only Mike Todd were alive, I'd be signing the contract to play Doolittle," she yelled at Fisher.

Eventually, Elizabeth took charge herself, summoning Kurt Frings, her agent, to the Villa Pappa. He was also the agent for Hepburn. He finally convinced her that "the contract with Audrey has already been signed."

Two views of **Audrey Hepburn** in the role Elizabeth coveted, *My Fair Lady.*
Top photo: Dancing with **Rex Harrison**

"Then it's your god damn fault for not getting me the part." She refused to speak to Frings for the next five days.

***

After the film's disaster in England, shooting on the "new" version of *Cleopatra* began in Rome in September of 1961, with the escalating costs estimated at $20 million spent so far.

Most of the filming of *Cleopatra* would be done at Cinecittà, a mammoth film studio originally constructed at the behest of Mussolini.

Dick got to see a Roman crew designing a Sphinx, 65 feet long and 35 feet high, to be used as a backdrop for Cleopatra's entrance into Rome. He also said that Plutarch's description was being used as a kind of instruction manual for the construction of two mammoth barges.

Hundreds of thousands of dollars would be needed to hire charioteers, bowmen, trumpeters, and acrobats who could whirl on their backs. Snake charmers were needed, as were white horses and elephants.

Fisher later claimed that he recommended Rex Harrison for the role of Caesar and Burton for Marc Antony. "I could have kicked myself afterward."

As production began, filming focused almost entirely on the first half of the screenplay, which consisted mostly of scenes between Elizabeth and Harrison in his portrayal of Julius Caesar. Even though Burton had been put on the payroll and flown to Rome, he really wasn't needed during the first half of the movie, He spent his time "boozing and boffing," as he graphically put it.

"Hell, I could have finished my run in *Camelot*," Burton told Harrison. "Wanger brought me to Rome months before I was actually needed on camera. But I was getting a paid vacation."

Chris Mankiewicz, the then-22-year-old son of the director, Joseph Mankiewicz, was assigned the job of getting Elizabeth to work every morning. On the first day of his assignment, he became familiar with the bizarre household at Villa Pappa. The first person he encountered was Dick Hanley. He was not impressed.

"Hanley was an angry, embittered, shrill *fagola*," Chris maintained. "When I walked in on him, I found him examining Elizabeth's underpants. At first I thought he was a panty sniffer. But he explained to me in his high-pitched voice that his first job in the morning was to inspect her drawers to see if she had the rag on. Her contract since *A Place in the Sun* always stipulated that she didn't have to work if she were having her period."

The producer, Walter Wanger, was already on the scene before Elizabeth had arrived in Rome, and Chris was not impressed with him, either. "He was a ludicrous old fop who had shot the balls off his wife's lover and had gone to prison for it [a reference to the night he shot Joan Bennett's lover, her agent,

Jennings Lang, in the testicles]. Even before Elizabeth arrived on the set, Wanger was showing up at noon, cracking a few jokes, and then wandering off to spend the rest of the afternoon and night chasing after hookers along the Via Veneto."

At Cinecittà on the sound stage, Burton was talking with Harrison when "Cleopatra" made her spectacular entrance, attired in a full-length black mink. She was preceded by her advance guard of Eddie Fisher, followed by Dick Hanley; her hairdresser, Sidney Guilaroff; her chauffeur; her wardrobe lady; her two sons; and her young daughter, Liza Todd.

Mankiewicz rushed to give her a big kiss. "How are you today, my little darling?"

"Ready to work," she said.

"My Queen, you leave me breathless," the director said.

"Of course, I do," she said. "I was born to leave men breathless."

Since Elizabeth seemed to be avoiding him, perhaps deliberately, Burton walked over to her, looking her up and down. "You're much too fat, luv, but you've got a pretty face."

Somehow she found this amusing and laughed, a laugh he later compared to "a horse's whinny." She walked over and plopped down on Fisher's lap.

She turned to Burton. "Everybody, including Roddy, has told me what a brilliant actor you are and an inveterate womanizer. On this film, I hope we'll see more of the former and less of the latter."

"Don't worry, luv," he said. "You can keep your panties on and save it for Eddie. I'm not interested." Turning his back on Elizabeth, Burton walked back to rejoin Harrison about fifty feet away.

Elizabeth told Dick and Fisher, "This is one leading lady that Burton will never fuck."

Mankiewicz came over to join the Fishers. He asked her what she thought of the revised script.

"I think it is the greatest woman's role ever written for the screen," she said. "It may become the most important film ever made, and I fully expect to win my second Oscar. As for you, I have to echo Marlene Dietrich's remark about Orson Welles. She said he was a genius. I feel the same way about you as a director. You're not all that hot in the hay, however."

"My other leading ladies had only praise for me," he said defensively.

She quickly assured Fisher that her intimate relations with Mankiewicz had occurred before her marriage to him, and not during the filming of *Suddenly, Last Summer* in London. He looked as if he didn't really believe her.

"And how do you see the character you're about to play?" Mankiewicz asked. "Theda Bara played Cleopatra like a vamp, Claudette Colbert played her like...well, like Claudette Colbert, Tallulah Bankhead played her like

Catherine the Great, and Vivien Leigh played her like a teenage vixen."

"She was more a tigress than a Brigitte Bardot sex kitten," Elizabeth said. "I think she was a very complicated woman—very ambitious, highly strung, fully aware that a great dynasty might end with her if she didn't maneuver carefully between Julius Caesar and Marc Antony. I identify with her. To me, Mike Todd was my Julius Caesar." She kissed Fisher on the lips. "Eddie is my Marc Antony."

Mankiewicz looked skeptically at Fisher.

Harrison joined Burton back in his dressing room, where he rethought his earlier assessment of Elizabeth's beauty. "This stuff about her being the most beautiful woman in the world is pure nonsense. She's a pretty girl, of course, and she has wonderful eyes. But she has a double chin and an overdeveloped chest—and she's rather short in the leg."

The following morning, she had to shoot her first scene with Burton. He arrived on the set battered from the previous night of carousing.

She immediately saw what bad shape he was in. "He was kind of quivering from head to foot and there were grog blossoms [skin blemishes] all over his face." Instead of turning her off to him, she became more sympathetic.

As she remembered it, "He ordered a cup of coffee to sort of still his trembling hands. I had to help it to his mouth, and that brought out my motherly instincts. He was so vulnerable, so sweet, so shaky. In my heart, I *cwtched* him—that's Welsh for 'hug'"

On location in Rome, the most famous woman of the modern world **(Elizabeth Taylor)** impersonates the most famous woman of the ancient world (Cleopatra) as she fine-tunes a doomed alliance with her future consort, Marc Antony **(Richard Burton)**

Even so, he pulled himself together until she felt he "had the grandeur of a Roman emperor's bust." The problem was, he kept blowing his lines.

In contrast, he found her "walking pornography." Fisher was on the set that day, handling her make-up man and costume personnel. As he described in his memoirs, "When she had emerged dressed in Cleopatra's golden gown, I was very, very sad. I had this premonition that I had lost her. She no longer needed me. I broke down and cried."

Earlier, when Elizabeth had been shown to her dressing room, she said, "It's not a dressing room, it's a god damn house. All five rooms of it, even a room just for my wigs and an office for Eddie. At least those cocksuckers at Fox are not being cheap with me."

Fortunately, Fisher was not at the studio on

476

January 22, 1962 when Mankiewicz directed Marc Antony and Cleopatra in their first love scene.

As Mankiewicz told producer Wanger, "Their succulent lips came together. He locked her into a deep, wet kiss. I ordered the scene reshot four times. I could feel their passion for each other. It was almost frightening, like an oncoming tornado. Finally, I had to say, 'Would you two mind if I say 'cut?'"

The following afternoon, when the sun went behind clouds and it started to rain, Burton guided Elizabeth behind one of the *faux* sets. There, one of the grips spotted Burton masturbating Elizabeth.

In about twenty minutes, when her hairdresser, Sidney Guilaroff, located her, she was adjusting her costume. The rain had stopped. She looked back at Burton and was heard to say, "You are a horrible, horrible wretch of a bloke."

"If I were twice as horrible, I'd be perfect for you," he shot back, licking his fingers seductively.

At Cineccittà one morning, after working with Elizabeth for five days, Burton appeared on the set. In front of Chris Mankiewicz and other members of the crew, he said, "Gents," in his most impressive stentorian voice. "Last night I nailed Elizabeth in the back seat of my Cadillac."

The day following Burton's seduction of her in the Cadillac, she stood nude before her dressing room mirror in front of Guilaroff and ordered him to get her a large bath towel. She then requested he pick up a blonde Marlene Dietrich type wig from wardrobe, which he did.

Returning, he fitted the wig perfectly onto her head. She told him goodbye, as she headed toward Burton's dressing room, where she found the door unlocked.

Once inside, she heard him taking a shower. She came into the bathroom and pulled the plastic shower curtain back.

At first, he didn't recognize her. Then she dropped the towel, standing completely nude in front of him.

"How much do you charge, luv?" he asked.

***

During the making of *Cleopatra*, Elizabeth adopted a little German girl. She had been born with a crippling hip defect.

"I think Elizabeth would have left Fisher sooner, but with the arrival of those adoption papers, she stuck it out a little longer," Roddy claimed.

When Elizabeth was first shown the child, she remembered, "Her legs were so twisted that one was practically facing around the other way."

The nine-month-old girl, Petra Heisis, was renamed Maria in hour of actress Maria Schell, who had guided the Fishers to the deformed baby.

The girl had large saucer-shaped eyes and lots of curls. But she required extremely expensive operations on her legs, which her Bavarian parents could ill afford.

After seeing a specialist, Elizabeth was told that Maria had a malformation of the pelvis. If not surgically altered, she would be crippled for life.

Although the recovery after surgery would require two years in a full body cast, Elizabeth ordered the surgery, which she insisted be performed in London.

For two years, the baby girl was known as Maria Taylor before her last name was changed to Burton when she was adopted by him as well. As Elizabeth recalled, "I fell in love with Maria the first day she was shown to me. I knew how much she needed me to give her a proper, happy, and fulfilling life."

The adoption, which was legally finalized in Catholic Bavaria, would later enrage the Vatican. Pope John XXIII was said to have privately denounced Elizabeth as an unfit mother.

***

Elizabeth got on reasonably well with Rex Harrison during her scenes with him. He was involved in his own romantic entanglements, and didn't want to get embroiled in what he called "the onrushing affair that Richard is having with Elizabeth."

He was sensitive to his billing on *Cleopatra* and didn't want her to have too many star advantages over him. As a special bonus, Harrison was offered ongoing access to a chauffeur-driven Cadillac to take him to the studio from his Roman house along Via Antigua. One morning, he emerged from his house to encounter a Mercedes-Benz.

At the studio, in front of Mankiewicz, he threw a fit, claiming that he'd been promised a Cadillac, not a Mercedes-Benz.

He also

HOLLYWOOD ON THE TIBER
(aka *ROMAN HOLIDAY*)
Denouncing Elizabeth as an unfit mother:
Pope John XXIII

REDEFINING FAMILY
Maria Heisig Taylor Burton *(left figure in photo above)*; her adoptive mother (**Elizabeth Taylor**); and her stepsister **Lisa Todd** *(right figure in photo above)*

478

learned that Elizabeth's chauffeur was being paid more than his driver. He threatened to walk off the picture if his chauffeur wasn't paid an equivalent wage. "Why the bloody hell should her driver get more than mine just because she's got a bigger chest?"

On March 22, 1962, Harrison in Genoa would marry Rachel Roberts, a friend of Sybil Burton's since their days as novice actresses in Stratford-upon-Avon.

On the set one afternoon, when Elizabeth and Burton weren't needed in front of the camera, she sat talking to him. She wanted to know anything he cared to tell her about his life, because all she knew was that he had been born in Wales. He liked talking about himself and filled her in on his early life, perhaps exaggerating to make a better story.

"Olivier, Noël Coward, John Gielgud, all the sods, criticized me in 1952 when I gave up my acting career on the London stage to go to Hollywood," Burton said. "They said I sold out. But I have this driving need to blot out all my years of living in humiliating poverty as a kid."

"I was the twelfth of thirteen children. We lived in a broken-down shanty with no running water. I never knew my mother. She died giving birth to her last child. My father was a rotter, a coalminer who was too drunk to work. We had to borrow ten pounds to pay for my mother's funeral."

Richard Burton's original name was Richard Walter Jenkins, Jr., named after his father, of course. His coalminer dad was more widely known as "Dic Bach," who took home the equivalent of $1.25 a week. Once, Elizabeth asked Burton why his father had such an unusual name. "I haven't a bloody clue," he told her.

Young Burton later learned four languages, but spoke only Welsh until the age of ten.

It was Philip Burton who took the seventeen-year-old into his home and taught him drama and literature, as well as details associated with homosexual sex. Burton always hated his biological father, Dic Bach, who died in 1957. Burton did not attend the funeral and proudly took the name of his mentor and older lover, Philip Burton.

Philip was a preparatory school drama teacher and an authority on Shakespeare. He was immediately attracted to Richard, who was a stunning male beauty in his late teens and

How Green Was My Valley?
Welsh schoolmaster **Philip Burton** *(right)* with his most brilliant pupil and adopted son, Richard Walter Jenkins, Jr.
(aka, **Richard Burton**)

early twenties.

A homosexual, Philip invited the teenager to come and live with him in comfort, removing him from the poverty-ridden town of Pontrhydfen.

"I always considered Philip as my true father. I met him in high school. He was the most wonderful schoolmaster. He taught me to speak English and lose my Welsh accent. He taught me drama, literature, Shakespeare. The sad thing is that he's madly in love with me. I'm his entire life. Of course, as a young boy, I had only sex to offer him in exchange for all the wonderful things he was doing for me. Without Philip, I would probably be dead now after a brief life as a coal miner suffering from tuberculosis and malnutrition."

"I just pretend I attended Oxford," he told Elizabeth. "I only got so far as high school. However, while based for six months in a Royal Air Force camp near the Oxford campus, I attended some lectures at the university."

"When I broke into the London theatre, there were so many established actors willing to give me a tumble on their casting couches—John Gielgud, Noël Coward, Larry Olivier, Emlyn Williams, you name him."

"My wife, Sybil Williams, gave up her acting career for me. She's a great woman, and also a mother to me. She reads my scripts, studies my contracts, picks out my clothes, worries about my whoring around, warning me, 'Don't pick up something with these whores you can't get rid of.'"

By his own admission, Burton was not strictly a heterosexual, although this didn't seem to bother Elizabeth a bit. She was used to bisexual men.

When Dick asked her about "the size" of Burton, she deliberately misinterpreted his question. "Oh, he's five feet, nine inches, the right size for me." Because of his large on-screen appearance, people who met him were astonished by how short he was.

One night, Elizabeth decided to invite the occupants of the "Villa Burton" to the Villa Pappa for dinner. Burton was living in the villa with Sybil, and also with Roddy McDowall and his lover, John Valva. As a favor to Roddy, Mankiewicz had cast Valva as "Valvus," a Roman soldier.

After dinner, Elizabeth and Burton got drunk on "Ivan the Terribles," a mind-bending blend of Grappa, Ouzo, and Russian vodka.

At one point over drinks, Fisher asked Burton, "Does a man really have to give a woman jewelry? Isn't that like buying a piece of ass?"

Burton lived up to his reputation as a marathon drinker. He gave a slobbering Shakespearean monologue that lasted for nearly an hour until Sybil ordered him to sit down. Once seated, he asked for more liquor and became more provocative than ever. He turned to Fisher. "Noël Coward told me you have the most delectable ass. Remind me to sample it before I finish this bloody picture."

"Mr. Burton, my ass is only for shitting and sucking by a beautiful woman

480

like Elizabeth here. You will never experience its pleasures. I am not a homo-sexual."

"Actually, I think all straight men should experience at least one good plug-ging up their arse so they'll know what it's like," Elizabeth said.

"I couldn't agree with you more," Burton said.

She turned to him and said, "I absolutely adore you in spite of that acne-pitted face of yours."

"And I think you're ravishing in spite of all that whale blubber," he coun-tered.

"With that voice of yours, you are a prince among men," she said.

"Actually, I'm more of a frog than a prince," he told her.

Sitting at the head of the table, Elizabeth would bark orders at her Italian waiters, who spoke no English. "Pass around the roast suckling pig, you moth-erfucker. We're ready for the spaghetti, asshole."

The party ended disastrously when a bored Fisher, a major musical star in his own right, walked over and started playing the piano and singing. "Shut up!" Elizabeth shouted at him. "We're trying to talk."

He slammed down the piano top and stormed out of the room.

"Time I took my drunken old sod home," Sybil said, rising and reaching for Burton's arm. "Elizabeth, you're a delight. The dinner was spectacular. What was that unusual appetizer, by the way?"

"The tongues of flamingos," she said.

"That was the creamiest custard I've ever tasted," Burton said.

"I asked all members of my male staff to whack off in a bowl," Elizabeth said. "Their combined semen was whipped into the egg custard mix and also used to make the whipped cream extra thick."

"Oh, I think I'm going to be sick," Sybil said.

"Male semen," Dick Hanley said. "No wonder it tasted so good. I've now discovered my favorite new dessert."

***

Word reached Hollywood that the filming of *Cleopatra* was costing mil-lions every week with little to show for it. Walter Wanger and Joseph Mankiewicz were said to have lost control of the budget.

Armed with a "flotilla" of accountants, Spyros Skouras himself made the long journey to Rome to find out what was going on.

Costs mounted, as Mankiewicz made outrageously bad decisions, includ-ing shooting scenes that would not be used and ordering sets constructed at ex-orbitant overtime costs that would sit idle for months—or else not be used at all.

Mankiewicz hovered on the verge of a nervous breakdown, as he took amphetamine shots to keep working on his uncompleted script, getting by on three hours of sleep most nights.

Everything from outraged Fox stockholders and rampaging elephants plagued him, as did the "epic" battles between the Italian and American crews. He constantly gnawed his knuckles and finally came down with a nervous skin disease on his hands, forcing him to wear gloves.

In Rome to confront the mounting problems of filming *Cleopatra*, Skouras met first with Wanger. "I told you Burton was trash. Remember I didn't want to hire him. It's your god damn fault."

"Actually, all this worldwide publicity about *Cleopatra* will make Burton a bigger star than ever, and Elizabeth a living legend," Wanger said.

"OK, I grant that about Miss Taylor, our resident whore, but Burton will never be a star," Skouras said. "Mark my words."

The next day, after watching the rushes of *Cleopatra*, Skouras changed his mind. He invited Burton for lunch and offered him contracts for two more pictures. "Make-up can fill in these hideous pockmarks," he told the actor.

Back in Hollywood, someone had tipped off Skouras about some romantic entanglement between Burton and Elizabeth.

It had been a peaceful luncheon. Actually, Elizabeth's name never came up. That's why Burton was shocked when he received a hot-tempered memo which was delivered to him in his dressing room later that day. The letter to Burton instructed him to "clean up your act."

On receiving it, the Welshman flew into a rage. He had learned that an equivalent letter was on its way to Elizabeth's villa. He called her and warned her to expect it.

She then flew into her own rage, calling Skouras' office and threatening to

Cleopatra
An *Über-Diva* checks her make-up.

walk off the picture if such a letter arrived at her villa. Skouras was able to contact the delivery boy just in time to intercept and retrieve the accusatory memo he'd sent.

Still saddled with unhappy memories about his star role in *Alexander the Great* (1956), which had been panned by critics, and now faced with studio disapproval about his involvement in *Cleopatra*, Burton ripped his copy of Skouras' memo into shreds.

Soonafter, he accidentally ran into a reporter from *Variety* who had been sent to Rome. He answered no personal questions about his private life, but he apologized for appearing in another "sex and scandal" epic. He announced to the reporter that his next picture would be a screen adaptation of Shakespeare's *The Taming of the Shrew* opposite Marilyn Monroe. When he'd had an affair with Monroe in Hollywood, she'd told him that her great dream involved appearing in a Shakespeare drama, although she had not yet read one of his plays or seen one performed on the stage.

Ironically, he would film *The Taming of the Shrew* (1967), but with Elizabeth as his co-star, as Monroe had been murdered in 1962.

Over dinner that night, Roddy discovered that Burton had never seen one of Elizabeth's movies. "I really can't judge her as an actress," he said. "All I know about her is she gets sick and she gets married."

When the first rushes of *Cleopatra* came in, Roddy invited Burton to come and look at them.

As he witnessed the magic relationship she had with the camera, he began to change his mind about her as an actress. "She surprised the devil out of me. She seemed to sleepwalk through our rehearsals. She doesn't come alive until the camera focuses on her. She sure knows how to turn it on then."

Back at the Villa Pappa, the talk was not of Elizabeth as an actress, but of Burton. Earlier in the day, she'd received a call from Monty, who had seen three of Burton's movies. "I'm not impressed," he told her. "He's self-indulgent. I feel that when he speaks, he is merely listening to the sound of his own voice—and getting off on that. To me, that is not acting. It's masturbation."

After the call, she was deeply disturbed. She'd come to believe that Burton was the greatest actor on the stage, even better than Olivier. But now, she feared that her romantic attachment to him was taking the place of her sound judgment. Would she, in fact, be laughed off the screen during her scenes with him?

She couldn't present any of these fears to Fisher, lest she tip him off about her growing sexual interest in Burton.

Besides, when she communicated with her husband these days, he was smoking a cigar, the kind Mike Todd always preferred, and wanted to talk about film projects subsequent to *Cleopatra*, now that she was no longer under contract to MGM. "We must decide what your next film will be after this session in hell called *Cleopatra*," he said.

"At that point in their relationship, Fisher seemed more like Elizabeth's business manager than her husband," Roddy said. "He hovered over her like a hawk. He allowed her only one glass of red wine at night. Imagine that allowance for Elizabeth, she of the hollow leg."

Personally, Elizabeth wanted to star in a movie based on the life of Isadora Duncan, the American dancer. The problem with that idea was that Elizabeth could not dance. She next told Fisher that she wanted someone to write a script for her based on the life of Sarah Bernhardt.

Fisher rejected such ideas as preposterous and beyond her range. He wanted something "sleazy and sexy" that would almost guarantee millions at the box office.

He was negotiating several movie deals for her, including *The Carpetbaggers*, based on Harold Robbin's steamy bestselling novel that was loosely based on Howard Hughes' involvements in Hollywood.

When Elizabeth rejected all of his ideas, he came up with another project that had more prestige, a vehicle that would cast her opposite Charlie Chaplin.

The film projected with Chaplin was entitled *The Gouffré Case*. It was based on a novel by German author Joachim Mass in which Elizabeth would be cast as a murderess in turn-of-the-20th-Century Paris. Chaplin was to come out of retirement to play the aging police inspector who goes after her.

Encouraged by Elizabeth, Fisher flew north to have lunch with Chaplin, who was in retirement at Vevey, Switzerland. Chaplin welcomed him with grace and listened attentively to the film proposal.

Assistant director Hank Moonjean and John Valva, Roddy's lover, accompanied Fisher to Switzerland. At Vevey, these men discovered Chaplin living in a house that looked like a miniature version of the White House in Washington, D.C. They were introduced to his pregnant and much younger wife, Oona

O'Neill Chaplin, the estranged daughter of the famous playwright Eugene O'Neill, who had strenuously opposed her marriage to Chaplin.

As Moonjean later reported, the lunch was interrupted by Chaplin every fifteen minutes, rising from the table and performing "a strange little dance" for them, in which he used the cane and top hat he'd worn in all those silent films as The Little Tramp.

Finally, at the end of the luncheon, Chaplin told Fisher, "You're a good salesman, and I'm flattered by the offer, an old man like me. But I must turn it down. However, I'd love to meet Miss Taylor. I've known Marilyn Monroe intimately, as have my sons, but I never had a chance to meet Miss Taylor and introduce her to the eighth wonder of the world."

It had to be explained to Fisher later that The

Charles Chaplin with **Oona O'Neill Chaplin** in 1975.

Little Tramp was actually referring to his legendary twelve-inch penis, which had been enjoyed by everyone from Mae West to America's most famous evangelist, Aimee Semple McPherson, plus dozens of bimbos in the countless brothels he used to frequent.

From Vevey, Fisher and his friends drove to the chic ski resort of Gstaad. He and Elizabeth had been advised to establish a residence in Switzerland as a means of avoiding painful American income tax. He had been told that a Texas oil millionaire had built the Chalet Ariel for his ballerina bride, but the marriage never survived the honeymoon.

The elegant Chalet Ariel was on the market for about $350,000. He called Elizabeth in Rome, telling her it was idyllic for both of them and their children, although he warned that it might cost another $100,000 in renovations.

"Buy the fucker!" she said.

Her neighbors would include the Aga Khan, Robert Wagner, Julie Andrews, and Peter Sellers.

After signing the papers, Fisher headed for Geneva for a final stopover. He liked to spend money as much as Mike Todd had done, even if it wasn't his own loot he was tossing about. In Geneva, he bought a $50,000 diamond necklace for Elizabeth from the prestigious jeweler, Vacheron Constantin.

Valva thought Elizabeth would "adore" the necklace, and he wanted to be at the Villa Pappa to see the expression on her face when Fisher presented her with the costly gift.

In Rome, Valva later asserted that Elizabeth examined the necklace very skeptically. "How much did you pay?" she asked. When Fisher told her, she said, "There's not one god damn good stone in it. You were taken."

Nonetheless, on his birthday, she presented him with another Rolls-Royce, this one a sports coupe in emerald green. In return, he purchased for her an ivory-colored Maserati as a means of celebrating Christmas of 1961.

After inviting Dick Hanley to go for a drive with her long the Appian Way in her new Maserati, she returned disappointed and skeptical to the Villa Pappa. "I detest this junk heap," she told Fisher on her way upstairs. Dick said that Fisher looked utterly humiliated, but later got his money back by selling it to actor Anthony Quinn, who was in Rome at the time.

When Burton heard about the purchase of the chalet in Gstaad, he told Roddy that, "The best gift Eddie can give Elizabeth is the ruby-tipped snake he keeps inside his trousers."

What Burton knew, or didn't know, about Fisher's penis at that time remains something of a mystery.

Roddy was among the first to realize how serious the love affair between Elizabeth and Burton had become. "Although she still wore Eddie's wedding ring, Burton asked her to take off the wedding band that had been retrieved from the wreckage of Mike Todd's airplane in New Mexico. Her removal of Todd's ring was a symbol of the influence Burton had in her life. I feared that Eddie's day as the consort to the Queen was nearing its end."

On January 26, 1962, Mankiewicz broke the news to Wanger: "I've been sitting on a volcano for too long. Burton and Liz are not just playing Antony and Cleopatra."

His announcement was the first of what became the most public adultery in film history.

Jack Brodsky, Fox's assistant publicity manager in Rome, became, in his words, "more sought-after than the Pope, at least for a while. Every reporter was trying to get the scoop from me."

Burton was consumed with such guilt he spent sleepless nights. He was especially concerned with Sybil and his family, including his young daughter, Jessica, who had been born mentally retarded. [She was later diagnosed as an autistic schizophrenic and was placed in a mental institution at the age of six.]

At a private meeting with Wanger, the producer urged Burton to go back to his wife, warning that "this thing with Elizabeth can ultimately harm everybody. Fuck Elizabeth on the side if you must, but don't destroy Sybil and bring harm to your family."

At least for the moment, Burton seemed to agree with this assessment.

Within his villa, Burton had a long talk with Roddy, who, while still one of Elizabeth's closest friends, was also extremely friendly with Sybil and wanted Burton to save his marriage and be a father to his two daughters.

Although he knew that Elizabeth would turn on him, feeling that he had betrayed her, Roddy nonetheless urged Burton to drive over to the Villa Pappa—"and put an end to this whole thing. It can only cause pain for everybody."

Burton finally agreed and, without warning Elizabeth, got into his car and drove to confront her.

On February 16, 1962, at 10pm, Burton walked into Villa Pappa. Elizabeth must have known something was wrong because he did not rush to take her in his arms, as he usually did. He had a stern look on his face. As he'd tell Roddy, "I wanted to make it short and sweet and get it over with."

To her stunned face, he said, "Our love affair was just one of those things that often happens between a leading man and a leading lady when they make a film together. It was fun, luv, while it lasted." Then he turned his back and headed for the front door. All he heard in the background were her sobs.

As Elizabeth confessed in a memoir, "I had to be with Richard. I knew it was wrong. I knew it would hurt people. I knew. I knew. But I also knew what I had to do. God help me. I had to be with Richard."

She became so upset that she raged through the villa breaking glass. Dick had to restrain her and called her doctor, Rex Kennamer, to give her a sedative.

He phoned Mankiewicz that Elizabeth would not be able to report to work.

At around noon of the following day, Wanger went to the Villa Pappa to check on Elizabeth's condition. He found her in bed but barely awake. She told him she'd taken a sleeping pill and hadn't eaten in twenty-four hours.

He went downstairs to ask the chef to prepare her a sandwich and pour her a glass of milk.

Suddenly, her upstairs maid came running downstairs and into the kitchen, holding up an empty bottle. "Miss Taylor...Miss Taylor. She's taken these pills."

Wanger ordered Dick to call an ambulance as he rushed upstairs and pulled a nude Elizabeth from bed. He practically walked her, dragged her, around the room until the ambulance arrived.

Someone in her household tipped off the newspapers. When the ambulance pulled up at the emergency entrance of the Salvator Mundi Hospital, at least thirty paparazzi were there.

Wanger put out a story that she'd consumed some "bad oysters and was suffering an acute case of food poisoning."

Roman newspaper editors were too savvy to fall for that line. That night, the entire world, it seemed, learned that LIZ TAYLOR ATTEMPTS SUICIDE OVER BURTON AFFAIR.

Sybil had already flown out of Rome heading for New York to tend to an ailing Philip Burton, her father-in-law. She faced reporters demanding to know when she was filing for a divorce. She dismissed such claims. "Elizabeth is one of my best friends. I absolutely adore her. There is no romance between Richard and her—no divorce coming up."

Burton was stunned at the newspaper coverage of their affair. "I've had affairs before," he said. "But how did I know she was so bloody famous? She knocks Khrushchev off the fucking front page."

After Burton's rejection, Elizabeth, in the words of publicist Jack Brodsky, "went coconuts. She wanted to junk the whole picture and bankrupt Fox. Imagine any guy turning her down."

Brodsky was asked if Burton were merely a beard for the Mankiewicz/Taylor affair. Jokingly, Brodsky asserted that the real story was "I'm the one in love with Richard Burton. Elizabeth is the cover-up for us. Send it out!"

Believe it or not, that comment from Brodsky went out on the Associated Press wire services.

Mankiewicz added to the gay rumors by standing in full view of a stunned journalist. Mankiewicz then grabbed Burton, placing his hand firmly on his crotch and tongue-kissed him for about a minute. He then turned to the journalist and said, "There you are. I'm the one having the affair with Richard here."

Time magazine reported that Elizabeth was merely using a rumored affair with Burton to conceal the real truth. "She is mad, mad, mad for her personable director, Joseph L. Mankiewicz, who is fifty-three years old."

Wanger greeted Burton when he returned to the set. In his journal, the producer wrote: "The romance is front page all over the world. Reporters are flocking like vultures to Rome from all over the continent. Burton on the set today—very gay, cocky, with a glass of beer in his hand. When he came to this picture some months ago, he was a well-known star but not famous. His salary was good but not huge. Suddenly, his name has become a household word. His salary for his next movie has skyrocketed. The romance has changed his life, but I don't think he realizes how deeply involved he is."

In New York, Monty told Marlon Brando at the Actors Studio, "Poor Bessie Mae. She's hooked up with a hustler. She's the most famous woman in the world, and he's using her to promote his own career. I am told that Burton wants fame at any price."

Hundreds of newspeople wanted interviews, but Burton rarely granted them. He did tell a reporter in Rome, "I will never leave Sybil. She loves and understands me."

The Cuban Missile Crisis of 1960 may have brought the United States and the Soviet Union to the brink of nuclear disaster, but the illicit love affair of Richard Burton and Elizabeth Taylor seemingly generated more headlines.

An extracurricular affair between two world famous stars would hardly merit such attention today—in fact, would be commonplace. But in a different time and place, "Liz & Dick," as they were called, were accused of sparking the sexual revolution that grew to fruition before the end of the decade of "free love."

When Truman Capote came to Rome for a visit and saw the affair up close, he was skeptical. "Elizabeth loved Burton. He didn't love her. He wanted her because he wanted to be an international movie star, far bigger than the picture actor he was. That was the career he wanted—money, money, and more money."

Sometimes, Elizabeth was enraged at the press coverage, screaming about how unfair it was. "The most famous man on the planet, John F. Kennedy, is fucking the second most famous woman on earth, Marilyn Monroe, and not a word gets into the press. But let me screw around with some Welsh actor and the media goes apeshit."

Distressed about his diminished importance within Elizabeth's emotional landscapes, Fisher didn't know what to do. He went and purchased a revolver which he carried with him at all times, planning at some point to assassinate Burton, perhaps even to shoot Elizabeth, too. He told Roddy, "In Italy, the courts are easy on crimes of passion."

When Elizabeth showed up on the set to film a love scene with Burton,

"The tension was so great that you could cut it with a knife," Mankiewicz said. "I told Burton he'd better go to her dressing room and work things out. He was in there for three hours, and I just assumed they'd made love. He later told me, 'I now know the truth: I can't live without her. We're back together again.'"

In the meantime, Sara and Francis Taylor had flown to Rome from California, although Elizabeth didn't really want them.

Throughout the filming of *Cleopatra*, a sleek white Roman ambulance was seen parked day after day outside the studio. Wanger had ordered it "in case Elizabeth tries suicide again." The crew referred to it as "the suicide mobile." A gleaming silver-colored stomach pump had been installed as part of its equipment.

The next day, Burton was accompanied to Bulgari, according to publicist Jack Brodsky, by a procession "of parents" (Sara and Francis), a hairdresser (Guilaroff), and other members of Elizabeth's court to purchase an emerald necklace for her for $150,000. Francis actually made the final selection.

"I introduced her to beer," Burton later said. "She introduced me to Bulgari."

When Fisher showed up on the set of *Cleopatra*, he went first to seek Burton instead of heading directly for Elizabeth's dressing room. He discovered Burton discussing a scene with Mankiewicz. Before Fisher could say anything, Burton moved menacingly close to the singer.

"You don't need her any more," Burton said to Fisher, standing so close to his face he was peppering the singer with his saliva. "You're already a star. I'm not, but she's going to make me one. I'm going to use her, that no-talent Hollywood nothing." Burton made this astonishing statement in front of Mankiewicz, who later revealed it in an interview long after *Cleopatra* had been released to theaters.

That night, over a private dinner with Roddy, Elizabeth shared her own feelings about Burton. She was surprisingly articulate: "He's a devious snakepit of contradictions. If a prefrontal lobotomy was performed on him, like what Katharine Hepburn wanted to have done on me, out of Richard's skull would emerge poisonous snakes, tadpoles, frogs, worms, and bats from hell. What a man! I get an orgasm just listening to his voice."

The next day, on the set of *Cleopatra*, Burton proved Elizabeth's point that he was a man of contradictions, coming up with a completely different set of feelings about her.

While Fisher was talking to a seated Elizabeth, Burton walked over and reached to fondle one of her breasts. "You know, old thing, I'm in love with your girl."

"She's not my girl." Fisher snapped. "She's my wife and she's going to remain my wife."

"Okay, *Dummkopf*, I'm in love with your bloody wife then."

Elizabeth sat silently through this exchange and made no attempt to remove Burton's hand from her breast.

At around five o'clock that afternoon, Dick and Roddy arrived at Burton's dressing room before Elizabeth and the entourage came to patronize what had become known as "Burton's Bar."

Sitting in the nude in front of his vanity mirror, removing his makeup, Burton told Elizabeth's two friends, "The woman who brings out the best in a man—who is good in bed—is very rare. In my entire life, I've enjoyed only four such women—Elizabeth Taylor, Marilyn Monroe, Jackie Kennedy, and an almost toothless middle age maid in Jamaica."

Although she didn't exactly announce it to the world, Elizabeth was attracted sexually to Burton as she had been to no other man, not even the aging Mike Todd, who had been her greatest lover before Burton.

Biographer Kitty Kelley wrote: "In this one man seemed to be all the men she had ever loved. As rich as Nicky Hilton, Richard Burton possessed Michael Wilding's quicksilver humor and Mike Todd's energy and command. He was as physical as Ingemar Johansson, as intellectual as Max Lerner, as mellifluous as Frank Sinatra and Eddie Fisher."

Elizabeth also wasn't satisfied just acting out dramatic scenes on the screen. She wanted a daily drama going on in her private life, too—and Burton was the man to do that.

A drunken Burton showed up unexpectedly at a dinner party at Villa Pappa at which Elizabeth and Fisher were entertaining twelve guests. Dick knew better than to turn him away, and therefore ushered him into the dining room. Burton immediately got into an altercation with Fisher.

The Ruin of Ptolmaic Egypt
Starring **Cleopatra** and **Marc Antony**

"Why don't you go back to your own home, you bastard?" Fisher said. "Go back to Sybil. She's your woman, not Elizabeth. Elizabeth is mine."

"Fuck you, you little faggot," Burton said. "They're both my women." He looked over at Elizabeth. "Are you my woman?" His voice grew louder. "Well, are you? If you are, get your fat ass over her and stick your tongue down my throat."

Elizabeth stood up and staggered toward Burton. In front of her other guests, she lip locked with him.

Fisher rose from his chair, staring in amazement and humiliation.

When Burton broke from Elizabeth's lips, he turned to Fisher. "Keep her warm for me, okay?"

Aided by Dick, Burton staggered toward the door, where Dick helped him into his car to drive him back to his villa.

"He was a total basket case," Dick later claimed. "He told me that Sybil was in London."

At his villa, Burton asked Dick to put him to bed. In his elegantly decorated boudoir, Burton told Dick that he had to "take an urgent piss" and asked him to "take me to the bathroom." Dick led him into the bathroom and directed him to the bowl. "I can't do it," Burton said. "Take it out for me."

Dick unzipped Burton's trousers, reached in, and removed his uncut cock, which he aimed toward the bowl. "After he took a horse piss, I shook it for him."

"He then ordered me to undress him and put him to bed. I did as I was told. Before I left, he grabbed me and held my face close to his and stuck his tongue in my mouth. The next morning, when I saw him, I don't think he even remembered my taking him home. I had never seen a man as wasted as he could get."

An even more intense drama was unleashed the following Sunday night when Burton once again arrived unannounced at the Villa Pappa.

On that occasion, Fisher was as intoxicated as Elizabeth and Burton. "It was the strangest and most unexpected night I ever spent at the Villa Pappa," Dick recalled.

On that particular evening, Burton seemed in a confessional mood. "I've heard that Elizabeth's friends, faggots, like that Capote and Monty Clift, even that cocksucker Marlon Brando, are claiming that I'm just a hustler, using Elizabeth here as a stepping stone to stardom."

"Are you?" she asked him.

In front of her guests, Burton admitted to her, "You're a good piece of ass, but I'm also becoming a household word around the world—and I was never that before."

"She burst into tears and ran from the villa," Dick said. "Two of her security guards chased after her."

Watching her leave, Burton said, "You know I don't give a fuck where she's going."

A drunken Fisher looked at him. "Neither do I. For the first time in my life, I don't give a hot damn."

"Eddie, tonight I'm going to do what had been my original intention," Burton told him. "When I got to Rome, I always planned to fuck your ass. I wasn't even thinking of Elizabeth's honeypot. Tonight, I'm going to fuck you. You can take it willingly, like a man, or else I'm going to rape you. Either way, you're going to get it. Your choice."

Dick searched Fisher's face, expecting him to put up massive resistance. He found none. If anything, Fisher looked like an abused, defeated man who might surrender to anything. "I always knew that's what you really wanted to do," Fisher said to Burton. "I knew it was going to happen sometime. I might as well endure it and get it over with. Let's go upstairs."

As Dick stood in semi-shock, watching Fisher head up the stairs with Burton, Fisher called back to him. "If word of this gets out, I'll claim that Richard raped me when I was drunk."

Roddy was a late arrival at Villa Pappa that night. When he came into the living room, Dick told him what was going on upstairs between Fisher and Burton.

"I'm not at all surprised," Roddy said.

"Eddie is always denying he's a homosexual," Dick said. "But he's one of us."

"He's bi," Roddy said. "I think Elizabeth likes bisexual men. Look at her track record. I've known about Eddie for a long time."

Roddy claimed that once, after Fisher had left Debbie Reynolds during their marriage, that he'd rented an apartment on Sunset Boulevard. "While he was there, his most frequent sleepover was that gorgeous little hunk, Ricky Nelson. Ricky is bi himself, and most of inside Hollywood knows that. Ricky has had two big crushes in his life—Eddie Fisher and Elvis Presley."

"That explains why Eddie went so willingly upstairs to his fate," Dick said. "The little shit is probably enjoying it."

Two hours passed before Burton emerged from upstairs. Fisher remained in the master bedroom.

Glenys Roberts, writing in London's *Daily Mail*, on the 20th anniversary of Burton's death in 2004, wrote: "Some claim Burton first tried to seduce Liz's then husband, Eddie Fisher, and turned to her only when he was rebuffed."

That was not exactly what Dick reported.

Outside, Burton got into a vehicle driven by his chauffeur and presumably headed home.

After telling Roddy good night, Dick drove to his own apartment. When he got there, he found Elizabeth sitting up in his bed having a drink. She had let herself into his apartment with a passkey he'd given her.

She told him that she'd called her bedroom telephone at Villa Pappa and was shocked when Burton picked up the receiver.

"When he heard who it was, he said, 'Hello, luv, I'm fucking your husband right now. One tight ass on our little Jew boy, a perfect bottom, and he's loving it.' Then the jerk slammed down the phone on me."

About fifteen minutes later, there was a pounding on Dick's apartment door. Burton was shouting, demanding to be let in.

Elizabeth ordered Dick to keep him out, but he disobeyed her, because he knew that Burton would break down the apartment's rather thin door.

"He came into my living room like a madman," Dick said. "He was calling her every name he could—some in Welsh. I recognized the word 'cunt' repeated endlessly. Like a caveman, he headed for the bedroom."

There, Burton discovered Elizabeth in bed by herself. In front of Dick, he ripped off her bedcovers. "You fucking sagging-titted, no-talent Hollywood cunt!" he shouted at her. "Eddie loves you so much, and you treat him like shit. From now on, I'll be fucking him instead of you!"

Of course, that drunken threat was never realized. Far from being offended, she seemed excited by this abuse.

As she told *Life* magazine in December of 1964, "I adore fighting with Richard. It's rather like a small atom bomb going off. Sparks fly, walls shake, floors reverberate!"

"He practically dragged her out the door," Dick said. "She seemed to love it. I knew she'd gotten off on Mike Todd beating the shit out of her. The pattern was being repeated with Burton. They disappeared for two days, and no one knew where they went. I was the poor sucker who had to call Mankiewicz the following morning. Did I ever get hell!"

***

Mankiewicz was asked what it was like to work with such temperamental stars. "When you're in a cage with tigers, you never let them know you're afraid of them—or they'll eat you." The director responded. "The one thing I could expect from them was the unexpected. If Elizabeth and Sybil weren't enough for Richard to handle, he showed up one day with a bimbo."

During his appearance on Broadway in *Camelot*, Burton had launched a torrid affair with Pat Tunder, a beautiful showgirl from the Copacabana.

From Rome, he'd sent her a ticket to join him during the filming of *Cleopatra*. "I'm importing a piece of ass," he told Roddy.

On the day after Tunder's arrival, Burton did not show up on the set until eleven the following morning. He arrived with a hangover and one arm protectively around Tunder. Elizabeth was forty feet away, surveying his arrival with the showgirl.

Publicist Brodsky later said, "Elizabeth just stood there, looking daggers at both Burton and the Copa-cutie. Ironically, those daggers were mixed with steamy, passionate stares. After make-up, Burton walked over to her. An angry Elizabeth confronted him. 'You kept us waiting.'"

"What a switch," he said. "It's about time someone kept you waiting for a change."

After being confronted with Elizabeth's anger, fueled by jealousy, Wanger ordered Tunder off the set. Two days later, he arranged for his office to provide her with a one-way ticket back to New York.

In addition to everything else, I didn't need three females battling over who was going to get Dick Burton's cock," he said. "I'm under constant attack from the offices of Fox in Hollywood and New York. They claim that the Taylor/Burton affair is like a cancer growing on us. If this budget keeps ballooning, I've been warned that there may be no 21st Century Fox."

With Tunder safely out of the way, Burton somehow got Elizabeth to forgive him for this indiscretion with a showgirl. It would become a pattern repeated often during the two times they would marry in the future.

Just as Elizabeth began to feel secure that Burton might divorce Sybil and marry her, an unforeseen event happened: Richard was summoned to Paris to appear in a cameo for Darryl F. Zanuck in his production of *The Longest Day*, a big-budget film epic detailing the D-Day invasion of Normandy during June of 1944.

From London, Sybil flew to Paris to rejoin her errant husband. Reporters spotted them having dinner at Maxim's. That night, Burton downed three stiff drinks of vodka and three bottles of champagne.

As he was leaving the restaurant, reporters crowded around him. "Are you going to marry Elizabeth Taylor?" one of them shouted at him.

"I'm already married to Sybil here," Burton said. "And I'm staying married."

This interchange was reported in the Paris newspapers the following morning, and Dick relayed the news to a disappointed Elizabeth.

Back in Rome after completing his assignment on *The Longest Day*, Burton claimed that the rumors of an affair with Elizabeth were "bloody nonsense."

Fisher seemed to realize that Elizabeth was still pining for Burton, and he volunteered to go to Switzerland to spend time there, allowing her to sort out her dilemma of which man to love.

"At that time, poor Eddie was grasping for straws," said Roddy.

"Oh, no Eddie," Elizabeth pleaded. "Don't leave me...ever!"

Richard Burton:
Re-enacting the Allied Invasion of Normandy was less stressful than filming *Cleopatra* in Rome.

"I talked with Richard when he got back from Paris," Roddy said. "He just couldn't make up his mind…Sybil or Elizabeth."

On the set the next day, Burton was hung over and so was Elizabeth. They'd spent the night together in Dick Hanley's apartment. At least for that one night, the choice had been Elizabeth. Burton tried to explain it to Roddy. "I need Sybil for emotional support and Elizabeth for sex."

For lunch, Burton and Elizabeth agreed to meet with scriptwriter Philip Dunne, who urged Burton to agree to accept the role of Michelangelo in *The Agony and the Ecstasy*, with Spencer Tracy playing the Pope. Burton promised to get back to him with a decision about that offer.

"They spent all their time with me fighting with each other, and I knew that Burton wasn't really interested in playing the difficult role of Michelangelo," Dunne said. "Of course, Charlton Heston was only too eager."

As the Burton/Taylor love affair heated up, the members of Burton's entourage who were loyal to Sybil, mostly those from England and Wales, bonded together to defend her.

Burton had hired Ifor Jenkins, his brother from Wales, as his bodyguard. Jenkins became so enraged at Burton for what he was doing to Sybil "that he beat the shit out of him," Roddy claimed. "Richard had a black eye, a cut lip, and a rip on his cheek. He missed several days of work until his face healed."

His fellow Welshman, the respected playwright and actor Emyln Williams, a former lover of Burton's and a great admirer of Sybil's, flew to Rome to chastise him. Williams and Burton got into a shouting match. "Elizabeth Taylor is just a third-rate chorus girl," Williams claimed.

Unfortunately, Williams delivered that assessment just as Elizabeth walked into the room. Consequently, he faced a stream of obscenities worse that any lorry driver could have delivered in any of the seedy pubs of Wales.

After confronting one attack after another, Burton became fed up with people telling him what to do. "So I said to Liz, 'Fuck it! Let's go out to fucking Alfredo's and have some fucking fettuccine.'"

When Burton complained about being hounded day and night by the press, Brodsky reminded him: "You can't deny an affair with Elizabeth and then be seen alone with her on the Via Veneto at three in the morning."

Burton referred to the relentless paparazzi who followed them day and night as "ravenous jackals." Their affair was viewed as an event of such international importance that it was written about by journalists who usually covered only politics.

Walter Lippmann, America's most respected journalist and winner of two Pulitzer Prizes, arrived in Rome to record his own impression of "the Liz & Dick saga." Elizabeth and Richard were friendly with the noted journalist, but gave him no insight into their private life.

He noted that the Nubian slaves who were hired as part of Cleopatra's grand entourage into Rome had to be painted black because Mankiewicz had decided that "they weren't black enough," Also, this costly scene had to be reshot for $155,000 because one member of the public had not been chased away. He was filmed in modern dress, among hundreds of extras, sitting on a stone eating an ice cream cone.

Elizabeth trusted her butler, Fred Oates, until he gave an interview to *Photoplay.* In it, he called her "a dictatorial empress, a true-to-life Queen of the Nile who treated her husband like a virtual slave, rejected telephone calls from her parents, invited guests for supper and then refused to dine with them." He referred to Fisher as "a submissive man" in the article. Needless to say, Elizabeth hired a new butler.

Max Lerner more or less agreed with Oates about Fisher. He wrote, "Elizabeth Taylor devoured men like Eddie Fisher for breakfast and spat them out at lunch. She couldn't stomach weakness in a male. Vulnerability, yes; sappiness, no."

Meanwhile, Fisher had flown to New York for recording sessions. He tried to put up a brave front.

In New York on March 30, 1962, Fisher held a press conference, denouncing claims of his wife's romantic involvement with Burton as "preposterous, ridiculous, absolutely false."

In front of reporters, he placed a call to Elizabeth in Rome. He said he wanted her to announce that there was no foundation to the Taylor/Burton romantic rumors.

"Well, Eddie," she said, as they listened in. "I can't do that because there is some truth in the story."

"Thanks a lot," he snapped at her before slamming down the phone. In full public view, in front of a coterie of journalists, he had been humiliated.

Le scandale, as it came to be called, drew fire from around the world. On the floor of Congress, Iris Blitch, a Democrat from Georgia, called for the revocation of Elizabeth's passport.

Ironically, Blitch sent her protests to Attorney General Robert F. Kennedy, not knowing that he found Elizabeth "desirable"

Congress Reacts as
Cleo Goes Global:

German-language poster for "Kleopatra." *Inset photo*: Crusading Georgia Congresswoman **Iris Blitch**

and not "undesirable," based on his own sexual trysts with her in Hollywood. Of course, RFK took no action on Blitch's demand.

"Blitch?" he asked his staff. "Now what does that rhyme with?

At the dedication ceremony of his library in Abilene, Kansas, Dwight D. Eisenhower denounced "the vulgarity, the sensuality, and, indeed, the downright garbage that Hollywood uses to promote its latest assault on morality and decency." He did not mention Burton and Elizabeth by name.

The world press began to denounce Elizabeth, Rome's *Il Tiempo* calling her "this vamp who destroys families and shucks husbands like a praying mantis."

Vatican Radio claimed the Taylor/Burton affair endangered the "moral health of society." *L'Osservatore della Dominica* called Elizabeth an "erotic vagrant."

Pope John XXIII himself, or so it was said, when reading the draft of the Vatican attack on Elizabeth, had personally written in the phrase "erotic vagrancy."

"Elizabeth didn't give a cup of rat's piss what the Pope or the Vatican had to say about her morals," said Roddy. "In fact, Richard and Elizabeth basked in their notoriety, heading off together for a weekend of romance and primal screams."

Elizabeth and Richard slipped away to the small coastal resort of Porto Santo Stefano, positioned some one-hundred miles north of Rome.

That night, Elizabeth and Burton got into a violent fight over his refusal to divorce Sybil.

In the bathroom, she grabbed a bottle of Seconal and swallowed all of them.

When he realized what she'd done, he plunged his fingers down her throat, making her vomit. "She was foaming at the mouth," he later said.

The reception desk was able to summon a local doctor to check her out, and the incident, at least for the moment, was kept out of the press.

According to Burton, the next day, a Sunday, "We drank ourselves to the point of stupefication and idiocy."

Another fight erupted. As it was later revealed, he beat her brutally, evocative of her fistfights with Mike Todd.

She suffered a black eye and facial contusions before he tossed her battered body into a Fiat and drove her back to Rome at the speed of one hundred miles an hour. One Italian patrolman pursued them, but Burton outran him as Elizabeth screamed for him to go faster.

She later confessed to Roddy, "I really wanted him to speed up and rush to our deaths. If he couldn't be mine, I didn't want Sybil to have him."

***

Back at Villa Pappa, Fisher discovered a badly bruised Elizabeth recovering from her weekend getaway north of Rome with Burton. Nothing had changed. If anything, she was more withdrawn from him than ever, and he reported, "We often ate our meals without saying a word to each other."

Fisher read in the tabloids the next day that he "looked as gaunt as a second-hand scarecrow." The tension over losing his wife was destroying his health, and he had been unsuccessful in New York in securing any singing engagements worth his while.

In response to Elizabeth's weekend getaway, Mankiewicz had to announce another costly delay in the filming of *Cleopatra* until her face healed.

It all became too much for Fox in Hollywood. "The heads rolled that weekend," said Roddy. "Elizabeth and Richard had to put their personal problems aside and deal with a major shakeup at Fox."

Millions were being spent on *Cleopatra*, and Fox was going bankrupt. Enraged stockholders fired Spyros Skouras as president. Walter Wanger was fired as *Cleopatra's* producer, and Mankiewicz was fired as its director.

[Although Mankiewicz had been ousted, he was later re-hired because no one else could piece together the extraordinarily long film during post-production.]

The enormous cost of completing *Cleopatra* more or less brought an end to the "sword and sandals" epics that had flourished during the 1950s, one of which had been Burton's own *Alexander the Great* (1956).

Mistress-collecting Darryl F. Zanuck, who had been ousted from the studio and had been temporarily living in Paris and planning a career as an independent producer, was reinstated as President of Fox. It was the company's stockholders who asked him to come back, believing that he might be the only executive who could save Fox from bankruptcy.

Zanuck's first move involved selling off Fox's back lot to real estate developers, who transformed it into Century City, a sprawling commercial and residential complex on Los Angeles' west side.

When Zanuck saw the rushes of *Cleopatra*, he was enraged, referring to it as "total chaos. The performers act like inmates in an asylum. The dialogue is overwrought."

Later, when he viewed a preliminary version of the film, which had been cut to a running length of five hours, he delivered a malapropism more suited to Samuel Goldwyn, who was famous for uttering them. Zanuck claimed, "If any woman behaved toward me the way Cleopatra treated Antony, I would cut her balls off."

A reporter asked him what were his regrets about his former role as the "chief honcho at Fox."

"I've got only two regrets," he said. "I didn't fuck Shirley Temple, although I tried, and I never got around to Elizabeth Taylor. I guess I never will because Fox is now suing Burton and the spoiled viper."

In Fox's lawsuit, Elizabeth was cited "for suffering herself to be held up to scorn, ridicule, and unfavorable publicity as a result of her conduct and deportment."

Zanuck was asking for fifty million dollars compensation from both Burton and Elizabeth, accusing them of "willfully and deliberately delaying production."

In time, Elizabeth settled with Fox for $2 million. In the final tally, she made $4 million from the picture, not the original, much-touted $1 million that she had originally asked for.

The Battle for Burton was also raging. On April 23, 1962, Sybil returned to Rome to deal with her marital situation directly.

Every day, Wanger pressured an increasingly unstable Fisher to abandon Rome and to not return to the set, especially when it was learned that he carried a loaded pistol. Before his final departure from the scene, Fisher decided to visit Sybil at Burton's villa, where she was in residence again. Roddy and Burton were at Cinecittà, but Roddy's companion, John Valva, was in the villa with Sybil at the time.

Fisher confronted her and told her the truth: "Burton's not coming back this time. Elizabeth is not like his other women. She's got her claws in him. He might come back for a brief reconciliation here and there, but you've got to face facts—it's over!"

Roddy later found out that Fisher spent about an hour with Sybil, who chose not to reveal the exact nature of their talk.

When Roddy returned to the villa, he found Sybil in tears.

"Fisher made me face what I had not wanted to face, what I could not even admit to myself—and that was that Richard loves Elizabeth more than me."

"He should not have done that," Roddy said, "but no one ever accused Eddie of being a gentleman. How did you respond?"

"After he made his case, I gave him the hardest slap in the face I was capable of giving and ordered him out of the house."

That same night, Fisher chose the moment to announce that he was driving north to Florence and Milan for no particular reason before returning to New York. "I'm leaving, perhaps for good," he told Elizabeth.

She yelled at him, "No one walks out on me, faggot. I'm more famous than the Pope, and the Queen of England, who always walks around like she's got a poker stuck up her ass. I'm even more famous than General Eisenhower."

But in spite of her fame, Fisher drove north the next morning in one of the Rolls-Royces she'd given him. He would later leave the Rolls at the Milan airport and would never see it again. Thieves made off with it.

From Florence, Fisher called the Villa Pappa in Rome, where Burton picked up the receiver. "What in hell are you doing there with my wife?" he asked.

"What in the bloody hell do you think I'm doing?" Burton said. "Fucking your wife—that's what! The only thing you're good at, Fisher, is sucking cock or taking it up the ass. You're not a man. I'm going to come to Florence and kill you."

"Stay where you are," Fisher ordered him. "I'm heading back to Rome to kill you, you mother-fucker."

Of course, these turned out to be two idle threats from two ego-driven performers.

Although Burton was with Elizabeth and making love to her at the time of Fisher's call from Florence, the next day found him with Sybil again.

Sybil convinced her husband, during a break in filming when he wasn't needed, to leave Elizabeth and travel to meet her and their two daughters at their home in Céligny, Switzerland.

Burton left that afternoon to join Sybil and their daughters, taking a train north from Rome. He made a decision not to confront Elizabeth with the news of where he was going. "It's all over," he told Roddy before heading out. "Sorry, old pal, but I'm leaving it up to you to pass the word along to our Liz gal. God damn it! At times I feel every fucking bitch wants my dick and all the cocksuckers, too. That includes you, my friend."

Both Dick and Roddy knew to be with Elizabeth when she comprehended the news that both her husband and her lover had deserted her.

"You can't go on being tossed around like a ball by Richard," Roddy said. "Let Sybil have him."

Dick urged her to send him an urgent letter to his villa in Céligny. In a drunken state, she agreed to do that. "I want him to know that I'm the one dumping him. I was hopelessly in love with him, but the affair is over."

Dick claimed that he mailed the letter, but he doesn't know if it was ever received.

Both Dick and Roddy slept over at Villa Pappa that night. At three o'clock in the morning, Dick decided to enter Elizabeth's room to check on her. He'd already removed all dangerous drugs, including her inventory of Seconal, from her suite. To his horror, he discovered a bottle, emptied of its contents, labeled as a container for that potent and dangerous barbiturate and sedative. He immediately summoned Roddy, who called an ambulance.

Once again, she was rushed to Salvator Mundi Hospital, where her stomach was pumped. An informant at the hospital called the newspapers, and word of Elizabeth's most recent suicide attempt was flashed around the world.

Her doctor told Roddy and Dick that, "Miss Taylor nearly died tonight. If she keeps doing this, she will succeed one night. That I predict."

When Fisher heard the news of Elizabeth's suicide attempt, he rushed back to Rome. She refused to allow him into her hospital room for an entire week. She only relented when he promised to bring her some cold beer.

Once inside her room, he made some attempt to kiss her, but she brushed him aside. "Open that beer can and get me a cigarette," she ordered him.

Burton, meanwhile, was with Sybil and their daughters at Céligny when he heard the news of Elizabeth's latest suicide attempt. He told he wife that he, too, was returning to Rome, even though she pleaded with him to stay.

Only hours after he drove away, Sybil attempted suicide. Mike Nichols later visited her and confirmed the report. He said, "I saw the scars. Two red razor blade scars on her left wrist."

When Burton arrived in Rome, she agreed to see him right away. She never told anyone what the two of them talked about, other than to say, "We have reached some understanding."

When reporters crowded around Burton as he was leaving the hospital, he said, "I have nothing to say."

When Roddy and Dick confronted Burton that night, each of them found him "wavering."

"He still hasn't made up his God damn mind yet," Dick said.

"The next morning, Burton told Roddy, "Elizabeth and I will be on the French Riviera together. We're also going to Gstaad. Our future is uncertain."

"My God, if you cut Sybil loose, she might take John (a reference to John Valva) away from me. They spend a lot of time together and seem to adore each other."

Roddy said that as a joke, but it eventually came true.

***

After her release from the hospital in the wake of her most recent suicide attempt, Elizabeth lived uneasily with Fisher at Villa Pappa. He tried to look after her, but mostly she attacked him, finding fault with almost anything he did, especially when he tried to control her drinking and pill-popping.

He knew that it was time to leave. But before going, he decided he would spend a final night with her. Even though she'd been hostile to him, she did not kick him out of her bed.

As he would partially relate in his memoirs, he planned to give her a "farewell fuck." When he moved on top of her, she did not resist him, but didn't reciprocate in his love-making. "I got off," he later claimed, "but she didn't. She was like a bored housewife having to endure an assault from her old spouse."

The next morning, he rose nude from her bed and stood looking down at her when she slowly opened her eyes. "Her face was a total blank. I looked for some kind of love or recognition. But I found nothing registered on her face. I could have been some waiter she'd brought back from a Roman restaurant for the night. I knew it was over."

"Just to let you know, I'm flying to New York this morning," he told her.

"If you go, you'll never see me again," she said.

"I'm going." He headed for the door.

Dick Hanley drove him to the airport at ten o'clock. Fisher told him, "My humiliation has been too great. I can't take it any more."

Fisher later recalled, "Before I got on that plane at the Rome airport, I downed three stiff vodkas with Seconals. I knew it was all over, except for the fight over money, which was likely to drag on for years."

He left for New York on March 19, 1962, and wouldn't see Elizabeth again for two whole years.

***

In June of 1962, after 225 days of filming at various locations in Italy, Spain, and Egypt, *Cleopatra* was wrapped. A mountain of film had been exposed, and the first rough cut ran for eight hours.

At the time of his departure from Rome, ten months after his arrival there, Burton said, "I never want to see this bloody place again—flashbulbs in the dead of night, lies in the press, Vespas racing after us, interference from the Vatican...To hell with it!"

At the time of Elizabeth's departure from the Rome airport, she turned to Roddy, who recalled her words to him: "I've won!"

"You mean he's promised to divorce Sybil and marry you?" Roddy asked.

"It's not that simple," she responded. "But I now hold the winning card. Dozens of offers for starring roles in films, as you know, are coming in. In the immediate future, I'm going to insist that Richard be my leading man in all of my upcoming films."

"My God!" Roddy said, "Sybil can't compete with that. Let me put it this way: You're making Richard an offer he can't refuse."

"You got that right, sweetheart," she said, before bidding him *au revoir*.

Aboard the jet plane, the captain came out to greet her personally and to tell her she was his favorite movie star and "the most beautiful woman in the world."

"Of course I am," she said to him, maybe only half in jest. "One question: Why do they call Rome 'The Eternal City?' There's nothing eternal about it."

POSTSCRIPTS TO CHAPTER 19
WHATEVER HAPPENED TO EDDIE FISHER?

Although the press was still on Fisher's trail, he managed to slip in an affair after leaving Elizabeth that reporters didn't discover. Checking into the Hotel Pierre in Manhattan, he occupied the room next to Audrey Hepburn's.

Along with Elizabeth, he had entertained her and her husband, Mel Ferrer, in Rome.

At the Pierre, they had rooms with connecting doors. Ferrer was out of town on business.

One night over dinner, Fisher admitted to Hepburn that Elizabeth had urged him to try to get the Eliza Doolittle role for her in *My Fair Lady*. "Audrey burst into tears and clung to me," Fisher later confessed to Dean Martin, Frank Sinatra, and others. "She felt terribly betrayed by Elizabeth. When you've got the delicate, lovely Audrey in your arms, something happens," Fisher said.

"I didn't feel all that sorry for him," Martin later said. "Here he was, shacked up with the most beautiful woman in the world, Elizabeth Taylor. He goes to New York and bangs Audrey, who some consider even more beautiful than Elizabeth. I'll shed no crocodile tears for Eddie."

In his memoirs, Fisher confessed, "There was never anything physical between Audrey and me, but I was in love with her." He was obviously sparing her reputation, since she was a married woman. At the time, he was still married, too.

Roddy McDowall, who later hooked up with Fisher in New York to talk about Elizabeth, later claimed he knew about his brief fling with Hepburn. "It was love on the rebound, a common occurrence."

Back in New York, Fisher was seen dating Maria Schell and getting endless shots of speed from Dr. Feelgood (Max Jacobson).

The gangster, Frank Costello, called him with an offer to have his henchmen in Rome break Burton's legs. "They'll even cut off his dick if you want that done, too," Costello said. Fisher declined this offer.

Fisher's sudden notoriety led to a series of nightclub appearances. He opened his act singing "*Arrivederci, Roma.*"

At the Winter Garden in Manhattan, he was both appearing with and "fucking Frankie's girl friend," Fisher claimed. He was referring to Juliet Prowse, the French *chanteuse,* who had been engaged for a brief, dysfunctional period to Sinatra. She appeared at the Winter Garden with Fisher, singing, "I'm Cleo, the Nympho of the Nile."

From the law firm of Louis Nizer in New York, a terse, coolly worded memo was released to the press on April 2, 1962: "Elizabeth Taylor and Eddie Fisher announced that they have mutually agreed to part. Divorce proceedings will be instituted soon."

After his divorce from Elizabeth, Fisher for a while dated voice coach Angela Sweeney. To author C. David Heymann, she praised the size of his penis, and also his ability to "have sex as often as a dozen times a night. It was unreal. He would reach climax and immediately he would have another erection. I attributed his sexual prowess to his speed addiction."

After his divorce from Elizabeth, he admitted in his memoirs to "taking Meth and drinking straight vodka all day. Life became blurred....Elizabeth was the one great love of my life," Fisher recalled. "but she treated me like a slave, and I spent most of my time attending to her various illnesses and ailments— that is, when not cleaning up dog poop."

Fisher blamed Elizabeth for destroying his career. In 1970, he filed for bankruptcy in Puerto Rico, listing debts of $916,000 and assets of $40,000. Actually, he could have blamed Elvis Presley. Fisher's style of crooning went out of fashion with the end of the Eisenhower administration.

As the years deepened, Elizabeth's contact with Fisher faded, except for an occasional call of desperation:

FISHER: *"The boys in Vegas are after me. If I don't come up*
              with $225,000 by tomorrow night, it's all over for me."
ELIZABETH: *"I'll wire you the money in the morning."*

After Elizabeth dumped him, Fisher would marry three more times.

In 1969, he wed the singer, Connie Stevens, and fathered two children with her, Joely and Tricia.

In 1976, he married beauty queen Terry Richard but the marriage lasted only ten months.

In 1993, he hit the jackpot, wedding a rich San Francisco night club owner, Betty Lin, who left him millions when she died of lung cancer in 2001.

Fisher himself died at the age of 82, based on complications associated with a broken hip, in September of 2010.

Three views of **Eddie Fisher** that prove that there was, indeed, life after Elizabeth:
Left photo, with singer **Connie Stevens**; *middle photo:* with **Terry Richard** (Miss Louisiana, 1973); and *right photo:* with millionaire **Betty Lin**

THE LONG-AWAITED *CLEOPATRA* FINALLY OPENS

In London, after Elizabeth sat anxiously through a private screening of *Cleopatra*, she later claimed "I rushed back to my hotel suite and vomited."

Cleopatra, at the time the costliest movie ever made, opened at the Rivoli Theater in New York City in June of 1963. It was also the longest, running four hours.

Critics had a field day, John Coleman of *The New Statesman* asserting, "Miss Taylor is monotony in a slit skirt, a pre-Christian Elizabeth Arden with sequined eyelids."

Judith Crist, writing in *The New York Herald Tribune*, said that "The mountain of notoriety has produced a mouse."

Not all critics agreed that Taylor and Burton had produced electricity on the screen. "Elizabeth showed greater passion for Lassie than she did for Burton's Marc Antony," wrote one critic in Rome.

In Hollywood, Elizabeth read daily reviews of the film. She called Peter Lawford. "How could the shits do this to me? This is the best work I've ever done."

"Then why did you vomit?" he asked.

She slammed down the phone.

David Susskind, a popular TV host of the day, saw *Cleopatra* and went on the air, claiming that Elizabeth was "overweight, overbosomed, overpaid, and undertalented. She sets the acting profession back a decade."

Time magazine was hardly kinder, claiming that "her screeching is like a ward healer's wife at a block party."

Ironically, the usually very critical Bosley Crowther of *The New York Times* liked it, defining it as "a surpassing entertainment, one of the great epic films of our day."

Referred to as a "Hollywood Edsel," *Cleopatra*, according to some sources, cost $45 million to make. Other accountants calculated the actual figure at $65 million. It would take years to recover the film's initial cost.

Even so, producers from all over the world wanted to immediately sign

Elizabeth, with Burton, as the stars in other films.

"We are the King and Queen of Hollywood," Elizabeth told Burton.

"I know, luv," he said.

"All you have to do is make up your mind: Do you want to sit on a throne with the Queen of Hollywood or bury yourself on some Swiss mountain with a devoted housewife?"

"I truly understand the dilemma of *to be or not to be*," he answered. "I know the question. But alas, what is the answer?"

CHAPTER TWENTY
The Elusive Pursuit of Love

After finishing *Cleopatra,* Elizabeth, with Burton, would embark on an illicit two-year relationship that lasted from 1962 to 1964, followed by a tumultuous marriage filled with grand passion and betrayal.

"I am not prepared to go forward with just the armor of my love to protect me," she told Burton.

"Armor of love?" he asked. "Did I hear right? You've been around me for too long. That sounds like something I would say."

Before there was any possibility of marriage between them, they headed for a "honeymoon" on the Côte d'Azur, a favorite stamping ground for both of them.

For one week, Burton and Elizabeth "disappeared from the radar screen," according to Dick Hanley. "Of course, I knew where they were." The romantic couple, pursued by the world press, was hiding out in a villa near Nice on the French Riviera. The German actor, Curt Jurgens, had lent them his vacation home.

But after days of isolation, Burton got bored and seemed to miss the media attention. He asked Elizabeth to put on her diamonds and a black mink coat and go with him to Monte Carlo. She agreed, and called Princess Grace at the Grimaldi Palace to alert her of her coming. The Princess invited Burton and Elizabeth for five o'clock tea.

That night at the Monte Carlo casino, Elizabeth made a spectacular entrance in a scarlet-colored Dior gown, mink, and diamonds. Suddenly the paparazzi knew where she and Burton were. When they left in the early morning hours, they caused a near riot, as all the press and photographers along the Riviera, and nearly half of the local citizenry, turned out to stare at them.

After leaving Nice, Elizabeth and Burton headed northeast to Switzerland. She invited him to spend as much time as he could alone with her in her new home in Gstaad before he rendezvoused with Sybil.

Elizabeth was all too aware that the Burtons' alpine cottage at Céligny, with Sybil living there, was only eighty-five miles from Gstaad. At the speed he drove, he could be there in an hour.

Even in seclusion in Switzerland, with no news coming out, Elizabeth and Burton were still a media event, their love affair being hailed as "the romance of the century."

Dick was put in charge of her mail, which arrived in bags from the local post office. "During that awful period," he said, "she got only a few fan letters. Most of it fell into two categories—either hate mail or else solicitations for money. A mother from Wyoming, or some place, would write, 'I have eight children and no husband and no money to feed them. Help me! Help me!' A number of aspiring actors wrote to her with requests for dates when she returned to Hollywood. The really eager ones enclosed nudes of themselves, some of which were quite impressive."

Before their return to America, Elizabeth invited John Valva and Roddy to visit with her. During her first days in Gstaad, she was living with Burton before he returned to his own home in Switzerland, where Sybil and his two daughters were waiting for him.

"Richard felt embarrassed to see us," Roddy recalled. "We'd lived in Rome in that villa with Sybil and him. Now we were in Switzerland, and we were seeing him as a husband to Elizabeth. Richard knew how close John and I were to Sybil. He was so uncomfortable that he left the next day and drove to his own home for a family reunion. I think Elizabeth was sorry she'd invited us because it threatened her love nest."

At one point, Elizabeth became convinced that Burton would never get a divorce. When he drove to Gstaad to have lunch with her, five days later, followed by a session in bed, she made him an astounding offer. "If you won't make me your wife, I'll be your mistress."

After Roddy and John Valva concluded their long visit with Elizabeth in Gstaad, Roddy thanked her for her hospitality, with the understanding that the two lovers were returning to New York via Geneva.

Later, she learned from Burton that Roddy and Valva had driven to his home at Céligny to stay with Sybil. "Those turncoats," Elizabeth said. "I thought that at least Roddy was loyal to me."

"He loves both of you fine ladies," Burton said.

"I'll never speak to the rat again."

Later, back in America, she heard that Valva had left Roddy and gone to live with Sybil as her lover on Staten Island. On hearing that, she called Roddy and made up with him because she had new common ground she shared with him. "Sybil turns out to have been competition for both of us," Elizabeth said.

[Sybil and Valva lived together for a while. When he grew tired of the relationship, he called Roddy and asked to be reinstated as his lover. Roddy refused to accept him back into his life, and Valva attempted suicide.]

During her stay in Gstaad, Elizabeth invited Peter Lawford to visit her for a vacation. Burton was fond of Lawford and often "popped in," in Elizabeth's words, without an invitation from his base in Céligny. During such visits, he never spoke either of Sybil or of his daughters.

One day, Elizabeth was checking out the designer boutiques in the center of Gstaad when she learned that Burton had arrived unexpectedly and unannounced at her house. When she returned home, she discovered a drunken Lawford giving a drunken Burton a blow-job. "Carry on, boys," she said.

But she got her revenge at dinner that night in the formal and very elegant dining room of the Gstaad Palace Hotel. She and Burton were already at table when Lawford entered the dining room. Raising her glass, she shouted, "Here's to the cocksucker!"

The next day, Burton left early to drive back home, and Lawford was still sleeping off his drunk of the night before at around eleven o'clock when Elizabeth received a surprise visitor. It was Princess Grace, who also maintained a vacation home nearby at Gstaad. To Elizabeth's amazement, she dropped in unannounced.

Elizabeth later told Dick Hanley, "The bitch did it deliberately. I didn't have make-up on, and she looked like she'd come straight from the hairdresser and a session with two make-up artists."

Years later, when Tennessee Williams came to visit Burton in Mexico, Burton reflected on his period of indecision and said, "I was trying to resist leaving my family for Elizabeth. I still loved Sybil. Yet I wasn't trying all that hard. I was less than a man should be. But Elizabeth proved too great a temptation to turn my back on. Perhaps I was fooling myself, but I became convinced that she would commit suicide if I left her."

***

The weather was cold and foggy on the English Channel as a night ferry crossed over from France. Two of its passengers, arriving at Victoria Station, were the most famous couple since Romeo and Juliet.

An armada of reporters and photographers had been alerted to their arrival. In separate cars and booked into separate suites, both of them headed for The Dorchester. They were to be married, but only on the screen in their upcoming movie, *The V.I.P.s* (1963).

509

Although she, like Burton, had been born in Britain, he took delight in introducing her to "my England." They attended rugby matches, drank at his favorite pubs, and watched the Oxford/Cambridge soccer match at Twickenham.

He met with the acerbic literary critic, Kenneth Tynan, who told him about his dysfunctional romance with Marlon Brando. Burton also talked of his own romance. "You must not use sex alone as a lever, as a kind of moral, intellectual, psychic crutch to get away from your wife. You can't say to her, 'I'm terribly sorry, but I can't sleep in the same bed with you any more because I simply have to run off with this infinitely fascinating girl.'"

Elizabeth knew that by Christmas, Sybil would be back in residence in Hampstead, and she wouldn't get to see Burton as much.

When he dined alone with his long-time friend, Vivien Leigh, Burton confessed, "I love both of them and want both of them, but I know in time I must choose between them."

There were mishaps along the way. When Burton left for Wales to try to mend strained relationships with his family, he was attacked. While hailing a taxi in Cardiff, he was set upon by a group of bully "Teddy Boys," one of whom stomped his boot into Burton's eye. It was black for days. "Thank God that boot was not a winklepicker—or else I might be wearing a black patch for the rest of my days."

For Elizabeth's thirty-first birthday, he gave her a $200,000 diamond necklace.

She purchased Van Gogh's *Lunatic Asylum, St.-Rémy* for 92,000 British pounds through the intervention of her father, Francis, who bid for it at a Sotheby's auction. For some reason, thirty years later, she was in possession of the painting herself and failed to sell it at another auction. Her asking price was $20 million, a price higher than the market at the time would bear.

***

Originally, Burton was to co-star with Sophia Loren in *The V.I.P.s.* Director Anthony Asquith had selected Loren for the female lead, as he remembered the box office success of her 1960 film, *The Millionairess.*

However, when Elizabeth heard of his choice, she became enraged. "Burton is a tit man," she told Roddy McDowall. "Loren has tits the size of mine, and I fear she'll lure him away from me." She went to Asquith and persuaded him to give her the role instead. "Let Sophia stay in Rome," she said.

The film was based on Vivien Leigh's attempt to leave her husband, Laurence Olivier, for the Australian actor, Peter Finch. During the peak of the affair's passion, Leigh and Finch made it as far as the London airport, which was fogged in, giving Olivier time to get there and talk Leigh out of leaving.

Unlike *Cleopatra,* shooting of *The V.I.P.s* was modestly budgeted at only $3 million.

Elizabeth was determined to complete the shooting of *The V.I.P.s* in just eight weeks. She claimed she was "pissed off" at Lloyds of London, which had refused to insure her.

In London, filming of *The V.I.P.s* had already begun, and producer Anatole de Grunwald lived in constant dread that Elizabeth would get ill. But except for a knee problem, she made it on schedule through a movie that featured Louis Jourdan as her illicit lover. Orson Welles, Rod Taylor, Margaret Rutherford, and Maggie Smith were also among the illustrious cast. In smaller roles were the sexy bombshell Elsa Martinelli, TV broadcaster David Frost, and Linda Christian, who'd married Tyrone Power.

The press still covered their every move, *Time* magazine writing that, "If Burton marries Taylor, he will become the fifth husband of the wife of Bath."

The British press became bored with the Taylor/Burton affair, and began writing of a torrid sexual tryst between Louis Jourdan and herself.

At the time, Elizabeth denied this, "I hate having to do love scenes with Louis," she told Asquith. "He always has bad breath." Later, she was enigmatic about a supposed affair. "My diary will tell the complete story," she said. "If anything is published, it will be only after both of us are dead. It's less embarrassing that way."

The V.I.P.s was the second of many films in which

V.I.P.s outgrosses *Cleopatra*

Top photo: **Elizabeth** with **Burton**
middle photo: Oscar-winning **Margaret Rutherford**
lower photo: **Louis Jourdan** with **Elizabeth**

Elizabeth would co-star with Burton: *The Sandpiper* (1965); *Who's Afraid of Virginia Woolf?* (1966); *The Taming of the Shrew* (1966); *Doctor Faustus* (1967); *The Comedians* (1967); *Boom! (1968); Anne of a Thousand Days* (1969); *Under Milkwood (1971);* and *Hammersmith Is Out* (1972).

Ironically, her last project with Burton would be entitled *Divorce His, Divorce Hers (1973),* which was made for ABC-TV as a two-part made-for-TV drama about the breakup of a 20-year-marriage.

In time, Asquith became one of the most successful of British directors, ranking alongside Sir David Lean and Sir Carol Reed.

One day at around noon, Burton asked Asquith to join Elizabeth and him for one of their "wet lunches." Burton was already aware that Asquith had had

Glorious and profligate icons of the British Theatre:

top photo: **Laurence Olivier**
lower photo: **Anthony Asquith**

a brief fling with Laurence Olivier during his 1934-35 filming of *Moscow Nights.*

Burton seemed to enjoy teasing Asquith. In front of Elizabeth, he said, "I understand that Larry has a nickname for you: Puffin."

"He calls me that," Asquith said. "But the nickname actually came from my mother. She said I looked like a puffin to her."

"Larry also told me something else," Burton said. "Forgive me for bringing this up, but he claimed I was better in bed than you were."

There was an awkward silence at the table until Elizabeth quickly changed the subject. "I've got a bone to pick with you. You need to make Jourdan act more masculine. I've seen the rushes. Many of his movements are effeminate. Please look into that. In contrast, Rod Taylor comes off as totally macho."

When it first opened, *The V.I.P.s* outgrossed *Cleopatra,* and Burton and Elizabeth took home a combined total of $3.5 million for their performances.

Actually, it would be the rotund and double-chinned Margaret Rutherford who would walk off with an Oscar for her portrayal of the "eccentric and poor" Duchess of Brighton.

***

Between films, Elizabeth made a TV special, *Elizabeth Taylor in London,* a tour of the British capital's cultural landmarks. She was given $250,000, the highest salary ever paid up until then to a TV performer.

One critic wrote, "Miss Taylor throughout the documentary was in competition with London—and she *won!* "

Back at The Dorch, Burton was getting more lucrative movie offers than she was.

Laurence Olivier had lobbied to play the lead in the film, *Becket,* but Burton eventually snared the role for himself.

Peter O'Toole and Burton filmed *Becket* at the Shepperton Studios in Middlesex, outside London. On most days, unless she was too hung over, Elizabeth ordered her chauffeur to drive her to the studio for lunch with Burton.

A heavy drinker himself, O'Toole often joined them.

"When O'Toole and Burton returned from lunch, they were often too drunk to appear on camera," Dick Hanley said.

Burton was said to have driven through the countryside of England and sometimes walked alone in its meadows. He slept at a bed and breakfast in the Cotswolds, where he woke up hearing the sounds of a meadow lark.

By the time he'd driven back to London, he'd made up his mind. He was going to divorce Sybil. Whether he'd eventually marry Elizabeth remained an unanswered question.

Hellraisers Acting Holy
and establishing Burton's precedent for roles as a frocked (or de-frocked) ecclesiastic

Left photo: **Richard Burton** as Becket, and
Right photo: **Peter O'Toole** as Henry II

For several weeks, Burton had not visited Sybil and his daughters. In January of 1963, he was seen entering the Savoy Hotel in London and going upstairs to one of the suites. A room service waiter noticed him entering the quarters of Zsa Zsa Gabor.

Three hours later, as he was making his way once again through the Savoy's lobby, he had one of those chance encounters that happens too often in life. He encountered Sybil leaving the Savoy Grill. During their brief dialogue, he bluntly "bit the bullet," as he later defined it, and asked her for a divorce.

"We'll let our attorneys handle it," she said, before rushing out and into a taxi. He was prepared to be generous, offering a proposed settlement of around a million dollars, which was all the cash he had.

After Burton left her, Sybil proved amazingly popular with *tout* London, and was seen dining with Princess Margaret and her husband, Lord Snowdon. Rex Harrison, although married, took her out dancing, as did gay actor Dirk Bogarde. Emlyn Williams was a frequent escort, as was actor Stanley Baker.

For the rest of her days, Sybil would have only one additional conversation with Burton, a two-minute dialogue about their children.

Tiring of London, she moved to New York. After her divorce, and after a brief involvement with John Valva, Sybil opened Arthur, "the mother of all discos," on 54th Street in New York. It quickly became "the disco" of the 1960s, attracting everybody from Bette Davis to Sophia Loren. Jackie Kennedy was seen dancing with Robert Kennedy, who was later caught in a phone booth liplocked with dancer Rudolf Nureyev. Truman Capote danced with Bette Davis, Princess Margaret, and Andy Warhol.

Sybil later shocked her fans by marrying Jordan Christopher, the handsome, sexy singer of the house band, "The Wild Ones." Most of her friends predicted that the marriage would not last. They were wrong. She was still married to the singer at the time of his death in 1996.

***

At The Dorch, Elizabeth constantly complained to Burton about Eddie Fisher's latest demands during their divorce proceedings. Fisher wanted all the jewelry he'd given to Elizabeth returned, even though he'd bought most of it with her own money.

When she wasn't complaining about Fisher, or making love to Burton, she read over film scripts that arrived. To her amazement, she was getting no really good film offers. In contrast, Burton had achieved the international stardom he coveted.

During one of their fights, she screamed at him in front of Dick, "I made you a star, and I can break you!"

Of course, that was an idle threat.

As a bankable movie star, Burton became increasingly demanding about the salary he'd expect for his acting performances. *Time* declared, "He is a kind of folk hero out of nowhere, with an odd name like Richard instead of Rock, or Rip, or Tab. He has outtabbed, outrocked, and outstripped the lot of them. He is the new Mr. Box Office."

It was time to return to America when Burton discovered a script he liked. It was the role of a defrocked priest in Tennessee Williams' *The Night of the Iguana*. It had been a Broadway play starring Bette Davis in an orange wig.

Elizabeth read the script and was intrigued by the role of the female lead, although the character who ran a small beachfront hotel in Mexico was "little more than a whore."

"I objected to playing a whore in *Butterfield 8*," she told Burton, "but I'm ready to do so now."

She called her friend Tennessee in Key West only to learn that the role had already been assigned to Ava Gardner.

"Talk about a whore playing a whore," Elizabeth said sarcastically.

"Ava's not all that bad," Burton later told her.

"If I hear you're fucking her, I'll tie you up and remove each egg of your testicles…very slowly and very painfully."

"Oh, luv, what do I need with a grandmother like Ava when I've got fresh quail like you?"

"Just to make sure, I'm hanging out with you to protect my investment."

***

"The arrival of the "scandalous" Elizabeth Taylor and Richard Burton in Mexico City occurred on September 22, 1963. As mobs descended on the airport, it became an international media event. Elizabeth was accompanying Burton to Mexico, where he'd be filming Tennessee Williams' *The Night of the Iguana*.

Losing her purse, part of her wardrobe, and even her shoes, Elizabeth made it through the crowd with the help of strong-armed security guards. "Fuck this!" she shouted at Burton. "They think we're the Beatles!"

Even before they left the airport, "The Liz & Dick" show entertained the masses by staging a big fight over a missing case of jewelry, each blaming the other for its disappearance. The box later turned up in a packed suitcase.

A press conference had been scheduled, but Burton refused to attend. However, he did issue a statement. "This is my first visit to Mexico. I hope it will be my last."

In a short time he would change his mind and buy a vacation home there.

Elizabeth had a different opinion. She told the press, "I have always wanted to come back to fucking Mexico. I like fucking Mexico." The Mexican reporters printed her remarks but left out the two adjectives.

Initially, there was a lot of misunderstanding in the press, headlines claiming that Elizabeth, not Ava Gardner, would be the female star of the movie.

John Huston, the project's director, had wanted Marlon Brando to play the defrocked priest, but Ray Stark, the producer, favored either Richard Harris or William Holden. Finally, they settled on Burton. Ava Gardner had been their first choice as the notorious innkeeper, but Melina Mercouri was also held out as a replacement.

For the role of Deborah Kerr's grandfather, Nonno, Huston wanted Carl Sandburg, America's most famous playwright, but he was in failing health. The role instead went to Cyril Delevanti.

According to Dick Hanley, who accompanied the famous pair, Elizabeth arrived "pissed off" at director John Huston. In fact, by the second day, she was already lambasting him as "an ugly, old, mean, withering fart," charging that he had mentally abused her friend Monty Clift during the filming of both *The Misfits* (1961) and *Freud* (1962).

In retribution, the director rather ungallantly chose to bring up the subject of how Elizabeth was "shameless" in stealing Mike Todd from Huston's former wife, Evelyn Keyes.

Zoe Sallis showed up in Puerto Vallarta. It was common knowledge that she was Huston's mistress.

In 1963, Puerto Vallarta was a seedy little fishing village lying three hundred miles north of Acapulco. Tacky and not very well known, it became instantly famous when Elizabeth and Burton arrived and put it on the international tourist map.

The actual shooting of *Iguana* took place on the isolated peninsula of Mismaloya, which had no road access to the mainland and could be reached only by boat. The only inhabitants on Mismaloya were Indians who lived in thatched huts and survived on fishing.

Elizabeth and Burton and all their massive amounts of luggage were taken to Puerto Vallarta and delivered to "Gringo Gulch," an upmarket section where Americans had purchased a number of vacation homes. Locals had another name for it, referring to it as *La Casa de Zoplotes* (the House of the Buzzards) because it lay near a garbage dump.

Whereas Burton had an actual part in the filming, Elizabeth was on site to see that he didn't go astray in the arms of any of his female co-stars, who included man-eating Ava Gardner, Deborah Kerr, and Sue Lyon.

Elizabeth also had to keep her eye out for at least fifty whores, some of them diseased, who had arrived from Mexico City to service the film crew. At least half of that number of male hustlers had also come to Puerto Vallarta to service homosexual members of the crew.

Arriving at the port, Elizabeth feared she'd be assigned to some shack, but was delighted by Casa Kimberley, the villa provided for her. In fact, she liked it so much she bought it for $40,000.

Burton liked the ramshackle port, too, and he eventually built a villa across the street, connecting the two properties with a footbridge that linked the two buildings. It was inspired by the Bridge of Sighs in Venice. "I can run across the bridge and escape from Liz when she becomes a raging harridan," Burton told Michael Wilding, who was all too familiar with her rages.

It would take almost a novel to untangle the past and present romantic entanglements that whirled around the cast and crew of *Iguana*. Before it was over, Kerr told the press, "I'm the only one here not shacked up with somebody."

She left out the fact that she was accompanied by her husband, Peter Viertel, the scriptwriter who had previously worked with Huston on *The African Queen* (1951) with Humphrey Bogart and Katharine Hepburn. Viertel had also been the former lover of Ava Gardner.

There were other sexual embarrassments unfolding. Huston had a reunion with Gardner, with whom he'd once had a torrid affair. Huston had also once pursued Kerr.

Elizabeth knew the Kerr had had a sexual tryst years before with Stewart Granger, but she was not certain if Burton had had an affair with her in Britain.

Elizabeth experienced her own walks down memory lane when Michael Wilding arrived in Puerto Vallarta. Her former husband was now the assistant to Burton's agent, Hugh French. Relationships between Burton and Wilding were still friendly, and Elizabeth had no animosity toward him. It had not been a bitter divorce. They were both involved in the rearing of their two sons, and both of them loved their boys very much, even though neither of them would ever win any awards for parenting.

Wilding was no longer lusting for Elizabeth. He showed up with a beautiful Swedish actress, Karen von Unge. She recalled, "Michael was a dear, sensitive man who should have been a great painter. Here he was, carrying suitcases of chili for Elizabeth from Chasen's in Los Angeles because she asked for

Puerto Vallarta: The Burton villas and their **interconnecting bridge**

them. She simply asked, and men did—it was that simple."

Huston looked upon Wilding as "a pathetic figure. He was once a big star in England, but he gave it up for Elizabeth. What did it get him? Now he serves her drinks and picks up dog poop for her. He's like the Erich von Stroheim character in *Sunset Blvd..* Formerly married to Gloria Swanson in the movie, he becomes her butler."

Anticipating feuds, Huston passed out derringers to key members of his cast. These were the kind of small pistols that card sharps used to wear up their sleeves. With the pistols, he gave each person a silver bullet with a name etched onto it. Even though she was not a member of the cast, the derringer he gave Elizabeth was gold-plated.

Unlike the others, Elizabeth received five bullets, each with a name on it— Richard Burton, Sue Lyon, Ava Gardner, and Deborah Kerr. The director also included one with the name of John Huston.

On seeing Elizabeth again over drinks, Gardner said, "Dear heart, you and Richard are the Frank and Ava of the 1960s."

Evelyn Keyes, though not in Mexico, was present at least in memory. Elizabeth had stolen Mike Todd from her following her divorce from John Huston. Keyes was now married to Artie Shaw, who had been Gardner's former husband.

The plot thickened when Budd Schulberg, author of the Hollywood novel, *What Makes Sammy Run?* and the screenplay for *On the Waterfront,* arrived to seduce Gardner. Viertel had once been married to Schulberg's former wife, Virginia Ray.

In a talk one day at the beach with Elizabeth and Dick Hanley, Viertel confessed that he had abandoned his pregnant wife to run away with Bettina, arguably the most famous French model of the 1950s. "She later dumped me for Aly Khan."

Deborah Kerr with Peter Viertel

"I know Bettina," Elizabeth said. "I know Aly Khan, too. Oh do I *know* Aly Khan!"

"Huston tried to console me when I lost Bettina, Viertel said. "He told me 'Aly Khan is one swell guy.' Then, when Aly Khan fucked Huston's wife, Evelyn Keyes, I told him, 'It's okay, John, Aly is one swell guy.' He punched me in the mouth. I love John, though. He's fucked everybody from Marilyn Monroe on the set of *The Asphalt Jungle* to Truman Capote on the set of *Beat the Devil* when they shared a double bed. He even screwed a neo-Nazi woman in London who gave him syphilis—something he later referred to as 'the Hitler clap.'"

When Viertel left to return to the set, he, as a man of the world, kissed both Elizabeth and Dick on the lips before departing.

When he'd gone, Elizabeth turned to Dick: "Put some suntan lotion on my back, honey love." She watched Viertel head to the waterfront to board a small ferry. "If he weren't married to Deborah, and if I wasn't messing up my mouth with Richard, I could go for that. Ava told me he's great in bed. I still might go for him if Richard ever gets out of line. Mark Peter down on that list I'm compiling—MEN I PLAN TO SEDUCE BEFORE I DIE."

Tennessee arrived in the small town with Frederick Nicklaus, a young recent graduate of Ohio State University. Tennessee told Huston, "Frederick is the world's greatest living poet, though not discovered as of yet."

Tom Shaw, Huston's assistant director, detested the volatile personality of Tennessee. In his bulldog manner, he said, "I hated the mean son of a bitch. I was having a drink at the bar, and he was berating the shit out of this poor Mexican bartender. At the time, I didn't recognize who he was. I said to myself, 'Who is this asshole?' He was a vicious kind of faggot."

One night over drinks, the key players were asked by Herb Caen, the San Francisco columnist, what they most wanted in life. Huston said, "Interest." Gardner wished for "Health." Burton opted for "Adventure," Viertel for "Success," and Deborah Kerr "Happiness." Elizabeth chose "Wealth."

James Bacon, the veteran Hollywood reporter who'd once seduced Marilyn Monroe, arrived on the scene. "I'm from Hollywood, and I knew John Barrymore and Errol Flynn, but I'd never seen such heavy drinking. One night in a tavern, Burton downed twenty-five straight shots of tequila, using Carta Blanca beer as a chaser."

The cast and crew were constantly besieged by reporters, Elizabeth claiming, "There are more press guys and paparazzi here than fucking iguanas."

Reporters from California relished writing about the heavy drinking and the behind-the-scenes romances, but the Mexican newspaper *Siempre* denounced the entire cast and crew of *The Night of the Iguana*. It attacked the "sex, drinking, drugs, vice, and carnal bestiality of this gringo garbage that has descended on our country." *Siempre* also cited "gangsters, nymphomaniacs, and heroin-taking blondes."

The local Catholic priest attacked Elizabeth as a "wanton Jezebel" and called on the President of Mexico to deport her as an undesirable alien.

A drunken Elizabeth was asked by a reporter one night how she'd describe the three women in the cast. She obliged: "Gardner is lushly ripe for a middle-aged woman; Kerr is refined and ladylike until you get her in bed, or so I'm told; and Lyon is...well, let's just say nubile. No wonder James Mason had the hots for her. When making *Lolita,* he temporarily gave up his interest in boys."

The reporter sent her remarks back to *The Hollywood Reporter,* whose editor chose not to print them.

When Tennessee, in a Puerto Vallarta tavern known as the Casablanca Bar, was asked for his opinion of the Taylor/Burton romance, he said, "They are artists on a special pedestal and therefore the rules of bourgeois morality do not apply to them."

Burton was sitting with Tennessee when he made that pronouncement. When Burton himself was asked for a comment, he said, "I am bewitched by the cunt of Elizabeth Taylor and her cunning ways. Cunt and cunning—that's what the attraction is."

Graham Jenkins, Burton's brother, was also in Puerto Vallarta, and he had a more sensitive view of the Taylor/Burton affair. "Richard discovered how much he really needed Elizabeth, and his surrender to her was total. Of course, they still fought like cats and dogs. Each of them was mercurial. But they truly loved each other, and that was so evident. That did not mean that each of them could no longer see with their roving eye. Rich especially would always have that."

Iguana Games:
Two views of **Ava Gardner**
lower photo: with **Richard Burton**

For the most part, Burton was pleased with his role, telling Huston, "After this film is released, those boys in the press will stop calling me Mr. Cleopatra."

The one thing Elizabeth liked about the script of *Iguana* was the dialogue. "It contained some of the most bitch wit ever recorded."

Over a private drink she had with Huston, she told him, "Believe me, no one adores Ava Gardner more than I do. Such a fine actress, if the role isn't too challenging. I think you'll make a good picture. Regrettably, if you'd chosen me for the role of Maxine, it would have been a great picture, and I would win another Oscar to give the one I have company."

"I'm sure you're right, my dear," Huston said. "Right on target. Forgive my mistake in casting."

***

In October, Tennessee kissed both Burton and Elizabeth goodbye before returning to New York. He told Elizabeth, "Please show up on the set every day, take Richard his lunch, and look after him. We don't want him to get so drunk he can't remember his lines."

She left her villa in late morning to go to the set, wading through chickens, naked children, and mange-encrusted mongrel dogs. Carrying a picnic basket with bottles of wine, Dick Hanley accompanied her. Both of them boarded a barge to take them to the remote peninsula where filming was occurring. Once there, reaching the set involved a sweaty and difficult climb up a steep hill.

One morning, Huston launched his day with five Bloody Marys. A reporter asked what he thought of having Elizabeth on the set, even though she wasn't in the movie. He said, "It's understandable. She and Burton are infamously co-habiting."

Elizabeth made it a point to show up on any day that Burton was shooting a steamy scene with Gardner. On those days, Elizabeth looked as sexy as possible, wearing form-fitting slacks in rainbow-hued colors, blouses that exposed at least three-quarters of her still firm breasts, and plenty of diamonds.

Her outfits on the set looked outrageous to Burton. He told Gardner, "She resembles a French tart working Place Clichy."

Huston's secretary, Thelma Victor, kept a diary relating details about the shooting of *Iguana*. In it, she claimed that Elizabeth arrived in Mexico with forty designer bikinis from Paris. "She was packing on the pounds around her middle and spent many an afternoon on the beach. She often was seen picking at her navel with her fingernail."

Thelma's entry for October 24, 1963 read:

"Elizabeth arrived on the set wearing a loose top and a bikini bottom of sheer white batiste trimmed with red embroidery. She had no bra on and you literally could see the complete upper structure of her tits. Imposing. She was also wearing a magnificent gold ring loaded with pearls and what looked like either pink diamonds or rubies. She said the King of Indonesia gave it to her. Richard said, 'She's seducing me again.'

"She turned to Burton, kissing him on the lips. 'I was dead when I encountered Richard again on the set of Cleopatra. It was a case of Prince Charming kissing the Sleeping Princess who'd slept through four years of marriage to that fucking schmuck, Eddie Fisher.'"

On the night of November 10, Burton's birthday, Elizabeth presented him with a library of calfskin-bound classics, priced at $35,000.

He thanked her by kissing her profusely. But later he got so drunk, he denounced her as a "scurrilous low creature," charging that she'd had sex on the beach with a lot of those Mexican beach boy hustlers. Actually, she had done nothing of the sort. From the fog of his intoxication, Burton blamed Elizabeth for what Gardner was doing.

The entire cast was shocked on November 22, 1963, when news reached them that John F. Kennedy had been assassinated. Elizabeth had known JFK intimately, and "she cried for two days," according to Dick.

The next day, Gardner got drunk long before noon and entertained the crew with tales of "my brief but memorable fling with Jack."

Burton was perhaps the first to connect the slain president to *Camelot,* wherein he'd interpreted the role of King Arthur. "Camelot symbolized for President Kennedy where America wanted to be. In a Kingdom of Grace and Righteousness, surrounded by monsters and dark enemies, but triumphing over them all, the Democracy of Good over the Empire of Evil, with a big sword and song."

In one of the most bizarre show-biz stories to emerge from the immediate aftermath of JFK's assassination, the following day, Kirk Douglas and his publicist visited Jackie Kennedy at the White House to express their sympathies. "Kirk," she asked. "Do you think Elizabeth Taylor will marry Richard Burton?"

Gardner learned that Burton had celebrated a birthday, and she'd been unaware of it. When she first heard of it around November 30, she presented him with a fifth of bourbon, a delayed birthday present.

"That's not all Ava gave him!" Huston told his cronies. "I couldn't get either of my two stars to emerge from her dressing room until the sun was high in the sky, and the heat was crushing. When they did emerge, they weren't really in condition to appear on camera that day."

As author Nancy Schoenberger wrote: "Ava seemed to come alive in Richard's presence. The press were not just covering a congregation of some of the world's greatest talents and personalities in a remote Mexican village, they were waiting—hoping?—that Burton and Taylor's vaunted love affair might founder on Ava Gardner's dangerous shoulders."

The coming together of the drunken, poetry-spouting, lust-filled Welsh actor and the Tarheel *femme fatale* and sex symbol had sparked "meaningful eye contact," as Huston described it.

One day before noon, both Gardner and Burton got drunk on a local moonshine known as *raicilla.* It was made from the agave plant. Gardner called it "cactus piss."

Huston defined it as "a cactus brandy stronger than tequila." Burton said the way to drink *raicilla* was straight down. That way you can feel it going into each individual intestine." When Elizabeth tried it, she said, "I hear it's made from cactus. Tell the fuckers who brewed it that they left the god damn needles in it."

One evening when Elizabeth was suffering from *"turista,"* Dick Hanley drove Burton to the Casablanca Bar. To Dick's surprise, a sultry Ava Gardner was waiting there for him. Burton turned to Dick, "I can always count on you for being discreet around Her Ladyship."

Actually, Burton was wrong about that.

"After Ava and Richard consumed enough alcohol to resink the *Titanic,* they retired to one of the hot-bed shanties out back, where they disappeared," Dick said. "I wondered if Richard could get it up in his condition. I sat in the bar with this beach boy hustler waiting for their return. They were gone for about three hours. Both of them came back into the bar hardly able to stand up. I literally had to toss them into the back of our car."

The next day, Elizabeth suspected that something had happened. Since Dick was loyal to her and not necessarily to Burton, she cornered him and pressed him for details about Burton's dalliance with Gardner.

She told Dick, "I won't say a god damn thing to the whoremonger. But when my first chance comes along, I'm going to get even. Be on the lookout for a handsome, well-hung charmer who'd like to fuck Elizabeth Taylor."

That day on the beach, her feet were attacked by *chigoes,* tropical fleas that burrow into the skin. If left untreated, they can invade a host's bloodstream. She had to have them removed with a surgical knife.

Knives were certainly not on her mind when she went with her two sons and daughter to the town square to watch a performance of the circus which had come to town. When one of the entertainers, Alejandro Fuentes, nicknamed "The Dagger Man," called for volunteers from the audience, Elizabeth, who had already consumed three Bloody Marys, cheerfully volunteered.

She stood before a wooden backdrop as the Mexican circus performer prepared to throw scimitars at her. The audience screamed when the first scimitar came within two inches of her face. Fuentes hurled three more, narrowly missing her. She stood almost fearless against the onslaught, later telling the press, "I've had daggers thrown at me before."

Fuentes later said, "Mother of God! I'm so grateful I didn't miss, because I'd had a little too much tequila that morning."

***

Elizabeth already had confirmation of Burton's brief fling with Gardner. But she also suspected that something might be going on between Burton and Sue Lyon, who played the rigidly chaperoned blonde nymphet in *Iguana*. In some ways, her selection as the actress in that role had been influenced by her involvement, in 1962, of Stanley Kubrick's *Lolita*, an adaptation of the novel by Vladimir Nabokov *(Lolita)* about a middle-aged man's sexual obsession with a young adolescent girl.

Burton, incidentally, had seen Lyon's film interpretation of *Lolita* three times, exhibiting a keen interest of which Elizabeth was emphatically aware.

In *Iguana,* Burton was cast as an alcoholic and defrocked priest tempted by the seductive teenager, as portrayed by Lyon, whose persona was in distinct contrast to Ava Gardner's portrayal of a fully mature, man-hungry whore cavorting with her agile and shirtless Mexican cabaña boys

In reference to the script, Elizabeth had said, "My God, how times have changed. It was only yesterday that Paul Newman and I had to face all those restrictions from censors troubled by Tennessee's script of *Cat on a Hot Tin Roof.* If this trend continues, Hollywood will be turning out homosexual love stories."

Elizabeth wasn't the only person struggling to keep Burton away from Lyon. She'd arrived in Puerto Vallarta with her boy friend, Hampton Fancher III. Huston's biographer, Lawrence Grobel, described the boy as "a tall, pale youth ravaged by love." Soon after his arrival, Fancher warned Burton, "I tend to be murderously inclined."

The circumstances which led to Burton finally being left alone with Lyon involved the fact that her boyfriend, as it turned out, was married. His young wife arrived unexpectedly on the set one day. Fancher would marry Lyon before the year ended, after his divorce became final.

As Lyon remembered it, "Richard drank so much at night that the alcohol literally oozed out of his pores the next day. It gave off a terrible odor."

Elizabeth did not learn about Burton's affair with Lyon until 1981, almost 18 years after it ended, when Eddie Fisher's first volume of memoirs was published.

In them, Fisher wrote: "I was surprised to discover that being dumped by Elizabeth had made me an extremely desirable man. I had gained a reputation for being an incredible lover— which is not a terrible reputation to have. There were many women like Sue Lyon, the very beautiful little girl who had starred in *Lolita,* who wanted to know if I was a better lover than Bur-

Two views of **Sue Lyon**

Heating up *Iguana* with **Burton** as her tour guide and (inset) as *Lolita* in 1962.

ton, so she slept with both of us. She was very upfront about her motives: This wasn't love, this was an experiment. Naturally, I rose to the challenge. "

Although the Burton/Lyon affair had burned out long before Elizabeth discovered that it had even happened, she flew into a rage when she learned, through Eddie's memoirs, about its existence.

"Michael Wilding was on the scene. Why didn't she fuck him, too?" If Mike Todd's corpse hadn't been incinerated, perhaps she could have dug him up, too. And I'm sure that when she returned to Hollywood, Nicky Hilton would have fucked her, too."

***

On December 5, 1963, Burton's divorce from Sybil was finalized, based on his "abandonment and cruel and inhumane treatment."

"At last Richard is free to marry me," Elizabeth told Dick Hanley. "This is the best Christmas present I've ever had in my life."

Simultaneous with that news, Elizabeth and Fisher were still fighting over money and possessions. He may have wanted all his jewelry back, but she wanted the second emerald green Rolls-Royce she'd given him. [The first vehicle had been stolen in Milan.] She also asked to keep the chalet in Gstaad and wanted all the profits from their jointly owned MCL Films.

His lawyers, however, finally forced her to make concessions with the understanding that Fisher would "refrain from embarrassing her publicly." Consequently Fisher's first memoir wasn't published until 1981, a delay based partly on his fear of lawsuits from both Debbie Reynolds and Elizabeth.

Regarding his feud with Elizabeth, Fisher told the press, "Elizabeth deserves the Oscar for sheer gall. Perhaps she's being advised by Richard the Lion-Hearted, who is hustling her, trying to jump-start a film career for himself, if he can stay sober long enough."

In Puerto Vallarta, Elizabeth constantly referred to Fisher as "that fucking *schmuck!*" She told both Burton and Dick that, "I'll never speak to the prick again."

At a dinner party at Casa Kimberly, she denounced him in front of her guests. "I never loved him. Marrying that *schmuck* was the biggest mistake of my life. I was trying to keep Mike Todd's memory alive. Mike once told me that if anything happened to him, I should marry Eddie and let him take care of me. I was in a state of shock. When I married the *schmuck,* I thought I did it because Mike wanted me to."

Elizabeth's petition for divorce from Fisher was filed in Mexico on grounds of abandonment. Its legalities were finalized on March 6, 1964, when she was in Toronto "chaperoning" Burton, who was starring in a stage production of

Hamlet. "The *schmuck,*" she said, "is gone from life forever."

Fisher, in contrast, celebrated his divorce in New York by seducing a series of beautiful girls—"eighteen in a row for eighteen nights. On the nineteenth day, I rested."

He told the press, "Elizabeth will marry Burton, but will eventually dump him. Then she'll marry someone else, and dump him, and the pattern will go on until she's old and fat. What Elizabeth wants, she gets. She is beautiful, the queen. But she uses up men."

***

Before his departure from Mexico for New York, Tennessee Williams hosted a party at his rented villa near Elizabeth and Burton in Gringo Gulch. He'd invited both of them to attend, but only Elizabeth had shown up.

There, she met Jose Bolaños, a Mexican screen writer who was enjoying a certain vogue. After the murder of Marilyn Monroe on August 4, 1962, he was getting a lot of press attention and being hailed as her last and final boyfriend.

Bolaños claimed that he and Monroe had mutually committed themselves to get married, although some of her friends said that Monroe had promised to remarry Joe DiMaggio.

Jose Bolaños with **Marilyn Monroe** only weeks before her murder

Bolaños was working on a TV commercial twenty-five miles to the south, but had come to Puerto Vallarta with the hope of meeting and ingratiating himself with Elizabeth as he had with Monroe.

Tennessee had been charmed by the charismatic young Mexican and had set up the meeting with Elizabeth, presumably without Burton.

She defined him as a Latin lover archetype, evocative of both Fernando Lamas and Ricardo Montalban. Bolaños was dark and handsome, with a magnetic personality. The night of their meeting, Bolaños told her that his dream involved coming to Hollywood and putting both Lamas and Montalban "out of business." Secretly, he hoped that by attaching himself to Elizabeth, she could use her influence to help him break into the American film industry.

Elizabeth might have paid scant attention to Bolaños except for two reasons: He was the only man she'd met in Puerto Vallarta who qualified for that "revenge fuck" she'd planned as a means of getting even with Burton for seducing Ava Gardner. Also, she was tempted by the idea of learning intimate secrets about Monroe's last lover, especially if the fallen star had considered Bolaños as marriage material.

At Tennessee's party, Bolaños exuded masculinity, and as Elizabeth would tell Dick Hanley, "He stood so close to me he was practically rubbing that big package up against me."

Dick didn't need to be told about that, as he, too, was at the party and could see what was obviously going on. "Bolaños was flirting with her, and Elizabeth was flirting right back."

On his own turf within Mexico's film community, Bolaños was known as a "star fucker," having previously seduced such aging screen divas as Merle Oberon and Dolores Del Rio.

On the patio of Tennessee's rented villa, lit by colored lights, Bolaños danced both the rumba and the samba with Elizabeth. Tennessee had hired a six-member band, each of the members appearing in tight white pants and shirtless, as per the playwright's request.

According to his reputation, Bolaños specialized in making a woman feel like she was the only female on earth.

The screenwriter mesmerized Elizabeth with his tales of working in the film industry in Mexico. He had been an intimate friend of the late, great modernist painter, Diego Rivera, and was also close to the Spain-born director Luís Buñuel, a towering figure in experimental cinema.

Bolaños also invited Elizabeth to see the Mexican historical epic, *La Cucaracha* (aka *The Soldiers of Pancho Villa; 1959),* whose screenplay he had written.

She pumped Bolaños for any details he could supply about Monroe's final weeks alive. Dick came over to join them. "Bolaños was very clever," he said. "He did not speak unkindly of Marilyn, but he placed Elizabeth on a higher pedestal. About three times, he told her that 'you are, of course, a far greater star than Marilyn, who possessed neither your talent nor your beauty."

"Your beauty is a natural beauty," Bolaños told Elizabeth in front of Dick. "Marilyn had to become Marilyn Monroe by acting the part, dressing up, and painting her face. With no make-up on, I'm sure you'd look stunning. Surely no one on the planet has eyes as beautiful as yours."

She was won over. Dick agreed to drive them from Tennessee's party back to his apartment, where he waited outside, in his car, for two hours.

When she finally came downstairs, she said, "Thanks for the use of your apartment. I hope you don't mind, but Jose wanted to stay over and not drive back to his motel along these impossible unlit roads at night."

"I don't mind at all," he said.

"All I will tell you is this: Marilyn died too soon. I understand completely why she wanted to marry Bolaños. He is God's gift to women, a great lover. Jose can be added to the list of many men Marilyn and I have shared. Richard Burton, John F. Kennedy, and Frank Sinatra come to mind. There were others."

"Peter Lawford, perhaps?" Dick asked.

"That goes without saying," she said. "Now take me home in case lover boy has straggled in."

She was, of course, referring to Burton, who had gone out that night drinking with Peter Viertel and Huston.

Back at his own apartment, Dick came into his bedroom. A nude Bolaños was asleep on his bed. Very gently, Dick slipped a sheet over him. "Lucky Marilyn, lucky Elizabeth," he later told Roddy McDowall.

"The next morning, I made breakfast for Jose," Dick said. "He also let me make love to him, but only in exchange for a big favor."

"I know you're her secretary," Bolaños said, "and you can arrange for me to have a rendezvous with her in Hollywood. I want to be in her life. She'll tire of Burton. He's an old man of failing powers, I heard. I want to be nearby when she replaces Burton."

"You've got yourself a deal, but I'll expect my pound of flesh."

He sighed. "All of you *mariposas* want that. So if you deliver Elizabeth Taylor to me, you can have me on occasion. After all, I'm the most sought after male in all of Mexico."

***

In *Becket* (1964), John Gielgud had played Louis VII, the effete King of France, beside Burton, who played a 12th-century archbishop in conflict with the English king. Over drinks together in a pub, both actors agreed that each of them should participate in some way to bring "the Bard to the masses."

Burton suggested that he'd like to perform *Hamlet* again if Gielgud would direct him. The project almost didn't get off the ground during its early stages when Gielgud informed him that, "Your first venture as *Hamlet* at the Old Vic offended my poetic sensitivity."

During the 1953-54 season at London's Old Vic, Burton had appeared under Michael Benthall's direction as Hamlet. Claire Bloom had been his Ophelia in more ways than one. She and Burton had one of the most torrid affairs of his career as a seducer when they starred together. His performance was viewed as successful, and even Winston Churchill came backstage to congratulate Burton as "My Lord Hamlet."

Burton had become the hottest male celebrity in the world. After his success in *Becket,* when he announced that he wanted to return to the stage as *Hamlet,* money was raised for the production in twenty-four hours.

One of Broadway's most successful producers, 43-year-old Alexander Cohen seemed only too eager to put up the cash. He didn't faint when presented with Burton's demand of $10,000 a week, plus 15 percent of every ticket sold. That was to become the richest deal for any actor in the history of Broadway.

Elizabeth agreed to follow "my man" to Toronto for rehearsals of *Hamlet.* Gielgud, who had seduced Burton when he was a very young man, had finally contracted to direct him.

Burton feared Gielgud would be patronizing and condescending, partly because the aging director believed, with some justification, that he himself had executed "the definitive Hamlet" already. [Gielgud had performed in six acclaimed productions and more than 500 spectacular performances of the Danish Prince on the stage and for British radio beginning in the late 1930s. No stranger to theatrical controversy, and highly opinionated, Gielgud had famously detested Laurence Olivier's film interpretation of the same role in 1948.]

Burton, with Elizabeth, checked into their five-room lodging ("the Viceregal Suite") at Toronto's King Edward Hotel on January 28, 1964. They were charged sixty-five dollars a night. Their suite had been occupied in years past by both Presidents, Eisenhower and Kennedy.

Immediately upon entering the hotel, they passed an evangelist minister who whipped out a prominent sign whose slogan was specifically, it seemed, directed at them: DRINK NOT THE WINE OF ADULTERY.

During rehearsals at Toronto's O'Keefe Theatre, whereas Gielgud passionately wanted Shakespeare's poetry to carry the play, Burton was "more interested in discovering the Bard's meaning."

As Graham Jenkins, one of Burton's brothers, wrote: "The result was an undisciplined and unpredictable *Hamlet* who, at times, had the rest of the cast running around in circles."

"The one thing that surprised me about them was that Elizabeth called Richard 'Fred' and he called her 'Agatha,'" said Gielgud.

Elizabeth noted that during trial runs, Burton wasn't clicking with the audience. She placed an emergency call to Philip Burton, an authority on Shakespeare and Richard's longtime mentor, and persuaded him to come to Toronto for additional coaching.

The appearance of this "second director" on the scene infuriated Gielgud. But Philip's magic seemed to work, and Burton delivered a more dynamic performance after his coaching. Philip had previously supplied behind-the-scenes direction to his star pupil at the Old Vic in London during the 1950s.

Whereas Burton may have believed that Elizabeth's legs were too short, like Errol Flynn, he didn't like the way his own legs appeared in tights, or in doublet and hose. "In tights, my legs look like a pair of stockings idly thrown over a bed rail," he told Gielgud.

In a wry and campy mood, Gielgud responded "Yes, but they'd look great wrapped around my head."

It was therefore agreed that *Hamlet* was to be performed in modern dress, and Burton subsequently appeared at every performance in a black V-neck sweater and black trousers.

Of course, during the run of *Hamlet,* as was to be expected, some members of the audience were put off by Shakespearean characters sipping martinis and puffing on cigars.

February of 1964 was a big month for Elizabeth, who was celebrating her thirty-second birthday and expecting jewelry from Burton. The month also saw the opening of Burton's stage version of *Hamlet* in Toronto.

Attending opening night, an elegantly dressed Elizabeth was booed viciously by the audience. This delayed the curtain for nearly half an hour.

Taking her seat, she sat with her head erect and her back straight, refusing to be intimidated by the hostile response to her presence. To those hissing her, Elizabeth had obviously become the *femme fatale* of the 20th Century. She represented vamp, vixen, she-wolf man eater, slut, tart, the devil incarnate in women's clothing, the Serpent of the Nile.

"My God, they viewed me as Gloria Wandrous in *Butterfield 8,"* she said, "the role I hated."

One night in Toronto, Burton played Hamlet as a homosexual, as Olivier had done in London on occasion. "I inserted a few lines from Marlowe, and no one noticed."

The Toronto Star called Burton "artistically impotent," but *The Toronto Telegram* hailed his performance as a masterpiece. During its entire run in Toronto, *Hamlet* sold out at every performance.

The production was interrupted when Elizabeth and Burton finally decided to fly away to get married.

***

Inconveniently, the province of Ontario, in which Toronto is located, did not recognize Mexican divorces as legally valid. Consequently, in the wake of her (Mexican) divorce from Fisher, Elizabeth flew with Burton to Montréal, in the more permissive French-speaking province of Québec, which did. It would be her fifth trip down the aisle of marriage.

Aboard a morning flight on a chartered Lockheed Jet, the couple was accompanied by America's most famous publicist, John Springer. En route, Burton revealed to Springer how he'd proposed to Elizabeth during the filming of *Becket* the previous summer.

"I proposed in front of Peter O'Toole at this pub in Berkshire near Windsor Castle. I looked straight into Elizabeth's eyes and said—'I want to marry Elizabeth, and I *will* marry her."

She responded, "You've said it, Richard."

Before 10am, aboard the flight to Montréal, Burton was already drinking heavily. "Why are you so nervous?" she asked him in front of Dick Hanley. "After all, you've been sleeping with me for two years."

In Montréal, she was married in two separate ceremonies on the same day, first in the Consulate of Mexico, for legal reasons, and again as part of a religious ceremony within the Royal Suite at the Ritz-Carlton Montréal.

As his best man, Burton made an unusual choice in Robert Wilson, his African-American dresser.

Elizabeth wanted to be married by a rabbi, but none was available. Other members of the clergy also turned down this request from "this wanton woman and home wrecker." Finally, the Rev. Leonard Mason, from the Unitarian Church of the Messiah, agreed to perform the ceremony at the Ritz-Carlton.

The Burton/Taylor wedding
in Montréal

Based on a costume she'd worn during her first scene with Burton in *Cleopatra,* Elizabeth arrived looking stunning in a canary yellow chiffon Irene Sharaff gown with lots of *décolletage.* Her hairdo was spectacular. Her own hair had been augmented by thirty-four falls priced collectively at $600. Hyacinths were woven into the resulting hairdo to create the effect of an elaborate diadem, halo, or circle of light, depending on who was looking at it.

Harry Winston would have been proud of her jewelry, which included a diamond necklace and matching diamond-and-emerald ear drop earrings, a gift from Burton.

After the first ceremony, Burton said, "It's a fairytale. The 'Boy from Nowhere' has just married the world's most celebrated beauty."

Back at the Ritz-Carlton, Elizabeth stayed in her bedroom preparing herself again and redoing her make-up. The minister, Burton, and the other guests waited for her.

"Isn't that fat little tart here yet?" Burton asked Dick Hanley. "I swear to you she'll be late for the Last Bloody Judgment."

Partly because of its dysfunctional timing, the second segment of the wedding in Montréal was a curious anticlimax to what had been one of the 20th century's most publicized romances.

A wedding party of ten, including her parents, had been flown in, as had Burton's agent, Hugh French. The actor Hume Cronyn, who had been cast as Polonius in *Hamlet,* was also a guest.

From afar, Elizabeth's longtime friend, Oscar Levant, who was not at the wedding, delivered the best quip—"Elizabeth is always a bride, never a bridesmaid."

Other commentators tried to match Levant's humor: "Imagine!" wrote Walter Winchell. "Marrying every husband you meet." Bob Hope quipped, "Want a steady job, gals? Try out for flower girl at Liz Taylor's weddings."

Before their departure from Montréal, Burton announced, "Elizabeth is like a mirage of beauty of the ages, irresistible, like the pull of gravity. She has everything I want in a woman. She is quite unlike any woman I have ever known. She makes men not want to know any other woman, believe me, sincerely. I think of her morning, noon, and night. I dream of her. She will be my greatest happiness—forever, of course."

Back in Toronto, Burton discovered his dressing room filled with gifts, mainly kitchen utensils. He picked up two rolling pins and turned to Dick. "These might come in handy if I have to beat the wench if she gets out of hand."

On the first night after his return from Montréal, just before another Toronto performance of *Hamlet*, Burton came out on stage to make an announcement: "Some of you have come to see Alfred Drake; some have come to see Eileen Herlie, some have come to see Hume Cronyn, and some have come to see Elizabeth Taylor." [Elizabeth virtually had to be pushed out from the wings at this point.]

Instead of boos and hissing this time, she received deafening applause.

Burton later referred to it as "orgiastic cheering."

At the end of that night's performance, Burton received six curtain calls. After the first three, he stepped in front of the curtain. "I would like to quote from the play," he said to the audience. "Act Three, Scene One. 'We will have no more marriages.'"

That comment produced another round of standing ovations.

***

From Toronto, Elizabeth and Burton headed to Boston with Gielgud's production of *Hamlet*. She told him that "Bostonians are more reserved than the more provincial Canadians. I don't think we'll attract such hysteria."

She was wrong. Never again in their lives would they be faced with such a massive onslaught of hundreds of fans. It became impossible for them to get off the plane. After waiting an hour, the pilot got permission to steer the plane into a hangar so he could unload his passengers.

Safely in the back seat of a limousine, Burton and Elizabeth were driven to the Copley Plaza Hotel. But as they entered the lobby, a mob of some one thousand unruly fans assaulted them. The police, hotel security, and private security guards could not control the screaming throng.

At one point, Elizabeth became surrounded by the mob. Someone shouted, "See if it's a wig!" A burly woman yanked out a hunk of Elizabeth's hair, while another tore at her diamond earring. Not succeeding at unfastening it, she nonetheless caused Elizabeth to bleed.

Burton fought his way back to her. With the help of two policemen, he managed to clear a pathway for her to the elevator. She'd been knocked down, falling against a wall, which dislocated her shoulder. In great pain, she was put to bed, and a doctor summoned.

The next morning, Burton was seen in a gun shop in Roxbury, outside Boston, purchasing a .22 caliber pistol and ample amounts of ammunition.

Burton was so furious, he even called Ted Kennedy, complaining, "Elizabeth was almost killed. You'd better talk to the Boston police." Kennedy obviously had some influence, especially on his "home turf" of Massachusetts. When the Burtons arrived that night at the Schubert Theater, a "police curtain" quickly materialized around them.

In Boston, Sammy Davis, Jr. came to see them and convinced her that Burton's wardrobe was not "mod" enough. She commissioned his tailor, Cy Devore, to design an entirely new wardrobe for him. "My aim is to have him known as 'the Sinatra of Shakespeare,'" a reference to Sinatra's stylish way of dressing.

While Elizabeth and Burton were still in Boston, before their invasion of Broadway, there were rumblings from Washington, D.C., attacking them.

Michael Feighan, a Roman Catholic Democratic congressman from Ohio, representing Cleveland, formally demanded that the State Department revoke Burton's visa and refuse his re-entrance into the United States. The request was denied. When Feighan learned that Burton would be bringing *Hamlet* to Broadway, he requested that the play be shut down because it was "immoral." When that initiative failed, he asked that all the lights on Broadway be dimmed on the play's opening night as a protest against its content. That final request was not honored, either.

***

In Manhattan, the Taylor/Burton brood was camped out in the Regency Hotel on Park Avenue at 61st Street, wrecking two separate suites.

By now, Elizabeth in particular was known for trashing every suite she occupied and paying damages. First, she allowed her dogs to run wild without being walked. The carpets ended up smelling like urine. Her children were often out of control. Draperies were ripped, and mattresses always had to be replaced because of the many drinks spilled over them. And for some reason, perhaps the result of drunken arguments, mirrors were often broken or cracked.

At *Hamlet's* opening at Broadway's Lunt-Fontanne Theater in April of 1964, masses turned out to catch a glimpse of Elizabeth and her latest husband. New York's finest were summoned to block off the street, as thousands of fans and onlookers flooded the streets around Times Square in ways that evoked the crowds of New Year's Eve.

"I left Broadway as King of Camelot, and I have returned as Prince of Denmark," Burton told the press.

On opening night, the biggest insult to Burton came from the famous Broadway producer, Harold Clurman, who got up and walked out in the middle of an important scene being performed by Burton as Hamlet. In the lobby of the theater, Clurman told a reporter, "Burton is the story of an actor who has lost interest in his profession."

But Walter Kerr of *The New York Herald Tribune* was kinder, claiming that Burton is "one of the most magnificently equipped actors living." Others used words such as "electric" and "virile" to describe his performance.

Burton himself defined his performance to critic Kenneth Tynan with irony and a touch of self-satirization: "I played it myself—that is, Richard Burton playing Richard Burton playing Hamlet."

Elizabeth had not seen Monty Clift in many months, and invited him to Burton's opening night on Broadway. Backstage, she masked the shock on her own face when she saw his ravaged face. He'd aged at least ten years since she'd seen him. "Oh, Bessie Mae," he said, falling into her arms and weeping.

She invited him to join her at the after-the-show party that Hamlet's producer Alexander Cohen was staging in the Rainbow Room at Rockefeller Center.

Newsweek reported that the party at the Rainbow Room, sixty-five stories above Manhattan's street level, "was the scarcest ticket in New York." Among the invited guests were Michael Wilding and Margaret Leighton. Wilding presented Leighton to Elizabeth with the words, "I have found renewed happiness with her. The old pain has gone."

In the Rainbow Room, Burton was seen dancing with Princess Lee Radziwill, sister of Jacqueline Kennedy. Even the Gish sisters, Dorothy and Lillian, showed up as ghostly reminders of the vanished heyday of silent films.

The next day, Elizabeth went to have drinks with Monty at his Manhattan brownstone, a building he had recently purchased. It had been almost four years since he'd faced the cameras, because no company would insure him. She asked him what he thought of Burton's *Hamlet*. "He's nothing but a reciter, a total phony running around the stage."

In spite of the insult, she was eager to put him back to work. She came up with the odd suggestion that they perform *The Owl and the Pussycat* together on stage. "A comedy together," she said. "It will be a sell-out." (Ironically, although after her experience with *Butterfield 8,* Elizabeth had vowed that she'd never again appear on screen as a prostitute, the female character she wanted to play in *The Owl and the Pussycat* was that of a hooker.)

She was convinced that if Monty didn't find work, he would die. Tennessee Williams had given her a copy of a novel written by a close friend of his. It was *Reflections in a Golden Eye,* written by Carson McCullers. The producer, Ray Stark, wanted to spearhead a film version, even though it clearly defined the leading male character as a latent homosexual.

Elizabeth told Stark she'd post a million dollars to insure Monty and herself.

For two full years, they continued to discuss and plot their dreams for *Reflections,* but Monty died on July 23, 1966. In the aftermath of Monty's death, Marlon Brando agreed to interpret the role of the homosexual, opposite Elizabeth, and the movie was finally released in 1967 by Warner Brothers, with John Huston called in to direct.

Burton suggested that Elizabeth, Monty, and himself remake the 1947 *The Macumber Affair,* which had starred Gregory Peck, Joan Bennett, and Robert Preston. Although such a film could have meant good box office, no studio expressed an interest.

Frank Sinatra came to see *Hamlet* one night, although he dozed off a bit. He came backstage, too, with kisses for both Burton and Elizabeth. "Even in my heyday with the bobbysoxers during the war, I didn't get crowds like you guys are getting. Keep wearing those sparklers, Liz."

Truman Capote also visited backstage and told them he was amazed at the masses gathering every night on Broadway at Forty-Sixth Street.

"That's because we're sex maniacs," Elizabeth said. "They're coming to see a pair of sinful freaks."

Capote put a different spin on it. He said, "It's the allure of wealth, diamonds, minks, exotic perfume—*intoxicating!*"

"During the run of *Hamlet,* Richard's drinking capacity continued to amaze," claimed Graham Jenkins in his memoirs, *Richard Burton, My Brother.*

"When I was with him, he always managed three or four powerful martinis before going on stage, and these were just a top-up of the day's intake. Nonetheless, he was there, on time, for every performance."

Actor Stanley Baker, an old friend, came to visit them at the Regency after placing at least twenty calls, finding it impossible to get either of them on the phone. Finally, he reached Burton, who invited him to come up to their suite.

Baker had a film proposal for an upcoming movie entitled *Sands of Kalahari,* a drama about five men and one woman stranded in the Kalahari Desert. He told them what they already knew: They were the most gold-plated couple in the history of show business. "Now is the time to capitalize on it."

Even though Elizabeth and Burton liked the script, and wanted to be part of it, they could not agree on terms. "Liz wanted a million dollars; Richard half a million, but they also asked a higher percentage of the gross than we could afford," Baker said. "Too damn bad."

During the run of the stage performance of *Hamlet,* the film version of *The Night of the Iguana* opened in New York. Ava Gardner, that onetime barefoot Tarheel girl from Grabtown, North Carolina, received the best notices. Bosley Crowther of *The New York Times* attacked Burton's performance as the defrocked priest. "He is spectacularly gross, a figure of wild disarrangement, but without a shred of real sincerity."

"He was impossible to live with for a week," Elizabeth told Dick Hanley. "I went one entire week without getting fucked."

Iguana, in spite of some attacks, turned out to be a blockbuster success. "If I ever run into that Crowther, I'll stick my Welsh fist up his ass," Burton said. "I've got the Midas touch at the box office."

In June of 1964, Elizabeth agreed to make her stage debut on Broadway at the Lunt-Fontanne Theater, the site of Burton's ongoing performances of Hamlet. She and Burton, as coached and rehearsed by Philip Burton, were commissioned to read poetry-and-prose selections for the $100-per ticket fund-raiser, *World Enough and Time,* a title inspired by the poetry of Andrew Marvell ("To His Coy Mistress"). It was understood that profits generated by the event would be donated to Philip Burton's nearly bankrupt school, the American Musical and Dramatic Academy.

Among the famous guests were Dina Merrill, Myrna Loy, Lee Remick, Kitty Carlisle Hart, Patricia Kennedy Lawford, Lauren Bacall, Anita Loos, Alan Jay Lerner, and Adolf Green. Drunk and drugged, Monty also showed up. Elizabeth believed that "the cream of the cream was turning out to see me fall on my face."

The event also attracted New York's handsome mayor, John Lindsay. Elizabeth told Dick Hanley, "I've always had a crush on this guy." She demonstrated that after her performance, when the Mayor came backstage to congratulate her. "She gave him a sloppy wet one," Dick said.

Burton read from a mélange of Shakespeare, D.H. Lawrence, and even "words of wisdom" from John Lennon. Also included was a rendering of the Twenty-Third Psalm, in Welsh (by Burton) and in English (by Elizabeth). Appearing in a Grecian gown with diamonds and emeralds, Elizabeth recited "Three Bushes" by William Butler Yeats, and "How Do I Love Thee? Let Me Count the Ways," by Elizabeth Barrett Browning. She fumbled several lines during her recitation of Thomas Hardy's *The Ruined Maid,* a poem selected as a means of poking fun at the Burtons' public image.

"And now you've gay bracelets and bright feathers three!
'Yes, that's how we dress when we're ruined,' said she."

"This is getting even funnier than *Hamlet,"* Burton said.

Sitting behind Bea Lillie (Lady Peel), Emlyn Williams heard Lillie say to Carol Channing, "If she doesn't get bad pretty soon, I'm leaving."

But Elizabeth recovered quickly from her fumble and finished the show with style. Later, the *New York Herald Tribune* said that Elizabeth "giggled her way through a series of bungled lines."

One night, she had the flu and remained in her suite at The Regency. That night, as Burton was delivering one of Hamlet's soliloquies, a heckler booed him, the first time that had ever occurred to him as a performer. He was furious. By the time the curtain went down, he was enraged. That led him to join two cast members in a heavy round of drinking. By the time he returned to his suite at The Regency, he was totally intoxicated and very belligerent.

When he walked into the living room, he found Elizabeth entranced by a Peter Sellers movie, *I'm All Right, Jack* (1959), the first one she'd ever seen with the actor.

"Cut off that fucking TV," Burton yelled at her. "I was booed tonight."

"It happens to all stage actors," she said. "Get over it."

"I said cut off that bloody TV!" he said.

He stormed into the bedroom and came out about fifteen minutes later, barefoot and clad only in his jockey shorts. He was infuriated to discover that she was still watching that Sellers movie. He gave the TV a kick, knocking it over, but cut his foot on the broken glass. Elizabeth was horrified when he couldn't stop bleeding.

That's when he revealed to her that he suffered from hemophilia. "It is the disease of kings," he told her, referring to the many inbred royal families of Europe who suffered from the same disease.

An ambulance rushed him to the hospital where he told her that he came from a family of "bleeders." Four of his brothers also suffered from the same disease.

At the hospital, Burton received a dozen stitches to stop the bleeding and he was forced to limp through *Hamlet* for the next two weeks.

Five nights after his hospital emergency, Burton encountered Eddie Fisher in a Manhattan restaurant, and graciously invited him to The Regency for a drink.

Fisher later wrote, "I arrived in the middle of an argument. Elizabeth's make-up was smeared, her voice loud and shrill. She was furious about something, and I thought, 'I was married to that woman, this wild thing,' Burton was trying to soothe her, as I watched him walk around their suite, apologizing, straightening up, retrieving things she dropped. I said to myself, 'There once went I.'"

"We agreed to bury the hatchet," Fisher said, "but there was no love lost." He was eager to let Elizabeth know that he had a new "high-class girlfriend" in Pamela Turnure, who was at the time press secretary to Jacqueline Kennedy. "But Pamela has made one big mistake in our affair. She's fallen in love with me. As for Jackie, I've met her several times. She's told the world that the public would lose respect for her if she ran off with Eddie Fisher. She may not run off with me, but I can tell she has the hots for me. The last time Pamela, Jackie, and I had dinner together, Jackie couldn't keep her hands off me."

Five nights later, the Burtons came together with Fisher and Turnure in Manhattan at the Copacabana for the nightclub act of Sammy Davis, Jr. Fisher's party included the Chicago gangster, Sam Giancana; producer Walter Wanger of *Cleopatra;* Mike Todd, Jr., and Jennie Grossinger. Fisher was still romantically linked to Turnure.

That night, Burton told Elizabeth, "*Hamlet* is coming to an end, and we should return to making films for big money. We'll co-star together in a movie called *The Sandpiper.*"

Burton's New York run of *Hamlet* was the most successful run of that play in theatrical history, with 136 performances. Ironically, it surpassed the previous Broadway record of performances, 132 in all, that Gielgud had chalked up in any of his single runs.

Burton became so carried away with the Bard that he contemplated directing Elizabeth as Lady Macbeth in some vaguely defined future enterprise.

His *Hamlet* played to standing room only for every performance for seventeen weeks on Broadway, grossing more that $6 million, of which he received fifteen percent.

"Deodorants come and go, but there's only one deodorant that works in this town. It's called Success." Elizabeth said.

***

The Sandpiper (1965)*,* some of which would be shot at Big Sur along the coast of central California at the end of 1964, would be the third film to star Elizabeth and Richard Burton, who was now her husband.

For the film, Elizabeth demanded her usual million dollars. "I always call it my 'giggly million' because I always giggle when I get a check with all those zeroes. It makes Richard happy, too, because he says he wants to be 'rich, rich, rich.'"

Burton drew a salary of $750,000, which he told director Vincente Minnelli "pisses me off. I want a cool million like Liz. After all, my dick is bigger than hers. Besides, let the record speak for itself. I am the world's leading box-office attraction."

He exaggerated. Although listed among the top ten, he was not number one.

Elizabeth's contract had granted her director approval and she had chosen Minnelli, who had helmed her in *Father of the Bride* and *Father's Little Dividend*, Burton wasn't thrilled with the choice of Minnelli. "Maybe he'll turn *The Sandpiper* into a musical and insist I do a soft-shoe."

She had known Minnelli during the course of his marriage to Judy Garland, and she also knew his young daughter, Liza Minnelli. But she immediately clashed with him by demanding that Sammy Davis, Jr., play her other love interest in the movie.

"I'm about the most liberal guy in Hollywood, but there was no way I could cast a black guy in 1964 to play love scenes with Elizabeth," Minnelli said. "She staged a bitter battle, but we had to give the role to Charles Bronson."

In his memoir, *Hollywood in a Suitcase,* Davis claimed that he had signed

Vincente Minnelli with his infant daughter, **Liza Minnelli**

a contract to do the film, but had to withdraw because of an early opening of *Golden Boy* on Broadway. This does not appear to be the case. "The racial issue was paramount," Minnelli claimed.

The Sandpiper had actually been conceived as a vehicle for Kim Novak, who in many ways would have been far better suited to the role than Elizabeth.

Originally, the producer and the scriptwriter, Martin Ransohoff, had wanted to film *The Sandpiper* eight months earlier, based on a screenplay that would have starred Elizabeth with Marlon Brando. [Ransohoff was the producer who had given the world *The Beverly Hillbillies* beginning in 1962.] Production was delayed, he claimed, "because Elizabeth wanted to hold Burton's hand during *Hamlet* and during the filming of *Iguana* in Mexico."

Minnelli privately told his friends that casting Brando and Novak might have generated more on-screen chemistry than Elizabeth and Burton. "If Sammy Davis, Jr., had also been cast as the second lover, that ebony-on-porcelain chemistry of the lavender blonde and the little boy from Harlem would have been something to see. After all, Sammy and Kim were rumored to have been lovers off the screen."

Minnelli also said he found the story "ludicrous and dated" and compared it to a watered-down version of W. Somerset Maugham's *Rain* which introduced the character of prostitute Sadie Thompson.

Dalton Trumbo, one of the original members of the Hollywood Ten accused of spreading communist propaganda to the American populace through the entertainment industry, worked on the script but didn't bring his usual magic to it. He said, "I didn't want to add an interracial romance to an already overburdened story," referring, of course, to Elizabeth's original insistence on casting Sammy Davis, Jr.

Exterior shots were filmed at Big Sur along the central California coast, but Burton and Elizabeth, for tax reasons, insisted that the rest of the film be shot outside Paris.

Frocked in *Becket,* defrocked in *The Night of the Iguana,* Burton was playing yet another ecclesiastic in *The Sandpiper.* He's willing to remove his "dog collar" with fewer reservations this time around as he surrenders to Elizabeth, a nature-loving unmarried mother living in a sea-fronting house near a coven of Bohemian artists at Big Sur.

In the film, the character of Elizabeth's illegitimate nine-year-old son, Danny Reynolds, was played by Morgan Mason, who was actually the son of James Mason. Minnelli had wanted to cast one of the Wilding teenagers [*i.e.,* one of Elizabeth's sons] in the role, but Elizabeth, perhaps for artistic reasons, refused.

Eva Marie Saint played the third lead. Cast as Burton's castoff wife in the film, "she was the stand-in for Sybil Burton," according to Minnelli. "The screenplay in some way and in some lines paralleled the real life drama of Burton and Taylor."

Burton and Minnelli did not get along and conflicted over the interpretation of several scenes. "The film was a bore," Burton said. "Minnelli had once been a good director, but he was past his prime. I didn't like the part, and it bored me, but as I told Minnelli, who wore lipstick every day, 'For the money, Liz and I will dance.'"

In the script, Charles Bronson portrays a bohemian sculptor who carves a life-sized nude of Elizabeth *au naturel*. Edmund Kara was commissioned to produce a voluptuous and anatomically correct nude of Elizabeth, but she refused to pose for it. He found a model whose body resembled Elizabeth's. As a means of replicating Elizabeth's face, Kara used a life mask. It took three months to transform a block of redwood into a nude replica of Elizabeth.

"I don't know what Elizabeth thought of my statue," Kara said, "but Burton had praise for it."

"Bravo!" Burton said. "Kara, you've even captured the dimples on her ass."

"I think nude scenes are absurd," Elizabeth said, "and I think it's really strange the way women, respectable women, will strip for magazines. The ones who don't need the money—it can only be a narcissistic complex, a vanity of the body so profound that they must show it."

When the filming was over, Kara got his sculpture returned from the prop room of MGM, although they demanded half the proceeds if he ever sold it. Instead of selling it, he decapitated the head to display as a work of art in its own right.

"THE SANDPIPER"

It was the 60s, and everyone went to Big Sur...
Two views of **Elizabeth Taylor**
as a bohemian precursor of the hippies

He then planned to use the block of redwood as the raw material for other sculptures. As he told author C. David Heymann, "I brought in a friend with a saw to decapitate it. He took off the head straight across the shoulders and then cut away the arms. He was holding the chain saw rather suggestively in front of his crotch. The blade protruded like a giant phallus. So I said to him, 'Go ahead, give it to her!' He plunged the blade deep into her vagina and ripped her. When he completed the cut, thousands of big army ants came marching out. They had been living inside the wooden love goddess's uterus for months."

Graham Jenkins, Burton's brother, said, "Allowed a free choice, I believe Rich would have turned down *The Sandpiper*. He knew from the beginning that it was a bad film."

Elizabeth got along with Minnelli much better than Burton, and she noted he still had a sexual interest in Tom Drake, who had a supporting role in the movie.

In *Raintree County,* Drake had played her brother. "To get a job in films, poor Tom is still having to drop trou for Vincente, just like he did when he played The Boy Next Door," Elizabeth said. "For god's sake, Tom was born in 1918."

The Boy Next Door reference was to his role opposite Judy Garland in the 1944 *Meet Me in St. Louis.* Minnelli had directed him in that, and had become sexually involved with the handsome young boy.

Elizabeth also confessed to Dick Hanley that "Tom and I were both in love with Peter Lawford at the same time."

***

Although Elizabeth and Burton had recently married, they had previously lived together for two years, which caused him to refer to her as "my old lady." Sometimes, in the British fashion, he referred to her as "old girl."

"I may be married," he told Minnelli, "but I'm not dead. I don't see much chance for me to knock off an extra piece. On this picture, I hear that Eva Marie Saint lives up to her last name."

At that point in his life, Elizabeth seemed to be fulfilling his heterosexual needs. But, as a bisexual, he had an eye out for a handsome, charismatic male. He found such a person in a talented architect, interior designer and decorator, Edward (Eduardo) Tirella, who had been hired to work on the movie's sets at Big Sur.

Born in Dover, New Jersey, Tirella was tall, charming, smart, athletic, and very good-looking. Growing up in an Italian family, he secretly wanted to be a singer. When he sang in clubs, his velvety voice evoked Mel Tormé.

Ransohoff had hired Tirella to design the bohemian artist's "shack" which Elizabeth's character would occupy as her oceanfront home in the movie. Tirella also made a brief appearance onscreen in a beach setting with Elizabeth and Bronson.

Ransohoff praised Tirella's artistic talent, claiming that "anything he touches can turn into something beautiful. He has hands of gold."

Like Burton, Tirella was a bisexual, and had lent both his professional and private talents to both Peggy Lee and the very closeted Alan Ladd.

As a hat designer at Saks Fifth Avenue, he had sold some of his more extravagant creations to Hedda Hopper, Elizabeth's friend and sometimes ally of long ago, and Mae West.

Soon after his work on *The Sandpiper,* he would begin a destructive and eventually fatal relationship with Doris Duke, the richest woman in the world.

Duke's biographer, Stephanie Mansfield, wrote: "A striking figure in his turtlenecks and in his sporty convertible car, Tirella was known as promiscuous in the homosexual world. But he never had any lasting relationships. They were only one-night stands."

Tirella got a weekend singing gig in San Francisco, and he invited Burton to drive with him there for the weekend, not only to hear him sing, but to see more of the city, of which he had only a passing acquaintance.

Technically, Elizabeth had been invited, too, but she told Dick Hanley, "I really think Tirella, and Richard, too, views me as so much extra baggage."

Actually, Elizabeth had a very good reason for not wanting to go. Deborah Kerr's husband, the sophisticated scriptwriter and novelist, Peter Viertel, was slipping into Monterey, close to the set of *Sandpiper,* and he wanted Elizabeth to come and visit him at his hotel suite.

"I adore the man," she told Dick. "We had such a grand time in your apartment in Puerto Vallarta...I'd like to see him again. Of course, we'll be very discreet."

While Tirella was away in San Francisco with Burton, Elizabeth had a secret rendezvous with Viertel.

During their short time together at Big Sur filming *The Sandpiper,* Tirella and Burton became "bonded at the hip.

This caused some jealous tension between Burton and Minnelli," Dick later said. "Minnelli soon tired of Tom Drake and wanted Tirella for himself. When Burton went off for a second weekend with Tirella to San Francisco, Minnelli seemed furious, but repressed his anger."

Dick later emphasized that during Burton's time away from her, Elizabeth did not embrace a self-image as an abandoned wife or lonely widow. During the second weekend that Burton was in San Francisco with Tirella, Jose Balaños showed up for a dalliance with her at a hotel/resort outside Monterey.

"He was still hoping that Elizabeth might jump-start a film career for him," Dick said, "but she was more interested in replicating the pleasures that Jose had managed to provide for Marilyn Monroe. She also wanted to gossip about the circumstances associated with the weeks prior to her death."

"In the end, Jose was very disappointed that Elizabeth did nothing for him in the film industry," Dick said. "After Richard and Elizabeth left for Paris, she told me not to put through any more of his calls or answer any of his letters. I felt a little sorry for the kid, as he had lost both Marilyn, because she died, and then Elizabeth, because she dropped him."

When his involvement with the filming of *The Sandpiper* was concluded, in early October of 1966, Tirella returned to the East Coast and began a "creative collaboration" with Doris Duke. He moved with her into Rough Point, one of the largest mansions in Newport, Rhode Island, where he was commissioned as her interior decorator during some of its renovations. But after growing tired of being both companion and nursemaid to the notoriously imperious heiress within her gloomy white elephant of an estate, Tirella became argumentative and consequently met a much worse fate than Bolaños.

In Big Sur, producer Martin Ransohoff had been so impressed with Tirella's contribution to *The Sandpiper* that he made him an offer for work on the set of *Don't Make Waves,* an ode to the go-go southern California beach culture of the 60s. Eventually released in 1967, with advertising slogans that included "It fills up the screen like she fills out a bikini," it starred Tony Curtis and Sharon Tate, the actress who would confront her own grisly death at the murderous hands of Charles Manson's gang.

Confronted with the reality of Tirella's upcoming abandonment, Duke argued violently, jockeying and maneuvering to convince him to stay by her side, but he remained firm in his resolve to depart from Rough Point.

At around five o'clock on the afternoon of October 7, 1966, in an event that would horrify local residents for years, Duke asked Tirella to accompany her on an errand in her white station wagon. Before they could drive away from the gardens surrounding the Duke mansion, she ordered him to exit from the driver's seat of the car and open the heavy iron gates separating her estate from the neighborhood that surrounded it.

As he was opening the gates, the station wagon roared forward at high speed, hit Tirella, and then crashed his body into the gate, breaking its heavy latch with its impact. The car then shot across the wide expanse of Bellevue Avenue, stopping only after it crashed into a tree on the avenue's distant side. Trapped under the car, and dragged for many yards at high speed under its chassis, the body of Tirella lay in a tangled bloody mess of torn flesh

How to Get Away with Murder:
Two views of **Doris Duke**
upper photo: With **Elizabeth Taylor** in 1981
lower photo: with **Eduardo Tirella** in the mid-1960s

544

and broken bones. His head had been smashed open like a melon.

Duke was almost immediately sedated and confined to her room, with only invited visitors allowed, by her doctors as a bevy of attorneys debated how best to handle the legal implications of this disaster. When she became available, many hours later, for interviews from the Newport police, the press was advised that Duke had "accidentally gunned the accelerator" from her position in the front passenger's seat. The police then ruled the incident as "an unfortunate accident," and dropped all semblance of a prosecution.

The resulting cries of foul play caused such a furor that the local police chief, Joseph Radice, was eventually forced to resign. Duke later settled out of court with Tirella's family when they brought civil charges against her.

When he heard about the accident, Burton told Elizabeth and Dick Hanley, "Doris Duke murdered Eduardo, and of that I have no doubt. When you have all the money in the world, you can get away with murder."

"Obviously, we can't go to the funeral," Elizabeth told Dick. "Send flowers."

Perhaps Elizabeth had many motives for not attending the funeral. First, she hardly knew Tirella, and resented his presence in Burton's life. Had she gone to the funeral, it might have caused speculation about those wild weekends Burton had spent with Tirella in San Francisco. Also, the appearance of either Burton or Elizabeth in Newport would have alienated Duke and focused even more light on embarrassments that the heiress wanted buried in more ways than one.

***

With the intention of filming the interior scenes of *The Sandpiper* in Paris, Elizabeth and Burton sailed aboard the *Queen Elizabeth 2*, booking all six first-class cabins except one. Ironically, that one was occupied by Debbie Reynolds, who had married Harry Karl, a shoe manufacturer.

Elizabeth and Reynolds met onboard for a Dom Pérignon toast, both of them agreeing, "Who in the fuck cares about Eddie Fisher?"

Regrettably, Reynolds' marriage to Karl ended in 1975 after she discovered him to be a serial adulterer who also gambled away all her money, forcing her at one point in her life to vacate her home and to live in her car.

Elizabeth, Burton, staff, and children checked into the Hotel Lancaster on rue de Berri, off the Champs-Elysées in Paris, renting twenty-one rooms for a combined fee of $10,000 a week.

From their digs at the Lancaster, Burton and Elizabeth were entertained by *tout* Paris, especially by the Baron Guy de Rothschild.

All of the interior scenes of *The Sandpiper* were shot at the Boulogne-Billancourt Studios in Paris's western suburbs. Wherever Burton and Elizabeth went, they were mobbed by thousands of fans.

Burton claimed that he was thoroughly mauled by the paparazzi at The Lido night club. "They were trying to get pictures of my wife's tits," he complained to his fellow guests, Aristotle Onassis and his mistress, the operatic superstar, Maria Callas.

A French reporter asked Elizabeth about her beauty and about Burton's sex appeal. "I am not a great beauty. I'm too short of leg, too big in the arms, one too many chins, big feet, big hands, too fat. For Richard, it's not about muscles. It is what he says and thinks."

Graham Jenkins, Burton's brother, claimed, "The couple lived in luxury. Outside Paris, they had a dressing caravan the size of a small hotel, and they were hauled around in a chauffeur-driven Rolls-Royce with a Welsh dragon engraved on it. The booze flowed from a ruptured brewery, and the parties were open-ended."

In Paris, Elizabeth shocked many of her most ardent fans by renouncing her American citizenship to become British. "It isn't that all of a sudden, I love America less. It's just that I love my husband more. Besides, I was born in England."

Most of the press viewed her statement as dishonest and self-serving. "It was done for tax reasons," said *Paris-Match*. At the time, British subjects who lived abroad had a far better tax deal than American expatriates in similar situations.

In Paris between takes, Elizabeth often entertained the crew. "She did the best Mae West and Marilyn Monroe impersonations known to mankind," Minnelli said. "When Burton was away one afternoon, she did an impersonation of him. But suddenly, he walked onto the set and heard it. For her trouble, he slapped her face, really hard."

"My eardrum did not function properly for one entire month," she said.

As Elizabeth and Burton were already painfully aware, one of the dangers associated with being rich and famous is that ghosts from one's past might suddenly appear.

Their adopted Bavarian-born daughter, Maria, had been assigned her own full-time nurse and governess. Born with birth defects, she was able to walk only after a large fortune had been spent on various orthopedic surgeries. Elizabeth had paid handsomely for the privilege of adopting Maria.

Unexpectedly, with fanfare, her biological parents, the Heisigs, flew in from Germany. Backed up with a lawyer in Paris, they claimed that Elizabeth owed them more money for the "sale" of Maria. Instead of defending the adoption in court, Elizabeth gave in to the extortion and settled more money on this German couple, the exact amount undisclosed.

Elizabeth, in a memoir, denied that she transferred additional funds to the Heisigs. She blamed the incident on a French tabloid whose editors had organized the Heisigs' visit to Paris. "The photographer wanted to take a picture of the mother standing near the opulence of my Rolls-Royce, her tattered coat contrasting with my fur coat—you know, a little woman standing out in the cold, waiting for days on end to get a look at her child."

That experience with the parents of Maria blighted their stay in Paris, and both Elizabeth and Burton were anxious to move on.

On the final day of filming, Burton completed his last scene and walked off the set. He said, "I'm bloody tired of playing fornicating clerics."

On viewing the lackluster *The Sandpiper* today, its best element is its theme song, "The Shadow of Your Smile," which quickly became a standard in almost any Tony Bennett concert.

The Sandpiper, because of the notoriety of its stars, made money, but garnered attack reviews. Elizabeth read one good review in a Los Angeles newspaper and threatened to sue for libel. "How dare this god damn writer falsely claim *The Sandpiper* is anything but total shit!"

***

After finishing *The Sandpiper* in that studio outside Paris, Elizabeth and Burton flew to Naples where a long limousine took them south to the coastal resort of Amalfi, perched on a cliff hundreds of feet above the sea.

Here, according to a story that appeared in *The New York Post,* Burton and Elizabeth staged one of their epic battles. Guests seated on the main terrace of their hotel heard Elizabeth's screams of rage, and witnessed a most unusual sight.

In Paris, she had purchased thirty-seven exquisite tailor-made suits for Burton. While still on their hangers, each of them was thrown from her cliff-hanging terrace into the sea. She also tossed a box of his jewelry, including two very valuable watches, some rings, and other items. The loss of the jewelry alone was estimated at $75,000.

What had sparked her rage was a report that Burton had been seen leaving the hotel bar shortly before noon with a big-busted Neapolitan girl who was, at least according to the manager, "a dead-ringer for Sophia Loren."

That night, when Burton returned to Elizabeth in her suite, she physically attacked him. According to Dick Hanley, "Burton fought back. There were cuts and bruises. The hotel doctor had to be summoned from his bed at around two o'clock in the morning."

"Believe it or not, when I was overseeing their breakfast service the following morning, I heard the sounds of their love-making through the bedroom door," Dick claimed.

***

After Amalfi, Elizabeth and Burton returned to Naples, where they caught a flight to Dublin. For $750,000, he'd been assigned the role of Alec Leamas, 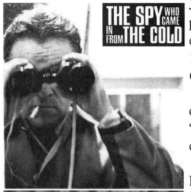 John Le Carré's disillusioned and joyless pawn in a Machiavellian game of Cold War espionage as laid out in Le Carré's bestselling 1963 novel, *The Spy Who Came in from the Cold.*

Burton got Le Carré on the phone, claiming that the screenplay's dialogue "lacked balls." Consequently, the British novelist flew into Dublin to "punch up" the script.

Elizabeth had met with the director, Martin Ritt, and urged him to cast her in the female lead, that of an innocuous and bureaucratic communist librarian. "I had to turn her down," Ritt said. "A star of Elizabeth's magnitude and brilliant glare would have totally unbalanced the stark tone of this *film noir*."

Cold War Espionage and the Comforts of the Damned

top photo: **Richard Burton**
middle photo: **Claire Bloom**
bottom photos: left **Rod Steiger**
right: **Elizabeth Taylor**

The role went instead to Claire Bloom, with whom Burton had had a torrid affair as recently as when he'd filmed *Look Back in Anger* with her in 1959. Their love had first blossomed when she had been Burton's Ophelia during his portrayal of Hamlet at the Old Vic in London.

Elizabeth was on the set every day to ensure that those old flames of passion weren't ignited again. "It was obvious that she was very uncomfortable in my presence," Bloom said.

Actually, Elizabeth need not have bothered, as those flames had been smothered years ago. Bloom was married at the time to actor Rod Steiger.

The columnist Sheilah Graham visited the set and interviewed Bloom, who was quite frank. "These days I find Burton boring," Bloom said. "A man is often boring when he's got what he wants—a beautiful wife, money, a great career. Burton is still drinking, still boasting, still reciting the same old poems and telling the same old stories."

When a written version of Bloom's comment was shown to Burton, he said, "Hell hath no fury like a woman scorned. I dumped the wench, you know."

Burton clashed several times with director Martin Ritt over his heavy drinking. "I can play any role with a big bottle of Irish whiskey in me," Burton boasted.

Ritt said, "I wasn't sympathetic to Burton's lifestyle. Nor to that of Elizabeth. She was there much of the time as an onlooker, constantly drinking from a champagne bottle which she'd open at eleven in the morning. Richard was fine until lunchtime, and then he'd join her in drinking. By the time he was back on the job, he had a buzz on."

When not consuming alcohol, the Burtons dined on such Irish game birds as widgeon, quail, and green-winged teal. On a few occasions, at Peter Parry's Soup Bowl Restaurant, Elizabeth dined with either Frank Sinatra or Laurence Harvey during their visits to Dublin.

Once, a fight broke out there between Harvey and Burton until the manager asked Harvey to leave.

The following week, Burton himself became *persona non grata* when he got completely intoxicated and tried to insert his index finger up a comely waitress's dress "to plug" her vagina.

A drunken Burton was just one of many problems Elizabeth had to confront in Ireland, even though she was not in the film. "Richard drank heavily, but Elizabeth was also sloshing around on brandy and champagne," Dick said.

During her time in Dublin, Elizabeth received a call from her mother. Sara told her that father, Francis, had suffered a stroke. "He may hang on for a week, or even a month or so, but I think it is the end."

Although she'd never been that close to her father, she flew all the way back to Los Angeles for a farewell visit.

When she returned to Dublin, she found that Burton had seemingly developed a sexual interest in Marya Mannes, a tall, statuesque beauty who had flown over from the United States to interview him for *McCall's* magazine. She also learned that Mannes and

top photo: Director **Martin Ritt**
lower photo: **Richard Burton**

Burton had headed off together into the Irish countryside on a pub crawl…or whatever.

Shortly after her return from the deathbed of her father, as Elizabeth was being driven in a Rolls-Royce by Burton's French chauffeur, Gaston Sanz, a pedestrian ran in front of the car and was struck, dying in four days.

Another tragedy followed soon after that. In St.-Jean-de-Luz on the Atlantic coast of southwestern France, Sanz's son had died in a shooting accident at a rifle range. Elizabeth flew with Sanz to Biarritz, where she was taken to the funeral parlor to identify the body. A grief-stricken Sanz could not bear to look at his son because half of his head had been blown off.

When Elizabeth returned to Ireland, she learned that a bandit had broken into her hotel suite and made off with $50,000 of her jewelry.

When *The Spy Who Came in from the Cold* was released, it was a big success at the box office, and critics hailed it as "the best Burton film ever." That critical acclaim manifested itself at Oscar time, when he received a nomination for Best Actor.

Although he didn't expect to win, he was still very disappointed when the Oscar went to Lee Marvin for his role in *Cat Ballou.*

Burton had chosen not to fly into Hollywood to attend the Academy Award presentations. In a hotel suite in Paris, he became drunk and belligerent waiting for an announcement of the winner. When he learned that he'd lost, he attacked Elizabeth, as if blaming her for his defeat. "The bloody fucking prize went to one of your lovers, Lee Marvin." He'd apparently heard about Elizabeth's brief fling with Marvin during their filming together of *Raintree County.*

"Did you also fuck my three other competitors?" Burton asked her, referring to Laurence Olivier, nominated for *Othello;* Rod Steiger for *The Pawnbroker;* and Oskar Werner for *Ship of Fools.*

"Did *I* fuck one of the nominees?" Elizabeth asked sarcastically. "Ask the same question of yourself." She was no doubt referring to Burton's long-ago affair with Olivier.

***

Before returning to America, Elizabeth wanted a vacation, and Burton booked her a luxurious villa at Cap d'Antibes on the French Riviera. They arrived together in Nice, where they were greeted by the paparazzi and reporters.

While in their villa, Ernest Lehmen sent them a film script. The Burtons had met Lehman during their filming of *The Sandpiper.* Previously, he'd written the screenplays for some excellent films, including *Somebody Up There Likes Me* (1956), *Sweet Smell of Success* (1957), and *North By Northwest* (1959). At the time he contacted the Burtons, he'd just completed the screenplay for *The*

Sound of Music (1965).

Burton was out on the beach that day, drinking far too much beer in the hot sun, and Elizabeth was suffering from a cold, and wanted to stay in bed.

Dick brought her Lehman's screenplay.

"I have to tell you," he said. "You're far too young and beautiful to play the lead in this."

"That's a switch," she said. "An actress is usually told she's too old." She took the script from him. "I need a refill on that champagne."

She picked up the manuscript and was surprised to see that it was a screen adaptation of Edward Albee's gritty three-hour award-winning play, *Who's Afraid of Virginia Woolf?*, which had played to sold-out crowds on Broadway beginning in October of 1962.

"They're offering this to me?" she asked in astonishment. "I read two days ago that Albee said the parts are going to Bette Davis and James Mason."

"Perhaps not," Dick said. "Why not Elizabeth Taylor and her consort, Richard Burton?"

***

Both Elizabeth and Burton wanted Mike Nichols to direct *Who's Afraid of Virginia Woolf?*. He'd been a cabaret entertainer and had directed plays on Broadway, but never a movie. Even so, Burton and Elizabeth insisted on him, and Jack Warner, who was releasing the movie, finally agreed.

Whereas Edward Albee's raw and raunchy dialogues had been acceptable as part of a live performance on Broadway, Warner feared that its obscenities would antagonize the Hollywood censors. He pointed out "thirteen god damns, three bastards, seven buggers, four screws, four sons-of-bitches or SOBs, and twelve variations of Christ's name taken in vain, as in 'Jesus H. Christ.' There were also references to scrotums and one reference to 'a right ball.'"

Ultimately, Warners decided to defy the censorship code and released the film with much of the original dialogue intact. Writing in *The New York Times,* Stanley Kauffman noted that when Burton delivered the line about "hump the hostess," old-fashioned Hollywood censorship came to an end.

When Albee's play had opened on Broadway, many critics claimed that it was really about two gay couples masquerading as straight. One critic wrote, "The dialogue should have been uttered by two gay queens, but Warner Brothers changed it to male/female relationship for the sake of the box office."

Elizabeth and Burton were offered a combined $4 million for their involvement in the shooting, which lasted from July to December of 1965. The first scenes were shot on location on the leafy campus of Smith College at Northampton, Massachusetts.

At first, the college's president did not want such a racy screenplay associated with his college, as he feared it would hold Smith up to ridicule. But after he received a $150,000 gift from Warner, and perhaps after realizing the literary and theatrical merit of the project, he changed his mind.

Initially, Jack Warner had thought that Elizabeth was far too young to play Martha and that Burton was much too strong to play such a spineless professor.

Ingrid Bergman was considered for the role of Martha, as were Rosalind Russell and Patricia Neal. "I got my hopes up," Neal later said, "but once again, I lost a choice role to Taylor, and I was still furious over losing *Suddenly, Last Summer.*"

Cary Grant was considered for the role of George, even Henry Fonda. Arthur Hill had created the role effectively on Broadway, and he was a candidate "for a day." Peter O'Toole agreed to do it, but Warner preferred Jack Lemmon, who refused. "This gutless creature would destroy my male image," Lemmon said.

"The fucker didn't mind dressing up like a girl with Marilyn Monroe and Tony Curtis in *Some Like It Hot,*" Warner retorted.

Connie Stevens, the future wife of Eddie Fisher, wanted to play the whiny second female lead, but the role eventually went to Sandy Dennis. Robert Redford was asked to play the second male lead, but notified Warner, "I wouldn't even read the script." The part eventually went to the very talented George Segal.

In preparation for her role as the middle-aged Martha, Elizabeth enjoyed packing on twenty-five pounds, devouring all the junk food and drinking all the alcohol she wanted.

Nichols had some reservations about the deliberate transformation of Elizabeth into the stout, vulgar, embittered, and frumpy Martha. "It's like asking a chocolate milkshake to do the work of a double gin martini. Wardrobe went through eight different wigs before Elizabeth and I could decide on the right one."

After the first week of shooting, and watching Elizabeth and Burton emotionally destroying one another during rehearsals and in front of a camera, Dick Hanley finally agreed that the roles were right for his employers. "Actually, it was type casting," he told Nichols. "All they had to do was transfer their off-screen battles onto the screen."

Of the film, Elizabeth wrote: "I think Martha is a desperate woman who has the softness of the underbelly of a baby turtle. She covers it up with the toughness of the shell, which she paints red. Her veneer is bawdy; it's sloppy, it's slouchy, it's snarly. But there are moments when the façade cracks and you see the vulnerability and the infinite pain."

One scene called for Elizabeth to spit in Burton's face. Not pleased, the director ordered take after take until she got it right.

"At first, I thought it was rather lewd," Burton said to Dick. "But eventually, it was a turn-on. It gave me a hard-on. But every day after shooting, I went back to my dressing room and fondled my balls. I wanted to make sure Elizabeth hadn't castrated me."

"During the filming of *Who's Afraid of Virginia Woolf?* our director, Mike Nichols, along with Burton and Elizabeth, privately entertained some super A-list guests," Dick said. "It was pure gossip, but members of the crew claimed that Nichols was dating Gloria Steinem, but that  he was merely using her as a beard to cover up his romance with Jackie Kennedy. He was crazy about the former First Lady. One day, he shut down production, leaving his superstars stranded while he flew to New York City to be with Jackie. When he returned, Nichols looked like the cat who'd just swallowed the canary."

As biographer Alexander Walker put it: "If *Who's Afraid of Virginia Woolf?* represented a

Two views of **Elizabeth Taylor as Martha** in
Who's Afraid of Virginia Woolf?
Lower photo: "Castrating George"

Marlene Dietrich
to Elizabeth Taylor: "My dear, you are brave. Imagine having the guts to perform with *real* actors."

Judy Garland:
"A bad moment onstage"

What not to say or do at a drunken dinner party: **Princess Margaret** with **Anthony Armstrong-Jones**, Earl of Snowdon

coming-of-age for Elizabeth in more than one sense, the experience of playing it did not leave Burton unscathed. In him, it sowed the seed of discontent with their relationship. Playing an unfulfilled man touched a guilty dread that all the star appurtenances, all the spending in the world couldn't extirpate. He needed to succeed as himself, on his own terms, and not as someone else's husband—be it Martha's or Elizabeth's."

On September 23, 1965, the crew left Northampton, Massachusetts and flew to Los Angeles to complete the film. On the sound stage at Warner Brothers, Burton celebrated his fortieth birthday, although he seemed none too happy about it. To cheer him up, Elizabeth presented him with a white Oldsmobile Toronado.

He received another gift too—a surprise visit from Marlene Dietrich. She appeared on the set in time to watch a drunken scene with all four actors—Elizabeth, Segal, Burton, and Dennis.

When Nichols called "cut," Dietrich rushed over to Burton and kissed him passionately on the lips. "Oh, darling, you were *vonderful,* so *vonderful.* How marvelous. I see an Oscar in your future."

Finally, she turned to Elizabeth and gave her a very light peck on the cheek. "Elizabeth, my dear, you are brave. Imagine having the guts to perform with *real* actors."

"Guts I have," Elizabeth said. "When I get home, Richard and I are going to fuck like bunnies."

Back at their rented home that night, Elizabeth said to Burton, "So you've fucked Marlene Dietrich. It was obvious to everybody that you two world-class whores weren't meeting for the first time. Marlene seems to get off fucking all my husbands—Michael Wilding, Mike Todd, Eddie Fisher, Richard Burton himself. I wonder if she ever made it with Nicky Hilton."

A week later, arrangements were made for Elizabeth to dine with Lord Snowdon (Anthony Armstrong-Jones) and Princess Margaret at Le Bistro in Los Angeles, where Judy Garland was scheduled to sing.

Whereas the A-list quartet sat together at a table for four, Dick Hanley and Roddy McDowall sat at an adjoining table in case they were needed.

Dick later revealed that Elizabeth and Burton were "about the drunkest I had ever seen them."

During one of his rambling monologues, Elizabeth loudly interrupted her husband in a style that evoked something Martha might have said to her husband George in *Who's Afraid of Virginia Woolf?*. "For *Chrissakes*," she shouted at him. "Shut your fucking mouth!"

"The most embarrassing point of the evening came when Burton reached in and fondled the breast of Her Royal Highness, Princess Margaret." Dick said. "I nearly fainted. The Princess got up and headed to the women's room. When she returned, Judy was singing but tripped on a microphone cord. In front of the entire bistro, Burton yelled, 'THAT JUDY—DRUNK AGAIN!'"

Princess Margaret and Lord Snowdon quickly made their excuses and left.

Burton called the next day to apologize, but the Princess would not come to the phone. Burton told Dick, "Oh shit, the next time I visit London, the Queen will banish me to the Tower."

Who's Afraid of Virginia Woolf? cost $7.5 million, the most expensive black-and-white movie ever released. It opened in theaters in June of 1966, challenging and changing forever the censorship standards of the industry's thirty-six year old Production Code.

Edward Albee's tense drama was both a financial and artistic success, earning Oscar nominations for both Elizabeth and Burton.

"Rarely in the history of the Academy has an actress of Elizabeth's stature faced such weak competition," claimed columnist James Bacon.

Other nominees for the Best Actress Oscar of 1966 included Anouk Aimée for her performance in *A Man and a Woman;* and Ida Kaminska for *The Shop on Main Street.* Evoking the competitiveness of two sisters, Olivia de Havilland and Joan Fontaine, two other sisters, the Redgraves (Lynn and Vanessa) were also nominated, Lynn for her role in *Georgy Girl* and Vanessa for *Morgan.*

Unlike Elizabeth, Burton faced stiff competition at the Oscars, and he knew it, predicting that Paul Scofield would win for his role in *A Man for All Seasons.* Burton resented all the adoring press reports that referred to Scofield as "one of the giants of the British stage."

Other nominees included Alan Arkin for his role in *The Russians Are Coming;* Michael Caine in *Alfie;* and Steve McQueen for his role in *The Sand Pebbles,* but none of those other actors was a favorite.

The Academy Award presentations were scheduled for the evening of April

10, 1966 at the Santa Monica Civic Auditorium.

Elizabeth and Burton were in the south of France at the time, filming *The Comedians* (1967), a politicized satire of Haiti under the repressive military regime of "Papa Doc" Duvalier. [Duvalier had refused entry into Haiti to the film crew.] Just so that she could be with Burton, she had agreed to appear in a supporting role, giving him—for the first time—top billing.

She wanted to fly back to Los Angeles for the Oscar ceremony, but he refused to let her go, despite her conviction, "I'm bound to win." She was therefore forced to call Anne Bancroft and ask her if she'd accept the Oscar in her absence.

Burton told Dick Hanley that he could not tell her the real reason he didn't want them to fly back to L.A. "I feel I'm going to lose, and I don't want to be humiliated in front of 150 million TV viewers while Elizabeth lords it over me with her Oscar. Instead, I told her that I'd had a bad dream, and that my dream was a premonition that she'd die in a plane crash like Mike Todd."

Shortly after the winners for the year's Best Actor and Actress were announced in Santa Monica, Peter Lawford put through a call to Elizabeth in France, telling her that she had won the Oscar, but that Burton had lost.

"I couldn't believe it," Dick later said to Roddy McDowall. "Instead of being overjoyed at her second Oscar, all I heard was this torrent of profanities. She was absolutely hysterically furious and in a violent rage that Burton had lost."

The majority of Academy members had been impressed with Elizabeth's bravery in abandoning her customary beauty as a vehicle for her portrayal of a sloppy, foul-mouthed, graying voluptuary like Martha. But a violent storm of criticism broke out when she didn't show up in person to receive her Oscar. Among other things, she was accused of not respecting the Academy.

The criticism was compounded when Sandy Dennis did not show up to receive her own Oscar as Best Supporting Actress either. Dennis was on the East Coast at the time, filming *Sweet November* (1968). She could have flown to Los Angeles, but confessed, "I have a fear of flying."

The evening's host, Bob Hope, quipped: "I know why Elizabeth couldn't come. Leaving Richard in Paris would be like leaving Jackie Gleason locked in a deli." The Oscar historian, Anthony Holden, said, "Burton was snubbed because he'd antagonized most of the men in Hollywood by sleeping with their wives."

Elizabeth seemed to know that with her Oscar for *Virginia Woolf,* she'd reached the apogee of her film career. More riches, more diamonds, more husbands would be in her future, but a role like Martha would never be offered again.

In their reactions to her lackluster future films, critics would often be vicious, as in the case when she appeared with Burton in *Doctor Faustus* (1967). The critic for *The New York Times* claimed, "Her eyeballs and teeth were dripping pink in what seems to be a hellish combination of conjunctivitis and trench mouth." Even more scathing attacks awaited her.

Biographer Kitty Kelley commented on Elizabeth's new persona in the years ahead: "With a raunchy laugh and *double entendre* lines, Elizabeth Taylor has become the cinema's quintessential shrew, cursing and castrating her way across the screen in a series of unsuccessful movies."

Even in reference to many of her future roles, Rex Reed referred to her as "a hideous parody of herself—a fat, sloppy, yelling, screaming banshee," sometimes giving the impression that he was writing about her performance as Martha.

In 1968, Burton was still married to Elizabeth, although he admitted to a friend, "I often experience the middle aged catastrophe of falling in love with some pretty little blonde for five minutes."

The year found him cast with Elizabeth in one of their biggest mistakes, *Boom!* (1968), in which they starred with Noël Coward playing "The Witch of Capri."

BOOM!

Boom! was based on the Tennessee Williams play *The Milk Train Doesn't Stop Here Anymore,* which had starred Tallulah Bankhead and Tab Hunter, and which had closed on Broadway, an abject flop, early in 1964 after only five performances.

Actually, Bankhead had recommended Elizabeth for the role. "Who better to play Flora Goforth, the richest woman in the world, a promiscuous, pill-ravaged, drunken slut who is the world's biggest joke than Elizabeth Taylor? She

Two views of **Elizabeth Taylor** in *Boom!* as the richest woman in the world. *lower photo*: In Kabuki costume with **Noël Coward** as the Witch of Capri need only play herself."

Also in 1968, Burton wanted to show his continuing love for Elizabeth by purchasing the world famous 33.19 carat Krupp diamond for her for $307,000. The diamond had a notorious association with the Krupp family, German industrialists who had been involved in the deportation and forced labor of Jews during the Nazi era.

Elizabeth, who had converted to Judaism in 1959, said, "I thought it perfect for a nice Jewish girl like me to end up owning the Krupp diamond. How ironic!"

To buy the diamond, Burton flew to New York and bid against America's most fabled jeweler, Harry Winston.

Back in London, he presented it to Elizabeth aboard their yacht, *Kalizma,* moored on the Thames River. She was thrilled with the diamond, later describing it as "so complete and so ravishing, like the steps leading into eternity and beyond."

But ten years later, in 1978, Elizabeth sold it to New York dealer Henry Lamberet for $5 million, admitting to friends, "I never really liked the damn thing."

Thirty-three years later, after her death on Wednesday, March 24, 2011, at the age of 79, the Krupp Diamond was worth $30 million. She had always regretted selling it.

Shortly after Burton's presentation to her of the diamond in 1968, she said, "I was wearing it at midnight when I had the best sex of my life. In fact, the best fuck before or after."

Aboard their yacht, *Kalizma,* one night in 1973, she stood with Burton and spoke what were perhaps the most melodramatic words she'd ever uttered. She sounded like Princess Alexandra del Lago, the fictional, spectacularly unfulfilled heroine of Tennessee Williams' *Sweet Bird of Youth,* a role she'd play on TV in 1989.

"That old enemy of time is marching in on me. I must inevitably face the final curtain, which is likely to come sooner than later." She turned to Burton. "You will always be at my side, won't you?"

"I'll never leave you," he promised.

"We will live happily ever after, won't we?" she asked.

"That we will, luv. Only problem is, what comes after they lived happily ever after?"

***

"Everything that I have done in my life that is a mistake, I will admit is a mistake and answer for it. But I am not going to answer for an image created by hundreds of people who do not know what's true or false. That would take me from here to Doomsday."

—Elizabeth Taylor

Elizabeth Taylor
1932 - 2011
REST IN PEACE

THANKS FOR THE MEMORIES

Over decades of meeting and talking with celebrities, Darwin Porter accumulated a vast trove of stories about Elizabeth Taylor. "Everyone who I came into contact with, from Mary Astor to Tallulah Bankhead, had a tale to relate about Elizabeth, either good or bad, often a combination of both," Darwin said.

Of the people sucked into the whirlpool enveloping Elizabeth, no sources were more insightful than actor **Roddy McDowall** and Elizabeth's secretary, **Dick Hanley.**

"I think these two men knew Elizabeth and her secrets better than anybody, and they were dear friends of mine," Darwin said.

As a child actor, Roddy bonded with Elizabeth on the set of the 1943 *Lassie Come Home,* and they remained "soul mates" until death.

Dick Hanley had been the private secretary of Louis B. Mayer for many years before going to work for Mike Todd. After Todd's death, Dick became Elizabeth's private secretary and "handler."

According to Darwin, "Dick and Roddy talked endlessly about Elizabeth, but not for publication. They loved her dearly, but were also aware of her vanities and foibles. Wherever they are today, I hope they forgive me for sharing their confidences about Elizabeth with her thousands of fans, though during my conversations about her at the time, they were 'off the record.'"

"For the insights of Dick and Roddy, and to countless others, including Peter Lawford and Janet Leigh, I remain deeply grateful," Darwin said.

Special mention should be made about contributions to this book by Van Johnson, Montgomery Clift, Stewart Granger, Sal Mineo, Shelley Winters, Peter Glenville, Ava Gardner, and Philip Burton, Darwin's neighbor in Key West. Also, Tom Drake, Judy Garland's "Boy Next Door" in *Meet Me in St. Louis,* shared experiences that have never before appeared in any book.

The first time Darwin ever saw "the violet-eyed goddess" was when he was a boy growing up in Miami. It was at a marina. Young and beautiful, Elizabeth was being escorted off a yacht by a handsome young man who turned out to be one of her first serious "beaus." It was William Pawley, Jr., who had hoped to marry her.

In later years, because of his world travels as a writer and researcher for *The Frommer Guides,* Darwin witnessed appearances by Elizabeth in such cities as Paris, London, Madrid, Rome, Monte Carlo, Cannes, and (most frequently) Los Angeles and New York.

His most memorable encounter with her was in Portofino, Italy, where Elizabeth and Richard arrived by yacht. As she made her way boutique shopping through the village, women came down from the hills, many holding up their *bambini,* hoping she'd purchase a baby boy or girl.

After surveying the hysteria she generated, Darwin, researching *Frommer's Italy* at the time, retreated to the pint-sized *La Grittà* American Bar along Portofino's waterfront. Author James Jones, who'd written the best-seller, *From Here to Eternity,* claimed that *La Grittà* was "the best waterfront bar this side of Hong Kong."

Within the hour, Elizabeth invaded the bar, accompanied by Richard Burton and Rex Harrison, each of whom had been key players in the recent filming of *Cleopatra* with her in Rome.

"My companion and I had planned to have a drink or two and then retire," Darwin said. "But we stayed until dawn and closed down the bar with the stars of *Cleopatra.* Seated only a few tables away from them, I eavesdropped on every word, although they ignored me. Much of what I learned that night, including insights into the offscreen *persona* of Miss Taylor, ended up in my chapter on *Cleopatra* within this book."

The only real social contact Darwin ever had with Elizabeth was in Puerto Vallarta, Mexico, where she had flown with Burton while he co-starred in *The Night of the Iguana* with Ava Gardner.

Darwin was a guest at the rented villa of Tennessee Williams where Elizabeth, without Burton, arrived as the guest of honor. "She had a wicked wit and amused us with outrageous stories told in 'triple X-rated' language. She was an amazing, fascinating woman."

Her escort that night was a young Mexican screenwriter, Jose Bolaños, who at the time was infamous throughout Hollywood as Marilyn Monroe's last lover.

"Thousands of fans adored Elizabeth, of course," Darwin said. "But at certain times in her life, she had almost as many detractors. I personally adored her. Her memory will remain forever. Incidentally, she had a wonderful smell. Even when she left Tennessee's villa that night, her aroma lingered. It was intoxicating."

ABOUT THE AUTHORS

Formerly a bureau chief and entertainment columnist for *The Miami Herald,* **Darwin Porter** is one of the world's leading celebrity biographers, the winner of almost thirty literary awards. He has explored the lives of such figures as Humphrey Bogart, Katharine Hepburn, Marlon Brando, Merv Griffin, Paul Newman, Steve McQueen, Howard Hughes, Michael Jackson, John F. Kennedy, Frank Sinatra, J. Edgar Hoover, and Marilyn Monroe. In *Damn You, Scarlett O'Hara,* the private lives of Laurence Olivier and Vivien Leigh were laid out in painstaking eloquence.

He is currently at work on *Linda Lovelace's Deep Throat: Degradation, Porno Chic, and the Rise of Feminism.* That book is scheduled for a spring of 2013 release, simultaneous with the release of an upcoming movie about Lovelace's tragic life and career.

Danforth Prince is a former staff member of the Paris bureau of *The New York Times.* With Darwin Porter, he has written more travel guides to more foreign countries than any other writer in history, specializing in the nations of Europe and the island nations of the Caribbean. He has co-authored four volumes devoted to film criticism, and has also co-authored four volumes within Blood Moon's popular Babylon series—*Hollywood Babylon, It's Back!; Hollywood Babylon Strikes Again!; Frank Sinatra, The Boudoir Singer;* and *The Kennedys, All the Gossip Unfit to Print.* As president and founder of Blood Moon Productions, he was honored in 2011 as "Publisher of the Year" at a consortium of literary critics and book marketers spearheaded by the J.M. Northern Media Group.

Publishing in collaboration with the National Book Network, he has documented some of the controversies associated with his stewardship of Blood Moon in more than 40 videotaped documentaries, book trailers, public speeches, and TV or radio interviews. Any of these can be watched, without charge, by performing a search for "Danforth Prince" on **YouTube.com,** checking him out on Facebook, or by clicking on www.BloodMoonProductions.com.

During the rare moments when he isn't writing, editing, or promoting Blood Moon, he works out at a gym, rescues stray animals, talks to strangers, and attends Episcopal mass every Sunday.

INDEX

569

205, 206, 207, 208, 209, 210, 211, 212, 246, 296, 444
Griffith, Corinne 135, 136
Grimes, Tammy 456
Grobel, Lawrence 524
Grossinger, Jennie 538
Grossinger, Tania 449
Grossinger's 325, 417, 442
Growing Up at Grossinger's 449
Grunwald, Anatole de 511
Gstaad (Switzerland) 429, 485, 501, 508, 509
Gstaad Palace Hotel (Gstaad, Switzerland) 509
Guilaroff, Sidney 52, 125, 142, 401, 424, 454, 475, 477, 489
Guinness, Alec 320, 456
Guys and Dolls 349, 355
Haggart, Stanley Mills 267, 279, 411
Hagman, Larry 64
Haines, William 73, 74, 75, 106
Hale, Barbara 202
Halliday, Richard 63
Hals, Frans "The Elder" 11, 221
Halsman, Philippe 166, 167, 168
Halsman, Yvonne 167
Hamlet 149, 526, 528, 529, 530, 532, 533, 534, 535, 536, 538, 540
Hammersmith Is Out 512
Hampton, Hope 203
Hanley, Dick 65, 67, 68, 72, 74, 76, 79, 80, 102, 108, 110, 120, 129, 139, 168, 170, 178, 203, 215, 225, 251, 257, 284, 300, 305, 320, 324, 325, 330, 334, 340, 347, 371, 375, 376, 377, 380, 381, 384, 385, 387, 398, 399, 400, 401, 403, 404, 408, 409, 411, 413, 415, 419, 424, 426, 428, 430, 437, 441, 444, 448, 450, 465, 466, 468, 472, 474, 481, 485, 486, 491, 492, 493, 495, 500, 502, 507, 508, 516, 519, 521, 523, 525, 527, 531, 532, 536, 547, 549, 552, 555, 556, 561
Harding, Laura 433
Hardwicke, Cedric 388
Hardy, Thomas 17, 537
Harlow, Jean 60, 106, 145, 222, 278
Harriman, Averell 397
Harris, Derek (see Derek, John)
Harris, Lawson 45
Harris, Richard 516
Harrison, Rex 307, 455, 473, 474, 475, 478, 514, 562
Hart, Kitty Carlisle 536
Harvard Lampoon, The 262
Harvard University 132
Harvey, Laurence 446, 549
Harwyn Night Club (NYC) 416

Hasty Heart, The 150
Haver, June 309
Hawks, Howard 193
Hawthorne Elementary School (Los Angeles) 33
Hayden, Sterling 328
Hayes, John Michael 445, 447
Hayward, Susan 152, 154, 199, 346, 413, 453
Hayworth, Rita 42, 72, 124, 229, 249, 278, 300, 301, 309, 349, 426, 427, 429
Head, Edith 63, 167, 183, 195, 196
Hearst, William Randolph 68, 70, 73, 74, 154, 289
Heaven Knows, Mr. Allison 367
Hefner, Hugh 46
Heiress, The 189, 190, 244, 365
Heisig family, the 546, 547
Hellman, Lillian 216, 244
Hemingway, Ernest 155, 271
Henie, Sonja 249
Hepburn, Audrey 299, 327, 390, 439, 473, 503
Hepburn, Katharine 47, 60, 102, 103, 126, 142, 145, 192, 213, 215, 300, 323, 432, 433, 435, 436, 437, 440, 489, 517
Herlie, Eileen 532
Heston, Charlton 495
Heymann, C. David 16, 244, 504, 541
Hickman, Darryl 58
Hidden Well Ranch (Pleasant Valley, Nevada) 422
High Heels 178, 179
High Noon 355
Hilda 177
Hill, Arthur 552
Hilton, Baron 204
Hilton, Conrad, Sr. 202, 203, 204, 214, 216, 219, 220, 223, 225, 226, 231, 245, 252, 255, 320
Hilton, Nicky 42, 64, 135, 166, 174, 175, 180, 200, 201, 202, 203, 205, 206, 210, 211, 212, 214, 215, 219, 220, 221, 223, 224, 225, 226, 227, 228, 230, 233, 234, 236, 238, 239, 244, 245, 246, 248, 249, 250, 251, 252, 254, 255, 256, 257, 258, 260, 267, 270, 281, 294, 342, 381, 405, 490, 525, 554
Hit Parade, the 79
Hitchcock, Alfred 156, 166, 270
Hitler, Adolf 13, 273, 316, 390
Hoffman, Charles 81
Hoffman, Dustin 194
Hogan, Jerry 373
Hold That Ghost 29
Holden, Anthony 556
Holden, William 56, 139, 199, 328, 380, 448,

Mann, Thomas 166
Mannes, Marya 549
Mannix, Eddie 400
Manouche 234
Mansfield, Jayne 256
Mansfield, Stephanie 95, 543
Manson, Charles 544
March, Fredric 218
Margaret Rose, Princess of England 18, 446, 514, 555
Marie Antoinette, Queen of France 183, 384, 458
Marina, Duchess of Kent (aka Princess Marina of Greece & Denmark) 382
Marlowe, Christopher 530
Marshal, Alan 46
Martin, Dean 136, 417, 462, 463, 465, 471, 503
Martin, Jeanne 463
Martin, Mart 72
Martin, Mary 63, 209
Martin, Tony 47
Martinelli, Elsa 511
Marvell, Andrew 536
Marvin, Lee 355, 356, 550
Marx, Samuel 34, 161, 236, 440
Mary Poppins 39
Mary's Bar (Malibu, CA) 294
Mason, James 23, 297, 299, 519, 551
Mason, Morgan 540
Mason, Pamela 299
Mason, Rev. Leonard 531
Mass, Joachim 484
Mata Hari 237
Mature, Victor 47, 308, 309, 310, 318, 320, 339, 340, 372, 374, 426
Maugham, W. Somerset 540
Maxim's (Paris) 42, 115, 230, 233, 234, 494
Maxwell, Elsa 229, 230, 232, 233, 234, 235, 246, 259, 277, 381, 388, 417, 428
Mayer, Louis B. 26, 27, 35, 40, 44, 48, 52, 55, 63, 65, 66, 67, 70, 73, 76, 78, 79, 81, 97, 105, 110, 111, 120, 122, 123, 129, 142, 161, 172, 180, 181, 191, 213, 214, 222, 249, 324, 348, 421, 427, 438, 561
Mayo, Virginia 137
Maytime in Mayfair 272
MCA, Inc. 296
McCall's magazine 15, 549
McCambridge, Mercedes 329, 370, 435
McCarthy, Eugene 205
McCarthy, Glen 226
McCarthy, Joseph 192, 305
McCarthy, Kevin 205, 216, 248, 358, 359, 360
McCarthy, Mary 205

McClintock, Patricia 256
McClory, Kevin 322, 323, 326, 330, 345, 346, 347, 349, 350, 356, 363, 379
McCullers, Carson 535
McDonald, Marie ("The Body") 307, 308, 364
McDowall, Roddy 15, 27, 34, 35, 41, 43, 44, 45, 46, 55, 58, 68, 69, 91, 93, 99, 119, 127, 130, 139, 153, 159, 178, 181, 195, 205, 210, 212, 246, 247, 278, 287, 300, 306, 322, 331, 335, 341, 405, 421, 452, 455, 456, 464, 475, 480, 485, 486, 492, 497, 500, 501, 502, 503, 508, 510, 528, 555, 556, 561
MCL Films 430, 525
McPherson, Aimee Semple 485
McQueen, Steve 194, 555
Me and My Gal 212
Meadows, Jayne 388
Medina, The 292
Meet Me in St. Louis 57, 170, 315, 542, 561
Menjou, Adolphe 216
Menninger Clinic (Topeka, Kansas) 419
Menzies, William Cameron 326
Mercouri, Melina 516
Merlo, Frank 244, 435
Merman, Ethel 267, 388
Merrill, Dina 446, 536
Merry Widow, The 88
Mertz, Egon 53
Meyer, Johnny 168, 175, 176, 181, 187
MGM, Inc. 34, 35, 36, 39, 40, 49, 72, 77, 78, 90, 91, 102, 106, 110, 118, 122, 125, 128, 135, 144, 145, 146, 147, 151, 161, 162, 164, 165, 168, 169, 179, 213, 214, 221, 222, 223, 235, 249, 251, 253, 261, 262, 263, 269, 275, 287, 307, 315, 321, 324, 351, 353, 357, 366, 368, 372, 393, 395, 400, 411, 424, 437, 438, 440, 447, 448, 541
Miami Herald, The 563
Mildred Pierce 61, 316
Milk Train Doesn't Stop Here Anymore, The 350, 557
Miller, Ann 137, 204, 223
Miller, Arthur 430
Miller, Steve 366
Millionairess, The 510
Mills, Freddie 451
Mineo, Sal 72, 329, 335, 448, 561
Minnelli, Liza 213, 539
Minnelli, Vincente 212, 213, 214, 539, 540, 542, 543, 546
Miranda, Carmen 97, 98
Misfits, The 198, 516
Mismaloya Peninsula (Mexico) 516, 521
Mistinguett 232, 235

Mitchum, Robert 229, 258, 328, 354, 440
Mocambo, the (Los Angeles) 275
Modern Screen magazine 71, 470
Moffat, Ivan 195, 256
Mohammed V, King of Morocco 231
"Mon Homme" 232
Monogram Pictures, Inc. 39
Monroe, Marilyn 41, 52, 88, 117, 127, 166,
    176, 179, 187, 198, 217, 243, 250, 251,
    252, 253, 259, 293, 297, 311, 315, 316,
    341, 364, 391, 406, 407, 421, 430, 439,
    448, 454, 462, 463, 464, 465, 468, 469,
    483, 484, 488, 490, 518, 526, 527, 528,
    543, 546, 552
Montalban, Ricardo 289, 526
Montbatten, Patricia 157
Monte Sano Hospital (Los Angeles) 111
Montez, Maria 154, 307
Montgomery, Elizabeth 286
Montgomery, Robert 32
Monush, Barry 29
Moonjean, Hank 484
Moore, Terry 131, 132, 175, 176, 177, 178,
    179, 180, 202, 256
Moorehead, Agnes 355, 422
Moran, Bugs 404
Morgan 555
Morgan, Jane 415
Morley, Robert 150
Moscow Nights 512
Mosley, Leonard 380
Motion Picture Herald 451
Motion Picture Magazine 470
Mountbatten, Lord 73, 150, 156
Movie Mirror magazine 470
Mrs. Miniver 120
Murphy, George 82, 87, 88, 132
Murray, Mae 88
Murrow, Edward R. 349
Mussolini, Benito 13, 474
Mutiny on the Bounty 453
My Cousin Rachel 298
My Fair Lady 307, 473, 503
My Husband, Rock Hudson 337
My Love Affair With Jewelry 347
Naar, Joe 136
Nabokov, Vladimir 41, 523
Naked and the Dead, The 216
Napoléon 390
National Book Network 563
National Velvet 28, 47, 51, 53, 55, 59, 65,
    69, 74, 87, 119, 131, 162, 168, 272,
    448, 461
Nazimova, Alla 4
Neagle, Anna 148, 157, 272, 278, 280
Neal, Glenda 128
Neal, Patricia 150, 152, 153, 221, 552

Nell, Susan 373, 383, 438
Nelson, Barry 133
Nelson, Ricky 492
Never Say Never Again 323
Neverland Ranch, the 471
New Statesman, The 505
New York Daily News 370, 417
New York Herald Tribune 125, 314, 424,
    505, 534, 537
New York Post, The 199, 418, 443, 547
New York Times, The 91, 314, 437, 457,
    505, 536, 551, 557, 563
New Yorker, The 169
Newman, Paul 194, 361, 362, 393, 395,
    402, 408, 411, 412, 524
Newspaper Fund, The 383
Newsweek 534
Niarchos, Tina (see Onassis, Athina
    Livanos)
Nichols, Mike 456, 501, 551, 552, 553
Nicklaus, Frederick 519
Night and Day 64
Night of the Iguana, The 515, 516, 517, 519,
    520, 521, 523, 536, 540, 562
Nightmare Alley 260
Nine Lives of Mike Todd, The 397
Ninotchka 26
Niven, David 104, 156, 190, 277, 304, 348,
    350, 380, 397, 413
Niven, Hjordis 397
Nizer, Louis, Esq. 503
No Highway in the Sky 273, 274
No More Ladies 107
"Norah" 443
North By Northwest 550
Novak, Kim 72, 415, 427, 454, 539, 540
Nude With Violin 383
Nureyev, Rudolf 444, 514
O'Brien, Margaret 31, 35, 39, 99, 126, 162,
    199
O'Connell, Jerry 36
O'Hara, John 440
O'Keefe Theatre (Toronto) 529
O'Neill, Eugene 484
O'Toole, Peter 433, 513, 531, 552
Oates, Fred 496
Oberon, Merle 349, 415, 427, 527
*Odd Man Out: A Memoir of the Hollywood
    Ten* 354
"Oh! My Pa-Pa" 414
Oklahoma! 350
Old Man and the Sea, The 413
Old Soldier's Story, The 121
Olivier, Laurence 5, 13, 24, 47, 122, 149,
    244, 249, 302, 304, 305, 372, 397, 453,
    455, 479, 480, 510, 512, 529, 530, 550
Olympic Winner 237

577

582

If you liked this book, check out these other titles from

BLOOD MOON PRODUCTIONS

Entertainment About How America Interprets Its Celebrities

Blood Moon Productions is a New York-based publishing enterprise dedicated to researching, salvaging, and indexing the oral histories of America's entertainment industry.

Reorganized with its present name in 2004, Blood Moon originated in 1997 as the Georgia Literary Association, a vehicle for the promotion of obscure writers from America's Deep South. For many years, Blood Moon was a key player in the writing, research, and editorial functions of THE FROMMER GUIDES, a respected name in travel publishing.

Blood Moon maintains a back list of 25 critically acclaimed biographies, film guides, and novels. Its titles are distributed within North America and Australia by the National Book Network (www.NBNBooks.com), within the U.K. by Turnaround (www.Turnaround-uk.com), and through secondary wholesalers and online retailers everywhere.

Since 2004, Blood Moon has been awarded dozens of nationally recognized literary prizes. They've included both silver and bronze medals from the IPPY (Independent Publishers Assn.) Awards; four nominations and two Honorable Mentions for BOOK OF THE YEAR from Foreword Reviews; nominations from The Ben Franklin Awards; two separate awards for Best Summer Reading from the "Beach Book Festival," and Awards and Honorable Mentions from the New England, the Los Angeles, the Paris, the New York, the San Francisco, and the Hollywood Book Festivals.

For more about us, including access to a growing number of videotaped book trailers, each accessible via YouTube, click on **WWW.BLOODMOONPRODUCTIONS.COM,** visit our page on Facebook, or refer to the pages which immediately follow.

Thanks for your interest, best wishes, and happy reading.

Danforth Prince, President
Blood Moon Productions, Ltd.

INSIDE LINDA LOVELACE'S
DEEP THROAT

DEGRADATION, PORNO CHIC, AND THE RISE OF FEMINISM
DARWIN PORTER
AVAILABLE IN JANUARY, 2013

A Bronx-born brunette, the notorious Linda Lovelace was the starry-eyed Catholic daughter in the 1950s of a local cop who called her "Miss Holy Holy." Twenty years later, she became the most notorious actress of the 20th century.

She'd fallen in love with a tough ex-Marine, Chuck Traynor, and eventually married him, only to learn that she had become his meal ticket. He forced her at gunpoint into a role as a player within hardcore porn, including a 1971 bestiality film entitled *Dogarama*.

Her next film, shot for $20,000, was released in 1972 as *Deep Throat*. It became the largest grossing XXX-rated flick of all time, earning an estimated $750 million and still being screened all over the world. The fee she was paid was $1,200, which her husband confiscated. The sexy 70s went wild for the film. Porno chic was born, with Linda as its centerpiece.

Traynor, a sadist, pimped his wife to celebrities, charging them $2,000 per session, It became a status symbol to commission an "individualized" film clip of Linda performing her specialty. Clients included Elvis Presley, Frank Sinatra, Milton Berle, Desi Arnaz, Marlon Brando, William Holden, Peter Lawford, and Burt Lancaster. The Mafia had found its most lucrative business—pornography—since Prohibition.

After a decade of being assaulted, beaten, and humiliated, Linda, in 1980, underwent a "Born Again" transformation. She launched her own feminist anti-pornography movement, attracting such activists as Gloria Steinem, and scores of other sex industry professionals who refuted their earlier careers.

Critics claimed that Linda's *Deep Throat* changed America's sexual attitudes more than anything since the first Kinsey report in 1948, that she super-charged the feminist movement, and that to some degree, she re-defined the nation's views on obscenity.

The tragic saga of Linda Lovelace is soon to be a major motion picture.

__Darwin Porter__, author of more than a dozen critically acclaimed celebrity exposés of behind-the-scenes intrigue in the entertainment industry, was deeply involved in the Linda Lovelace saga as it unfolded in the 70s, interviewing many of the players, and raising money for the legal defense of the film's co-star, Harry Reems. In this book, he brings inside information and a never-before-published revelation on almost every page.

Softcover, 430 pages, 6"x9", with photos
ISBN 978-1-936003-33-4; Available everywhere in January of 2013

At last, the story that Hollywood has been waiting for:
Inside Information about those "Man-Eating Magyars,"
those "Hungarian Hussies from Hell,"

THE GABORS

Those Glamorous Gabors

Bombshells from Budapest

Great Courtesans of the 20th Century

DARWIN PORTER

Born in Central Europe during the twilight of the Austro-Hungarian Empire, three "*vonderful vimmen*"—Zsa Zsa, Eva, and Magda Gabor—transferred their glittery dreams and gold-digging ambitions to Hollywood. They supplemented America's most Imperial Age with "guts, glamour, and goulash," and reigned there as the Hungarian equivalents of Helen of Troy, Madame du Barry, and Madame de Pompadour.

More effectively than any army, these Bombshells from Budapest conquered kings, dukes, and princes, always with a special passion for millionaires, as they amassed fortunes, broke hearts, and amused sophisticated voyeurs on two continents. With their wit, charm, and beauty, thanks to training inspired by the glittering traditions of the Imperial Habsburgs, they became famous for being famous.

"We sold the New World high-priced goods from the Old World that it didn't need, but bought anyway," Zsa Zsa said.

In time, they would collectively entrap some 20 husbands and seduce perhaps 500 other men as well, many plucked directly from the pages of Who's Who in the World.

At long last, Blood Moon lifts the "mink-and-diamond" curtain on this amazing trio of blood-related sisters, whose complicated intrigues have never been fully explored before.

Orson Welles asserted, "The world will never see the likes of the Gabor sisters again. From the villas of Cannes to the mansions of Bel Air, they were the centerpiece of countless boudoirs. They were also the most notorious mantraps since Eve. I can personally vouch for that."

THOSE GLAMOROUS GABORS, BOMBSHELLS FROM BUDAPEST

GREAT COURTESANS OF THE 20TH CENTURY

Darwin Porter

Softcover, 400 pages, with photos

ISBN 978-1-936003-35-8

AVAILABLE IN MAY OF 2013

J. Edgar Hoover's FBI Vs. Hollywood

Darwin Porter's saga of power and corruption has a revelation on every page—cross dressing, gay parties, sexual indiscretions, hustlers for sale, alliances with the Mafia, and criminal activity by the nation's chief law enforcer.

It's all here, with chilling details about the abuse of power on the dark side of the American saga. But mostly it's the decades-long love story of America's two most powerful men who could tell presidents "how to skip rope." (Hoover's words.)

Winner of 2012 literary awards from both the **Los Angeles** and the **Hollywood Book Festivals**

INVESTIGATING THE SEXUAL SECRETS OF AMERICA'S MOST FAMOUS MEN AND WOMEN BY DARWIN PORTER

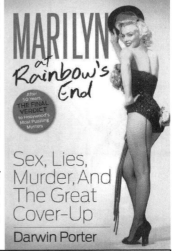

Less than an hour after the discovery of Marilyn Monroe's corpse in Brentwood, a flood of theories, tainted evidence, and conflicting testimonies began pouring out into the public landscape.

Filled with rage, hysteria, and depression, "and fed up with Jack's lies, Bobby's lies," Marilyn sought revenge and mass vindication. Her revelations at an imminent press conference could have toppled political dynasties and destroyed criminal empires. Marilyn had to be stopped...

Into this steamy cauldron of deceit, Marilyn herself emerges as a most unreliable witness during the weeks leading up to her murder. Her own deceptions, vanities, and self-delusion poured toxic accelerants on an already raging fire.

"Darwin Porter is fearless, honest and a great read. He minces no words. If the truth makes you wince and honesty offends your sensibility, stay away. It's been said that he deals in muck because he can't libel the dead. Well, it's about time someone started telling the truth about the dead and being honest about just what happened to get us in the mess in which we're in. If libel is lying, then Porter is so completely innocent as to deserve an award. In all of his works he speaks only to the truth, and although he is a hard teacher and task master, he's one we ignore at our peril. To quote Gore Vidal, power is not a toy we give to someone for being good. If we all don't begin to investigate where power and money really are in the here and now, we deserve what we get. Yes, Porter names names. The reader will come away from the book knowing just who killed Monroe. Porter rather brilliantly points to a number of motives, but leaves it to the reader to surmise exactly what happened at the rainbow's end, just why Marilyn was killed. And, of course, why we should be careful of getting exactly what we want. It's a very long tumble from the top."

—ALAN PETRUCELLI, Examiner.com, May 13, 2012

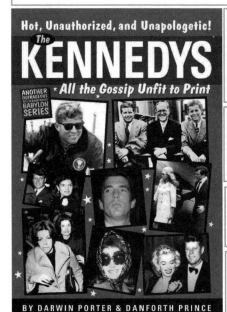

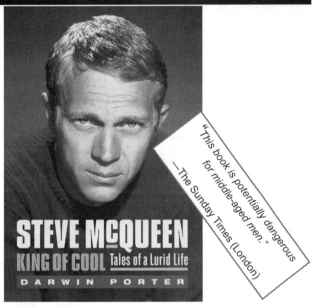

PAUL NEWMAN
THE MAN BEHIND THE BABY BLUES
HIS SECRET LIFE EXPOSED

Darwin Porter

THE MOST COURAGEOUS AND COMPELLING BIOGRAPHY OF THE ICONIC ACTOR EVER PUBLISHED

Drawn from firsthand interviews with insiders who knew Paul Newman intimately, and compiled over a period of nearly a half-century, this is the world's most honest and most revelatory biography about Hollywood's pre-eminent male sex symbol, with dozens of potentially shocking revelations.

Whereas the situations it exposes were widely known within Hollywood's inner circles, they've never before been revealed to the general public.

If you're a fan of Newman (and who do you know who isn't) you really should look at this book. It's a respectful but candid cornucopia of information about the sexual and emotional adventures of a young man on Broadway and in Hollywood.

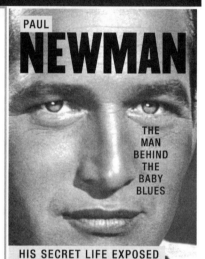

Hardcover, 520 pages, with dozens of photos. Also available for E-readers
"One wonders how he ever managed to avoid public scrutiny for so long."

ISBN 978-0-9786465-1-6

PAUL NEWMAN WAS A FAMOUS, FULL-TIME RESIDENT OF CONNECTICUT. SHORTLY AFTER HIS DEATH IN 2009, THIS TITLE WON AN HONORABLE MENTION FROM HIS NEIGHBORS AT THE NEW ENGLAND BOOK FESTIVAL

This is a pioneering and posthumous biography of a charismatic American icon. His rule over the hearts of American moviegoers lasted for more than half a century. Paul Newman was a potent, desirable, and ambiguous sex symbol, a former sailor from Shaker Heights, Ohio, who parlayed his ambisexual charm and extraordinary good looks into one of the most successful careers in Hollywood.

It's all here, as recorded by celebrity chronicler Darwin Porter--the giddy heights and agonizing lows of a great American star, with revelations and insights never published in any other biography.

Humphrey Bogart
The Making of a Legend
Darwin Porter
A candid overview of the rise to fame of an unlikely
and frequently unemployed Broadway actor

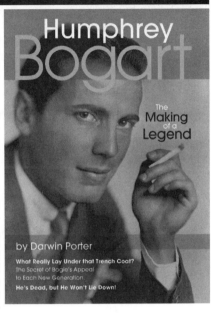

Whereas **Humphrey Bogart** is always at the top of any list of the Entertainment Industry's most famous actors, very little is known about how he clawed his way from Broadway to Hollywood during Prohibition and the Jazz Age.

This pioneering biography begins with Bogart's origins as the child of wealthy (morphine-addicted) parents in New York City, then examines the love affairs, scandals, failures, and breakthroughs that launched him as an American icon.

It includes details about behind-the-scenes dramas associated with three mysterious marriages, and films such as *The Petrified Forest, The Maltese Falcon, High Sierra,* and *Casablanca.* Read all about the debut and formative years of the actor who influenced many generations of filmgoers, laying Bogie's life bare in a style you've come to expect from Darwin Porter. Exposed with all their juicy details is what Bogie never told his fourth wife, Lauren Bacall, herself a screen legend.

Drawn from original interviews with friends and foes who knew a lot about what lay beneath his trenchcoat, this exposé covers Bogart's remarkable life as it helped define movie-making, Hollywood's portrayal of macho, and America's evolving concept of Entertainment itself.

This revelatory book is based on unpublished memoirs, letters, diaries, and often personal interviews from the women—and the men—who adored him.

There are also allegations from colleagues, former friends, and jilted lovers who wanted him to burn in hell.

All this and more, much more, in Darwin Porter's *exposé* of Bogie's secret life, with startling information about Bogart, the movies, and Golden Age Hollywood you won't find in other books.

Humphrey Bogart, The Making of a Legend

Hardcover, 542 pages, with hundreds of photos. Also available for e-readers

ISBN   978-1-936003-14-3

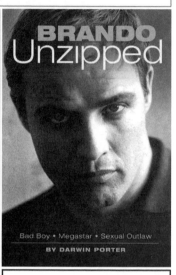

MERV GRIFFIN
A LIFE IN THE CLOSET

Darwin Porter

Merv Griffin, A Life in the Closet

Merv Griffin began his career as a Big Band singer, moved on to a failed career as a romantic hero in the movies, and eventually rewrote the rules of everything associated with the broadcasting industry. Along the way, he met and befriended virtually everyone who mattered, made billions operating casinos and developing jingles, contests, and word games. All of this while maintaining a male harem and a secret life as America's most famously closeted homosexual.

In this comprehensive biography—the first published since Merv's death in 2007—celebrity biographer Darwin Porter reveals the amazing details behind the richest, most successful, and in some ways, the most notorious mogul in the history of America's entertainment industry.

HOT, CONTROVERSIAL, & RIGOROUSLY RESEARCHED

HERE'S MERV!

Hardcover, with photos. ISBN 978-0-9786465-0-9
Also available for E-Readers.

JACKO
HIS RISE AND FALL

The History of Michael Jackson

Darwin Porter

He rewrote the rules of America's entertainment industry, and he led a life of notoriety. Even his death was the occasion for scandals which continue to this day.

This is the world's most comprehensive historical overview of a pop star's rise, fall, and to some extent, rebirth as an American Icon. Read it for the real story of the circumstances and players who created the icon which the world will forever remember as "the gloved one," Michael Jackson.

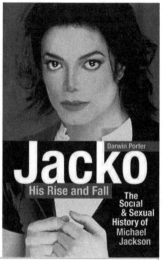

"This is the story of Peter Pan gone rotten. Don't stop till you get enough. Darwin Porter's biography of Michael Jackson is dangerously addictive."

The Sunday Observer   (London)

"In this compelling glimpse of Jackson's life, Porter provides what many journalists have failed to produce in their writings about the pop star: A real person behind the headlines."
Foreword Magazine

"I'd have thought that there wasn't one single gossippy rock yet to be overturned in the microscopically scrutinized life of Michael Jackson, but Darwin Porter has proven me wrong. Definitely a page-turner. But don't turn the pages too quickly. Almost every one holds a fascinating revelation."

Books to Watch Out For

This book, a winner of literary awards from both *Foreword Magazine* and the Hollywood Book Festival, was originally published during the lifetime of Michael Jackson. This, the revised, post-mortem edition, with extra analysis and commentary, was released after his death.

Hardcover 600 indexed pages with about a hundred photos

ISBN 978-0-936003-10-5. Also available for E-readers

HOMOSEXUALITY IN THE MOVIES
A Book of Record, Reference Source, and Gossip Guide
to 50 Years of Queer Cinema

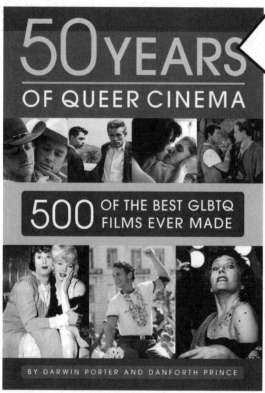

"In the Internet age, where every movie, queer or otherwise, is blogged about somewhere, a hefty print compendium of film facts and pointed opinion might seem anachronistic. But flipping through well-reasoned pages of commentary is so satisfying. Add to that physical thrill the charm of analysis that is sometimes sassy and always smart, and this filtered survey of short reviews is a must for queer-film fans.

"Essays on Derek Jarman, Tennessee Williams, Andy Warhol, Jack Wrangler, Joe Gage and others—and on how *The Front Runner* never got made—round out this indispensable survey of gay-interest cinema."

RICHARD LABONTÉ
BOOK MARKS/QSYNDICATE

Are you, like us, bored to death with the ho-hum celebrity gossip
in today's mainstream newspapers and tabloids?
ALL OF THAT HAS CHANGED FOREVER.

Blood Moon proudly announces its commitment to an ongoing series of
FREE monthly newsletters wherein Darwin Porter, America's
most literate muckraker, meets the 21st century's tabloids.

"Dirty Laundry is putting the *oooomph* back into
editorial coverage of celebrity gossip and the entertainment industry."

FREE CELEBRITY DISH LIKE YOU'VE NEVER SEEN IT BEFORE

WHY? *BECAUSE DIRTY LAUNDRY MAKES WASHDAY FUN!*

The water's hot, but you won't get it
unless you sign up for it first, from the home page of

WWW.BLOODMOONPRODUCTIONS.COM

What's New at Blood Moon?
**Follow us on Facebook.com/Blood Moon Productions
and on Twitter.com/ BloodyandLunar**